# IMPRESSUM

**Released by Publishing House / Veröffentlicht im Verlag**
ÉDITIONS MOUSTACHE
↘ *www.editionsmoustache.net*

**Address / Verlagsanschrift**
Marco Siedelmann
Eintrachtstrasse 41
52134 Herzogenrath
Germany / Deutschland

**Copyright © 2016** Marco Siedelmann, Nadia Bruce-Rawlings, Stephen A. Roberts

**ISBN**-9783960340133

**Cover Artwork**
Christian Struzan

**Book Jacket Design / Umschlaggestaltung**
Christian Schmalohr

**Layout-Design**
Tobias Gossen

**Editor-Director**
Marco Siedelmann

**Mai / May** 2016

**Printed by CreateSpace,**
↘ *An Amazon.com Company*

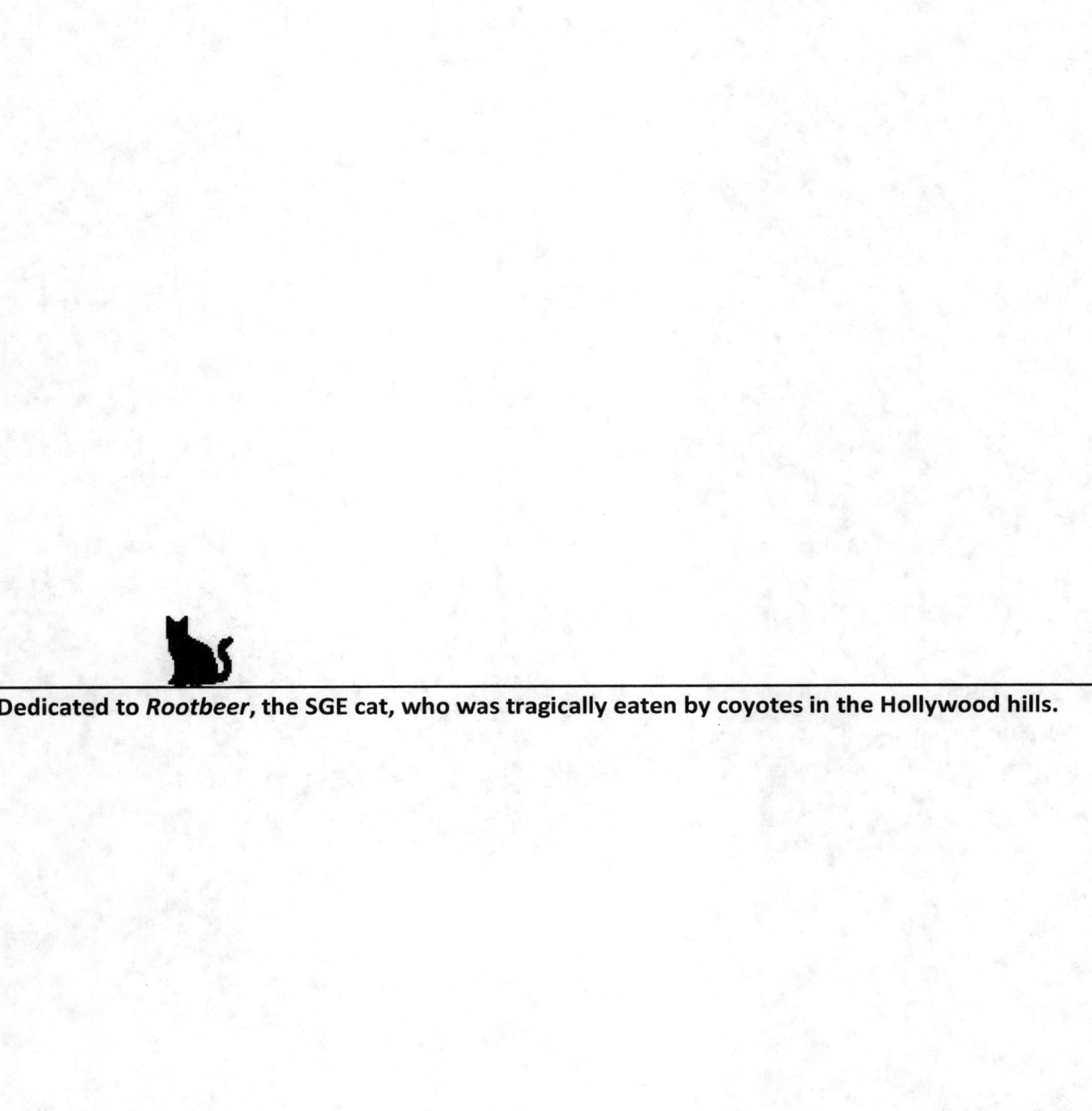

**Dedicated to *Rootbeer*, the SGE cat, who was tragically eaten by coyotes in the Hollywood hills.**

Marco Siedelmann ★ Nadia Bruce-Rawlings ★ Stephen A. Roberts

# The Untold, In-Depth, Outrageously True Story of Shapiro Glickenhaus Entertainment

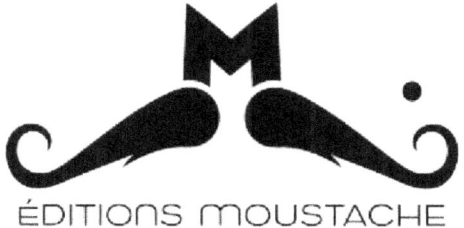
ÉDITIONS MOUSTACHE

|     |                                                                         |
| --- | ----------------------------------------------------------------------- |
|     | Introduction ............................................................. 3 |
|     | Editor's Preface ......................................................... 5 |
|     | Foreword ................................................................. 8 |
| I.  | **Let's get this Party started: SEC becomes SGE** ....................... 10 |
|     | Leonard Shapiro (Part I) ............................................... 22 |
|     | Stephen A. Roberts ..................................................... 49 |
|     | Sonoko Sakai ........................................................... 66 |
|     | Ted Rosenblatt ......................................................... 91 |
|     | Lewis Horwitz ......................................................... 109 |
|     | John Alexander ........................................................ 134 |
| II. | **SGE as a Production Company:   Hiring Creatives was cheap then** .... 143 |
|     | William Lustig ........................................................ 149 |
|     | Frank K. Isaac ........................................................ 164 |
|     | Frank Henenlotter ..................................................... 183 |
|     | Kevin Tent ............................................................ 202 |
|     | Jefferson Richard ..................................................... 222 |
|     | Cynthia Cirile ........................................................ 238 |
| III.| **The VHS Explosion:   SGE Goes Nuclear in Home Video** ............... 253 |
|     | James Glickenhaus (Part I) ............................................ 255 |
|     | Andi Elliott .......................................................... 285 |
|     | J. Christian Ingvordsen ............................................... 301 |
|     | Jalal Merhi ........................................................... 326 |
|     | Jacqueline Palmiere ................................................... 339 |
|     | Cynthia Rothrock ...................................................... 346 |
| IV. | **Expansion and The Red Scorpion  Experiment** ........................ 359 |
|     | Joseph Zito ........................................................... 361 |
|     | Stephanie Denton ...................................................... 367 |
|     | Bob Berney ............................................................ 373 |
|     | Marilyn Moore ......................................................... 384 |
|     | Robert Chapin ......................................................... 396 |

| | |
|---|---|
| **V.  The Remains of the Day: Life after SGE** … | 404 |
| Nadia Bruce-Rawlings | 410 |
| James Glickenhaus (Part II) | 424 |
| Leonard Shapiro (Part II) | 432 |
| Afterword: A Song of Solomon | 439 |
| **I N D E X** | 465 |
| … Moustache's ***NEXT*** | 474 |

# Introduction

*"All those moments will be lost in time ... like tears in the rain."*

– **Rutger Hauer,** *BLADE RUNNER*

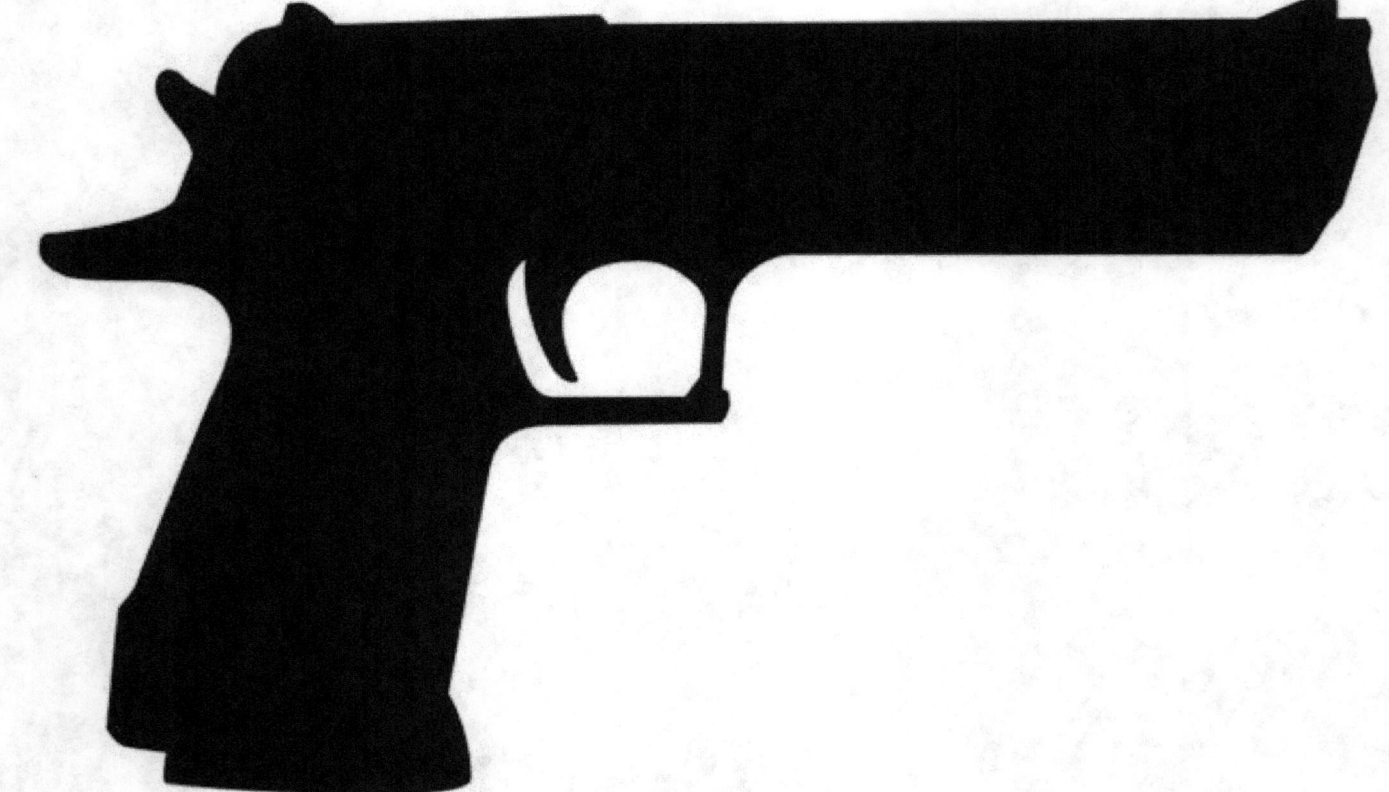

# Editor's Preface

*by Marco Siedelmann*

Shapiro Glickenhaus Entertainment was in the right place at the right time. The American Film Industry of the mid-1980's was awash in iconic images, new highs (and lows) of exploitation, and a radiant fascination for mythological hard-bodied heroes pumped up just like the 'GoGo' 80s themselves. It was an adrenalized era of perceived plenty, when Ronald Reagan's trickle-down economics inspired and fueled the USA and her disciples in an American 'anything is possible' spirit that tempted many worldwide to follow in its wake. From this atmosphere of boundless opportunity, facilitated by the VHS boom, exploded a vibrant rush of independent film companies that reached for the sky. A huge number failed, but in its own way, SGE succeeded. Why? That is the key question this book will attempt to answer.

SGE made schlock films with bravado, pride, dignity and above all fun - but also with economical savvy. However, unlike better-known companies of the era like The Cannon Group, SGE remains largely unsung as a production and distribution company. The iconic films of James Glickenhaus, Frank Henenlotter, William Lustig's MANIAC COP and cult favorites like MOONTRAP are well known to cinema buffs worldwide. But how many fans know that all these films were made, marketed and distributed by one and the same company?

The voluminous pages of this publication include 24 deep-focus conversations with many of the key players who made SGE 'go' before, during and after its heyday. It discusses how FRANKENHOOKER was pitched and born as a project; why SGE did not produce the sequels to the highly acclaimed MANIAC COP, and MOONTRAP; how producing alliances worked with partners like Sultan Films and Film One; details of the value of marketing; specifics about international licenses, theatrical, home video and foreign releases; and what happened afterward with the filmmakers. It includes all this and much, much more, including rare, previously unheard anecdotal stories that in many ways humanize and crystallize the era itself. Like nowhere else, here you'll find factual, perspective-based analyses of what was really happening in the movie industry in those crazy, hazy days directly from the lunatics who were actually running the asylum.

This book is not intended to be some kind of "official" studio history, nor is it something "complete" by any means. It's an intentionally messy mixture of different points of view and personal memories from the financial, creative, marketing and distribution components of filmmaking at one iconic company.

There is complexity and ambiguity here; there are emotions and personalities; hopes, dreams and aspirations -- but above all these pages prove that there is no such thing as one single truth.

The missing man, the now and forever silent partner of SGE, is Alan M. Solomon, who passed away in 2010. He is acknowledged here with an Afterword, written by Nadia Bruce-Rawlings and Stephen A. Roberts, both of whom initially came into this project as interview subjects, but quickly grew into Co-Editors, which is how this publication became an inside job. The book started as a simple, single interview with James Glickenhaus that evolved into a wide-ranging journey through different decades of independent filmmaking and morphed into a snapshot of the times themselves to arrive at what you are now reading...a veritable 'brick' 'o knowledge that you will find absolutely nowhere else in the world. Guaranteed. And, despite its voluminous length, and ambitious scope, in many ways this interview-collection only scratches the surface. But if you've got the guts to go for the glory – it's certainly here for the taking...dig in deep, hang on tight, and definitely fasten your seatbelts!

*All interview questions were derived from a master set written by Editor-in-Chief Marco Siedelmann to form the original vision that gave rise to this book. Each interviewer was encouraged to deviate off script, when and if, the conversations led there.*

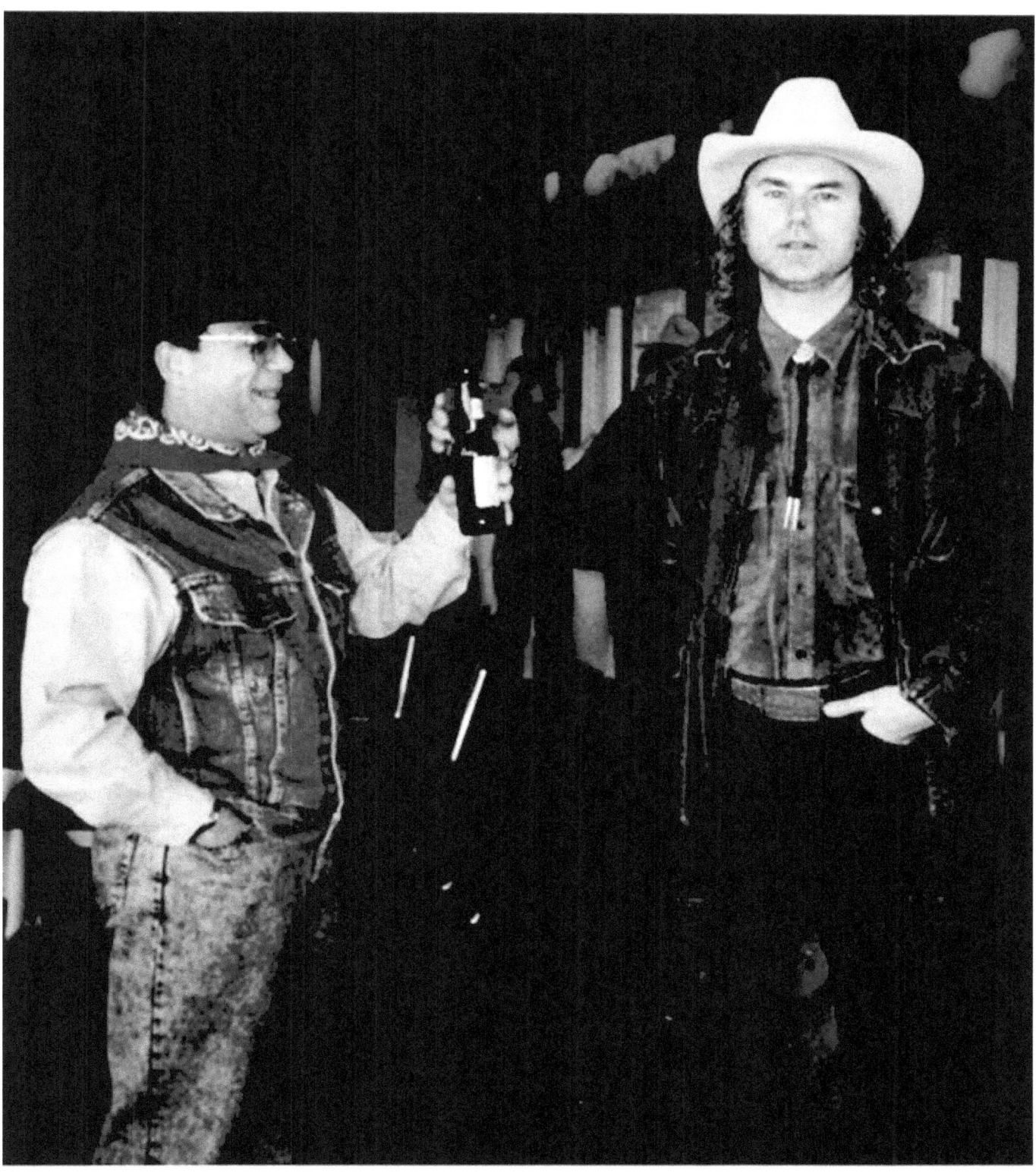

# Foreword

*by Charles Band*

There were only a few key players in the exploding 1980's indie scene that really stood out: Cannon Films, Shapiro Glickenhaus Entertainment, and Empire Pictures. Back then, I think many of us measured the success and strength of each other's companies by how many full page ads were taken out in the weekly trades: Variety and Screen International magazines were tied to the foreign sales markets such as Cannes and MIFED. Combined, there were literally hundreds of pages spread out between just these few companies. Unreal!

These were the "Go-Go" days of the early to mid-80's, fueled by the then-booming home video industry. We independents suddenly had a new amazing revenue source, and we were all punch drunk. Shapiro Glickenhaus broke through with some big mainstream hits. I remember that we would usually be stationed next to each other at the various international markets. And while my Empire Pictures didn't have those theatrical gems that Shapiro Glickenhaus did, we did have numerous home video hits. Our bombastic promo reels were blasting my friend Lenny Shapiro right out of his sales office! Today, most of my memories of that period are just a mad blur. But Lenny – who is still a good friend after all these years - and Shapiro Glickenhaus were amongst the few who really stood out and really made an impact during those crazy days.

Together these mad companies took the industry by storm. Shapiro Glickenhaus had RED SCORPION and SHAKEDOWN. They had some good luck and some strong films, but they also had a heart that set them apart from some of the others. Lenny Shapiro, Alan Solomon, Jim Glickenhaus and the rest of the team behind the scenes – they worked hard and had a lot of fun doing it. One thing you'll hear voiced throughout these interviews is that this company was a family. And that's why they moved forward with such success.

*Enjoy the ride...they sure did!*

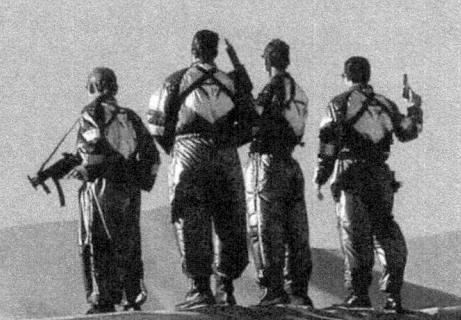

# BEYOND TIME, BEYOND SPACE...

# THE ULTIMATE ADVENTURE IS ABOUT TO BEGIN.

# I. Let's get this Party started: SEC becomes SGE

*" Roads? Where we're going, we don't need roads."*
— **Christopher Lloyd,** *BACK TO THE FUTURE*

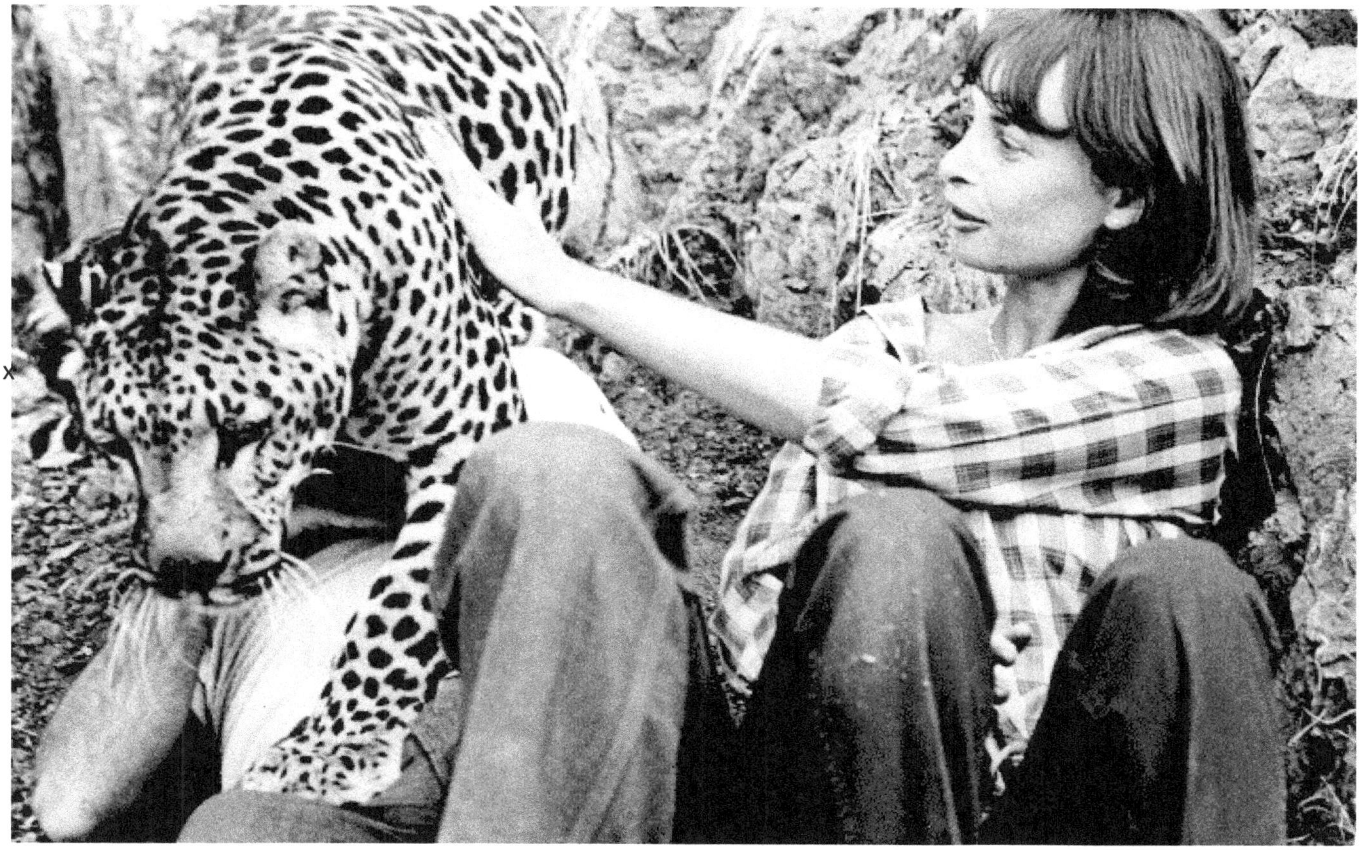

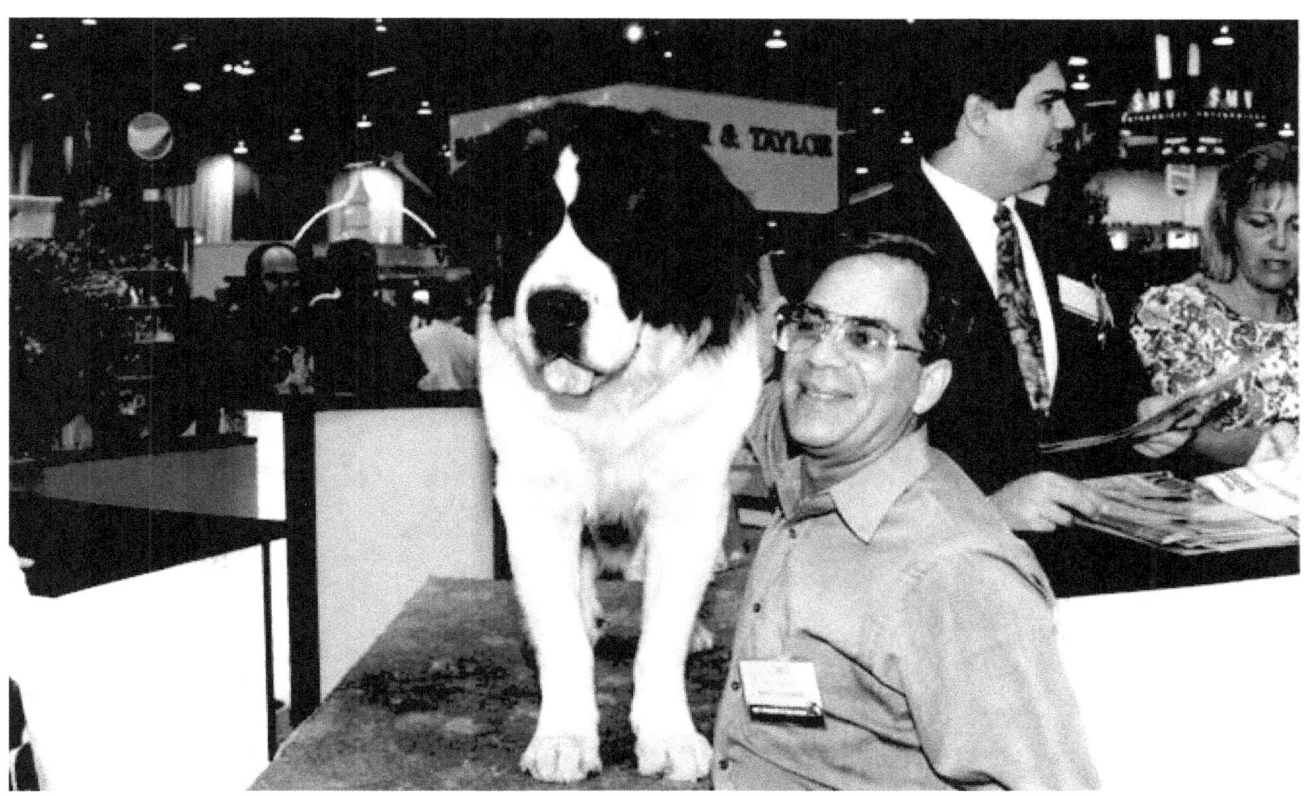

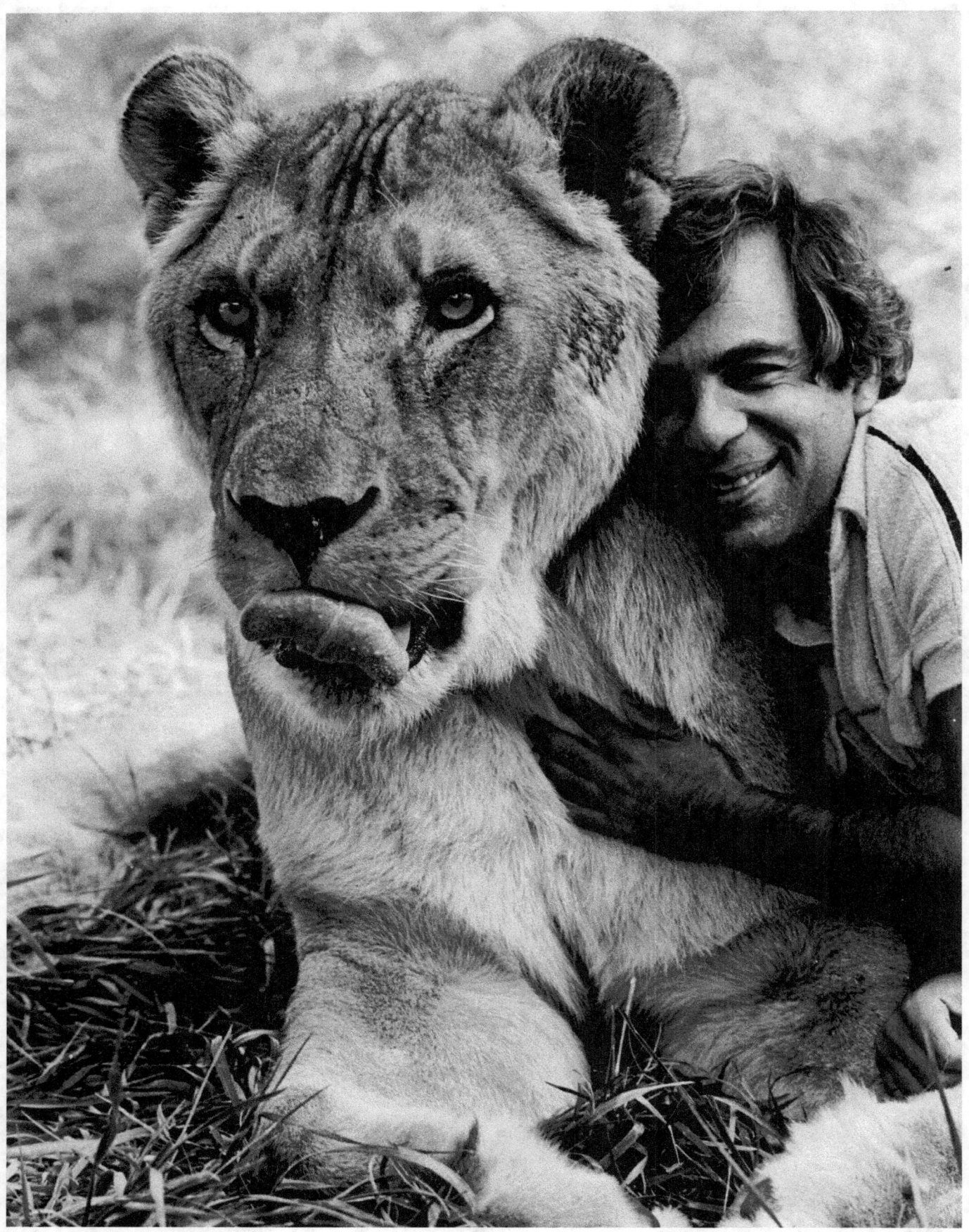

# CBS' CABLE DESIGNS CHALLENGED

## Migden Warns Against Strike Mentality In Upcoming Talks With Writers And Directors

By WILL TUSHER

Unless something dramatic is done to reverse the industry's strike mentality over upcoming negotiations with writers and directors, the emotionally charged atmosphere could provoke a self-fulfilling prophecy.

That warning was sounded yesterday by Chester L. Migden, national executive secretary of the Screen Actors Guild, which itself recently went through a nine-and-a-half week strike that extended to 13 weeks before a new contract was ratified by SAG and the American Federation of TV & Radio Artists.

The view that another strike is a virtual fait accompli is widely held in the industry. Early attempts to initiate talks on a new agreement between the Writers Guild and the Motion Picture & TV Producers Negotiating Committee have foundered amid signs of prenegotiating polarization over the same issue that precipitated the actors' walkout — home video residuals.

Already, there have been ominous signals that differences over pay-tv residuals have placed management on a collision course not only with the Writers Guild, whose current pact expires March 31, but as well with the Directors Guild, whose agreement runs out June 31.

Outlines of impasse already are sharply defined. The word is out that the writers and directors have no intention of settling for as little of the home video pie

(Continued on Page 44, Column 1)

## Ashby To Direct 'Coffins' For United Artists

Hal Ashby will direct United Artists' film version of Truman Capote's "Handcarved Coffins," Daily Variety has learned. Judith Rascoe is writing screenplay for producer Lester Persky, and lensing is skedded to commence in Colorado in March.

Bought by UA in January, 1980, for a reported $500,000, property appeared in the Christmas, 1979, issue of Andy Warhol's Interview magazine and deals with a series of bizarre midwestern murders in which intended victims received miniature coffins in advance of their demise. Story is said to

(Continued on Page 44, Column 3)

## LEONARD SHAPIRO GETS V.P. STRIPES AT AVCO EMBASSY

Leonard Shapiro has been named film acquisitions and marketing services veepee for Avco Embassy Pictures Corp. effective immediately, according to prexy-chief exec Bob Rehme.

A 10-year vet at Avco, Shapiro

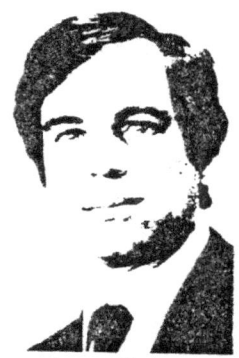

Leonard Shapiro

moves up from his position as director of marketing services and research, a post he has held for the past year.

In his new slot, Shapiro will be responsible for determining, with Rehme to whom he reports directly, the independent features that Avco will acquire for distribution, coordinate the marketing and research campaigns.

(Continued on Page 42, Column 3)

## Pix, People, Pickups

Oscar-winning composer **Maurice Jarre** will score "Don't Cry, It's Only Thunder" for producer Walt deFaria and director Peter Werner. Sanrio Communications pic stars Dennis Christopher and Susan Saint James.

• • •

**George Peppard** has changed the name of his company from Long Rifle Prods. to Lime Tree Prods., currently prepping two action pix, "Gambler's Luck" and "The Smugglers."

• • •

Producer **Myrl Schreibman**

(Continued on Page 4, Column 3)

## Coalition Of Minority Orgs Files FCC Protest Aimed At Blocking Net's CATV Entry

By MORRIE GELMAN

Coalition of minority actors, writers, directors and community groups, banded together under the name Appeal, yesterday filed a protest with the Federal Communications Commission seeking to block CBS from entering the cable tv field as a system operator.

The Appeal (Actors & Artists to Promote Effective American Broadcasting Laws) coalition — the actors and artists were joined by 10 minority and community organizations — contends that entry of CBS into cable tv amounts to merely an "opening wedge," a sort of "Trojan Horse," that will ultimately "diminish creativity, interfere with the free exchange of ideas, and continue a subtle form of network censorship in which minorities are under-represented and or misrepresented."

The protest petition, filed before the FCC, is in direct response to the CBS petition to the FCC of Dec. 9, 1980, seeking "limited entry" into the cable tv area. Specifically, CBS asked for a waiver of the FCC's ban on network ownership of cable tv.

Appeal wants the FCC to declare a 180-day moratorium on implementation of the CBS petition.

Coalition also wants the Commission to force CBS to alert its audience, via radio and tv spots, that it is attempting to crack the cable tv biz so groups that will be affected can express their views.

Finally, Appeal is asking the FCC to hold public hearings before CBS or any other commer-

(Continued on Page 46, Column 3)

## Showbiz Stocks In Big Plunge; 71 Issues Down

Entertainment stocks plunged with the rest of the stock market yesterday in record N.Y. Stock Exchange trading of 93.75 shares. The market was besieged with sell orders from investors taking profits on recent increases which had seen the Dow Jones Industrial average pass the 1000 mark Tuesday.

In showbiz yesterday, 71 stocks lost ground while only three gained and 11 remained unchanged. Showbiz volume was a huge 5,550,400 shares, led by Eastman Kodak with 705,400 shares traded.

The DJI average fell 23.8% yesterday as the Amex Index

(Continued on Page 4, Column 3)

## LITTLE CHANCE FOR CO-TENANCY AS SAG, AFTRA HUNT NEW H.Q.'S

A generally sympathetic, but far from immediately compliant, response has greeted a demand from the Caucus of Artists for Merger (CAM) that the Screen Actors Guild and the American Federation of Television & Radio Artists pool separate searches for new and larger quarters.

SAG, which owns the building it occupies on Sunset Blvd., and Los Angeles AFTRA, which leases its premises, have been shopping individually for new homes. Each is considering building from the ground up.

CAM regards the separate efforts to relocate as a default on commitments by both performing unions to early amalgamation. The pro-merger group is gathering signatures on petitions asking the two performing organizations to validate their pledges by starting with combined new headquarters.

Coincidentally — not through consultation or coordinated planning — SAG and AFTRA each moving unilaterally, are considering new Studio City locations in close proximity to one another.

SAG is mulling the construction of a new office building on a vacant site on Ventura Blvd., near Tujunga. Los Angeles AFTRA is conducting a feasibility study on a new building at a nearby North Hollywood location.

AFTRA's Los Angeles executive secretary, Allan Davis, says the projected site — under "very active consideration" — probably is closer to the possible new home of SAG than present AFTRA headquarters on High-

(Continued on Page 42, Column 4)

## CBS WINS NIELSEN WEEK DESPITE A STRONG SHOWING BY NBC-TV

NBC had a good primetime ratings week over the New Year's holiday period, taking Monday, Tuesday, Wednesday and Thursday nights in succession and 22 of 44 competitive half hours, yet CBS won the week by a full rating point.

How come? For one, "Dallas," in its last half-hour on Friday, did a 50 share (compared to an 8 share for "Run America" news spec on NBC).

The problem for NBC and ABC? How to compete with a CBS Friday lineup that takes the night by 14 and 18 rating points and a Sunday night lineup which consistently winds up in the win column.

Friday and Sunday are the only two nights CBS won last week. The network is barely competitive on Saturday (a night, as usual, taken by ABC). Of the 44 competitive half hours CBS won 14, nine of them on Friday and Sunday.

Just how important is Friday night to CBS? The week before last, as an experiment to expose the new series to a wider and different audience, "The Secrets Of Midland Heights" preempted "Dallas" in the Friday 9 p.m. time slot. It did a 21.7 rating, 41 share, basically retaining the audience delivered by its lead-in series, "The Dukes Of Hazzard."

Last week, back into an even heavier than usual time slot Saturday, 9-10 p.m. instead of 10 p.m. (up against ABC's continuing monster hit "Love Boat"), the new CBS program reverted to form, limping in with a 11.1 rating, 18 share.

Is there anybody in tv today

(Continued on Page 46, Column 1)

BEACON

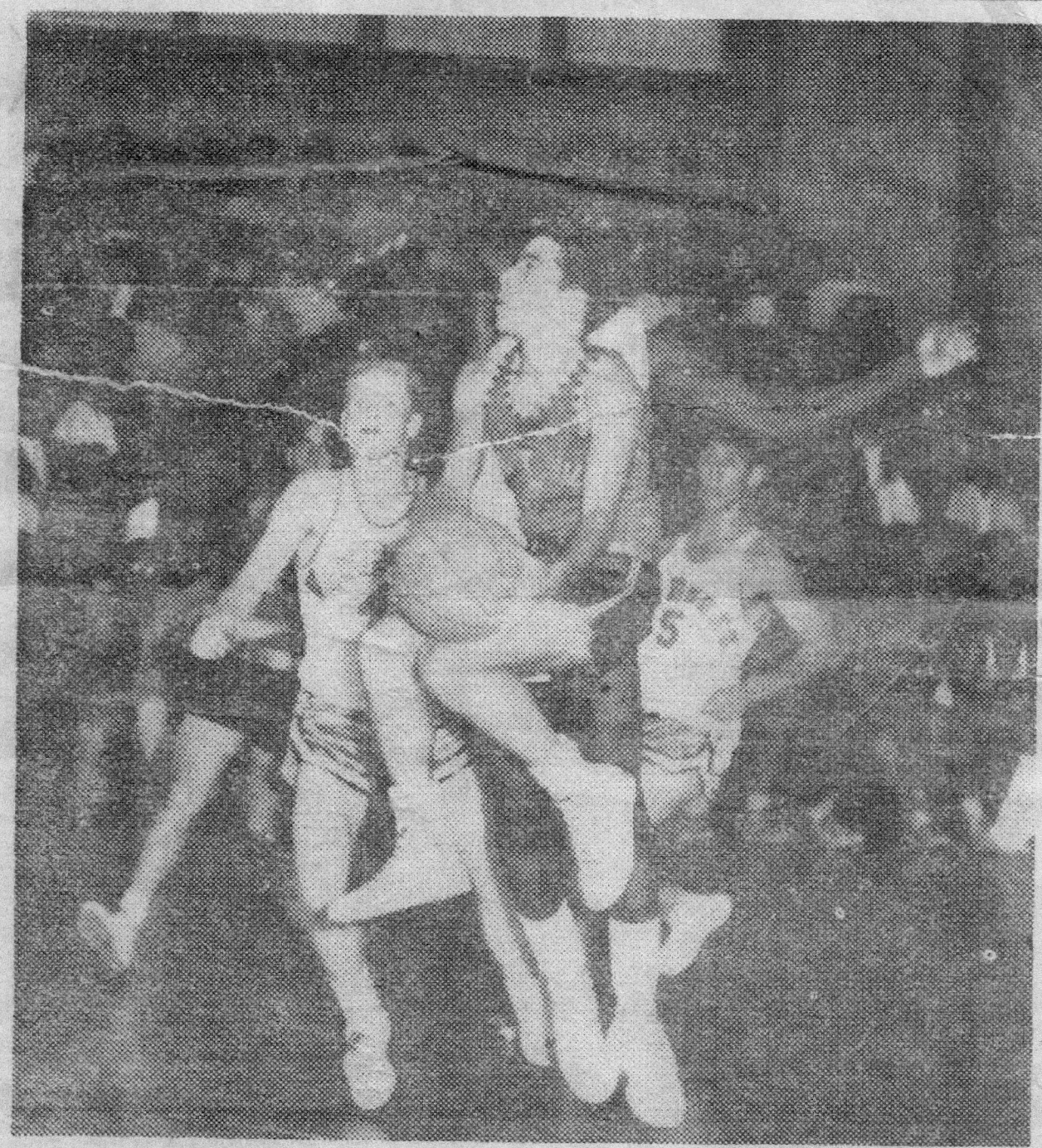

Lennie Shapiro drives for two points against Van Buren. Rangers lost 73-57.

# EXTRA

**COMPLETE RACING**

### Los Angeles Times

MONDAY
FINAL

Copyright © 1968
Los Angeles Times

DAILY 10¢

VOL. LXXXVIII — FIVE PARTS—PART ONE — MONDAY MORNING, JULY 21, 1969 — 54 PAGES

# WALK ON MOON

## 'That's One Small Step for Man... One Giant Leap for Mankind'

### 'Moontrap' Springs In Time For Moonwalk's 20th Anniversary

LOS ANGELES—Twenty "MOONTRAP" channels

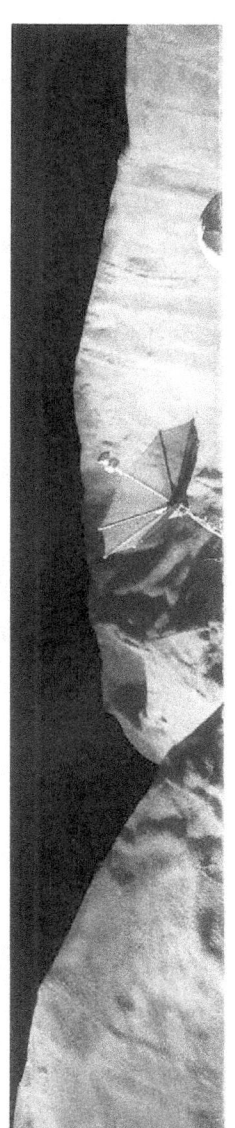

years ago, man first landed on the moon. Next year, man will land again...and discover that he was not the first.

It's all in "MOONTRAP," SGE's epic new science-fiction film, featuring "Star Trek's" Walter Koenig and "Evil Dead's" Bruce Campbell as contemporary astronauts who encounter the remains of an ancient civilization on the lunar surface—and a race of self-propagating robots bent on the earth's destruction.

Timing of the feature comes at the height of "Moon Mania," celebrating the 20th anniversary of the first manned space landing by Neil Armstrong and Edwin Aldrin, Jr. Already the world's eyes have returned to the heavens, with the recent dedication of the world's largest telescope, joint U.S./Russian probes to Mars and Jupiter, and a new space shuttle launch scheduled for 1989.

successfully into our lifelong fascination with the cosmos, a thrilling science-fiction story told with chilling contemporary credibility. Lingering images of the Apollo missions provided the starting-off point for producer-director Robert Dyke. "We thought, 'What if something was discovered up there tomorrow? How would we as contemporary people respond to it?'"

The answer makes for breathless adventure combining the action of "Alien" with the imagination of "2001." Topping the lavish production values (including accurate large-scale recreations of the lunar surface and space shuttle) and state-of-the-art optical effects are malevolent robots certain to rank among the screen's most terrifying monsters.

Celebrate Moon Mania with "MOONTRAP." The heavens will never look the same again.

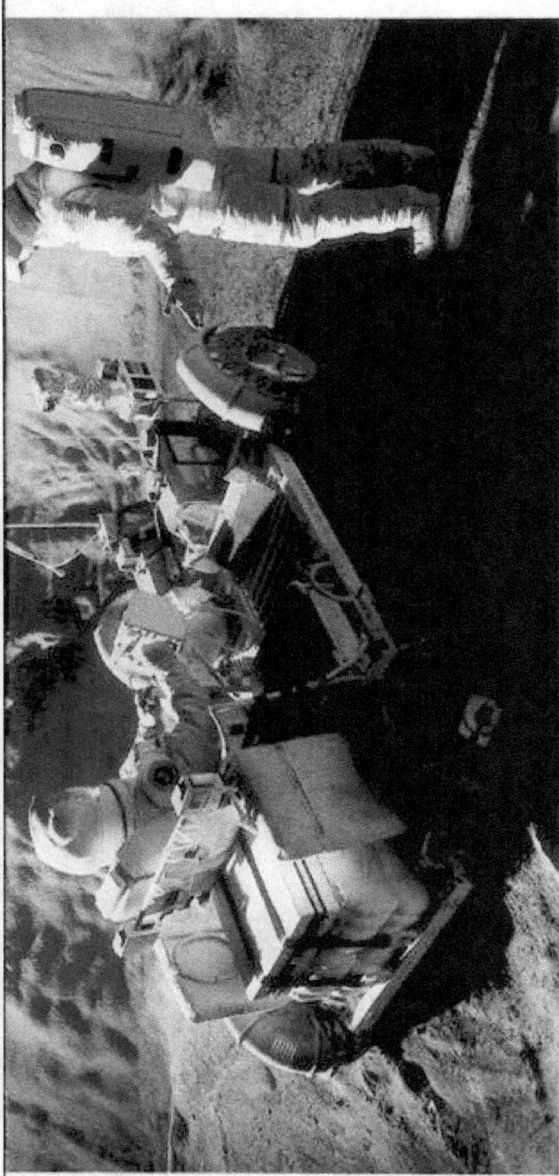

ARGO MISSION ASTRONAUTS JASON GRANT (WALTER KOENIG) AND RAY TANNER (BRUCE CAMPBELL) ABANDON THEIR LUNAR ROVER, UNAWARE THAT A "MOONTRAP" LIES JUST AHEAD.

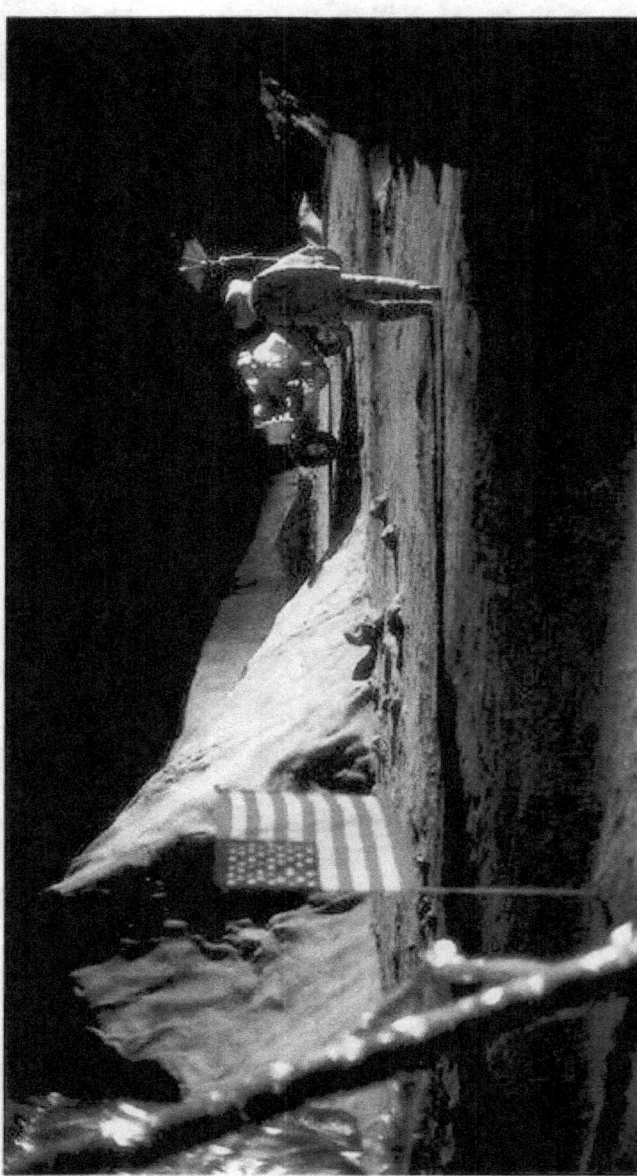

GRANT TAKES ONE SMALL STEP TOWARD ALIEN INVADERS.

## Fans React With Raves

Already "Star Trek" fans on both sides of the Atlantic are helping turn "MOONTRAP" into the movie event of 1989. A six-minute promo reel of selected scenes continues to raise the roof at "Trek" conventions both in the U.S. and overseas, winning the picture lengthy feature stories in the major American science-fiction magazines, CINEFANTASTIQUE and STARLOG. Reactions follow:

"An absolute must-see"
— *Kathleen McKown*, Honey Brook, Pennsylvania

"It's going to be a hit; it has all the elements of an exciting, gripping movie."
— *Rosemary Rackham*, Great Britain

"I'm excited. And I'll be the first person at home to see it when it's released."
— *Laurie Torrez*, West Germany

"Absolutely fantastic! The robot with the rotor blade was decidedly nasty!"
— *Howard Jones*, North London

"Really looking forward to it."
— *Bruce Hyde*, Los Angeles, CA

The word is out. Make no mistake: Moon Mania is here. And "MOONTRAP" leads the way.

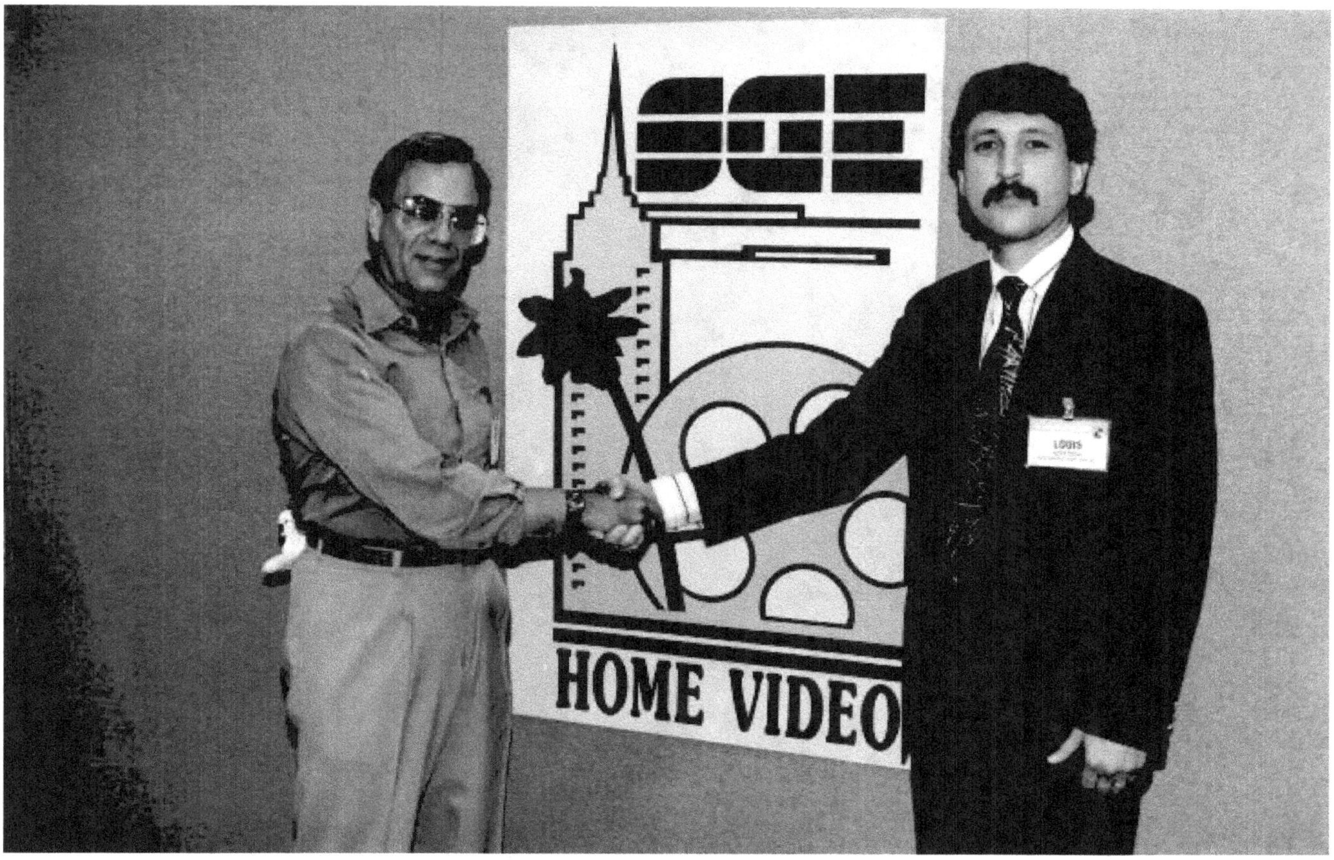

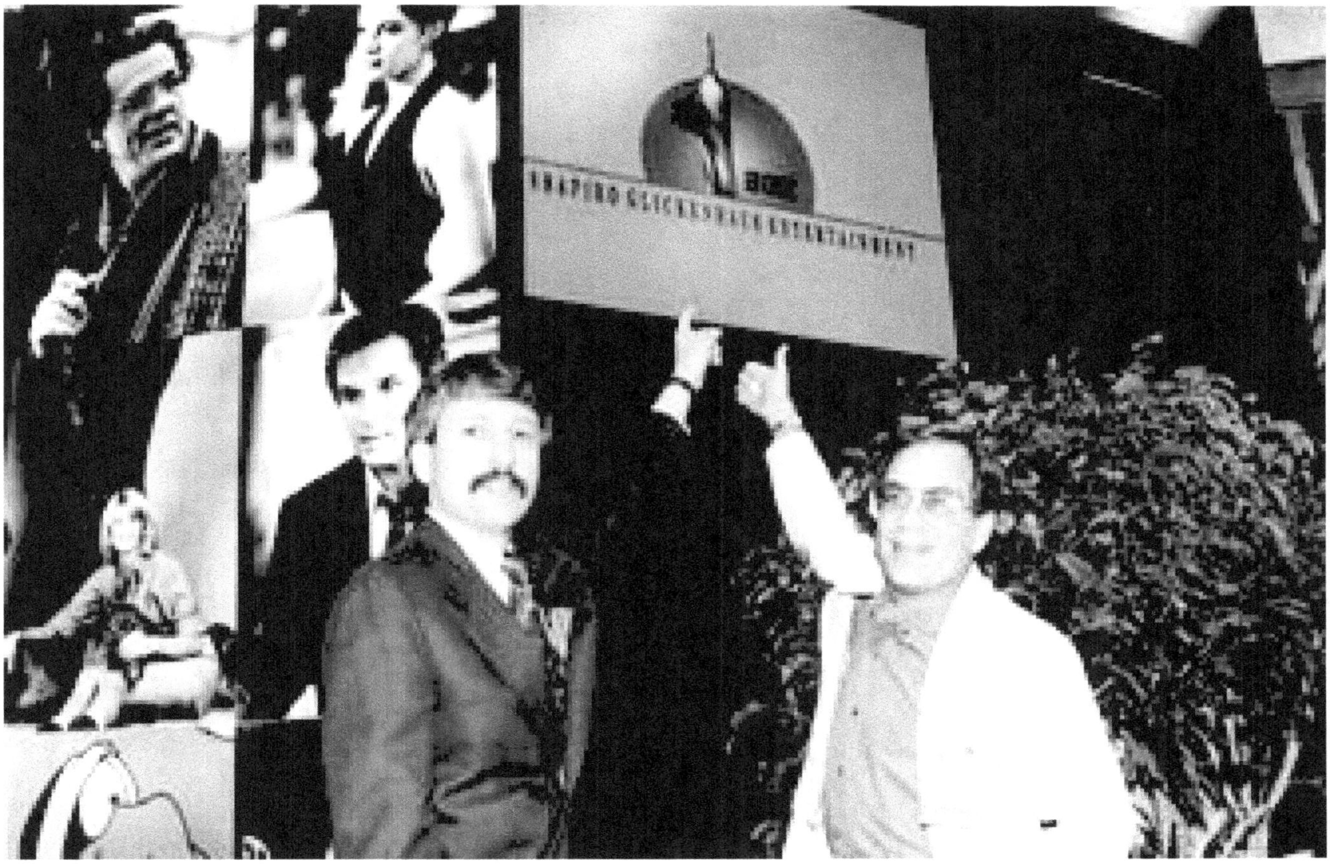

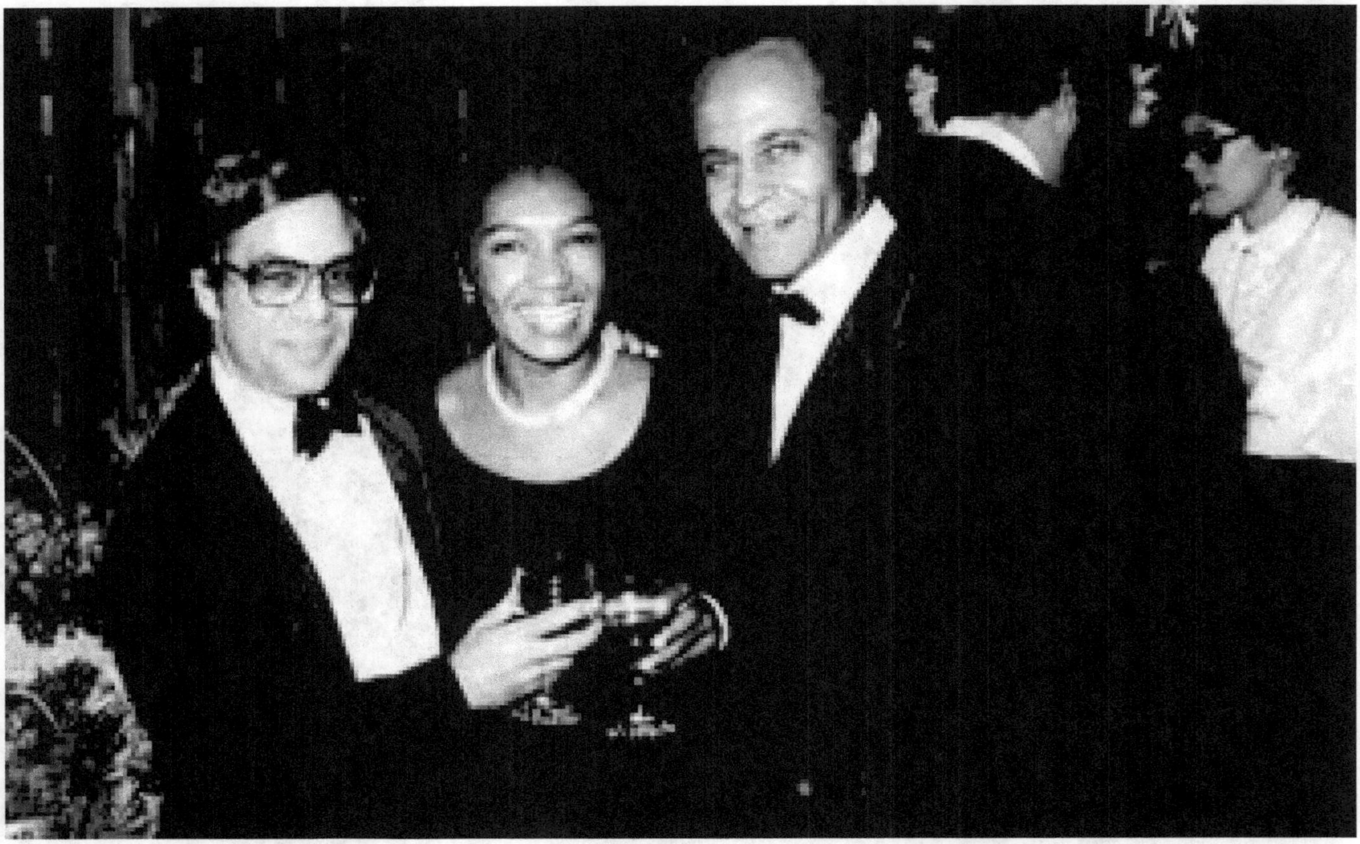

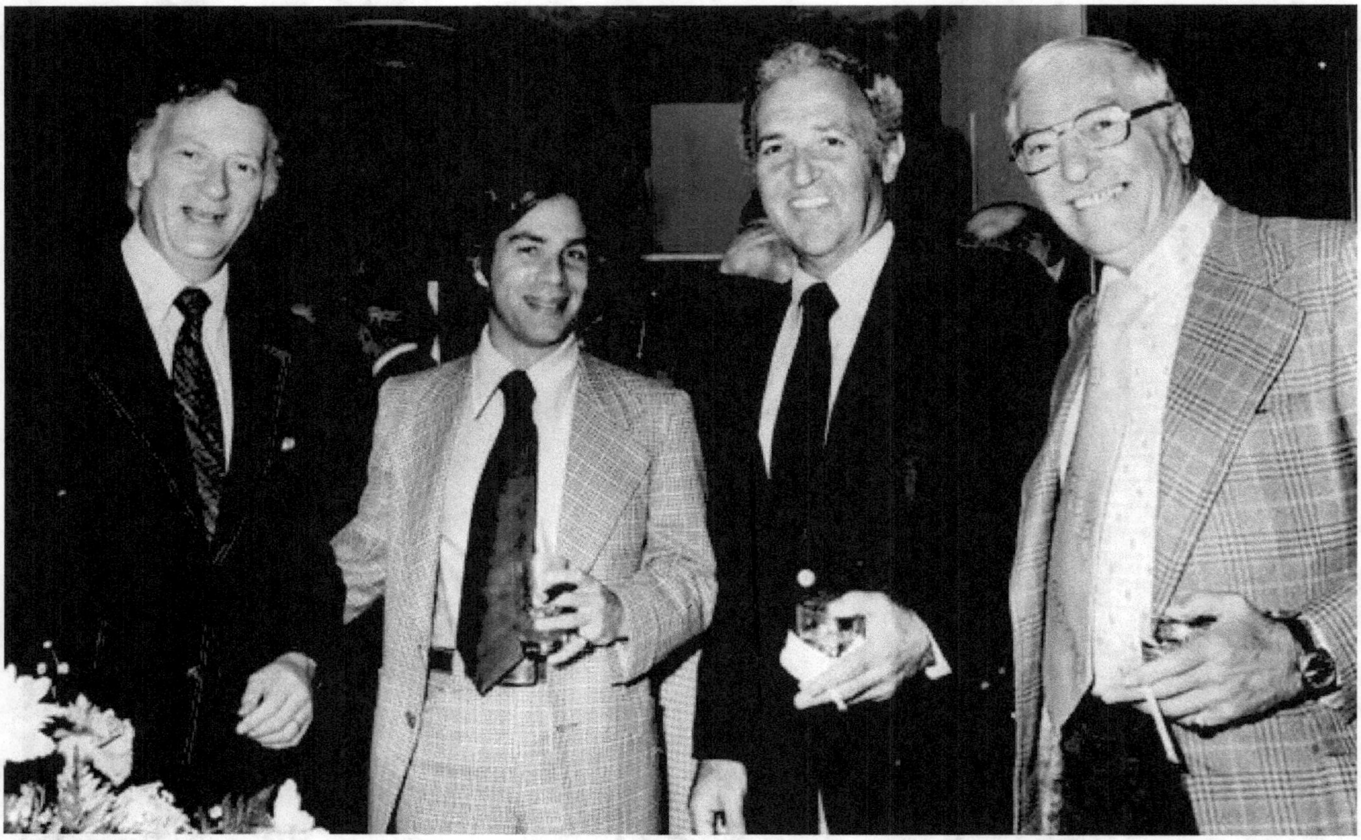

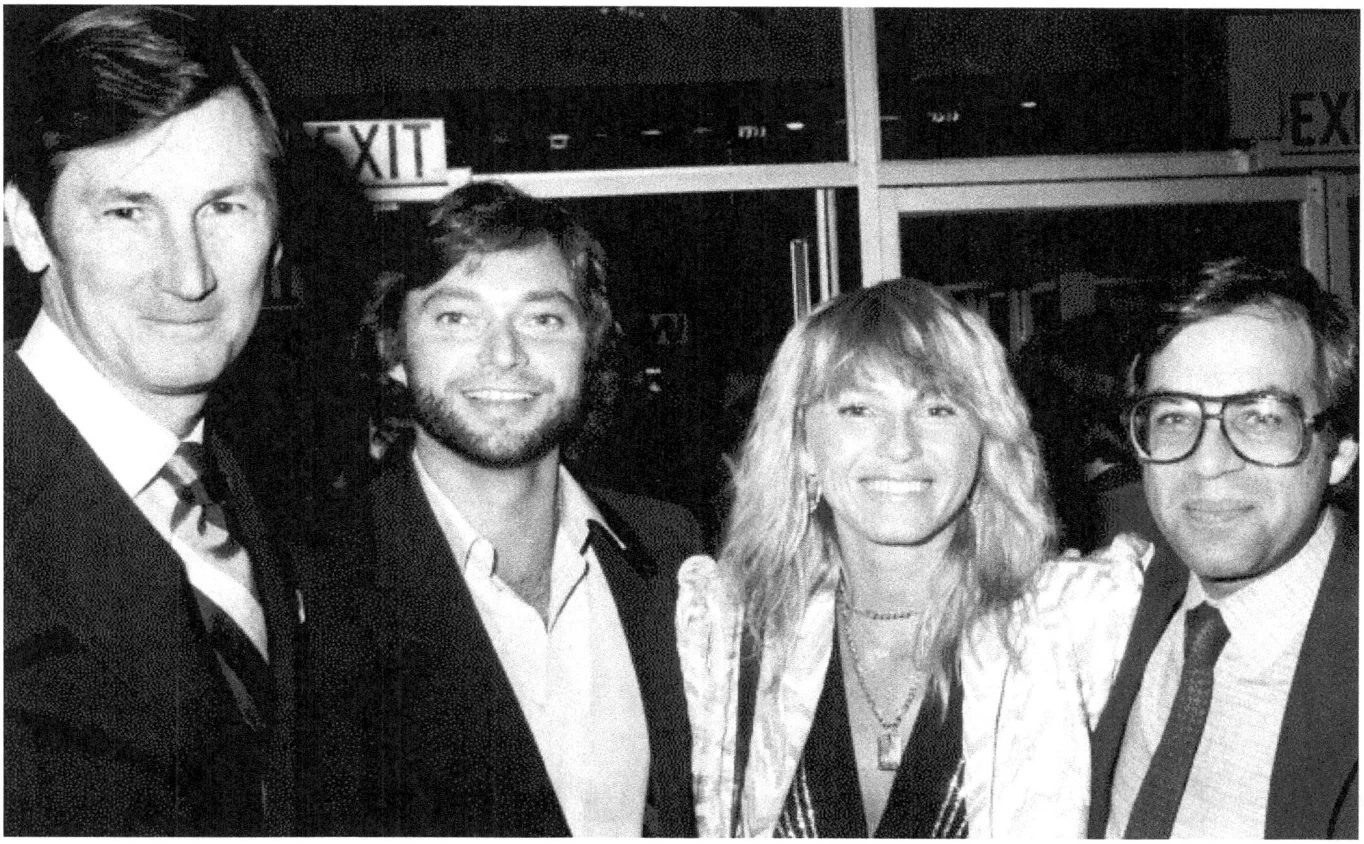

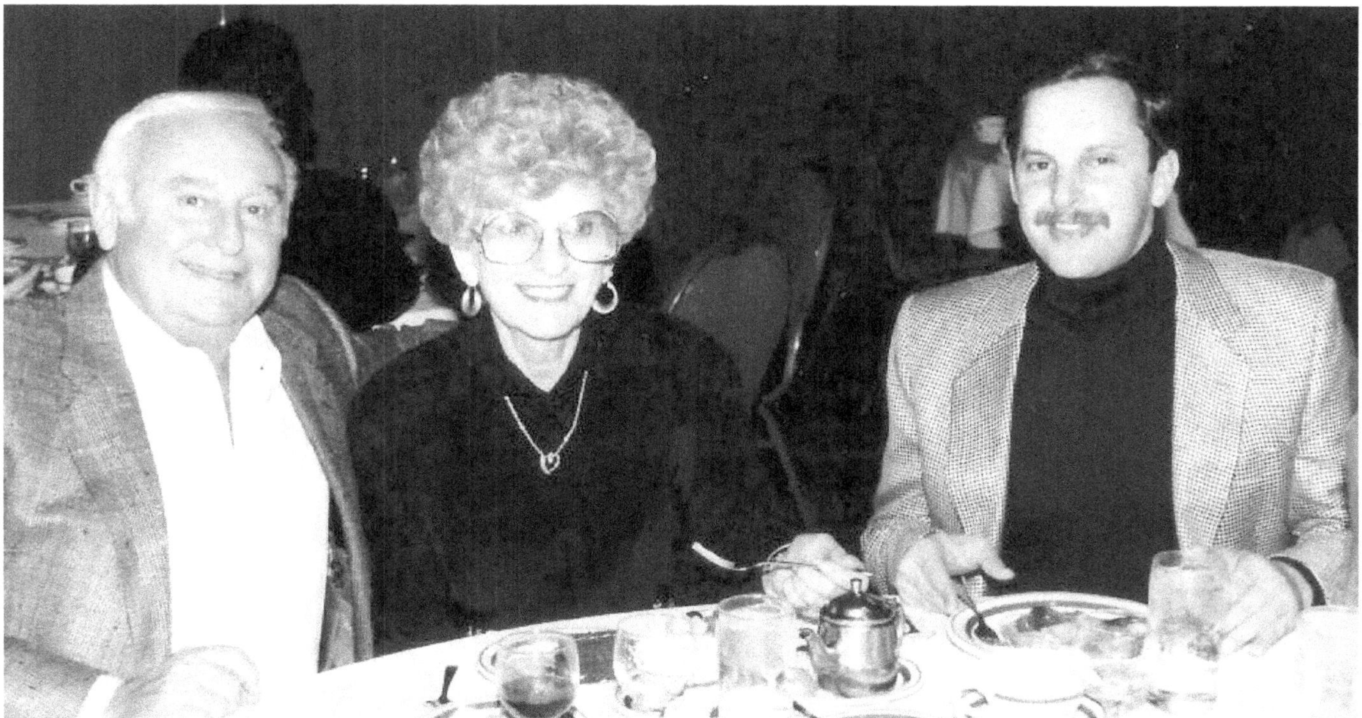

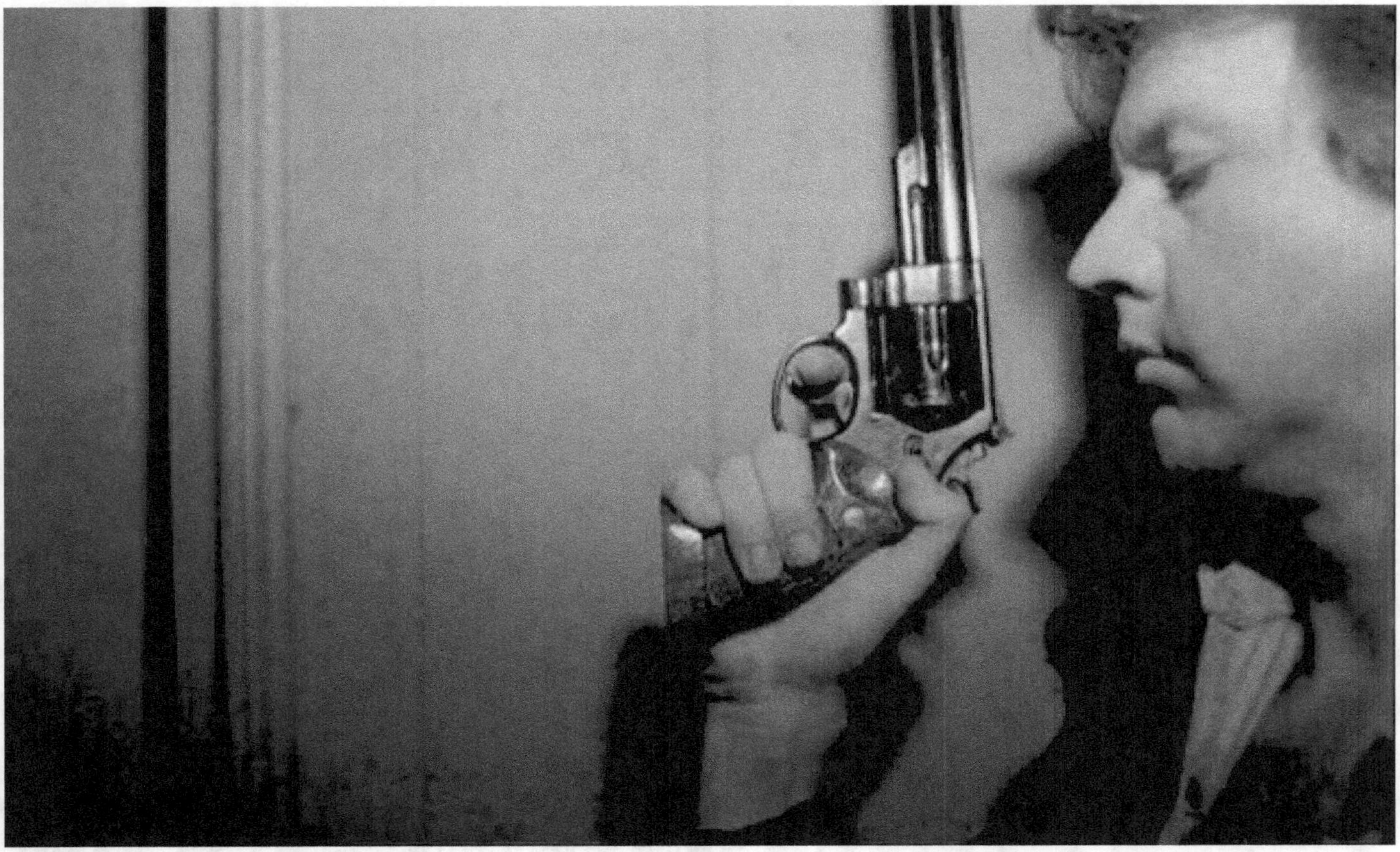

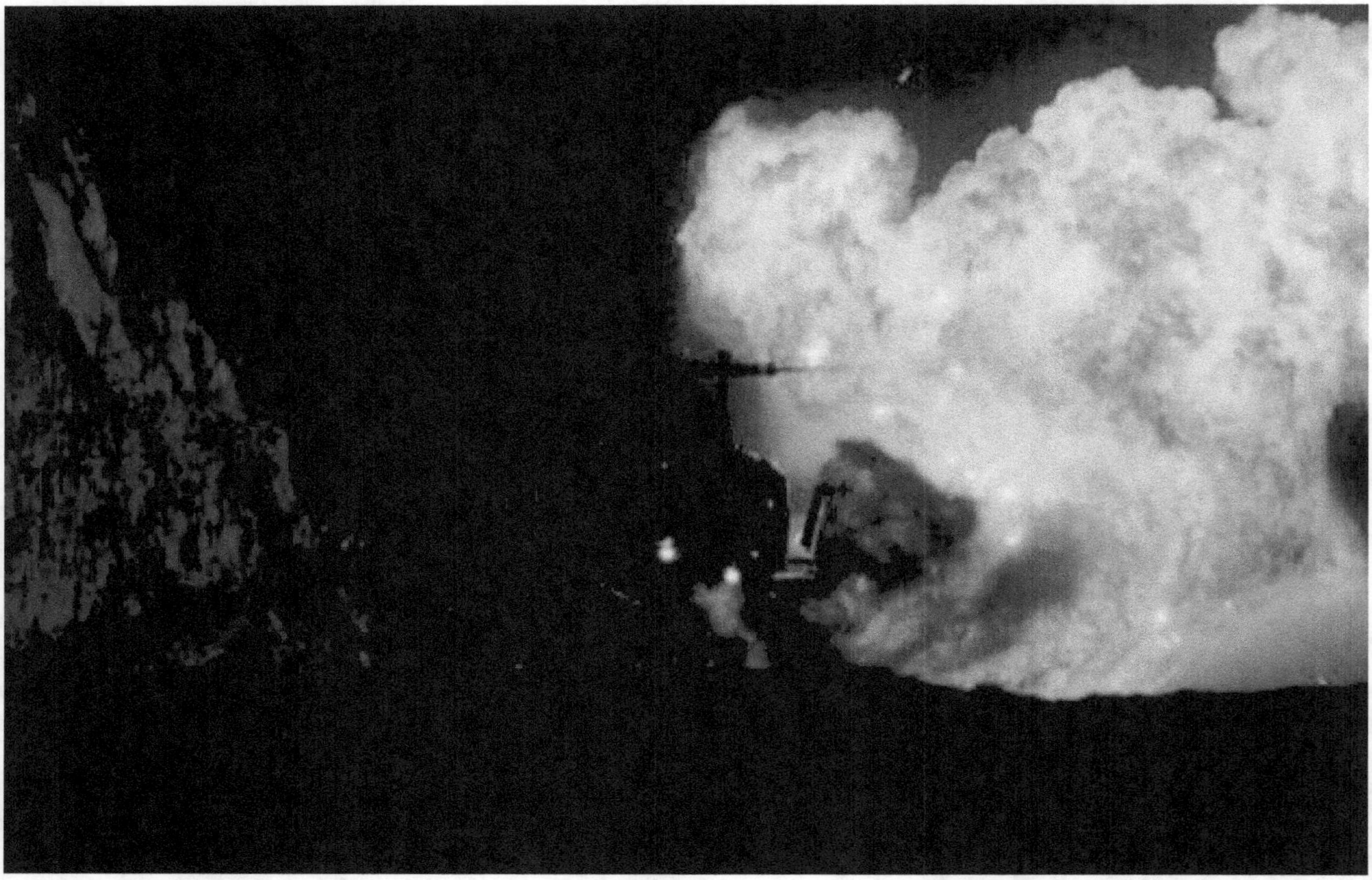

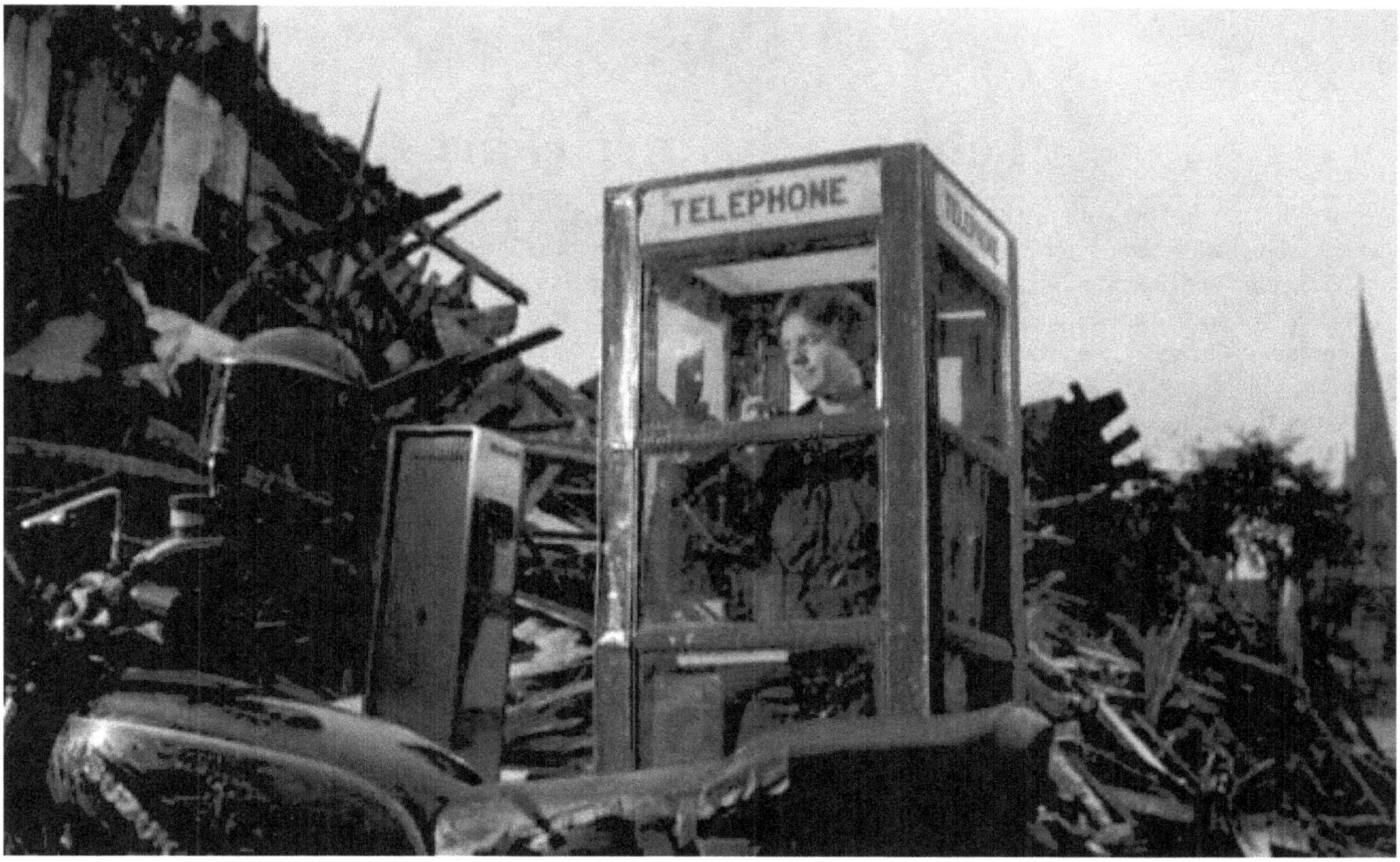

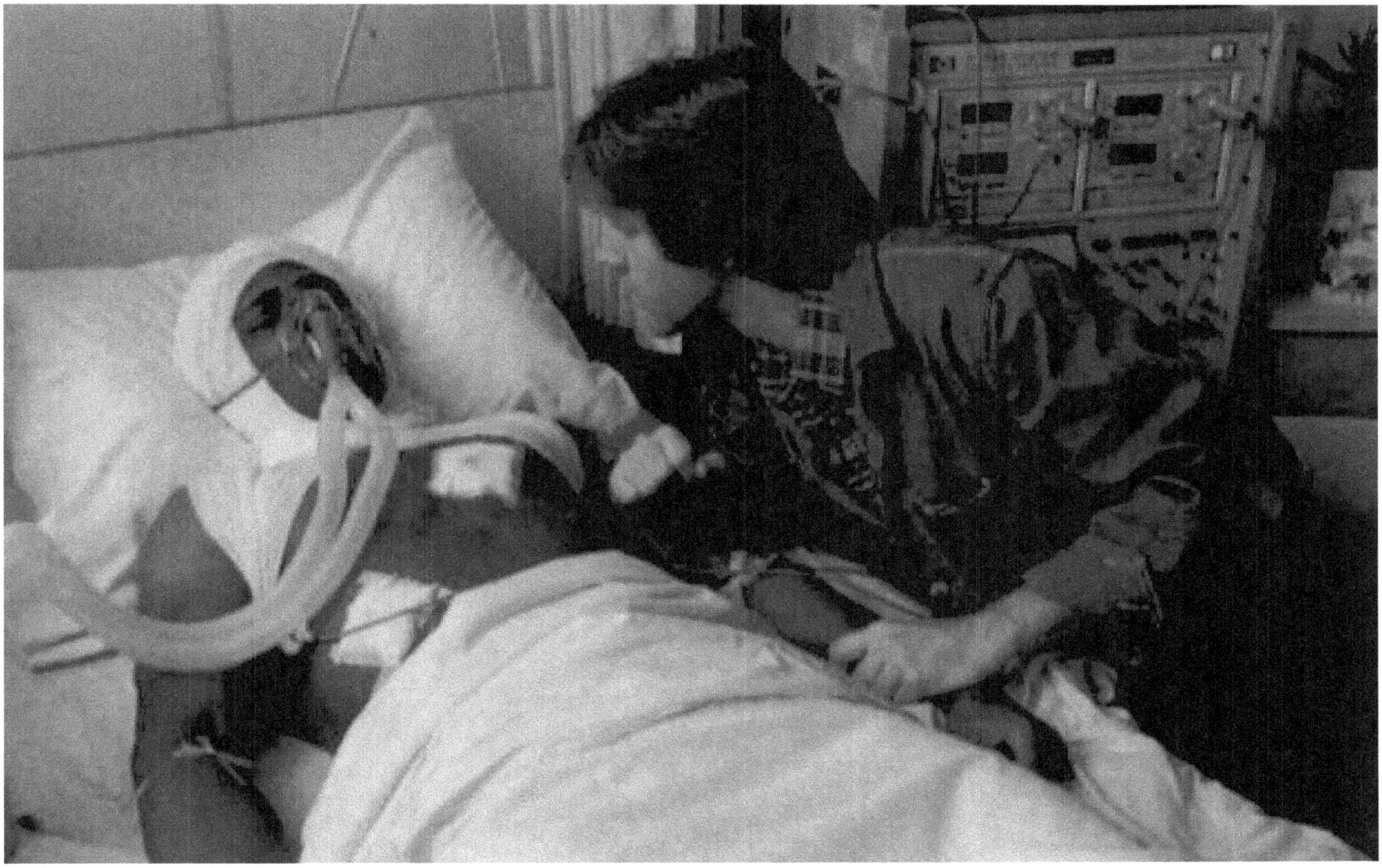

# Leonard Shapiro (Part I)

Born in Brooklyn, New York in 1947 Leonard Shapiro is a seasoned industry veteran. After working at Avco Embassy for many years, he formed Shapiro Entertainment, which then became Shapiro Glickenhaus Entertainment (SGE). The boom of VHS, plus the partnership with cult-director-turned-luxury-car-designer James Glickenhaus and producer Alan Solomon led to a tremendous library of some 76 films, directed by cult filmmakers such as William Lustig, Frank Henenlotter, Christian Ingvordsen and James Glickenhaus himself. Leonard Shapiro is widely respected and beloved by countless colleagues in the business. Never missing a beat since SGE's shutdown, Shapiro has served on the IFTA board of directors, has spent 14 years teaching film production and distribution for the UCLA Extension program, and is currently President and COO of Good Deed Entertainment, an independent studio with several films under its belt.

**Stephen:** It's Sunday April 26, 2015 (in) Calabasas, California. A beautiful—

**Lenny:** At Marmalade...

**Stephen:** ...at Marmalade Café with Lenny Shapiro, the one, the only, the legend. In his own jeans/genes.

**Lenny:** Drinking, what are these?

**Stephen:** These are Bloody Marys, so far... And so we're going to get started. So here we go, Lenny, all right...

**Lenny:** I just want to back up one thing on books. So it was interesting, like about ten days ago the CEO/Founder, Scott Donley, at my new company...

**Stephen:** ...Good Deed Entertainment...

**Lenny:** Right, (he) says to me, "Lenny you should do a book on the history of the industry. You started in the sixties, in the mid-sixties, in the entertainment business. You've been in it for fifty years. And there's fifty years of changes of technology, changes of marketing and distribution techniques. You taught at UCLA for fourteen years on all these changes right, can you do an outline of each ten years since you lived it in marketing and distribution more than anything else, and then into acquisitions in your own company, can you write the fifty years, every ten years, of the changes?" So what I did, Steve, was I wrote it out and made a blueprint of it and I used it when I was a guest speaker recently at a UCLA class. So, up on the PowerPoint was every ten years all the changes for fifty years. You know, so, it was very cool...

**Stephen:** I'd like to read that.

**Lenny:** It's basic but very cool there's nothing in there that you don't know, but it was, for new students to know the progression of the technology and the changes. Anyway, I wanted to say that.

**Stephen:** All right here we go, Lenny... Question one: In what time interval were you Vice President of Acquisitions and Marketing for AVCO Embassy Pictures? Was it before you partnered with James Glickenhaus?

**Lenny:** Yes.

**Stephen:** Ok. What period of time was that?

**Lenny:** From 19...uh...... *(pauses, thinking)* I was at AVCO Embassy Pictures moving up the ladder for 13 years. My last job there was Vice President of Acquisitions and Marketing Services. And that was from 1969 to 1982.

**Stephen:** In 1987 Shapiro Entertainment transformed into Shapiro Glickenhaus Entertainment and you started with a handful of employees. You had worked with James Glickenhaus before, back to the year 1976, is this correct?

**Lenny:** Yes.

**Stephen:** What did you work with him on?

**Lenny:** When I was at AVCO Embassy as Head of Acquisitions I acquired the film [THE] EXTERMINATOR, that Jim uh..., the domestic rights for EXTERMINATOR, the foreign rights were handled by a company named J & M. The first names of Julia and Michael who owned their own company. And Patrick Wachsberger who now is the Chairman of Lionsgate, he was part of J & M at that time.

**Stephen:** Believe me I didn't write this next question, Marco wrote it, thank you Marco *(sarcastic laugh)*. All right, do you remember the hiring of Stephen A. Roberts in 1985? Be honest, be honest.

**Lenny:** All I remember is that there were three partners who started Shapiro Entertainment at that time. And the three partners were Kelly Ross, Alan Solomon and myself. And Kelly Ross said I have this kid, from the AFM, bugging me. He wants an interview, and he wants to work with the company. Are we ready to hire somebody to do everything: to be an office manager, to do marketing, to do delivery? You know there were a million areas that we were scrambling in. And the background, and I did look at the resume, and the background looked fantastic with USC and all the other information. And then, I think, then Steve came in for an interview, but I had already made up my mind that we needed somebody and this sounded good. I don't think I had to do anything else other than to say, "You're hired." Is that correct Steve?

**Stephen:** Absolutely!
Everything he just said. Ok, nice job Lenny thank you. It's a little weird hearing you talk about me while I'm sitting right here. Alright, so question four, you talk about yourself as a businessman - do you like working with so many creative people a lot or is it stressful and annoying sometimes?

**Lenny:** I came from a company where I coordinated acquisitions with marketing, with sales, with the lawyers with the finance people... when I got into that whole world and I had the opportunity, after they were sold and a lot of changes were made on the new company that bought them, I had the opportunity to go on my own. Or maybe you could say I was forced to go on my own, but I did have the contacts in distribution and marketing and acquisitions and it was at the same time very much a lucky situation where video technology and [the] video market was starting to open up.
And that was the biggest boom of all time

for independent companies. Prior to that and after that there was no bigger boom than 1982 to 1995 in the video market because it was new revenue, new technology, new players in every country in the world. And if you could acquire product, and market product, which was what a new company would do, especially a new company without financing, that was a bonanza that you could never ever duplicate. It was also a false confidence that you would get as a film company because you thought it was going to go on like this forever... which the marketplace changed technology-wise and where product gets distributed and what gets theatrical and what doesn't, and what gets VOD and what doesn't. So it was a changing marketplace, but, prior to that it was a bonanza for any company that thought they were a distributor internationally, domestically... there were just a million ways to go and a million deals and opportunities to benefit from.

**Stephen:** Specifically regarding creative people; when you work with creative people...do you like that or not like that?

**Lenny:** I was more in the marketing, distribution, the deal-making side of it. I had two partners that were in the selling and the creative side a little bit. Of course in the marketing/distribution you have to also know a little bit about what you're selling, what the creative, what the marketplace wants. So our biggest objective was, what is the marketplace looking for, who are the players who could bring that to us...for a price. Because we had zero capital to finance films. So everything was dealing with producers on a one-on-one basis. All over Canada, many, many films coming from Canada. All over the United States where we had the distribution potential and the distribution channels to get pictures into the marketplace. Alan Solomon, who was the Head of Foreign, had all the foreign contacts to sell our films overseas. We had a great in-house staff, like Steve Roberts on the servicing, with the great memories of Steve going through that process, and everyone that worked for the company growing as I was learning and growing at the same time, as Alan was, as Kelly Ross the other partner was, we could find product, we could get it to the marketplace.

My concern was closing the deal and getting the material as good as we can and getting the rights sold worldwide. I handled most of the domestic, Alan handled all of the foreign and it was growth and learning at the same time.

**Stephen:** Throughout your career you have been involved in the financial aspects of film production and distribution. Even though you always worked with films as financial products, do you have some personal love of movies, of cinema?

**Lenny:** Can I be frank on this?

**Stephen:** Well I would prefer you be Lenny, but, if you want to be Frank too *(laughs)* – that's a joke.

**Lenny:** I was interested in the deal making process and how to make money for the company.

I really wasn't... because the films that I

loved are not films that I bought or made. When I was at AVCO I was involved with PHANTASM, PROM NIGHT, THE EX-TERMINATOR, THE HOWLING... you know many, many hit independent films that got theatrical releases and got into the market-place with theatrical.

When the '80's started, you didn't necessarily have to get into the market with theatrical you know when the video started hitting, but back at AVCO I never went to see these films. I wasn't a horror fan. I wasn't a low-budget exploitation fan. But I had an eye for what the marketplace wanted in these films. And if there were kids in the film, there was horror, there were a couple of actors in the film like a PROM NIGHT with Jamie Lee Curtis and a very good producer that I was very close with at that time, Peter Simpson...I went after those films because I felt we could make money on those films. They were all, the deal making process, even PROM NIGHT which turned out to be a bonanza for AVCO-Embassy, we made a lot of money in theatrical, video, television, foreign. And we got the picture for a very low guarantee that wasn't due for a year ... so it's all the deal-making philosophy. I had not only been marketing these films but I was also doing the deals on these films. So, I wore those two hats, at different times, with a whole group of people, the lawyers, the sales people, the foreign people. So I got my training at AVCO to be involved in bringing in product and understanding the business side of it in every single area. And that was my expertise that I learned with a lot of very, very good people and associates at AVCO.

**Stephen**: Good training for running your own company eventually, wouldn't you say?

**Lenny**: Exactly, exactly.

**Stephen**: You have joined many sets in person, on location - do you have any anecdotal stories, you would like to share with our readers?

**Lenny**: My role wasn't really to really know what was going on, on the sets. Certainly on our own films that we were producing, I certainly dropped by to see how things were going. I certainly went to see rough cuts and how the post was going but basically with the people we had in the company, and after Jim came aboard, you know I took a back seat to all of that. I did show up because I was very interested in how it was going, but I did not put any of my creative thoughts or muscle into it. I let the filmmakers do their thing. I let our company do their thing. We had very good people around the picture[s]. Again, some of these pictures in those times, in Canada, we did a lot of deals in Canada, we were not really the creative force in it. We were just going to distribute and handle the rights without a financial investment in the production budget.

Now we brought money, we promised what we could bring to the table, we did pre-sales, we had foreign companies like Gaga in Japan, and companies in Korea, and companies in the UK that would advance us money knowing that the film was getting made, because we had a very good reputation. As we built our reputation in the independent marketplace through exploit-ation commercial films that were great for video, we would ask for, I remember in different cases, for money to give to the producers so that they could finance their films so we gave guarantees. We put up some money as we got a little stronger, and we used our foreign sales ability to finance some of these films. So there was no perfect formula, but, we did not really, other than the overall concept of the film, we didn't get involved that much in the production-creative.

**Stephen:** Asked about the most difficult scene he ever shot, when Jim Glickenhaus was interviewed, his response was the shoot-out in SHAKEDOWN. Were you on the set for that scene? Do you remember it? Do you remember anything about that situation?

**Lenny:** The picture was shot in New York City for 51 straight days, we closed down, these are the things I remember Steve, we closed down 42nd Street for one full week from 12 at night, midnight, until 5 in the morning – 42nd Street was 100% ours with shootouts, with the buses, and car crashes...

**Stephen:** And the hookers and the deviants...

**Lenny:** All we had to do was feed anybody that showed up - we had a very big budget for catering. And there were a lot of action scenes, and I stayed for a week, but I don't...and there were just major, major action scenes all through the shoot. I did stay on a couple of days on the 42nd Street shoot. I remember the DP, John...do you remember the DP? Look it up... [the DP on SHAKEDOWN aka BLUE JEAN COP was Mr. John Lindley]. The DP is a big DP now, that this was his first important film. He went on to do major, major action pictures for studios. He did a brilliant job as his first opportunity to do a theatrical level budget. And so the footage that we got from the DP, who was brilliant and turned out to be a superstar, so there were spectacular scenes. But I don't remember any specific shoot out. I remember the bus crashing...

**Stephen:** The rollercoaster.

**Lenny:** The rollercoaster stuff was fantastic; I wasn't there for that. But, so we did a lot of firsts for an independent film. That really was the film that started the company and transitioned it from Shapiro Entertainment to Shapiro Glickenhaus. That was the picture that was part of the transition where Jim wanted to come in and own the film with Shapiro Entertainment, change the name of the company to Shapiro Glickenhaus and that was our first film.

Basically it was a 13 million dollar budget, 51 day shoot, Peter Weller and Sam Elliot, action scenes galore, great tight script, great...Boyce Harman Jr. produced the show, and he was always Jim's Producer, on THE EXTERMINATOR and other projects. And it was fully financed by investors that came in with Shapiro Glickenhaus, with us, and it was a major action film that got a Universal release in domestic...

**Stephen:** Universal Pictures the studio?

**Lenny:** Yes. And that deal was made after the film was in production, and we made huge sales in foreign. So, it was a great way to kick off not only a relationship...a full relationship with Jim, which I already had from his other films, but, it put us [Shapiro Glickenhaus Ent.] on the map.

**Stephen:** Continuing with the thread of early Shapiro Glickenhaus films and ones that may have gone on to financial success, which films have been the best-selling titles at SGE? Is MOONTRAP among them for example?

**Lenny:** Absolutely.

**Stephen:** Can you talk a little about some of the other ones?

**Lenny:** MOONTRAP was a picture that we put in some financing on. At that time, we were starting to finance films. We guaranteed a certain amount with the Producers that had a special effects company in Michigan, in Detroit. And they were bringing in the effects and some of the money. And we were bringing in the rest, and we were also using their special effects – a sci-fi film with action, a couple of good names like...

**Stephen:** Walter Koenig, Bruce Campbell...

**Lenny:** ...that were very good independent film names, at that time, on a sci-fi film. And with those names and with our foreign positioning, and foreign relationships we were able to start to promote the film campaign-wise and position the film in foreign with some of the buyers which turned out excellently. The overall budget at the end of the day cost a million four right? Because the Producers ran out of money and couldn't meet their obligation we took over all the financing, and restructured the deal and all the marketing and everything else. And the person I'm sitting here with, that's doing the interview, was all over this film from day one, and that's where staff comes into play, where even though there were owners of the company... but we did rely on all our people and they did have an opportunity to push the buttons and make films work and get films delivered to the marketplace, and support in any way they wanted. There were no like real "rules", I don't think, Steve could answer that better, but, I don't think there were any rules where there was any ground that you couldn't go into and participate in. Whether it was sales, marketing, trailers, Steve did all those things, and at the end of the day he used all those areas to become the superstar he is today.

**Stephen:** All right, we're cutting you off now. Hang on a second, I'm going to pause just for a second, I want to change the umbrella, it's getting sunny.

**Lenny:** You do have to do some creative [editing] on this. But I'll give you the essence of it which you'll like.

**Stephen:** All right, this is an unscripted question... Lenny just wants to give me the secret of... what is it?

**Lenny:** Of everything that we're talking about.

**Stephen:** All right. Bring it on.

**Lenny:** Because there was new ground for everyone in the company, because there were new relationships for everyone that worked for SGE, when SGE closed down, wound down, in 1996 I went on to produce a few films, consult with several companies and start another company with some investors, while all that was going on, all the people that worked at SGE or Shapiro Entertainment have remained friends. Once a year we have a reunion. There's total camaraderie and great memories that we're talking about now, everybody went on with their own careers. And what I'm most proud of is that they all became very successful in their own endeavors after SGE. Sonoko Sakai who will be interviewed became (employed by a) major, major Japanese company, Gaga. After those successes, she went on to Nippon Herald to become the head of Nippon Herald Acquisitions and Marketing, Production Services.

**Stephen:** She also produced some films.

**Lenny:** Yeah, she produced some films and was the person most involved in convincing Nippon Herald to buy the LORD OF THE RINGS series, all three of them. First one with an option on the other two books. LORD OF THE RINGS became the number one grosser of all time in Japan due to Sonoko buying it and having the deal on all three of them.

**Stephen:** There are other examples of people going on and having big careers as well. For example, John Alexander?

**Lenny:** Yeah.

**Stephen:** Who also agreed to be interviewed.

**Lenny:** Yes, I'm going to talk a little about, I'll just mention the names Steve and you can fill in everything they've done. And I certainly know everything they've done. But the friendships, the camaraderie, the root interest in everybody being successful, for all of these people that worked there at that time, it's still a very close union. And John Alexander, as Steve mentioned, comes to mind, who became the President of Hallmark International, he's going to be interviewed. Sonoko is going to be interviewed. Steve Roberts who became the head of marketing and creative advertising at Universal that now has his own independent company, doing major, major studio films, credits that go on forever. Nadia [Bruce-Rawlings] with her own marketing / sales company. Stephanie Denton who was the President of Lakeshore, a major, major independent company she became the President of International on...

**Stephen:** Also going to be interviewed...

**Lenny:** ...yes hugely successful, hugely successful. On and on and on, so, my biggest claim to fame is the people that I worked with at the company. The energies and the fun that we kind of remember today. And all of them going on to be successful and wanting to stay in touch with each other. And wanting to get together once a year and wanting to know what each other is doing. To me, way more than the whole analysis of everything going on, to me, that is my 'claim to fame' way more than any other accomplishment.

**Stephen:** Well said. Ok, now here's another question.

**Lenny:** Ok.

**Stephen:** All right. MCBAIN.

**Lenny:** Right.

**Stephen:** MCBAIN was the most expensive production in the history of SGE, is this correct? And if so, and even if it wasn't, can you talk briefly about the experience of making that particular film MCBAIN?

**Lenny:** Up until MCBAIN there had been no disagreements between the production and the creative side that Jim was running, and the marketing/distribution side that I was running. There's no question that Jim had the creative control, and I remember that I had problems with the script. I'm just being totally honest. Sometimes the time a picture goes from creative into a preparation timetable into a pre-production timetable, sometimes you can't stop the momentum of a film going, and I think this film hit the marks where... the creative and the marketing weren't coming together on this like it had on other films. Like on MANIAC COP, like SHAKEDOWN, like the Henenlotter films. And this one, there was some concern, and at the end of the day those concerns came to be a reality where the picture didn't perform well. So, at what point could you make the changes, at what point could you change directions? I had my concerns, but, I never did enough to stop the momentum.

**Stephen:** Ok, let's move on. After TIMEMASTER, SGE was shut down for personal reasons. Have you continued to work with any colleagues from SGE? If so, whom?

**Lenny:** I stayed in touch with everybody. Certainly Nadia controlling the library for the Glickenhaus family...

**Stephen:** That's Nadia Bruce-Rawlings right?

**Lenny:** Yes. The Glickenhaus family put up all the money and was entitled to recoupment from the library. So Nadia and Alan Solomon, who was the Head of Sales, and Nadia, who for many years worked for Alan, as assistant General Sales Manager, so first Alan and then Nadia, kept all the films in the marketplace both in Video on Demand, international re-issues, there's a couple of classic films in there that we had bought and got made like RED SCORPION which was a huge budget...

**Stephen:** We're going to get to RED SCORPION in a minute.

**Lenny:** Ok. So the library had value, and Nadia oversaw that. So, Nadia, from that standpoint I stayed in touch with. Steve Roberts from the marketing and trailers and things that I may need outside from my new company or new ventures that I'm involved in, I called on Steve. John Alexander who ran sales for Hallmark, I called on John. And they were all very comfortable in helping in any way they could. They all looked at me a little bit as their mentor while they were growing in the industry, and I looked at them as personal friends. Frank Isaac went on to run a couple of major insurance companies, who was the Head of our Production...

**Stephen:** Completion bond companies right?

**Lenny:** Yeah. And I look at all these people as part of SGE, Shapiro Entertainment, part of my great, great experience; great, great relationships. And maybe during the time when everything was happening they became very, very close friends.

**Stephen:** Compared to many other action films from the 1980s, SGE was non-partisan when it came to political statements in their films, generally speaking. But RED SCORPION was highly controversial in the media. Thinking back on RED SCORPION, and its release, what comes to your mind first?

**Lenny:** What comes to mind first is knowing that picture was available to be purchased, as a picture in production that the bond company took over. And I knew all the people in the bond company. And I knew the director very well, Joe Zito, on a personal basis. I strictly looked at it as an opportunity for SGE to make some money on the distribution of the film. Because of the asking price and what Alan and I were estimating the foreign value was and the domestic opportunities that it could bring to the company, it was a very big investment on a very interesting deal structure and worth the risk. But I was strictly looking at it as the potential for marketplace sales. I never even thought of or looked at it as a political issue.

**Stephen:** In 1996, you founded Root Beer Films, a consulting company, specializing in different aspects of marketing and distribution of independent films. Can you talk a little bit about Root Beer Films and the films it dealt with?

**Lenny:** The first film it dealt with was a picture called TRIGGER HAPPY. And Alan [Solomon] was an independent, who kept overseeing the SGE library, and started acquiring other films for his own company Amsell, and working with his son Elliot. And so the deal on that first picture was: a friend of mine came to me, Richard Dreyfuss, wanted to do his own film. He had just made MR. HOLLAND'S OPUS. And his production partner was Judy James, and they wanted to go after actors, and they wanted to do a film with a longtime, lifetime friend of Richard's, Larry Bishop, Joey Bishop's son, who he went to high school with.

**Stephen:** And what was that movie called?

**Lenny:** TRIGGER HAPPY or retitled MAD DOG TIME. It was a good independent. My friend who brought it to me said they needed two and half million dollars in pre-sales out of foreign. It was going to have a major cast, besides Richard coming off MR. HOLLAND'S OPUS, and there were several 'wish list' cast names mentioned, all 'A' level actors. And Richard was promising that the actors would come in for scale and own the film with Richard as the production company and the producer of the film, and Larry Bishop the producer/writer and director of the film. The actors would come in as partners, but work for scale. Those deals are very rare; they very rarely happen today. But Richard coming off a worldwide hit at the top of his career, international hit, American, United States hit, I think it did 70 million box office in the United States and at least that much overseas. On an independent film, that's considered a break-through hit. So he wanted to star in this film, produce it; he wanted his friend Larry Bishop to direct and write the script. Larry had already written several very, very good scripts that were in the marketplace. And my role as one of the Executive Producers was to bring in 2 and ½ million in pre-sales. And I partnered with Alan Solomon and his new company. And Alan said let me go to the market with the names that Richard is saying he can get, and bring in pre-sales at that level, and then we'll go from there. Because the budget was going to be a controlled budget since the actors weren't getting salaries.

**Stephen:** Right, right. Ok, great, so that was the first major production out of Root Beer and you did others beyond that. We'll talk about some of those in a moment. At UCLA you taught independent film production and distribution for 14 years. Which year did you start this work, and how did it happen at all? And also, did you enjoy working with students, and do you enjoy working with young talent in general? So when did you start teaching the UCLA class?

**Lenny:** I want to say around 1990.

**Stephen:** How did it happen? How did you find out about it?

**Lenny:** One of the courses that was being given there was a producing course by one of the top professors at UCLA, Myrl Schreibman, who did a book on directing and a book on producing that got published.

**Stephen:** And did you guest-speak at his (Myrl Schreibman's) class?

**Lenny:** Yes.

**Stephen:** And that's how you found out about it?

**Lenny:** Yeah. So he said, "Lenny, you have to come in the last week of [class]." I had met him earlier at AVCO Embassy Pictures, and he had produced some films in the 70's. So anyway, he had this theory that any producer making a film today in a tough challenging marketplace has to know the end results about marketing and distribution after they learn all the nuts and bolts about producing. So he asked me to come in as his guest speaker...

**Stephen:** To show how it really all worked in the real world?

**Lenny:** So I had the last week of his class, I think it was a UCLA Extension Class, and I had the last week to come in and talk about what happens when you finish your film. What is the marketplace looking for? How do you navigate the marketplace?

**Stephen:** When the dream is dreamed, what do you do then?

**Lenny:** Right. And he thought that was really important that they hear somebody talk about an independent world after you make your first film. And what you have to look at while you're making it, after you make it, and who are the players and what are the opportunities to get your film picked up and seen and marketed and so forth. So I gave that class because I had experience in all those areas, and so I did that for the first year and the second year. And then he comes up with a brilliant idea, since he was key faculty at UCLA, he comes up with the 'brilliant' idea, "Lenny why don't you give a marketing / distribution / acquisitions / finance class as the second part of my class on producing." So I did that for a couple of years. I started with a class with a syllabus that took it from part one of producing to part two of marketing/distribution and financing, and then he stopped giving his class after a couple of years, and I continued on for the next ten or twelve years. And, why it was fun and what made it interesting is I came up with a formula that was really every day practice. Guest speakers because I'm not that great a public speaker, but I always wanted my friends to come in as guest speakers in marketing, in foreign sales, in the banks and the finance. Every way that I put together a film, I wanted those people as experts in marketing research and marketing to come in and talk about their areas while the students are working on their own project; doing a business/marketing plan on their own project that they would pitch to the class at the end of the semester. And during the semester, they will meet with all these people to work on their marketing plan, and when they do pitch the class at the end, it would be to the acquisition executives at the different independent companies. So it gave incentive for the class members to work on their plans. Each film that got presented at the class had a producer that wanted to produce a film, it had a creative person, it had a marketing person, and it had an administrative / finance person. So those four people would put their plan together. It took me a couple years to figure out that that formula is a good way for people to learn the business for people wanting to know every aspect of the independent business. And then, since I was a member of the American Film Marketing Association [AFMA] where all the independent pictures got marketed and sold and presented, I was on the Board of Directors of the AFMA, so I was able to get these kids from the class all into the AFM [the American Film Market] for one day toward the end of the AFM, one day for free, with all the marketing material and the bags they give out, and have total access to every company and all the screenings. And one thing I thought was important to set up, because in ten weeks you can't learn the whole business in ten weeks, unless you are really functioning properly. So I would take four meetings at the Market with the entire class, you know usually 20 to 30 people showed up for the free badge and the free day at the Market because AFM was a big deal for the independents. And so I would take four companies where I knew the owners, and I knew the people, and since it was towards the end of the Market they would spend time, and I could get the whole class in there, and basically I always used this terminology about students learning and filmmakers learning, all you could do as a teacher is sharpen their instincts. So when they came out to the AFM toward the end of the full year of the class, their instincts all of a sudden clicked in. I could see the faces when the different executives of the film companies were talking. They didn't get it during the whole class, but the instincts when they started to hear it in reality—

**Stephen:** The dots would start to connect?

**Lenny:** ...it was amazing. And that was my...then I felt, okay I'm not—this is not for nothing, I'm helping these kids out. They kind of enjoy learning. They're enjoying coming to the Market. They're enjoying meeting people in the industry. And it's not just go sit in the classroom and be told what to do, they're working on a project, they're meeting people, their instincts on what phase of the business they like or don't like [are being honed], that was my gratitude, and it really came home in their analysis of the class.

**Stephen:** Right. And was one of the guest speakers Stephan Manpearl during that period?

**Lenny:** Yes.

**Stephen:** And doesn't Stephan now teach a version of what you started?

**Lenny:** Yeah.

**Stephen:** The next level of that and do you sometimes speak at that class for Stephan?

**Lenny:** Yes. I'm now the guest speaker!

**Stephen:** Well as it turns out I was the guest speaker in his second week.

**Lenny:** I know that! I know that!! I'm a little reluctant to do it because I'm not as up-to-date on everything as maybe some of the speakers he would have, but he always calls on me to come in. And more of an overview type of thing. But Stephan was a guest speaker in my class on marketing and research, and he's playing it more of a syllabus of the Studio Game.

**Stephen:** Marketing for the Global Marketplace is how he plays it.

**Lenny:** Yeah, and more studio players.

**Stephen:** You were involved in the movies DAHMER and GACY as an Executive Producer. Do you think the fascination with serial killers is an American phenomenon, or were these films, both of which were about legendary serial killers, sold worldwide?

**Lenny:** Maybe a touch more American, but it certainly had worldwide appeal on DAHMER with the actor being Jeremy Renner who became a superstar, and that was his first film. But the marketplace dictated that film to get made. There were a couple of serial killer films done for video before DAHMER that went straight to video and hit a giant home run. Two or three of them. I've forgotten the serial killer's names, but they were as famous serial killers of their time as Dahmer was. DAHMER [the film] was a lot more successful than GACY [the film]. Basically they were low budget films with good young filmmakers that captured the story, and there were big buyers who wanted to come in the video world.

**Stephen:** Let me ask the question in a different way, the typically formula for how the indie movies breakout, and sometimes the studio movies too, is that 50% of the gross is domestic and 50% of it is foreign, that's a general thumbnail formula. It's different for different movies, of course. Like the Bond movies do huge business overseas, and they do great business domestically [USA domestic box office], but they do more overseas than domestically, for example. So, in the case of both of those serial killer movies, let's just take the first one for example, DAHMER, would you say it was about ½ as successful total gross, half as successful US versus foreign?

**Lenny:** Two thirds to three quarter domestic, a quarter foreign.

**Stephen:** I see. So it was more successful domestically than foreign?

**Lenny:** Yes.

**Stephen:** So the fascination with the serial killer thing, if you use that as a measuring stick, you could say perhaps the audience's serial killer fascination in movies is an American phenomenon?

**Lenny:** Yeah.

**Stephen:** Five years ago, in 2010, Alan Solomon - one of the key people of SGE - passed away. Were you in contact with Mr. Solomon after SGE? You've mentioned already the Dreyfuss movie as one example of doing business with him.

**Lenny:** I was always interested in whatever Alan was doing. He was a key reason for Shapiro Entertainment, and then he was my first partner, with Kelly Ross, at Shapiro Entertainment and then after that Alan went on to start his own company. We had a couple of films that we had done under Alan's banner together, and I always, if I had any foreign questions, or if he had any questions on deals — I think we collaborated, stayed friends and respected each other with his new company and everything he was doing.

**Stephen:** In 2013 you became President and COO of Good Deed Entertainment. Do you still work every day? Can you please describe a regular day at work?

**Lenny:** My hours, I do come in everyday, we have a nice young creative team. The owner of the company works from out-of-state on other businesses, but he comes in every other week. I run the day-to-day. We've made three films since we started. And we're in development on several others. And we're looking to acquire finished films. We're also in development with a big, big Canadian production company which has a very good subsidy and a very good way to make films. All people that I've known for years, trying to tap in on some of those relationships that really started with the Shapiro Entertainment and then Shapiro Glickenhaus eras. These are people that are raising money for productions and working with us.

**Stephen:** So is it fair to say that you're still working because you want to work? And you enjoy the work?

**Lenny:** Yes.

**Stephen:** How much difference is there between your contemporary work, the work you're doing today, and the way you did it during the days of SGE? You know it ended twenty years ago, right? But it began in '81, '82. So, how has it changed?

**Lenny:** Technology, the marketplace conditions, what pictures are made today for. Basically it's the video not being as effective as it was back then. And the digital, VOD internet market not replacing the revenues that the video brought in to the Independents.

**Stephen:** So it [digital/VOD] is a new revenue stream but it's not the same dollar…

**Lenny:** Right. And even for the studios it has changed their makeup on how they make films. Because if you ask a studio, do they want to make a 30 or 40 million dollar film and spend 30 to 40 million dollars in marketing the film, is that riskier, or is making a 100 million dollar film with a brand name riskier? They're going to say the safeguard is the brand name, and the 100 million dollar film is more risk than a 30 million film than there is in the 100 million dollar brand. So everything's become tent pole, branding, major, major productions like the FURIOUS 7…

**Stephen:** The FAST & FURIOUS series.

**Lenny:** Yeah. They're up to probably $200 million dollar productions, but, $250, production budget on those, and that's less risky, because that's over a billion dollars and going strong in gross, that's less risky at $250 million dollar budget than a $40 million dollar film the experts will tell you. So, you take that down to the Independents, they now can't get into theatrical obviously. They can't get into VOD meaningfully. So they have to then adjust their budgets, adjust where the revenues are coming from, so, the math absolutely does not work anymore without subsidies, without production partners, without investors taking more risks. Because of the time in the '80's and '90's the video corrected any mistakes. So you could throw a dart at anything, which we did, and figure out a way how not to lose money. I can't say that today.

**Stephen:** There is not the safety net that there once was?

**Lenny:** Right.

**Stephen:** Back to your workday, or the way you work today, do you spend much time on business trips these days or do you work mostly out of your office locally?

**Lenny:** We work out of the office, but we're trying to expand, and we'd love to go to Cannes but the only way you'll go to Cannes is you have a couple of finished films and you're working with Sales

Agents. At Good Deed Entertainment we don't feel that we need our own foreign selling organization at this stage. Because it's really a mathematical figure that's...what's your overhead going to cost and what is a top, top foreign sales agent going to take in fees? So you have to evaluate...

**Stephen:** You're talking about your business model at Good Deed Entertainment?

**Lenny:** Right. Right. So you have to evaluate what is it going to cost a full operation in foreign with limited product? Or when do you push that button that you want to be into foreign sales where you're doing enough to cover your overhead? So we haven't reached that point yet, so I'm dealing with all the foreign sales agents on a 'one-off' basis.

**Stephen:** The focus in present times appears to not be on low-budget action movies like during the time of SGE. From an economical viewpoint, how much do you think has changed around genre films?

**Lenny:** I think there's very little change from the standpoint of genre films whether it be horror, action or sci-fi – good quality genre films with good filmmakers, bringing it in for a price ... the only difference now is the price is very, very critical. And you've still got to get the quality, which is also tough to marry up. But, if you can marry up those things, the independents are still most successful on a genre basis. And at a budget conscious basis. So much tougher – tougher to get the whole budget covered – but those are the goals that you have to try and go for.

**Stephen:** Over the years you've worked with more than 100 different companies in the film industry. All in all, do you like it better working with the majors or with the indies?

**Lenny:** I don't think there's any really "like" or "dislike" on that. I think it's very tough to get studio deals today. And get them to focus on an independent product, so, you're really pushed into a place where you have to work with the independents. When we had SGE rolling on all cylinders, our partner was Universal Home Video. So we had an output deal and a label deal with Universal Home Video. Like for instance, SGE had Universal, so it was a perfect relationship where we had the majors for video, we were a label deal, we were the only label deal that Universal had at the time. SGE would release basically one film a month with Universal...

**Stephen:** I think, just to digress on SGE Home Video for a second, the premiere release was RED SCORPION, followed by MOONTRAP and then I think THE WIZARD OF SPEED & TIME? And then there were a string of them.

**Lenny:** Yeah. It set up the brand of SGE as a home entertainment company, and then we moved on to Universal at some point during that period. I think it was a five-year relationship with Universal handling our home entertainment, which was hugely successful, hugely successful.

**Stephen:** Here's a 'retrospective' question: looking back 20+ years to the approximately 13 years that SEC/SGE was active, from

| | about 1982 to 1995 – '96 ... so that's fourteen years, so 1982 to 1996, what would you say it was that made SGE unique among the independent producer / distributors of indie movies of that particular era? What was different at SGE? |
|---|---|
| **Lenny**: | I really think if you look back and kind of like sum it up on what made it unique, and what made it different, and what made it work, I would have to say it's the people, the energies, the camaraderie and the caring of everyone in the company. Because when I look at all the people that we talked about in this interview, they're all hugely successful, they moved into huge careers – almost all of them. And they gathered their experiences and their camaraderie and their friendships, and they took it on to new levels, new opportunities.<br><br>And I would have to say having that group of people together at that time in the changing industry where the independents were really getting relevant -- I think it's the people, and it's hard to ever duplicate that. We all came together at a certain time and it was growing and learning together, so it wasn't [that] anybody had the answers, it was like "trial and error" and let's get better at what we do and grow with the situation. But it wasn't like there were any super-masterminds creating the situation, the marketplace created it. |
| **Stephen**: | After a career that has spanned decades and multiple specialties in the entertainment business, what would you say are the three most important things you've learned about this business? |
| **Lenny**: | There are two key words that I kind of use today, and I realized they were used back when I was making decisions and growing with the industry and the different companies I grew with. It was teamwork and the energies and the atmosphere of each of these individual companies. When they have it right, the companies grow and they do really well. When they don't have that energy and teamwork and camaraderie right at all levels of the company, at all levels, the middle and the higher levels, when that is not jelling, companies do not work. So what I learned is: be a team player and work with the talent around you and try and be part of making everybody better. |
| **Stephen**: | All right, those are the questions I have; now it's your turn. What do you want to add? |
| **Lenny**: | The only thing I'll add, and it really comes home to roost, is that in my whole career, and I guess it's the magic part of anybody's career, is the relationships that you build, the relationships that you remember and your friendships in the business. Because everything moves on and on and on but those things, I always treated that as really critically important because I needed very good people around me at all times to try and compete in the marketplace and somehow that seemed to work. So the friendships from my different companies that I grew up in all the way back to my early days I still know and stay engaged with the people |

that I worked with whether I see them every year or not. The camaraderie and the friendship and the years together. I never kind of lost that. So to me I take away from whatever I accomplished or didn't accomplish is the people I still know, remember, and can call on.

**Stephen**: Wonderful.

**Lenny**: I mean it's a little soapy, but it's kinda true...

---

**By Stephen A. Roberts, in person
in Calabasas, California at Marmalade Café
26April, 2015 - 07June, 2015 - 03July, 2015**

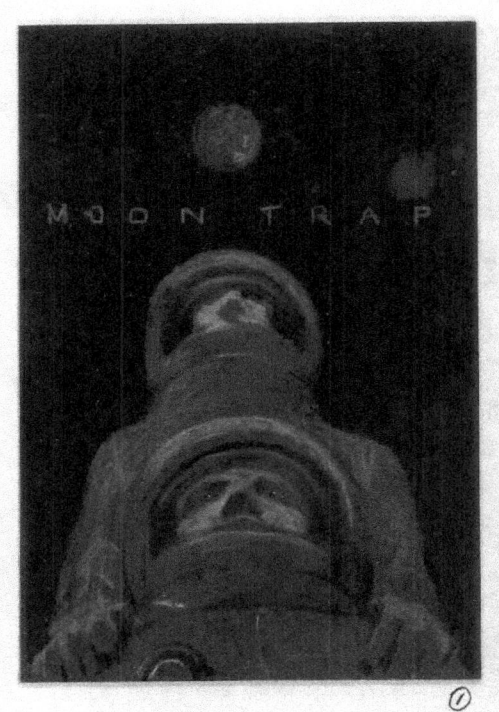

①

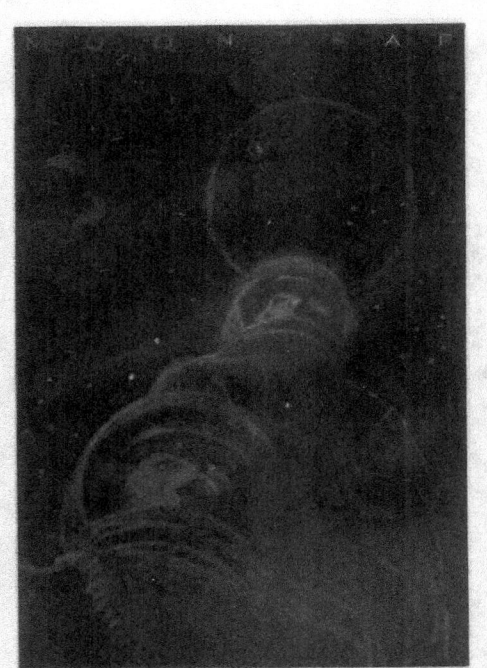

②

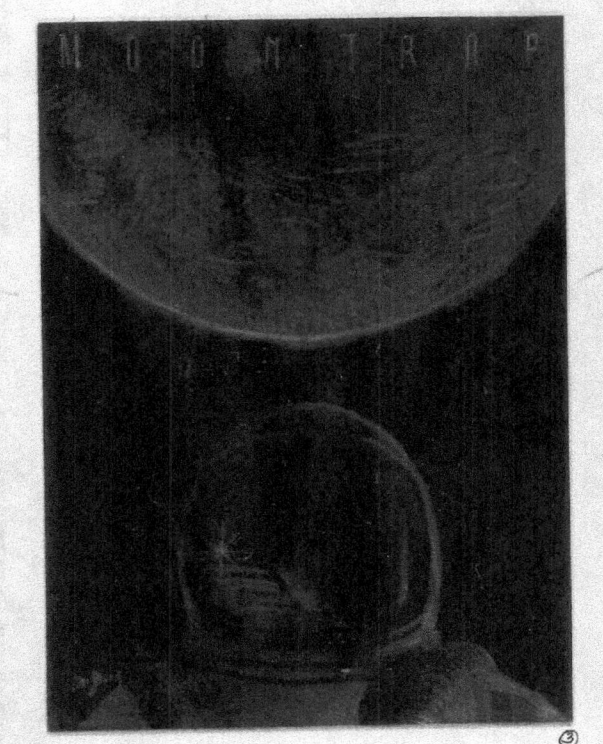

③

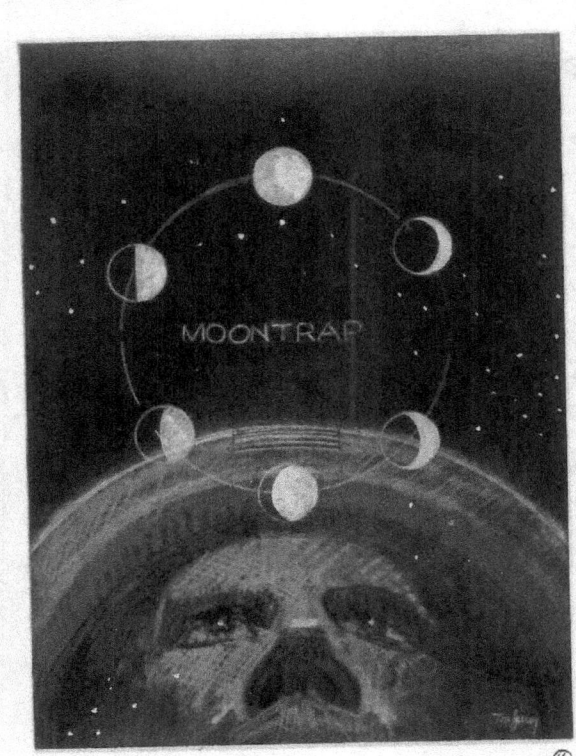

④

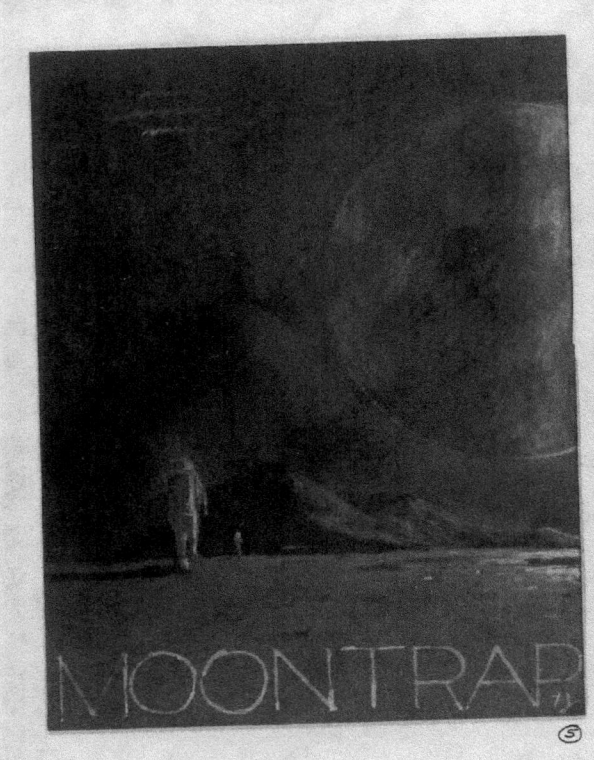

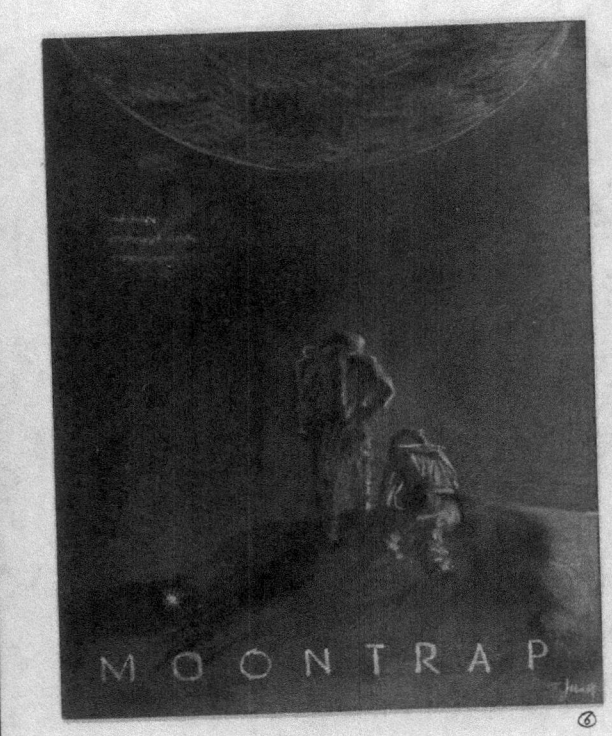

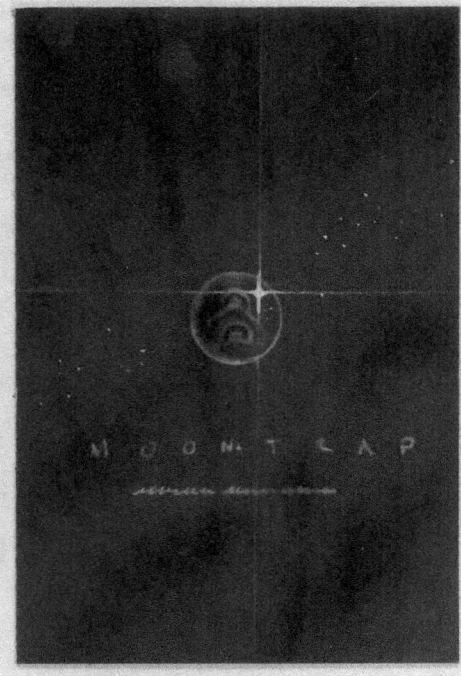

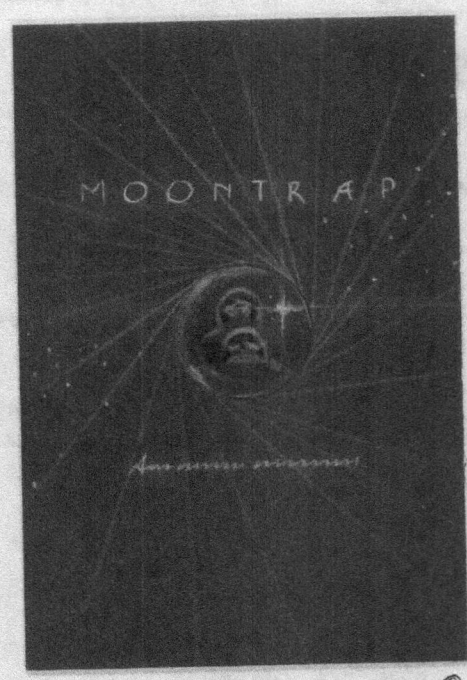

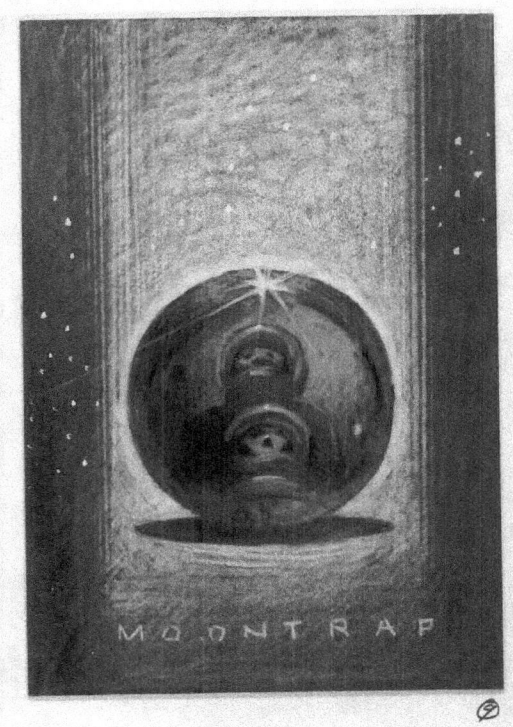
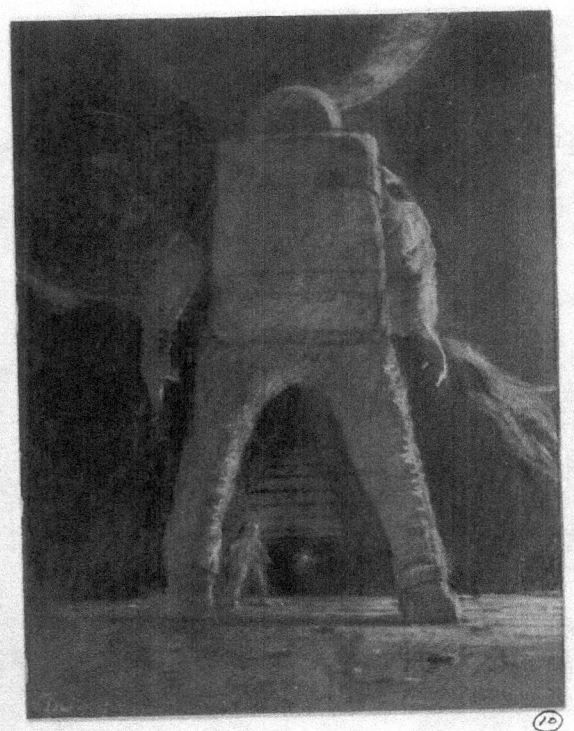
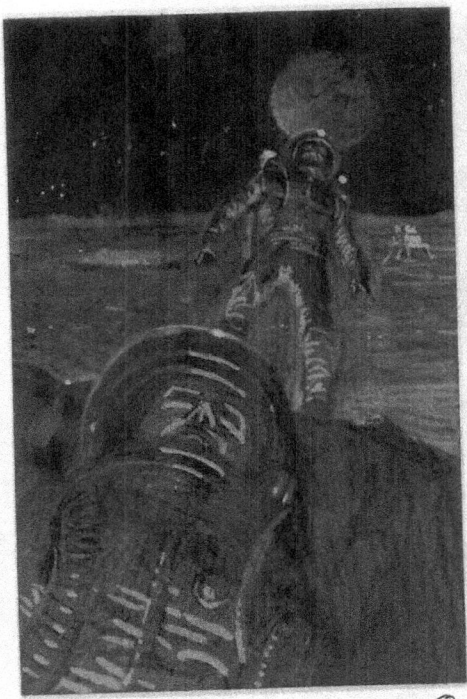
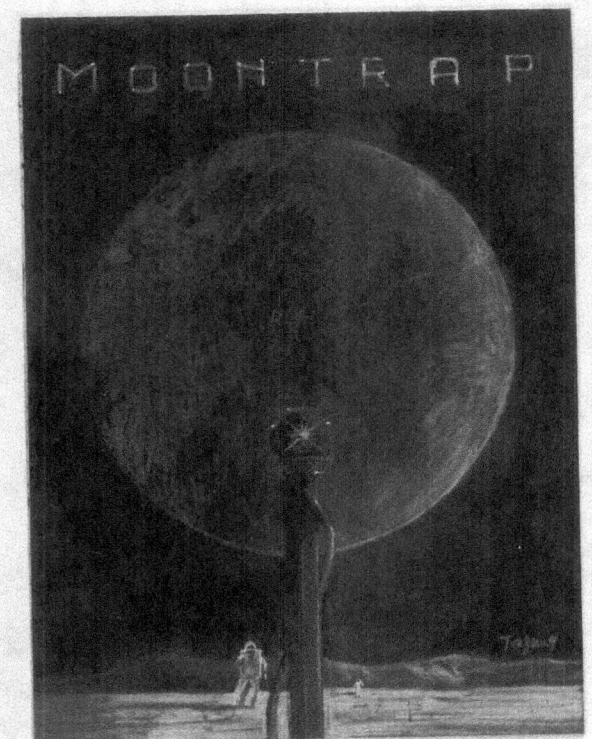

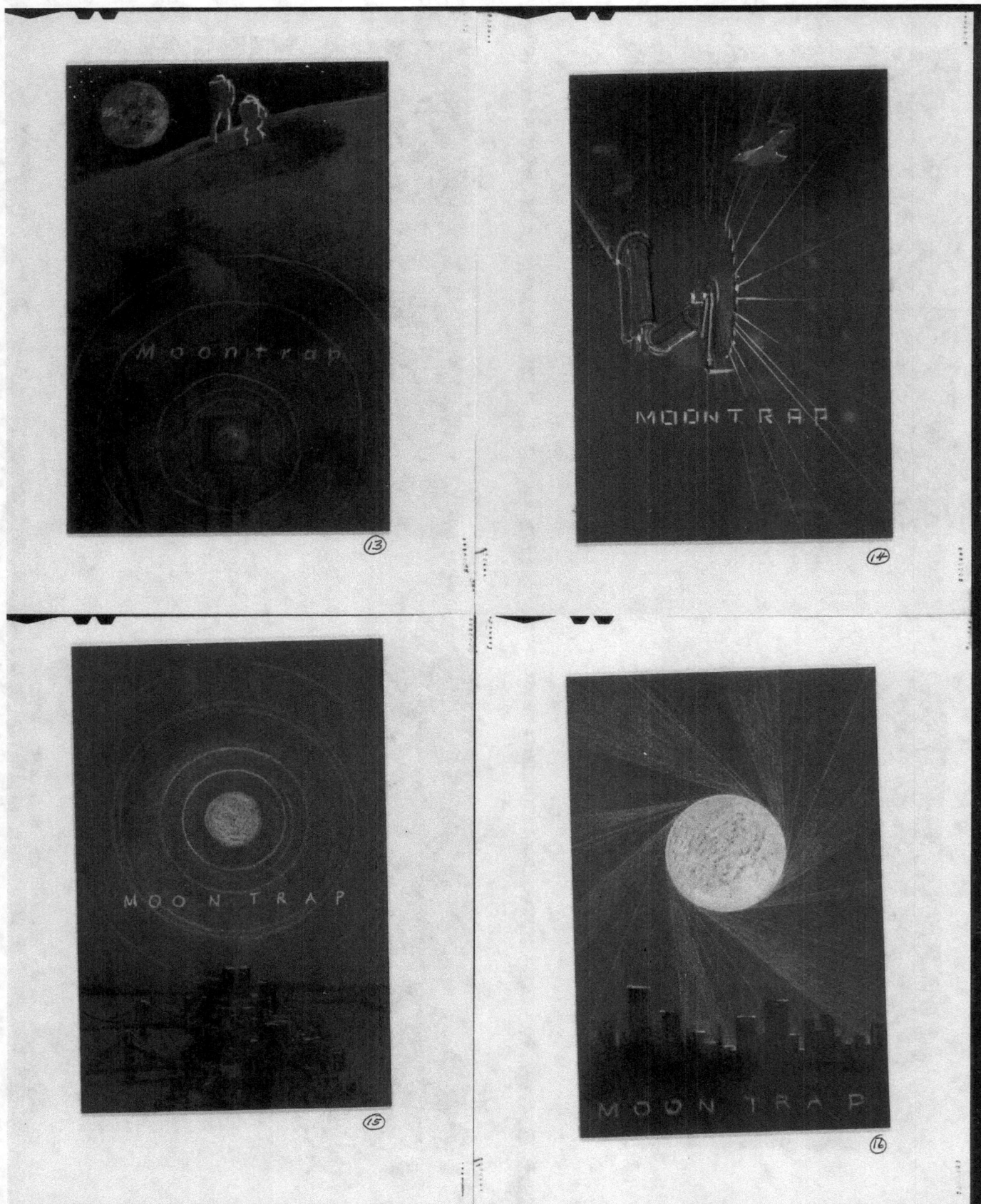

# LIGHTS! ACTION! STUDY! THESE FILM STUDENTS ARE BATTLING FOR TOP BILLING IN HOLLYWOOD

It's a big-budget extravaganza with a cast of thousands, and it's shooting all over Los Angeles. As the clock strikes midnight at the University of Southern California, a neophyte director in an excess of zeal scales a chain-link fence, unlocks a window in a darkened building, and risks life, limb and expulsion to reach his off-limits destination: the editing room. At the University of California, Los Angeles, a 20-year-old auteur instructs a movie crew outfitted with state-of-the-art equipment that rivals the goods over at Universal. In screening rooms around town, studio execs pick through student films in search of the next Steven Spielberg. And somewhere in the city, Professor Jay Bernstein, better known as Farrah Fawcett's former manager, is preparing to teach a course in "Stardom: the Management of, the Public Relations for, and the Maintenance and Survival in." Seriously.

In the reel world, film schools are enjoying their biggest booms since sound came in. Inspired by the successes of such A-list alums as George Lucas and Francis Coppola—four of the five top-grossing movies of all time were directed and/or produced by film school grads—students who used to dream of writing the Great American Novel are now clamoring for a chance to make the Great American Movie.

Since the late 1960s the number of film and television students at UCLA has nearly doubled, to 527. Enrollments are climbing at New York University, Columbia and the California Institute of the Arts in Valencia, while over 100 other colleges have established undergraduate film study programs. In five years, there will be 20,000 film school grads vying for only a handful of jobs, says director John Milius. "The concept of the hot young cinema student is part of the language."

Nowhere is the competition more keen than in Hollywood's own back lot. In Hollywood B.C. (Before Coppola), a director broke into the business by hanging around the studio instead of the campus. But in the 1960s a new movie-mad generation began to take filmmaking more seriously. Film freaks now debate the relative merits of the USC and UCLA programs in the kind of heated discussions usually reserved for the Hitchcock oeuvre. Forget the football field. The real battle between the Trojans and the Bruins is on the cutting room floor. "The competition is not vicious," says UCLA junior Scott Tygett, "but it is definitely there."

Among USC's biggest boosters is Lucas, whose senior thesis, a 15-minute sci-fi short called THX-1384EB, paved the way for Star Wars. "USC made me what I am today," Lucas says. "I knew nothing about films before I got to USC. Every waking hour was something new and exciting."

The grads of USC and UCLA have created a powerful new-boy network in the movie business. USC's all-star team includes Lucas and his colleagues from the legendary classes of

CONTINUED

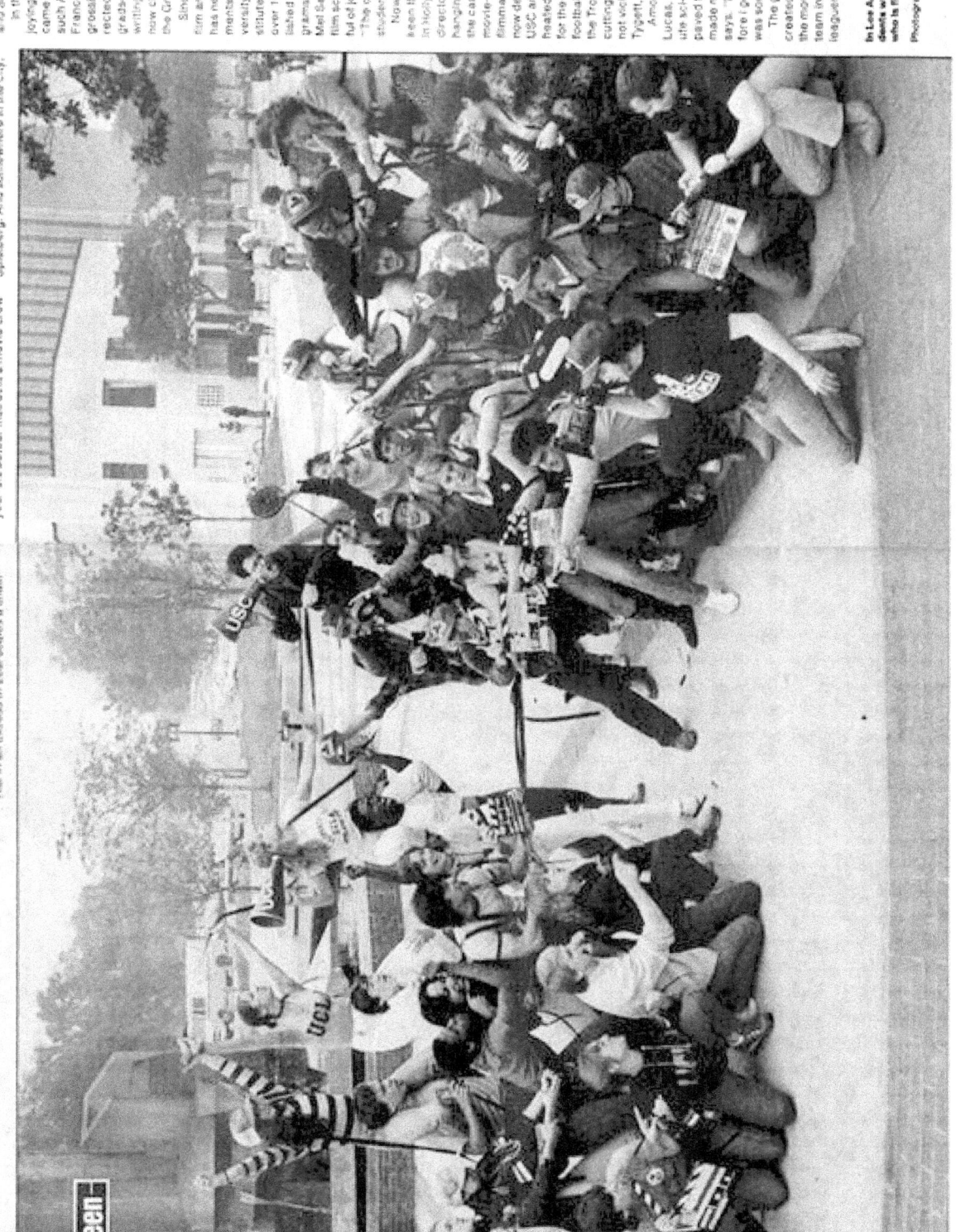

In Los Angeles, rival USC and UCLA students wage a seventeen-tug-of-war over who is first in the Hollywood class.

Photograph by Mark Sennet/Gamma-Liaison

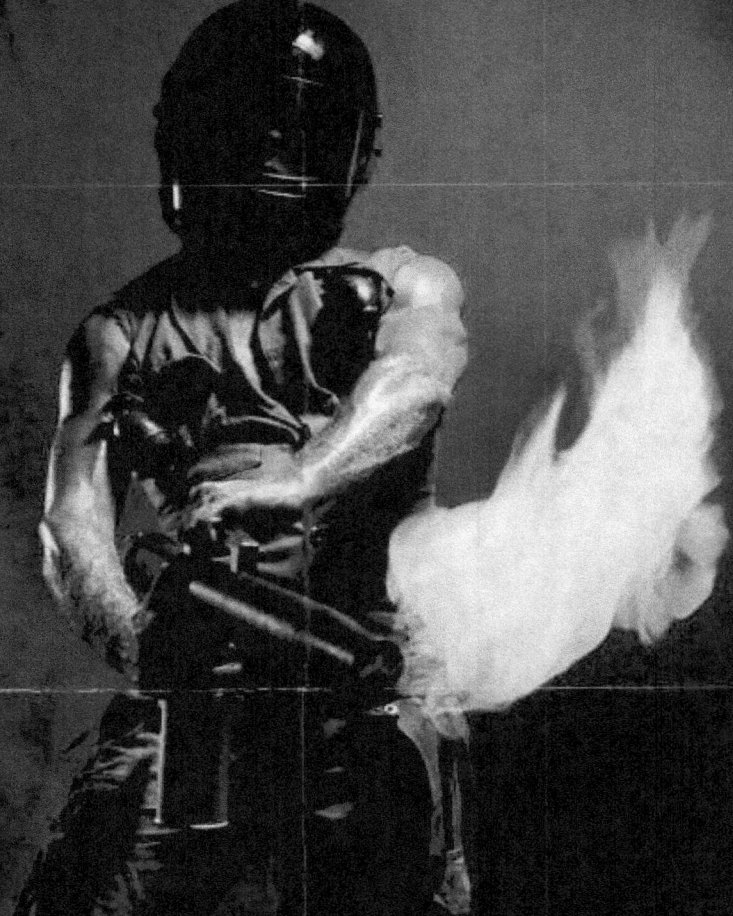

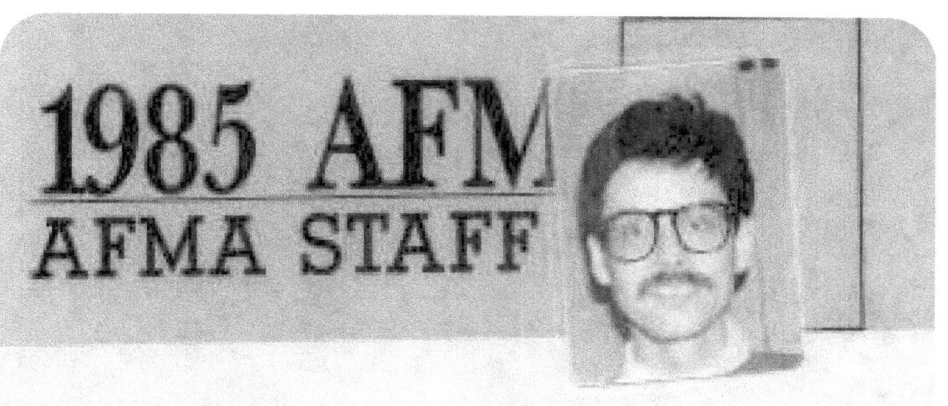

STEVE ROBERTS

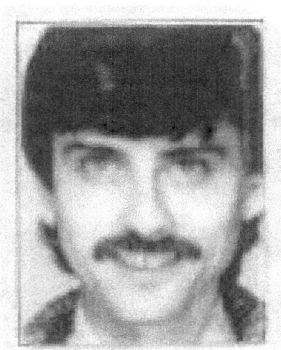

Stephen
Roberts
Shapiro Entertainment Corp.

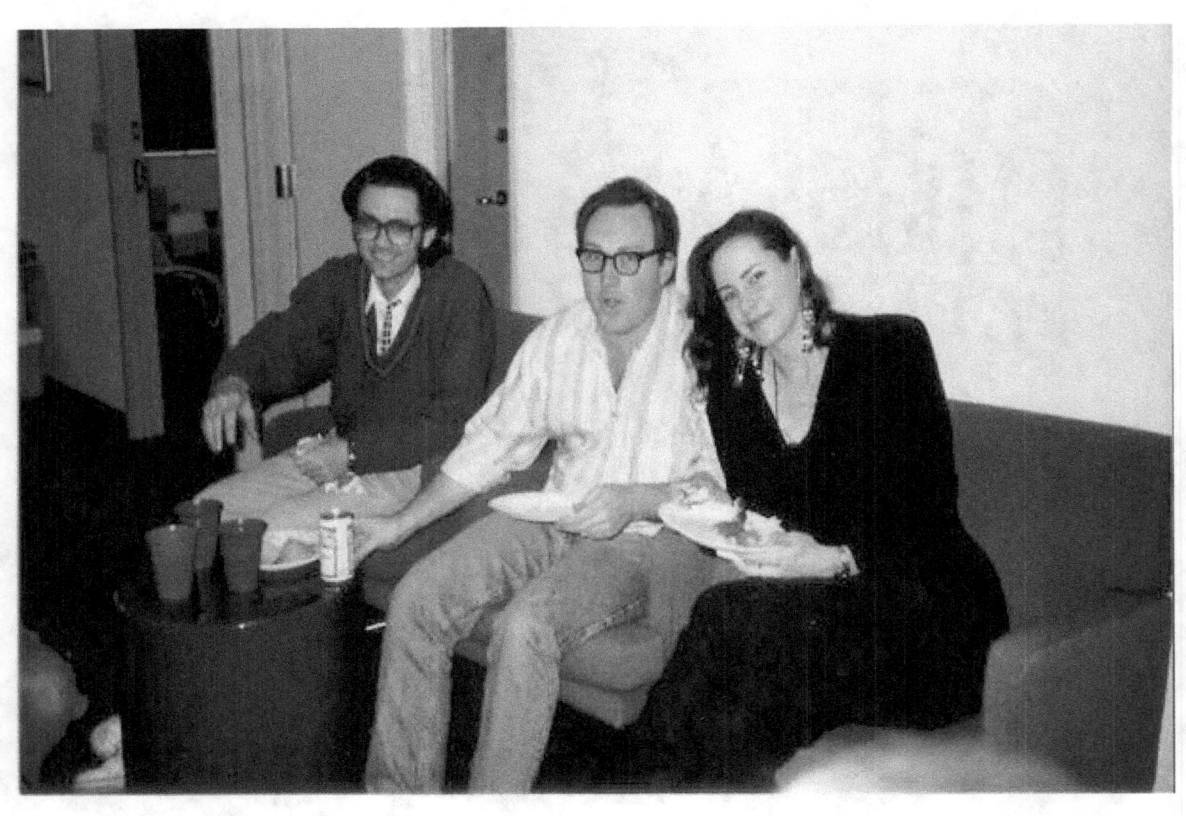

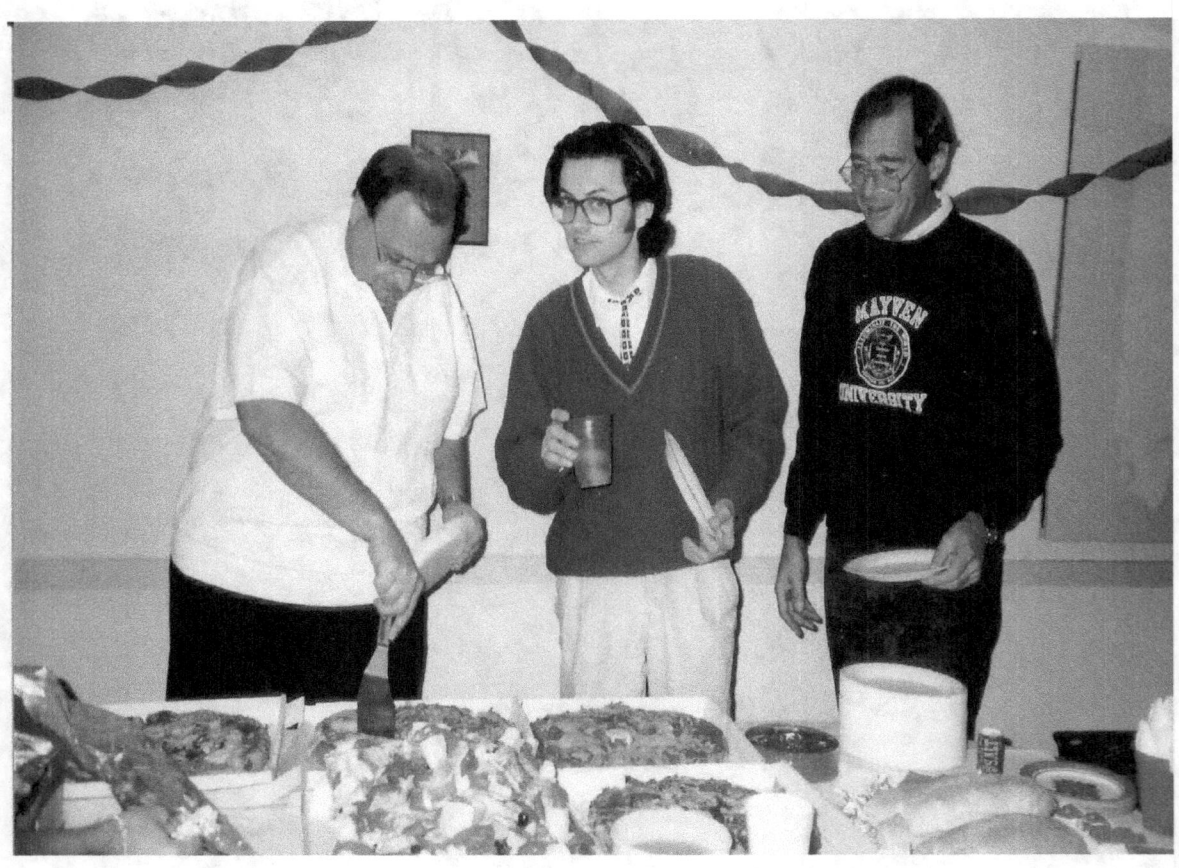

SHAPIRO GLICKENHAUS ENTERTAINMENT

April 6, 1992

Via Federal Express
2-day Standard delivery
AWB#0902604765

Ms. Shirley A. Williams
LIBRARY OF CONGRESS
Documents Unit, Cataloging Div.
Washington, D.C. 20559

Re: "BASKET CASE 3: THE PROGENY", "VOODOO DOLL"

Dear Shirley:

Further to your telephoned request and your fax dated April 2, 1992 enclosed please find our check #15011 in the amount of USD$35.00 which should pay the balance due for the registration of the contracts for the a.m. pictures.

Thank you for your assistance on this matter.

Kindest regards.

Sincerely,

Stephen A. Roberts
Director Int'l Servicing

encl.
cc. Alan Solomon

THE EXTERMINATOR                    REEL TWO (1B)              Page 3

CUT TO: FRUIT & VEGETABLE WAREHOUSE in the USA where MICHAEL and
JOHN are working. Their boss, MR. HOFFMAN, makes up the wages in
his office...he mutters to himself as he writes the wage envelopes
(A lot of it is unintelligible)

20      303.4     307.4     4.0      ...amount $207...
HOFFMAN

21      307.8     313.10    6.2      ...State Tax 17 dollars
HOFFMAN

Two 'hoods' enter HOFFMAN'S office to collect protection money. Not
a word is exchanged, he just pays up and the 'hoods' leave. HOFFMAN
makes his way to the loading bay and hands MICHAEL his money

22      538.14    543.8     4.10     Here you go, Michael. This week
HOFFMAN TO MICHAEL                   there's a little raise.

23      543.12    547.12    4.0      You're a good worker. I wish it
HOFFMAN TO MICHAEL                   could be more.

24      548.0     550.12    2.12     Thank you, Mr. Hoffman.
MICHAEL TO HOFFMAN

At this moment, JOHN comes over to MICHAEL

25      553.0     556.0     3.0      Hey, Michael, what's going on.
JOHN TO MICHAEL

26      556.4     559.12    3.8      Hey, how're you doing, John boy?
MICHAEL TO JOHN                      How about some coffee, man?

27      559.14    562.0     2.2      Who's buying?
JOHN TO MICHAEL

28      562.2     566.12    4.10     Well, er, I will, if er...
MICHAEL TO JOHN

29      567.0     570.14    3.12     ...you push this down to stall 34.
MICHAEL TO JOHN                              (Loaded barrow)

30      571.10    573.10    2.0      All right.
JOHN TO MICHAEL

31      573.12    575.12    2.0      I knew I could convince you.
MICHAEL TO JOHN

32      576.0     579.12    3.12
JOHN TO MICHAEL   2 titles in 1      -Okay, I'll meet you over there.
MICHAEL TO JOHN                      -Yeah.

JOHN takes hold of the heavy barrow and struggles to get it moving

33      580.9     582.12    2.3      Come on!
JOHN EXCLAIMS

34      584.0     587.14    3.14     He didn't tell me it was this heavy!
JOHN EXCLAIMS

In another part of the warehouse, 3 men break open the locks to one
of the bays containing canned beer and start loading cases into the
boot/trunk of their car. JOHN sees them and confronts them

# Stephen A. Roberts

As a child, Stephen A. Roberts emigrated to Texas from England with his family. He received his BA in Radio/TV/Film from North Texas State University and then continued on to earn a Masters in Film from the University of Southern California, graduating in 1987. He started his entertainment career at SGE in 1985, working his way up over an eight year tenure there to VP of Marketing Services. Roberts worked in several aspects on most of the films SGE produced over the years, including Associate Producing MOONTRAP. After leaving SGE, Roberts went on to Imperial Entertainment as Sr. VP Special Projects. A talented and successful writer, he has authored several screenplays, and has written, directed and produced an acclaimed play based on John Lennon's life. Since SGE, his marketing career grew with high-level creative positions at companies such as Seiniger Advertising, Creative Domain and Universal Pictures Marketing. After four years as Co-President of the boutique marketing company ThinkTank he recently accepted a position as a Creative Director at leading Los Angeles firm Petrol Advertising.

**Marco:** Mr. Roberts, please give me some background information about your origins. Which road led you into the film industry?

**Stephen:** I was born in March 1960 near Liverpool, England (Birkenhead) and was drawn to the arts at a very early age. At about age 4 I remember being in the audience for a school-sponsored puppet show and finding myself watching the audience as much as the show. I was fascinated by the way 'performance' affected people. The power of that dynamic took seed in my tiny brain later growing through live theatre into a fascination with film. My family and I emigrated from the U.K. to Fort Worth, Texas in 1966. I remained active in live theatre through my youth, developed an interest in still photography in high school, and eventually attended college at North Texas State University (Denton, Texas) with a dual major in Theatre and Radio/TV/Film with an emphasis in Film. In 1981 I moved to Los Angeles to attend graduate school at the University of Southern California Film School from which I earned a Master's Degree in Cinema in 1987.

**Marco:** How did it come you joined SGE? Do you remember the year and how many productions you participated on?

**Stephen:** I talked myself into a temporary job as the copy room clerk for the American Film Marketing Association's 1985 American Film Market held at the Sunset Hyatt (Jonas Rosenfeld, President of the AFMA was an instructor of mine at USC.) At the market I met Kelly Ross, one of the three key executives of Shapiro Entertainment Corporation at the time (SEC was the precursor to Shapiro Glickenhaus Entertainment). After the AFM ended, I inundated Lenny Shapiro, President of SEC, with telephone calls until one day, he finally picked up the phone. I'll never forget what he said to me: "Kid I can't afford to hire you, but I wanna be your agent!" He obviously thought that with a master's degree in cinema I was vastly over qualified to work at an entry-level job at SEC.

He was right, but I had two very young children at the time and desperately needed an income... any income. I told him I had no problem answering his phone, picking up his laundry and fetching his coffee. So........... on April 1st, 1985 (April Fool's Day!), Leonard Shapiro hired me – and, at first, those menial chores were exactly what I did at SEC. I started, quite literally, at the rock bottom as perhaps the most overqualified Boy Friday in the history of the movie biz... and I was eternally grateful to have the gig. I replaced a guy named Frank Occhipinti, who had replaced Ted Rosenblatt. Ted had been with SEC from its inception.

**Marco:** Which functions did you have over the years at SGE? Were you on location during any shoots?

**Stephen:** At the time I joined SEC in April of 1985 (SEC would very soon become SGE), we were a company of six full-time employees: three Company Principals – Leonard Shapiro (President & CEO), Kelly Ross (VP, COO, Head of Acquisitions) and Alan M. Solomon (VP, CFO, Head of International Sales); and three Support Staff – Sonoko Sakai (Alan's Assistant), Regina Cheung (Accountant) and last, me (receptionist / everyone's assistant.)

Over the course of my eight-year tenure with SGE, from April of '85 through approximately Spring / Summer of '93, the company grew exponentially. We went from being a Foreign Sales Agent on movies owned and produced by others to actually funding our own productions and releasing product through a variety of in-house divisions. For example, SGE had a domestic theatrical distribution operation, a home video distribution company, a domestic TV sales arm, a development/production unit and so on. Because I had a number of skills that the company needed, and was young, ambitious and willing to take on more responsibility (without much pay) I was given the opportunity to expand my involvement. It was like a Film School 2.0 for me. Initially, once other staff was hired to handle the more menial chores, I became a Script Reader...charged with plowing through the dozens of scripts SEC/SGE was sent for consideration (we accepted unsolicited [meaning not sent by accredited entertainment agents, managers or lawyers] materials -- and it avalanched in constantly. Then, as the company took on more movies as sales agent, I was put in charge of International Servicing. Once sales contracts, both international and domestic, were made I was responsible for gathering and creating all of the contractually specified physical delivery items named in the contract and delivering same to the licensee. I serviced a library of over 100 titles on a global scale. If I didn't do my job properly we didn't collect on the contract... so it was an important job that directly affected cash flow.

Gradually, because I said I could do it (and was available and cheap), and Lenny et al. allowed me to, I created (sometimes personally, other times in a supervisory role) audio-visual trailers, promo reels, 1-sheet posters and ad/publicity materials (ads, bios, photos, press-kits etc.) for our growing library of movies. This is how I taught myself movie marketing – by trial and error. While performing my primary jobs, I was still encouraged to 'bird-dog' for projects, and in 1988 I was sent a script (by producer Mary Petryshyn [STANDING IN THE SHADOWS OF MOTOWN [2002] ) for a movie entitled MOONTRAP that was to star Walter Koenig (STAR TREK) and Bruce Campbell (EVIL DEAD). At the time Mary was not yet a full-time movie producer but instead a very persuasive sales person for a Michigan-based film to tape company called Grace & Wild Studios. She had previously convinced me to use G&W to do SGE's film to tape transfers and duplication and her husband Robert Dyke owned a Detroit-based commercial/special effects house called Magic Lantern Productions that was interested in making the leap to feature films. Once Lenny, Alan and Jim greenlit MOONTRAP (Kelly didn't stay with the company after the Glickenhaus merger), MOONTRAP became my first feature film credit. I earned an Associate Producer credit and was on location for a portion of the shoot, which took place in a pair of warehouses in Troy, Michigan. I also have a vague memory of being on the set of MANIAC COP, but, would have only been an observer...with no real job/function per se.

**Marco:** Are you still in contact with many colleagues from back then?

**Stephen:** Yes. I am in frequent contact with Leonard Shapiro. Len was a very important mentor in my movie biz life and over the years has become a close friend. We're even trying to get a project made together, which is a really cool thing to try and pull off all these years later. I am also in close touch with Nadia Bruce-Rawlings (International Sales). And occasionally in touch with John Alexander (International Sales) and Frank Isaac (Executive in Charge of Production) and Darby Walker (Receptionist). I also speak with Marc Meeks (my assistant) and Stephanie Denton (International Sales) from time to time. I even met with Jim Glickenhaus in NYC about 12 years ago when I was seeking funding for a more expanded version of my John Lennon play ONE NIGHT ONLY.

**Marco:** MOONTRAP was a success at the box office, correct? Were there plans for a sequel? If yes, why were the plans spoiled?

**Stephen:** MOONTRAP was released into the world-wide marketplace over twenty-six years ago. The global entertainment marketplace has changed much since then. In order to fully understand and describe the relative success of MOONTRAP, it's important to qualify the circumstances and also to view it in historical perspective. If memory serves me correctly, when MOONTRAP was pitched to SGE by Robert Dyke in 1987-'88, it was budgeted (including deferments, goods & services donations, favored nations deals etc., etc.) at around USD$700,000 cash, as I recall. Once the film went into production and post-production the budget increased to around USD$1.2million, and, in order to get it completed and presented to the marketplace in a timely manner, SGE raised and invested the additional money required. By the time the film had run its distribution course from all revenue streams worldwide, my recollection is it grossed somewhere in the neighborhood of USD$5 million. So, mathematically speaking (on paper anyway), the figures make it appear as if the film was a big money maker... proportionate to its cost that is. It did cost significant sums of money to distribute and market the film as well, so, it certainly didn't make a profit of USD$3.8M by any means. But still, by nearly any logical, thumbnail measure MOONTRAP was indeed a financial success. And I am very proud to have played my part in bringing it into the world and positioning it for success. If, however, you are referring to 'box office' in the strictest and narrowest definition of the phrase to mean USA Domestic Theatrical Box-Office, then no, MOONTRAP was not a success...in first-run theatres in America that is. I recall that in order to secure a shipment of a certain number of VHS cassettes in the US market there had to be a 'token' theatrical release. It was a regional release, as I recall, that was somewhere in the neighborhood of 80 – 100 screens. It may have moved from region to region across the country in a phased roll out, but I'm not certain of that. In any event, the film didn't make its money (in America at least) from theatrical box office receipts. It made its money in VHS sales, and cable and syndicated TV license fees. But really the big success story for MOONTRAP was how it faired in the foreign marketplace.

The first indication SGE got that we had something special on our hands was when the film was pre-sold to two key territories: Germany and France, for big license fees that included sizable minimum guarantee payments. Those were the days (the late 1980's) when pre-sale deals were commonly done in foreign. We created a great poster and a hot trailer that piqued interest, and, across-the-board buyers responded very favorably. In my opinion the reason for the film's success has to do with a number of factors. The main cast (Walter Koenig and Bruce Campbell) was a big positive due to their fame from the hugely successful movies STAR TREK and EVIL DEAD respectively. Also the setting: landing on the moon was something that the marketplace really responded to. It's important to remember that 1989 was the thirty-year anniversary of Neal Armstrong's 1969 moonwalk. It was a very hot marketing hook that resonated deeply in multiple territories around the world. Another plus was our key art (movie poster). We hired Tom Jung to do the MOONTRAP poster as an enigmatic 'teaser' illustration. Tom is a very famous illustrator who is probably best known for his first STAR WARS poster. Also we created a very high quality trailer. And finally, quite frankly the film itself LOOKED like a big studio movie – its sets, effects and so on (at least when presented in short form e.g. trailers etc.) made it appear as if it could hold up to higher budgeted motion pictures – and we capitalized on that association wholeheartedly. As to why there was no

MOONTRAP sequel involving SGE, the short answer is: I'm not sure. I do recall that SGE's original agreement on MOONTRAP may not have definitively secured sequel rights, so, that was a deal-point that required negotiation with Mr. Dyke and his investment group located in Detroit, Michigan. I was not directly involved with any of those negotiations, so, I have no first-hand knowledge of how they did or did not proceed.

Suffice-to-say, evidence would suggest that no agreement was arrived at between the parties – hence no SGE-sponsored MOONTRAP-sequel ever materialized. I remember there being interest and efforts to make it happen, but like many things in show biz... unfortunately, it was not to be. Final word, I am partially aware that there was a lawsuit between the producers and SGE, but all of that occurred without my knowledge and participation. I had moved on from SGE by the time that unpleasantness occurred. I do not know the resolution to it. But here we are nearly 30 years later and a sequel (with the participation of Mr. Dyke and Mr. Ragsdale) does appear to be eminent. So, even in movies, I suppose patience is indeed a virtue.

**Marco:** MOONTRAP has become kind of a cult favorite, have you noticed that? Which films by SGE has remained most popular, do you think?

**Stephen:** I am somewhat aware that MOONTRAP has gained a degree of cult status...probably due in no small part to the inclusion in the cast of Walter and Bruce. Also, for their time (and certainly considering the low budget) the sets, costumes and effects aren't too shabby for a 'genre' movie. Nadia Bruce-Rawlings is far more qualified to speak to which of the SGE films are most popular since she I think she is still involved with Jim Glickenhaus in sales of some of the old catalogue. I've heard FRANKENHOOKER still pops up here and there. Also MANIAC COP.

**Marco:** Bruce Campbell starred in MANIAC COP and also in MOONTRAP - did you get in touch with the cult actor and how do you remember working with him?

**Stephen:** Bill Lustig already had Bruce Campbell cast in MANIAC COP when the film came to SGE. Also, I was not very involved in the MANIAC COP production. As for MOONTRAP, when Robert Dyke pitched the project to SGE he had his cast (including Bruce and Walter) totally committed. It was a major reason SGE was interested in becoming involved with the project – it just seemed to have so much already going for it. The story I recall on the Dyke / Campbell connection leads back to a close-knit Detroit production community in the 1980's. The filmmaker Sam Raimi (THE EVIL DEAD and SPIDERMAN) and Bob and others all started out together in Michigan. Bruce was also part of that group. I remember Bob telling me that Bruce was just a Production Assistant coiling cable on set when he first met him. Apparently after Bruce gained his THE EVIL DEAD success (which Sam wrote and directed), he was willing to continue his relationships with others in that community to whom he

**perhaps** felt indebted for some of his success. As to my personal relationship with Bruce, he was not on-set during the time I was in Detroit for principal and effects photography, so, we did not interact much at all. Although I do recall meeting him a couple of times (perhaps it was socially) and he was very approachable, genuine and friendly. I'm told that people from Michigan tend to come off that way.

**Marco:** What's your favorite film done by SGE?

**Stephen:** Since I 'touched' (in some cases quite literally), in varying ways, every single movie SGE handled for nearly a decade, it's very hard to single out just one movie as a 'favorite'. There are many favorites, for many reasons. For selfish reasons, my obvious choice is MOONTRAP since I had so much to do with its raison d'être. But MANIAC COP has to be a close second though.

The MANIAC COP production company was physically located inside our SGE corporate offices, so it was a real treat seeing the day-to-day MANIAC dramas playing out daily. And third place has to go to... FRANKENHOOKER. It was just such an out-there wacky concept and execution, and so much fun to market... what's not to love?!

**Marco:** The office was in Los Angeles?

**Stephen:** By then it was located at 12001 Ventura Place, Ste 404, Studio City, CA 91604; the company's original location was at 3880 Fredonia Dr., LA, CA 91604.

**Marco:** Networking has always been one of the most important things in the movie business. During your time at USC, did you meet a lot of the people with whom you work today?

**Stephen:** I agree that networking is a very, very important part of the entertainment business. Always has been, always will be. You can't always work with people you like, but, as often as possible it's nice to work with people you know. So there are as few surprises as possible...both good and bad. The devil you know dynamic.

To properly answer your question, I have to define what the word "working" means for me personally today. I have an ongoing business (with a partner, and also on my own) that operates in the advertising and branding spheres. That's my 'day job'. I polish other people's apples. Whether the 'apple' is a Movie, a TV show, a product, a service etc. I sell things to strangers – through advertising, promotion and such. Separate and concurrent with that I also develop long form projects including movies, television series and video games. Both of these activates sometimes present opportunities to interface with colleagues from my USC Film School days. And when those opportunities arise, I seize them. I like those USC guys (and gals) – they're smart and imaginative. And I will forever share the 'foxhole mentality' borne of having dodged coming-of-age bullets together with them... that builds a blood bond that isn't easily broken.

**Marco:** Tell me about the importance of marketing (posters, flyers, ads and trailers and promos) for SGE. Were you responsible for that during your time there?

**Stephen:** When the movies are of 'questionable' quality, marketing has to be A+; it's your only shot at crossing over into the mainstream or near-mainstream. The idea being, if you can't be a big movie at least you can try and look like a big movie. So the importance of marketing is huge for the 'B', and the significantly less-than-B, product Shapiro Entertainment handled prior to merger with Jim and the birth of SGE.

I was not initially responsible for marketing at the company. That was handled exclusively by Ms. Kelly Ross, who was a founding partner of Shapiro Entertainment. But Kelly didn't make the transition into the partnership that included Jim Glickenhaus, I'm referring to SGE now, and that created an opportunity for me.

The thing about trailers, let's take that first, is that because of my film school education (and personal chutzpah) I had acquired, for lack of a better phrase, a "filmic sense". I felt in my bones what made a story tick from a visual perspective. And had been schooled (at actual educational institutions [first in Texas and then in Southern California]) in how to edit movie footage, so I possessed the rudimentary skills. Also, because I was answering the phones, and hanging around the office listening to Lenny and Alan and Kelly, hour-after-hour-after-hour I figured out pretty quickly what it was that made these films appeal to buyers, simply put: it was people hitting people... and breasts.

So it was just a matter of putting the best of that (and sometimes there was precious little of it mind you) into one shiny, sexy, semi-pro package. And it didn't hurt that I was exceedingly cheap and always available. As for posters, that came much more slowly to me. Even though I'd been an amateur still photographer, making 1-sheet posters wasn't a craft I'd had any training or experience in. But, once you've seen enough exceedingly bad, and I mean BAD, posters, and if you have a modicum of taste...at least you learn what NOT to do. So eventually I got somewhat involved, in a supervisory capacity, in creating posters as well.

**Marco:** SGE produced and distributed movies in the heyday of VHS. Were these deals much more important than theatrical releases?

**Stephen:** Yes. It's important to understand that in the earliest days of SEC, the company was not capitalized and functioned almost exclusively as a 'Sales Agent' which meant we took already produced films, made by outsider producers with nothing to do with SEC/SGE, and sub-licensed them to distributors throughout the world. For the most part our biggest 'buyers'/licensees were in the foreign territories. And, with some exceptions (African countries, the Philippines, Lebanon etc.) these deals were all about VHS. Most contracts were 'all rights', meaning that Theatrical Distribution was part of the sales contract, but, for the most part the subdistributors didn't need

**Marco:** What about the Foreign Market, was it more important for the success of an SGE production or was it mainly the American Market?

**Stephen:** Once again, in the earliest days of the company (prior to Jim, when we were still SEC) it was mostly about the foreign deals. Although at that time Lenny did do his thing in domestic sales, packaging some of our films together to make domestic rights deals both in TV and home video. I recall three domestic deals in particular that were noteworthy. All of these deals involved packaging up to twelve (12) movies bundled together, it seemed like a classic example of strength in numbers, we had the 'bulk' and sometimes that made doing business with us more logical than with another company. I recall three (3) package deals that worked very nicely for the company from that era. The first is a TV deal with The Samuel Goldwyn Company for a package of a dozen titles that Goldwyn named "The Dynamite Dozen" or something catchy like that, movies like KILL ZONE, KING OF THE STREETS, FRENCH QUARTER UNDERCOVER, and other titles lost to time (and my memory). This deal happened because of Lenny's long-time relationship with Meyer Gotlieb at Goldwyn. Another was a deal Lenny did with New World Pictures, once again because of a relationship he had with Bob Rehme (whom he knew from Avco Embassy Pictures). And last there was a major deal with Vestron Video that included movies like DEATH SPA (aka AEROBICIDE) and others. So, yes the foreign market was a mainstay for the company pre-SGE, and continued into the SGE-era itself, but Domestic revenues were very much a part of the financial picture all along. Percentage-wise it's hard to say what the split was...but, if I had to guess I'd say it was 60-40 favoring foreign. In some cases, as much as 70-30 foreign.

Now, once we moved into the SGE-era, things changed. Domestic revenues, especially in the case of RED SCORPION (and MOONTRAP too, to some extent), became a big deal. But in the case of both of those two films it wasn't domestic theatrical b.o. that made money, it was the VHS shipment number. And also the US cable and syndicated TV sale numbers.

**Marco:** Who picked up the films for the SGE distribution catalogue? Were the criteria for the selection of a particular movie mainly economical in nature?

**Stephen:** In the early days, everybody was bird-dogging films. Everybody. And that idea that anyone in the company could find and promote a film to be an SGE library picture never really lapsed during my nearly eight years with the company.
Lenny was particularly open to the idea that product could come from anywhere. In my personal experience at SGE, MOONTRAP was the perfect example of

me introducing a movie to the company (in script form) that I thought would make an excellent SGE movie. Luckily (for the company and me) I was right.

As to the criteria for selecting films, yes it was primarily economical. But that's not to say that art (or quality) was consciously shunned at SGE. The goal was to create or be associated with a commercial product first, and, as long as commerciality wasn't compromised, if the movie happened to be GOOD too (or as Lenny liked to say was a, "movie, movie"), then that was totally cool.

In my opinion one of the strengths of SGE, and an enduring 'difference maker' when one considers the other indie companies of the '80's-90's VHS era', is that SGE didn't focus on just ONE genre. We weren't the 'horror company', or the 'action company', or the 'sci-fi company' or the 'martial arts company'…we did it ALL. And ultimately that strengthened our profile, and now, all these years later it has contributed to cementing the SGE legacy. At least that's what I like to think.

**Marco**: Please share some information about your stage work. Were these jobs exceptions, or do you still continue this kind of work?

**Stephen**: Entertainment-wise, my first love was the stage. At a very young age I was interested in live theatre. But the short answer to this question is, yes, involvement in live theatre is very much the exception in both my professional and personal lives at this time. And I regret this. But the end to that story isn't yet written.

I am very proud to have written, directed and produced my John Lennon one act musical ONE NIGHT ONLY, back in 2002. And part of me still keeps my creative radar up in search of my next stage production. But no, live theatre is not my primary focus these days. It was the exception, but was thoroughly exceptional.

**Marco**: You are Co-President at the company ThinkTank. Are you a Co-Founder as well? What's the story behind the company?

**Stephen**: I co-founded ThinkTank four years ago in partnership with a long-time friend and associate whom I met when I was working on staff at Universal Pictures Marketing about thirteen years ago. ThinkTank makes advertising and promotional materials for movies, TV shows, brands, products and services. We also develop long form projects including feature films, television programs and video games.

**Marco**: What's the business philosophy of Think-Tank and with which parts of filmmaking and distribution does the company deal?

**Stephen**: Our focus is two-fold. On the one hand, we make advertising and promotion for both studio and independent clients. On the other, we create long form projects that we own 100% which we pitch to studios, networks and independents. So we are in both the marketing and content creation business – essentially we polish other people's apples and we grow our own. We are not involved in distribution.

**Marco**: Chris Ingvordsen and others who worked with SGE remember the parties thrown

**for the film markets. As a final question, do you have a favorite party story from those days?**

**Stephen:** Yes...our parties. There were epic parties of many types thrown all around the world. Some involved parades, fake gun battles, live bears on chains, naked ladies wrapped in boa constrictors and much, much more. The two main party locations were in Cannes and Los Angeles. The parties were timed to coincide with the Cannes Film Market and the American Film Market and were aimed at attracting buyers to notice our product. Since I was Alan Solomon's 'man back home' I never had the 'pleasure' of attending any of the soirées in France. But I have heard plenty about them. I'm sure those who did attend will speak of them at length in these pages.

There was one party in particular thrown in Los Angeles that I will never forget however. It had to be AFM 1986, I think; and Kelly Ross was the ringmaster of that particular circus (as she was of most of them in the early days.) She rented a Country Club up in the Hollywood Hills which she had decked out floor-to-ceiling as a Las Vegas Style 'casino' complete with poker tables, blackjack tables, roulette, wheel of fortune - you name it. There were hot girls walking around serving drinks, selling cigarettes and cigars, giving away all kinds of movie-themed chotskies ... it was Hollywood Babylon to the max! The Asian buyers in particular loved all the 'fake' gambling, everyone was issued a brick of pretend money to use, as I recall. There was a rumor that toward the end of the night people had substituted real cash for the fake cash. It's a good thing we didn't get busted. But, oh what a night!!

---

**By Marco Siedelmann, in writing
from West Hills, California
22Feb, 2015 - 25March, 2015 - 28June, 2015**

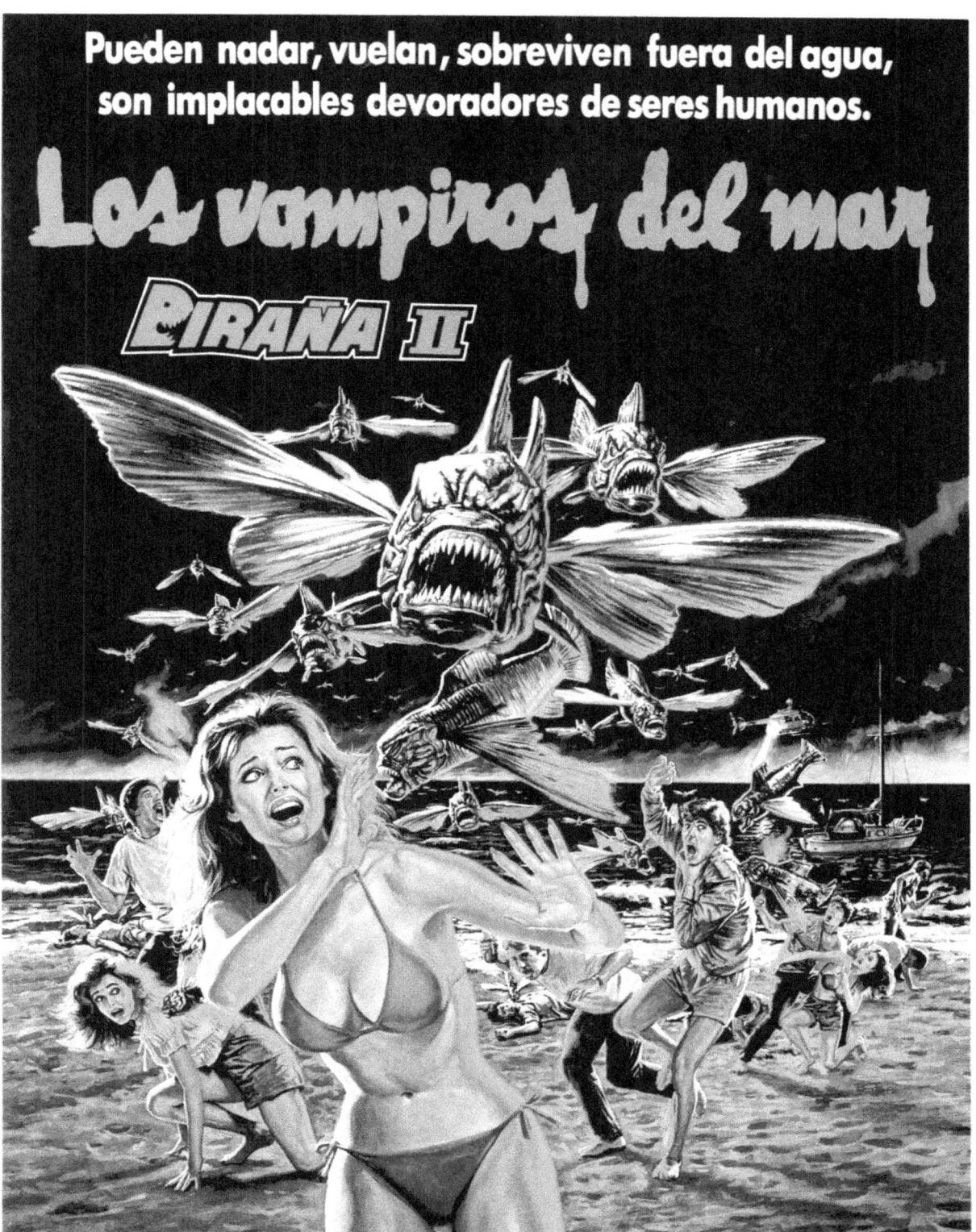

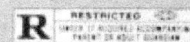

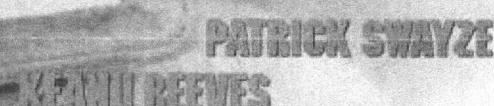

IN A WORLD GONE BLIND, WHAT IF YOU WERE THE ONLY PERSON WHO COULD SEE?

JULIANNE MOORE  MARK RUFFALO  DANNY GLOVER  GAEL GARCÍA BERNAL  ALICE BRAGA

FROM FERNANDO MEIRELLES DIRECTOR OF CITY OF GOD AND THE CONSTANT GARDENER

# BLINDNESS

BASED ON THE NOVEL BY THE NOBEL PRIZE WINNING AUTHOR JOSÉ SARAMAGO

FALL 2008

When he said I do,
he never said
what he did.

# Schwarzenegger
# True Lies

A JAMES CAMERON FILM

TWENTIETH CENTURY FOX PRESENTS A LIGHTSTORM ENTERTAINMENT PRODUCTION A JAMES CAMERON FILM ARNOLD SCHWARZENEGGER JAMIE LEE CURTIS TRUE LIES TOM ARNOLD BILL PAXTON ART MALIK TIA CARRERE MUSIC BY BRAD FIEDEL EDITED BY MARK GOLDBLATT, A.C.E. AND CONRAD BUFF AND RICHARD A. HARRIS PRODUCTION DESIGNER PETER LAMONT DIRECTOR OF PHOTOGRAPHY RUSSELL CARPENTER SPECIAL VISUAL EFFECTS BY DIGITAL DOMAIN EXECUTIVE PRODUCERS RAE SANCHINI ROBERT SHRIVER LAWRENCE KASANOFF SCREENPLAY BY JAMES CAMERON BASED UPON A SCREENPLAY BY CLAUDE ZIDI, SIMON MICHAEL AND DIDIER KAMINKA PRODUCED BY JAMES CAMERON AND STEPHANIE AUSTIN

SOUNDTRACK AVAILABLE ON LIGHTSTORM/EPIC SOUNDTRAX

DIRECTED BY JAMES CAMERON

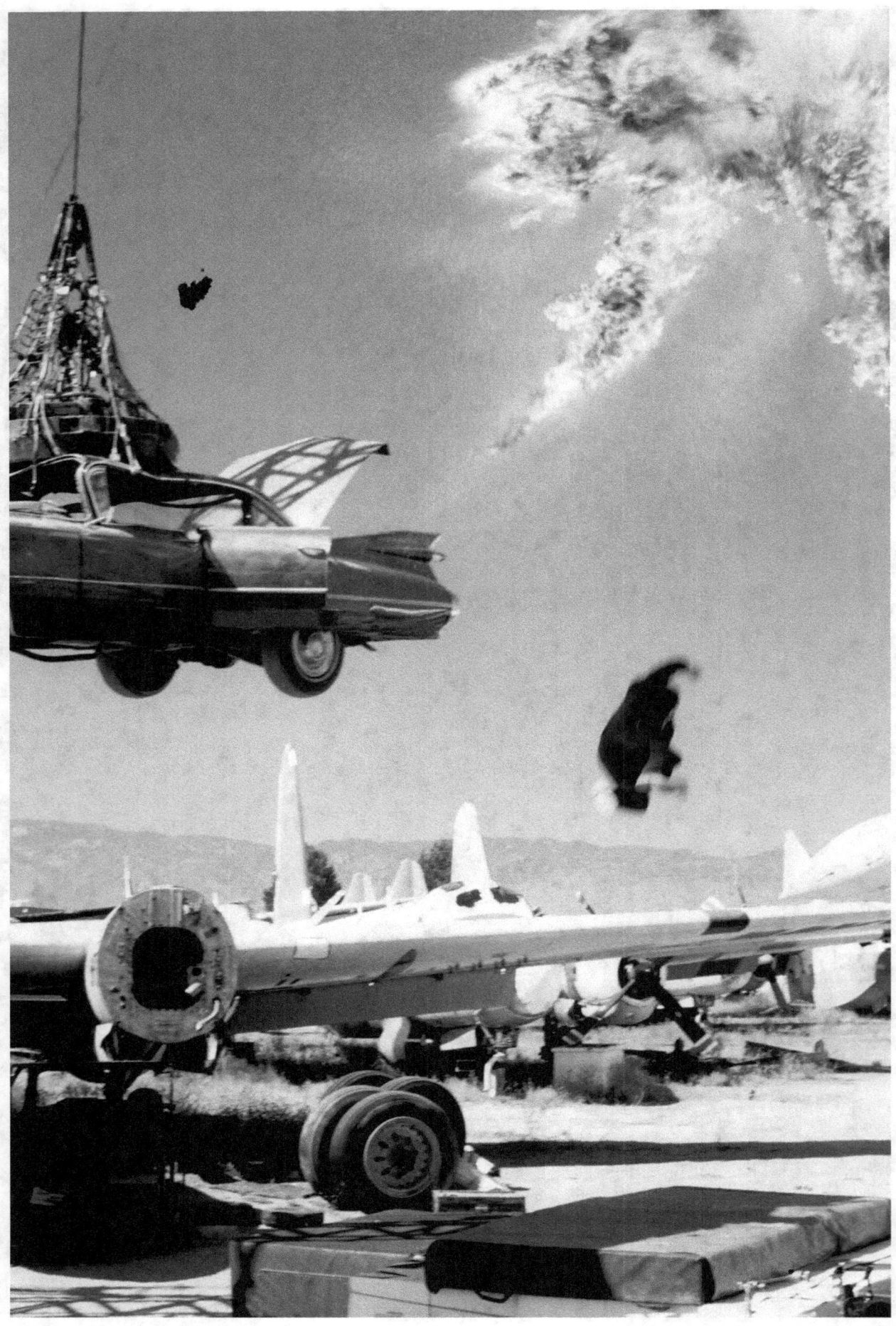

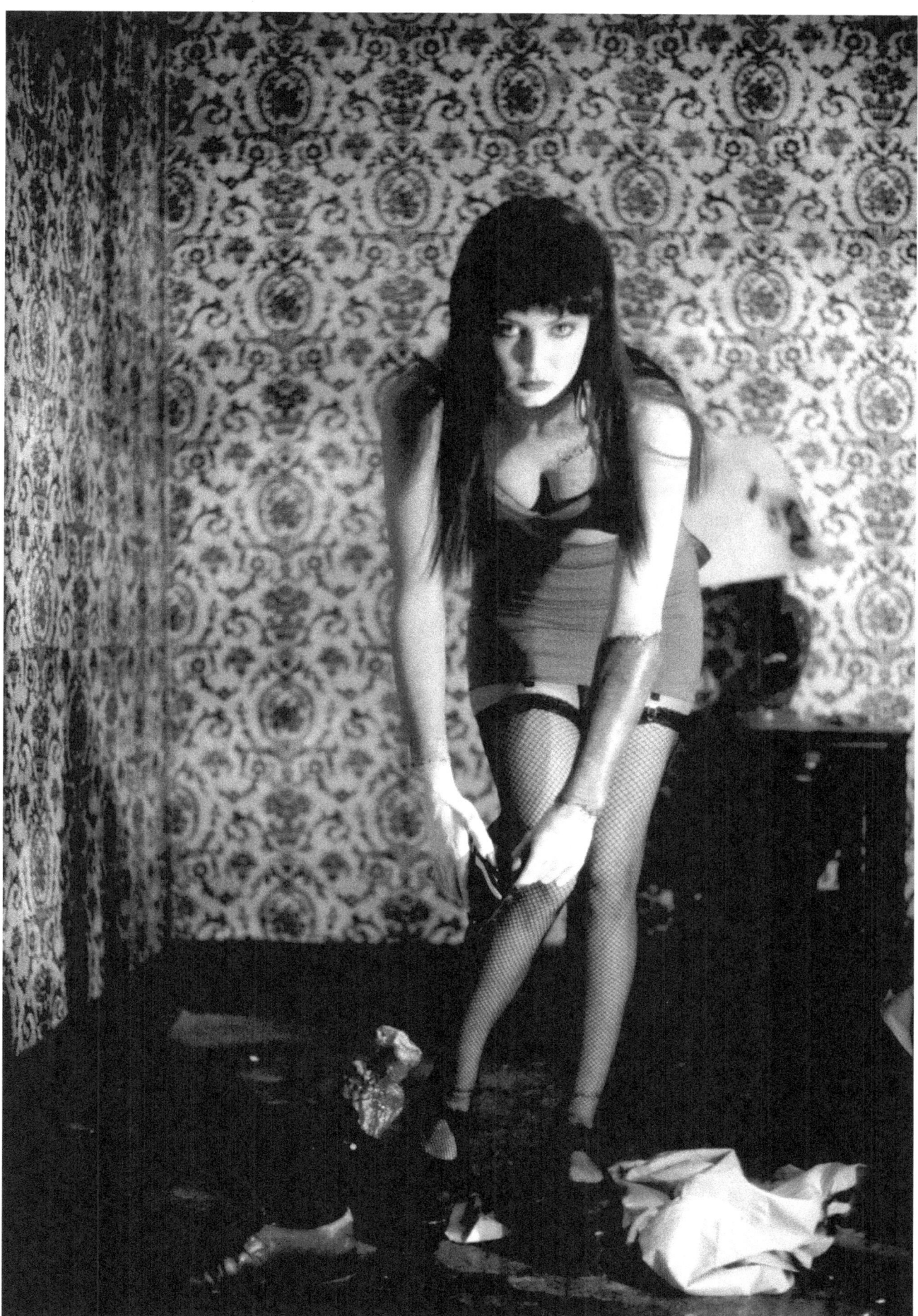

# Sonoko Sakai

Sonoko Sakai was born in New York, and lived briefly in Mexico City, Tokyo, Kamakura, Los Angeles and San Francisco. Her first cookbook, *The Poetical Pursuit of Food: Japanese Recipes for American Cooks*, was published by Random House/Potter in 1982. She has written articles for the Los Angeles Times, Chicago Tribune, San Francisco Chronicle, as well as several Asian publications. One of her most passionate projects is the Southern California Heritage Grain project. Sonoko was also a key member of the team in the early years of SGE (when it was still called SEC), working closely with Executive Vice President Alan Solomon. After her time at SEC she developed a very successful career in international film sales. She also produced theatrical releases such as SILK, starring Kiera Knightley, and BLINDNESS, starring Julianne Moore. Currently she's working on a film about the French chef Bernard Loiseau, a project that combines two of her passions: movies and the art of cooking.

**Stephen:** It's Monday May 11, 2015 and I have on the line with me the beautiful and talented and very cooperative Sonoko Sakai. Thank you for doing this, Sonoko, I very much appreciate it.

**Sonoko:** Well thank you very much for inviting me to be on this interview.

**Stephen:** Absolutely. So let's just get started; these are questions by Marco Siedelmann who is the publisher and writer and mastermind behind this book. I've done a little bit of editing and augmenting. We can just freestyle a little bit too, depending on how much time you have. So don't feel like we're tied down to these questions. Feel free to digress to the extent you wish [to] or feel comfortable [doing].

**Sonoko:** Okay.

**Stephen:** So let's start at the beginning, where were you born and raised?

**Sonoko:** I was born in New York and raised in Tokyo, San Francisco, Mexico City and Los Angeles.

**Stephen:** Lovely. Quite a cosmopolitan trip there.

**Sonoko:** Right. A multicultural upbringing.

**Stephen:** Let's just get right to cinema, has cinema always been important to you? And if it has been, since when would you say?

**Sonoko:** My father was a real film buff, and just before the war he had seen so many films, and this is back when you'd go to a theater to see a movie, and he was looking at movies, skipping school to go to films before the American movies got banned from Japan because they entered into WWII. And he had produced a lot of these paper movies. He would go into the cinema and photograph a whole Western movie and do this paper movie in his photographic albums, and some of those survived the war. And I grew up listening to him tell us about these movies, and so there was always an interest in films. He took turns taking his five children to go see films. We couldn't all go at once so he would choose one kid at a time to go the movie cinema with him. So I've always been interested in movies because of my father but I never thought I would go into the film business; that was just something that just happened.

**Stephen:** Let's talk about that, that's a perfect segue, how did you get into the movie industry? Was it your plan after university?

**Sonoko:** No, I was actually going to grad school at UCLA in Education and I had no idea that I would work in films. While I was trying to work through grad school, my parents, who ended up going back to Japan, said, "We're not paying for grad school. You figure that out yourself." So I started working for a professor in the Theatre Arts Department and Film School. And I did that for like a year and half and I just really got interested in film. And I thought, "Wow, that's another way of maybe connecting to the international marketplace."

I was always interested in the international arena because of my upbringing. And I also thought maybe I could find a voice. I was trying to figure out my voice, trying to find my identity, and I thought that maybe the visual arts could be something that would help me. And since I couldn't sustain a living being his assistant, being a darkroom assistant, I started looking for a job. And I landed basically as sort of a gopher/assistant for Frank Konigsberg who is a producer that did a lot of these hit television series and stuff. I don't know if you remember GUYANA TRAGEDY: THE STORY OF JIM JONES (TV Movie 1980)? He was a pretty major TV producer who worked at Fox. So that's how I got my entry-level position and basically I was a gopher delivering scripts back and forth to Warner Bros. and to different studios. Before the computer was discovered.

**Stephen:** And then did you segue straight away from that to Shapiro Entertainment, which later became Shapiro Glickenhaus Entertainment?

**Sonoko:** What happened was we had a mutual friend named..., uhm-- Lenny's cousin actually, I forgot his last name but his first name is Gary. And I was working for Frank Konigsberg, but I didn't make a very good secretary. I was a good gopher but...You know this is the crazy world of the studios, and at a TV studio basically you had to take in like twenty phone calls in one minute. And figuring out how to use the intercom system... I was just not trained as a secretary, and I was just coming out of grad school, and I just could not keep up with the 24/7 kind of demanding hours and demanding producer, and I was burning out before I even started. That's when Gary told me that Lenny was looking for an assistant, and he was looking to get into the international market. So I thought well maybe I could go work for him, and that's what I did.

**Stephen:** This is a two-part question, how many years all told did you spend at Shapiro Entertainment, and while you were there how would you describe your journey within the company; what was your first position and what was your last position? And then the second part of the question is, did you work for that entire time for Alan Solomon? So tell me who you worked for and when?

**Sonoko:** When I started working for Shapiro, Alan was already there. There were like Kelly and Alan and there was this other gentleman, I forgot his name, and it was just like these four executives who had left the studio system to form this independent company. And they needed an assistant to answer the phones and to do the contracts. So it was working out of the apartment that Lenny had rented, and I think he was living upstairs. I mean it was really as "indie" as you could get. And I was sort of the assistant for everybody. But mostly for Alan.

**Stephen:** Was that the condo on Fredonia Drive, Sonoko?

**Sonoko:** Yes, on Fredonia, that apartment. And I think for a time Lenny just had that one apartment. And he had a sofa bed, because he was separated from his wife, so he would make the bed in the morning and then we would come in and work in the office. He had left Embassy Pictures and was just getting started. It was really an independent situation.

**Stephen:** Take me through how you segued over to working mostly with Alan.

**Sonoko:** Alan was the one who needed the most administrative or secretarial work because he was the one that was selling. He was the 'lawyer' of the company that was going through the contracts. They were both, Lenny and Alan, were both making the deals but somebody had to put it down on paper, and that was Alan's job. And I was there to administer or to help with the contracts. And mailing things out or taking dictation and faxes was it faxes?

**Stephen:** Yes, we had faxes back then. But that wasn't the extent of it, we had telexes too.

**Sonoko:** Oh yes, that's what it was, telexes, yeah. I remember pulling off the long scroll of telexes that would come in in the morning and then bringing it to Alan to go through.

**Stephen:** Oh yes. I remember that very well myself. Speaking of Alan, why don't we talk about Alan for a minute? What kind of person would you say Alan was? Did you guys become personal friends would you say at all?

**Sonoko:** There's something about Alan. I'd have to say that he was a really intelligent man, an intellectual. He had a great love for music. He would go to the record store that still exists in Silverlake. Rockaway Records or somewhere. And he would tell me about something that he had acquired or something. That was something that he loved doing and he would share that with me on occasion. But he was a very shy person in some ways. Remember he had a little stutter?

**Stephen:** Yes.

**Sonoko:** And when he got really nervous he would kind of stutter a little bit. And he was very meticulous about his note taking. You know I don't think I was his best secretary and I think if he had a choice he would've gotten someone who was native in English. You know being British, he was very particular about how he expressed himself. And I learned a lot from him. He would write out everything he wanted me to type, nearly everything, and for me it was like going to school to learn English. He was sort of very patient with me and was willing to teach me about film contracts, and I learned a lot from him because otherwise I would not have a clue.

**Stephen**: Would you describe him as a mentor of yours?

**Sonoko**: Not really, not a mentor. He was a boss. He was often difficult and sometimes he was not very open. He was shy not open and sometimes he had a very difficult personality. And he wasn't trying to teach me to become a sales person. I never really had a chance to get into sales, I didn't get to really sell anything. I was just always going to be just his secretary. If I had stayed there, just organize and do the contracts. So I was just basically a contract administrator, and that's basically where he wanted me to be.

**Stephen**: If you had to think of one characteristic or story, just one, when you mention Alan Solomon, what's the 'bumper sticker' that describes him?

**Sonoko**: I think he was a good salesman.

**Stephen**: Ok, I'll take that.

**Sonoko**: I mean considering the tough movies we had — I'm telling you the kind of movies that we were handling were what you'd call "B" movies, right? And it was not exactly my cup of tea, they were sort of low budget action movies, and what we were selling to tell you the truth was not really very high quality. I didn't really get to the level of the Glickenhaus films, because I left before Glickenhaus really came on board, and I have never seen his movies. But we were handling very low budget action movies and selling basically off of a promo reel. Cutting a really good promo reel, doing the marketing. I learned a lot about marketing from Alan and Lenny and Kelly. And how to put a film market together and how you presented product. Even if we didn't really have big budgeted movies, I think they really gave those little pictures the best shot they could get. I mean they really cared about the movies, and I like the way they nurtured them. Even though what we were selling was really "B" level films, I was happy to go to the market with them. They took me with them. The one thing that Alan did which was so generous, I still remember, it was my first market to Cannes — you know I never thought I would go the Cannes Film Festival to attend the Soiree, you know the red carpet event. But somehow, some Japanese producer decided that he wanted to invite me, and he had an extra ticket. But I had nothing to wear. I had no clothes. I mean I was just making $200 a week right? I had just enough to get there to do the work for Shapiro Entertainment. But Alan said, "Go out and get yourself a dress." He gave me a hundred dollars to go out and get a dress.

**Stephen**: Wow.

**Sonoko**: And I actually went out and got a red dress. And it was a Costarella, and I still remember it.

**Stephen:** Oh that's so sweet.

**Sonoko:** That was really sweet of him. He just gave me a hundred dollars, it was beautiful.

**Stephen:** You know what, he could be that way, couldn't he?

**Sonoko:** Yeah, he could be very generous like that, and also he could be not very open and not very generous. But that day it was a mood you know? He was in the right mood, and he really wanted to send me off to this thing. And that so sweet of him.

**Stephen:** That's nice. You mentioned the movies generally in terms of quality level but is there one that you remember, and go, "Oh I remember THAT movie." from your time there?

**Sonoko:** Oh yeah. There was an art film we sold: GOODBYE...It was about one of the groupies that hung around, what's that famous artist, the conceptual artist?

**Stephen:** Andy Warhol?

**Sonoko:** Andy Warhol yeah. What was it GOODBYE...? It was a movie that we handled that was about one of the groupies of Andy Warhol, the woman.

**Stephen:** I'll look it up there were a few women. [the movie is CIAO MANHATTAN (1972)]

**Sonoko:** So that was one that we took to the market and some kind of high end art house buyers came to buy it, and that's how I got exposed to the art house market. That was very interesting. And I think she, the woman in the movie, had overdosed, I think it's the story of her life I can't even remember that one—

**Stephen:** Was it Edie Sedgwick?

**Sonoko:** Yeah Edie Sedgwick. So I thought, "Oh this is good, we're actually handling something that belongs in an art house and not just these 'B' action movies." So that was one. And the other one was James Cameron's movie, THE PIRANHA.

**Stephen:** Oh, PIRANHA PART 2: THE SPAWNING (1981).

**Sonoko:** Yeah. I remember Jim Cameron did a poster for that. I remember that big piranha eating into the thigh of that woman.

**Stephen:** Yeah where it's below the water line?

**Sonoko:** Yeah, yeah it was, kind of—*(laughs)*

**Stephen:** Yeah, I know. Well it was that time right? Do you remember meeting any of the filmmakers? Did you ever meet Jim Cameron for example?

**Sonoko:** Yes. I was the secretary that would greet people, and Jim was the person who used to come and deliver the posters and the trailers that he cut. If it wasn't for that – he also used to hang out a lot because I think Lenny did things for him when he was really struggling while he was writing THE TERMINATOR (1984). It wasn't like he had a lot of money. He was doing this [making posters and trailers] to just get by so he could write THE TERMINATOR. So he was in and out—

**Stephen:** He actually painted some of those poster paintings didn't he?
He painted the PIRANHA 2 painting.

**Sonoko:** Yeah and he did these big helicopter, big bombs exploding kind of posters. You know those typical "B" movie posters. So James Cameron did those just to get by. And it was so funny because after I left Shapiro, I went on to work with Gaga Communications and some others and as an agent for Gaga. And then I went to work for Nippon Herald, and when Nippon Herald was bidding on James Cameron's films I had lunch with him. You know as part of the interview he decided to invite some Japanese buyers to see which buyer he would want to be in business with, before he went to work exclusively with Fox. So he wanted to go independent and do this whole thing – produce and distribute these films through independents. So I had lunch with him, and I shared our memories of working at Shapiro Entertainment. He was basically working as a freelance employee, and I was working there as a secretary. And we connected because of that.

**Stephen:** Oh that's great!

**Sonoko:** Yeah and he would say, "You know some of those movies I couldn't even watch the whole thing but I would make sure there were enough explosions, you know to really make it commercial." And it was kind of funny because I remembered exactly which movie he was talking about. And I didn't watch most of those movies because I only watched the trailers. I mean we had so many of them. But he would just churn them out. And I was the one churning out the contracts and handing out the pamphlets. You know we would mail everything. Mailing out all these flyers and things before the market to reach the distributors overseas. A lot of my work entailed handling the mail and the faxes and those kinds of things. What happened, which was amazing was, Jim and I hit it off really well and even though he actually had an exclusive, outright relationship with Toho-Towa, that year he decided to do the deal with us. We actually got the deal, and we did the movie TRUE LIES (1994) and we did another movie with him that Kathy Bigelow did about the surfer with Patrick Swayze, I forgot the name…

**Stephen:** POINT BREAK (1991).

**Sonoko:** Yeah POINT BREAK. And then we were going to do more movies, but then the term ran out and he went and did TITANIC (1997) which was not part of our deal. And then he just decided to go with the majors. And TRUE LIES made a lot of money at the box office. In Japan it made like $65 million dollars and that was a huge hit.

**Stephen:** So you left Shapiro Entertainment before the merger with Glickenhaus Film that then formed Shapiro Glickenhaus Entertainment. What was your first job after leaving Shapiro Entertainment?

**Sonoko:** I went to work as an agent for Gaga Communications.

**Stephen:** In 1992 you were credited as an Associate Producer of the romance film called THAT NIGHT.

**Sonoko:** That was when I was at Nippon Herald.

**Stephen:** I see, so that was further on. So you moved on from Gaga to Nippon—

**Sonoko:** In 1990 I moved on from Gaga to Nippon Herald.

**Stephen:** And two years later you received your first Associate Producer credit on THAT NIGHT. So how did that happen? How did you get your very first job as a producer?

**Sonoko:** Nippon Herald was buying movies from New Regency. What was the name of that producer? He's an Israeli producer. [the producer's name is Arnon Milchan] Anyway, so I came across a script that I thought was really interesting. And I thought, "Well you know this is maybe something I would like to buy for Japan but it's not produced. So maybe I could take it to an independent producer who has some clout and get it produced." And it had a director. He had done some shorts but he written BLACK RAIN (1989) so I said, "Okay, well maybe it's a good enough package." So I just casually took it to this producer at New Regency, and they jumped on it. Basically I was going to stay on as a producer, and I was going to have the Japanese side put in part of the money, but after negotiating with them we decided that we didn't want to be the real producers on it. So I just took a back seat and took Associate Producer credit.

**Stephen:** Shapiro Entertainment or Shapiro Glickenhaus didn't have anything to do with that project, did they?

**Sonoko:** No nothing, nothing. That was years after I had left Shapiro. I didn't do any producing there [at Shapiro Entertainment] or take any projects from Shapiro.

**Stephen:** Was the movie THAT NIGHT a box-office success in its time?

**Sonoko:** It was a Warner Bros. release. It was originally budgeted for like six million dollars. They ended up producing it for more than ten million, I think. But it had a good cast. It had a decent cast, and it was an okay movie, but I wouldn't say it was a box office hit. It was just okay. I think it made its money back.

**Stephen:** Well, hey – that's good enough sometimes. So shifting gears away from movies for a second, besides cinema, cooking has been your personal passion and is now actually your profession. How long has cooking been important to you and have you been cooking since you were young?

**Sonoko:** I've always been a home cook. I love to cook because my mother and my grandmother were really good cooks and entertained a lot. And my sister ended up going to pastry school in France, and she's a professional chef. I am actually surprised I didn't follow that path, but what's interesting is when I started at Shapiro, it was also the year that my first cook book came out. And so I was just finishing up my cookbook while I was still working there. I started my cookbook while I was a graduate student at UCLA. And I was just working on it for three years, and then I found a publisher, and so what Lenny did was he bought all these books. That was sweet of him, right? To help me promote the book he bought the books to give away. And I did my cookbook tour while I was still working at Shapiro. I was already interested in food then. My husband is an artist, and I needed a steady job. You can't have two people with unsteady income. So my film career sort of took off even after I left Shapiro, and I got recruited to work on the Japanese distribution side. It was a good run. I went to work with Gaga which was a great company. And then I worked for Nippon Herald which was a really great company, and I spent almost twenty-five years working for the Japanese companies before I went independent. It just gave me the kind of financial stability that I needed to raise a family, and I cultivated my eye in films and got to the see the world. It was a really good run and it was the days when independent films were highly regarded – there was a good market for them. I had fun being a buyer.

**Stephen:** Back to cooking for a second, there are many examples of the subject of cooking in the history of cinema; can you name any all-time favorite movie that has cooking as an integral element in its story? For example, what did you think of the Meryl Streep, Amy Adams movie JULIE & JULIA (2009)?

**Sonoko:** Of course those are always fun, and Meryl is a great actress, so I enjoyed that. I loved her, she played Julia Child so well, so that was good. My favorites are BABETTE'S FEAST (1987), and I also loved TAMPOPO (1985), the ramen story that was made by a Japanese filmmaker. I also love LIKE WATER FOR CHOCOLATE (1992). I actually bought that film for Nippon Herald, and we had a bit hit with that film in Japan. Remember that one, LIKE WATER FOR CHOCOLATE?

**Stephen:** Yes of course.

**Sonoko:** It was directed by Alfonso Arau. We took the filmmakers to Japan, and we recreated the recipes. We actually went wide with the film even though it was just an art film. And that was a fun film to work with. As a buyer, I'd have to tell you that when I go through all the films to buy, I was 'smelling', you know I was always looking to see if there was anything related to food. BIG NIGHT (1996) is a good film too, but I lost the bid on that one. Yeah, I've always been interested in movies about food. But there aren't so many good ones.

**Stephen:** You know what I just had a memory of something, tell me if I'm making this up, I mentioned Meryl Streep... didn't Meryl go to school with someone in your family?

**Sonoko:** Oh yeah with Sakai.

**Stephen:** With your husband?

**Sonoko:** Her husband Don Gummer and my husband, they were all students together

**Sonoko:** at Yale University, in the same sculpture department.

**Stephen:** Let's talk about another one of your films, the blockbuster SILK from '07. It's among the most popular projects that you produced, would you say that's true?

**Sonoko:** No. I think my favorite film is BLINDNESS (2008).

**Stephen:** We'll get to BLINDNESS in a second—

**Sonoko:** I mean they're all different films. And I wouldn't say they're— none of these are big box-office winners. In some territories they did better than others. Like SILK did really well in the Spanish-speaking territories - interesting. Like Spain and Mexico. But I think in Japan we could've done better, but we took the film way too wide, so it performed differently in different territories.

**Stephen:** Let's talk a little bit more about BLINDNESS then, did you find that it was hard to bring that film to the screen?

**Sonoko:** They're all hard. It's grueling; it's so much work. But it was a lot easier when Fernando Meirelles came on board. He was the director of CITY OF GOD (2002). When he came on board everything else started to come into place. It was not the easiest picture to produce. That project had been around for ten years, and it was only after he came on board that we were able to put the financing together. But even that was hard.

**Stephen:** Were you involved in the casting and crew selection?

**Sonoko:** Yes. Especially in the casting.

**Stephen:** When did you read that novel for the first time?

**Sonoko:** When the Canadian producer gave me the script, I read the book at the same time. The book is a pretty well-known book. It's been translated into many languages. It's from a Nobel Prize winning writer, José Saramago. And the message is very universal. But it's very bleak at the same time. It was not an easy subject matter to produce a movie for.

**Stephen:** So when it came to you it had already been adapted into a screenplay?

**Sonoko:** Right. But then the writer and the director, Fernando and Don McKellar, they both sort of did another rewrite of it, that part went pretty quickly.

**Stephen:** Let's talk about both of those films together and some similarities that they have, BLINDNESS and SILK. The biggest one being that they both have strong female lead characters. Would you say that was an important aspect in your career at that time, or was that just a coincidence that both of those films had strong female leads?

**Sonoko:** It's a total coincidence. As a matter of fact, it's very difficult to produce a film of that budget scale with a strong female lead, because you don't know if you can recoup your investment. A strong male lead; if you had Johnny Depp then it's just so much easier to sell the movie. Movies with strong female leads were a challenge. We had Julianne Moore in

BLINDNESS, and Keira Knightly in SILK; these are really good actresses that can carry a film, but still it was pretty tricky. You know if you really go to the individual territories it's all a negotiation and it's a lot harder with females in the lead unfortunately. But I think these two movies helped change that pattern, but movies for the most part work better at the box office when you have big male actors.

**Stephen:** Let's talk about a genre that male stars are really strong in, which is action genre movies, have you had much contact in your career either as a buyer or as a producer with these big action genre films?

**Sonoko:** Yes, with James Cameron, I did TRUE LIES with Arnold Schwarzenegger in his heyday so that was a very big box-office hit.

**Stephen:** Do you enjoy watching those action movies as an audience member or is that just not your 'thing'?

**Sonoko:** I actually like a good action movie. If you consider an action/adventure movie like the Kurosawa films or any of those old Westerns, or I like Michael Mann's movie HEAT (1995) – an action/thriller. Those are films I was involved with - THE LORD OF THE RINGS there's a lot of action and adventure. At Nippon Herald we distributed all three films. They're entertaining and full of action and thrills. I actually like a movie that has mass appeal, when it's done well. But if I have a choice, I'd rather see a drama or a good romantic comedy, I would go for that. But when you're a buyer you can't just be too choosy, you have to find what works for the market.

**Stephen:** How long have you been out of the movie business now?

**Sonoko:** Since 2008.

**Stephen:** What's your main focus now in your life?

**Sonoko:** Food and food education. I'm working with farmers in Southern California to restore some of the ancient grains.

**Stephen:** What's the name of your company?

**Sonoko:** My project is called Common Grains. And I'm trying to find a common ground with farmers and bakers and chefs by introducing these heirloom grains back into the soil. And fighting this big agricultural machine that is causing the depletion of our resources, I don't know if you are familiar with that but industrial agriculture is one of the culprits of climate change. My role is maybe so small because I'm really just a cooking teacher but even a cooking teacher can do a lot by being a conduit to bring seeds to farmers. I have a network of farmers and chefs, food educators and scientists that I work with trying to promote sustainable agriculture. So that's one of my life missions right now. And to make a living I teach cooking classes, and I'm writing a book on rice, and that's really exciting. And I do event producing. So some of the things I learned in film I am actually applying - like the marketing and the production I am applying it to the producing of food events.

**Stephen:** This is one of those 'back over the years' questions, looking back the thirty or so years since your time at Shapiro Entertainment, if you had to pick one main thing, how would you say that the independent movie business has changed since those days?

**Sonoko:** The reason why I left was because the financing dried up. There are ways to finance a film together among the independents but I noticed that it dried up in Japan and then I saw that the European market was drying up. And the kind of films that I used to love, I just saw less and less in the marketplace. I don't know how the market is right now, maybe some of those quality independent movies are coming back, but I just felt like the whole film world was changing. I don't know if I answered your question.

**Stephen:** Yes, I think you did. Financing is a very good answer, and that just happens to coincide date-wise with the onset of the Great Recession as well – perhaps not an accident.

**Sonoko:** Well you know my movie BLINDNESS opened on the day that the stock market crashed. I don't know if you know this. And people did not want to see a movie about that very message— because you know, we went blind because of money and greed right? The whole economy crashed because of that. And if you look at the underlying theme of this movie, it's about that. It's about seeing but not looking. You know this whole metaphor was about that. It was timely, but yet it was a tough movie to release when people had to deal with this in their real lives. Yeah, financing, and also I noticed that the quality of films wasn't there. And as a buyer that was tough. And as a producer trying to bring quality movies to the marketplace, it was even tougher as the financing dried up. But I hope that's coming back, I don't know. I'm not up to date with it anymore.

**Stephen:** Are there any anecdotal stories that we haven't touched on that you'd like to share about your Shapiro Entertainment days whether they be meaningful to your career as a producer or the enrichment of yourself as a person? What is something you can remember that happened back then that you think is worth mentioning?

**Sonoko:** Lenny is a wonderful person you know? And he cared about people. Even though we were all struggling as a company he had a way of nurturing people. I think what I really learned from Lenny and Alan and Kelly and all those people that were trying to put this company together is how industrious and creative you could be with the resources that you had. Even though the resources were very limited. I really learned how to be independent. I had never worked in a real American company. I did some, at Frank Konigsberg, but that was just scratching the surface. But when I went to work with Lenny I just got to learn all the ropes. And I told him, because I would sit in the living room and hear all the conversations that Lenny was having. Alan would just close the door so I never knew who he was talking to. But with Lenny, he was just really open, and I would just sit and listen.

And I said, "One of the training lessons you gave me was how to wheel and deal, just by listening to you." And you know, in his New York kind of accent, he would wheel and deal. And that's something that I couldn't have gotten working in a Japanese distribution company or production company. So I think it was like going to film school in some way. That was an invaluable lesson. And about how he treated people. I have to say there are still some things that I apply to what I do today. So I really appreciate the short time that I was there, I'll always remember that.

**Stephen:** I'm not sure if it was the first Cannes or the second Cannes that I went to, but, Shapiro Entertainment had a movie about Marilyn Chambers. She did these X-rated films, and this movie was her 'moving on' and not doing an adult movie. Maybe it was an 'R' rated film, I didn't even get to see the film. [the film was probably MY THERAPIST (1984)]. But anyway so Marilyn Chambers was going to come, and they were going to put a big hot air balloon and fly it at the beach. And they did this parade. Remember Kelly used to come up with all these crazy ideas?

**Sonoko:** Yes.

**Stephen:** So Marilyn Chambers is coming, and what happens is Kelly's father, or someone else in her family, passed away, and she had to leave Cannes before Cannes started. And she left me to manage this event -- with Marilyn Chambers! I was like, "What am I going to do?! I don't even know how to handle the talent." And she says, "And make sure you get that air balloon up!" And there was too much wind, and the Fire Department said we couldn't get the balloon up, so the balloon had to come down. I was under so much pressure.

**Sonoko:** My God.

**Stephen:** And I was crying and everything - I remember that. But somehow we managed to get through it. And I think it was a really successful market. So that was one incident. But another incident which was too much was, when I had my son, at six months I could not leave him at home. So Lenny says, "Why don't you bring your son with you and just get an apartment? Or just stay at a hotel." And I had my mother, and my 84-year-old grandma, come from Tokyo to watch my baby son. And one day I wanted to give them a break, because this is a two-week event. So I hired a babysitter to take care of my son. But guess what happened? After they had left the hotel the babysitter never showed up.

**Sonoko:** Oh no!

**Stephen:** So what happened was Alan and Lenny got a little baby bed and put it in one of the meeting offices and let me keep Sakai in there for the whole day. Can you believe it?

**Sonoko:** You know what? Talk about family right?

**Stephen:** Talk about family! And you know what he did not complain. Neither of them. They sympathized with me and they said, "Look, we understand. We are the ones that said you could bring the baby and we were happy that your mother and grandma had a little break from the market." And we managed. I mean we always managed. Even in these chaotic times they didn't lose it. I mean I was nursing my son, my God. But I got through that day, and my mother and my grandma came back, and everything was ok. But that babysitter did not show. It was a 'no-show' case; it was horrible. So that's what I mean by family right?

**Sonoko**: Absolutely.

---

**By Stephen A. Roberts, via telephone**
**From Los Angeles, California**
**11May, 2015**

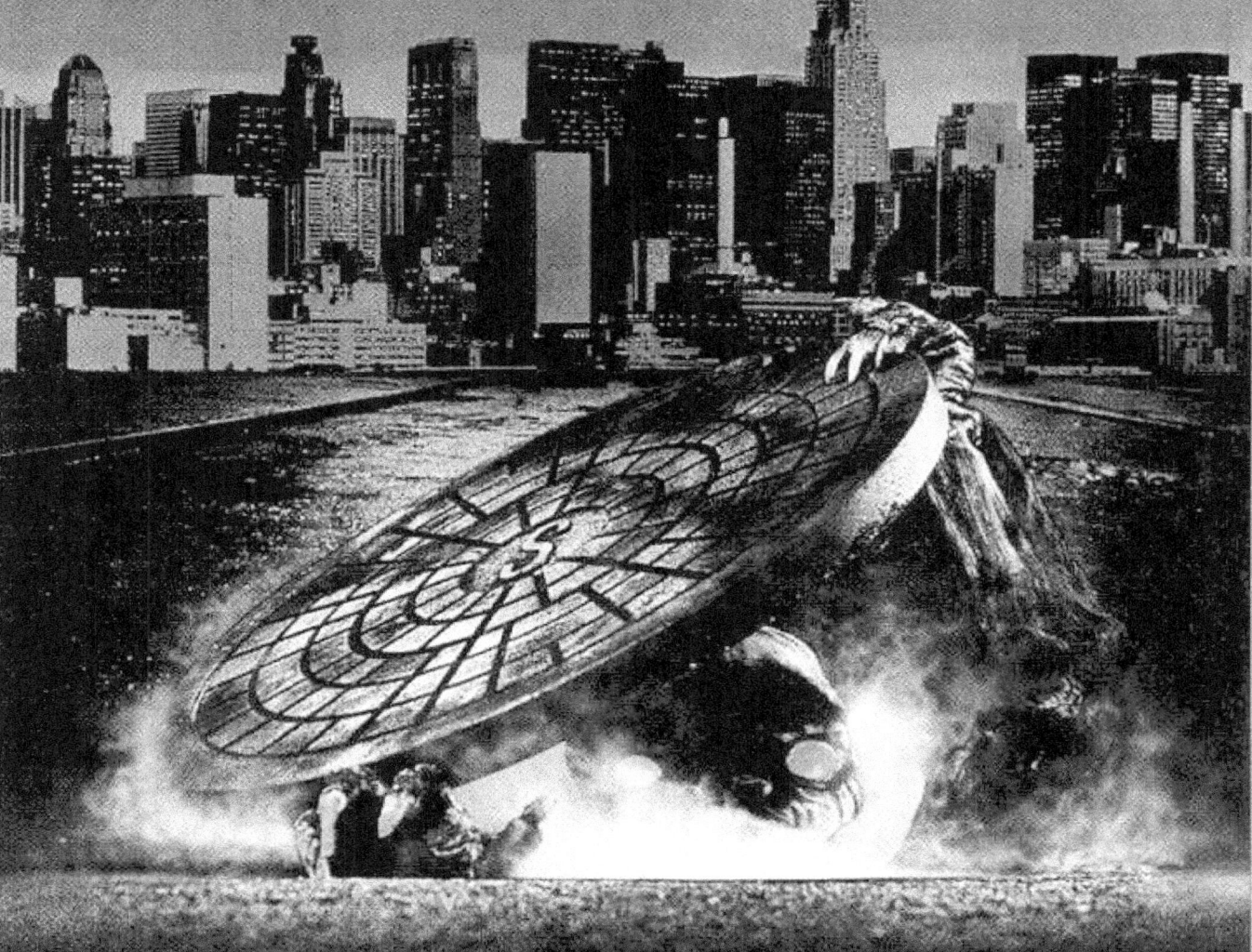

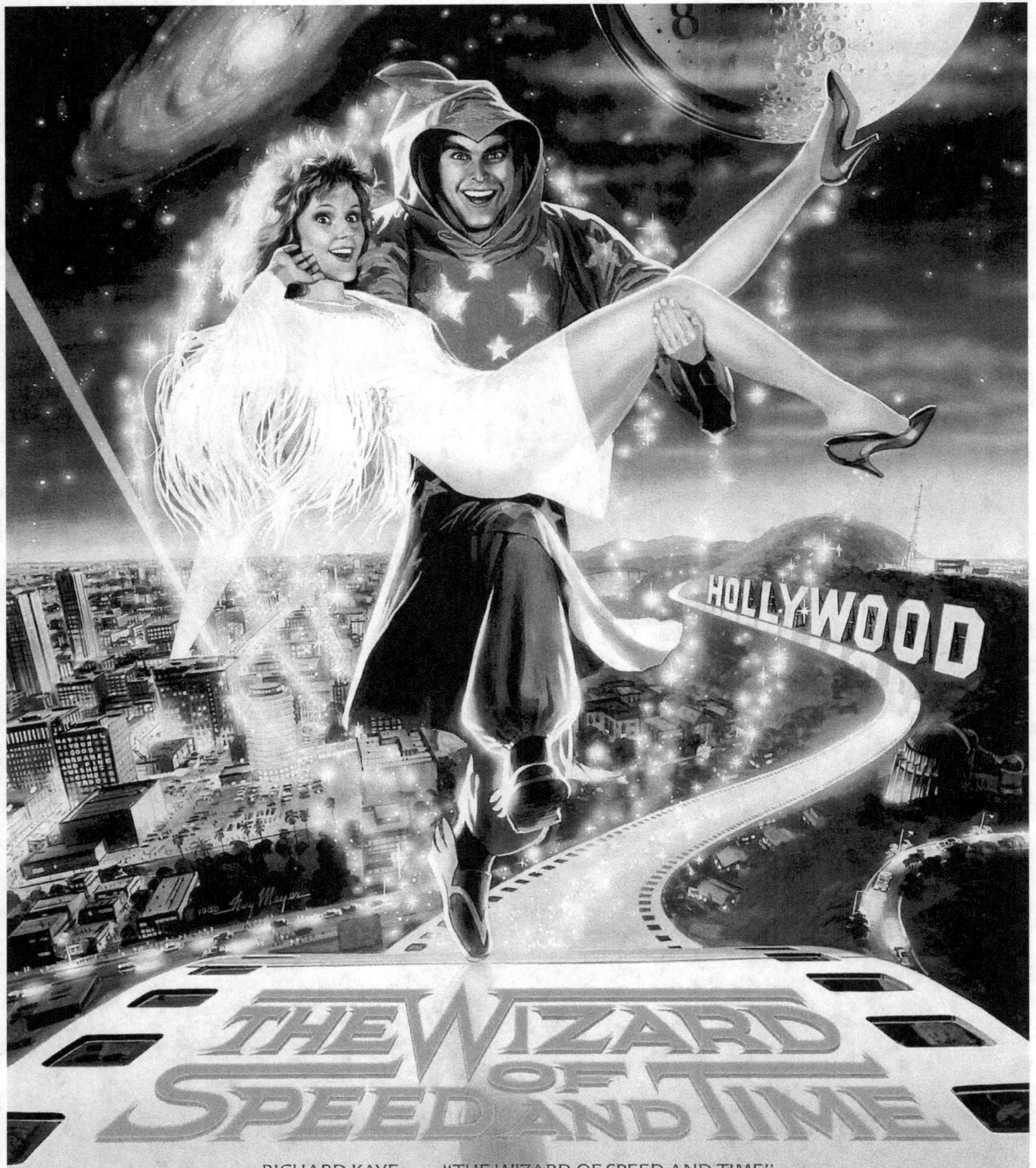

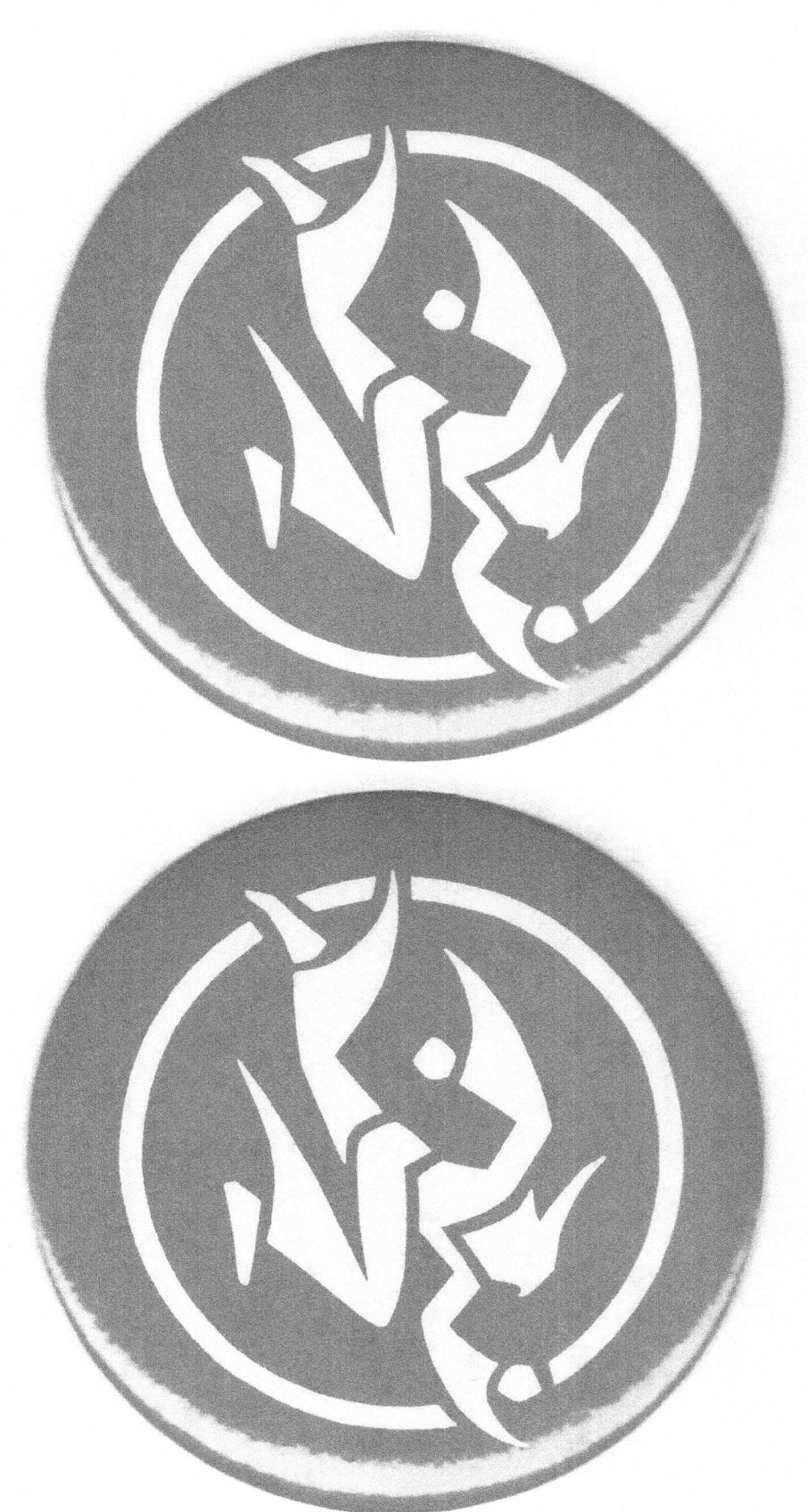

**SHAPIRO GLICKENHAUS ENTERTAINMENT CORPORATION**
12001 VENTURA PLACE, FOURTH FLOOR
STUDIO CITY, CA 91604

15011

16-21/1220
137

PAY TO THE ORDER OF __Library of Congress__   Apr. 2, 19 92   $ 35.00

__Thirty Five and 00/100__ DOLLARS

First Interstate Bank
First Interstate Bank of California # 137
4605 Lankershim Boulevard
P.O. Box 7067
North Hollywood, CA 91609-7067

TWO SIGNATURES ARE REQUIRED FOR ANY AMOUNT EQUAL TO OR ABOVE $5000.00

FOR "B.C.3 and Voodoo Doll"

⑈015011⑈ ⑆122002181⑆ 13740736811⑈

# MUSIC CUE SHEET

Production: THE EXTERMINATOR

Music Producer: MURRI BARBER

Recording Date: 5 MAY 1980

| | | |
|---|---|---|
| COMPOSITION: | "Opening Case" | TIM |
| COMPOSER: | Joe Renzetti | PART |
| AUTHOR: | | INST |
| PUBLISHER: | Napolis | BKGI |
| CLEARANCE: | BMI | SOUR |
| COMPOSITION: | "Bullits in Pocket" | TIM |
| COMPOSER: | Joe Renzetti | PART |
| AUTHOR: | | INST |
| PUBLISHER: | Napolis | BKGI |
| CLEARANCE: | BMI | SOUR |
| COMPOSITION: | "Closing Case" | TIM |
| COMPOSER: | Joe Renzetti | PART |
| AUTHOR: | | INST |
| PUBLISHER: | Napolis | BKGD |
| CLEARANCE: | BMI | SOUR |
| COMPOSITION: | "Leaving House" | TIM |
| COMPOSER: | Joe Renzetti | PART |
| AUTHOR: | | INST |
| PUBLISHER: | Napolis | BKGD |
| CLEARANCE: | BMI | SOUR |
| COMPOSITION: | "Fried Pimp" | TIM |
| COMPOSER: | Joe Renzetti | PART |
| AUTHOR: | | INST |
| PUBLISHER: | Napolis | BKGD |
| CLEARANCE: | BMI | SOUR |
| COMPOSITION: | "Freed Chicken" | TIM |
| COMPOSER: | Joe Renzetti | PART |
| AUTHOR: | | INST |
| PUBLISHER: | Napolis | BKGD |
| CLEARANCE: | BMI | SOUR |
| COMPOSITION: | "Kali Au" | TIM |
| COMPOSER: | Chuck Loeb | PART |
| AUTHOR: | | INST |
| PUBLISHER: | On Stage Music | BKGD |
| CLEARANCE: | BMI | SOUR |
| COMPOSITION: | "Ghoul Dies" | TIM |
| COMPOSER: | Joe Renzetti | PART |
| AUTHOR: | | INST |
| PUBLISHER: | Napolis | BKGD |
| CLEARANCE: | BMI | SOUR |
| COMPOSITION: | "The Chase of the Ghouls" | TIM |
| COMPOSER: | Joe Renzetti | PART |
| AUTHOR: | | INST |
| PUBLISHER: | Napolis | BKGD |
| CLEARANCE: | BMI | SOURC |

# CERTIFICATE OF COPYRIGHT REGISTRATION

OFFICIAL SEAL

This certificate, issued under the seal of the Copyright Office in accordance with the provisions of section 410(a) of title 17, United States Code, attests that copyright registration has been made for the work identified below. The information in this certificate has been made a part of the Copyright Office records.

REGISTER OF COPYRIGHTS
United States of America

**FORM PA**
UNITED STATES COPYRIGHT OFFICE
REGISTRATION NUMBER

PA 477 439

PA / PAU

EFFECTIVE DATE OF REGISTRATION

July 12 1990

DO NOT WRITE ABOVE THIS LINE. IF YOU NEED MORE SPACE, USE A SEPARATE CONTINUATION SHEET.

**1. TITLE OF THIS WORK ▼**

BASKET CASE 2

PREVIOUS OR ALTERNATIVE TITLES ▼

NATURE OF THIS WORK ▼ See instructions

MOTION PICTURE

**2. a NAME OF AUTHOR ▼**

FRANK HENENLOTTER

DATES OF BIRTH AND DEATH
Year Born ▼   Year Died ▼

Was this contribution to the work a "work made for hire"?
[ ] Yes
[X] No

AUTHOR'S NATIONALITY OR DOMICILE
Name of Country
OR { Citizen of ▶ New York City, NY USA
    { Domiciled in ▶

WAS THIS AUTHOR'S CONTRIBUTION TO THE WORK
Anonymous?   [ ] Yes [X] No
Pseudonymous? [ ] Yes [X] No
If the answer to either of these questions is "Yes," see detailed instructions.

NATURE OF AUTHORSHIP Briefly describe nature of the material created by this author in which copyright is claimed. ▼

SCREENPLAY - DIRECTOR

**b NAME OF AUTHOR ▼**

DATES OF BIRTH AND DEATH
Year Born ▼   Year Died ▼

Was this contribution to the work a "work made for hire"?
[ ] Yes
[ ] No

AUTHOR'S NATIONALITY OR DOMICILE
Name of country
OR { Citizen of ▶
    { Domiciled in ▶

WAS THIS AUTHOR'S CONTRIBUTION TO THE WORK
Anonymous?   [ ] Yes [ ] No
Pseudonymous? [ ] Yes [ ] No

NATURE OF AUTHORSHIP Briefly describe nature of the material created by this author in which copyright is claimed. ▼

**c NAME OF AUTHOR ▼**

DATES OF BIRTH AND DEATH
Year Born ▼   Year Died ▼

Was this contribution to the work a "work made for hire"?
[ ] Yes
[ ] No

AUTHOR'S NATIONALITY OR DOMICILE
Name of Country
OR { Citizen of ▶
    { Domiciled in ▶

WAS THIS AUTHOR'S CONTRIBUTION TO THE WORK
Anonymous?   [ ] Yes [ ] No
Pseudonymous? [ ] Yes [ ] No

NATURE OF AUTHORSHIP Briefly describe nature of the material created by this author in which copyright is claimed. ▼

**3. a YEAR IN WHICH CREATION OF THIS WORK WAS COMPLETED** This information must be given in all cases.
1990 ◀ Year

**b DATE AND NATION OF FIRST PUBLICATION OF THIS PARTICULAR WORK** Complete this information ONLY if this work has been published.
Month ▶ February   Day ▶ 23   Year ▶ 1990
Los Angeles, Ca. USA ◀ Nation

**4. COPYRIGHT CLAIMANT(S)** Name and address must be given even if the claimant is the same as the author given in space 2. ▼

1989 SGE ENTERTAINMENT CORPORATION
12001 VENTURA PLACE, SUITE 404
STUDIO CITY, CA. 91604

APPLICATION RECEIVED
JUL. 12 1990
ONE DEPOSIT RECEIVED
JUL. 12 1990
TWO DEPOSITS RECEIVED

REMITTANCE NUMBER AND DATE

**TRANSFER** If the claimant(s) named here in space 4 are different from the author(s) named in space 2, give a brief statement of how the claimant(s) obtained ownership of the copyright. ▼

By written agreement

**MORE ON BACK ▶**
• Complete all applicable spaces (numbers 5-9) on the reverse side of this page
• See detailed instructions
• Sign the form at line 8

DO NOT WRITE HERE
Page 1 of ___ pages

## Show Cue Sheet Report

**Series Name:** Not available or a standalone Program
**Program Title:** BASKET CASE III (1992)
**Program Number:** 0000
**Expected Air Date:** 1900-01-01
**Program Duration:** 000:00:00

**Printed:** September 29, 2010

### Usage Code Description:
V V: Visual Vocal   V I: Visual Instrumental   B V: Background Vocal   B I: Background Instrumental

| Cue # | Title | Time | Usage | Entitled Party Type | Entitled Party Name | O. Shares | C. Shares | Member Society |
|---|---|---|---|---|---|---|---|---|
| 0001 | BASKET CASE III CUES | 000:50:16 | BI | COMPOSER V | RENZETTI JOSEPH | 50.00 | 50.00 | BMI |
|  |  |  | BI | ORIGINAL P | MUZETTI INC | 25.00 | 25.00 | BMI |
|  |  |  | BI | ORIGINAL P | NAPOLIS MUSIC CORPORATION | 25.00 | 25.00 | BMI |
| 0002 | GROWING BELIAL (MAIN TITLE) | 000:01:34 | BI | COMPOSER V | RENZETTI JOSEPH | 50.00 | 50.00 | BMI |
|  |  |  | BI | ORIGINAL P | MUZETTI INC | 25.00 | 25.00 | BMI |
|  |  |  | BI | ORIGINAL P | NAPOLIS MUSIC CORPORATION | 25.00 | 25.00 | BMI |
| 0003 | PERSONALITY | 000:01:34 | VI | COMPOSER/ | LOGAN HAROLD | 25.00 | 25.00 | BMI |
|  |  |  | VI | COMPOSER/ | PRICE LLOYD | 25.00 | 25.00 | BMI |
|  |  |  | VI | ORIGINAL P | IRVING MUSIC | 50.00 | 50.00 | BMI |
| 0004 | OPERATIONAL FLASHBACK | 000:00:44 | BI | COMPOSER V | RENZETTI JOSEPH | 25.00 | 25.00 | BMI |
|  |  |  | BI | COMPOSER V | SANDS ROBERT | 25.00 | 25.00 | BMI |
|  |  |  | BI | ORIGINAL P | MUZETTI INC | 25.00 | 25.00 | BMI |
|  |  |  | BI | ORIGINAL P | NAPOLIS MUSIC CORPORATION | 25.00 | 25.00 | BMI |
| 0005 | PERSONALITY (END CREDITS) | 000:02:55 | BI | COMPOSER/ | LOGAN HAROLD | 25.00 | 25.00 | BMI |
|  |  |  | BI | COMPOSER/ | PRICE LLOYD | 25.00 | 25.00 | BMI |
|  |  |  | BI | ORIGINAL P | IRVING MUSIC | 50.00 | 50.00 | BMI |

EXHIBIT F

Date: April 12, 1991

CERTIFICATE OF AUTHORSHIP

I hereby certify that I co-wrote the manuscript hereby attached entitled "BASKET CASE 3", based upon Basket Case 1 and 2 as an employee of Full Moon Films, Inc. which furnished my services pursuant to an employment agreement between Frank T. Henenlotter and Full Moon Films, Inc. in performance of my duties thereunder and in the regular course of my employment and that Full Moon Films, Inc. is the author thereof and is entitled to the copyright therein and thereto, and all renewals thereof, with the right to make such changes therein and such uses thereof as it may, from time to time, determine as such author.

IN WITNESS WHEREOF I have hereto set my hand:

*Frank T. Henenlotter*
(Frank T. Henenlotter)

Date: 4-12-91

NOTARIZED:
STATE OF Georgia )
COUNTY OF Fulton )

BEFORE ME, the undersigned Notary Public personally appeared Frank T. Henenlotter on this 12th day of April, 1991 he personally known to me he proved to me on the basis of satisfactory evidence to be the person who executed the within instrument as Co-author or on behalf of the corporation therein named, and acknowledged to me that the corporation executed it.

WITNESS MY HAND AND OFFICIAL SEAL

*Becky E. Herring*
NOTARY PUBLIC
In and for the State of Georgia

Notary Public, Fulton, Georgia.
My Commission Expires October 12, 1991

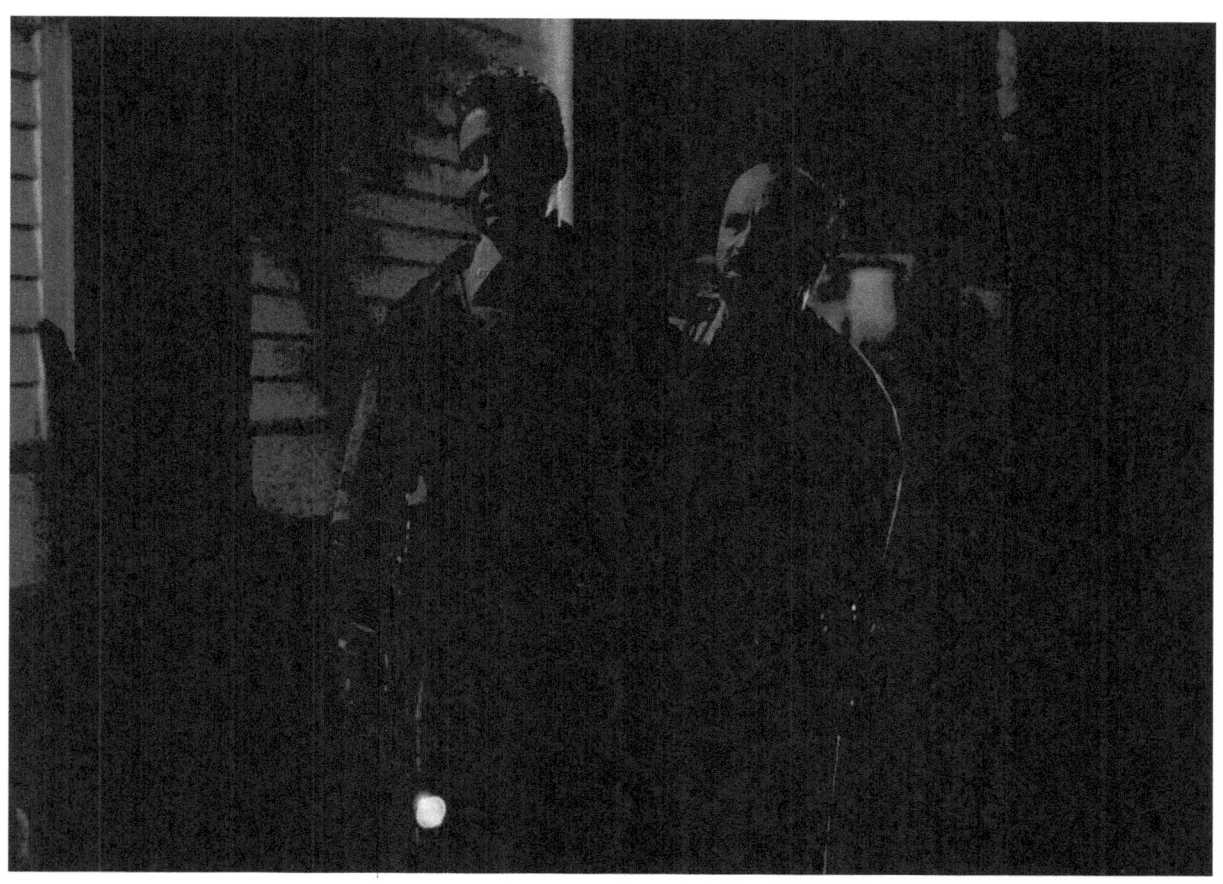
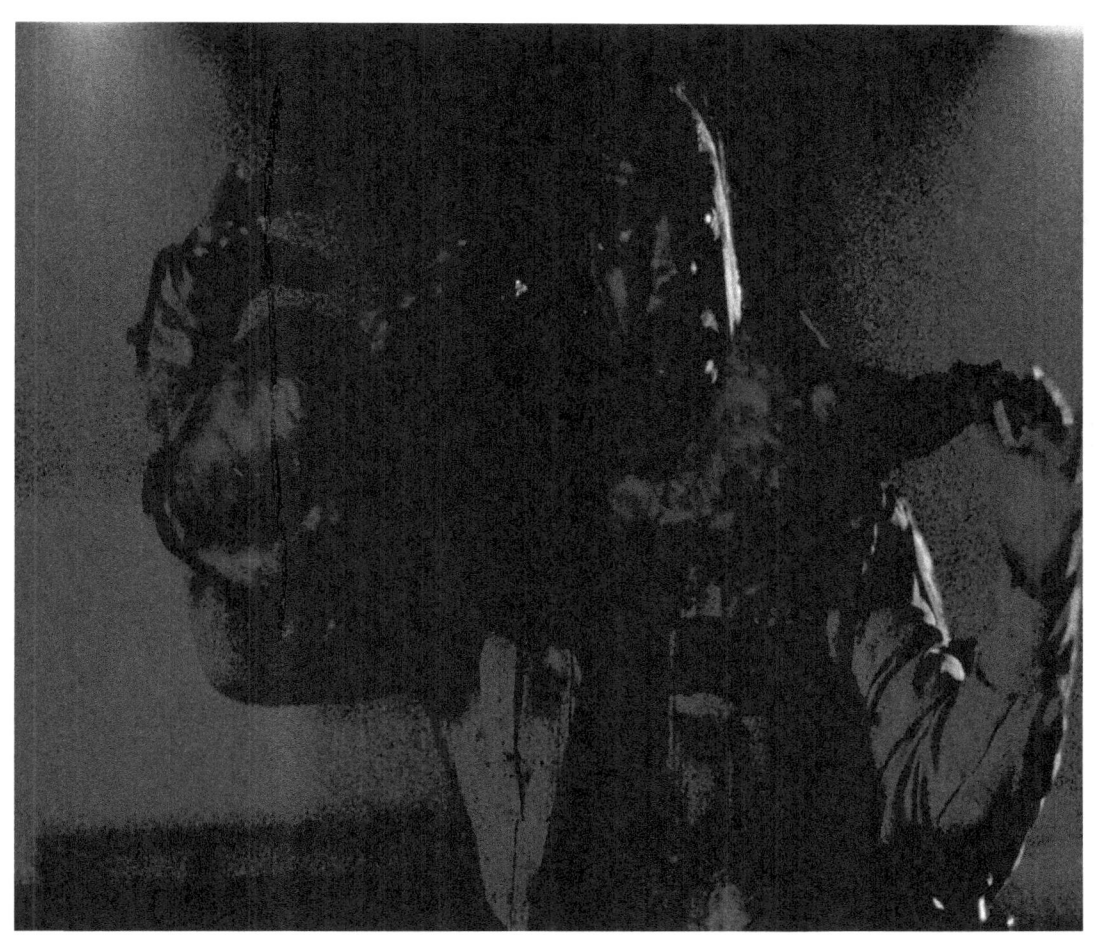

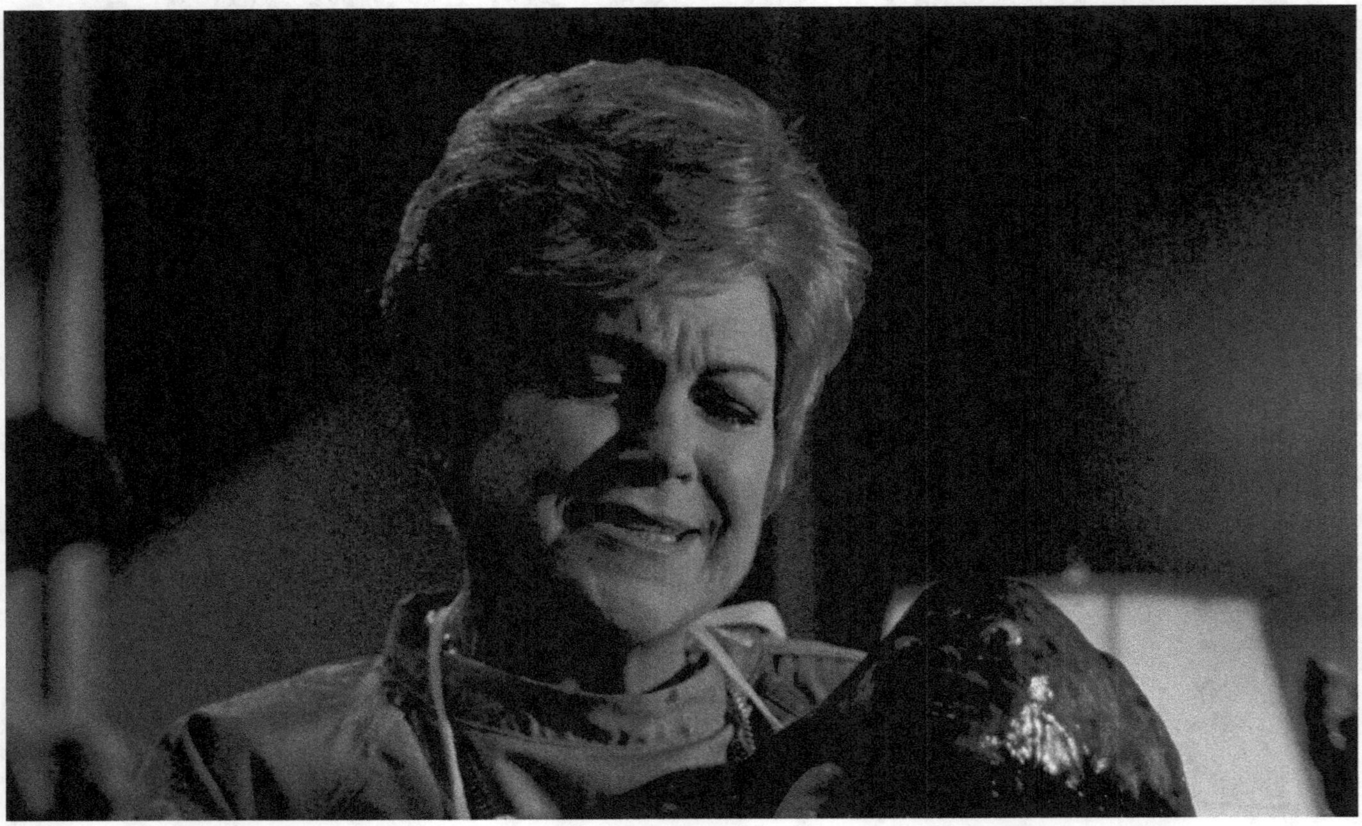

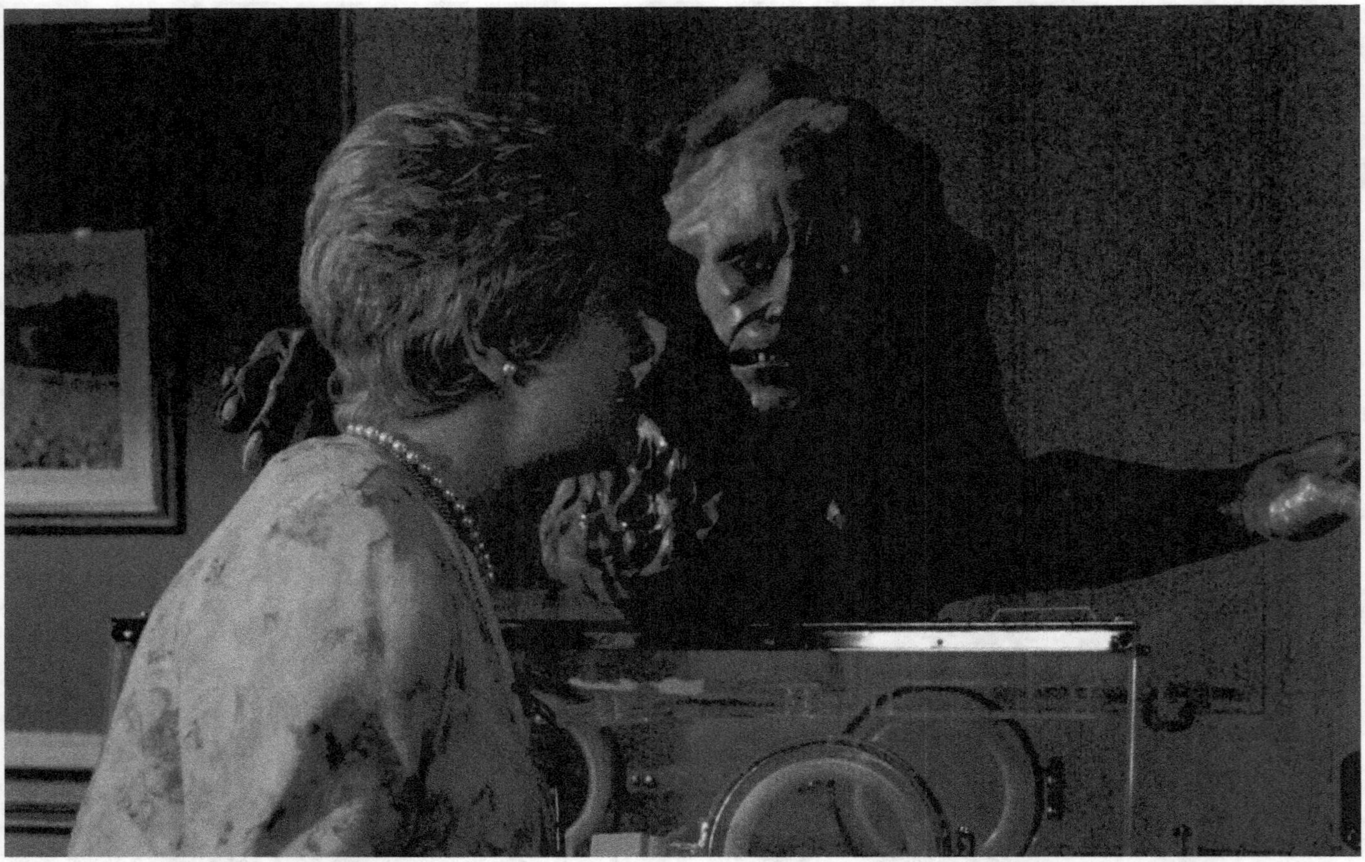

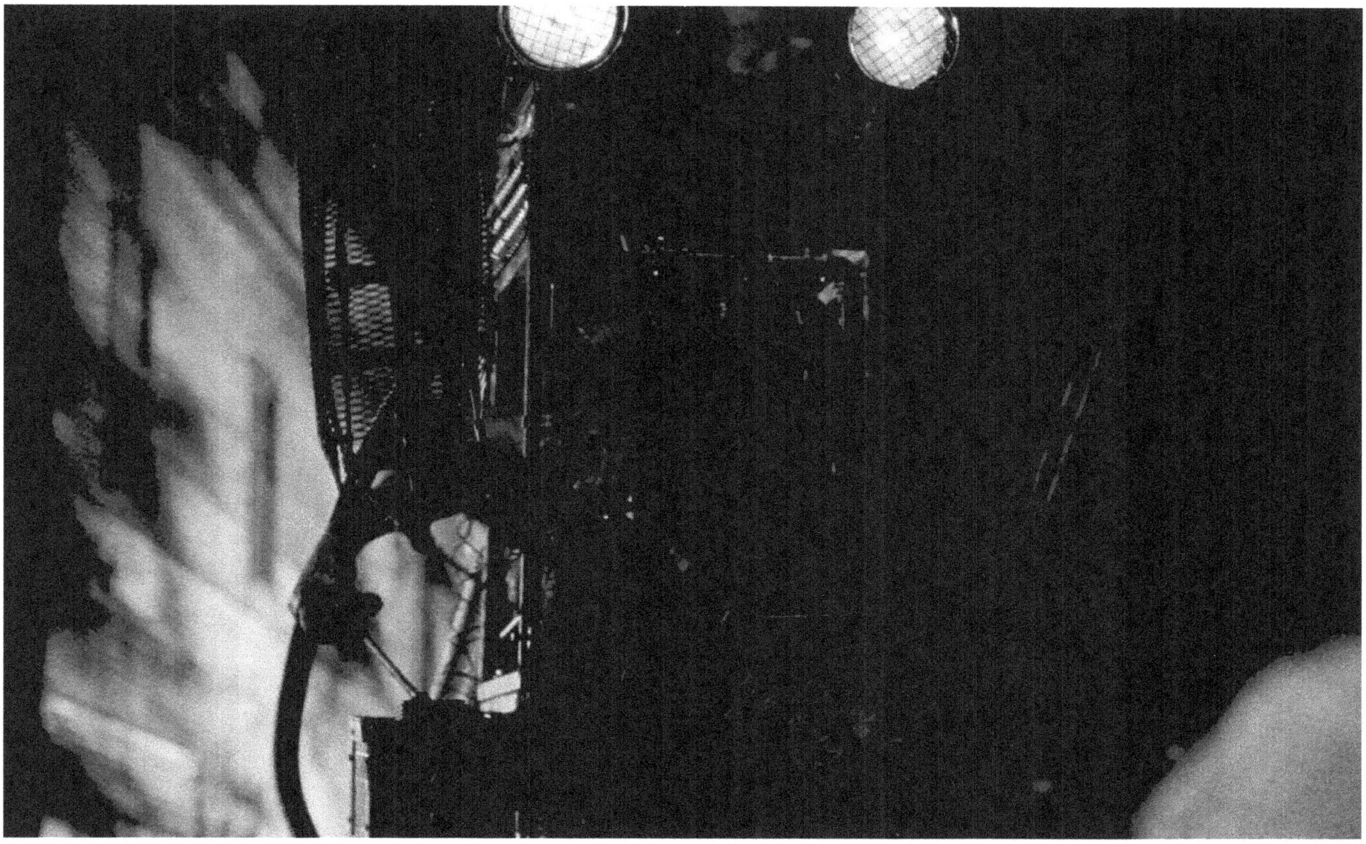

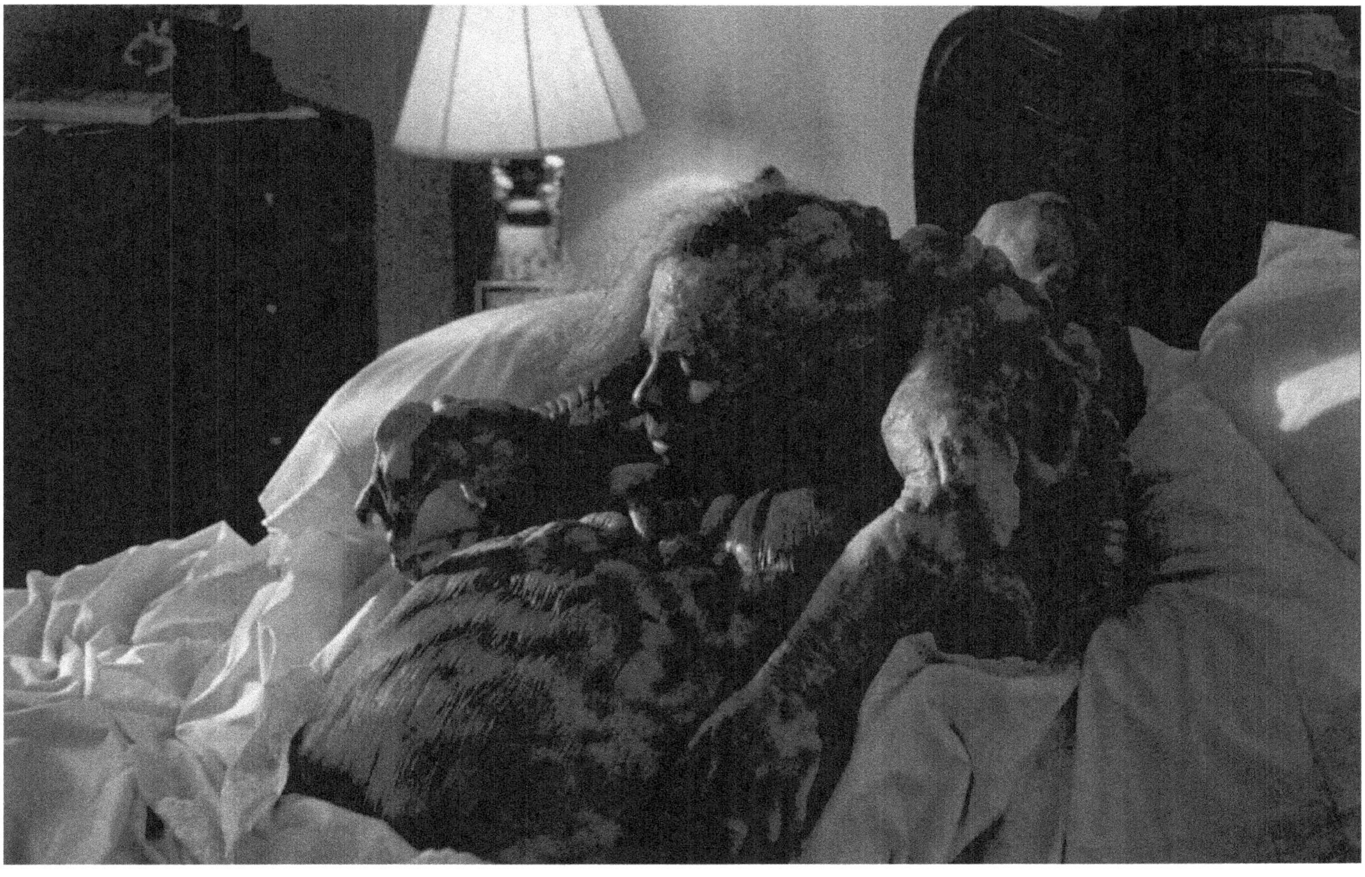

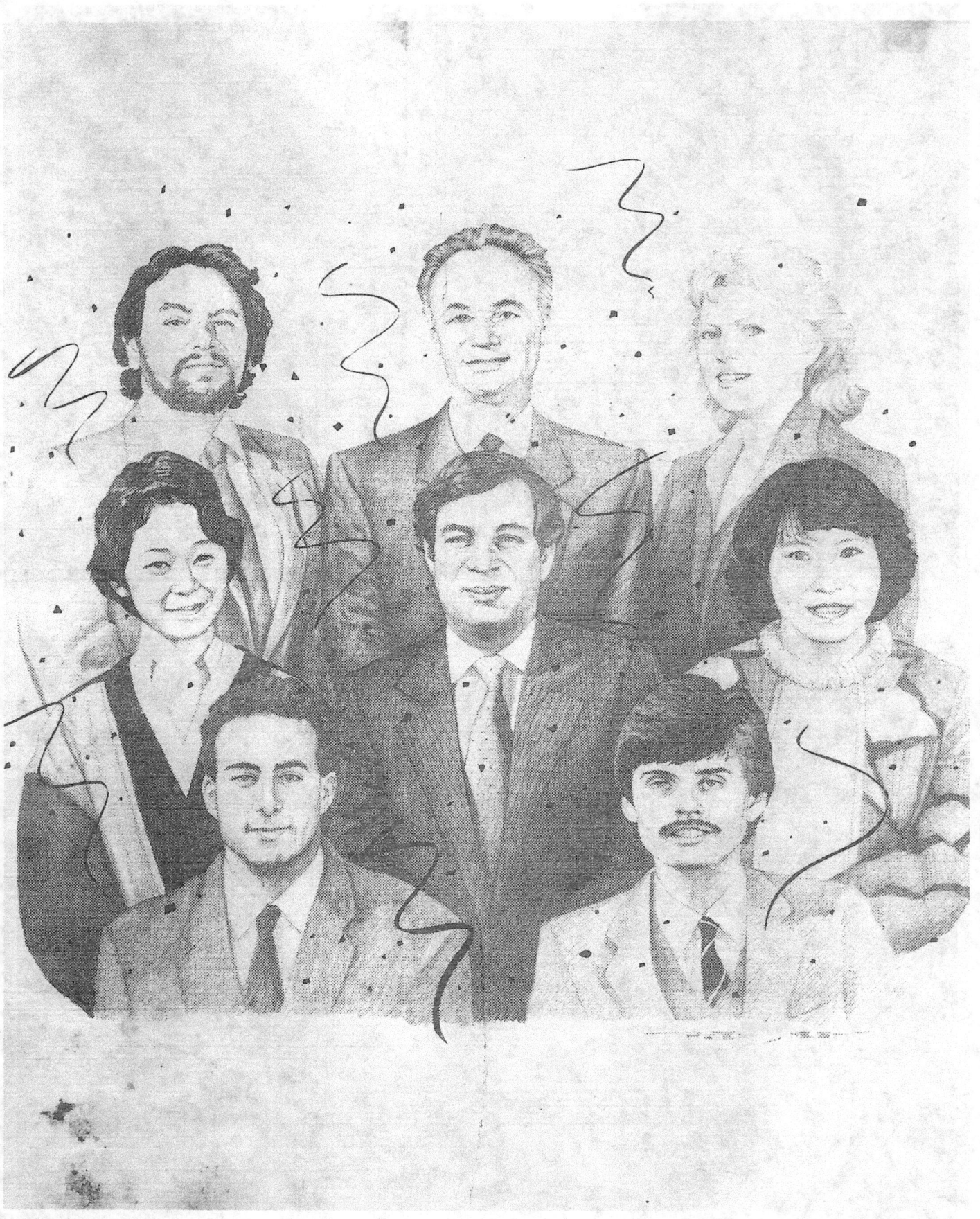

# Ted Rosenblatt

Ted Rosenblatt earned his Bachelor's Degree in Political Science at the University of California (Los Angeles), graduating in 1978. He, along with Sonoko Sakai, worked closely with both Leonard Shapiro and Alan Solomon at SGE's precursor, Shapiro Entertainment. After leaving Shapiro Entertainment, he founded PFG Entertainment Inc., which he still runs as President. He has executive produced several feature films and television series, including Tom Holland's acclaimed tv series TWISTED TALES and several films.

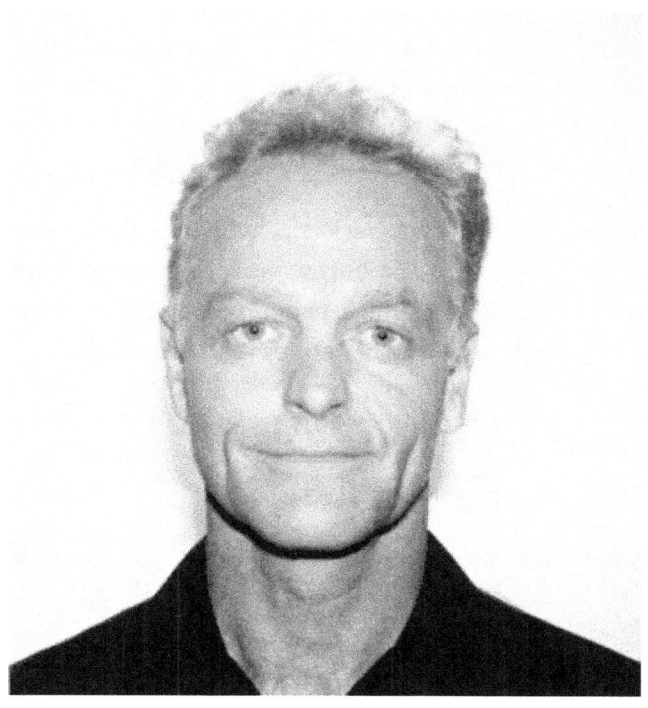

**Stephen:** It's Monday April 27th, 2015, and this is Mr. Ted Rosenblatt who has generously agreed to an interview, and he's on the line, right Ted?

**Ted:** Here I am.

**Stephen:** Ok he's there, and I have here the questions that Marco Siedelmann has written that I've already sent to Ted. I don't know if you've had a chance to look at them or not...

**Ted:** I perused them briefly.

**Stephen:** All right, so he's had the chance to check them out a little bit. So I've got them in front of me here so let me just read them off, Ted. just to give it some kind of structure here. All right I'll start with question number one, Mr. Rosenblatt, let's start at the beginning. Would you like to share some information about your origins? Where were you born and raised?

**Ted:** I was brought up [in California], both my parents were native Californians and one, my father, was from San Francisco, my mother from Los Angeles. And I grew up in a town called Whittier, which is in the Greater Los Angeles Area. And then I went to university in Santa Cruz and finished at UCLA.

**Stephen:** At what point did you develop an interest in the film industry? Was it always your plan, to participate in the movie business?

**Ted:** Honestly I had no plans other than I wanted to graduate on time and then figure out what to do. So I had not developed an interest in any particular field or profession while I was in college. Having said that, one of my first jobs out of college was an intern for a film festival called Filmex, which would today be The

Los Angeles Film Festival. And after that it just so happened that I got a referral to Lenny's company through my brother-in-law and that started my career in the film business.

**Stephen**: And Lenny's company at that time was called Shapiro Entertainment right?

**Ted**: Correct and there was a writer friend named Gary Drucker who I think might have been a relative of Lenny's, who was a colleague of my brother-in-law, who was also a screenwriter.

**Stephen**: And I believe Gary Drucker is also a friend of Sonoko Sakai's, isn't he?

**Ted**: I believe so, I'm not sure how that came about. I think that friendship was forged after Sonoko started working there.

**Stephen**: Actually I think I know the answer to that. I believe her husband Sakai went to Yale University with Gary.

**Ted**: Oh ok, there you go. And my brother-in-law was writing, and Gary was a writer at the time, and so I was told to get in touch with Lenny's company and go for an interview.

**Stephen**: And just a little side-light: Gary Drucker was the ghostwriter on an SGE title called THE BRAIN.

**Ted**: And my brother-in-law's first big hit was REVENGE OF THE NERDS.

**Stephen**: Oh that's fantastic. Wonderful. Ok great so you answered the third question, which was "How did you get into your profession?" Let me just read the question to make sure there isn't something in it that we didn't touch on. Which is, how did you learn about your profession? Did you go to business school/college or was it more or less a lateral entry?

**Ted**: The irony is that my education benefited me after the fact because being involved with international/ foreign distribution complimented my field of studies at UCLA, which was political science with an emphasis on international relations.

**Stephen**: Thinking back on working at Shapiro Entertainment, what comes first to your mind? Which people were important or close to you besides Alan Solomon?

**Ted**: The first part that came to mind was the drive...to work. The length of time it took to get to work.

**Stephen**: You don't mean the motivation to work. You mean the actual time in the car?

**Ted**: Yes! With the time it took we used to joke that you don't wake up until your off ramp, because my drive was about an hour.

**Stephen**: Wow!

**Ted**: Which, I would argue, today would be closer to two hours.

**Stephen**: Yeah, welcome to living in LA.

**Ted**: Yeah because I lived in Pacific Palisades at the time so there was no quick way to get there.

**Stephen**: The second part of the question now: which people were important and close to you besides Mr. Solomon at Shapiro Entertainment, can you recall?

**Ted:** Well, to be honest with you, I learned Alan's organizational technique, if you will. I still set-up files in a similar way, where there is correspondence on one side and contracts on the other. In the sense of when we used to have paper files. Having said that, I liked paying attention to Lenny and seeing how his...he had a unique rapport with producers and other interested parties. So I always enjoyed his, I don't know how to describe it – lack of formality, if you will.

**Stephen:** Very good. Who else was working at Shapiro Entertainment at that time?

**Ted:** The 'Witch in Residence' -- Kelly Ross.

**Stephen:** I see, the 'Witch in Residence'?

**Ted:** I could never really understand what she actually did for the company. Other than to impose herself into situations that made everybody else have to accommodate her.

**Stephen:** I see. So who else other than Lenny, Kelly, Alan? Was Sonoko there when you joined?

**Ted:** Yes, Sonoko worked there while I was there, and we developed quite a nice friendship together. She was really smart and capable and very helpful to Lenny.

**Stephen:** And that was it at that time--?

**Ted:** Yeah, and then after she left I believe there was one other guy that came after her, I can't remember his name?

**Stephen:** Would that have been Frank Occhipinti?

**Ted:** No, there was another one. Tall, mild-mannered and Kelly ragged on him all the time.

**Stephen:** Right.

**Ted:** Can't remember his name but he was, he just got beat up by her all the time.

**Stephen:** Right. Ok, so, moving on....as an audience member, what kind of pictures do you prefer today? That is part one of the question, and part two is: did you like action and horror films back when you worked at SEC?

**Ted:** I did not have an affinity for either one. The odd part was that I didn't ever consider myself a "film fan" per se. I ended up becoming very much aware of films being, as I call them, "pieces of business". So in a weird way it kind of warped my appreciation for movies in general. So now I look at them as exercises in marketing.

**Stephen:** And so what kind of films do you prefer? Are you a movie fan today?

**Ted:** I am in the sense that I like the movies I like. I wouldn't say that there's a particular genre. I will say that I don't like big special effects movies, because I really prefer them as 'productions' more than films. If you said to me at a dinner party, "Which are some of your favorites?" It would be, you know, YOUNG

FRANKENSTEIN, DR STRANGELOVE, the first DIE HARD... There are plenty more, but there isn't a particular genre that I'm devoted towards. Other than my aversion for the overly produced special effects films.

**Stephen:** Would you describe yourself as a 'very' cinematic guy just in the general sense? Or do you like other types of entertainment in addition to just movies?

**Ted:** I think movies are more of a part of what I would consider my areas of interest. If I told you I read the newspaper every morning and that I like sports and I like movies... I don't watch series television. So current events are really important to me. Sports. I play tennis, and I like all the other sports that I used to play. And I like movies. Sometimes I like movies, not because they're new, just because they're movies I haven't seen before. Or movies I like seeing again. It's not the kind of encyclopedic knowledge that some people have with regard to knowing every director's films and which cast members are in every movie. I couldn't claim to be that.

**Stephen:** Do you enjoy watching a film you have been involved with in a 'special' way? Meaning do you get more pleasure out of films that you had something to do with creating as opposed to ones that you've had nothing to do with creating?

**Ted:** I can tell you that the ones that I have been involved with, I don't watch them thinking they're any better than somebody else's movies. It's only a matter of whether I have good stories about how the movie actually came to fruition. Especially if it was, you know, one where we were involved in raising the financing and that kind of thing. And so sometimes the stories about how many deals it takes to get a movie made are more interesting than the film itself.

**Stephen:** Right exactly, I have the same stories. Going back to again into the past to SEC, what would you say the most important deal that you worked out for SEC was? That's the first part of the question, second part: how many films did you work on while you were employed by SEC?

**Ted:** I would say looking back, although not knowing it at the time, was obviously the Media Home Entertainment deal. By virtue of that deal, that's how I ended up getting asked to work at Media Home Entertainment.

**Stephen:** Can you explain a little bit about that Media Home Entertainment deal?

**Ted:** Yeah they... if I recall correctly Lenny or Alan had sold titles to Media Home Entertainment. The woman at the time in acquisitions was Barbara Javitz, who had a nice relationship with Lenny. I don't recall what the nature of that relationship was, but it was very good.

**Stephen:** I believe that Barbara may have been his Executive Assistant at one time at Avco.

**Ted:** Well, maybe that was it. Because you could tell it was one of those relationships that wasn't based on a particular title. And so having serviced that deal, and I

| | |
|---|---|
| | guess developed a little bit of a rapport with her, through Lenny. And by virtue of me being there, it provided for the opportunity for me to be hired at Media Home Entertainment. |
| Stephen: | And what year would that have been? |
| Ted: | That I believe was in '84. |
| Stephen: | In general, how many films were in the library at SEC at the time. |
| Ted: | That I can't remember. I just remember that there was one instance where we had a selection of movies that I had been asked to show to Showtime at the time because another good friend of my brother-in-law's was Greg Nathanson, and he was Head of Acquisitions at Showtime. And that's when Hal Richardson was his second in command over there, so they were pretty good guys to be able to say, "Hey, I have a connection at Showtime." And I believe it must've -- I don't know if it was the whole library but I believe it was about twelve films at the time. |
| Stephen: | Can you remember some of those titles? |
| Ted: | No..... ah, I'm not saying this one was in it, but, I do remember C.H.U.D.! |
| Stephen: | Yes, that was, uh.... |
| Ted: | CANNIBAL HUMANOID UNDERGROUND DWELLERS or something like that? |
| Stephen: | I can't believe you remembered that. Yeah that one slipped my mind. But that was a big, big movie for Shapiro Entertainment as I recall. |
| Ted: | Yeah. And that ultimately was sold over at Media Home Entertainment as well. |
| Stephen: | Very good. I'm going to mention the name of a film, and, if you want to tell a story about it feel free, and that is: NOT FOR LADIES ONLY |
| Ted: | Oh yes! I think the idea there was, how could they come up with some key artwork. And I don't know what the actual event was where they broached the topic, but, they had the fortunate circumstance that my wife was also a photographer. |
| Stephen: | Right... |
| Ted: | So, between her being a photographer, and my incredible physique! They decided that that would be the way to come up with the artwork for the best film ever from Shapiro Entertainment. |
| Stephen: | Right, and as I recall it was a triptych of photos that was you, in sort of a FULL MONTY outfit with a cowboy hat. |
| Ted: | Yeah, my Speedos were put to good use absolutely. I think it gave more enjoyment to the printers down there on Ventura Blvd.... |
| Stephen: | You want to know a little story, when I came in and flew your desk after you left, that's how they introduced me to who used to fly the desk. They held up a flyer and said, "This guy used to sit in that chair." And of course I sprang to my feet like John Cleese in a Monty Python sketch and said, "My God! Have you had it cleaned!??!" |

**Ted:** Yeah, well, they set the bar pretty high there then, didn't they?!

**Stephen:** You are a very brave man. Thank you for telling that story.

**Ted:** I mean I don't know if actually it provided an opportunity for Kelly Ross to lust at night when all the boys were gone.

**Stephen:** Goodness gracious! All right...if you happen to have a piece of that artwork, I don't know where that flyer is, and I mean I've looked on the web and it's not—

**Ted:** Oh my God, you mean I'm not— Do you mean I might be the only person to have been on a poster artwork that can't be found on the web?

**Stephen:** Yes, I think that's true. So if you have that—

**Ted:** Maybe that's an indication of something that some things are better left not found.

**Stephen:** Well we'll just let that out there and let's see if you can find it, or if perhaps one of our readers can.

**Ted:** It's probably under Kelly Ross's pillow.

**Stephen:** Very nice. Ok, moving right along, let's talk a little bit about Media Home Entertainment. And what it was like for you to work there. Just describe that a little bit, tell us what you learned there, and tell us when you joined, what year did you join them?

**Ted:** In 1984 I took over as the Director, or Manager I guess, Manager of International, or Foreign Sales and Administration. And what that meant was that every morning I called RCV Benelux, Otger Merckelbach was the gentleman's name, who was in charge of all of Media Home Entertainment's foreign distribution. And they had distribution set up in virtually all the European, Scandinavian, Australia/New Zealand territories and they did all the duplication out of Benelux. And my job was to make sure that the elements they needed to do all of their servicing and to keep track of which deals were shipping which titles, that was my responsibility.

**Stephen:** And if you could describe in a nutshell, what would you say you learned at Media Home Entertainment?

**Ted:** How to run... back then when home video was just a growing – and getting bigger and bigger -- business, we had incredible relationships with what proved to be really good companies at the time, and thereafter it turned into some of the bigger companies beyond just home video. So I was charged with running the administration, overseeing the distribution, the contracts the deliveries, all of the aspects of what it takes to license titles, multiple titles, on a territory-by-territory basis.

**Stephen:** And then in 1991 your company PFG Entertainment was born. So, which circumstances led you to found a business of your own at that time?

**Ted:** It went from...I got asked by a sales company that was called Film Star if I wanted to work for them. It was a significant increase in salary. And I knew one of the other employees there. Not great, but enough to...I knew who he was; he was a New Line executive. And so I went there, and within a year their financing was not consistent enough to sustain the company. So it provided, ironically, an opportunity for two other colleagues and myself to start PFG from what would have been somewhat the remnants of Film Star. Meaning that we took a couple of titles that Film Star had and got the Producers to assign them to us. And we literally took some of the office furniture and set up shop at a new office in Santa Monica.

**Stephen:** Your specialty for many years has been international sales. Now and then, does your job include a lot of business trips all over the world?

**Ted:** Well it used to in the days where you would go and if you were trying to pre-sell. I remember with Film Star I did a world tour with the boss there, trying to promote, or trying to pre-sell a series of films that Fox was releasing domestically. And then at PFG we had a Brian Bosworth film where I went and traveled Europe trying to get that pre-sold.

**Stephen:** Ok. So this is part two of my interview with Mr. Ted Rosenblatt. It is Wednesday April 29th, 2015. And we left off with a question that he started to answer, but I'm going to re-ask it now, which is... your specialty for many years has been international sales. Now and then, does your job include a lot of business trips all over the world? And also has there been one territory or area in which you've been mainly focused? So do you travel a lot for your business?

**Ted:** Not as much, not nearly as much as in the days past. And also what's evolved is that you have to, on certain pictures, be more focused on the domestic deal as opposed to the international territories. So they're not mutually exclusive in terms of the importance of the domestic to the international.

**Stephen:** I see.

**Ted:** With regard to whether there's a particular territory, other than if you want to call the US a particular territory, yeah everybody concentrates on that but in the general sense, on the international side, no, there isn't one particular territory.

**Stephen:** Do you work very closely with the creative people, meaning the filmmakers? Do you visit the set or participate in casting often? If yes, can you describe what that's like for you?

**Ted:** I will give you that there's no one approach. On certain films that have already been finished, obviously we were not a part of the creative process other than to give comments about editing and things of that nature. On other projects, we are more involved at a much earlier stage and we are asked to be consultants, without even being a sales agent, as to certain casting choices and the viability in the marketplace connected to those choices. In other instances, we might even be involved with comments regarding the script. So, with relationship to the creative side, on certain projects, when we're brought in at that stage yes. On other projects where we're hired simply to review a finished film and make a determination as to whether we'd be interested as a sales agent, we didn't have input from the creative side, no.

**Stephen:** So just continuing with the idea of, if you're brought in on a project before it's made, would it be typical for you to be asked by a producer, "Does actress 'A' mean anything in France?" - type of question?

**Ted:** Right, on a typical basis, we'll have a series of actors, you know choices, on a menu if you will, and they'll ask us to say, "If you had, best case scenario, which ones would you pick? And if we couldn't get those, which ones would be your second choice?" and things of that nature.

**Stephen:** Is your personal life strongly connected to your job? Would you say for example you've made a lot of friendships in the entertainment business?

**Ted:** I have made a lot of friends in the entertainment business. And having said that, my personal life is somewhat segregated from my professional life. So, put it this way, there's only a few guys that I'm friends with in the industry that play tennis, so there's one place where it would cross over. I have other friends that I see only as a result of the business relationship. And there's a few that I see socially as well and as business-wise.

**Stephen:** Looking back, or thinking back to Shapiro Entertainment Corporation for a moment, are you still in contact with any of the people you worked with during the SEC era?

**Ted:** Occasionally in contact with Sonoko, but more as a result of her current involvement with food-related endeavors. And she's involved with some Japanese cuisine promotion. She's always has an affinity for the culinary arts so stayed in touch a little bit there. But on a more regular basis, always stayed in touch with Lenny – still do.

**Stephen:** Flashing forward thirty years now. Can you describe a typical workweek in your job? Like for example, do you work 24/7?

**Ted:** No I've always made a habit of trying to, when I do leave the office, to try and actually stop that part of my day and turn towards something that would be more conventional like going home and hanging out and talking about current events or watching the news or exercising. I really try not to become one of those guys that all they do is think about work the whole time.

**Stephen:** So it's fair to say that you keep your real R-E-A-L life separate from your R-E-E-L life?

**Ted:** Very much so and have made an effort to do so from the very beginning.

**Stephen:** Great. So the second part of the question is, would you call yourself a workaholic or do you reward yourself with vacations once in a while?

**Ted:** Not a lot of vacations per se, but also not a workaholic. A lot of times I take Friday afternoons off, that type of thing.

**Stephen:** So PFG...what does PFG stand for by the way?

**Ted:** Originally when we started the company it was Pangea Film Group.

**Stephen:** And now it's just PFG Entertainment isn't it?

**Ted:** Yeah it was a little bit cumbersome. And then after about three years we also had some, what was it, Sting's company Pangaea Records made an issue about our name even though we didn't spell it the same. And so rather than fight it we just went to the initials, and it proved to be much easier for everybody.

**Stephen:** Can you describe something like the business philosophy of your company, of PFG?

**Ted:** I would say we've always tried to be a boutique. And we like the producers to produce the movie rather than claiming that we have to be the producers. For the most part we also like to have an eclectic choice of films that we like to represent.

**Stephen:** Now going broad for a moment; many things have changed during the digital revolution. Celluloid is fading away; piracy is more easy and prevalent than ever. Have things worsened from the view of a distributor and producer and sales agent, in your view?

**Ted:** I would say yes.

**Stephen:** In what way specifically does it impact your business?

**Ted:** I think the simplest was, how did we say it, in the 80's and 90's DVD sucked up virtually all titles. And after that, television was a great medium for requiring a lot of bulk product. After that the reality of the declining physical DVD business being replaced by the digital business has been a real problem for virtually everybody in order to calculate revenues by virtue of exploitation of home entertainment. VOD activity is fantastic except that you can't put a number next to it like you could in terms of calculating what conventional DVD business was.

**Stephen:** OK. Shifting over to what is often a sore subject for a lot of business people in the film business: film critics. Do you ever care what they might write about your films, at all?

**Ted:** Well, if it's a certain kind of movie that requires there to be an appreciation for what we would call, you know, a 'smart movie' or a 'select audience film,' yeah, it can be advantageous to have great reviews. They give confidence to certain distributors. You also maybe get more invitations to certain kinds of festivals that you think would be of benefit to the film. Having said that, regular commercial fare I don't think depends on reviews. For the most part it has much more to do with how easily marketable the title is.

**Stephen:** I'd like to ask a question about your experience at Shapiro Entertainment and just a real general question. What about what you learned there? And you've mentioned a couple of things already in the first part of this interview, about Alan Solomon's organizational system that you picked up, but what would you say in a broader sense – what did you learn there, so many years ago, that you think has benefited you or that you've carried forward in your business today, in a more sort of global sense?

**Ted:** I can think of a few things: that no matter how may deals that you think are going to come to fruition, that they don't come to fruition as fast as you would like them to or in the order that you anticipated. And I think also that it's an important aspect about knowing which producers are able to tell you more accurately what the status is of their project as opposed to other producers. And to develop a reputation amongst the industry that you are, how do we say it, more transparent or, what's the word, credible...something of that nature? And hope that those things provide a reason for why certain producers would gravitate towards the company. And also develop good relationships with the legal and banking community as well.

**Stephen:** I'm going to mention a couple of names here and I'd you just to give me just your snapshot, what comes to mind about that person... these are from Shapiro Entertainment Corporation. Just your first thoughts, when I say Alan Solomon, what comes to mind?

**Ted:** Very focused Sales Guy. Took the job very seriously.

**Stephen:** Ok, Lenny Shapiro.

**Ted:** Multi-talented. Knew how to, how do I say, develop rapport with producers as well as any of the other people. Very good with people and very good at engaging himself into whatever the situation was.

**Stephen:** All right Ted. Is there anything you'd like to say? That's the end of my questions. Is there anything you'd like to throw in that we may not have covered that is something that you think is important?

**Ted:** I always felt great about being able to speak at Lenny's classes when he was teaching at UCLA Extension. I enjoyed it very much and felt like it was a kind of a karma thing. Where here I am speaking at my original first boss's, my first boss, and now I'm speaking at his class. I thought it was great.

By Stephen A. Roberts, via telephone
in Los Angeles, California
27April, 2015 and 29April, 2015

C'est une machine à tuer. On lui a appris à traquer, entraîné à tuer, programmé à détruire.

UN FILM DE JOSEPH ZITO

# DOLPH LUNDGREN
# LE SCORPION ROUGE

SHAPIRO GLICKENHAUS ENTERTAINMENT présente une ABRAMOFF PRODUCTION — FILM DE JOSEPH ZITO — DOLPH LUNDGREN dans "RED SCORPION"
avec M. EMMET WALSH • AL WHITE • T.P. McKENNA • CARMEN ARGENZIANO • ALEX COLON et BRION JAMES
et avec REGOPSTAAN musique JAY CHATTAWAY photo JOAO FERNANDES producteurs exécutifs ROBERT ABRAMOFF • DANIEL SKLAR • PAUL ERICKSON
scénario ARNE OLSEN d'après ROBERT ABRAMOFF • JACK ABRAMOFF • ARNE OLSEN produit par JACK ABRAMOFF réalisé par JOSEPH ZITO

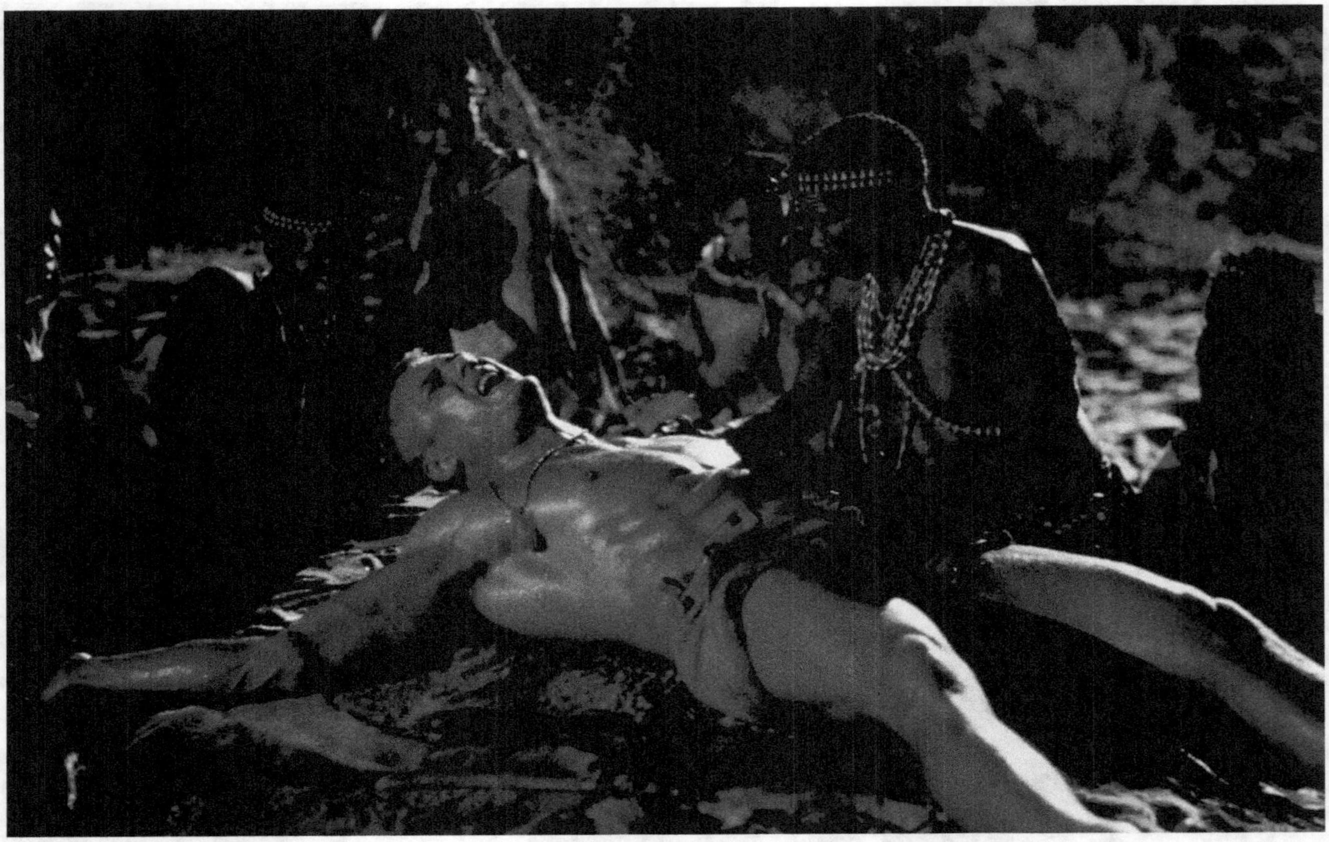

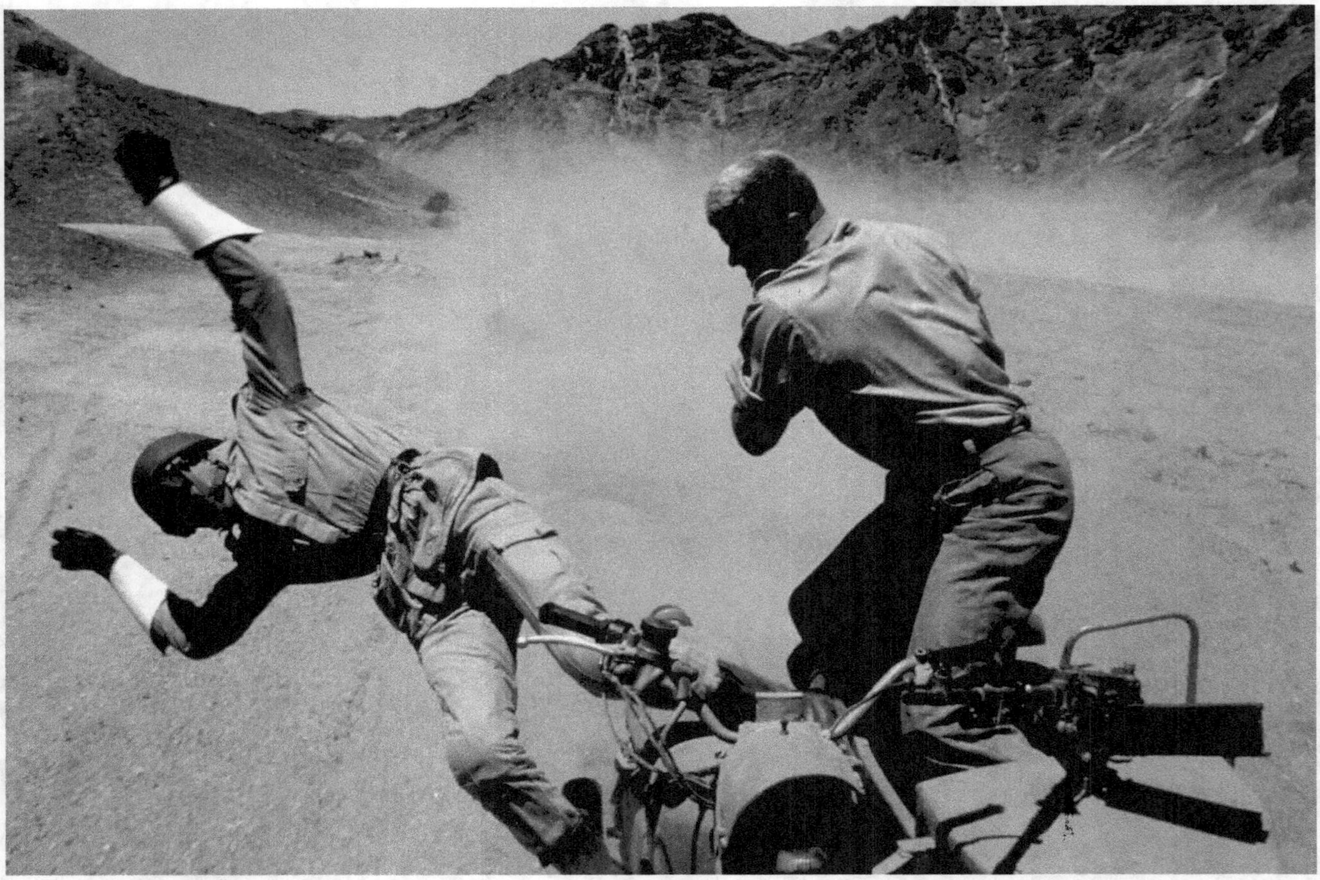

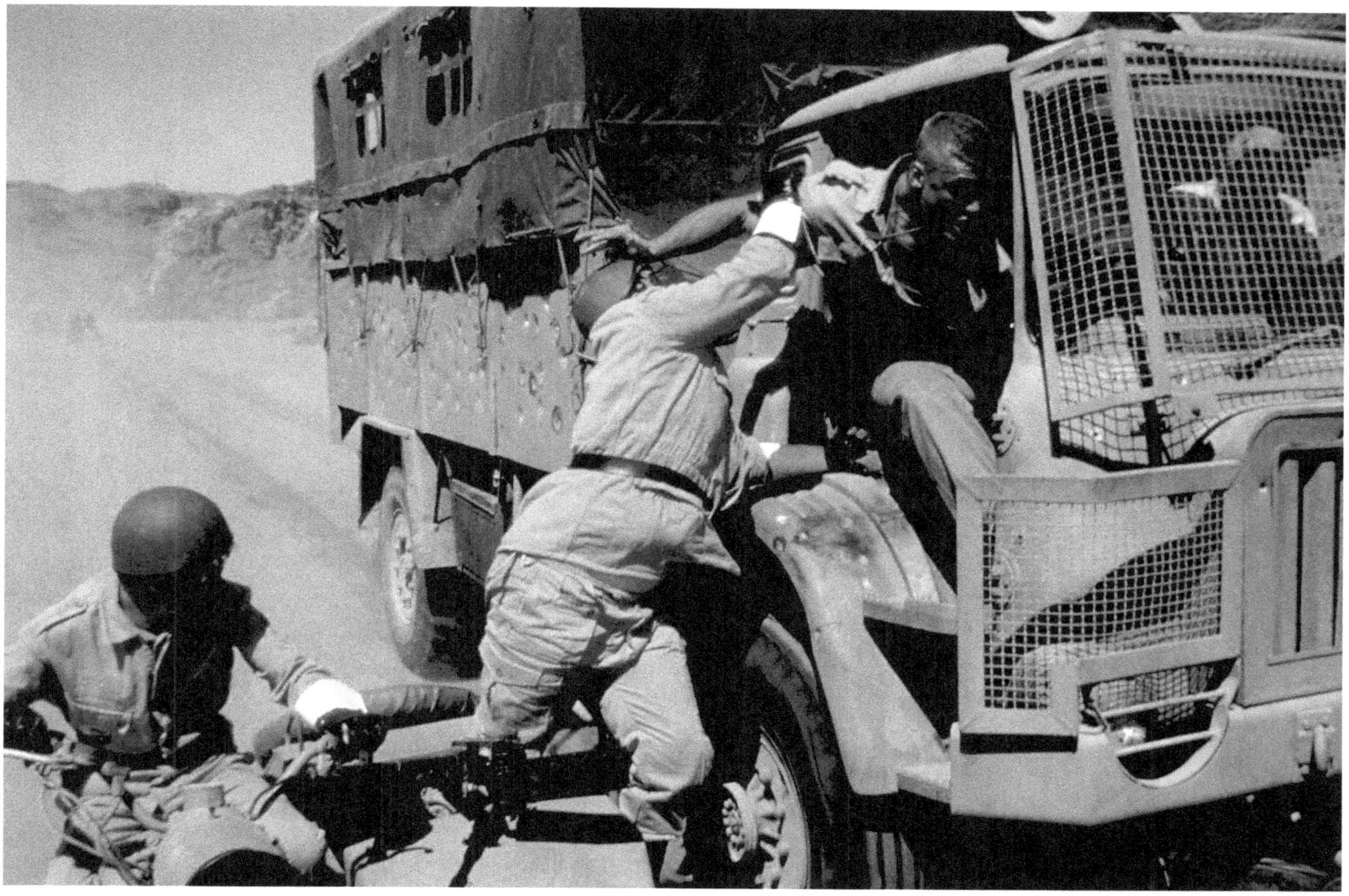

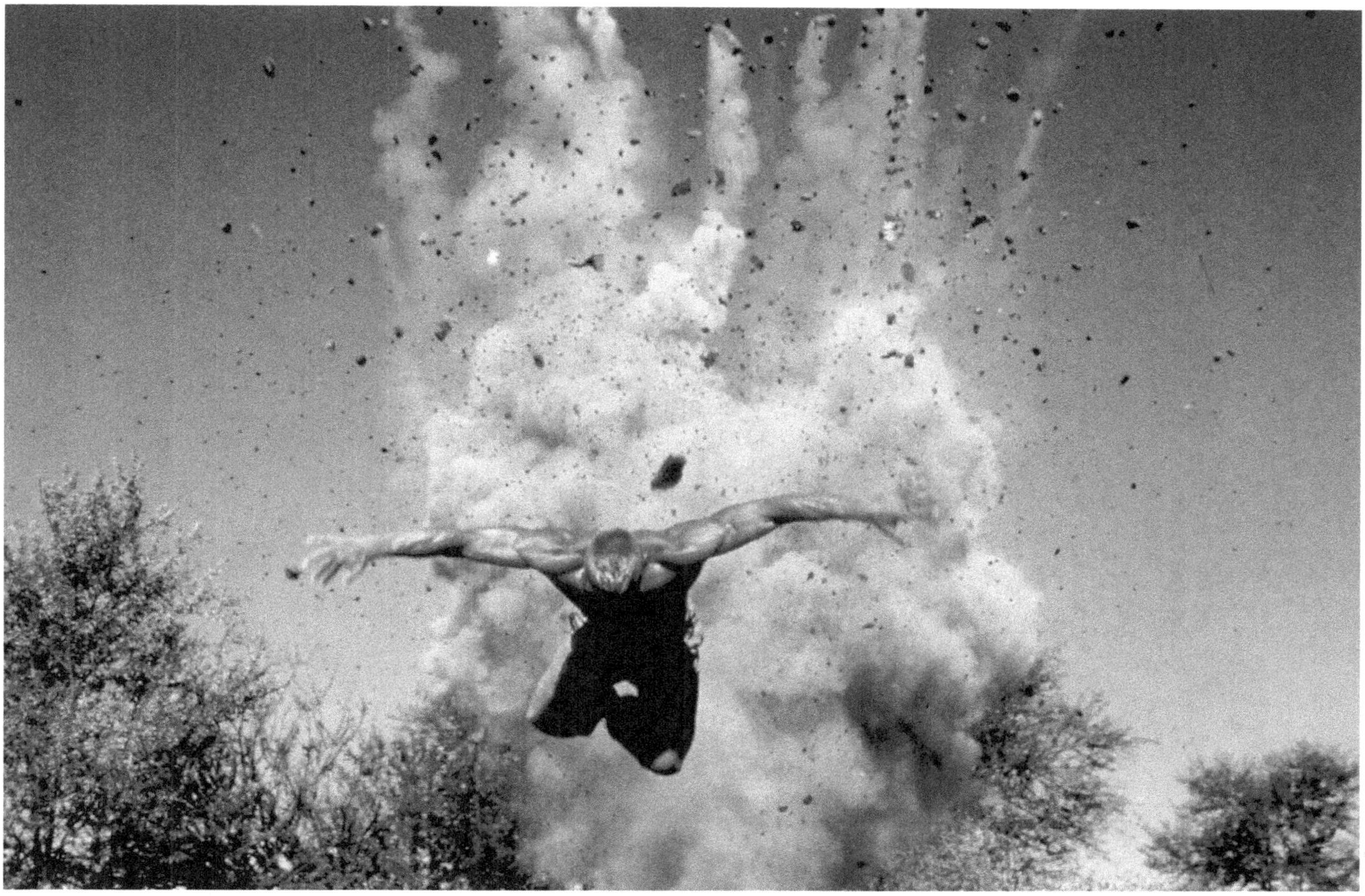

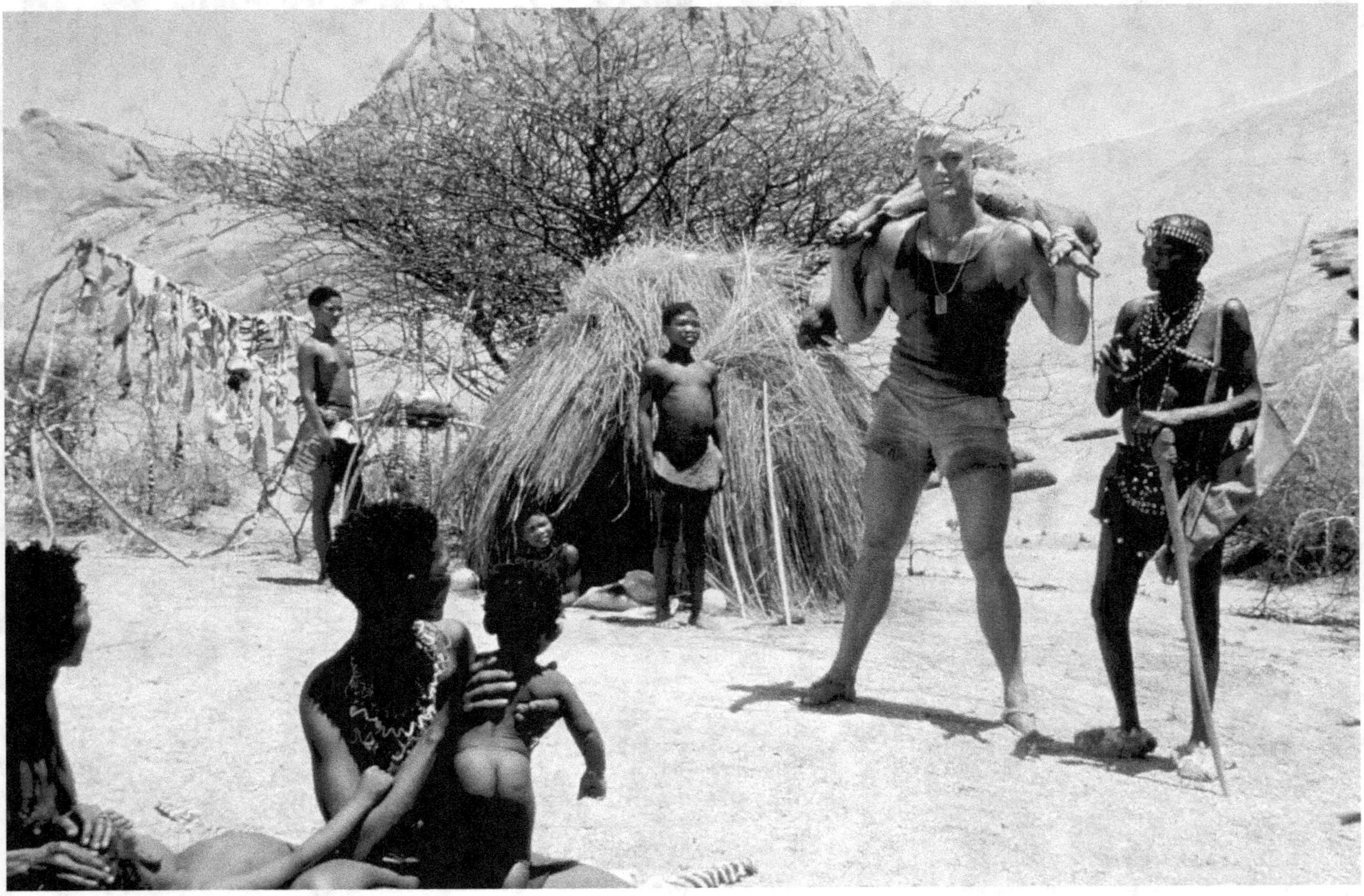

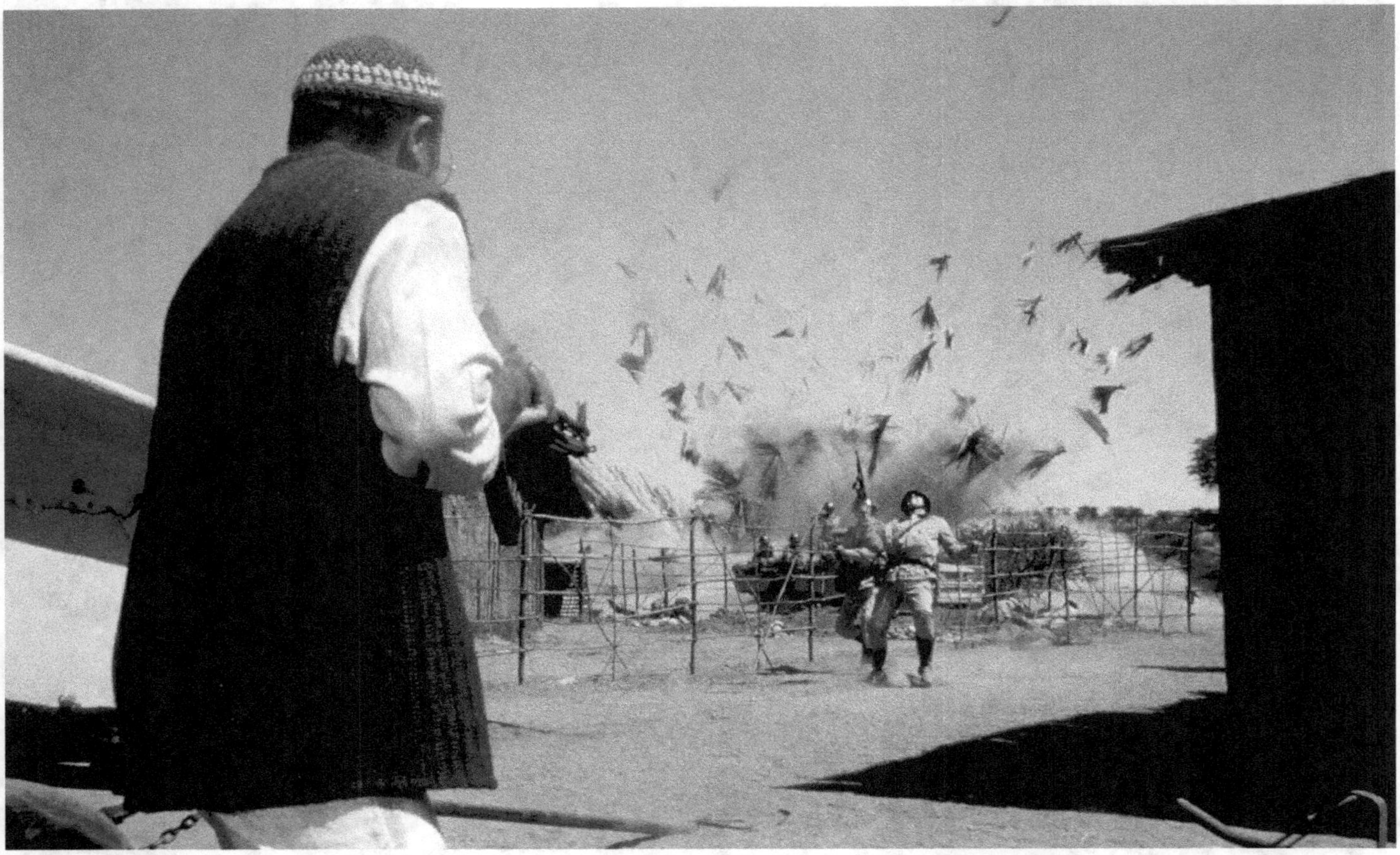

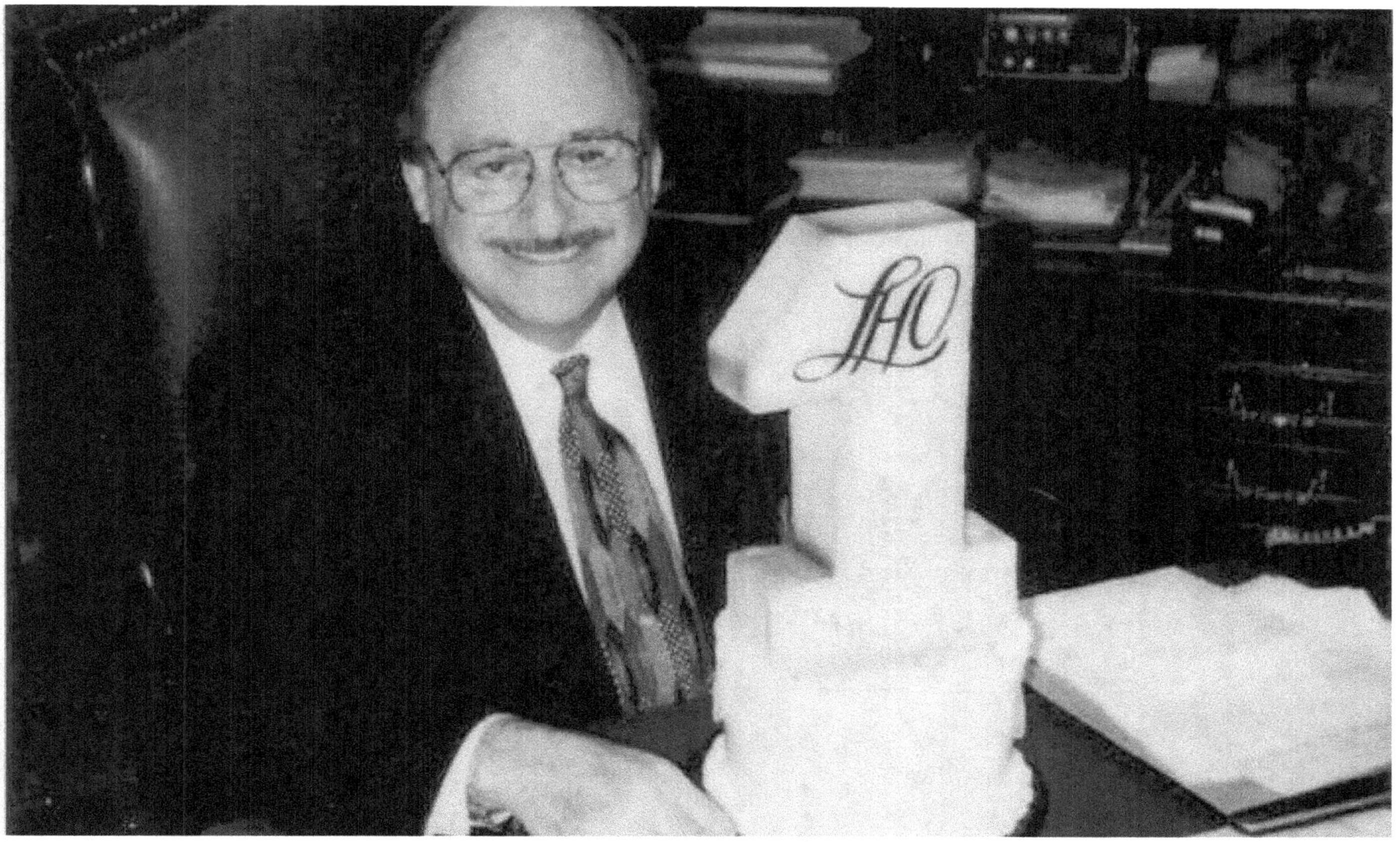

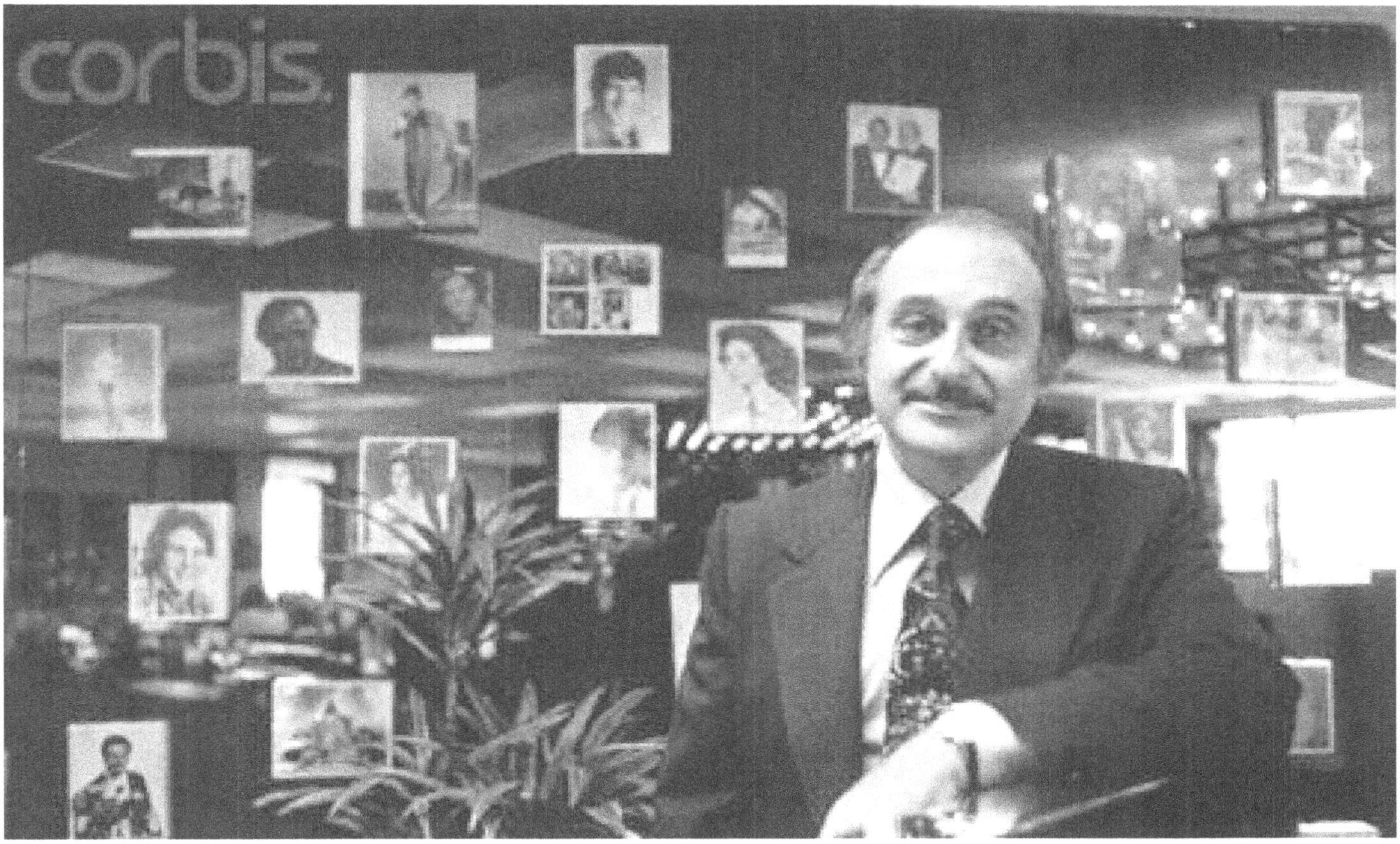

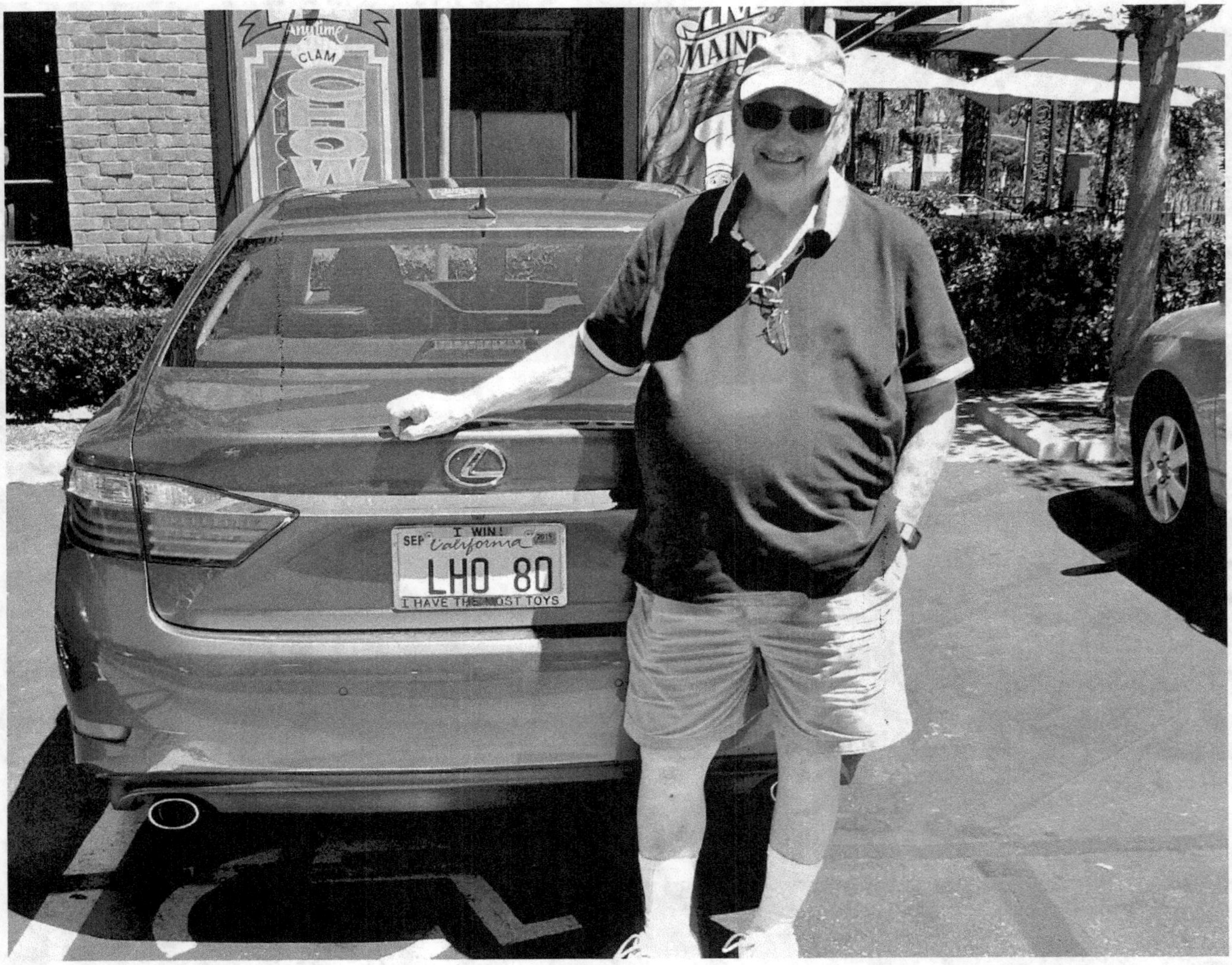

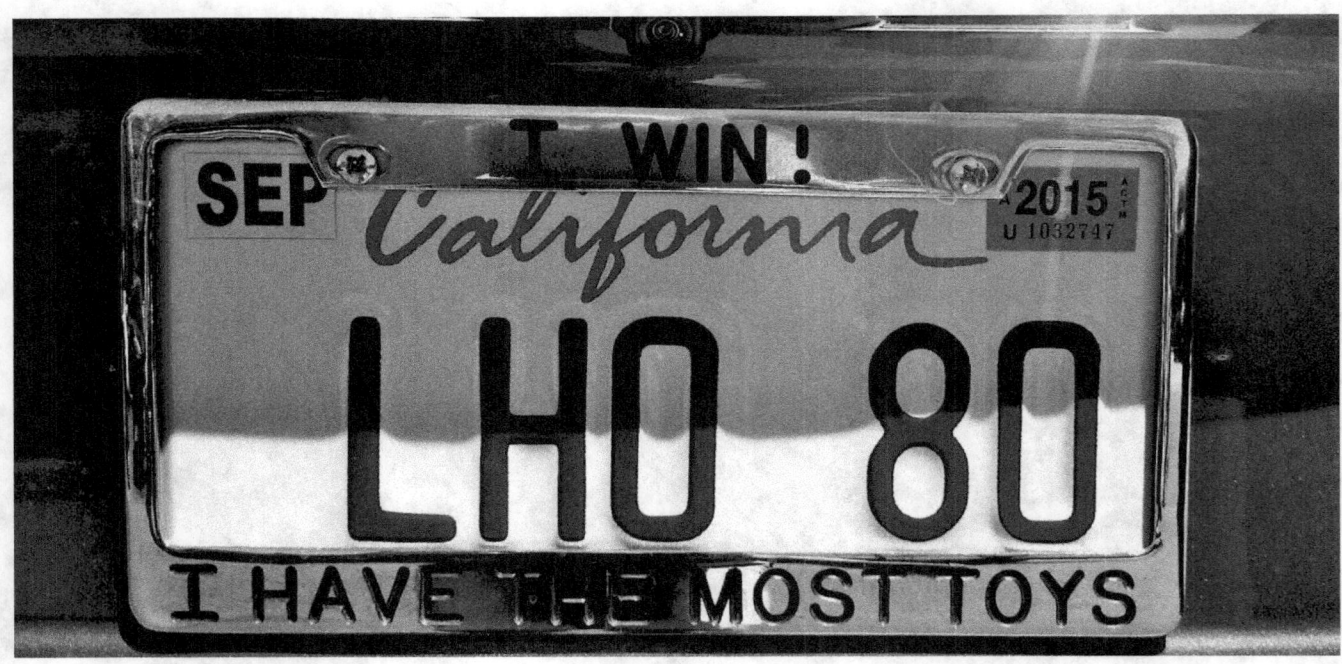

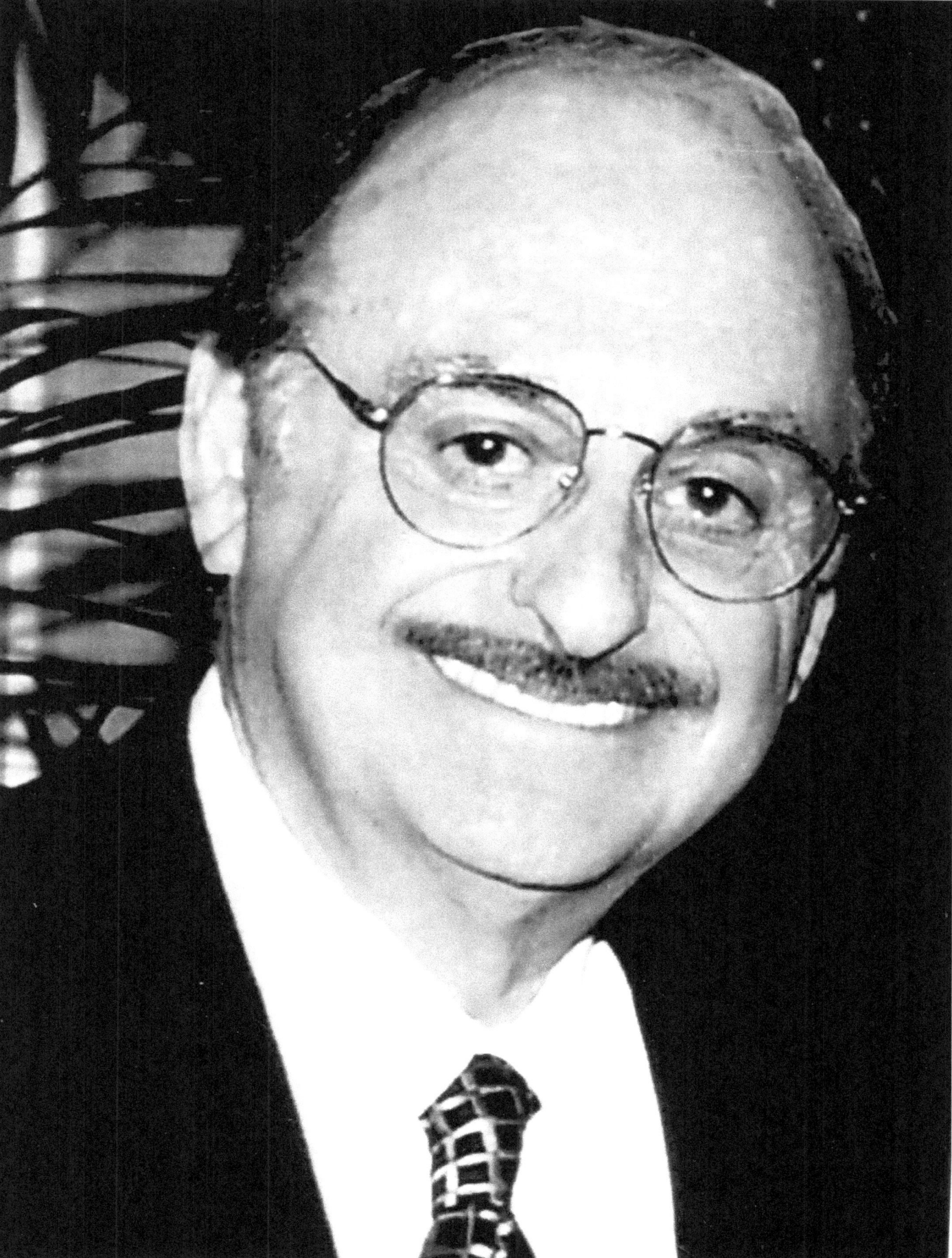

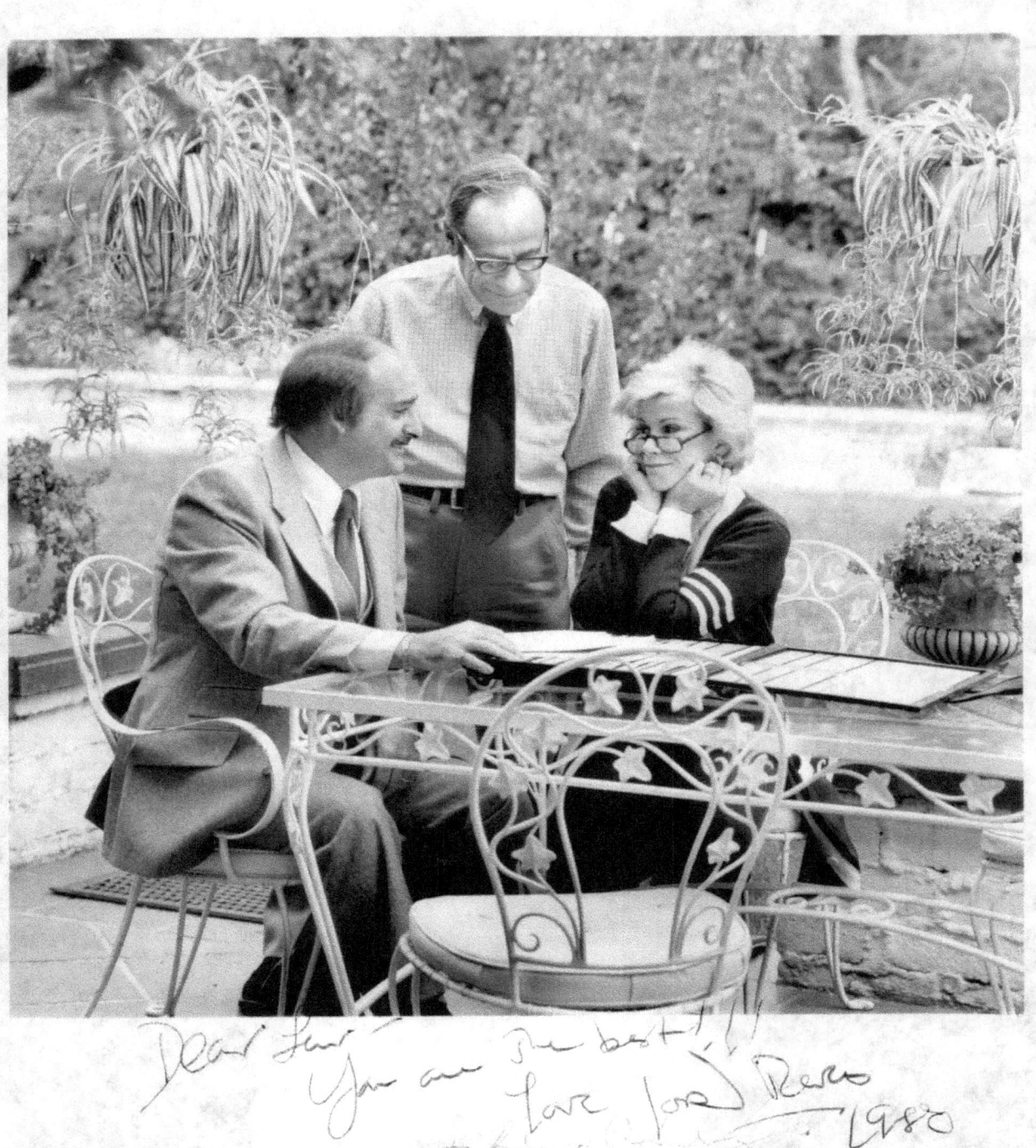

# Lewis Horwitz

Lew Horwitz is a film business legend if ever there were one. "The Magic Banker" was a pioneer in entertainment industry financing. He developed revolutionary financing concepts and made it possible for countless film makers to produce their dream movies. After years at BMI, he entered the movie industry and quickly became famous as a reasonable, trustworthy and open-minded banker. He formed the legendary company The Lewis Horwitz Organization (LHO), which was involved in some of the most recognized commercial independent films of the time, directed by acclaimed filmmakers like Boaz Davidson, David Worth, Peter Berg, E. Elias Merhige, Patty Jenkins, Tobe Hooper, and many more. In 2004, Horwitz retired from the banking industry and formed Horwitz Entertainment Financial Services, Inc. In 2014 Horwitz released the book Memories Are For Tomorrow, which gives a deep insight look into the world of independent filmmaking as well as his compelling personal story.

**Stephen**: I'm sitting here with Mr. Lewis Horwitz. We're at Marmalade Café where I interviewed the wonderful and talented Lenny Shapiro before. I just want to thank you, Lew, for being part of this. I really appreciate you spending your valuable time doing this. Your voice is something that's not really well represented in the book yet. So I'm really looking forward to everything you have to say today. Thank you. Let's just jump right in. The first question is a little bit about your background and your education. When did you develop an interest in film, music and in the arts? And how did you become one of the most prominent bankers in the independent film field?

**Lew**: Well, that would take two and a half hours just to explain that to you. Because it wasn't something that happens immediately. I started out, when I was about ten years old, learning about magic. And I always was interested in entertainment, because of the magic. My father used to whisper to me in his thick Russian-Yiddish accent: "I vant you to be an actor." And my mother would say, "You be a doctor, don't listen to your father!" So I always had that inclination. As a matter of fact I enjoyed doing a little acting roles and so forth, so, this was an area I always was interested in. But not something that I ever thought I was going to do from a vocation point of view. It's just that I was interested in it. How I started out doing entertainment lending was actually by accident. A little history: I was Vice President and Branch Manager of a little bank called Beverly Hills National Bank, later bought out by Wells Fargo, right in the middle of Beverly Hills on Wilshire Blvd. and Highland. It just so happened that at that particular time which was about 1968 that I went there, or something like that -- people would come in from the industry, because they lived around there. And so they opened up their accounts at that bank. I became their banker and we would talk about the industry, because I always was so interested in it. One day a man walked in and asked for a home improvement loan. Which certainly has nothing to do with the Entertainment Industry, except that he was in the music industry. He said, "I don't want to give you a second mortgage on my house. I would prefer to give you a contract that I have with BMI (Broadcast Music Inc.)." And I said, "I don't know what a BMI is." ...so we started talking. His name was Dominic Frontiere, a very famous [music/soundtrack] composer. Long story short: I learned enough about the BMI and I made my first loan based upon a contract coming from the Entertainment Industry. In this case the Music Industry. I became absolutely fascinated in that. I was always a very creative banker, and kind of a maverick. I didn't always obey the rules; I wanted to see things done. I loved to make things happen. You can't really make things happen if you're going to be just a nice straight banker. And so being a little maverick banker I decided, "Jee I should learn more about the music business and this BMI." I learned enough about it; I interviewed them, that I became BMI's banker here in Los Angeles. I developed a method of lending money for their composers, which was something that BMI had never been able to do before. And now they became competitive with ASCAP [the American Society of Composers, Authors and Publishers] who were giving minimum guarantees, but BMI could never do it. Now I showed them how I could lend against their contracts. Therefore they could be competitive with ASCAP and they really started growing a great deal from that.

**Stephen:** You actually just answered the second question. You segued very smoothly to how you really got into entertainment through the record business.

**Lew:** Yeah, I started in the music business. You couldn't lend anything to television in those days, there was no syndication at that particular time. Not much of anything in the independent film business: in '68/'69 or the early 70s - nothing to speak of at all. Because [home] video hadn't come about yet. So I was lending in the music business. Because of BMI other people came in, and we started talking and I became quite well known as the only lender in the music business in the United States. That part of the business grew a great deal. Then one day the President of the bank had a little meeting with all the officers. And he was saying, "You know we have to specialize. Just lending money at random when people come in was very nice, but we should develop certain specialties." It was a very good talk, and he was very motivated. Then I started thinking; maybe this is my chance to live vicariously in the entertainment world. In my mind I was going to do something that has never been done before ever in the United States - or any place. I wanted to start a division, because of his comments I go thinking about this, I wanted to start a division in an independent bank for Independent Entertainment people, and to lend to them in a way that had no other bank had ever done before. And have a division dedicated just to those people, because I loved that business so much, and I wanted to do it in a way that showed my own personality and character. I wanted it to be just a friendly, beautiful business, filled with integrity. I took this idea to the President of the bank. I showed him what I had done so far in the music business. And they said: "Ok. Do it!" -- which was very surprising to me. That was 1972. I was branch manager, and they found another person to take over the management of the branch, and I went upstairs. They gave me $5,000 dollars to build my own division. Now today you couldn't put wallpaper on for $5,000 dollars! But in 1972 I built a beautiful office. It was a small office - totally from glass, so that anybody could see me when they came in. My secretary sat right in front. The rest of the office was like a living room. I had couches; I had overstuffed chairs, end tables, lamps. I had, in those days it was called a stereo. *(laughing)* Which confused the purchasing department a great deal, because they had never done that for a bank. I had music playing. And I started a division that catered to those people who were afraid of regular bankers, who didn't understand banking, and bankers didn't understand them. So they'd come in, they'd sit in my living room. We would talk about their needs, and I would try to figure out a way to lend them money.

**Stephen:** You created a comfort zone.

**Lew:** Yes, yes. And it became extremely popular. As they came in I asked them for pictures. People in the music business, people in the film business. And pretty soon I had posters and pictures on the walls all over. They all felt at home coming in there. It was upstairs, so it was private. That was the beginning of my interest, and starting out in the Entertainment Business.

**Stephen:** So is it fair to say that you had found a way to please both your mother and father?

**Lew:** I guess you're right. I didn't think about that, but I guess that's right. *(laughing)*

**Stephen:** That's wonderful! How much time passed in between what you just described to me, and the founding of the Lewis Horwitz Organization [LHO]? And also tell me about the main idea and business philosophy for LHO.

**Lew:** LHO didn't begin until 1980. I think it was August, I'm not totally sure.

**Stephen:** So about eight years passed?

**Lew:** Yes, it took me that much time. But I was lending in the Entertainment Business. When that bank was purchased by Wells Fargo I wanted to stay with independent banks. At a big bank I could never gone to the President of the bank, and say I want to do this. You couldn't even know who the President of the bank was. So I wanted to stay with independent banks. And so I went to another bank – actually they asked me to join them – a bank called First Los Angeles Bank. They were later bought out by City National. At any rate, I started with that bank. Usually when the President of a bank calls you and says, "I'd like to interview you, I'd like to leave the bank you're at and come with me." -- usually you go to their office. I said to him, "Would mind coming to my office, and there was a reason for it." And so he did, and I showed him the office. I said, "If I come to your bank I want to have my own Entertainment Division." I explained to him what we were doing, he had heard about me because my name was getting around with bankers now. He said, "I'll build you a beautiful office just for your business." So I started there as a Senior Vice President. I built that division tremendously. As a matter of fact, I was still doing mostly music, but then in the early '70's probably '75, I'm not sure about the dates exactly - the music business then started collapsing, for a number of reasons. And I saw this - and don't forget as a lender I had to be careful and not lose the bank's money - and so I started switching over from music to television, because now there was syndication there were ways to lend money against...

**Stephen:** Thanks to Lew Wasserman [Chairman of MCA/Universal]. Another Lew. He invented syndication, essentially, didn't he?

**Lew:** Yeah. Yeah. Then somebody came to me. It was the same man from the music business, Dominic Frontiere who was interested in making a movie. The television studios in those days could not own the product. They could only license it, they couldn't own it. Today they could own it again unfortunately. So they would license it for a million [or] $1.2 million, something like that. But [the question was] how do you go about lending money? People who wanted to make these movies for television - the Producers - had to come up with their money themselves. They had a contract from the Television Network, but they couldn't finance it. I figured out a way to finance [their productions]. That's kind of a long story itself... So, I figured out a way to finance what we called Movies of the Week. I started the Movies of the Week for all the television networks. I lent, at one time every movie you saw on Movies of the Week on television was financed by my division!

**Stephen:** That's impressive.

**Lew:** Yah. So it started growing a great deal, and then it continued to grow in other areas as well. And then this incredible thing happened. It was called video! VCR's came out. I remember a videotape cost $25. The beta-tapes, they were the first ones. Anyway, I saw that there was a huge business there. Because now, all of the sudden, the distributors throughout the world that had only had the movie theaters to depend upon to get their money back now had another source! At the same time television, in various countries all over the world, was not public. It was all owned by the governments. One after the other they started de-governmentalizing them - if that's a word... *(laughing)*

**Stephen:** Privatizing.

**Lew:** Yes. So I saw, now wait a minute, now there's video, there's the theaters - of course, which were always there, and there is television. There was going to be a huge business in the Independent Film Business. I never wanted to deal with the studios, 'cause they're the big bad wolf and they tell you what to do. I always wanted to be more creative. I stayed with the independents. And I said, "I want to start lending money in the film business as well, using video contracts, et cetera." I had a huge division. I had 22 people working for me. I was doing a huge percentage of the bank's business, I had so many deposits, the money that I was lending was significantly less than the deposits that I had so I was making a bundle for the bank. I went to the President of the bank and I said, "I'm dying here. I never go home. I'm working so damn hard because my business is growing so fast. I'm not making enough money. Don't pay me a salary anymore. Just give me a percentage [of what I'm earning]." I started feeling a little entrepreneurial. *(laughing)* - He says, "Lew I can't do that." I never forget - and I absolutely loved this man, because he gave me a break and let me do all these things! But I said, "I have to do this." And he said: "I can't let the tail wag the dog." -- I never forgot that. It bothered me so much. That I decided I wanted to leave the bank, and start my own business.

**Stephen:** What year would that have been?

**Lew:** 1980. I forget what month...June, July, August - something like that. I had a client who was a real entrepreneur. He asked about how much money I might need. I said, "I could start my company with $320,000." - and I couldn't lend that money. But I would broker deals because

**Stephen:** everybody knew me. The investors would then be supposed to - within the next 1-2 years - raise enough money to get me the millions that I would need to lend. But in the meantime I would broker deals. Because of my reputation people would take my loans once I put them together. So I started a business with $320,000 in 1980 and that was LHO.

**Stephen:** Describe the business philosophy of LHO please.

**Lew:** It's very simple: I love the business. I wanted to build a lending business based on integrity. That was the first thing. Because, bankers are bankers. If I made a promise, if I said I would do something - I would do it. I wanted to build the business based on integrity, on caring for the client and on caring for the project. I was a lender, not an investor so I couldn't pick and choose film and television deals that I fell in love with. That would be very dangerous. What I did was I lent against collateral, etc. cetera. But for every deal that I did everyone was as important as the next one. If it was a tiny little loan, or if it was a giant loan. Whatever I put together I cared about. I did this without ego. In other words, I didn't build a business that would be like, you walk in and somebody would be sitting there just saying like: "Ok, tell me what you have. If I don't like it get out of my office." It was nothing like that at all. I remember one person this happened to be in the music business. I said, "I wish I could help you, but I don't know how. You help me to help you. Bring me a shopping bag full of every piece of paper you have that might have anything to do with some form of collateral that I could have." He brought me in box of paperwork. I got went through it, and I found a contract that I could lend against and I started the man's company. So this is what I build it on. It's just that simple.

**Stephen:** You're talking about a real, genuine, personal connection to...

**Lew:** ...to every client that we had. Almost every client became a friend, like Lenny [Shapiro], and like all the others. That's what it was built on.

**Stephen:** So let's talk about Shapiro Glickenhaus Entertainment and the people behind the company. Did you have a relationship with the principals of SGE - Jim Glickenhaus, Lenny Shapiro, or Alan Solomon - prior they became SGE? For example, did you do business with Lenny at Shapiro Entertainment Corporation?

**Lew:** I'm not sure what company it was. I know the first deal that I did with Lenny. He came in, and he asked for a loan that he needed for - let's call it: working capital - for his trip to Cannes. He needed money for publicity -- for this, for that. So I went ahead and I lent him this money. It was for working capital he would require. But it was there. Now I go to Cannes - I was going every year - and I was on the Croisette, and I see this incredible parade coming down the street! With this gal - I remember she had a snake around her if I'm not mistaken...

**Stephen:** The Naked Snake Lady! She's mentioned by interviewees often in this book!

**Lew:** Well...... I see that parade. And I see that it is Lenny! This is what he used my money for! For this parade! I remember seeing him there saying, "You shit! You told me about working capital! You put together this parade that I just paid for?!?!"

**Stephen:** That would have been sometime between 1984 and 1986.

**Lew:** You're right yeah. That was the first loan.

**Stephen:** That would have been Shapiro Entertainment Corporation, the immediate precursor of SGE. Before Lenny started business with Jim.

**Lew:** Ok. But I knew the other guys. I did business with all of them. There was a very cute thing: I financed a little movie called BASKET CASE.

**Stephen:** The first one?

**Lew:** No, the third one.

**Stephen:** OK, BASKET CASE 3 which is subtitled: 'THE PROGENY'.

**Lew:** I have in my office at home a plaster cast of BASKET CASE.

**Stephen:** His name is Belial by the way. I happen to know these things. *(laughing)*

**Lew:** I remember lending him for that. There must have been other loans I made too. I know that I lent money to Solomon separately when he left...

**Stephen:** Yes, Alan formed his own business after SGE called Amsell.

**Lew:** Then over the years - Lenny gets involved with so many different things – I remember he brought me a deal that he was involved with. I remember putting that together and it was very successful. Throughout the years Lenny often made business together either directly or indirectly even up to a few years ago. I would refer something to him; he would refer something to me...

**Stephen:** So it was an ongoing relationship over the years. Let's focus SGE for now. During that period which would have been since 1986 - I know that because I was there - up until the company officially ended - which was between '94- '96, how would you characterize SGE? Is there anything about it that you could say, "This is what that company did differently." versus other leading independents of that era?

**Lew:** As far as I can recall the personality of the company was Lenny's personality - which I liked! Creative. Lenny felt passionate about every deal he did. It wasn't just, "I got another deal!" It always was something that was very important to him. That's the way I remember the company. I placed all my trust in Lenny; in his abilities, his knowledge and his honesty and integrity.

**Stephen:** Can you remember some of the other movies besides BASKET CASE 3?

**Lew:** I thought about it when I came here. I truly do not remember.

**Stephen:** This is part two of my interview with Lewis Horwitz. Let's just pick back up where we left off. I think you may have answered this next question, which is: When SGE was shut down in 1996 and then Jim Glickenhaus stopped making movies you did continue working with Alan and Lenny right?

**Lew:** Yes.

**Stephen:** Did you work with any of the other Filmmakers from the SGE era that you can remember?

**Lew:** I can't recall.

**Stephen:** Talk a little bit about your work after SGE - which would have been after 1996 - with

Lenny and Alan. Can you remember any of those deals?

**Lew:** No, no. I do have a memory of a transaction with Alan, which I didn't like.

**Stephen:** You can talk about that, too.

**Lew:** I don't remember it. I'm sure we all have that sort of thing. You have a memory that you know happened; you know it was either pleasant or unpleasant. I think there was something with Alan that was unpleasant, but I don't remember anything more about it.

**Stephen:** All right, that's fine. Let's move forward. Talk about a moniker that has been attached to you throughout the years, and I happen to have a little insider information on this. But speak for yourself. Which is the idea of The Magic Banker? The second part of the question: Besides making money - which is what bankers do for themselves, or they're no longer bankers, they're ex-bankers; do you find something special about investing in these projects involving artists and what they do? Talk about that a little bit.

**Lew:** Most important: I don't invest. I have not invested I've only lent money -- big difference. A loan is something that you expect to get back and you have collateral to help you to get it back. An investment is something in which you take a chance on, and you may make a whole bunch of money - or lose some or all of your money. With a loan you don't anticipate that and you only earn an interest rate. And that's all. So I was a lender and not an investor. The only thing special with me in that regard as I've mentioned previously: [is] the way I lent it, and the way my staff learned to lend from me. And that is to be creative. I never looked at a project as something that couldn't be done. I would listen to my client, or potential client, and sometimes of course it's just impossible, you can tell in two seconds. But if there were an opportunity to do this [meaning make a loan] I would try to be as creative as I could and still make a prudent loan that I would get paid on. But I was willing to bend, and twist, and do whatever was necessary to try to get that [project] made. I could give you examples, but that would take too much time. But for example with the Movies of the Week, I figured out a way to do it by actually holding back money from the network, on various things that they would allow the Producer to spend on. For example: they would give the Producer the money right in the budget for the various monies he'd have to pay for the Screen Guild, and so forth. And I would hold that back, and I would hold back the other contingencies that they would put in, and a number of other things. And my attorneys told me that would be impossible I would be committing fraud against the network. I actually called the business affairs people of all the networks, and told them what I was doing. And I said, "Now would you rather have the Producer take this money and buy a new car for his new girlfriend, or use it for a down payment on a new home; or would you rather have me hold that money, and make sure that the film gets made in case it's necessary, and once it's made I would release it. But until it's made I am going to hold on to it, in the case I need it." -- because they go over budget or something like that. And they said: "Hell yes, hold that money!" And so the attorney almost fell off his chair and I was able to lend money on

**Lew:** MOWs. So it's that kind of thing that I would do.

**Stephen:** Let me just interject, and phrase a semi-question that's perhaps more a statement. That's to say that, "No." is easy. Whether you're a lender, whether you're someone green lighting a project. There are a thousand reasons to say no. All of would be really smart, actually. *(laughing)* But the "Yes." is the hard one.

**Lew:** Right.

**Stephen:** Would you say that more often or, when it could have been a "No" you'd say "Maybe", and you'd find a way?

**Lew:** Yes. If it should have been a "No", then it's a "No". But if it could have been a "No" I would try to find a way.

**Stephen:** That's the creative part.

**Lew:** Yes. And I would not just say, "I won't try." For example, I had a very good crew. I remember dozens and dozens of times throughout the years where I'd say, "Okay this is how I want to put this deal together." And my top men would say to me: "You can't do that. It isn't gonna work. It's not safe." And I would say: "No, first let's try to make it work, and then if we find that we can't make it work - then we'll say no." That was the way I worked, and that was the way I wanted LHO to be as well.

**Stephen:** That was what made you different, really.

**Lew:** Exactly right. And there were a number of deals that we made, because of it. And some of these deals we had difficulties with, but we were always able, or almost always able to come out of it because people were willing to work with us, because we never said, "We are going to foreclose on this if you won't do the following." We worked with people.

**Stephen:** So it was atypical banking.

**Lew:** Yeah. Now, as far as how I got to be called The Magic Banker is: I love magic and anybody who was going to borrow money from me had to sit there and watch me do some magic or else! *(laughing)* And then what would happen was, it got around so much that wherever I went, like I'd be in Cannes - or any place in the world - and I'd be in a restaurant somewhere and somebody would say, "Do some magic!" So I always carried some with me, and I would start doing magic and the waiters would come out, and once we even had the chef come out of the kitchen – and they were all watching me do magic.

**Stephen:** What was your favorite type of magic?

**Lew:** Close-Up magic.

**Stephen:** Prestidigitation?

**Lew:** Yeah, the real magic. But I also did some larger things so that more people could see it.

**Stephen:** More David Copperfieldy / Doug Henningy?

**Lew:** Well, that's too big. But if I were doing it here I couldn't just work with cards. So I did this all over, if I were giving a lecture I would do magic while I was giving the lecture. People remember that. People would maybe forget my name, but they remember: The Magic Banker.

**Stephen:** So that was your shtick? *(laughing)*

**Lew:** That's exactly right. And everybody started calling me The Magic Banker.

**Stephen:** That's great. So it's actually not just a metaphor, it's a truism?

**Lew:** Yeah.

**Stephen:** Have you ever thought about going into the process of filmmaking itself, or have you been happy with just handling the financials? Do you have any dream of making a movie, of writing a movie, directing a movie...?

**Lew:** No, no. I thought about maybe Producing a film, but I never learned to be a Producer. I was a financial man. And to be frank with you I enjoyed that so much, and, with a little modesty, I was very good at it. And so I said: "Stick with what you know!" So, I never thought of making a picture.

**Stephen:** Fair enough. So you financed all kinds of movies and supported various creative people, and all different kind of films. Did you make some projects just because you thought it's a good deal, or is there a passion beyond the financial aspect?

**Lew:** There were some films I really had a passion for...

**Stephen:** ...can you name them?

**Lew:** No, I don't think so. I'm terrible with names. Usually I have a whole list of films that we made, because when I would be interviewed while I was working as a banker and one of the Trades would interview me, I'd have to get the list out in order to give them the names.

**Stephen:** We all need notes, Lew. There's no shame in it.

**Lew:** So, however, I never made a loan because I loved it. There were times when I didn't make a loan because I thought that it was not the kind of loan I wanted to make. But I never made a loan just because I had a passion for the film - and I had a passion for many films, because it wasn't prudent. It was only going to hurt the person... If I lend you money for something that I know is going to be a problem - even though it's something that I love - I'm hurting you as well as myself. Because you're going to end up with nothing for that film, you're going to end up by maybe losing the film, and I'm going to end up by losing my business. So I was passionate about many projects, but I only lent against those projects that [made good business sense].

**Stephen:** But business aside for a moment and talk a little bit about the films you like to watch.

**Lew:** I am completely eclectic. I love romance, science fiction, horror films, especially if it has to do with little heads and no bodies!

**Stephen:** This is part three of Mr. Lewis Horwitz's interview. We are sitting in the same dining and shopping complex called the Calabasas Commons and today we're at the Corner Bakery. It's a lovely California day, slight breeze, it's hot as the devil but we'll soldier on through. So when you think back on the heyday of SGE, which we are loosely defining as 1983 to about 1993, about 10 years or so, the Home Video Market was just huge in the entertainment industry as a whole but particularly in the independent industry. And it really created enough space for a lot of different kinds of films. If you look back on this, and you talk about this in your book [], would you describe this as like a 'Golden Age' for independent commercial films? And if so, why?

**Lew:** It was definitely a "Golden Age" and primarily because of [home] video. Everybody at home in all of the various countries around the world as well as the USA wanted to try out this new thing. Wanted to be able to go out and buy a movie and see it at home. And stop it and start it and go forward and backward and all of that. And it got to the point where you could – there were companies that I lent money to that just bought product. They didn't care anything about the product they just bought it. And based upon the title they invented a cover for the VHS box and it sold like crazy. Everybody was buying on covers – "Oh that looks good let's get it!" There was a company that I did business with that was purchased for a small amount of money but they had a <u>huge</u> library, which of course had never been exploited for video. And based upon the value of the library, that they had purchased some years before, now that video was out they were able to get all kinds of debt, which of course wasn't a good idea, and they formed a huge company. It was Cannon as a matter of fact. And so it was truly a Golden Age. For me as a lender it was most definitely a Golden Age because everybody was buying. I made loans based upon on nothing more than what I conceived the value of, not the titles, but the amount of product that they had. And they were getting contracts from everyplace. And the contracts were being fulfilled because it was easy for them to do it and the Distributors were paying because they were making money on it. So it was an excellent time to lend money, an excellent time for the Distributors, an excellent time for the Independent Producers because they made a lot of crap! Just as long as it looked good on the cover [it sold.]

**Stephen:** So marketing was a huge part of making that work?

**Lew:** Oh, definitely.

**Stephen:** Why do you think that most small companies from that 'Video Era' let's call it, including SGE, closed up shop in the early and mid-1990's?

**Lew:** After the 'Gold Rush' *(laughs)* when Distributors had purchased all this product, and they had done this for years, their customers, the consumers, were saying, "You know what? It was fun in the beginning but this stuff is terrible!" And so what happened was the Producers were making a lot of junk and all of a sudden, well not all of a sudden, but slowly but surely the Distributors didn't want to buy junk anymore because they couldn't sell it to their consumers. The time of the 'Gold Rush' was over and good product was necessary. Foreign Distributors were not doing well if they bought product that wasn't selling so everybody got choosier. So what happened was a lot of the Independent Production Companies didn't do well because they couldn't change their methods. To sum it up, after a period of time, several years, the Foreign Distributors found, and the American Video Distributors found that the public no longer wanted junk. They wanted decent films that they could enjoy and so the business changed and some companies were able to change with it and some were not. And what I mean by changing [is] better product had to be made. Many companies just weren't capable of handling the better product for whatever their reasons.

**Stephen**: Some financial, some creative perhaps?

**Lew**: Mostly creative. However, in those particular times there truly was not the same amount of money available as there was a little bit later. More money became available because, while I started this and I was the only lender, when other bankers found that this was a profitable business they got into it as well. And there's an interesting factor, there must be an economic term for it I don't know what it is, but the more money that is available the more expansion there is in the entire business. So while I was able to lend six inches, [and] that's all I could lend because that's all the money that I had, Producers that didn't get in within that 6-inch area that I could lend in couldn't get the money. Now, more bankers came in, more lenders started lending, even non-bank lenders, what happened is that grew from 6 inches to 12 inches to 18 inches and now there was more money available and more people could come in and start borrowing money. So the business grew exponentially. And when it grows that fast you there's going to be a time in which it stops because there's too much product number one and number two people want better films. I'll give you an example of how wonderful the business was at that time. I happened to be at the American Film Market talking to one of my clients in their offices and they were making at that time very low budget really bad science-fiction-horror films. And they were selling them like crazy. They had a group of maybe four or five films that they were working with. There was a Japanese Distributor that came into their office and they saw that he was really chomping at the bit wanted to buy all that product. So one of the partners turned to his partner in front of the Japanese Distributor and said, "Okay, go ahead and sell him these films for the amount you're talking about, fine, fine, fine that's just great. But I am not going to agree to let him buy—" I don't know [what he actually said] I'm just going to make the title up, "—'The Ant That Killed The World' I'm just not going to let him buy that film, I am not going to let you do it. It's just too good, you've got to get more money if that's the film that you want to sell him along with the others." The Japanese guy says, "Wait a minute, wait a minute what are we talking about?" And his partner said, "Well this is a special [movie] but if you'll pay X+ for it I'll let you have it." The [Japanese] guy says, "Absolutely! I want it!!" And he leaves after they made the deal. I'm in their offices and I said, "So tell me what kind of film is this 'The Ant That Killed The World'?" He said, "I don't know! We haven't made it, we haven't even got a script, but when I heard that he was chomping at the bit for all of this I just made it up!"

**Stephen**: Oh my God!

**Lew**: "And now we're going to go write a script and do it!!" And <u>that's</u> how wonderful the business was.

**Stephen**: That is a great story. Talk about moguls. That's how a mogul thinks right? A mini-mogul in this case.

**Lew**: Oh yes. And that's how the business was being done then. Of course it couldn't continue on that same basis.

**Stephen**: It was a combination of things it sounds like, there was just too much money and people were making films of lower and lower quality and at the same time consumers wised up and so obviously Distributors wised up along with them. And so it just matured and ripened and eventually got to a place where it was just not feasible to continue that way anymore.

**Lew:** Right.

**Stephen:** Let's move into the Digital Era. Flashforward to present day and talk about some of the modern advances in distribution; for example: streaming, downloading, file sharing. If you think about that, and describe it as the Digital Age, do you think it's killed any parts of filmmaking in terms of ruining the market in a way where because anybody can do it, that product that's being made today is of a lower quality? Put another way, have modern technological advances where anyone with a phone can make a movie has ruined filmmaking, meaning the market/business side of it?

**Lew:** I'm not as up on that as I was about the other information but I can tell you from still being involved with the business being a consultant and seeing what's happening I don't think it's changing anything. There are more outlets for film. You can make a film with your [consumer] camera and will your cell phone and there are ways now that you can get it sold. Whether you can make any money on it is something else. There's always the odd one that comes along that becomes something that all the young people are interested in and that makes some money. But basically it's another way of seeing films that has not hurt the business and I don't believe the business has been increased by it at all. NetFlix is a wonderful example of it doing very well and helping the business. But for the entrepreneur young Producer wanting to make a film on his own, no, I don't think [digital] changes anything.

**Stephen:** Although you retired from LHO you still stay very busy. What kind of projects do you work on these days? What are you doing?

**Lew:** That's what my wife wants to know too! *(laughs)* Actually I've been retired for a little bit over 11 years now in June. And it's been absolutely wonderful and I have been extremely happy with what's happening. I have done a little bit of everything. I have consulted for banks that want to get into the business. I have consulted for non-bank lenders that raise their money from investors that want to get into the business. I have done work for Independent Producers in just guiding them in what they should do with their film to get it financed. I don't seek out investors. I don't know investors. But I can be helpful to Independent Producers and have been in telling them why their film can't be made or how they go about arranging a loan to get it made, and then helping them raise the money, through loans rather than investors. One other thing I have been doing is I work with attorneys as an expert witness, that's the most fun I enjoy that a great deal. The last four years I have worked exclusively as a consultant for a non-bank lender who was investing as well as lending money in the Independent Film Business. I was not involved in the investment portion, I stayed away from that. But in the lending portion I consulted for them in how to make the best deal, doing the negotiations, closing the deal. Closing the loan for a film is one of the most difficult and time consuming and stressful events that you can imagine. And that's what I'm pretty good at because I had done so many over the years, about 500 or so, and so that's what I did over the last four years.

**Stephen:** Is it fair to say that maybe you're doing less in terms of clock hours in your day but you get to do a lot more of every different thing that you've had contact with in your career?

**Lew:** Yes that's exactly true except for one thing. It is less clock hours. Being a consultant is wonderful because I don't have to do any work. I have to read documents and I have to understand the deal. I have to take time [to soak it all in] but otherwise I just consult and give people my opinions and then they have to do the work *(laughs)*.

**Stephen:** So it's more reactive?

**Lew:** Exactly.

**Stephen:** Well you've earned that right! *(laughs)*

**Lew:** You bet!!

**Stephen:** You are considered as a revolutionary key figure in Independent Film financing especially when it comes to the term Gap Financing which is different from Bridge Financing. Try to summarize Gap Financing in terms for people who are not familiar with the financial intricacies of lending in general and lending for independent films in particular. Can you put into layman's terms what Gap Financing is?

**Lew:** Gap Financing, or 'The Gap', is the difference between the collateral that a lender has and the actual budget of the film. For an example, let's assume the budget of a film, just to make things simple, is a million dollars. And the Producer has $500,000 in collateral, the collateral could be contracts from Distributors, it could be cash from investors, it could be anything that the lender feels comfortable with. So what's the difference? There's $500,000 in collateral, the budget however is a million dollars, the difference between the two, $500,000 is the gap. So that's the amount of money that in previous years borrowers couldn't get, Producers couldn't get. Okay so that gives you a brief explanation. Let me give you a tiny bit of history that leads it into there. We had the '80's in which anything was selling etc. And you could lend a 100% of the money for the production of the film just on your pre-sales. And at that time I thought, "Oh, what a tough business this [is]!" Ha! I didn't realize how easy it was. *(laughs)* And that made life very simple. But now what was happening, as I said, was the Distributors were now getting a little anxious, they weren't making all the sales. They were buying dreams and getting nightmares! So what they wanted to do was they wanted to see more of the film. Well you can't make more of the film unless you've got the money to put it into the film. This kept getting more and more important to the Distributors and of course to the Producers. The Producers also realized that you don't get quite as much money from a pre-sale as you would from a [finished] film that everybody wants. And so if it's not pre-sold you could get more money because the Distributor's going to discount the pre-sale because he's putting the money up in advance – he hasn't seen the film. Now of course that could work two ways: the Producer could want to get more money by going to the Distributor saying, "Fine I don't want to do this with your contract I'll wait until I get the film done and then I'm going to sell it to you." If the Distributor doesn't want it after the film is made now you've made a gross error — it might have been better to get a pre-sale for less money. Because of the Distributor's needs and wants and because of the Producer's needs and wants I saw that there was a need for [a special kind lending], and after all that's what lending does you've got to find a need and then fill it. So I said, "Wait a minute, maybe there's a way to lend on this gap." Because what I had found was there is a value to the unsold rights. Let's take that first example: $500,000 in collateral — a million dollar budget, there is a value to the rights that are not licensed yet. Now that value is kind of nebulous, you really can't put a number on it exactly, however, I found that by working with the Sales Agents, not the Producer, but the Sales Agents, and saying to them, "What do you think the 'ultimates' would be? What do you think we could get for this film if it were finished and it were not great and it were not terrible and it was just a film what do you think the values would be?" I did a great deal of experimenting and I did my own calculations and I found that if I took a percentage-- Well first what I would do is I would break down the individual values of the individual territories and then I would put my own value on it. Now you can't do this if you don't know the business. But I had been involved for many years. I knew the buyers as well as the sellers and I knew the Sales Agents. I made a point of being very much involved with Sales Agents. I joined AFMA, the American Film Marketing Association and later became a Director of AFMA. So I was very much involved. And so I would take their value, I would usually discount it — I never went up! *(laughs)* I discounted a certain amount and then I worked out a formula and now that I discounted it then I'll only lend a certain percentage of the budget and I'll only lend on those, what I call 'primary territories', the larger territories, not on the smaller territories. And by combining all of that into a spreadsheet I found that I could come up with a reasonable evaluation of what the unsold rights would be worth. And on this film of a million dollars where there was $500,000 in collateral, if I saw there was another, let's say, million dollars of collateral [monies for unsold territories] and I said, "Okay, I'll lend half of that." using my formula, I then filled the gap. I then lent on that portion that nobody else had ever lent on. And I was able to make the loan. That was something that I found that I needed to do as well because the business was slowing down because we couldn't make enough loans just on pre-sales. That ended. Where you could lend 100% against only pre-sales previously you couldn't do it anymore. So Gap Financing started. Obviously it was rather difficult to get the bank that I was partners with to agree to do that. But once they saw that it was very successful financially because I charged a significant rate for lending on that gap portion. So it became profitable for the bank and very important to the Borrower, the Producer. And that grew to the point where today there are four ways you can get money for a film and if you can't get them you can't make the film independently, forget about going to a studio. You need pre-sales because that's the cement that holds everything together. You need Gap [Financing]. You need whatever tax incentive is available. And you need probably an investor for the portion that the lender won't give you to fill the gap. The reason it evolved into the point where you now need an investor as well as a lender for Gap is that the business became even more difficult because we found that Gap Financing was very dangerous unless you really were specifically so careful. So it got to the point where myself and other lenders that were in the business then said, "Fine, we'll do these deals but I'm not going to give you as much for Gap as we used to." And so the only way to fill that, aside from your tax incentives, was to find an investor. Today, almost every single independent film financed uses those four streams of financing.

**Stephen**: One of which you essentially invented.

**Lew**: Yes. Yes. Without Gap you couldn't do it.

**Stephen**: You're known for being a caring, communicative, hard-working businessman. Everyone says so including Lenny Shapiro.

**Lew**: *(laughs)*

**Stephen**: And many others. Would you say that the interaction between you and those human beings-- because even though it is balance sheets and spread sheets and Bank Managers and investment funds and all the rest of it, it does come down to people in many ways. The people whom you lend money to, the Producers. The people like the Sales Agents you know. The Buyers who you may happen to know personally. These are people with spreadsheets and balance sheets too but they're also human beings. And you get to know them over the years. And you get to know them from their actions not just their words if you know them for a long period of time, so there's that human connection. Would you say that that's something that makes the job interesting for you?

**Lew**: Well, yes. People are really fun. When I started as a teller in banking in 1955--

**Stephen**: Were we using Confederate money then? That's a joke, obviously! *(laughs)*

**Lew**: *(laughs)* I was just a teller. It was a lot different than it is today I'll tell you that. I just loved meeting the people. The same thing with these deals. The Distributors are so interesting. You may not trust what they say but you might enjoy being with them anyway. I made so many friends whom I might not lend money to but I would enjoy their company. I met so many friends who were absolute scoundrels but with the best personalities and the biggest hearts. And what I found is that, not all, but a good many – I won't say 'most', but a good many people of all walks of life of every color and religion, basically are very loyal. And if you don't screw them they won't screw you. Of course being a banker gives you an added touch there. [If] you screw your friend, okay; your friend's never going to talk to you again. [But if] you screw your banker, okay, that's the end of the money. And I always made sure that people understood that if they screwed me the rest of the banking world would know about it. What I found was, aside from the fact that I made money; most of the clients that I did business with were extremely loyal. That was true for the music business, television business and the film business. Loyal. They might take advantage of other people but not of me. 'A', because they needed me. And 'B' because we had a form of camaraderie where they knew that I would take care of them if they would take care of me. For an example, one of my clients had a problem with their film and they couldn't pay me because it wasn't doing well, I wouldn't just say to them, "Okay, I'm foreclosing tomorrow you're going to lose the film!" for two reasons. Number one it doesn't make sense because what am I going to do with the film? But the other reason, and truly more important, is if I work with them they'll find ways to get it paid. I would work with my clients, I wouldn't place all my trust with them, but I would certainly work with them. And I have formed many wonderful relationships and have helped a great many companies because I could've put them out of business but I kept them in business and they grew larger and larger.

**Stephen:** Is it fair to say that Lenny Shapiro is one of those guys who you connected with over the years?

**Lew:** Yes! Yes.

**Stephen:** With 3D, digital projection and all the technological gimmicks like D Box and so on, I'm sure you're generally aware of what's going on with modern technology in theatre exhibition these days — trends and progressions let's call them. Do you think these advancements are making theatrical exhibition more interesting for consumers? Not from just an audience standpoint of seeing a clearer picture and so on, but also for Producers and Filmmakers. Are these advancements changing the business in a good way do you think?

**Lew:** I don't think at this particular time that it's doing much changing. The kids like 3D if you can have hands coming out of the screen and all sorts of fun things like that that the young people want to see and that makes the film perhaps more enjoyable. Although, because the studios are charging a great deal more for it I don't know whether the kids can afford to go. But as far as adults go, in all my conversations with the independent Producers and Distributors and Sales Agents, nobody has talked about it. It is not something that is making a big difference right now. I think the only reason the studios are doing it a lot is because they can charge more money; the theatres can charge more money. The other day I went to see a film and I didn't realize I was buying a ticket for a 3D viewing, I just saw what time it was playing. I got to the theatre and the guy told me what the price was I couldn't believe I was paying that much money. I said, "Why is this so much?" He said, "Oh you're here to see the 3D version." And the 3D version was the same thing as the 2D version because it wasn't the kind of film where you have hands reach out and animals flop around and all that. I don't think the adults care that much. Now it's going to make a big difference in the sale of television sets if the price ever comes down. I think it's going to take a while before it becomes [something impactful].

**Stephen:** You've already told a very funny story about one particular thing that happened in Cannes when you walked out and saw the parade with Lenny and you knew what the marketing advance he needed was for at that moment. So did you go to Cannes often?

**Lew:** I went to Cannes for twenty-two straight years.

**Stephen:** Have you been in a while?

**Lew:** No, since I retired I haven't gone because there hasn't been any need for me to go. And, to be honest, if you're in Cannes and there's nothing for you to do there— I've seen it, I've seen all of the beauty and all of the fun and interesting things. So it just becomes a lonely place. So no, I haven't gone since I retired.

**Stephen:** There are two Cannes events that happen pretty much side-by-side; one is the official Festival, including the competition, the Director's Fortnight and all of those things. And then there's the market, The Marché du Film, which is where the films are being sold.

**Lew:** Yes, that [The Marché] is what I have always been interested in.

**Stephen:** Did you ever attend any of those festival screenings and see any of those?

**Lew:** Oh sure.

**Stephen:** And what was that like?

**Lew:** When you go to the big screening in the Palais it's wonderful. You wear a tuxedo and you walk down this huge red carpet, or I should say you walk up these stairs. There is music playing, actors and actresses all walking around. It's very glamorous and very nice. But it's 'their' evening. See I've never been the type to go and say, "Well – I just walked up the red carpet. And I've just seen this film with so and so and oh boy!" Naw, that's not my thing. So it was a nice glamorous thing to see, and, then you've done it. It's their evening not your evening. Unless you're representing a film there. I went there once to the Palais on a film that I financed. Oh, oh, oh! That was a whole different thing. That made it much more fun. It didn't change the glamour any but it just made it--

**Stephen:** Made you more part of that glamour?

**Lew:** Yeah, yeah. But nobody looked at me. They didn't care about me.

**Stephen:** But if they only knew that the film wouldn't exist if not for you?

**Lew:** That's the truth.

**Stephen:** You become a far more 'important' person the more people know about you.

**Lew:** I have recently financed, or helped finance as a consultant, about nine films coming out at various times. My name is on the very bottom of the list as a 'financial consultant' that's all. I don't take any big part of it [credits-wise].

**Stephen:** Back in the era that this book covers there were three main sales festivals. In 'order of appearance', it used to be AFM was first in February and then it was moved to November, then came Cannes, which was in May, then there was MIFED--

**Lew:** MIFED in October where it rained all the time!

**Stephen:** All the time! It was the 'gray' festival. AFM was the red, white & blue festival; Cannes was just exceedingly French in any color and those colors changed; and MIFED was the gray festival. When you compare those three markets and think of them from the businessman's perspective in terms of volume of business done, in terms of where the important deals got made – comparison-wise, which of those three main festivals when they were all operating 'big guns' would you say was the most important of the three?

**Lew:** I went to all the festivals. I went to MIFED until they closed down. And of course I've been going to AFM since 1982 until now. I go every year. I can tell you the most important deals and the biggest deals start out in Cannes. MIFED and AFM both did the same thing. They took on the opening of smaller films. Most importantly they took on the closing of the deals and finishing up the deals for the films that started in Cannes.

**Stephen:** Why would you say that is?

**Lew:** I don't know. Just my own thoughts, could be completely wrong, Cannes is the big glamorous place where all the big films go. The studios go there. The studios don't go to AFM because they have their own sales group. So I think [Cannes] with its big festival, and it was France, and being in Europe of course.

**Stephen:** Don't forget the Naked Snake Ladies!

**Lew:** And the half-naked ladies on the beach. That was what drew, that was the glamour--

**Stephen:** The magnet?

**Lew:** The magnet, that's the best term thank you. And the other two markets were very important but they closed the deals and they opened the smaller deals. Unfortunately, the AFM and MIFED did the same thing and— and MIFED, I loved MIFED first of all.

**Stephen:** So did Alan Solomon by the way. That was his favorite market and reason why was he felt like he could get more business done.

**Lew:** That's interesting because I found that if I could stand at a certain part of the hallways, [MIFED] was a maze, I would see everybody! And I saw so many more people there than I did in Cannes. In Cannes I had to walk around a lot more. It was very hot although it was very beautiful. I liked MIFED a great deal. But [AFM and MIFED] did the same thing and when it got to the point where AFM wanted to change its date, that hurt MIFED very much and it closed, ultimately that was the reason for it.

**Stephen:** So now instead of three sales markets there are two?

**Lew:** Yes. Well no, now we've got Toronto [The Toronto International Film Festival]. Toronto started as a small film festival and is now getting very, very, not getting IS very, very important.

**Stephen:** Switching gears into TV, tons of high quality TV series changed the face of productions made for television. I know you started out in Movies of the Week. In terms of LHO's business, you didn't just focus on motion pictures did you? Talk a little bit about where you did your business, movies vs. TV.

**Lew:** I was involved in the TV area before film. I moved from music, which stopped being a good business to lend into, to television; and then from television, which stopped being a good business to lend into, to film. I not only lent on Movies of the Week but there was at that time a great deal of syndication throughout the world and throughout the United States. So I lent on a number of syndicated deals for the US. There were only two ways you could lend: you lend against syndicated contracts or lend against Movies of the Week because as a lender I have to lend against some collateral that I feel comfortable with and that turns out to be contracts. So it was either contracts with various television stations for the syndication of a film or lending money to a syndicator, in turn [we lent on] his contracts. Or lent money for Movie of the Week.

**Stephen**: Just to talk about the mechanics of lending for a moment. From my own personal experience of sitting at Lenny Shapiro's elbow for years, so many years ago, I remember that when LHO would lend against contracts, that that contract, whatever was due on that contract, would not be paid to SGE, it would be paid to LHO. Essentially it was assigned to you. So is that really how that worked?

**Lew**: Yeah. Oh yeah. I took an assignment of whatever the monies were from that particular contract.

**Stephen**: Let's say a film was sold to Germany for $500,000 which was a very big number for those little movies, but that happened.

**Lew**: Uh huh.

**Stephen**: So that money when it was due and payable, it was due and payable to LHO?

**Lew**: Yes. Exactly.

**Stephen**: So that German buyer would no longer be paying SGE they would be paying LHO.

**Lew**: There were documents, which we used to get that.

**Stephen**: Last question, and it's one of those retrospective questions that is very open-ended so feel free to answer it however you choose to. Being very well known and acclaimed within lending in the independent motion picture business, by anyone's measure you succeeded. Looking back over the years over your career do you have any regrets? Is there anything that you did you wish you didn't, or anything that you wish you've done but you haven't?

**Lew**: You know, I've been a very lucky person, very fortunate. I don't have any real regrets and I don't have a bucket list believe it or not. But if I had to go back and do it again I would have become more involved with investors. Because, for my later years, so that when I left banking, like now as a consultant, if I had arrangements with investors I could have put together a lot of deals using investors. But I truly made no arrangements with them. And I don't know one investor from the other. So that would have been another avenue for me to pursue. But I have never done it.

**Stephen**: It was certainly logical, banking was where you came from and it's what you knew: lending. So you went with what you knew and you invented new ways to do it.

**Lew**: That's right.

**Stephen**: Is there anything that we haven't covered that you think is relevant?

**Lew**: You've been extremely thorough. I don't have any other thoughts except on a personal basis. Lenny has always been one of those people I told you about that you make a friendship with. Except with him it was one where there was trust as well as liking him. And knowing that, unless the roof fell down on his head and crushed him to pieces, he would do what he could to pay me and to be loyal and to make certain that I was taken care of. Therefore, I always did everything that I could to help him.

**Stephen:** You are talking about integrity I think.

**Lew:** Yes integrity.

**Stephen:** And that is a theme that you began with when we first--

**Lew:** Yeah it's a good way to close isn't it? Yes, a nice bookend.

---

By Stephen A. Roberts, in person
in Calabasas, California, At Marmalade' Cafe
09June, 2015 and 16June, 2015

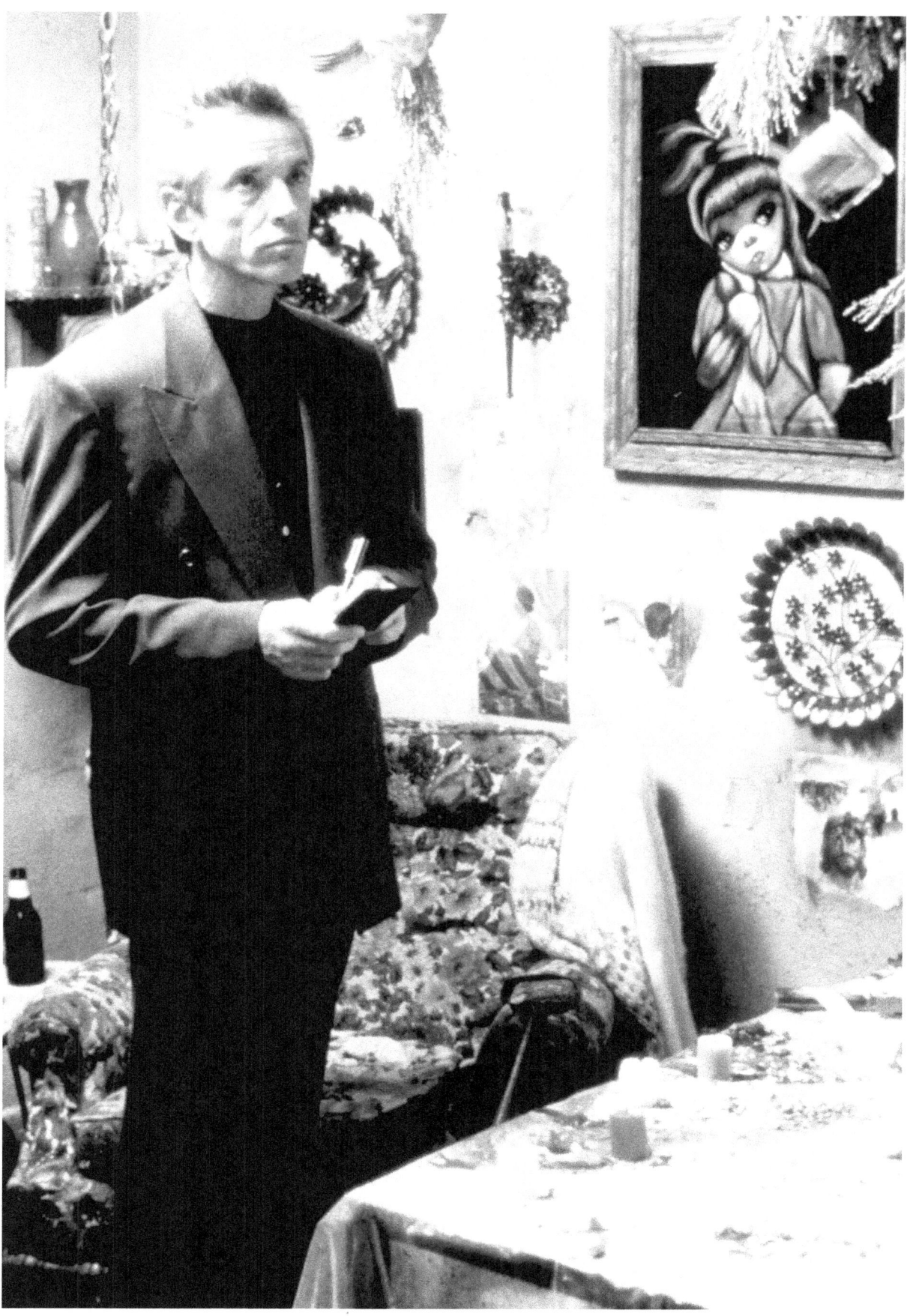

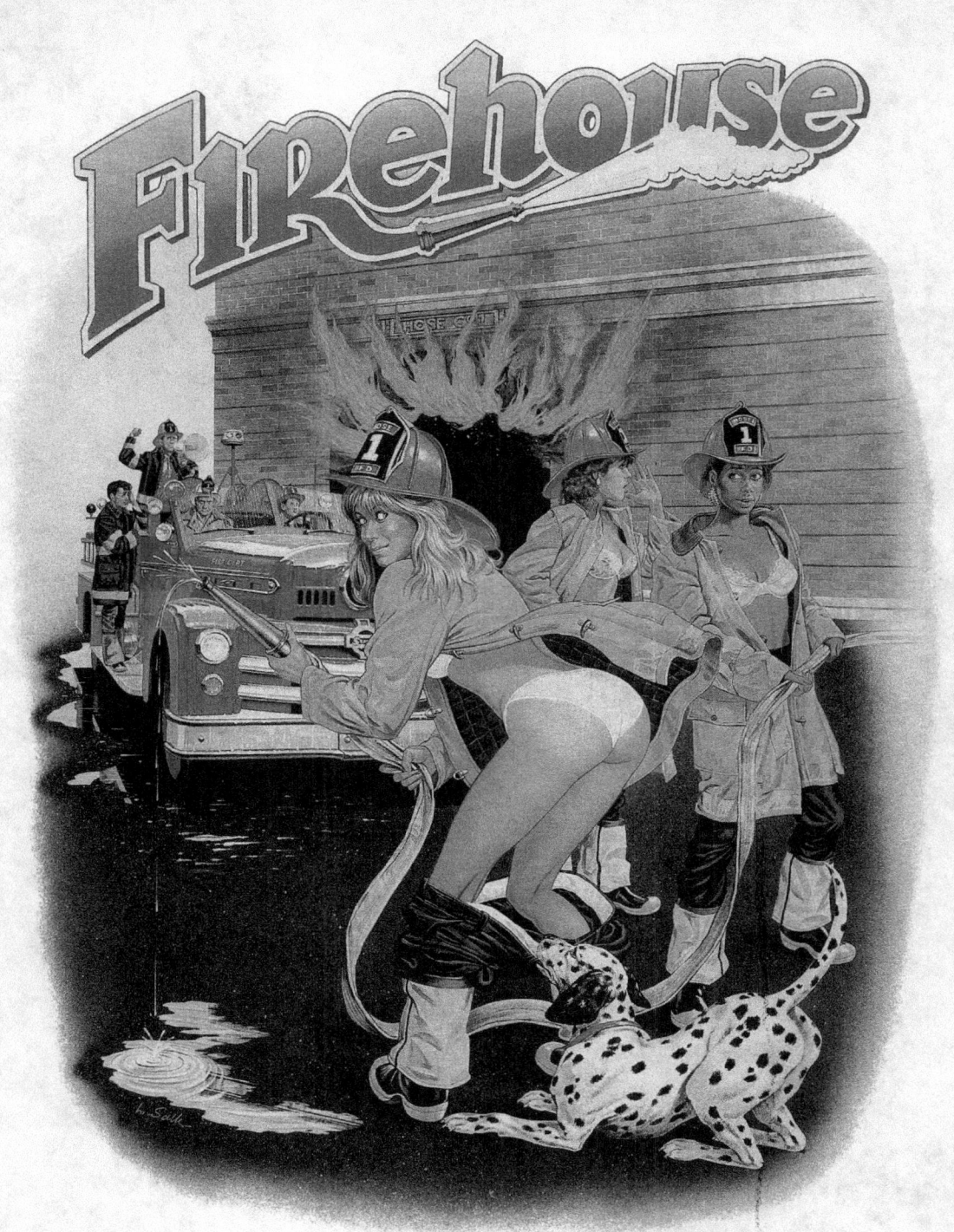

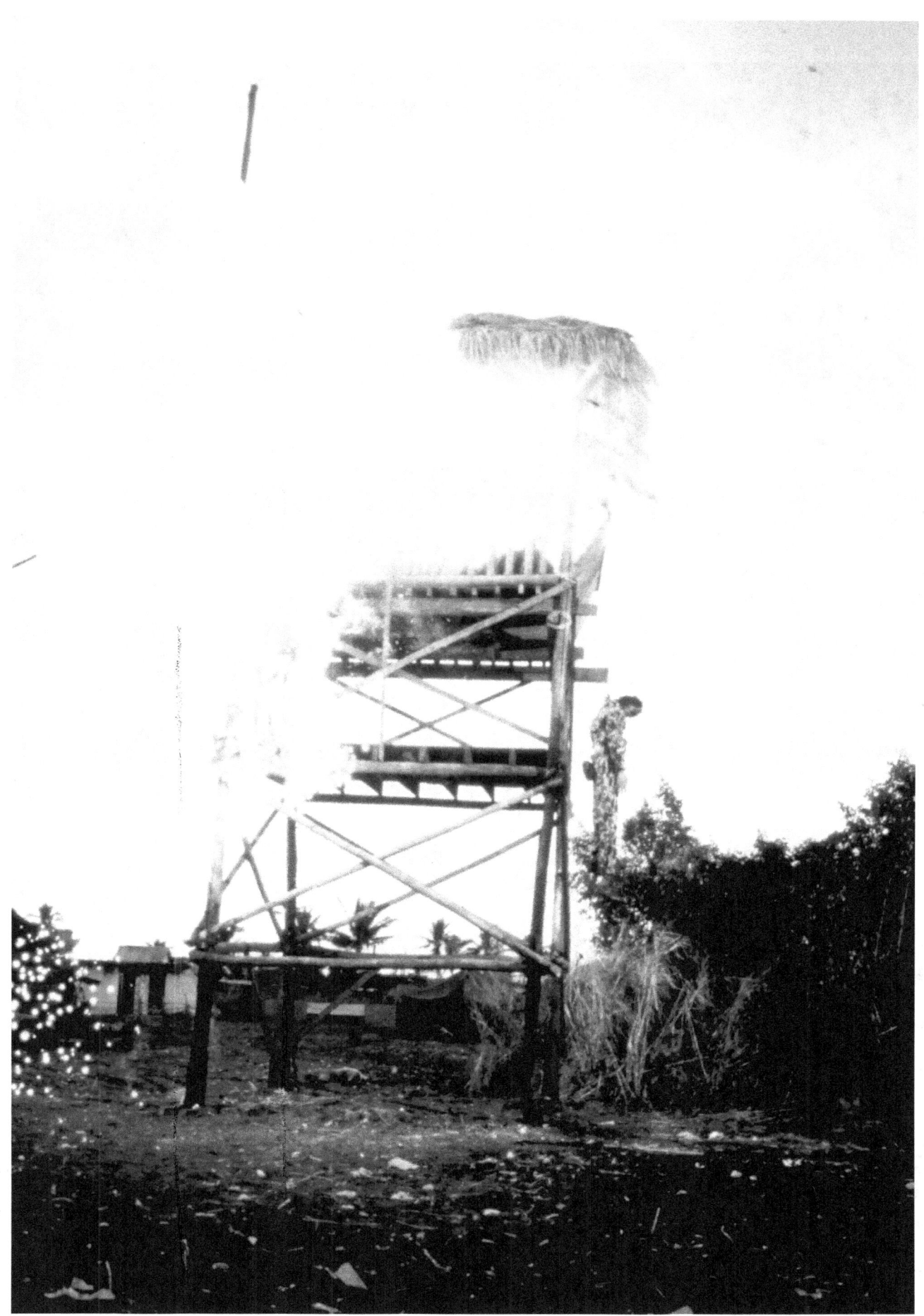

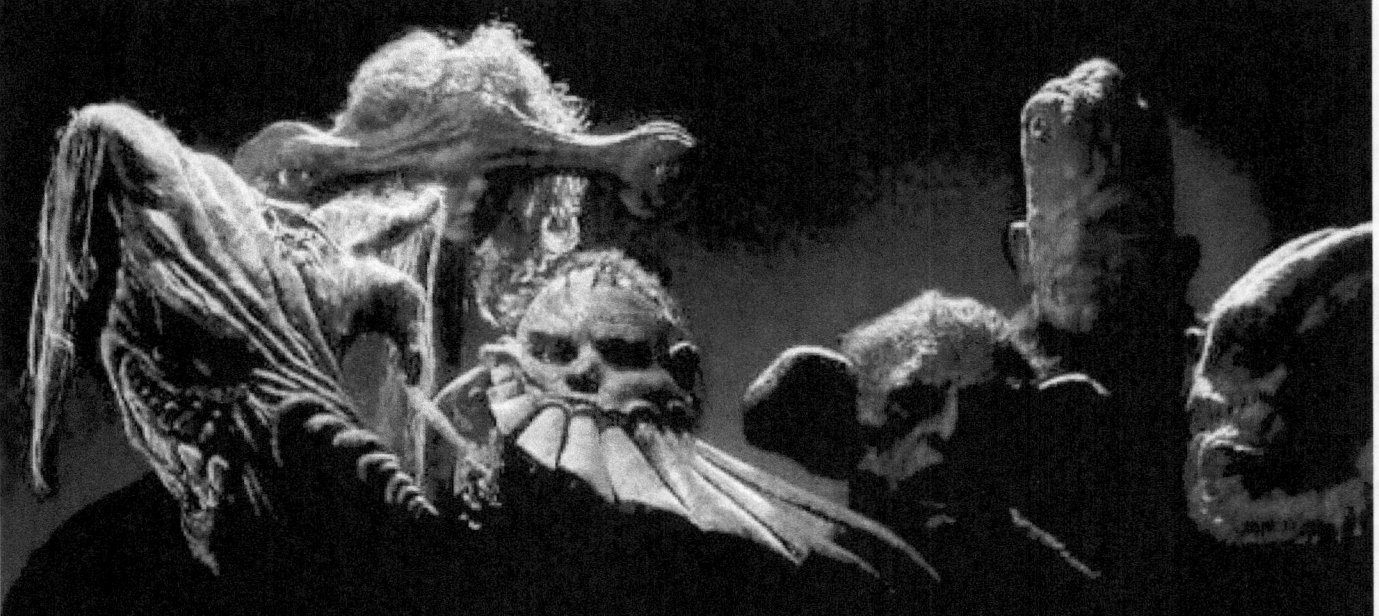

It's time to build a bigger basket!

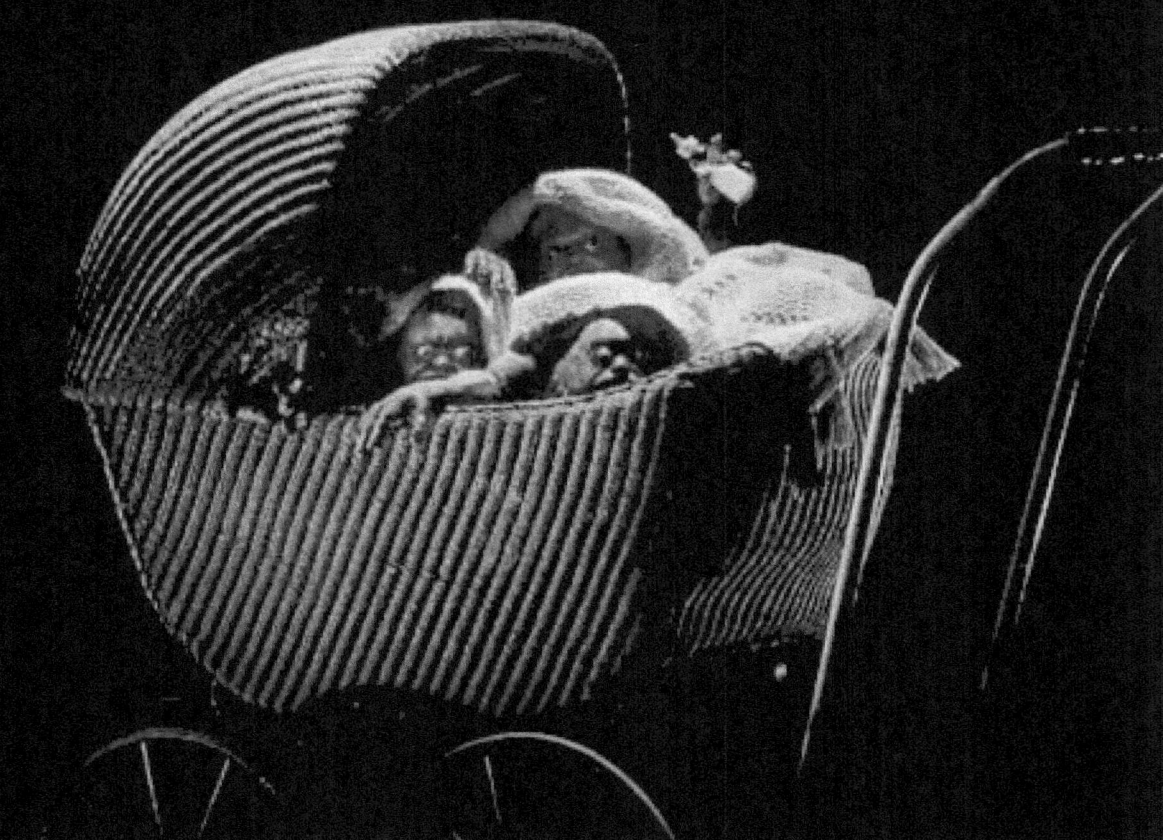

IN THIS WORLD NO ONE IS INNOCENT AND IF YOU WANT TO LIVE, YOU'VE GOT TO BEAT THE HANGMEN.

# HANGMEN

CINEMA SCIENCES CORPORATION PRESENTS "HANGMEN" STARRING RICHARD R. WASHBURN, JAKE LAMOTTA, DOG THOMAS, KOSMO VINYL, KEITH BOGART PRODUCED BY J. CHRISTIAN INGVORDSEN AND STEVEN W. KAMAN AND RICHARD R. WASHBURN DIRECTED BY J. CHRISTIAN INGVORDSEN DIRECTOR OF PHOTOGRAPHY STEVEN W. KAMAN SCREENPLAY J. CHRISTIAN INGVORDSEN AND STEVEN KAMAN ORIGINAL SCORE MICHAEL MONTES ASSOCIATE PRODUCERS MARC BAILIN AND PEGGY JACOBSON EXECUTIVE PRODUCERS C. STEVEN DUNCKER AND ROBERT ANDERSON

© 1987 Cinema Sciences Corporation

# John Alexander

Like many of the SGE employees, John Alexander grew up all over the world, in such places as Peru, Libya, Spain, the Caribbean and the United Kingdom. Fluent in several languages, he also plays piano and sings. Graduating from Ithaca College, John then moved to Los Angeles and began his career at Shapiro Entertainment working with Alan Solomon. John left SGE to continue a hugely succesful career in film sales, first at MCEG, then on to Hallmark Entertainment, which became RHI Entertainment, and then Sonar Entertainment. He currently is President of Worldwide Sales at Great Point Media Ltd.

**Marco:** Mr. Alexander, you were born in Argentina - how did it happen that you joined the Film Industry? Where did you spend your childhood and youth?

**John:** I was actually born in darkest Peru, like Paddington Bear, and because of my father's job, we lived all over the world in countries like Colombia, Argentina, Libya, India, Norway and several other places including a couple of sun soaked years in the Caribbean. High school was spent in Italy and college in the UK and the US. I studied Film and Television in the US graduating with a degree in Communications and was referred by a professor to Tim Kittleson who, at the time, was the head of the AFMA in Los Angeles. He in turn referred me to a small independent Italian company that worked as a sales agent for independent movies, and while it was a short stint after which I gratefully moved on - it was the starting point of my career in the film and television business.

**Marco:** Do you remember how it happened, that film became such an important thing for you? Were you interested in the arts, music and books before you got into motion pictures?

**John:** I was always interested in movies, the arts, music and books as well as drawing, acting and writing and came from a creative family that was into all those areas. I have played piano ever since I can remember and composed my own music as well as playing in a classic rock and blues cover band called The Indies (as in independent film companies) for a number of years where we played gigs and raised money for homeless children charities. Some of the highpoints of the band, for me at least, was playing at the House of Blues in LA to a packed house, Jimmy Buffet's Margaretville in New Orleans and performing at the Cannes Film Festival a couple of times. PolyGram even funded a week in the famed Olympic Recording Studios in London where we recorded about 12 songs and made a CD. In fact - a six degrees of separation reference here - ex-Shapiro employee Ted Rosenblatt's business partner played for a stint as the band's drummer!

**Marco:** You joined Shapiro Entertainment in 1986 just before it changed to SGE. How do you remember those days, was it an important time in your own career?

**John:** It was an exciting time, and it was where I was able to tap into my international background and languages and really learn the ropes of the international film distribution business, a subject that back then they did not teach in school or university. Video was exploding around the globe, and it was exciting to be working in the business with this new medium, while learning about the existing theatrical business as well. It's funny how when you are young, you just want to run and adapt and be part of something, so you miss a lot of things in your haste. As you get older, you become more reflective and observant about your surroundings. I often wish I could time travel back and be more aware of some of the people and places I was around and some of the history I lived through. I have always been fascinated by old Hollywood, the classic era of the studio system, MGM in particular during its heyday, and how Los Angeles evolved during those years from a dusty semi-desert area of land to the teeming metropolis it is today. Sadly, much of that history has been mowed under to accommodate mini-strip malls and apartment buildings, but if you read and delve deeply enough below the surface, there is wonderful history in all those places along with the characters who came in search of a dream or just to find work in a sunnier environment. I love stories like the city of Tarzana being named after Edgar Rice Burroughs' famous cartoon and movie character Tarzan. Back in 1919, Burroughs bought founder of the LA Times General Harrison Otis's tract of land in the valley and named it Tarzana Ranch. He also allegedly built one of the first swimming pools in the Valley. As his time passed by, he sold off parcels and eventually the area where the Borroughs estate was became the city of Tarzana. Pretty cool and very Hollywood from a bygone era. I recall another time exploring an abandoned estate in the Hollywood Hills that used to belong to a string of luminaries, some immortalized and others long forgotten except in books focused on that time in the city's history. For me is was a fascinating, mysterious place filled with secrets not yet revealed, and a feeling that what had been before still had a tremendous allure and pull, particularly as I devoured book after book on Hollywood, Los Angeles, the film industry and the characters that populated that world over the decades. Going even further back I loved something I had read about the California oak trees and how in Spain they are called encinas. I assume that this is also where perhaps the Los Angeles town of Encino with its protected oak trees got its name. When the Spanish first came to California they missed their famous Jamon Iberico which is made from pigs that are allowed to graze on the fallen acorns of Spain's oak trees. The Spaniards logically thought to bring their own oak trees to California so that they could enjoy Jamon Californiano using the same technique. Later on I read something suggesting that not that many years ago, you could walk under the shade of the oak trees all the way to the Pacific Ocean. All very romantic.

**Marco**: At SGE, you worked closely with Alan M. Solomon. Can you describe your duties while assisting him in sales and contracts? How do you remember him as a boss? Was he a mentor?

**John:** Alan Solomon was a true taskmaster who demanded complete thoroughness and attention to detail in his employees. I learned a tremendous amount from Alan, and what I learned from him formed the basis of my legal, contractual and sales knowledge which I built upon as I have moved through my career in this industry. Alan was a tough boss but he appreciated those of us who rose to the challenge, inspiring us to be better and achieve greater goals on the work front. I think a lot of ex-Shapiro employees who worked for Alan feel the same way - he effectively gave us some very useful tools to forge our own careers after we left Shapiro and yes, I would definitely say he was a mentor for me in those days.

**Marco:** On which titles did you work at SGE, and do you have a favorite now, looking back on those days? For how many years did you work with Mr. Solomon?

**John:** I worked for Alan for about four years before being offered a job at Manson/MCEG at a substantially higher salary and an elevated position. Re titles the ones that come to mind foremost are RED SCORPION and BLUE JEAN COP aka SHAKEDOWN. As I was given more freedom by Alan to deal with clients where language was a substantial roadblock for him, I was able to build a great client base as well as to generate my own sales for the company in territories like Spain, Italy, France and Latin America. I remember doing a very big deal in Spain with Record Vision for a package of films including RED SCORPION and sitting there listening to the Spaniards discuss their intended negotiation strategy in Spanish right there in front of me. Once they had finished their internal dialogue, I replied in Spanish that we should cut to the chase and agree on a figure a little north of what they said they would ultimately propose. Needless to say, there was much uproar and mild-mannered indignation that I had not divulged to them my ability to speak Spanish, after which we shook hands and agreed to the first of many deals. We are still friends and colleagues to this day. I also remember a certain German distributor grandly writing us a cheque for $1M for RED SCORPION and flourishing it in front of Alan as he outbid the other German contenders. In the end I seem to remember the cheque was no good or we were asked not to deposit it and after some period of time, another German distributor ultimately picked up the title. However, the Hollywood theatrics, albeit with a German flair, were hugely entertaining to an impressionable young man like me, and it has been one of those industry stories oft repeated around dinner tables across the globe. I remember some of the movies we used to handle including C.H.U.D. (the sequel to which was sold by Vestron I believe), BLOOD MONEY, which we repped for Jack Murphy and his young accomplice Gavin Reardon, with whom I still have a great friendship and has had a good long career in our business. I must admit I was frequently less interested in our movies than I was the parade of dazzling young ladies walking through our marble lobby entrance that either worked on many of our films or wanted to star in them. My taste in movies skewed more towards the Film Noir classics of the 40's and 50's and well-written thrillers. For a while the big action titles were appealing in their blockbuster novelty, but then they became one long stream of explosions, gun fights and non-stop pace that lost any peaks and valleys where one could catch one's breath and appreciate the overall story, and I lost interest. Needless to say, in those days with video, action-action-action was what sold, and the more guns and explosions the better, so putting my sales hat on, they were the movies I wanted to be able to sell.

**Marco:** After leaving SGE, what happened next? What was your next career step? Did you stay in touch with some colleagues from that era?

**John:** As mentioned above, I took a job as VP of Sales for MCEG - Management Company Entertainment Group - which was helmed at the time by Jonathan Krane who had previously worked with Blake Edwards and had formed a company that managed talent, produced films and had its own sales distribution department as well. Jonathan Krane managed talent like John Travolta, Brooke Shields, Kirstie Alley, Robert Duvall and others, and I remember we had films like CHAINS OF GOLD, starring Travolta. We had other movies with big names in them as well, and my background at Shapiro Glickenhaus served me very well at MCEG where I had higher profile mainstream product to sell and a great bedrock education and client base to apply at the new company. The company then acquired Richard Branson's Virgin Vision and we expanded our international network to encompass overseas offices in the UK, Germany and Australia. With all this expansion I was promoted to Head of Sales for the company. Unfortunately, like many independent companies of that time that grew quickly and then spent far too much against contrastingly low revenue generation, the company went bust after a couple of years. However, it was a great experience while it lasted, and I remember lavish offices on top of the Martinez Hotel in Cannes during the Film Festival where we threw big parties and flew out a lot of our stars to promote movies and mingle with the international buyers. That also reminds me of a party Shapiro Glickenhaus had in Cannes to promote a movie we were involved with, called GRIZZLY ADAMS. The party was held at the Carlton Hotel replete with lithesome French wannabee starlets scantily dressed as Indian squaws prancing around a large manacled bear that somehow - and I doubt this would be allowed to happen today - the "powers that be" at that time were able to get into the Carlton as a centerpiece to the whole party! If memory serves, I don't think the movie ultimately got made but it was a hell of a party, and I remember suddenly being everyone's best friend because they all wanted to get into the party and I handled the tickets! They don't throw parties like that in Cannes anymore.

I have stayed in touch with quite a few people from my Shapiro days including Alan until his unfortunate passing, Lenny, Stephen Roberts who has been a friend consistently throughout the intervening years, Ted Rosenblatt and Nadia Bruce-Rawlings. I hear stories about other colleagues who worked there at the same time as I did but have not been in touch as much with that crowd. When I lived in the Woodland Hills/Calabasas area in Los Angeles, Lenny used to come down to my house, ring the doorbell and ask "Hi John, is Riley here? I've come to take him for a walk!" Forget about me, it was all about my lovable Labrador that everyone adored - including Stephen Roberts who was his favorite uncle and loved that dog as much as I did. Sorry to digress. But the other great Lenny story was one year when we were all at the now defunct MIFED market in Milan, Lenny and I and a number of other people from the industry were having dinner. Having attended high school in Rome and reasonably fluent in Italian, I was the resident translator. We were eating at Baguta, one of the industry's favorite dining spots right next to the famous Milan cathedral and as I was going around the table telling the waiter what people wanted, I was saying "And for her (lei)... such and such. And for him (lui - which sounds like Louie in English) such and such." When it came to Lenny, I repeated... "E per lui...", and Lenny, not understanding that 'E per lui' meant 'and for him' promptly interrupted, stating... "NOT Louie, Lenny!" Of course the whole table erupted in cackles of laughter and while the written retelling of the story lacks the spontaneity of the moment, it was truly a memorable and hysterical moment. I have really enjoyed the many years of laughter with Lenny complimented by his many years of experience in the business and his confidence and support in me and my career. He most certainly has been one of my great mentors, and like Ted Rosenblatt, Lenny asked me to speak at his UCLA extension course on international distribution, another series of memorable experiences that I have always remembered.

**Marco:** Did you work closely with the creative people, like filmmakers, composers, writers? Were you in charge of all the contracts?

**John:** Over the years I have had the opportunity to be involved with creative people on their projects, and this is an area that personally I really enjoy because of my own creative interests in writing and music and the technical side of filmmaking. However, I have also really enjoyed the building of businesses and the financing side of putting together films through international subsidies, pre-sales and other forms of financing.

**Marco:** Now and then, do you join the set while filmmakers are shooting? How much are you involved in the creative process?

**John:** I have been on sets during production, and while initially an exciting experience, there is a hell of a lot of waiting around before a shot is finally set up and a scene is filmed. That can get tedious as a visitor, particularly when you have no other involvement other than to watch the goings on. My creative involvement over the years has been more on the evaluation side of projects as they are being developed and considered for financing. My job is to put a sales hat on and gauge whether or not, in my experience, a project with whatever elements are attached, will be able to recuperate its budget and make a reasonable profit for the company. This is always a tough thing to do because you base your evaluation on historical data you have, but at the end of the day the final proof is in the finished production, and even then there are variables beyond your control that can adversely affect a film's performance. As a result, blind luck has to be included as one of the many elements of what makes some films work and others not.

**Marco:** Hallmark Entertainment became RHI Entertainment and finally became Sonar Entertainment. What's your part in this company history/evolution?

**John:** I transitioned from the film world into the television world when I took my job at Hallmark Entertainment eleven years ago. Hallmark was the biggest independent producer of TV movies and miniseries in the business starting with their huge success with LONESOME DOVE and transitioning from that to producing high budget miniseries for the American networks and establishing a Hallmark Channel internationally. We had tremendous relationships with international broadcasters who at the time had voracious appetites for this kind of programming. Over the years the business has changed with increasing local production, and over-production of the so-called event miniseries we originally created so that they were no longer events because so many were being produced.

I was with the company through the transition from Hallmark to RHI and finally to Sonar where, without the stewardship of the Halmis, the company has taken a different direction by relocating their headquarters to Los Angeles, reducing the company's output of TV movies and miniseries and plunging head long into the world of scripted one-hour series.

Going back to what makes projects work and the importance of strong writing and scripts, I worked on a series called TABOO which will be produced this year by Ridley Scott's Scott Free Productions, will star Tom Hardy and has been commissioned by the BBC in the UK. I remember hearing the pitch of the story and not being all that impressed and then reading the first hour of the series and being blown away by the writing. On the basis of that first hour script by Stephen Knight (PEAKY BLINDERS, EASTERN PROMISES, LOCKE), the highly regarded production company, and a rapidly rising feature film star all combined made the odds of this show performing extremely good. As a result of these elements, my team and I provided very optimistic estimates that greenlit the project, and, fortunately, our gut feeling was confirmed by the number of aggressive presales we were then able to make in multiple territories even before the series starts production. Pre-sales of TV series is something that happens very rarely, so this was very much the exception rather than the rule.

**Marco:** Since you became an executive, how has the business changed?

**John:** Similar to the impact of Video and DVD when they first arrived on the scene, the impact of the Netflixes, Amazons, Hulus, etc today I believe will have an even greater impact on the future of distribution and how product/films are delivered to their audiences. When I think back on companies like Shapiro Glickenhaus and MCEG, the world was a far simpler place in those days compared to all the windowing and multiple platforming that is required today in order to correctly and efficiently exploit the rights to a movie. I also think that today the bar has been set far higher, particularly in the world of television where the audiences expect the production values they see in shows like GAME OF THRONES and HOUSE OF CARDS. This is television that is produced like a feature film with those production values and very often theatrical names in their casts but over a 6 - 10 hour period of time. That is an expensive proposition and if the stars don't align, that very expensive series can end up being cancelled and that's it. Of course when something does click with the audience, it is the ultimate goal, the Shangri-La of the business, a veritable money printing machine that, with spin-offs and sequels, becomes the gift that keeps on giving. As long as those select few projects come along every so often, there will always be talented and creative people striving away behind the scenes trying to produce the next evergreen title.

**Marco:** As the Head of International Sales, do you concentrate mostly on the European market?

**John:** Currently as Head of Worldwide Sales, I have to oversee all markets, but the European market (outside of the US), particularly the five big territories, is a very important one for generating the most revenue out of the international market place. However, all the other territories add up too and it requires a lot of hard work and diligence to tap into the multiple platforms that exist today in order to maximize your potential revenue from movies or television product in this increasingly changing and fragmented market.

**Marco:** As a sales person, do you agree with Cecil B. DeMille, that the audience is always right?

**John:** As a sales person, yes, because at the end of the day you are trying to sell a product one way or another, and, logically, if an audience likes a certain genre of product (in this case film) you want that audience to buy your product. If they like it, they buy it; if not, they won't. That said, there are audiences and audiences, and programming for both groups. There is product that is big and flashy with lots of colors and pictures and few words and that appeals to a broad and general audience which means lots of tickets/revenue. There is other product that is more complicated and requires paying close attention in case you miss nuances in the story. These can quickly lose the interest of a broader more general audience but this sort of movie is more often what garners the critical acclaim even if the dollars are far fewer on the ground.

**Marco:** Have you ever thought about switching from the Film Industry to something different? Which parts of your job do you enjoy most?

**John:** I think we all have, at one point or another, but it is an industry built on relationships, knowledge and experience, and at a certain point it is often too late to be able to build that in a completely different business or industry. That said, I have known many people who have left the business for other businesses and never looked back. While the film business can be glamorous and exciting and creative and lucrative, it also chews people up and spits them out on long forgotten broken boulevards that lead to nowhere. Not to sound too cliché but this business is littered with shattered dreams of people who wanted to make it and for various reasons, did not, and instead eked out an existence pursuing the ever elusive dream while subsisting on wages from day jobs that were always meant to be stop gaps to the big time. That said, I also known people who have scaled the great heights of this business and become Academy Award winning producers, so as long as those few achieve their dreams, millions more will be inspired to pursue their own dreams and spawn the future greats our children will know.

**By Marco Siedelmann in writing
from the South of Spain
06May, 2015**

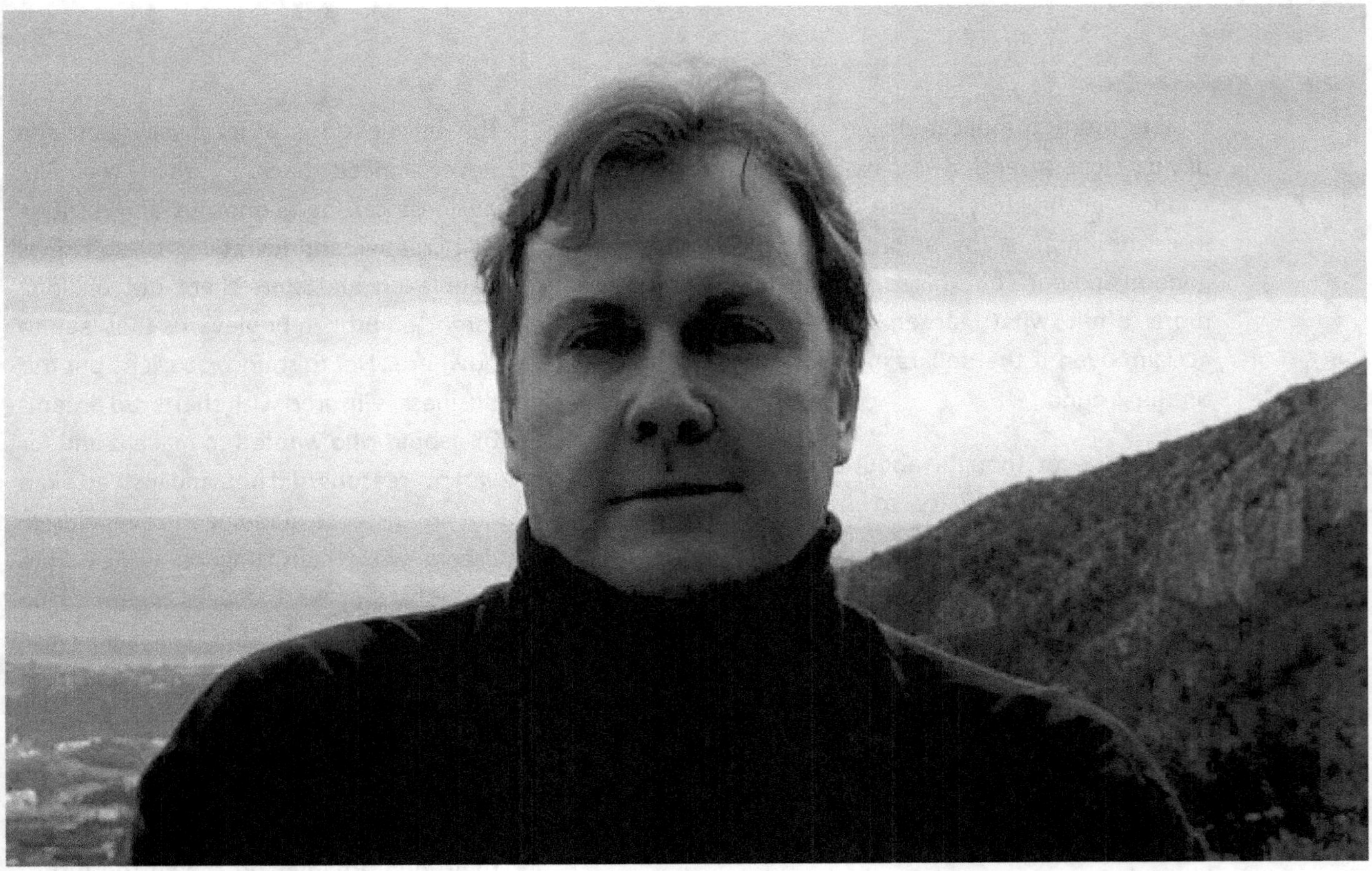

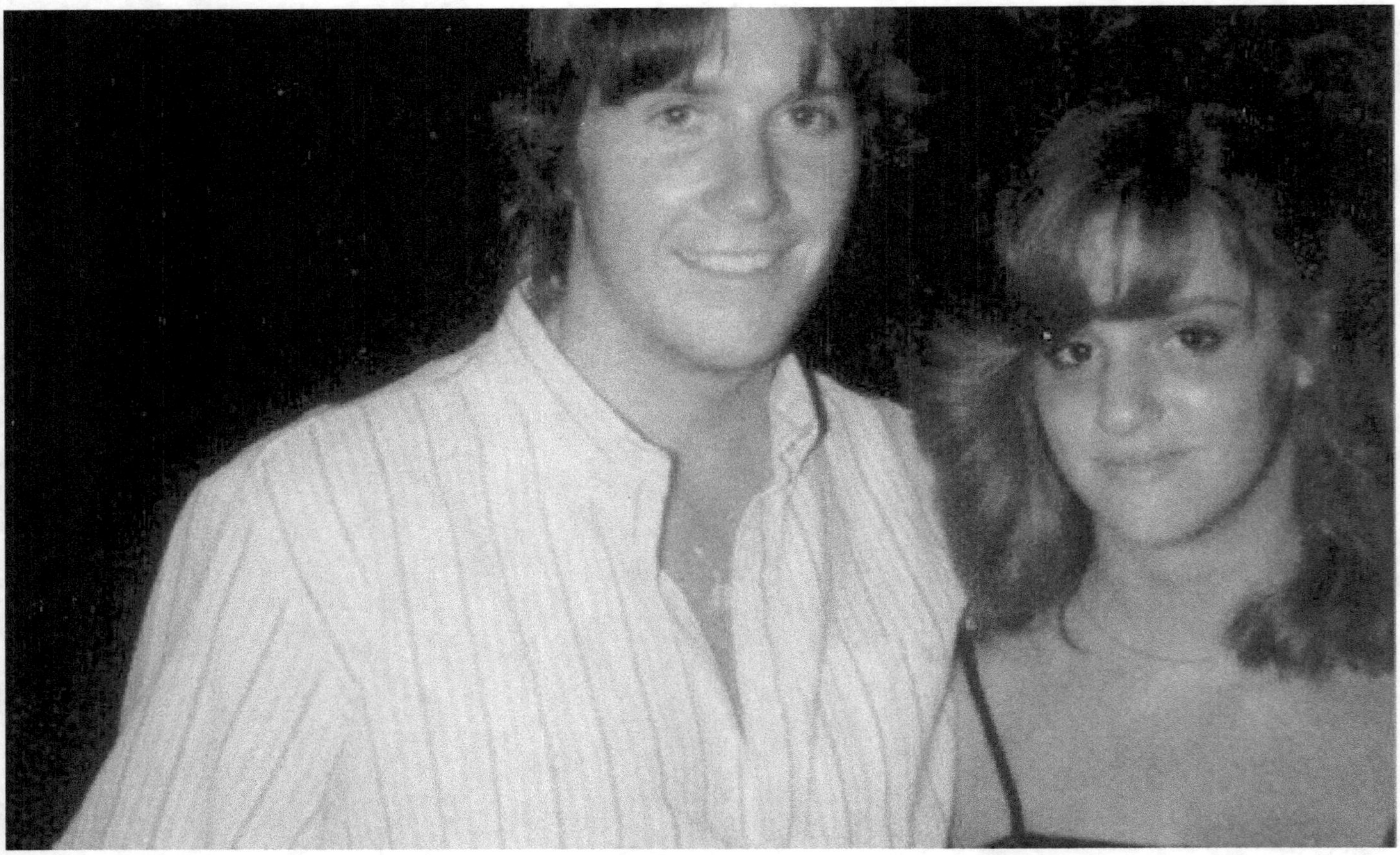

# II. SGE as a Production Company: Hiring Creatives was cheap then

*"If you can't make it good, at least make it look good."*

– Bill Gates

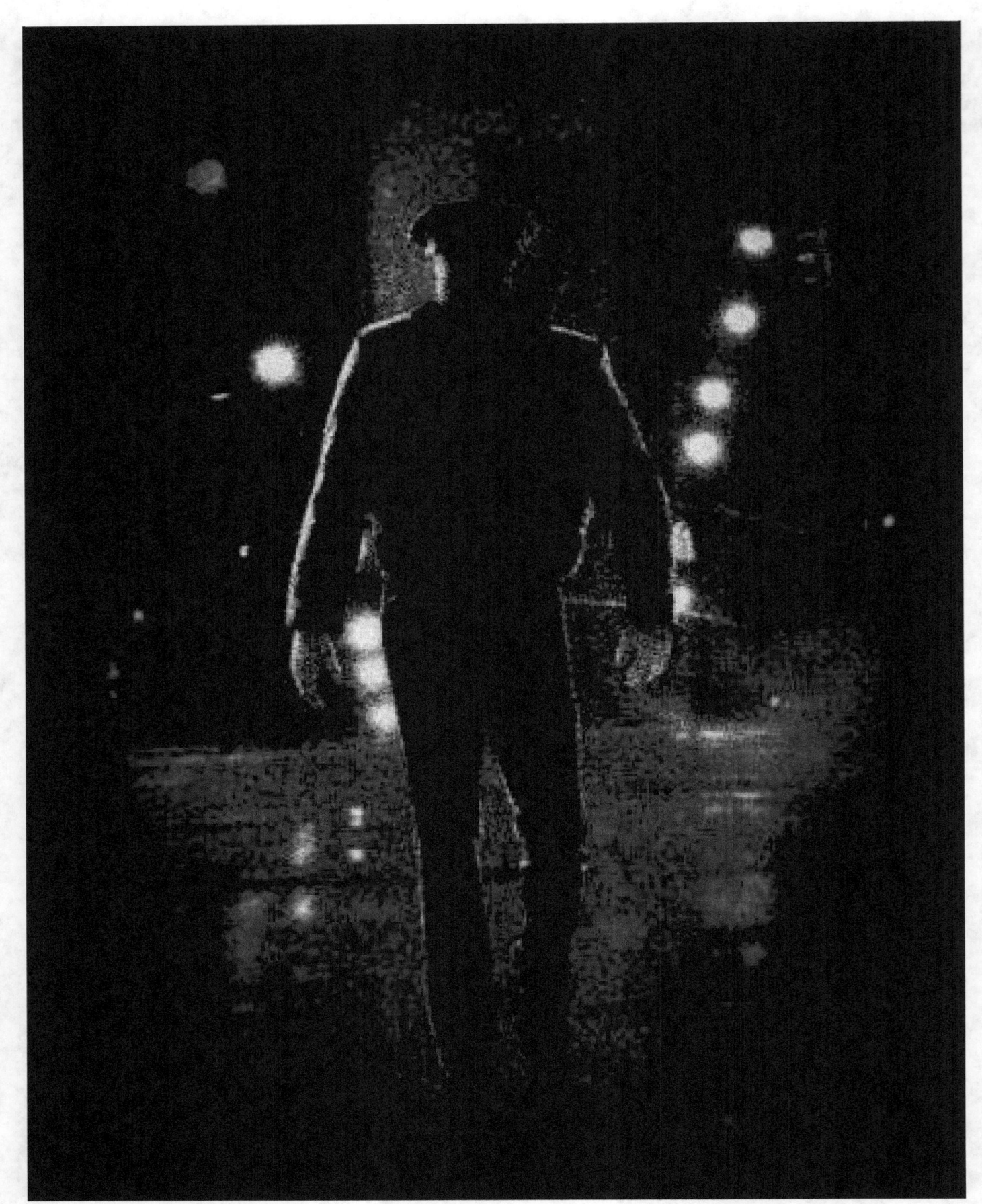

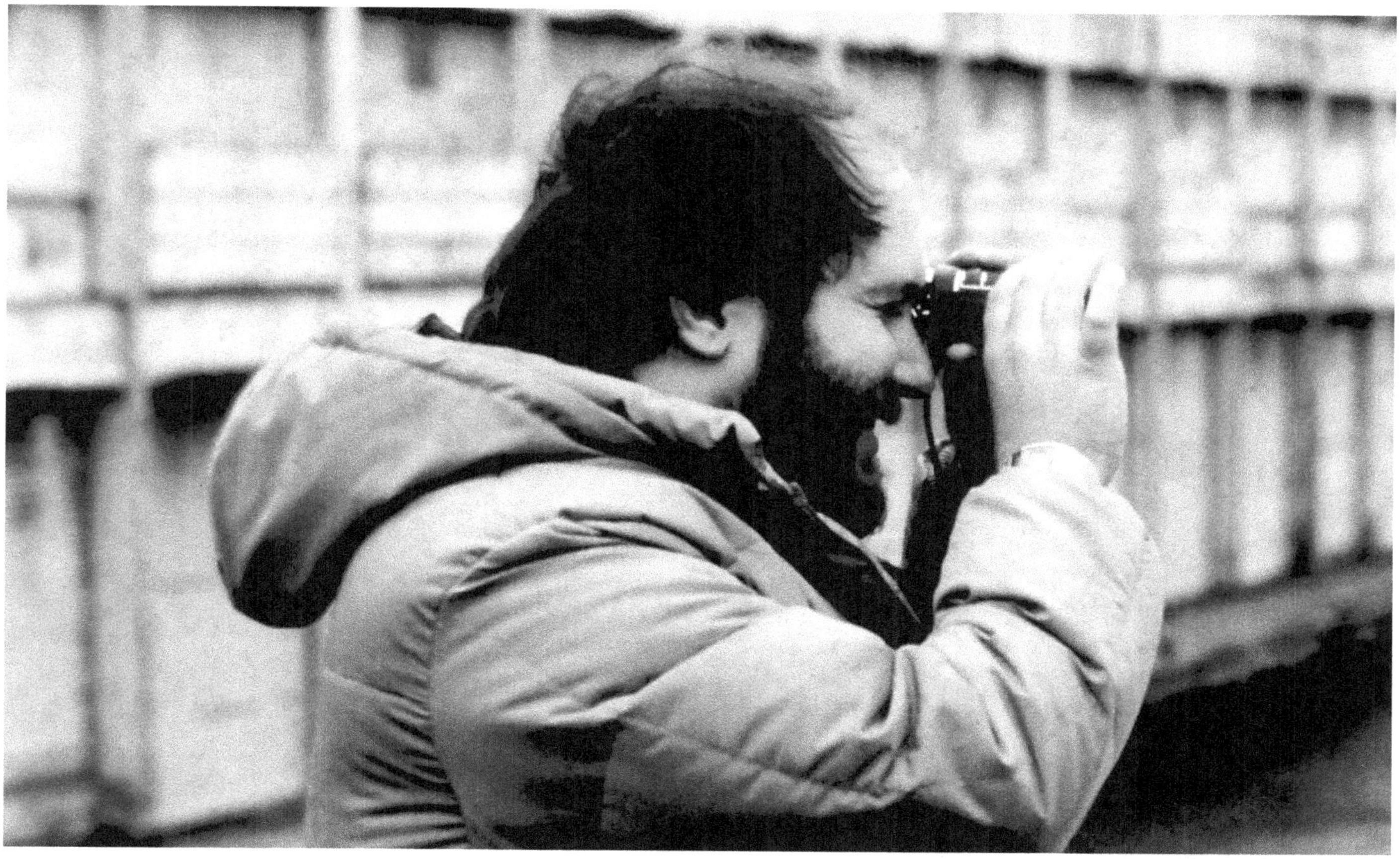

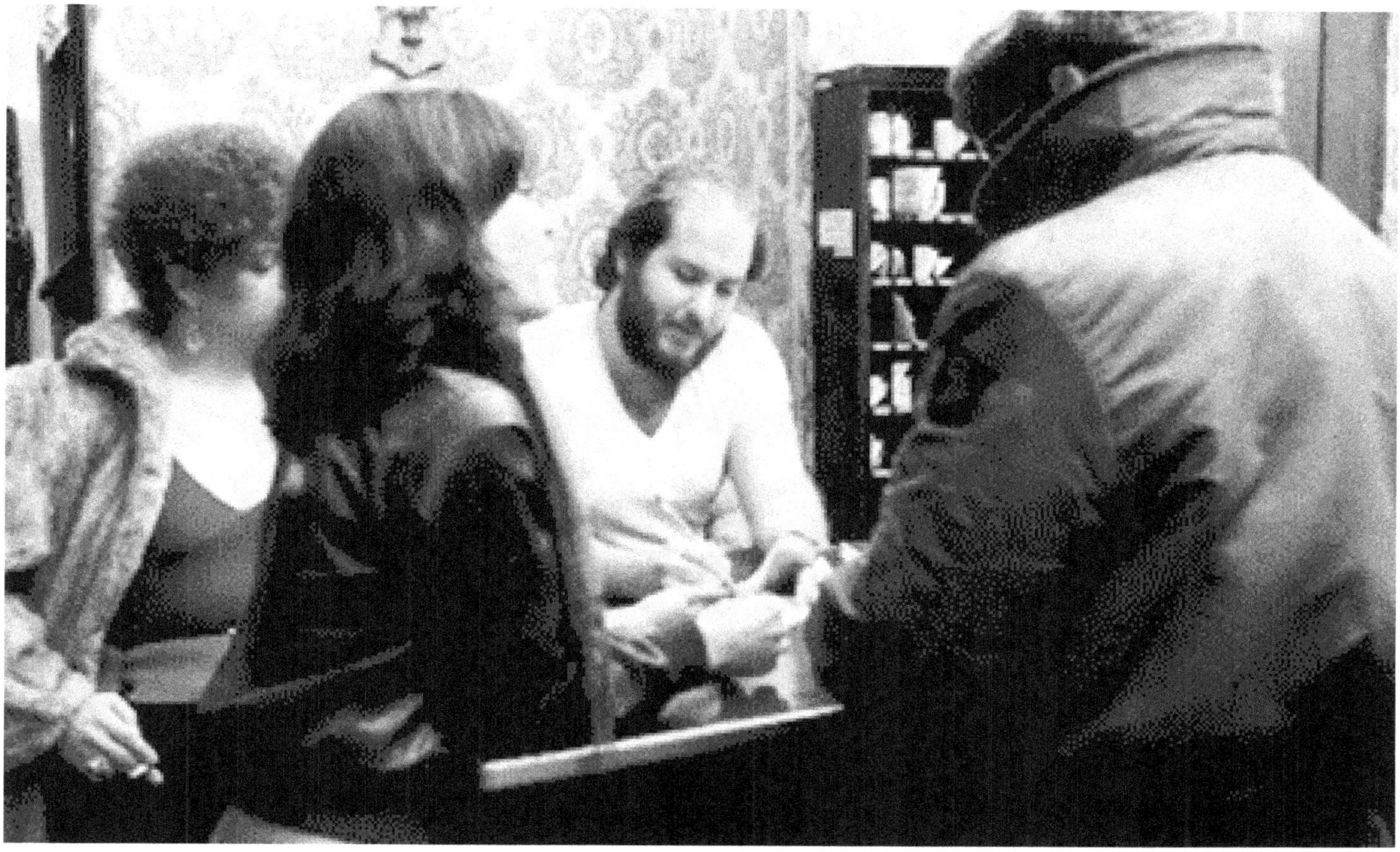

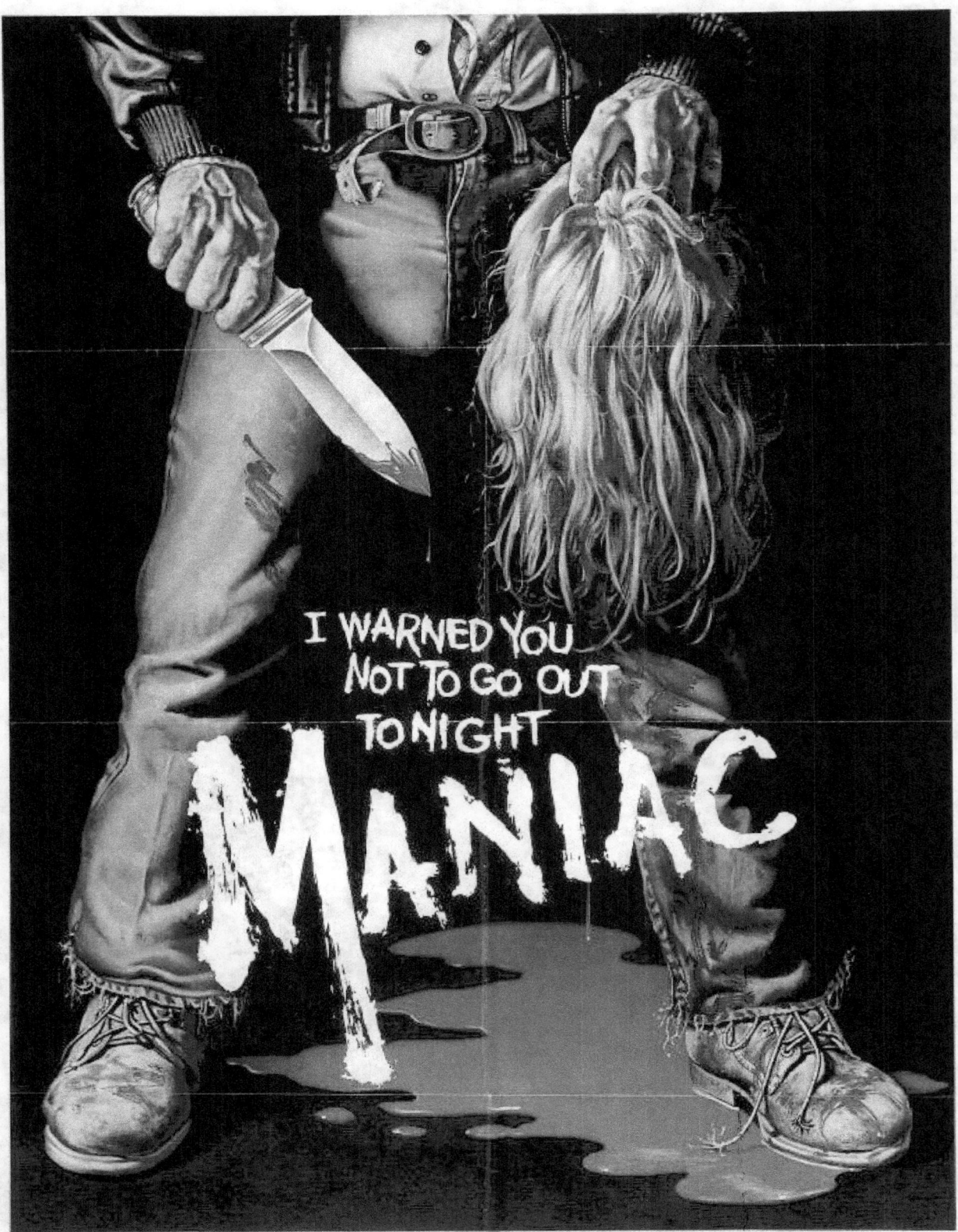

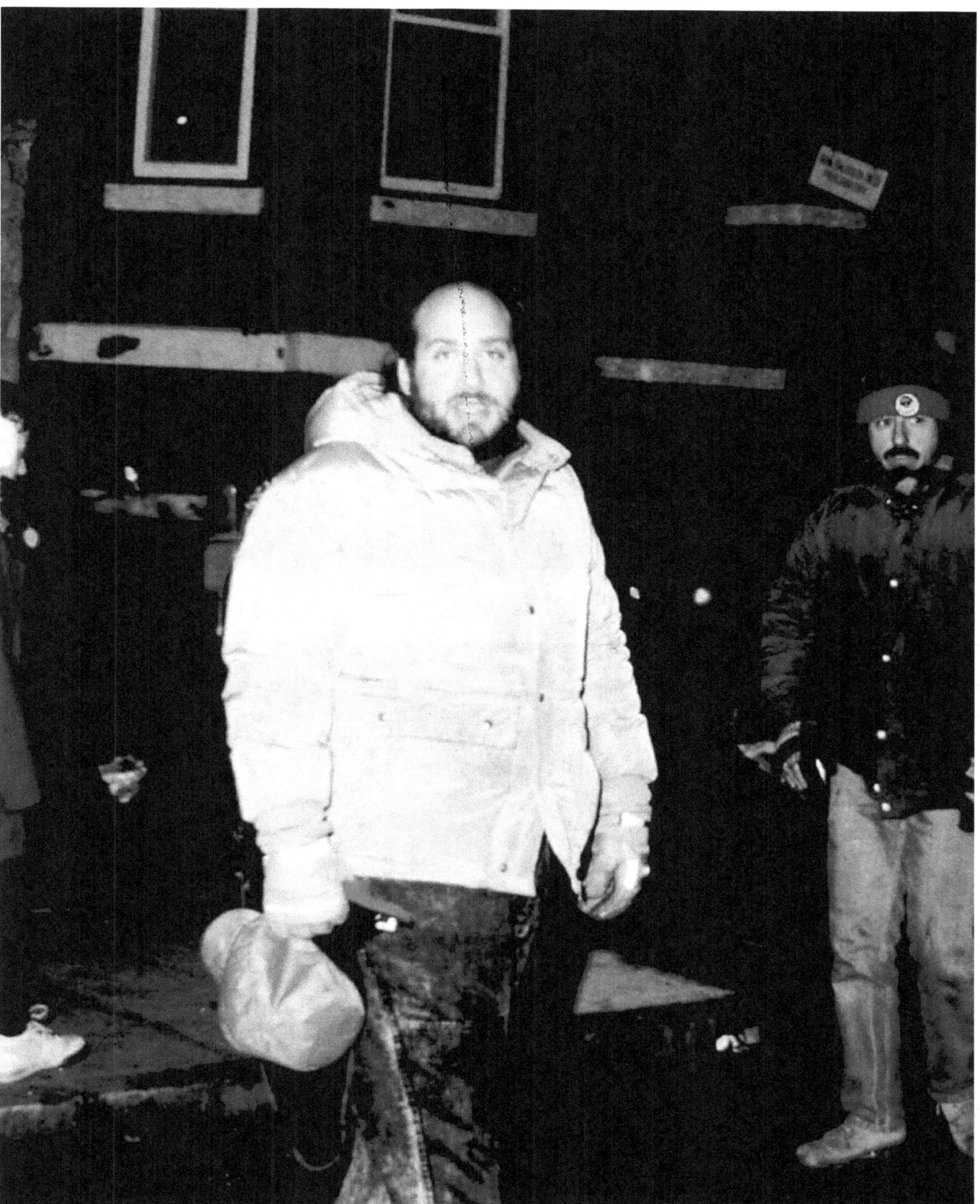

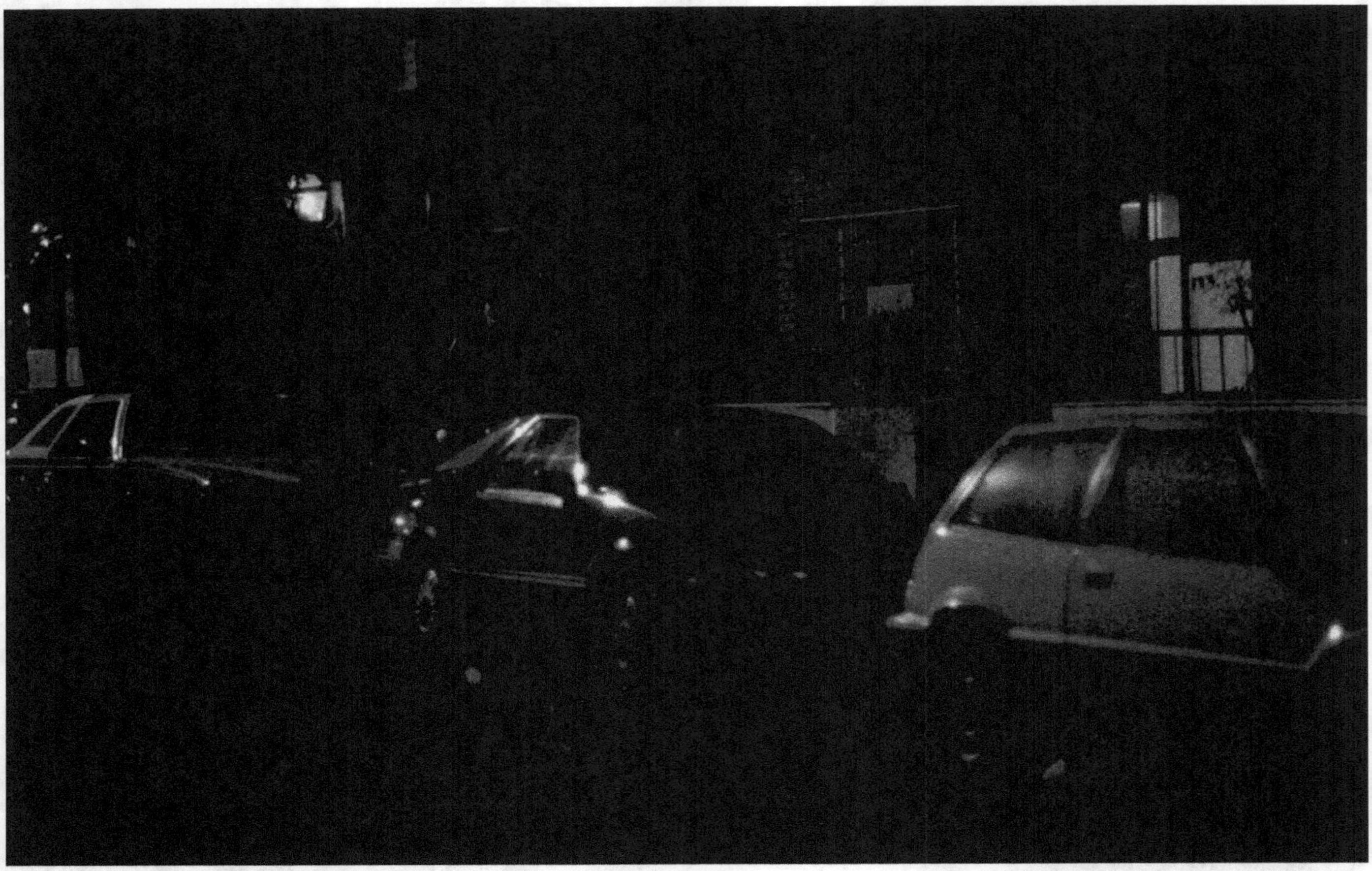

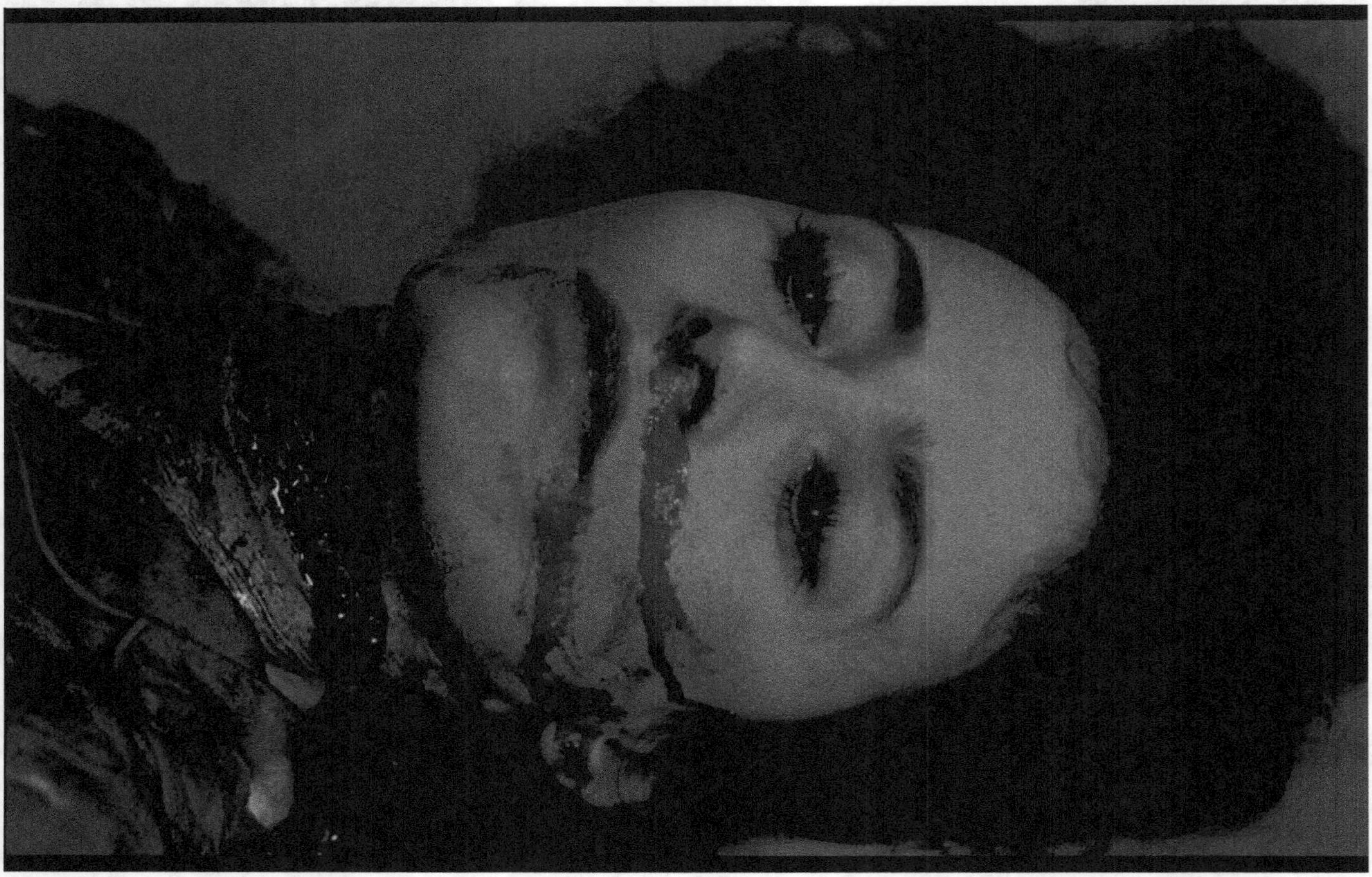

# William Lustig

William Lustig is a widely respected filmmaker to horror and grindhouse enthusiasts alike. Lustig skipped film school and jumped into the adult film business, where he learned all aspects of filmmaking and distribution. Later, he created the legendary gruesome masterpiece MANIAC. With SGE, Lustig worked on just one single film, but MANIAC COP - his third non-adult feature - became a key movie for the distribution company. William Lustig went on to direct the action film HIT LIST and the serial killer themed RELENTLESS, and two sequels for MANIAC COP. Finally, he directed the slasher movie UNCLE SAM before another chapter opened in his career. After working with Anchor Bay producing bonus features for DVD-Releases, William Lustig's own company Blue Underground established itself as one of the finest DVD labels focusing on European and American cult classics.

**Nadia:** In the late seventies you directed two adult films: THE VIOLATION OF CLAUDIA (1977) and HOT HONEY (1978). Let's talk about the times of Billy Bagg - do you like those films today?

**William:** Actually this name was given to me when I was a truck driver for an autoparts company. And I used to complain when they handed me the dirty parts. I'd put them in a bag, and they called me Billy Bagg, I don't know. Anyway, do I like those films today? Those films represent my film school. I am proud that I made them. They were widely distributed. I was 21 years old when I made THE VIOLATION OF CLAUDIA. It played pretty much every market in the world, it was dubbed in many languages and everything else. They're porn films; they are not films that I look at as particulary being good, but they were commercial and the recent DVD release to those films I did an audio commentary with no less than Nicolas Winding Refn, who is a fan of those films. Go figure!

**Nadia:** So you learned about filmmaking while shooting adult films?

**William:** As I said, those films were my film school. I learned all the various technical aspects of filmmaking as well as distribution and everything else by making those films. Which enabled me to go on to do low budget films later, because I knew how to work efficiently in a budget. I'm proud of having produced and directed those two films.

**Nadia:** Today we call it The Golden Age of Porn. How do you remember working with huge adult stars just like Jamie Gillis, Serena, Sharon Mitchell and others?

**William:** Besides my two films with Jamie Gillis, I have worked on several other films starring him, including a gay porn. Serena was kind of aloof, I didn't really get to know her. And Sharon Mitchell, we became friendly. I saw her not too long ago. She came from being a heroin junkie when she was working on my films. A functional junkie but she was a junkie nonetheless. Then she went to school and became a doctor. Today she services the adult film industry by doing HIV and other tests for the performers. She is really remarkeable, she was always smart. There was no doubt when I first met her

**Nadia:** that she is very intelligent, unfortunately she had the drug dependent thing. I really do like her, she's the one I admire the most.

**Nadia:** That's a great story.

**William:** Yeah, it's a good story, It's true.

**Nadia:** It's a hard road out of the adult film business if you want to enter the so-called regular movie industry. Was this possible for you because MANIAC was kind of an underground film?

**William:** The adult business really enabled me to make MANIAC. I had an investor with a small fortune of 30,000 dollars, together with Joe Spinell's $6,000 and my producing partner Andrew Garoni's 12,000 we were able to start shooting the movie. From a practical standpoint it financially enabled me to start MANIAC but also from what I learned in the adult business, it enabled me to do many roles on the film, to get it done for the budget we - well, it was some money available but it wasn't really a budget - to make the picture. So the adult industry was a great training ground, I never turned my back on it. I think it was fantastic, better than going to film school. Because, you go to film school you become a 27 year old graduate, with no experience but making coffee, your parents are gonna support you. You wind up, just kind of drifting.

**Nadia:** HIT LIST and RELENTLESS were your entry into mainstream cinema and both were distributed by Cinetel, correct? Please compare this business relationship to your experience with SGE and MANIAC COP.

**William:** That's kinda complicated because I don't believe that HIT LIST and RELENTLESS were my entry into mainstream. My entry into mainstream was really MANIAC. I think that the difference between MANIAC and VIGILANTE and MANIAC COP and say, those two films was: HIT LIST and RELENTLESS were kind of vanilla movies, whereas movies like MANIAC, VIGILANTE and MANIAC COP had an edge to them. They really reflected my personality. HIT LIST was a product and RELENTLESS was a product. Interestingly enough, in the test of time it's really just like these three personal movies still endure and the products are long forgotten. Although RELENTLESS probably made more money, than all the prior films combined.

**Nadia:** Was that the one with Judd Nelson?

**William:** Yeah, it was a huge hit. It made a lot of money for Cinetel. We made the film for like 2.2 million dollars, and you know what, the first shipment on VHS at that time was? 115,000 units at a wholesale of about 50 bucks.

**Nadia:** Right. Oh my God, that's right.

**William:** And it was profitable theatrically, which was something of an anomaly in that time. They made three sequels from it. You do know that the script of RELENTLESS was handed to me from that guy Howard Smith, who Lenny [Shapiro] introduced me to. It was called SUNSET KILLER.

**Nadia:** I remember that!

**William:** Lenny didn't want to make it, and so I took it to Cinetel, they grabbed it within hours. Literally in an hour, not even!

**Nadia:** Howard Smith was the older gentlemen with grey hair? I remember that.

**William:** Yeah, he gave me the script, I read it and thought, boy, there's a movie in here. I don't know what Jim [Glickenhaus] thought. Boom, Cinetel grabbed it. Anyway, about the different business relationships. Well, let's take Cinetel: on HIT LIST, Cinetel was firing me every other day, although they never did officially, and I shot the entire movie. But we kind of butted heads, because it was the first time in my career that I was a director for hire and there were producers on the movie. And I am not a good employee, that I can tell you. After the success of HIT LIST, we immediately did RELENTLESS, and on this film I was left totally alone. We had our budget, and we agreed on cast, and although there were producers I was sort of the de facto producer. I made the picture, and the only time I ever heard of Cinetel was when they heard I had a cold -- they brought me chicken soup one day on set. And that was it. On MANIAC COP with SGE: Jim already knew I was a producer and so, for the most part, I was really left alone. The only time there was somebody who came in on that, what was that guy's name?

**Nadia:** Frank Isaac?

**William:** Sometime late in the production or maybe in the post-production, this guy showed up at dailies with a clipboard and a little light, starting to write notes to us. And so I neutralized him by giving him a big credit in the main title with the provision that he should go and take a walk. And that was it, there was an attempt to collaborate and it was quickly neutralized. I'll give a credit - go away! - He has this big credit in the main title and he was never there for production. Welcome to show-business! But the great experience of making MANIAC COP I'm not really touching on. This really relates to this interview. VIGILANTE was not a financial success initially, for various reasons. The US distributor went bankrupt, there was a big problem of foreign exchange at the time, so my foreign contracts had been de-valued. I'd kind of taken a downturn in my career, at the golden age, of, well I was 25 or 26 years old and I went through a cold streak. I was in New York, I was offered opportunities in L.A. but I didn't want to go to there - I'd eventually changed that but initially I didn't want to go to LA. The projects I was working on, I just couldn't get any traction. One day I had lunch with Jim Glickenhaus and, you know, he comes from inherited wealth. He was always very forthcoming, especially as broke as I was at the time. He told me about how much money he recently made out of family business, and I used to get so damn sick over it. So one day something happened with his family business and he had just got 50 million dollars. I said, "Well, Jim, why don't you give me a million of it? If I had 50 dollars on me, I'd give you a dollar. You made 50 million, give me a million. I'll be the happiest guy in the world, anytime you talk to me you will always hear that I'm happy." And he laughed, and he said, "I'll give you a million dollars to make a movie."

**Nadia:** Cool!

**William:** That was interesting. I said, "Well, I have this project MANIAC COP that I want to make." He was just about form this business with Lenny Shapiro, which became SGE. This lunch actually took place 2 or 3 months before they formed the company, but they were in the process of doing it and so MANIAC COP became their first picture. So I am forever grateful to Jim Glickenhaus, without him I don't know where my career would be today. I was really... I had lost traction, I couldn't anything done. Along came MANIAC COP, and it kinda put me on a streak and that was fantastic. As I said making the film, we agreed on budget, it was really kind of a cool thing. I remember being with Leonard Shapiro, we happened to be on the same plane going to New York where I was doing pick-up shots for MANIAC COP. I said to him, "I really would like to put some helicopter shots in MANIAC COP, I think it would really open the film a lot." He said, "How much will this cost?" and I said, just a number off the top of my head, "$7,000 dollars." You know, I didn't want to say $10,000 because it sounded like bullshit, $5,000 as well. $7,000 sounded like I thought about it and I had actually budgeted it. He handed me $7,000 on a handshake on a plane. That was the spirit in which the film was made. Well, what was interesting, cut from Leonard Shapiro to Alan Solomon, the sales person. They had not seen the movie, except from a promo reel we cut, they had gone to MIFED and pre-sold the movie. Meanwhile, when he asked me about the movie, I always said, I think it's ok, it's gonna work, it's commercial. - I would always downplay, and I did that to anybody I worked with. I wouldn't overpromise and underproduce. I'd rather underpromise and overproduce. And then they would be happy. So, finally, I'll never forget when I finished the movie, and I screened it for Lenny Shapiro and Alan Solomon in Hollywood, and I'm sitting there with the editor. Just the four of us in the screening room. They were sitting by themselves a few rows ahead. After the movie screening ended, they didn't say a word to me, and they just bolted out of the screening room. I was thinking, what did I do wrong, what happened? I really thought, maybe they thought I stole the money and it wasn't all up on the screen. All these things were going through my head, so I ended up following them. Several cars were in the parking lot and I kind ran up to them, and I'd seen them kind of arguing. I looked at them and they were dead serious when they said this to me: "Why didn't you tell us the movie was going to be good?"

**Nadia:** *(laughing hard)*

**William:** They were like, "We sold Germany for this but we could have gotten that. Japan for this, we could have gotten that. We sold Italy..." and Alan Solomon, he was really angry, because they undersold the movie. That was the basic substance of it. "We undersold the movie." But it was the

**Nadia:** weirdest way of people saying congratulations, it was the first and only time, anybody came to me like that.

**Nadia:** That's Alan Solomon for ya! *(laughing)*

**William:** That's exactly what happened, he was really angry at me. And that was a weird thing, to ask, why I didn't tell them the movie is gonna be good. I mean, what the fuck you think I was doing all the time, I was trying to make a shit movie? The weirdest kind of upside down compliment that you could get. That's the absolute truth.

**Nadia:** MIFED was my first Film Market. I don't remember a lot of it, we were so busy because of MANIAC COP and BLUE JEAN COP. And it was crazy. It was like, I've never been to a market, you know? I thought, oh my God, these people are just bidding on these films! It was crazy and wonderful.

**William:** It kind of created a weird rift because you would think, that if you made a picture that they really thought was good, the next thing you know, is to hear, why don't you make a home here and make more movies? Instead of that I was being pushed out the door. And I really didn't understand it. *(laughs)* So when asked the questions about, why didn't I work with them on MANIAC COP 2; they didn't want to do a MANIAC COP 2. It was the weirdest thing. I know Jim had some issue with me, I don't know exactly what it was but I thought I did everything I was supposed to do.

**Nadia:** I had not understood that, to be honest.

**William:** I didn't understand it, I sort of became a persona non grata. There was one thing Alan Solomon once showed me. I don't know, he showed my a fax or email, and he showed me a thing from a distributor, saying they wouldn't buy BLUE JEAN COP if they couldn't get MANIAC COP. I also know for a fact that MANIAC COP out-performed BLUE JEAN COP, and MANIAC COP was made for far less. But again, it's weird, but as the owner of the company. It's something like they are stacked against you, you are almost embraced if you under-perform. A strange upside down situation. I really can't blame him, I mean I have a personality that maybe was a problem, but at the end of the day I did the best thing the company ever did. I can't think of another movie that performed so well, thinking of costs and performance. They're selling it still to this day.

**Nadia:** Absolutely. I just did a deal for Germany.

**William:** So it's a film that has longevity. If Shapiro Glickenhaus had made MANIAC COP 2 and 3 it would have given them a franchise. Every distributor longs for a franchise because it becomes a tentpole for the company. That's why it makes no sense to me, from a business standpoint why they passed on their option to be able to do a MANIAC COP 2. And it was even more successful than MANIAC COP 1. Strange.

**Nadia:** Actually, on this whole topic. Robert Z'Dar [who played the Maniac Cop] just passed away. I remember him as the kindest and sweetest man.

**William:** I know. I do too, he was, definitely.

**Nadia:** After releasing MANIAC COP, there was HIT LIST - it seems to be your least popular title, or am I wrong? Don't you think it's somehow underrated/overlooked?

**William:** Well, it was a very successful movie. It was made for 1.3 or 1.4 million dollars, and Warner International, they pre-bought the foreign video and theatrical, not even television, for 1.2 million. So, everybody was extremely happy. There was $200,000 exposed on the picture and they had foreign television and all the rights in US and Canada. So, it was very successful film, financially. It's just that HIT LIST, it was kind of a vanilla action film. Those films don't really stand the test of time. It's always the edgier films that have the longevity. HIT LIST could have been made by anybody. It was just kind of a vanilla, run of the mill, no name action film. That's probably, why it's today overlooked. It just doesn't have the legs.

**Nadia:** All your films are very urban, many key scenes were shot on location. What's your relationship to New York City?

**William:** New York City is were I was born, I lived there all my life. It's in my DNA. Also, what I love about New York, is anywhere you shoot - unlike L.A. - you have texture everywhere. It always can make an interesting shot. When you are in NYC versus LA, in LA you kinda have to work a little harder to make it interesting, visually. It's just a great gritty city. For those two reasons I always gravitated back to NYC.

**Nadia:** How did it come you went from filmmaking to distribution?

**William:** Um, survival! Filmmaking for me started to become very difficult. Surprisingly the projects just became less interesting to me, so I sort of stumbled into distribution from my hobby, being a film preservasionist. I was preserving films and creating extras while I was directing movies for laserdisc. From that I sort of segued into distribution. Well, I have a distribution label, I'm not a distributor, I would say.

**Nadia:** Since 1999 you produced tons of exclusive interview and bonus stuff for Blue Underground. Do you feel like an archivist, doing this important historic work?

**William:** Yes, I do, and one of the reasons is, so many of the people I've interviewed have died. So I wind up with a storage room filled with tapes and recordings and everything else, of people who are no longer with us. I serve them a certain importance, doing that kind of work.

**Nadia:** The obvious question: Will there ever again a feature film directed by William Lustig?

**William:** Perhaps. Not sure.

**Nadia:** What do you think of vigilante action films? Were you referencing any particular films in VIGILANTE?

**William:** Firstly, VIGILANTE was really inspired by the Italian police movies of the seventies. There weren't a lot of vigilante movies made in New York, but there were a lot made in Europe that inspired movies like DIRTY HARRY, DEATH WISH, FRENCH

CONNECTION. VIGILANTE took its inspiration both storywise and stylisticly from those Italian movies. In fact I shot and scored the film like a spaghetti western. *(laughing)*

**Nadia:** It's unusual, when Fred Williamson talks directly to the audience in the opening of VIGILANTE? Did you want to leave a comment about the reactions such films provoke?

**William:** That opening scene with Fred Williamson talking to a gun club and ultimately directly talking to the audience, was shot, actually, before we started principle photography. It was shot as a promo. I got all the equipment for free because I told the camera company I was doing a camera test. I got film stock for free because I told Fuji that I was testing their film and I got the labs and processing for free. I got Fred Williamson to fly in and do the opening scene. All the people in the audience are friends and one of them was the lighting technician for the film. We shot it as a promo for MIFED in order to start pre-selling the movie. Then we shot the film afterwards.

**Nadia:** Composer Jay Chattaway was in charge of the mesmerizing scores of MANIAC, VIGILANTE, MANIAC COP and others. How did you meet him and how do you work on a film soundtrack? Is he involved from the beginning?

**William:** Jay Chattaway, what in our collaboration worked the best, was when he was involved from the beginning. My first choice for the score was Goblin but they dropped out, and I was racing to find a composer. I was introduced to Jay, who had really never scored a movie before. He worked on the score of a cheesy, Euro, action film called FIREPOWER, he arranged the score for Barbieri [LAST TANGO IN PARIS] - Jay organized the score for this movie but wasn't the actual, official composer. He came to meet me, and he was anything but what I would have expected for someone to look like who was going to do MANIAC. I expected more of a punkrocker, Jay Chattaway was a suburban family man, living in Connecticut. He didn't watch horror films. Wasn't really too into horror films. And that's what made his score for MANIAC great, he didn't score it entirely as a horror film. What he did was, he ignored my direction and focused on character. And what he did was absolutely brilliant. It gave our audience empathy for the killer's character. We worked very closely on the MANIAC score but I was just sort of giving him an idea of what I had in mind, and he would kind of go off and do it. He would be invited to dailies, he knew what he was doing. It's so often in American movies, they look at scores as an afterthought. Whereas, in my style of filmmaking which has been influenced by the European movies, music comes into the forefront. Music is a very, very important element to me, as well as sound and things like that. I noticed when I was working with Cinetel, when I was forced to work with another composer on HIT LIST, and again it was just an afterthought. The scores became very TV-like and very generic, often boring and kind of play to heightening what they perceive to be the visceral part of the scene. Kind of sad, or happy, or action, or scary, but not really tapped in creating a fully encapsulated score. Because of my efforts of the European film, and the influence of someone like Ennio Morricone, my films have a full-bodied scores on them. The ones that I consider my personal films have full-bodied scores and that's why I think Jay and I complimented each other very well. It showcased him, and of course it also was a tremendous attribute to the films.

**Nadia**: Another important crew member is cinematographer James Lemmo. Do you pick locations with him?

**William**: I met Jim Lemmo when he has shooting a movie called MS.45 for my friend Abel Ferrara. When I saw MS.45 I contacted Abel, I asked him how it worked with the cinematographer, he gave me high recommendations. I hired Jim to shoot VIGILANTE, and we did many films after that. He's a enormously talented cinematographer, he worked with some of the great New York cinematographers like Arthur Ornitz and some of these other legendary people. I mean, he was just an amazing collaborator. So much of the films I can't emphasize enough that Jim was my brush. He really did just an incredible job on shooting these films. One of the things is because I am a big fan of the film noir, and I always looked at MANIAC COP as being a film noir and it was fun to have him shoot the film like that, like an old film noir. That was the kind of stuff we had fun doing. He was really stylizing the films, so they really didn't look like low budget independent films, that was the thing Jim did. He knew how to take it and make it not look like a run of the mill, low-budget generic movie. He gave it style, that little extra edge, that just made it look like something slick and a little bit more professional. Of course, we picked locations, you know, they are important for me.

**Nadia**: Before shooting, do you make storyboards? Are you a very visual filmmaker?

**William**: I've never done storyboards. I did some kind of shotlist but only for myself, I never show it to anybody. So, no.

**Nadia**: MANIAC COP is one of the very few films blending action and horror half and half. Do you think there are intersections or are they incompatible?

**William**: Well, I think that's the thing that makes MANIAC COP unique, it was a blend of action and horror. It's sort of... I call it FRENCH CONNECTION meets FRANKENSTEIN. It kinda played in both fields. I think in MANIAC COP 2, because I had more money I was able to amplifiy that more than I could on MANIAC COP 1, where I was working with very limited money. Also, in MANIAC COP 1 I really hadn't figured the movie out. I was figuring it out as I was shooting it. It hadn't really gelled in my head. Maybe it was there, but I wasn't in touch with it. In MANIAC COP 1, I was still finding the picture, in MANIAC COP 2 I had a very definitive approach to it. You know what's interesting, I don't know if you know this. One of the deal points on MANIAC COP that became a real sticky thing was that Lenny wanted to change the title.

**Nadia:** Really?

**William:** It's in the contract, he wanted to change the title. And we fought over it. I said, are you crazy? That's the whole fucking movie! It's the title! He said, "It makes it sound so down", or words to that effect. And I said, "That's the fun of the movie, it's MANIAC COP!" Oh God, I was so happy I was able to keep it. He really put it in the contract before we had started shooting.

**Nadia:** In UNCLE SAM (1996) you had another script by Larry Cohen, it's a sarcastic version of a slasher film. Was there a theatrical release?

**William:** As far as I know, UNCLE SAM never got a theatrical release anywhere in the world. It did get an extended video release and a cable release, but it was a weird set of circumstances. It was financed by a wealthy guy, who had no experience in the film business and he was listening, too much, to a Beverly Hills entertainment attorney who knew jackshit about the film business. But heavens if I could say that. He was an expensive Beverly Hills entertainment attorney with celebrity clients. So, on UNCLE SAM, you know what he did? You would appreciate this: He pre-sold all foreign rights to the film for $750,000 dollars.

**Nadia:** Oh, lord...

**William:** Yeah. And it was a budget of a million and a half...and he pre-sold it for $750,000 because his attorney told him, that's the way the film business works, 50 percent of revenues comes from foreign market, 50 percent comes from domestic. There was nothing I could push to tell him don't pre-sell it! And he just didn't listen to me. So, before we had shot a foot of film, I knew the film would never recoup its money. It was like working in defeat. So all I did when I shot UNCLE SAM was, I just relaxed in the country, I cashed my checks, and I didn't invest myself in the picture because I knew it wasn't gonna go anywhere. Imagine that, isn't it like the text book thing you would tell somebody?

**Nadia:** Yes!

**William:** And yet, it's like if you're sitting there, just thinking of Roy Scheider and JAWS, the shark coming to shore, and the people swimming, you tell the people to come in and they are not listening to you. It's just total frustration. The more he was bound with what the guy was saying, the more it caused this attorney to be antagonistic to me! The most fun thing is that the attorney said, "You got to watch out for Bill Lustig. He may not deliver our idea of a movie. I hear that he makes these bloody movies. And it's not going to be an R-rated movie." So, what did I do? I didn't shoot any violence, I implied everything in the movie. It became like a thing over my head, like if you see any blood in the dailies, you know, it won't get an R rating. Well you know what? I had to go back three months later to shoot violence, to put it into the movie. Because they showed it to the company and they'd go, "Where's the blood in the movie?" And we had to get all the people back out and shoot again, I had to go and do everything, so we can shoot the blood for the film. I mean, at the end of the day, the reason I looked back at movies like MANIAC, VIGILANTE and MANIAC COP is, there was nobody there saying stupid things, who had control of you. There was nobody! You made the fucking movie! That was it. You made the movie, you delivered it. I made MANIAC COP 2, I produced it, I directed it, I delivered the movie. Nobody's there making stupid fucking remarks the whole time. The reason UNCLE SAM was my last movie is, at that point I gave up. I said, if this is where I'm headed with my career, that I've got to sit here, listen to this stupidity when I had more experience than any of these people. No matter how much money they have, no matter how much they get paid, no matter what their address is, I knew more than these people, why am I here sitting and doing this. As you see, I'd rather just have my own company and that's it.

**Nadia:** Your films are still cult favorites among fans all over the world. Are you thankful, that there is such a bright horror community or are you annoyed sometimes, talking about your early works?

**William:** No, I was never annoyed by horror fans, I embraced them, they put food on my table, they also feed my ego, and I absolutely appreciate any people that appreciate my work. I really do. I work hard for them....I'll give you an example. Do you know, out of my own pocket, I spent over 16,000 dollars, fixing MANIAC COP. Just so, I didn't have to look at that fucking Synapse Films version that looks like an episode of LAW AND ORDER. I was so sickened when I saw what they had put out, that I actually spent my own money to go back and re-grade the movie the way it's supposed to be. Go back and get rid of it. I saw it last night on Chiller, I was curious what master had been used. It doesn't look like the movie we shot, what we put in there. This is not the movie we shot.

**Nadia:** Too slick-ish?

**William:** No, what it is, when you transfer a movie from the original negative. Well, you know that the process known as an answer print right? Would you ever consider an answer print without the director or the cinematographer there? No! Because they are the ones who know what the movie looks like. And Synapse transfered the movie from the original negative, which is like making an answer print, color grading in the original negative. They colorgraded it and what usually happens when you let the people in the facilities do their own grading, no one ever complains that a movie is too bright. Never. Always complain, however, that it's too dark. So it's the fault of an unsupervised colorgrading, that the movie would always be brighter than what the filmmaker intended. What you have with MANIAC COP today, and the version that's out, is you have that version that literally looks like an episode of television, versus it looking like a movie. And also, we shot the film in the summer, but the movie takes place in the winter. So as a result we graded everything when we did the prints, to be cold. Meaning to bring up the blue. What they did, they graded it for when it was, August, when we shot, When you have people, and it's subliminal, and they are bundling themselves up in the cold, it looks warm outside!! It's ridiculous!! The thing that kills me is, that forever - or at least the near-future, maybe even in my lifetime - there is this version that people are gonna see, that doesn't reflect what we did. It's the horror at the end of the day. You put all that work in, and in the end it's not there. You look at it side by side, it's a serious difference. What you see at the original version, it looks colder and darker. Also the reason it has to be darker is, we were trying to cover up his make up. There are scenes where he's not wearing make up. Yet you could see it in the Synapse version, could they not even darken those scenes. So in those shots, he doesn't have make up on!!! And they don't know it because they weren't there when we shot it. So you don' t have dark where it should be. In high definition you see everything, it's actually dark in the sections where you see his face. So there are scenes watching the blu-ray you see a guy who has no make up on. God, almighty, it's torture!

**By Nadia Bruce-Rawlings, via telephone from New York**
**13May, 2015**

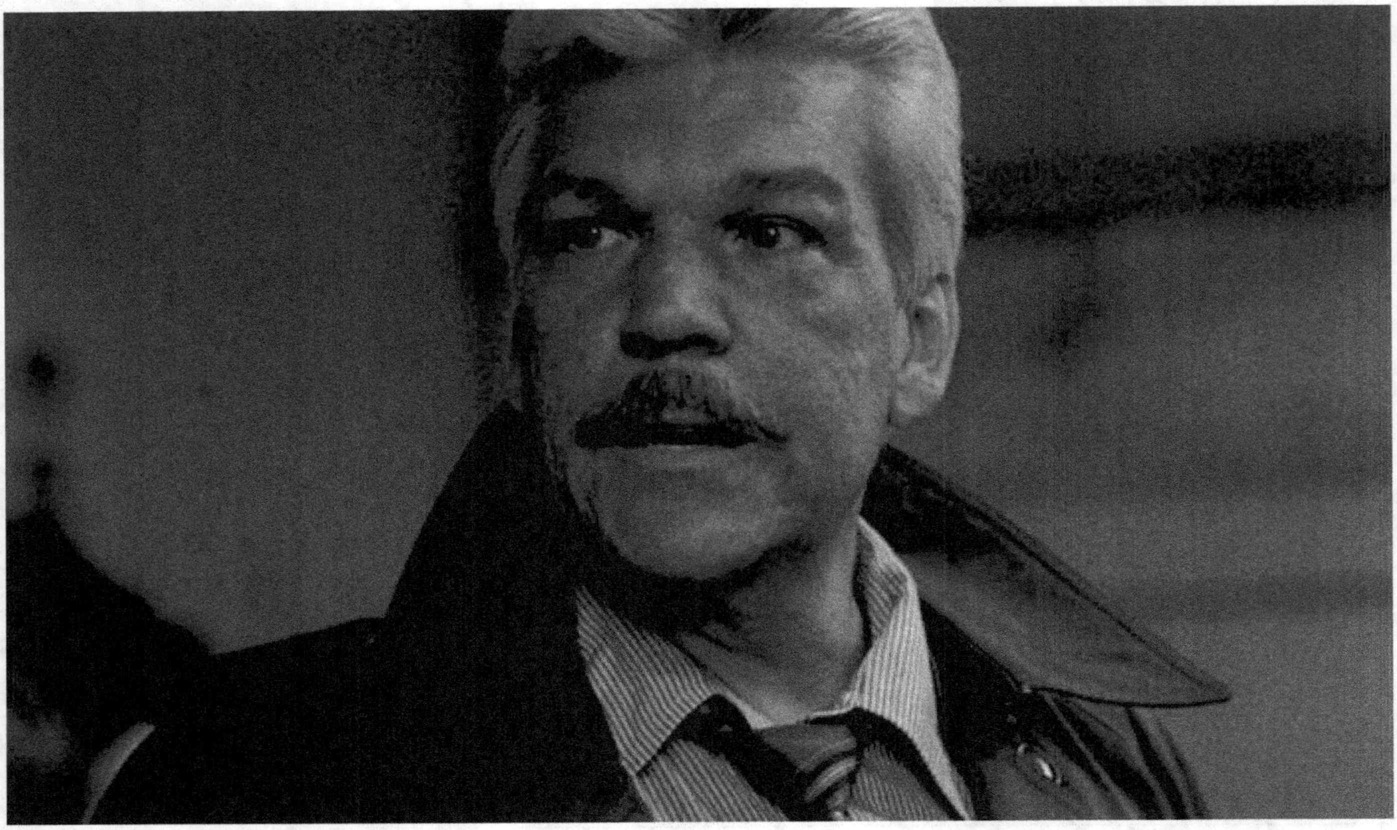

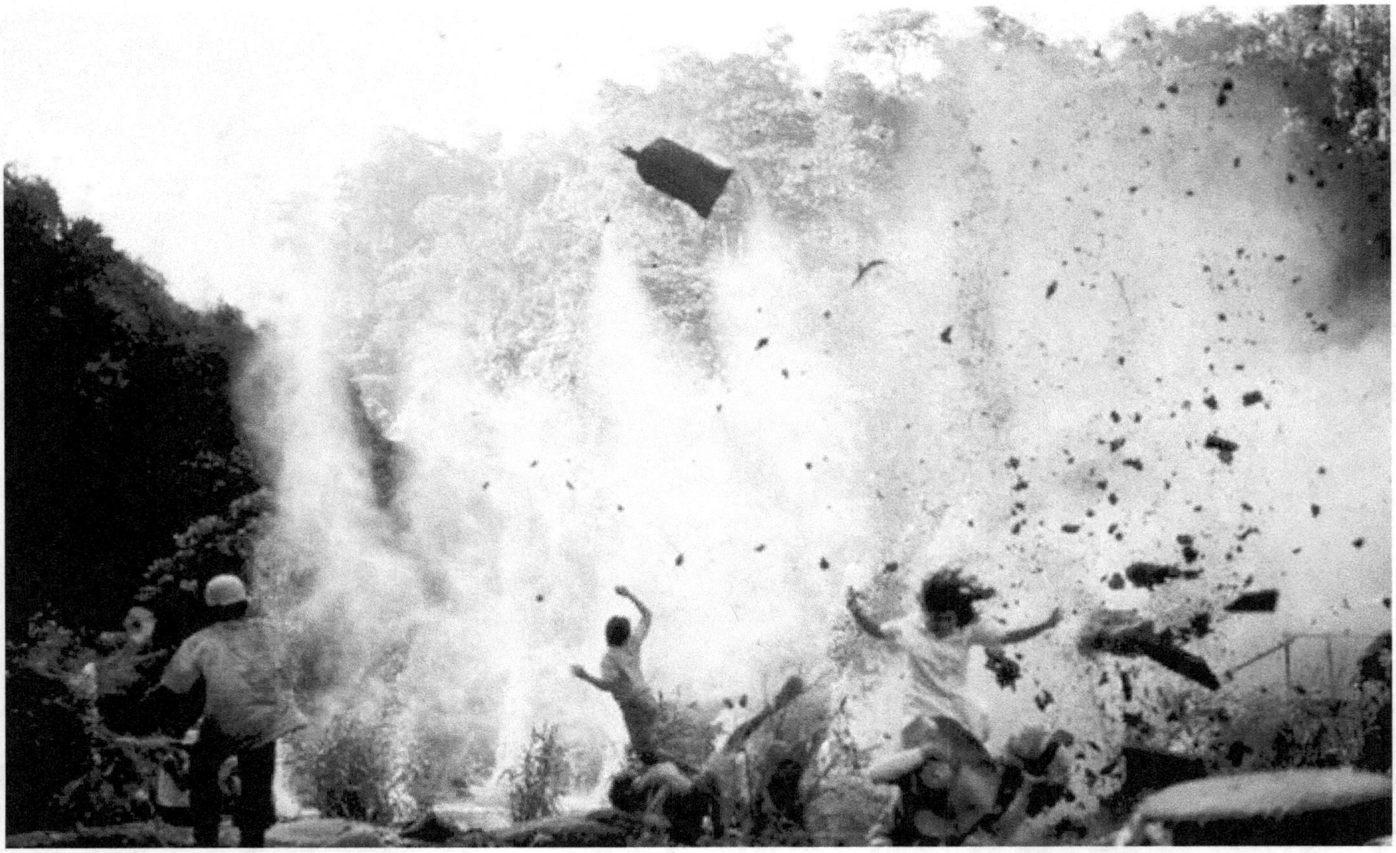

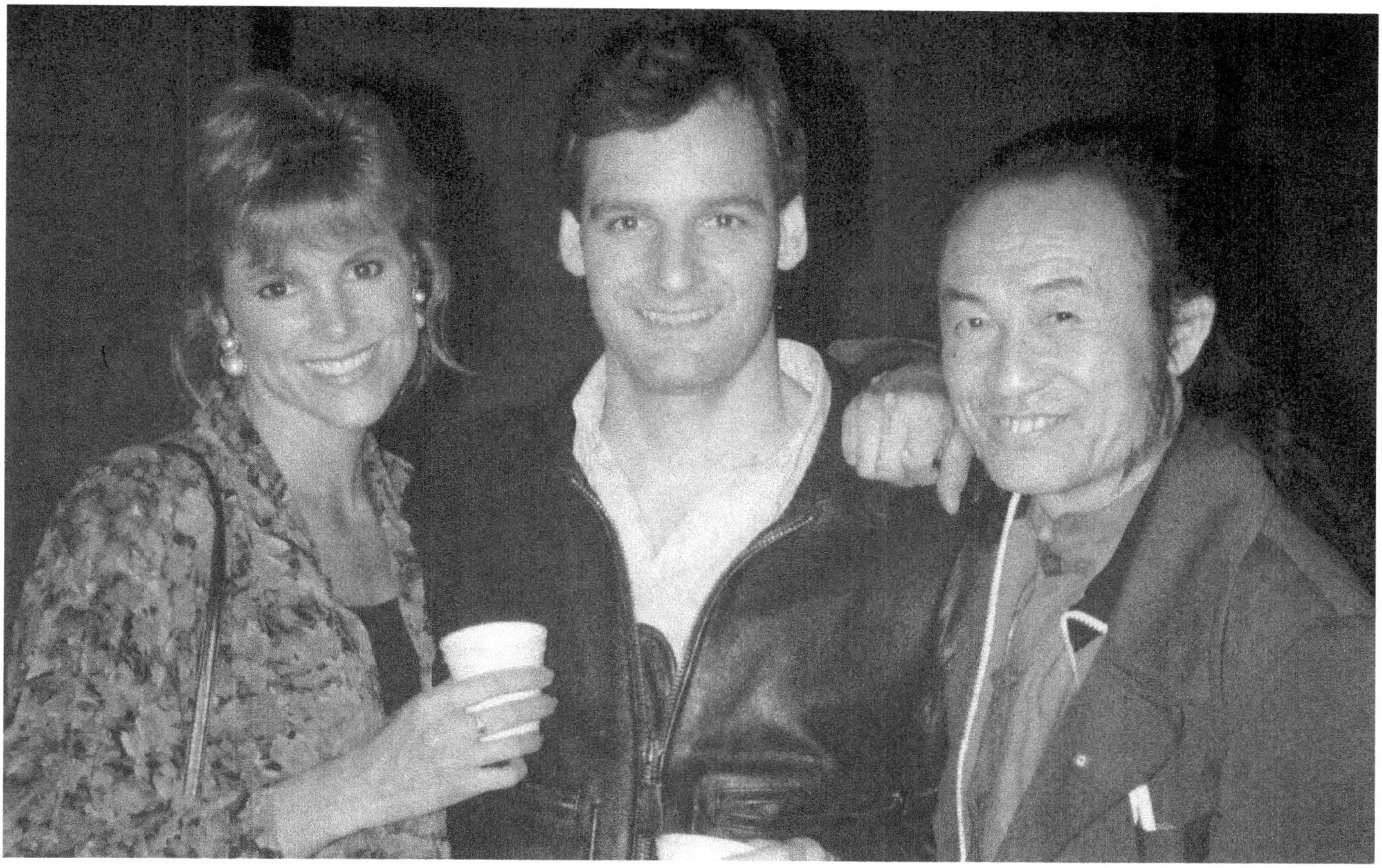

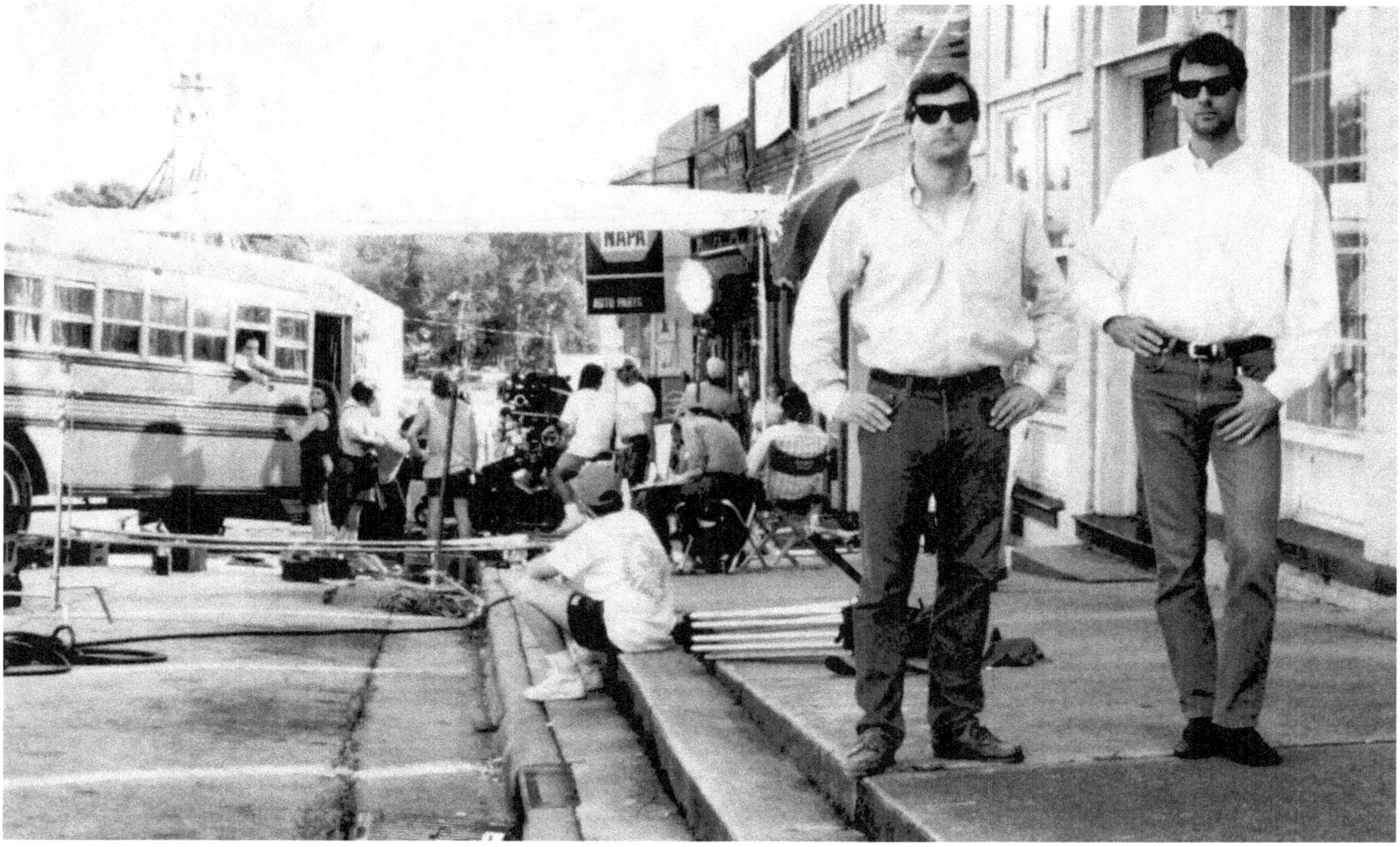

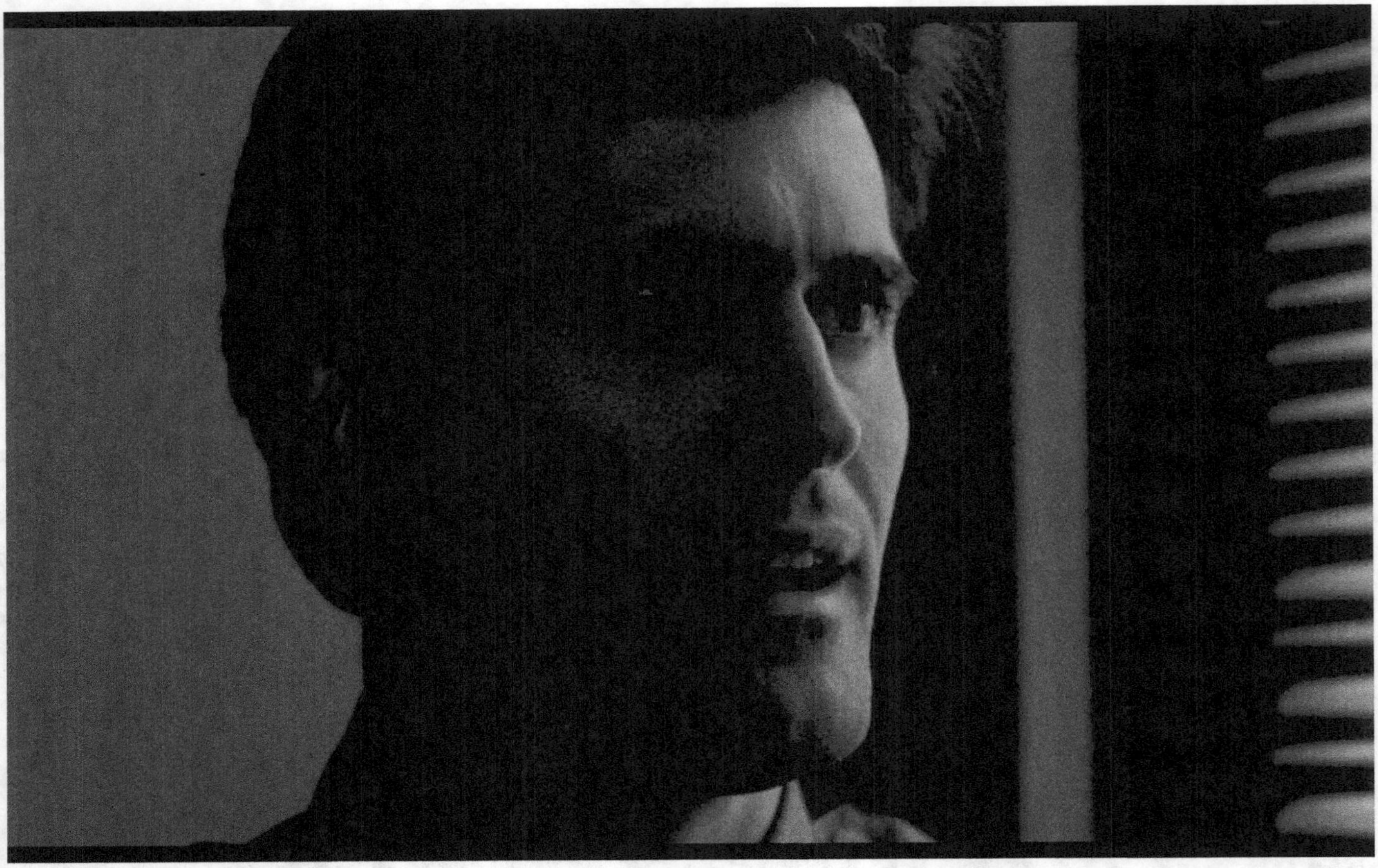

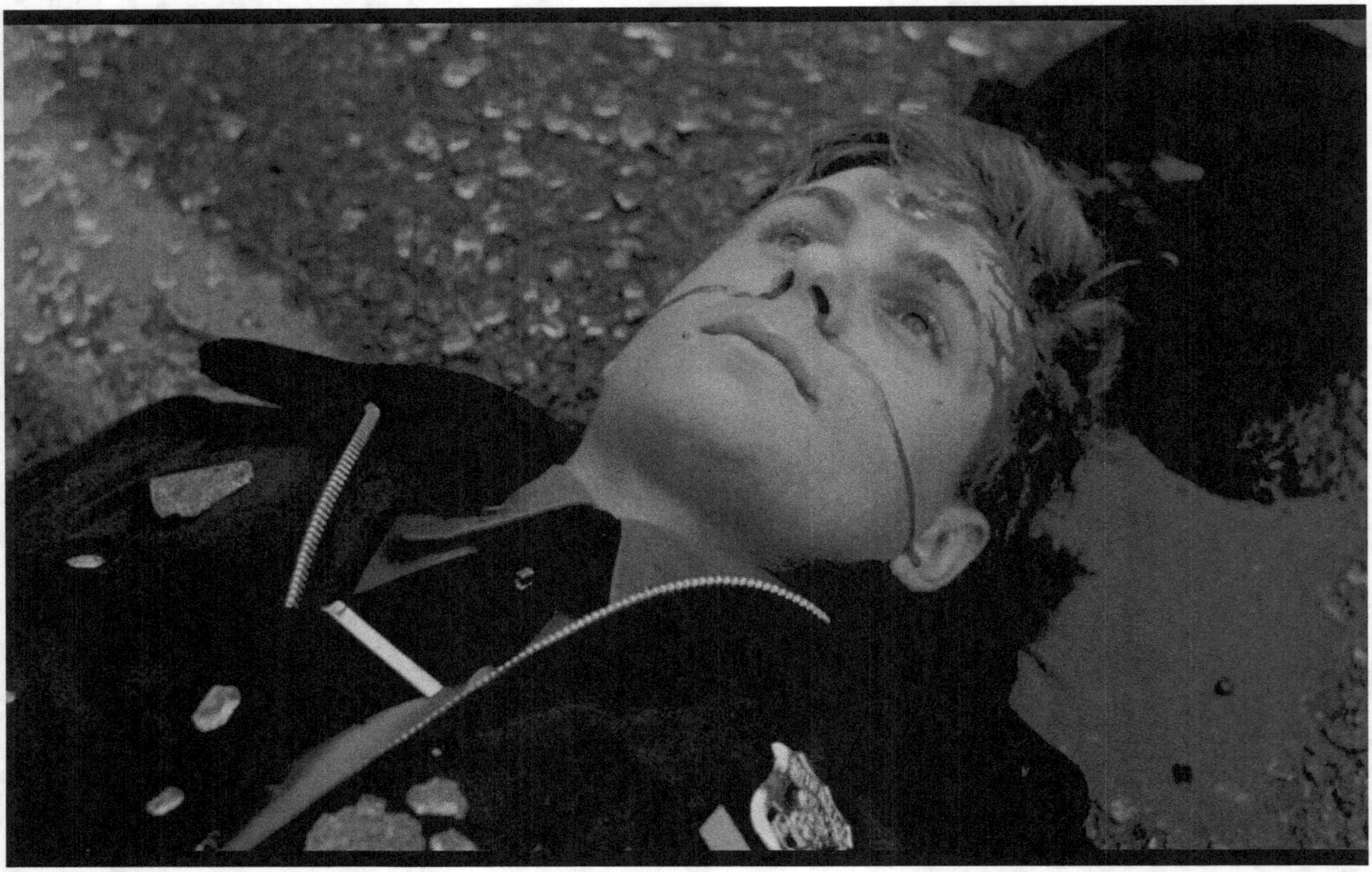

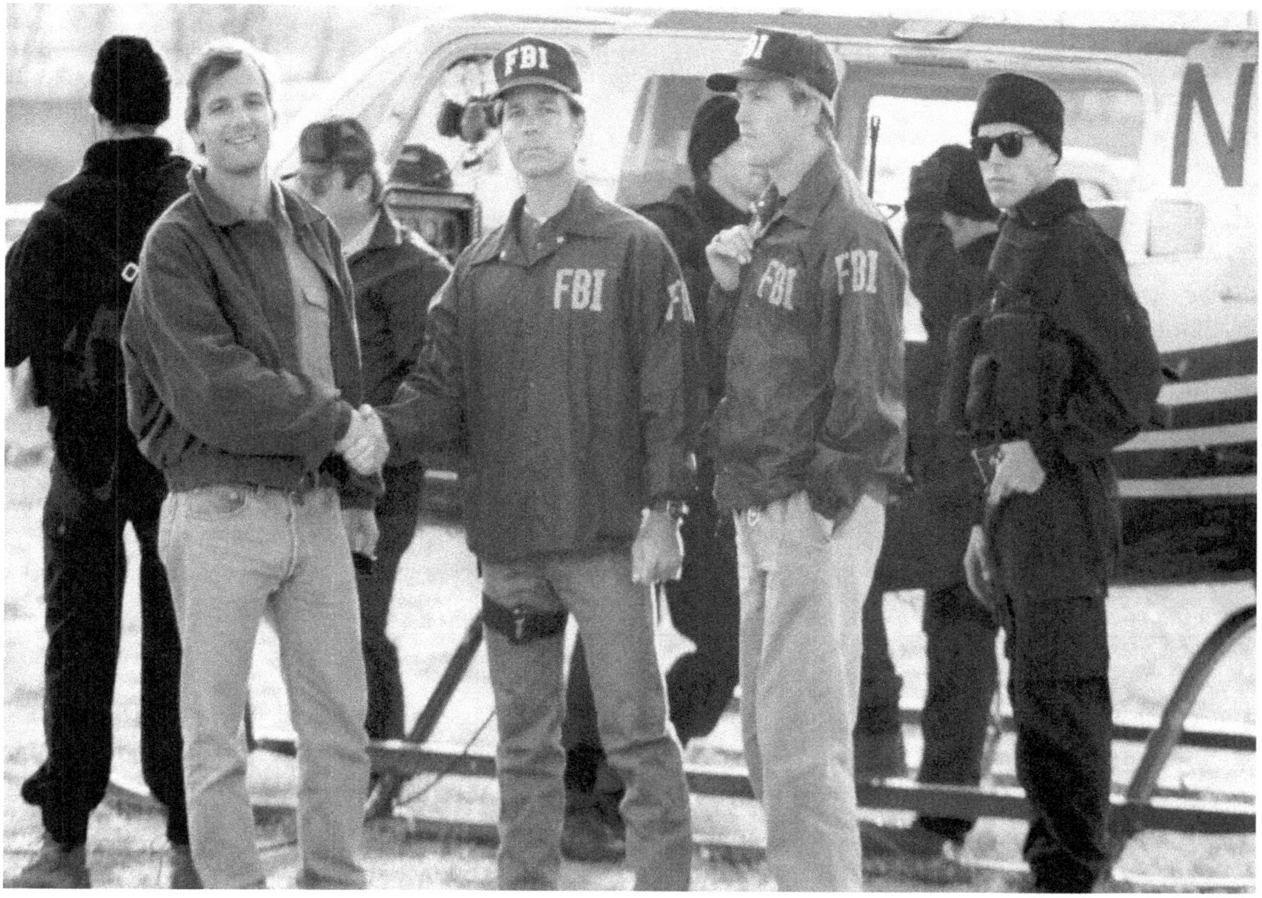

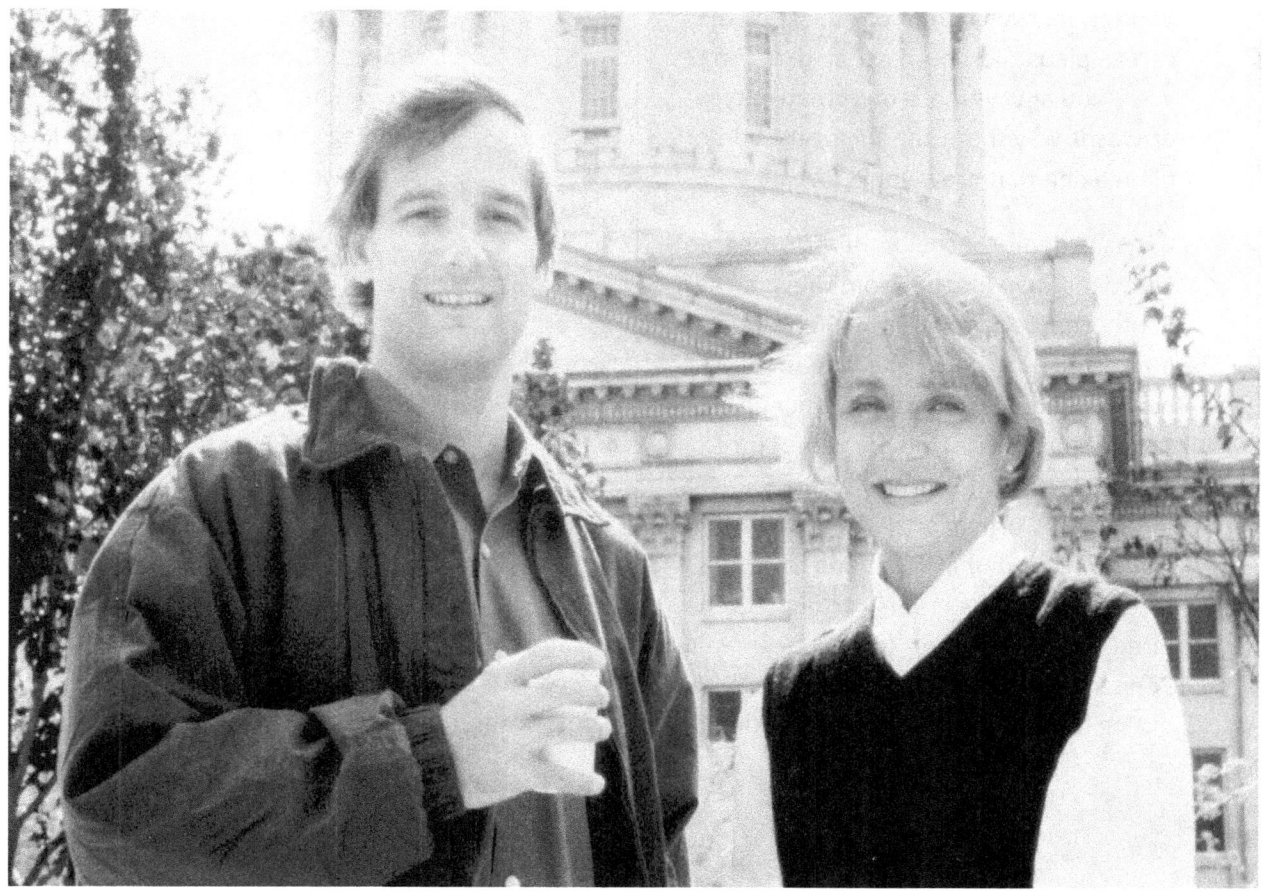

# Frank K. Isaac

Frank Isaac currently serves as SVP Production for Film Finances, the industry's leading completion bond company. His responsibilities include the review and approval of all production elements including shooting schedule, budget, post production plan & key personnel for films that Film Finances bonds. Recent films and series that Frank has supervised include POINT BREAK, DEMOLITION, SICARIO, TED 2, PAWN SACRIFICE, NIGHTCRAWLER, SENSE8 and MAKING A MURDERER. Notable films that Frank supervised during his similar tenure at International Film Guarantors from 2000 to 2013 include IRON MAN, TOMB RAIDER, TERMINATOR 3, THE AVIATOR, THE GOOD SHEPHERD, ALPHA DOG, SISTERHOOD OF THE TRAVELING PANTS, and DIARY OF A MAD BLACK WOMAN. From 1996 - 1999, Frank served as Vice President Production for Largo Entertainment, a wholly owned subsidiary of JVC. While with Largo, Frank co-produced CITY OF INDUSTRY, THIS WORLD, THEN THE FIREWORKS, UNDER PRESSURE, SHADOW OF DOUBT, FINDING GRACELAND and AFFLICATION, which earned James Coburn an Oscar as Best Supporting Actor. Frank received his BA in Cinema / TV from USC in 1981.

**Nadia:** Mr. Isaac, first of all thanks very much for sharing some memories about SGE. What was your first job in the film industry? Before SGE, you served as a co-producer on THE BEASTMASTER and some other films. How old were you when you first started in the film industry? Did you go to film school? What kind of education and career plans did you have at that time? Were you always more of a creative type, or was it way more the financing side of filmmaking that drew you?

**Frank:** I received my Bachelor of Arts degree with a major in Cinema from University of Southern California in 1981. I was Interested in both the creative and business side of filmmaking while in film school, and as I started my career on THE BEASTMASTER in 1982 and as a producer on Roger Corman's slate of sword-n-sorcery films shot in Argentina from 1983 through 1986. I was very fortunate to be hired as an assistant to producer Paul Pepperman and director Don Coscarelli during the early days of pre-production of THE BEASTMASTER. Paul & Don assigned me quite a lot of responsibility in helping to plan the production, and it was a wonderful learning experience that lasted almost a year and a half and through the release of the film in 1982 by MGM. As a result of my experience on THE BEASTMASTER, I was hired by Roger Corman to oversee a slate of six sword-n-sorcery films to be shot in Argentina. Beginning in 1983, I worked on DEATHSTALKER, THE WARRIOR AND THE SORCERESS, WIZARDS OF THE LOST KINGDOM, BARBARIAN QUEEN, AMAZONS, and DEATHSTALKER 2. Roger Corman recognized the popularity of the sword-n-sorcery genre after the successes of CONAN THE BARBARIAN, THE SWORD AND THE SORCERER and THE BEASTMASTER. He was approached by Alex Sessa and Hector Olivera of Aries Cinematografica to take advantage of the production values that could be achieved in Argentina largely due to the strength of the U.S. dollar vs. the Argentine peso at the time. Relative to the low below-the-line budgets, Alex &

Hector were able to deliver skilled Argentine crew, build substantial period piece sets and provide unlimited "extras" for large crowd scenes. For each film, Roger sent me to Argentina with just the screenplay and a few key American cast & crew, including a director. Roger financed the films entirely and it was my responsibility to physically produce the films in collaboration with Alex & Hector's Aries Cinematografica. The advent of home video began in the early 1980's, i.e. booming videocassette rentals and sales, was taking place. There was a tremendous need for new titles to stock the shelves of the video stores that were popping up all across the U.S. and rest of the world. Roger Corman knew that he could drive the sale of the videocassette rights for the sword-n-sorcery films that we made in Argentina on shoestring budgets by releasing them theatrically around the U.S. through his own distribution company first. So, these films that we made on budgets well under a million dollars started showing up on Variety's weekly box office charts! At the time that we started DEATHSTALKER, Roger was in the process of selling his original company, New World Pictures, and starting up a new company, Concorde / New Horizons. Roger hired me as Associate Producer on DEATHSTALKER and told me that if things went well, he would make me the full producer on subsequent films. He kept his promise, and during a four-year stretch from 1983 through 1986, I was handed a great opportunity to learn how to produce low budget films and problem solve production challenges without having a lot of money. In fact, the experience that I gained from those films would directly lead to my hire by Lenny, Alan & Jim a few years later.

**Nadia:** How did you come to join SGE? It was in its very early days, correct?

**Frank:** I met Lenny for the first time while I was working on THE BEASTMASTER. Lenny worked for Avco Embassy at the time. Since Lenny knew both Paul Pepperman & Don Coscarelli from the work they had done together on Avco's release of their earlier film PHANTASM, he naturally wanted to buy THE BEASTMASTER. As a promotional event to attract Avco's interest in the film, Paul & Don arranged for Lenny & Roger Burlage to visit the set in Simi Valley. Since we were shooting a scene in front of a massive pyramid that had been built, there was a need for many extras. So, Don & Paul invited Lenny & Roger's kids to be extras in the film. They asked me to coordinate the visit, so on the Friday afternoon prior to the shooting day, I phoned Lenny and Roger at Avco. Lenny put me on the speakerphone as he typically likes to do. I explained to Lenny that his kids would be villagers in a big scene in front of the pyramid. Lenny let out one of his patented laughs, and asked if his kids should wear togas. It was the first time I heard Lenny's laughter, which really is one of a kind. In fact, it's one of Lenny's many characteristics that makes him so endearing and charming to people. MGM, which was headed by David Begelman at the time and still located on its historic lot in Culver City, bought the domestic distribution rights for THE BEASTMASTER. But, I got to meet Lenny, and to this day, we laugh about our first meeting on the set of THE BEASTMASTER. Also, Alan Solomon worked in business affairs for a short time for the executive producer of THE BEASTMASTER shortly after the film began post production. So, I got to know Alan also at the time I was working on THE BEASTMASTER. I found Alan to be a very smart executive, and very genuine and kind, so we established a friendship. Once I returned from Argentina in 1987, I wanted to explore opportunities to work on films in the U.S. I made some phone calls to the various contacts that I had established since starting my career, including Alan. Shapiro Entertainment was in the process of merging with Jim Glickenhaus' company to become Shapiro Glickenhaus Entertainment. Alan invited me to visit the office and meet with him and Lenny to discuss an opportunity to join the company as Executive In Charge of Production on the upcoming slate of films they were planning. Lenny, Alan & Jim recognized the value of my experience in working for Roger Corman, and felt I would be helpful to them with their production plans. A week later they hired me, and I started in August, 1987.

**Nadia:** What was your position, what was the main part of your job? It was primarily production logistics, correct?

**Frank:** When I joined SGE in August 1987, Lenny, Jim & Alan assigned me the responsibility of overseeing the physical production of SGE's slate of films. Although it was Jim, Lenny & Alan who ultimately chose the film projects that were put into production, once they began pre-production, principal photography and post production, I directly supervised all phases of production. The first four films that went into production were Jim's film, BLUE JEAN COP aka SHAKEDOWN, MANIAC COP, LETHAL PURSUIT and BLACK ROSES. It was a very exciting time when Shapiro Entertainment merged with Glickenhaus Films to form Shapiro Glickenhaus Entertainment. Lenny & Alan brought the marketing & sales know-how to the company. Jim had fantastic production experience and a reputation as a maverick writer - producer - director who especially knew how to make action-adventure films that found success in the worldwide independent marketplace. Lenny, Alan & Jim hoped to build a successful company based upon the concept of making genre films smartly and efficiently and being able to sell the international and domestic rights through either pre-sales or after completing the films. Alan had excellent relationships with film buyers from around the world who attended AFM, Mifed & Cannes. Lenny had great knowledge and experience in domestic distribution and had strong contacts. Jim was very well-regarded in the independent film community because of the films he had made in the past, and brought production expertise to the new company. At the time that SGE started up its home video division, Lenny asked me to help with the acquisition of titles. So, my responsibilities expanded to screening films and meeting with filmmakers and producers who had projects in need of distribution. This was a wonderful opportunity to learn from Lenny about the "acquisitions and distribution" side of the business, and I enjoyed it a lot.

**Nadia:** One of the first films you participated in was MANIAC COP, then? How did you get along with Bill Lustig, the director? Is it true there were some tensions between you two?

**Frank:** Yes, MANIAC COP was one of the first films I worked on at SGE. In answering your question as to whether there was tension between Bill Lustig, the answer from my perspective is no. In fact, I was very impressed with Bill's skills as a director and producer. And, I really enjoyed working with the line producer Jef Richard and stunt coordinator Spiro Razatos. Relative to the budget, the film looked very polished and was quite well done. If someone has suggested that there was tension, it may be because I didn't initially understand the type of film that Bill was making and its intended audience. The title should have been my first clue! So, after seeing the first cut of the film, I came back with a creative suggestion or two that, in hindsight, were off target given the fact that this was meant to be a horror film with some intermittent laughs from offbeat humor. MANIAC COP was tremendously successful as a genre exploitation film, so Bill's vision for it was spot-on correct. Later, Bill and I went out to lunch, and he gave me one of my first Laser Discs, which was ROBOCOP. So, he must not really have felt that there was much tension either. In regard to the term, "exploitation film," many of the projects that SGE did fell into this category. The word "exploitation" may seem to have a negative connotation. But, what I think it really refers to is the filmmakers attempt to produce a certain type of film that has a very specific and time-tested appeal to large segments of the potential marketplace. In the case of the films that SGE made, action films and horror films with a bit of offbeat humor were staples due to their appeal and commerciality in the indie marketplace at the time, especially given the booming global videocassette business. Lenny, Alan & Jim's approach was to make films for a price that had the requisite "exploitation" elements to drive sales internationally and domestically.

**Nadia:** What about your early SGE film contributions (FRANKENHOOKER, MOONTRAP, LETHAL PURSUIT, etc.) – were you always on location? Did you mostly get along with directors like Frank Henenlotter, and others?

**Frank:** Jim Glickenhaus became aware of Frank Henenlotter because they were both part of the New York independent world. There is no question that Frank Henenlotter possessed an original style and skill as an independent filmmaker, and Jim recognized that. However, since the budget level that SGE was providing for the first two films that Henenlotter would direct was much higher than what he had ever had to work with before, Jim thought it would be a good idea to have me come to New York to oversee the films on behalf of SGE. I had a lot of fun working on FRANKENHOOKER and BASKET CASE 2, because of the manner and style in which Henenlotter mixed humor and horror. And, lead actor James Lorinz was a great pleasure to work with and very funny. Jim and I would watch the outrageously graphic and offbeat humorous dailies together in a screening room, and Jim would laugh and say something to the effect of, "I know I'm going to be disinherited because of this!" While mixing FRANKENHOOKER at Sound One, the fine comic actor Bill Murray, who was working there on another film, would sometimes walk in and watch the work being done on FRANKENHOOKER. He must have greatly enjoyed what he was seeing, because we asked him for a quote, and he offered this one, which we included on the FRANKENHOOKER videocassette box: "If you only see one movie this year, it should be FRANKENHOOKER." ~~ Bill Murray

**Nadia:** There were some problems during the production process of MOONTRAP, can you share some details?

**Frank:** MOONTRAP was an interesting production in that it was undertaken by a director - producer, Robert Dyke, who was based in the Detroit area. I enjoyed working with Robert and his team. John Cameron, who worked on the film as the production manager, has gone onto produce some very impressive films. Stephen Roberts is the SGE executive who brought the project in based upon his prior working relationship with Robert and Mary Petryshyn. Given the production budget, the film possessed high production value in large part due to the resourcefulness of Robert in getting NASA to ship the inside of an actual space shuttle to Detroit for use during the filming. Robert and Mary also obtained some great stock footage of actual NASA moon expeditions, which also enhanced the story. If I recall correctly, the estimated costs of production may have increased somewhat after production began. Ultimately, however, I think the film was successful and helped to launch SGE's video company.

**Nadia:** What about the movie SHADOW DANCING, released in 1988? Was it an in-house production by SGE, or did the company just do the distribution & marketing?

**Frank:** SHADOW DANCING was shot entirely in Toronto and produced by Kay Bachman, who resided there. I visited the set once or twice, but SGE had very little to do with the film creatively.

**Nadia:** One of the in-house productions was ONE MAN FORCE, which covered a lot of veterans in front of, and behind the camera. How was it to work with Dale Trevillion, who also had experiences as a producer?

**Frank:** Dale Trevillion and his wife Sharon Farrell, who starred in the film, were both great to work with. ONE MAN FORCE was Dale's first theatrical feature film as a director, and he worked very hard and responsibly to make the film as successful as it could be. After we had just completed post-production, I remember getting the news that the film's star, John Matuszak, had passed away of heart failure. John, who was also a former NFL star, was a "larger than life human being" in more ways than one. He was very kind and generous to the cast and crew. It was a great pleasure to have gotten to know him during the making of ONE MAN FORCE.

**Nadia:** How do you remember the production process of TIGER CLAWS?

**Frank:** Jalal Merhi, the Canadian producer and star of TIGER CLAWS was a very smart, serious filmmaker who really knew how to make martial arts-themed movies for a price. I enjoyed working with Jalal and getting to know Toronto while working on the films that SGE made with him. It was a very nice experience overall.

**Nadia:** In the later phase of SGE, you received a credit as a producer on James Glickenhaus' serial killer movie SLAUGHTER OF THE INNOCENTS. Were you on location in Utah? Any particular stories about that film?

**Frank:** It was a privilege to work with Jim Glickenhaus on SLAUGHTER OF THE INNOCENTS in the capacity of producer. Much in the same way that I consider Lenny to have been a mentor, I think of Jim the same way. Lenny & Jim knew that I wanted to produce a film that Jim was directing, and they offered me that opportunity on SLAUGHTER OF THE INNOCENTS. Jim had previously chosen Boyce Harman to produce his SGE films (SHAKEDOWN, MCBAIN), so I was very happy to have the opportunity to work with him in that capacity on SLAUGHTER OF THE INNOCENTS. The best part of the entire experience for me was getting to know Jim well personally and having the chance to see him work on the set every day. Jim is highly intelligent and conversant on so many different topics. He always speaks his mind and lets you know exactly what he's thinking. Another way to put it is that he doesn't pull punches. I always thought Jim would make a great talk radio host because he's not only articulate, but he's very entertaining and colorful. Jim worked really well with actors and chose interesting ways to cover the material creatively. And of course, his forté is setting up and executing exciting action sequences, so it was fascinating to see him do that on SLAUGHTER OF THE INNOCENTS and I'm glad I had the chance to help produce one of his films while at SGE.

**Nadia:** Did you join the legendary SGE parties? Did you go to the American Film Market, and the Cannes film market?

**Frank:** The SGE party that I remember most vividly took place at a nice venue overlooking Hollywood Boulevard and The Chinese Theater. The party was meant to be a celebration of the theatrical release and opening weekend of RED SCORPION. Unfortunately, instead of looking outside the window at a line of people waiting in line to see RED SCORPION, we viewed a long line stretching around the block for PET SEMETARY. Jim & Lenny had committed a great deal of money for prints & advertising to help ensure the success of

**Frank:** RED SCORPION and help launch SGE's new video division. The preview of opening weekend results that we viewed along Hollywood Boulevard during the party that night did not bode well.

**Nadia:** Did you stay friends with many of the SGE key people? Do you miss those days sometimes?

**Frank:** Since Lenny and I live in the same community, we have the opportunity to see each other regularly. In fact, as my kids were growing up, we would visit Lenny & Harriet's house every Halloween. They always had special treats or toys for the kids, and they became known as "Uncle Lenny & Aunt Harriet." When one establishes strong friendships with former business colleagues, it's a very nice outcome. I consider Lenny a close, lifelong friend. And, although I haven't stayed in touch with Jim, I'm very appreciative of the opportunities that he provided and the friendship we formed during the six years I worked for SGE.

I enjoy seeing Nadia, Stephen and other wonderful SGE staff members and associates at the occasional get together, especially during American Film Market. SGE was a great place to work because the people who worked there were very smart, kind and energetic. Lenny, Alan & Jim offered the staff opportunities to develop their skills and take on more responsibility and as a direct result, some have gone on to do some very interesting and impressive things post SGE.

**Nadia:** Thinking back about SGE - was it a significant step in your personal career? What's the key thing you learned there?

**Frank:** Shapiro Glickenhaus Entertainment was a wonderful and unique company. Lenny & Jim brought a tremendous amount of energy to the company. It was a truly bi-coastal company, financed largely through equity, which offered a great deal of autonomy and independence. So SGE was an independent production company in the truest sense. What makes companies special and nice places to work are the people. SGE had an amazing staff of people such as Nadia Bruce, Stephen Roberts, Chris Bunney, Kirsten Bates-Renaud, John Alexander, Marilyn Moore, Elliot Solomon and the rest of the team. Most importantly, Lenny, Alan & Jim were fine leaders. I learned a lot from all three of them and as a result of their confidence in me, I was provided an excellent opportunity to develop my skills as a film executive and producer. Throughout my career, I have been very fortunate to have had some excellent mentors. I consider Lenny, Alan & Jim to be amongst the finest. One of the most important things that one does as an executive is to solve problems. Lenny once passed along some advice that he received or heard about from one of his mentors, Joseph E. Levine, founder of Avco Embassy. Lenny recounted that Levine always said, "I would rather commit an error of commission than omission." What that meant was that Lenny believed in exploring new ideas and innovative approaches as a film executive financing, producing and distributing independent feature films. He preferred to risk making decisions and being proactive, rather than holding back and not doing something because of a fear of it not working. You learn a lot about the people that you're working with when you are facing challenges and difficult situations. Lenny, Alan & Jim always kept their cool and collaborated to find solutions to the kinds of problems that inevitably occur when you run a business (especially one as difficult as a film financing, production and distribution entity). In particular, I recall the many long distance conversations that Lenny & Jim in which they discussed strategies for the company or specific films. It was a pleasure to listen to Jim and Lenny discuss their respective views, which sometimes conflicted but were always well thought out and stated. It was during those types of conversations and debates that I learned the most. So, I feel extremely fortunate to have had excellent mentors in Lenny, Alan & Jim while I worked at SGE.

**By Nadia Bruce-Rawlings, in writing**
**from Los Angeles, California**
**22August, 2015**

JOURNEY TO AN AGE OF AWESOME MAGIC

The Might of the Sword…

The Evil of the Sorcerer.

# Deathstalker

**YOU HAVE THE RIGHT TO REMAIN SILENT...**

**FOREVER.**

# MANIAC COP

GLICKENHAUS FILMS, INC. PRESENTS A LARRY COHEN PRODUCTION A WILLIAM LUSTIG FILM "MANIAC COP"
STARRING TOM ATKINS • BRUCE CAMPBELL • LAURENE LANDON • RICHARD ROUNDTREE
WILLIAM SMITH • ROBERT Z'DAR AND SHEREE NORTH  MUSIC BY JAY CHATTAWAY
CO-PRODUCER JEF RICHARD  EXECUTIVE PRODUCER JAMES GLICKENHAUS  WRITTEN AND PRODUCED BY LARRY COHEN  DIRECTED BY WILLIAM LUSTIG

RECORDED IN ULTRA-STEREO
© 1987 GLICKENHAUS FILMS, INC.

NO MAN CAN TOUCH HER NAKED STEEL.

# BARBARIAN QUEEN

Starring LANA CLARKSON · KATT SHEA · FRANK ZAGARINO · DAWN DUNLAP
Produced by FRANK ISAAC and ALEX SESSA   Screenplay by HOWARD R. COHEN
Directed by HECTOR OLIVERA

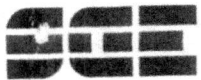   SHAPIRO GLICKENHAUS ENTERTAINMENT

A SHAPIRO GLICKENHAUS ENTERTAINMENT PRESENTATION

OF A

JAMES GLICKENHAUS FILM

STARRING

SCOTT GLENN

# "SLAUGHTER OF THE INNOCENTS"

JESSE CAMERON

SHEILA TOUSEY

DARLANNE FLUEGEL

ZITTO KAZANN

MUSIC   JOE RENZETTI

EDITOR   KEVIN TENT

COSTUME DESIGNER   SHAWNA LEAVELL

PRODUCTION DESIGNER   NICHOLAS T. PREOVOLOS

DIRECTOR OF PHOTOGRAPHY   MARK IRWIN, CSC

EXECUTIVE PRODUCERS   LEONARD SHAPIRO, ALAN SOLOMON

PRODUCER   FRANK K. ISAAC

WRITER AND DIRECTOR   JAMES GLICKENHAUS

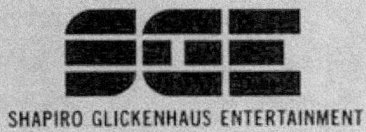

**SHAPIRO GLICKENHAUS ENTERTAINMENT**

Dear Frank,

I personally want to thank you for the loyalty, energy & integrity that you brought to our company.

It gave me great pleasure to have had the opportunity to have worked with you & see the tremendous growth in your leadership & business acumen in our many years together.

LEONARD SHAPIRO

(over)

I wish all the best & I want you to know that I will always be there for you if you need me.

Your Friend

Lenny

# FRANKENHOOKER

## Synopsis

James Lorinz tears up acres of scenery as Jeffrey Franken, a neurotic electrician and aspiring mad scientist, who goes completely 'round the bend after his slightly pudgy girlfriend (former Penthouse pet, Patty Mullen) is shredded by his latest invention, a remote-control lawn mower. Preserving her head in his mom's freezer, he sets out to acquire shapely female parts to rebuild the rest of her, focusing his search on the city's red-light district.

After watching a news feature on crack addiction among local prostitutes, Franken hits on the solution and invents a formula for "supercrack," which triggers the spontaneous detonation of anyone who smokes it. After blowing apart a hotel roomful of unfortunate ladies, he spirits their scattered limbs home to his garage laboratory, where his patchwork creation is eventually brought to life in a hilarious lift from The Bride of Frankenstein. Apparently, her brain spent too much time bobbing in the same preservative bath used for the hooker-parts, since she is instantly compelled to peddle her assets on every street corner in town, resulting in the high-voltage deaths of several johns (who are not entirely dissatisfied with their choice of demise).

Frankenhooker's exploits reach the attention of sadistic pimp Zorro (Joseph Gonzalez), who, obsessed with finding the person responsible for blowing up his women, tracks her back to Franken's lab for the inevitable (and quite disgusting) confrontation.

"FRANKENHOOKER"

STATE OF _Georgia_ )
) ss.
COUNTY OF _Fulton_ )

On this _30_ day of _April_, 199_1_, before me, _Becky E. Herring_, a Notary Public in and for said County and State, personally appeared _Edgar P. Ievins_, personally known to me (or proved to me on the basis of satisfactory evidence) to be the person who executed the within instrument as the _V.P. Corporate Secretary_ of The Full Moon Company, the corporation therein named and acknowledged to me that the corporation executed it.

Witness my hand and official seal.

Notary Public, Fulton, Georgia.
My Commission Expires October 12, 1991

_Becky E. Herring_
Notary Public in and for said
County and State

EXHIBIT C

INSTRUMENT OF TRANSFER

Dated  December 23, 1988

For One Dollar ($1.00) and other good and valuable consideration, the receipt of which is hereby acknowledged, the undersigned ("Grantor") hereby assigns solely and exclusively to Shapiro Glickenhaus Entertainment ("SGE"), by means of this instrument of transfer, all rights in and for the Territory (as defined below) which are possessed, or which have been or may in the future be obtained by any means whatsoever, by Grantor in and to the motion pictures presently entitled "HOUSE OF FREAKS" and "FRANKENHOOKER" including, but not limmited to, the following:

> All rights to exhibit, distribute and otherwise exploit such motion picture and all of the elements thereof, forever and throughout the United States and Canada, and all of their respective terrritories and possessions, including without limitation, Puerto Rico and Quebec (the "Territory"), and all foreign countries, in all media, whether or not now known, including, without limitation, merchandizing rights, video cassette and video disc rights, and theatrical sequel and remake and standard and non-standard (including free, pay, cable, satellite and broadcast) television program and series rights.

This instrument of transfer is executed in connection with and is part of and subject to an agreement between Grantor and SGE dated December 23, 1988.

THE FULL MOON COMPANY

BY: _Frank T. Henenlotter_
TITLE: _Pres._

BY: _[signature]_
TITLE: _V.P._

NOTARY: _____

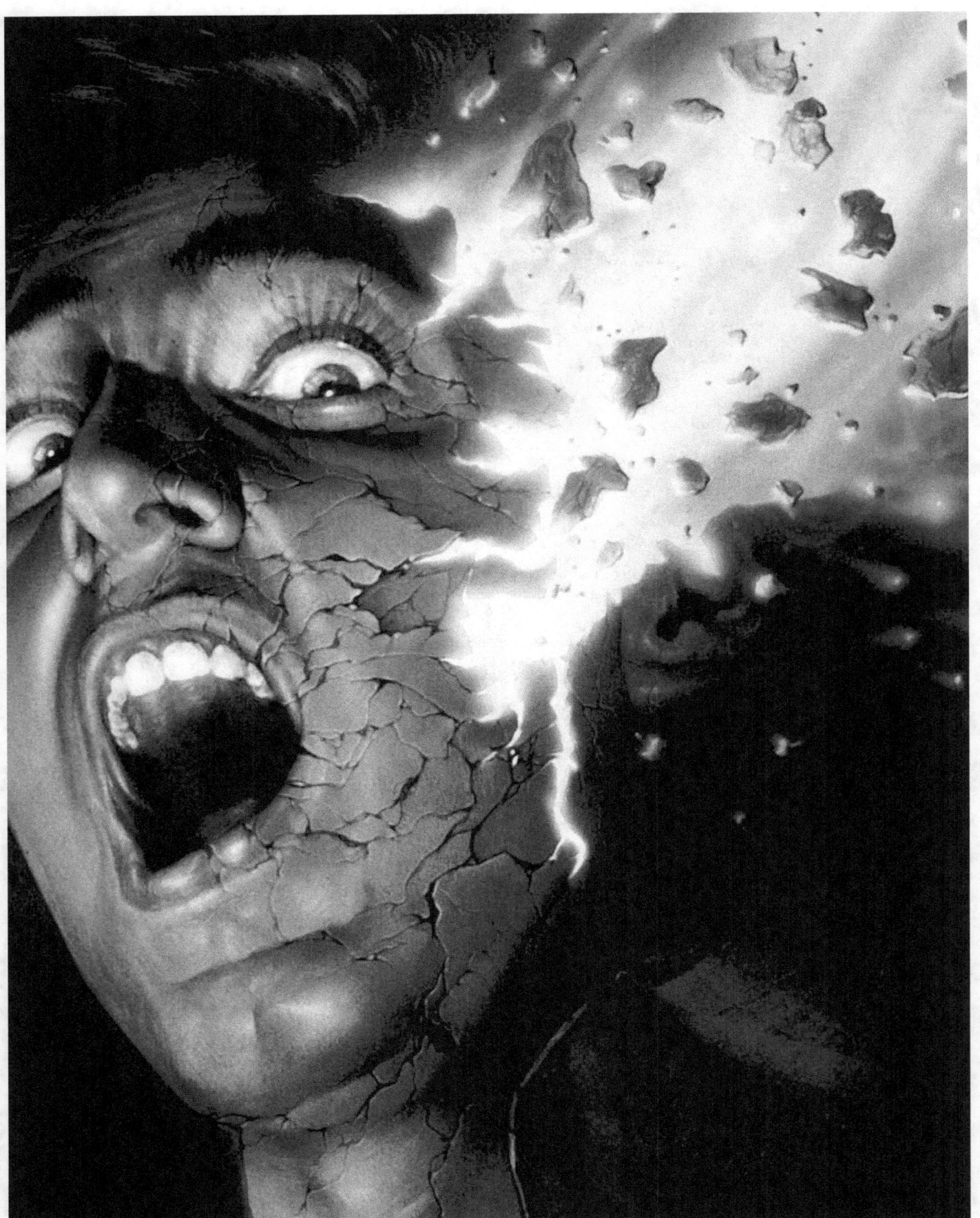

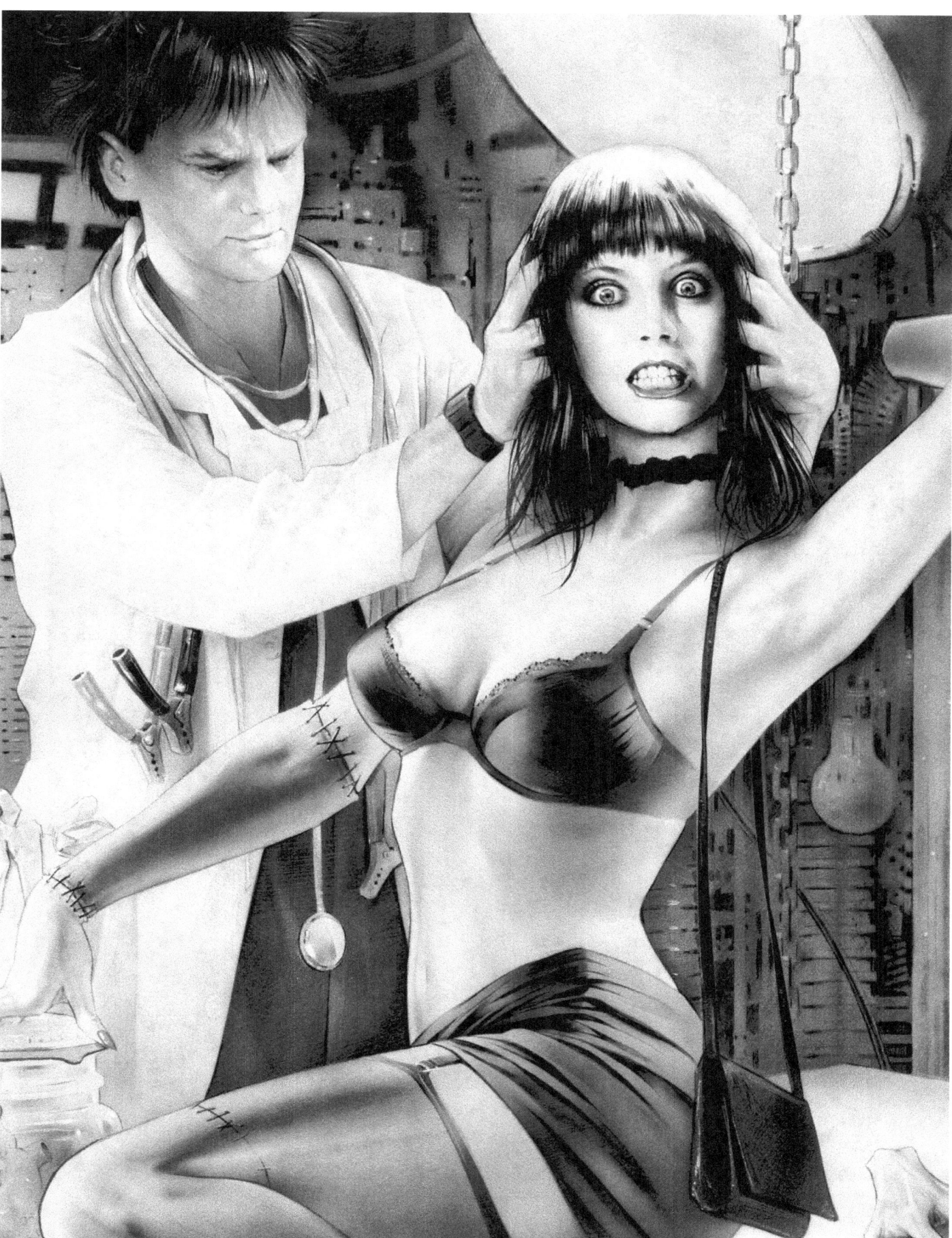

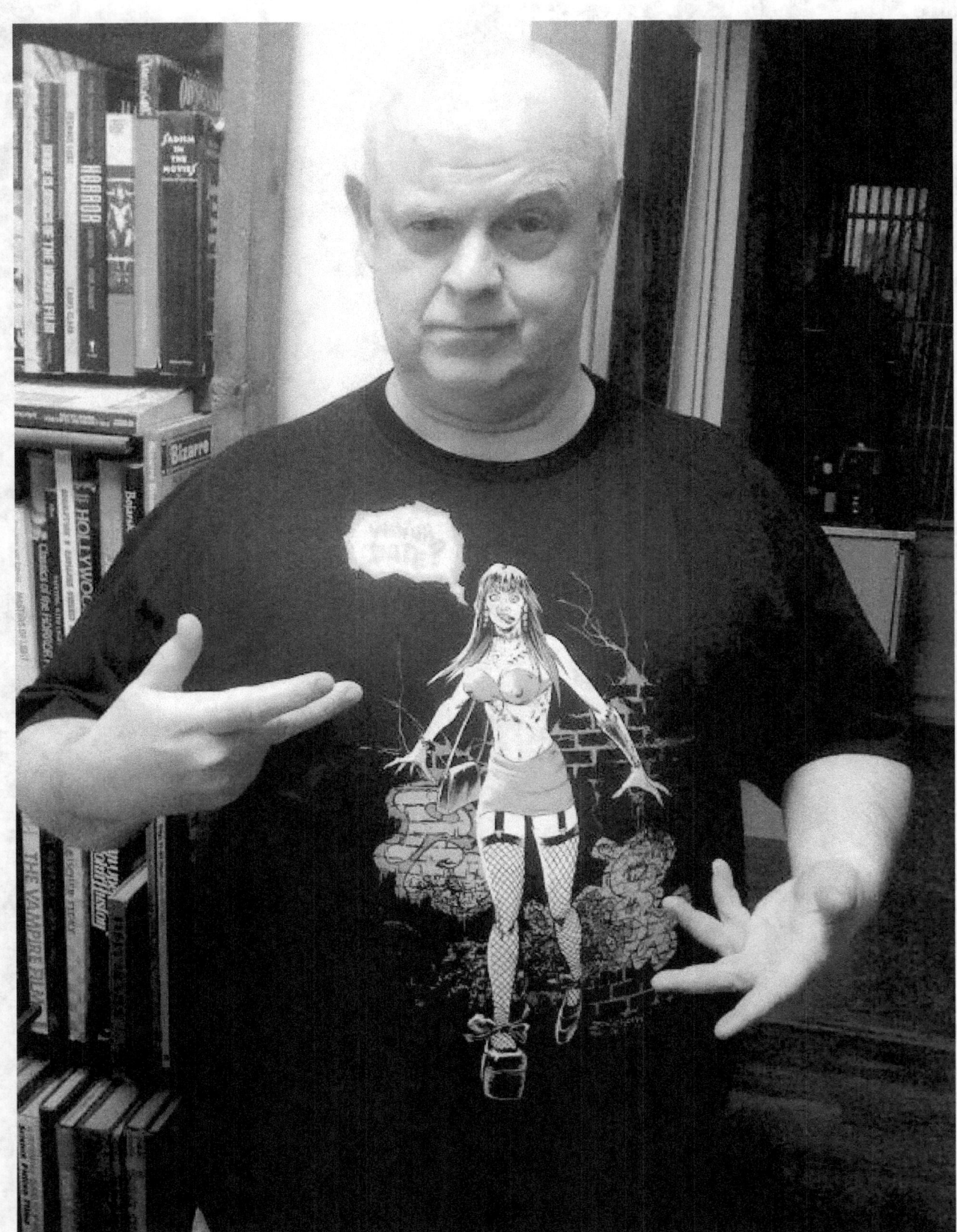

# Frank Henenlotter

At a very young age Frank Henenlotter began filmmaking with Super-8, then switched to 16mm, when the black and white short film, SLASH OF THE KNIFE, was screened at a midnight show at 42nd street. His theatrical debut feature BASKET CASE gained cult status over the years. He went on to direct BRAIN DAMAGE in 1988. Afterward, he found that SGE was the perfect fit for his films. He made three films during their partnership, including both sequels to Basket Case and the outrageous FRANKENHOOKER. Henenlotter then changed direction and became an important contributor for the special interest label Something Weird. In 2008 he returned as a filmmaker and delivered a true Henenlotter film, BAD BIOLOGY. After BAD BIOLOGY, he directed two profound and extensively thorough documentaries: THE GODFATHER OF GORE (2010) about the life and work of H.G. Lewis, and THAT'S (S)EXPLOITATION.

**Nadia:** So, how did you meet Jim Glickenhaus and Lenny?

**Frank:** Well, after I did BRAIN DAMAGE in the late eighties. I guess it was about 1989, don't remember exactly now. But I revived an old script I had, called INSECT CITY, that nobody wanted to make. Everybody thought it was too crazy. And it was. But at the time I wanted to do something radical. Even more than BASKET CASE and BRAIN DAMAGE. It was at that time when I heard that Jim Glickenhaus had started SGE, he had his SGE office in New York City.

**Nadia:** Right.

**Frank:** I thought, I've never met Jim but I loved his movies so well, if anybody sees any merit in my script it might be him. It was that simple. I sent it to him, and asked him to speak to me about it. We met, and in this first meeting he told me why he loved the script, and why he would never spend a penny making it. *(laughs)* Because nobody would ever pay to see that. He said it was crazy, yes, but completely uncommercial. And it really was. You know, so Jim had this phenomenal office on the sunny side of the Brill Building that faced Times Square. It was just beautiful. And he just said, "I don't want that script, but I want to work with you. What else do you have?" Well, I didn't have anything else. I didn't even have one script written, but you know, you have all these ideas in your head. One of the ideas I was playing with was a Frankenstein film about hookers and stuff, that would be pretty funny. I said to Jim, "Well, I've got this one idea but it's not totally finished yet." I started to tell him the idea, and he started laughing and then prompting me. I said, "This guys girlfriend dies." and he'd go, "How did she die?" [To which I replied,] "...in a tragic lawn mower accident...And he works at ConEd, that's where he gets all the equipment..." So, Jim was fueling this with me, and I was talking like a mad man. You know, when you're creating something, adrenaline is really flowing. Basically, in this office, on the spot, the blueprint for the first 45 minutes of the film was written like that! I didn't know how it was going to end but that was ok, and I told him, "I don't know if there's much more I can do on this script," and he was laughing. He said,

"Great, I like it, what do you want to call it?" And when you're on the spot, you know how fast your brain can work, and immediately my brain started going, "Frankenprostitute - no! Frankenslut - no! Frankenwhore - no! FRANKENHOOKER - YES!" *(both laughing)* So, I said "FRANKENHOOKER!" and he just died laughing. Then he said "Wow, maybe we should make this." And I said, "Ummm, yeah!" And he said to me: "What else do you have?" Well I couldn't do this a second time. The room smelled like toast from my brain cells that were already fried. I said, "Well, there's always a sequel to BASKET CASE." because I knew, this was a commercial property, that they could sell. I didn't have an idea what the plot was going to be, but, it's funny: he did not care either. He did not ask, what's all about, he knew if we call it BASKET CASE 2, that it would make money.

**Nadia:** Yeah, sure.

**Frank:** And that's really what happened. I guess it was two or three days later, he sent over an agreement. It was that fast. Before that, when we were still in the office he said, "If you have a choice, which one do you want to make?" And I said "Let's do them both back-to-back." It caught him by surprise, but he said, "Yeah, why not?" That's what we did. He basically gave us, I think it was three million dollars to make these films. A million and a half each was good money back in 1989 to make these films with. They have production value, the most expensive films I ever made. They look good, and I was able to hire Gabe Bartalos with all these freaks and creatures. That's what you spend the money on, it's what you can put on the screen.

**Nadia:** They are fantastic, both of them. I remember Jim and I did the contract for them, because I was Alan's assistant but I did all the legal stuff. I just remembered meeting Gabe, looking at his portfolio, what he had created. That was amazing.

**Frank:** Absolutely. We had more. The only reason we didn't have a spider-boy to put in, [and] the other stuff, time constraints were pushing on top of us. And we realized, ok, we can't do everything. And I wanted to put all the freaks in every scenes, and it was Gabe who said to me, "You can't. I need a couple freaks in rotation, so we can repair them." And I was like, "No problem." We made - well, he made them, and I'd only come up with the bad jokes. He made creatures like, like the singing Opera Head scene. You know, it never appears again but it didn't need to, it achieved what it was gonna do. That was right at the beginning of the film. That's where that stuff needed to be. They were each six-week shoots. We started with FRANKENHOOKER first, then in the three weeks we converted everything to get ready for BASKET CASE 2. We did it at a pier here in Manhattan, like only ten minutes away from where I live and that's walking slowly. Very convenient. And it was these giant cinderblock rooms, no windows. So it was perfect for sound. You had diesel trucks out there you could not hear, and there were enormous rooms. Because we knew we were doing two films, we planned everything for that. You

**know,** we did the casting for both. So, while we were shooting FRANKENHOOKER, Gabe's people were already making the masks for BASKET CASE 2. Because we would pre-cast a lot of those actors for that. Same with the sets. we knew we were going to need elevated sets for both. So we designed the sets, like Jeffrey Franken's laboratory was raised, so we could animate the creatures at the end. That became Granny Ruth's attic. So all those designs, that's why we could flip them so quickly in three weeks. There was a lovely and cool way of working. I remember at the end of FRANKENHOOKER. I was pretty much exhausted and I said, Jesus, another one right away? But at the end of BASKET CASE 2 everybody wished we had a third one to do! Everybody was – so, it was such a fun assembly line machine, that we was just wishing we had a third one to do.

**Nadia:** How did you cast James Lorinz? I loved him...

**Frank:** I had seen him, he has a small part in a movie called STREET TRASH. Also shot in NY by a friend of mine, Jimmy Mural, who since became one of the major Steadicam operators in Hollywood. Lorinz had a small part in STREET TRASH, but I thought he stole the move, he was so damn hilarious. I had trouble envisioning the mad doctor. What kind of person he'd be. I thought of James, I thought, "My God I can even make him crazier." You know, I think it's only someone like Lorinz that could make drilling holes in your head make sense!

**Nadia:** Yes. And I can never forget when he was, like my favorite line in the movie is "Bunions!" and he's throwing the legs over his shoulder!

**Frank:** He absolutely did, that's an ad lib he did. What we were doing with that, he always was trying out dialogues and lines, never while the camera was running. Always before. And the agreement was, if I cracked up, if I laughed at it, we kept it. If I didn't, he didn't want to use it. That's what we did, and it worked out fine. The beauty of what he did with that, he also made the scripted lines sound like he was making them on the spot. You know, that beautiful speech he says to his mother. I'm going insane, this and that...

**Nadia:** Oh, yes!

**Frank:** That was heavily scripted, and he didn't miss a line, but the balance, he was able to put that quality there. The way he spoke, he made it all sound like it was blooming from his head at the moment. That was fun. And I wanted for the girl a traditional – not a scream queen. I didn't want a big breasted... - you know that scream queen type. No offense to that type, we love them but I really wanted someone who was believeable as the girl next door. Who Jeffrey unfortunately turns into a scream queen, but into my office one morning came Patty Mullen, and she has just been the Penthouse Pet of the year. I couldn't believe it. I was thinking, this sweet and wonderful little girl, she was just a delight. There were a lot of really good people who were helping me make that one who deserved, if not the same credit that I got but even more so. The reason we shot FRANKENHOOKER first, was because we still had no CGI effects. So the post production effects that we needed to do, like the creation scenes - it was going to take time. That was made first, although BASKET CASE 2 was released first.

**Nadia:** And BASKET CASE 2, except for one other film, is absolutely my favorite film in the world. I watch it periodically, and I'm just blown away. It has the best monster-sex scene ever made!

**Frank:** You know, I didn't want to remake part 1, it's as simple as that. That was the first concern, I came back from Jim's office, I thought I'll write FRANKENHOOKER with my friend Bob Martin, but I'll do BASKET CASE 2 by myself. But I thought, well, first thing I don't want...I couldn't do the story from the first one. They'd killed the doctor, I'm not going to have them hangout in another fleabag hotel in NY, so I thought let me go the opposite direction, let's find a mansion or something. We found a great place in New Jersey – it was a club for elderly women called The Tuesday Afternoon Club, and it was exactly what we needed. And then about a year after we finished, there was a murder or something there, a handyman had a dead woman's hand, some strange story, but on all the newscasts, the anchor people would make a point of saying, "...and this was the scene of the movie, BASKET CASE 2." *(laughs)* Cause and effect, you know!? That was insane, that production, the poor extras who were playing the freaks. Every freak had a freak-wrangler who was there to help them get the mask off in a hurry or if they needed help getting where they were going, or needed air! So they all had little fans to blow into their masks, I mean it was an army! It was crazy. And it was so....you needed all this coordination. And there were days when Gabe and I would walk on set, and they'd all be there, and you'd see them all. Gabe and I would just start laughing! How beautifully insane it all was. Once Jim read the scripts, Jim said we'd never get away with that with the ratings board, and really I knew how that works, so fine. You know what happened with FRANKENHOOKER, right...

**Nadia:** Yes, they rated it S for "shit".

**Frank:** Valenti, that fucker, amazing, right? That the MPAA would even dare to pull that crap, I've always felt they were a corrupt organization, but whatever, they're funded by the majors so they stick it to the independents. And Jim went on the attack, I hope he talks about this in the book, to really embarrass them. To the point where, when we were recording sound effects for FRANKENHOOKER, I think, and I remember Jim came rushing up to me, and said, "The MPAA just approved BASKET CASE 2 for an R without a single cut!" and we knew why, because they were just embarrassed with what happened with FRANKENHOOKER and just wanted to get us the hell out of there. Much to SGE's credit, they stood behind the film and put it out un-rated. And the other thing I should mention about it, is when it came out on video, I think the entire success of the film was not because of the movie, but because of the talking box they marketed it in.

**Nadia:** That talking box was fantastic! We had a giant one in the SGE office, like 7 foot tall, that would play "Wanna date? Going out?" over and over, it was great!

**Frank:** The impact it had, was fantastic – right across the street from Jim's office, from the Brill Building, was a store called Video Shack, and it was the first store of its kind that only sold VHS and Betamax tapes, and when they had the display of FRANKENHOOKER, that's all you heard in the store all day, were those video boxes squawking. It drove me crazy!! *(laughs)* 'Wanna date, wanna date??' As we were finishing BASKET CASE 2, that's when SGE was suggesting, why don't we do a third one. I was going to do two more films back-to-back. I'd written a film called VOODOO DOLL, and that was going to be back-to-back with BASKET CASE 3. There were problems with the script that I knew about, but I knew I could tap dance around them once I had a little more time. But what happened was SGE ran into – well by now it was like 1993, and the whole market, the whole industry was collapsing, and the whole exploitation market was dying because the theatres were closing, and once the theatres disappeared, you know. America lost like three-quarters of their theatres in the 90s, and once the theatres died, the ones that survived were under control of the majors. So all these exploitation companies, distribution companies, that I grew up with, were all dying, one after another. All these video companies that I grew up with were dying, one after another. So the writing was on the wall. So SGE said maybe we shouldn't do two. It made more sense to do BASKET CASE 3 because of the masks were already made, we just had to fix them up. That was why we made BASKET CASE 3 over VOODOO DOLL, which would have been a difficult script to make, I think. Part three was relatively simple to do, but unfortunately at the time BASKET CASE 3 was done it had a very limited theatrical release. You know, it was a grim time.

**Nadia:** Yes, it really was. It's like now. *(laughing)*

**Frank:** Yeah, yeah, yeah, yeah. There were even less options to think about then though. After BASKET CASE 3, I still wanted to do stuff that was a lot more radical. Horror films that were more shot like an art film, or more like avant-garde and underground stuff. But you know, there was just no more market for low budget horror movies. At least very little on the stuff I wanted to make. And also SGE did not last not much longer. So the end was in sight. I was just banging my head against the wall, and I got involved with a video company named Something Weird, and I was able to instead of making exploitation films, finding them, restoring them, and putting 'em out. All that crap from the past, probably almost anybody would wish had stayed unseen. *(laughing)* We just loved this stuff, you know. Tons of 60's exploitation which had no commercial value on television, and therefore hadn't been seen in years. And we were packaging them on DVD like it

**was a party tape. We were extraordinary successful, because we were the only ones doing it back then. So that's where I was all those years of not making a film. I was getting this stuff out and having a great time.**

**Nadia:** That sounds fantastic.

**Frank:** Yeah, here's how successful we were – at Tower Video, the buyer would buy our all stuff nationally - they bought so much from us that on street date, we were already shipping in profit.

**Nadia:** Wow!

**Frank:** That's extraordinary. And the reason is, for whatever reasons, kids weren't returning these discs. I wrote all the copy on them, all the liners, all that stuff. I put the extras on it, and basically I sold it. I envisioned my key customer as a 15 year old, who wants to see some tits and blood. "I got the perfect double feature for you, right here!"

**Both:** *(laughing)*

**Frank:** So that was the fun of that.

**Nadia:** So how did BAD BIOLOGY come up after all these years?

**Frank:** At that point one of my friends said he might get a small sum of money, would I be interested in making a film again? I said, "Why not?" I never debated about whether to do it again or not to do it again. I just always took the path of least resistance in life. So if there's a film on the horizon for me, I'll do it. If not, I won't. We decided to do BAD BIOLOGY and spend the budget we had basically on 35mm. To make it look really, it was more of a sexual comedy than anything...but this one was even more insane. I was afraid If we shot it on video it would just look dirty. Shooting in 35mm kinda confused the equation because boy, this really looked slick and beautiful but it was certainly not acting that way. So we shot that. During that time, Gabe Bartalos and I always wondered where was Jim!? We heard that he was working in the family firm, but we didn't know where. We were wondering "What's Jim up to?", and we always said to each other we should give him a call someday. Gabe was doing something for the extras of BASKET CASE 2, for the DVD. He said, "I want to look up Jim." Jim invited us to his office, and it was like we hadn't seen each other in just 2 days. It was like back to normal, you know what I mean? It was the Jim we knew way back when, and so immediately I thought - I don't remember how I asked him about this – I thought he would be great to play the editor, because he was once my boss. When he read what I wanted to do on the film, he got, not mad, but he got quiet. He said, "Frank, you can't do this."

**Both:** *(laughing hard)*

**Frank:** And I was very happy he played the editor in it. And Jim also does a cameo in my new film, which I just finished but hasn't been released yet. He plays an art critic in the new film I did, which is called CHASING BANKSY.

**Nadia:** You did it with Gabe Bartalos, right?

**Frank:** Yes, but here's the problem: It's not a horror film, it's not even an exploitation. It's a true story about three hipsters who go to New Orleans and attempt to steal a Banksy piece from the side [of] an abandoned building. I thought, "This would not be much fun, there ain't gonna be any blood." But on the other hand, Gabe has just produced a film that hasn't been released for some reason that's called MERCY MAN. It started as a five million dollar production and mushroomed into eleven million. It had to do with the director, who was also his own investor. It has nothing to do with being a regular producer. So the guy who did was the one who created Airborne. So I said to Gabe, "Listen, I got nothing for you to do on this, no creatures, but do you want to produce it?" He said "Hell yeah!" And he was a perfect hands-on producer. It didn't matter, if a lightbulb needed to get changed, he would be the one changing it, he wouldn't even ask somebody else to do it. You know what I mean? If stuff needed to be done - all he was doing the whole day was doing what needs to be done. This is exactly what a producer should be doing. So he was terrific. And Jim plays a New York art critic in it. He gets to say... - I wrote his dialogue that morning. I had something else in mind but I thought this would be great to give to Jim. In all seriousness, he's saying to this woman in the art gallery. He said, "It's all art. Everything is art. Scrambled eggs is art."

*(both giggling and laughing)*

**Frank:** So he's hilarious in that. He has two scenes in the film. Whenever Jim was on the set of these, he was always, well...I think he's still testing the waters to see if he'll ever do another one. We'll see. I hope so. About exploitation films, all I can say is when I was 15 I used to cut high school, get on the railroad and came to 42nd street in Manhattan. See the movies - not just horror, everything that was there woman-In-Prison-Films, blaxploitation, actionfilms, crap films. I just loved the diet of exploitation. That's where I think I was made. I think my films are not just horror. They're meant to be sold as horror films, but I think the mixture of comedy, and craziness...

**Nadia:** ...tongue-in-cheek...

**Frank:** Yeah! I think it's a more balanced diet. That's where my love was. And that's why it was very easy for me move into working with Something Weird. Because I grew up on 42nd street, and I knew exactly the kind of films we wanted to put out on DVD. So that's about that. I think this is the story of my sad life.

**Nadia:** That's fantastic!

**Frank:** *(laughing hard)*

**Nadia:** I just remember the BASKET CASE films, and FRANKENHOOKER! BASKET CASE 2 **was** fantastic!

**Frank:** Part 3 is a disaster! For a couple of reasons: When we started the film - well, I'm a little unsure of this now. But I had it in my head that when FRANKENHOOKER went out Unrated we would do the same with BASKET CASE 3. It surprised me, what they really wanted was a PG. And that changed a lot of stuff. The schedule changed, instead of being a six-week-shoot it became a four-weeks-shoot. A bunch of other stuff, and as a result: Um, it's easy to shoot comedy if you have time. So I was frantically re-writing the script on the set. Oh, and another thing: I don't remember whose decision this was - Lennys, or Alan's, or anyone's at SGE... - but my version of the film was about pregnancy. There were eleven pages in the script about her giving birth. They thought it would be disrespectful, or offensive to woman. And I thought, they're the ones who appreciate these scenes the most. But they said, no - we want them out.

**Nadia:** Really? *(laughing)*

**Frank:** Yeah, yeah.

**Nadia:** There was someone who had a problem with FRANKENHOOKER — that it was so misyoginist. We were all going, of course it is! It's called FRANKENHOOKER!

**Frank:** You know, how many woman are fans of these films?

**Nadia:** I know! They're fantastic!

**Frank:** I think the whole point in Jeffrey's punishment in the film...He didn't try to bring his girlfriend back to life. He tried to improve her. He tried to make her into a centerfold. That's what his mistake was, that's what he got punished for. And I had the same accusation thrown at me about BAD BIOLOGY. And whenever that film is screened at Festivals, it's the women that come up to me after the film, not the guys. The women saying, thank you for that film! I was in Argentina and Brazil, one month, and the next month. The women would came up to me and thank me for making a film about the female orgasm. And thank me for making a female character that's so empowered. And I'm going, "You do realize she's also insane?" They would go, "Yeah, but that doesn't matter. She knows how to deal with it." *(laughing hard)* You know when you're playing with that kind of material some people will not get it. Anyway, I didn't understand about the pregnancy scene but it meant gutting the film by eleven pages, so it meant my page count was down by eleven. This happened like the day before we started shooting, there was really no time to re-write something. So I was frantically writing to extend scenes I could shoot fast and quick that didn't involve special effects. So that we bring up the page count, and the running time. Part of this was turning it more, and more, and more into a comedy. It's not the film I wanted to make. But on the other hand when you accept the money of someone to make a film you have to ... make it. I'm disapointed with that but I certainly would not take my name off it.

**Nadia:** I love it. And the baby Belials are awesome!

**Frank:** Yes, they are. Oh, I tell you something about that scene. I really only had two shots. One shot was Annie Ross popping the babies out of Eve. The other shot was her son, Little Hal, watching it all and making comments. Before the scene, Jim O'Daugherty, who plays Little Hal - said to me: "Hey, I got a funny idea. What if everything I say is a rhyme? That would be funny." So he writes this elaborate speech that's all in rhyme. And he's on the set, we're ready to go, and he's so nervous that the sweat on his neck is peeling off the make-up if you look carefully. We were ready to go, and he screws up his first line, which means the rhyming is off. I wouldn't cut, I just wanted to see what he was gonna do. So that whole sequence he does is panic, because he's making it up as he goes along. And he doesn't understand why I'm not stopping. That's one of my favorite scenes. When he sighs at the end, that was real! We did a take two. And he said, "Please let me do it my way." We did it his way, and as soon as he got done he said, "Yeah let's go with the first one!" All in all I loved those films, it was an incredible experience! When we started FRANKENHOOKER I would have happily turned out films for SGE for the next 20 years.

**Nadia:** Yeah, I loved working there. I started at SGE when I was 21, worked there for 8 years. Oh my goodness, I learned a lot. *(laughing)* It was fantastic, and my best friends have come from SGE.

**Frank:** Sad...How can you sell a film when there's no place to sell it? *(sighs)*

By Nadia Bruce-Rawlings, via telephone

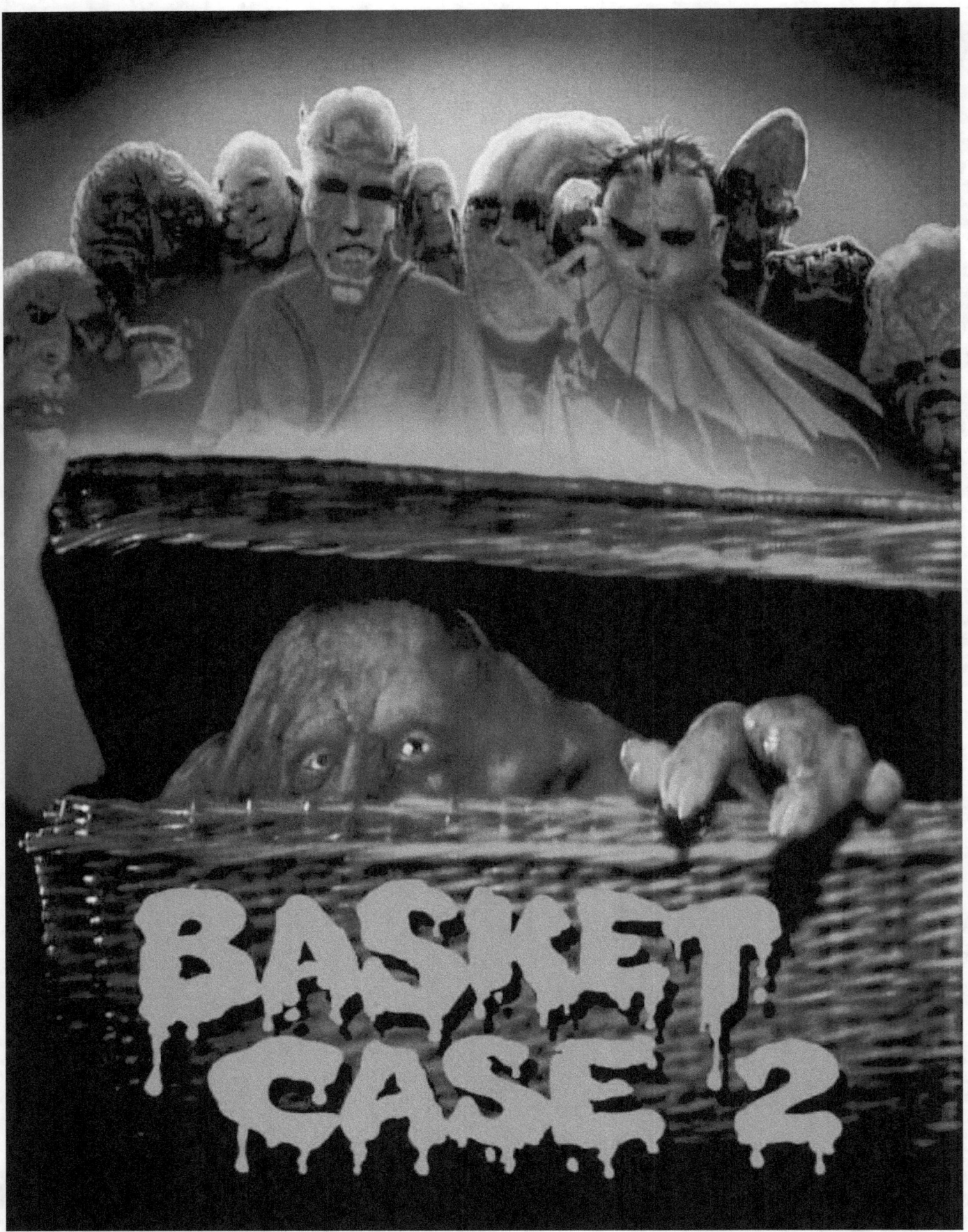

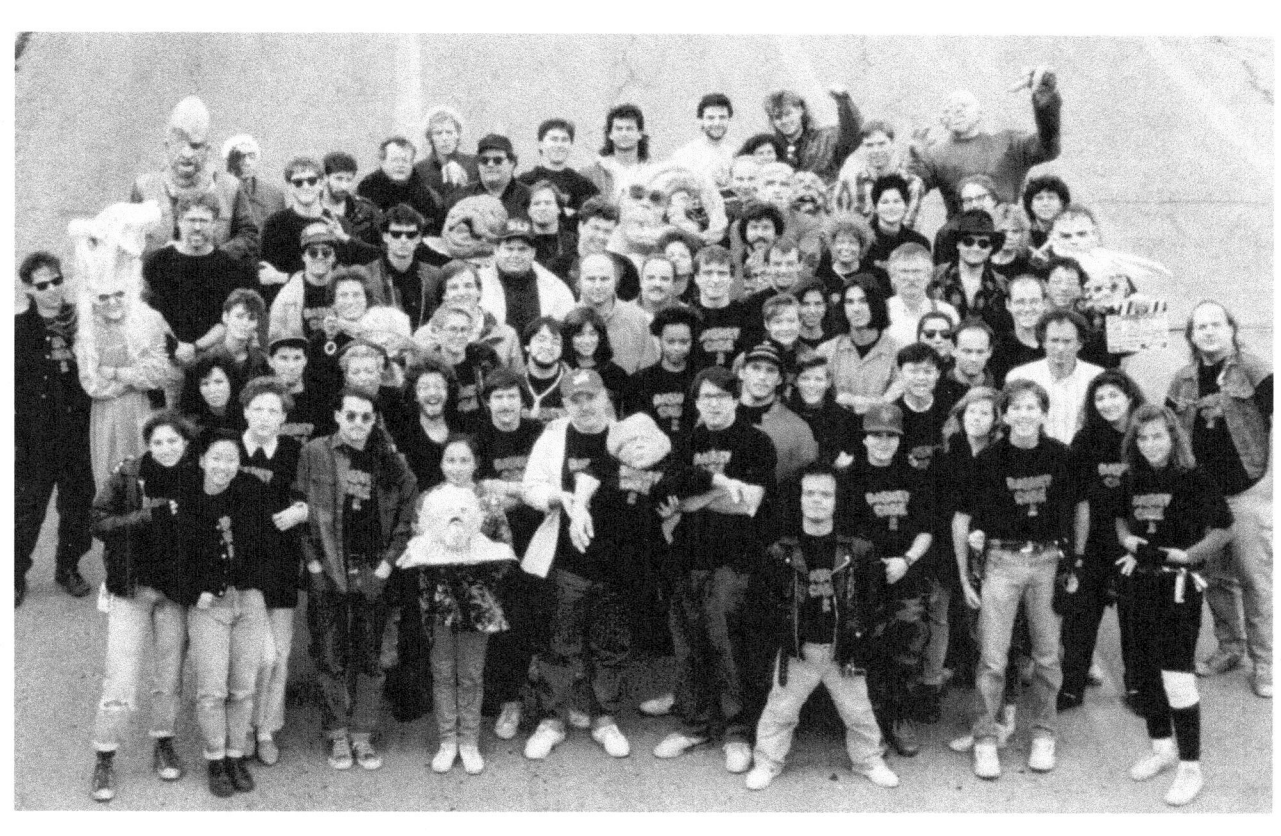

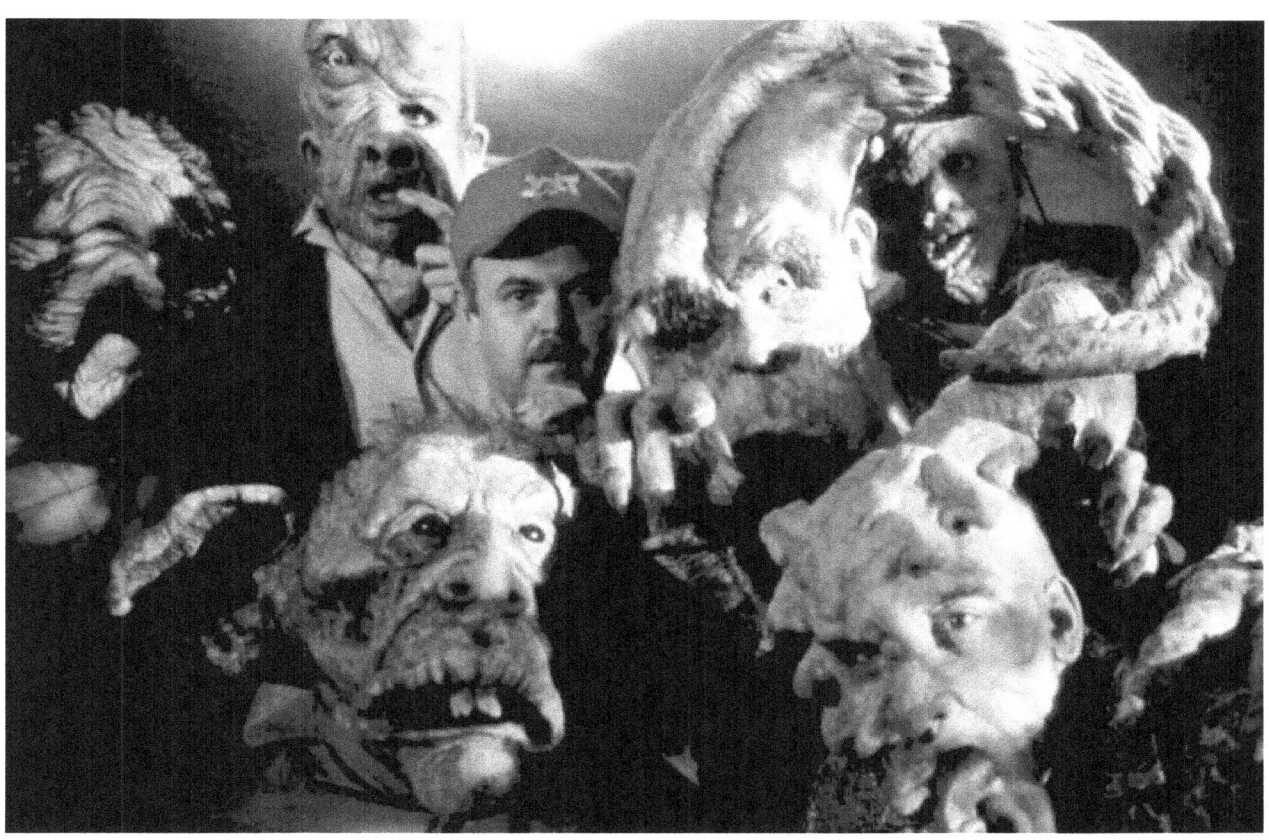

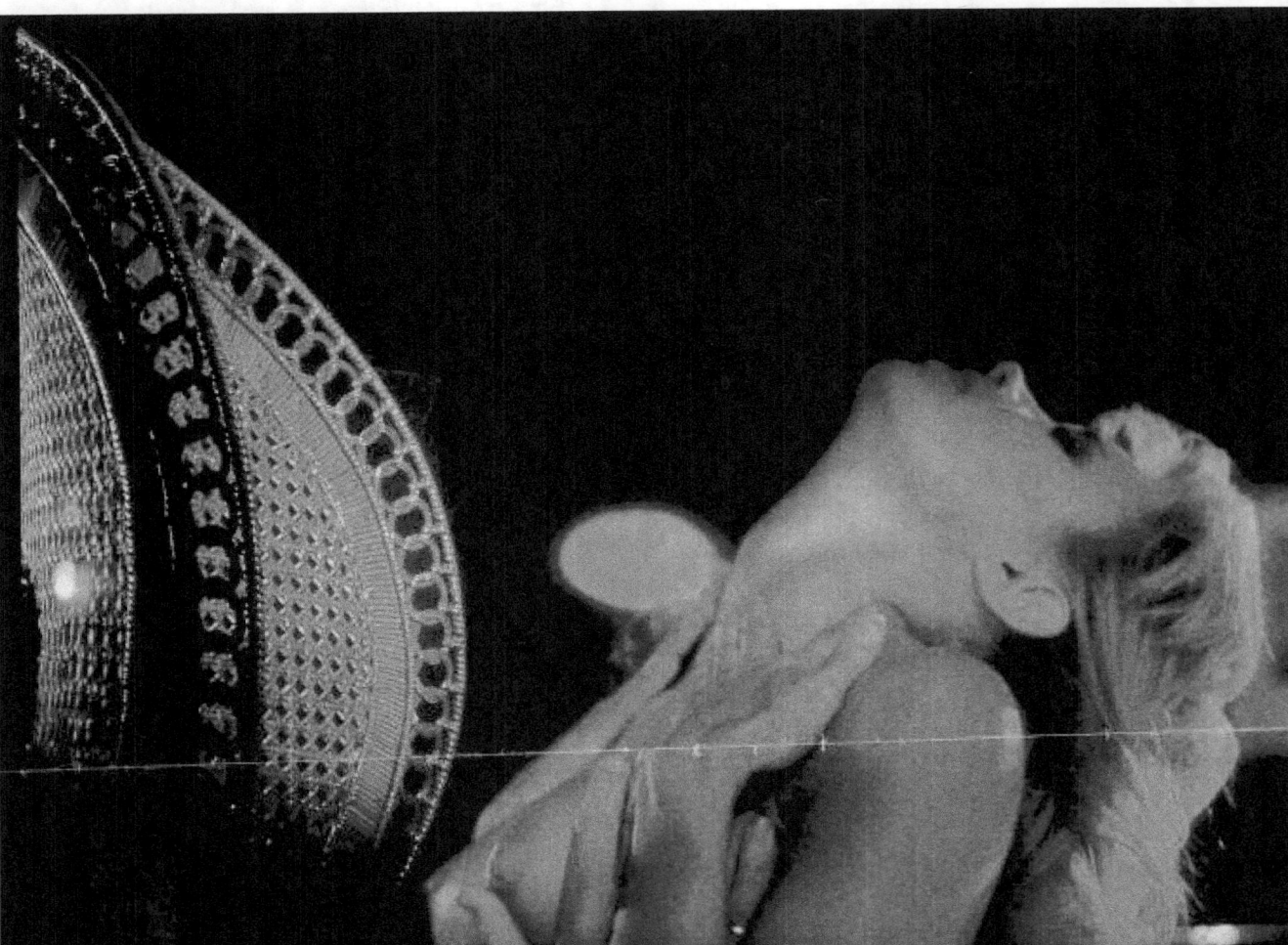

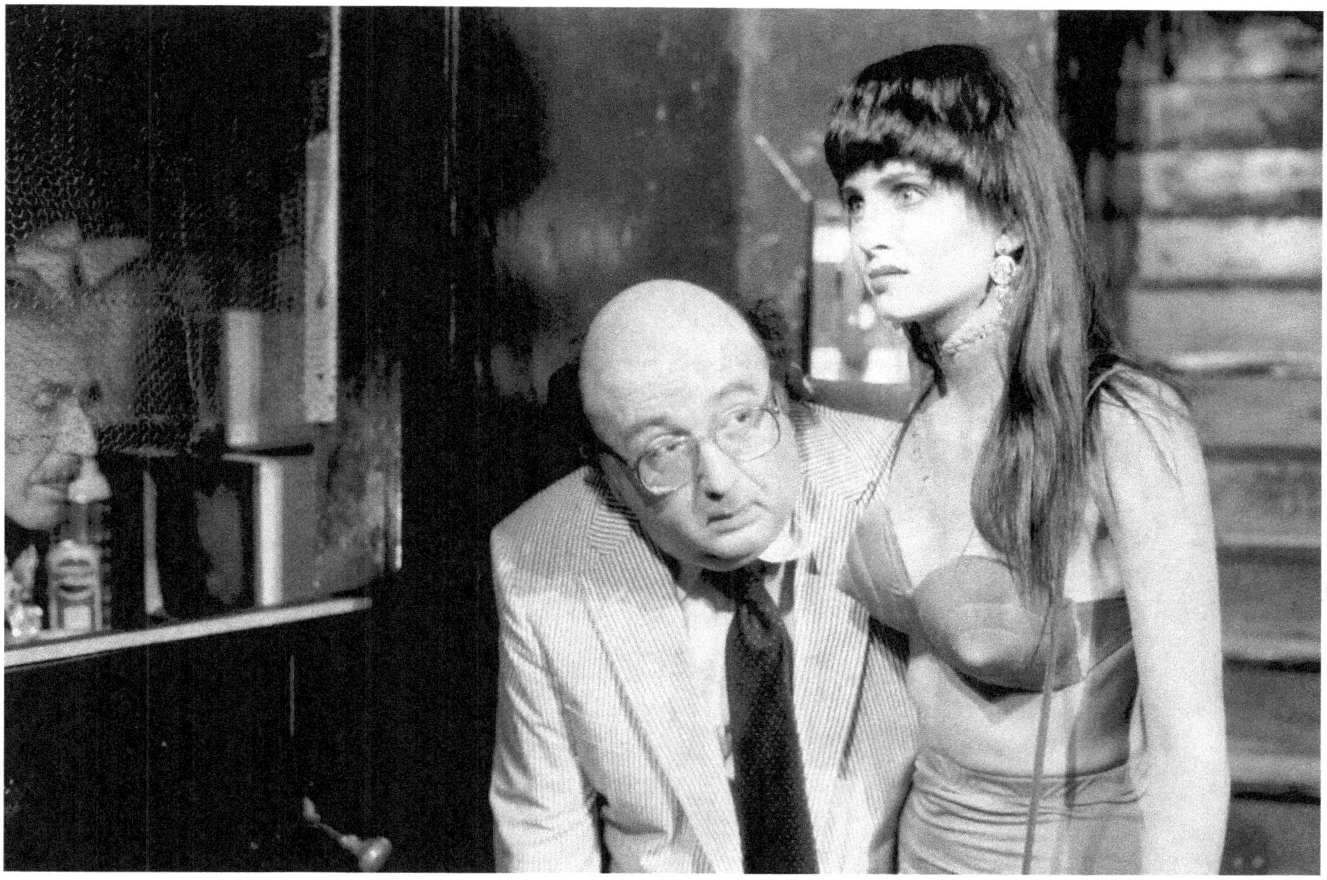

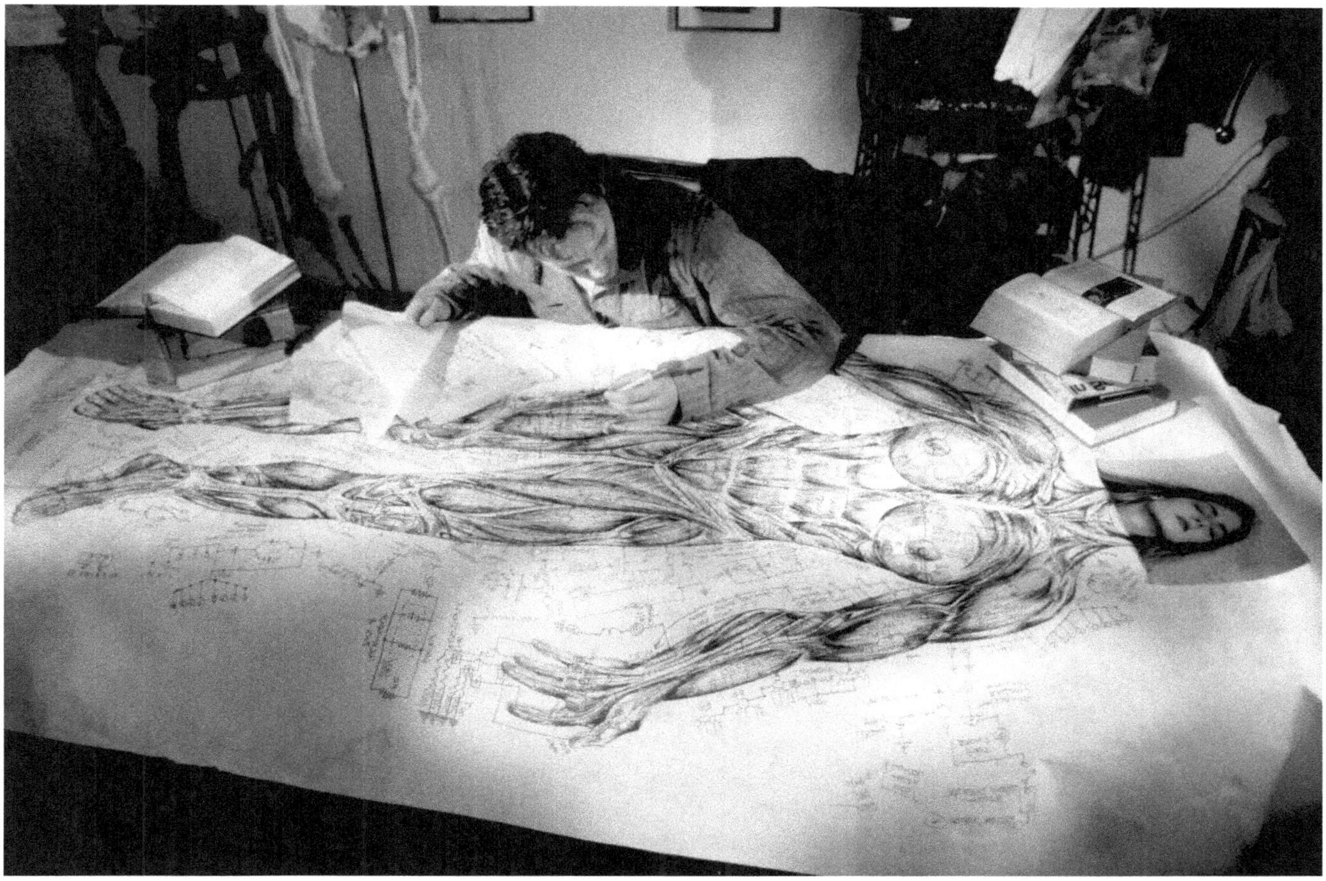

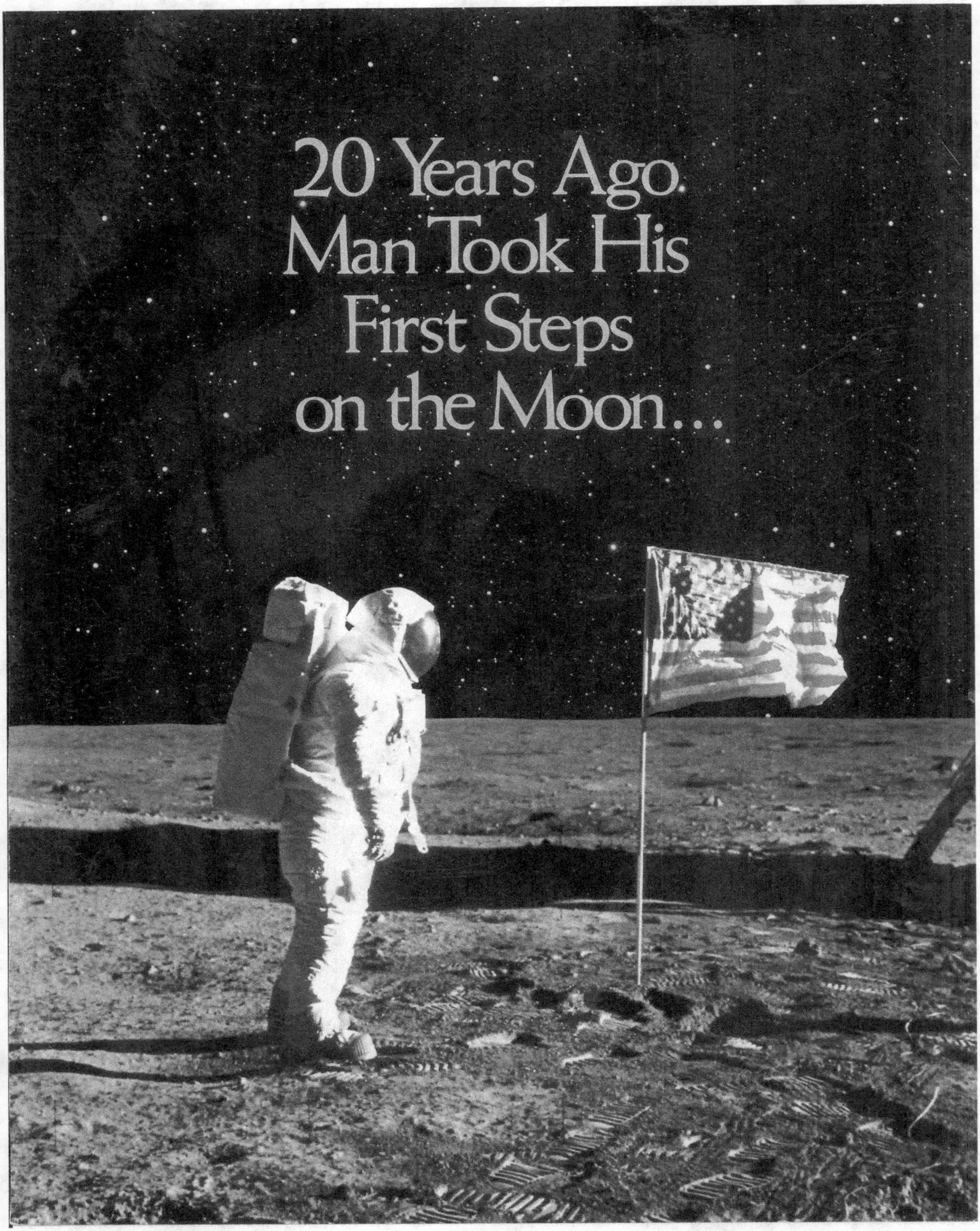

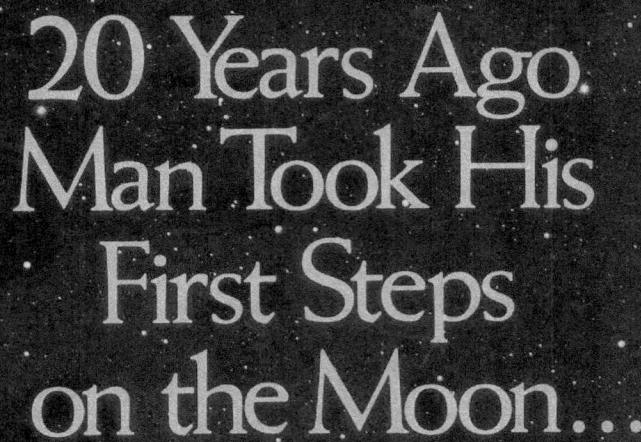

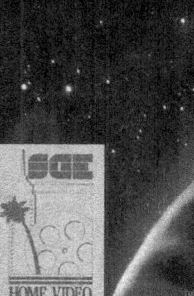

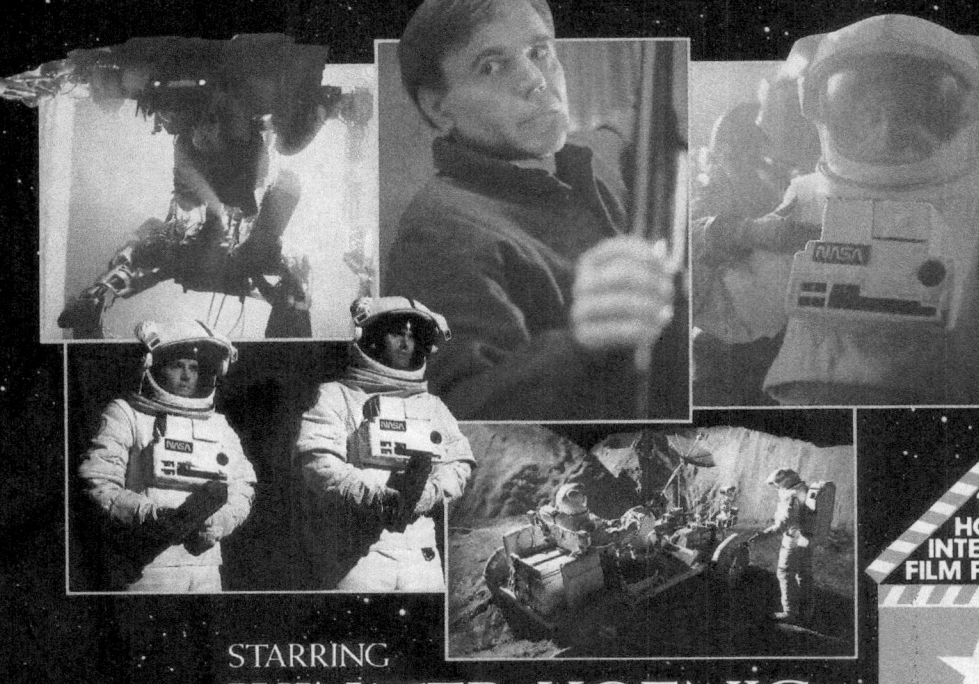

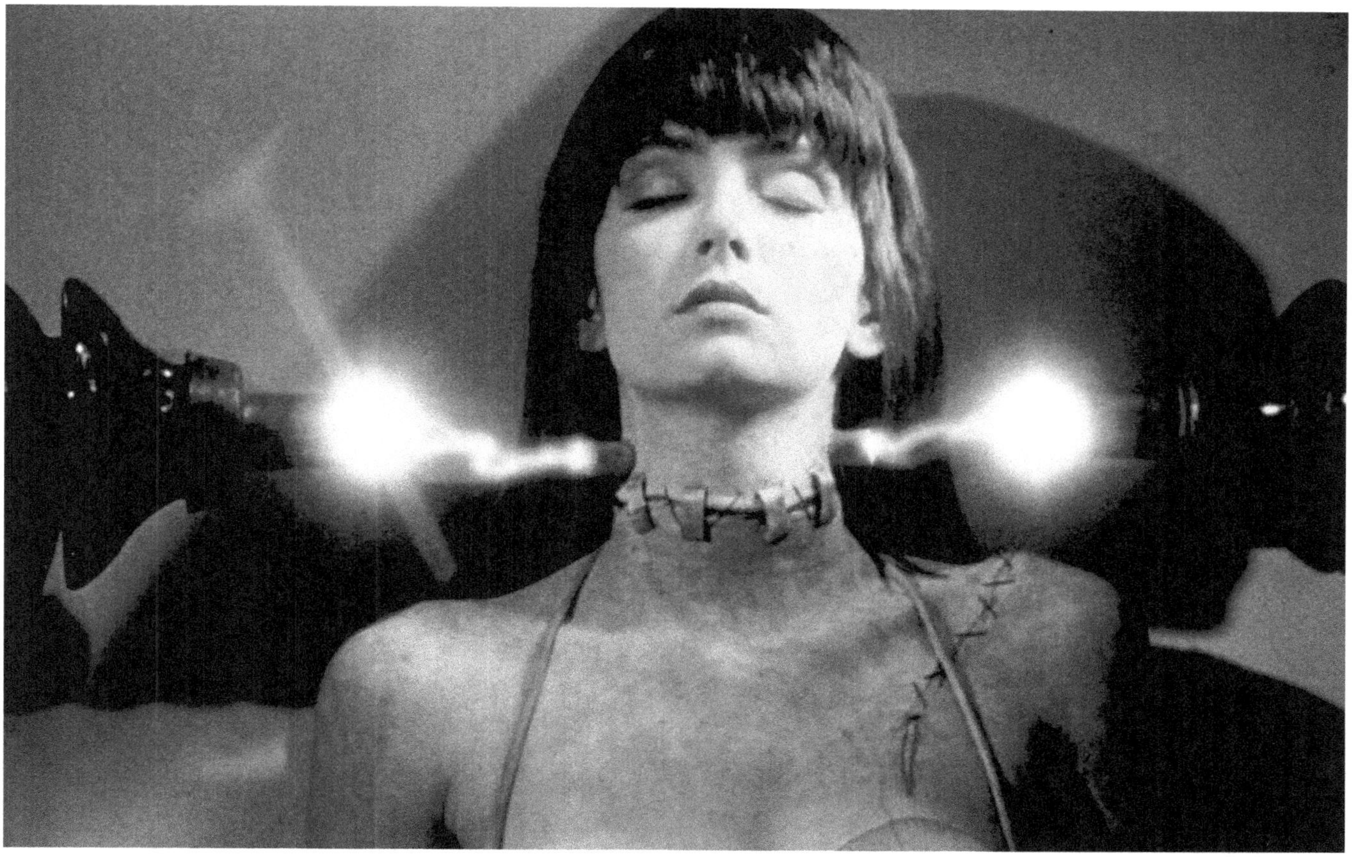

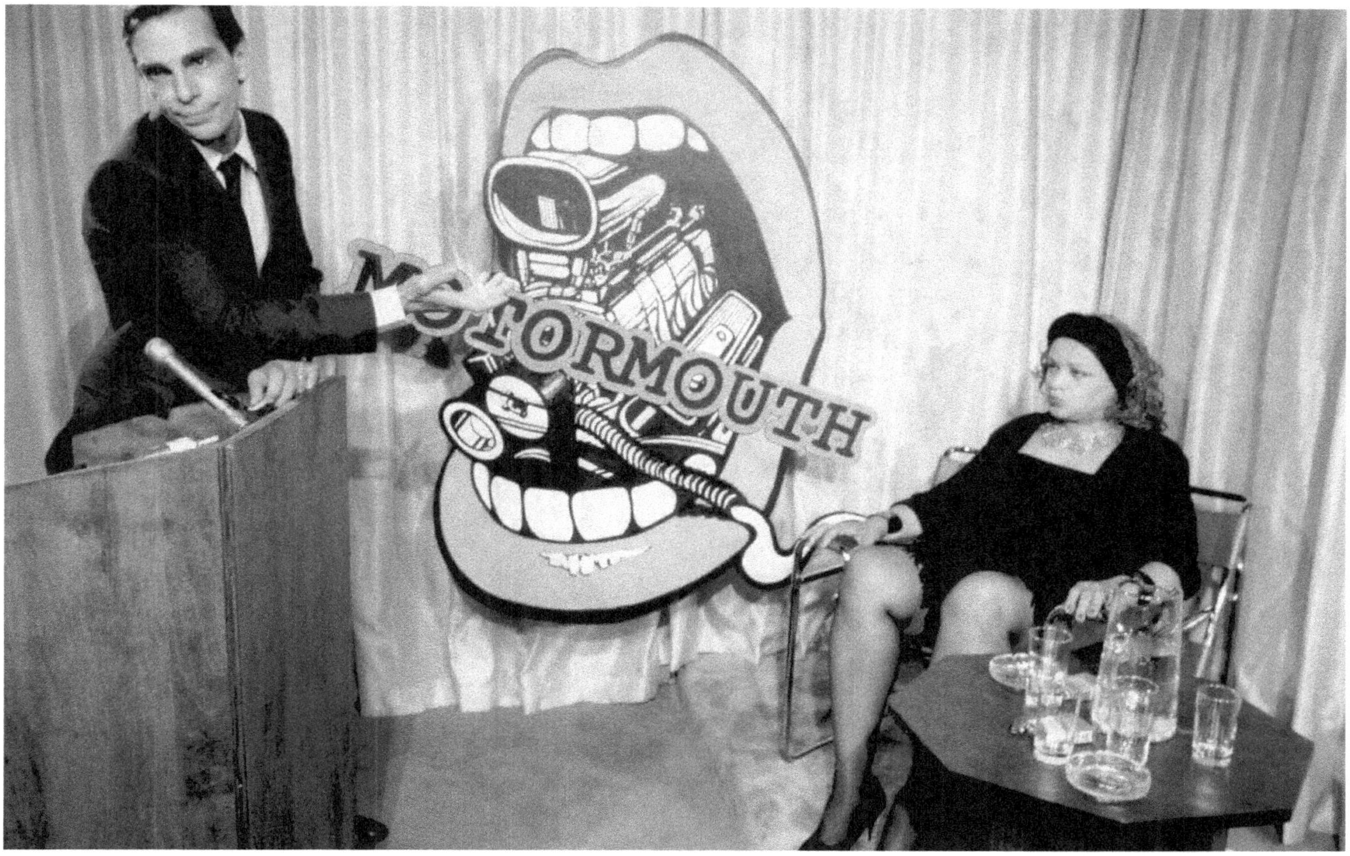

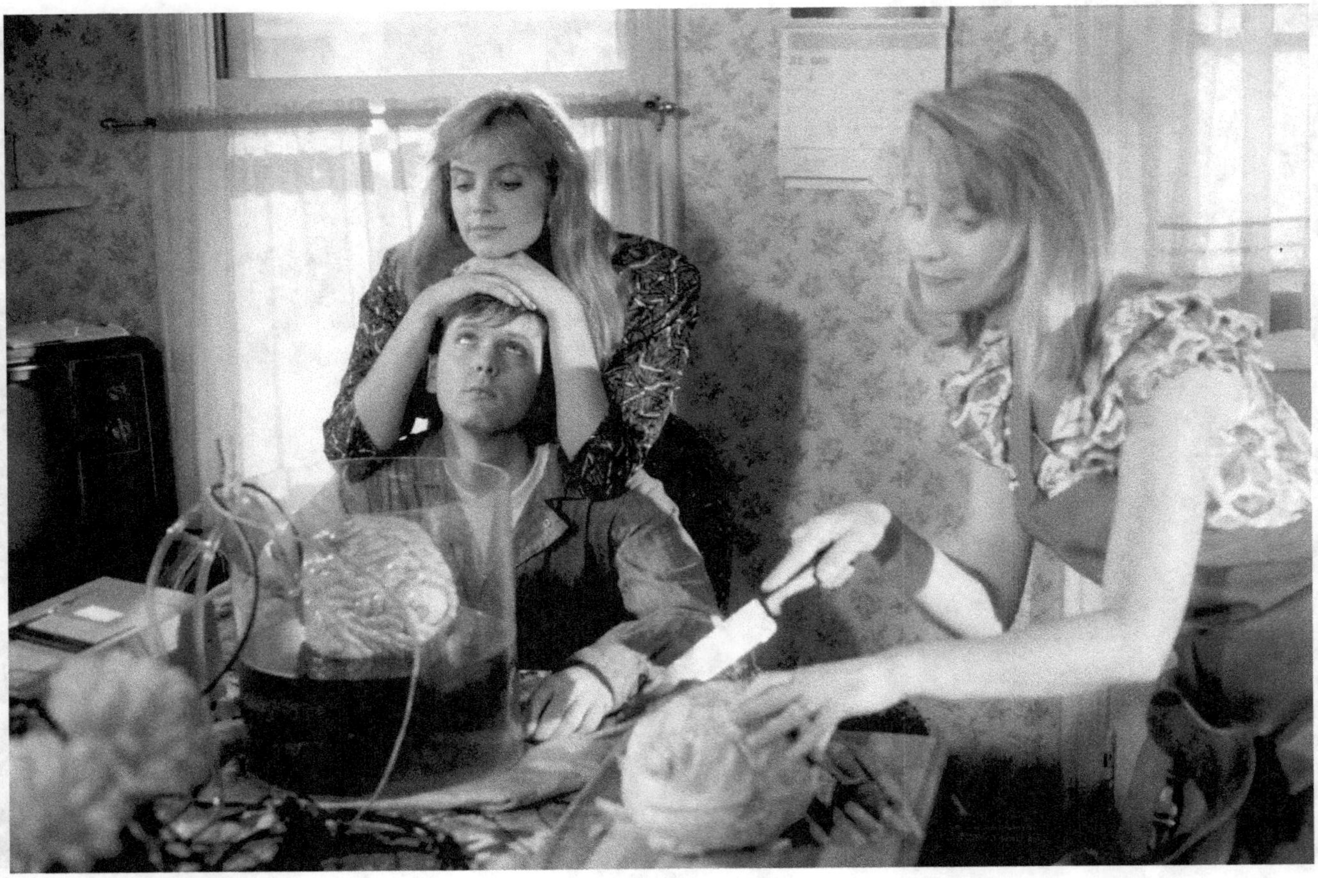

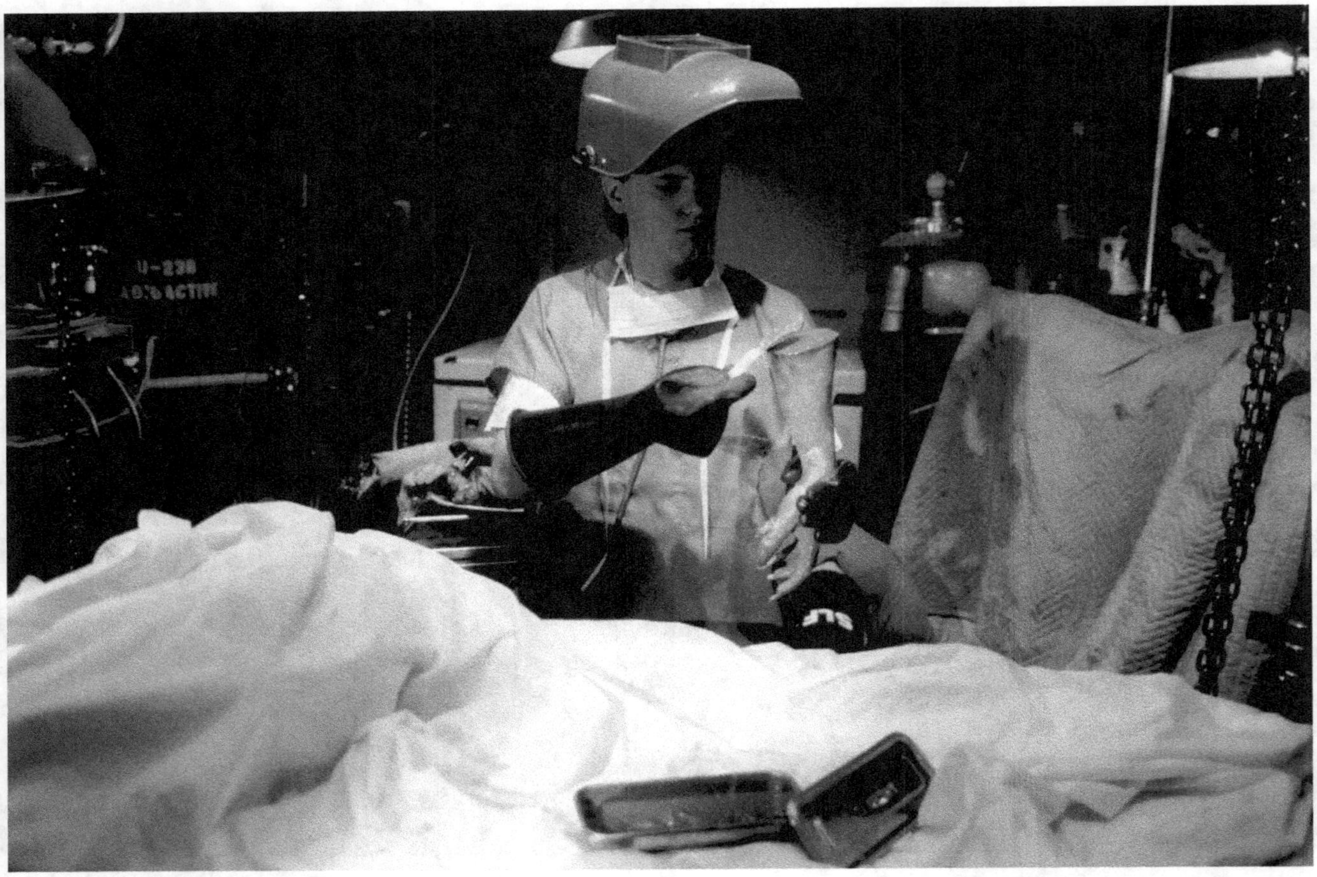

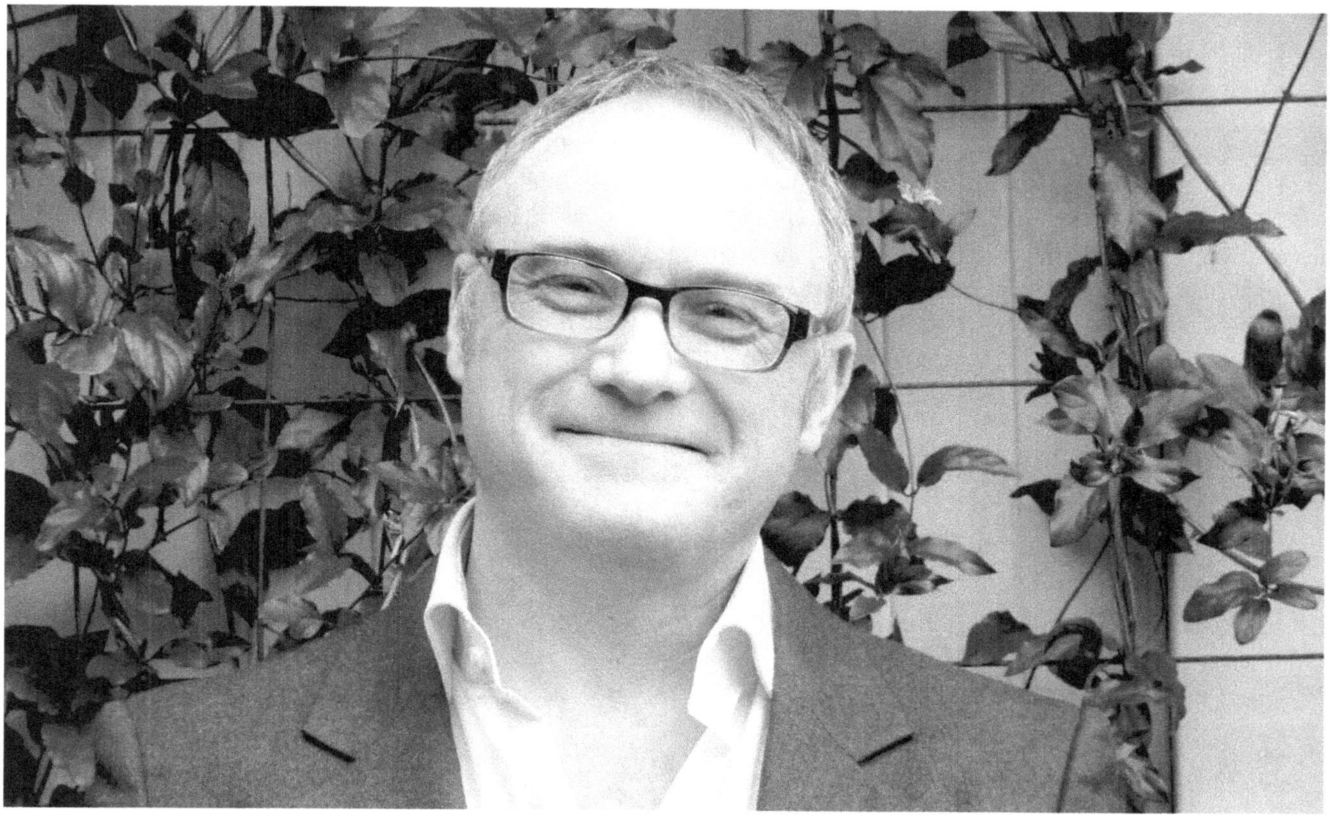

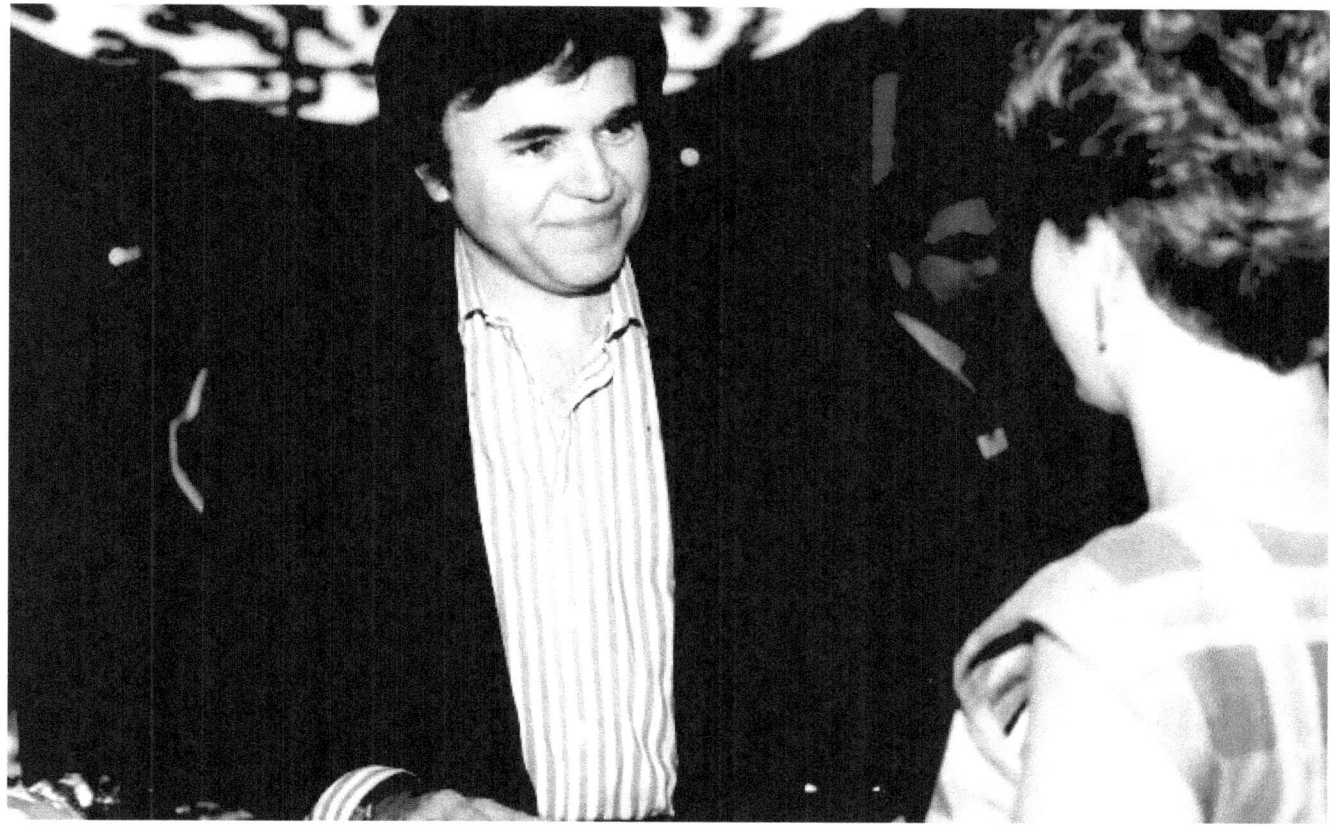

# Kevin Tent

Kevin Tent was trained as an editor while working for no less than Roger Corman, and then went on to SGE where he edited four pivitol movies produced by the company: MOONTRAP, BASKET CASE 2, FRANKENHOOKER and SLAUGHTER OF THE INNOCENTS. In a very rare interview, Kevin Tent goes into deep focus on nearly all phases of his successful career, from Corman and SGE to collaborations with James Mangold, Ted Demme, Jonathan Payne, Martin Scorsese, and other star directors. He is widely known as one of the most esteemed and talented editors in the business. He was nominated for an Academy Award for THE DESCENDANTS and won an ACE Eddie award for the same film. He received three other ACE Eddie Award nominations for ELECTION, SIDEWAYS and ABOUT SCHMIDT.

**Stephen:** Houston, I think we have recording. It is Wednesday, May 6, 2015, and I have on the line the beautiful and talented Mr. Kevin Tent, who has graciously agreed to an interview. Are you there Mr. Tent?

**Kevin:** I am here. Kevin Tent is here.

**Stephen:** Fantastic. So anyway let's just jump in, get it going here. First off, thank you for agreeing to do this Kevin it really means a lot. And I'm sure you'll have many brilliant things to say.

**Kevin:** Well I'm happy to do it. It's fun.

**Stephen:** Awesome. Okay, well, right I'll just go down the list of the questions here and we can improvise to the extent we wish to as we move along. It's not that kind of strict thing. So if a question takes us in a certain place and you decide you want to say something...feel free. So here you go. What's your background? How long has cinema/movies, how long have they been an important part of your life, assuming they have been, and I think they have been given your profession -- did you always want to make movies?

**Kevin:** Yeah, when I was about 16 or 17, I started the idea... some friends of mine were making little Super 8 short films, and they were soccer buddies, and we were riding home on the bus one night, and they were saying that they had shot a western with their brothers and sisters and I thought, "Wow, that's so cool!" and so I said, "Can I help you on your next one?" or...I forget how we got it together. But then we decided to start making these little Super 8 films, so I guess I was a junior in high school or something like that. So that's where I got the bug, way back then. And then I slowly kind of worked my way to Los Angeles and fell into basically editing. One of my first jobs out of film school, I went to LA City College, which was a 'free' school, and I made a couple of short films and then my first job straight out of film school was working for this guy that made educational films. And so I did a ton of those. They were all 16 millimeter, and they were really cheesy and really stilted and boring and kind of hilarious '50's-like educational films. And the guy who made those '50's-like educational films, he was elderly, and he continued to make them the same into the 80's and 90's, and that's where I got my start. And then fortunately also my short films that I had done at LACC wound up getting me my very first job recutting a movie for Roger Corman. And that really got me editing in a big way and that was really fun and exciting and I wound up doing a number of pictures down there. And I recut one, and, because I did such a good job on it I got to cut a feature on my own pretty quickly which was great and that was NOT OF THIS EARTH.

**Stephen**: Very good. You just plowed through the first three questions.

**Kevin**: That's so good.

**Stephen**: I love it. I love it. You've done your homework. Very good. All right. These don't necessarily go in chronological order so, as you'll notice probably, they jump around the timeline of you a little bit. Can you name your biggest filmmaker influences, especially among editors that you admire?

**Kevin**: Editing Gods? You mean Editing Gods that I have?

**Stephen**: Yes, your "Editing Gods" Kevin...

**Kevin**: My Editing Gods? Oh there's quite a few... There are a couple that are still with us today and working. Alan Heim is one of them, who did all of Bob Fosse's movies. And I think those movies are so amazingly edited and so fun and they really use editing as an element...a 'snazzy' element, in those films. And he's still around. And then Dede Allen was a huge Editing God to me; she was amazing. Just recently I watched DOG DAY AFTERNOON again, and I just think – the movie works on so many levels – great characters, great story, everything... but the editing is really good I think. And then there are many others, there are lots of others that I think are just amazing editors.

**Stephen**: You answered the second part of the question without me having to ask it. I love this! This is great.

**Kevin**: Efficiency that's what we're all about.

**Stephen**: Editing?

**Kevin**: Right exactly.

**Stephen**: Your very first credit, at least on IMDB and other databases, shows as EMMANUELLE 5 by legendary director Walerian Borowczyk. Since there are three different editors named, what's the story behind that?

**Kevin**: That was my very first job. That was a Roger Corman movie. It was one that Roger bought or co-financed, I don't know what the heck happened. And they needed someone to kind of just take it over and recut it and finish it. And they didn't really want to deal with it, and it was sort of pretty much incomprehensible and didn't really make any sense. It was really kind of a tough crazy, weird film. So basically they hired me, and it was again it was like a weird thing like I don't know...I guess it was because I was cheap or something they hired me to just kind of get it done. In any way possible. So I did a whole recut on it. And I found scenes rolled up in a box that had never been even looked at and fortunately those scenes were plot points in the story.

**Stephen:** You've got to be kidding me? Nobody had even looked at them?

**Kevin:** They had not even been run through a Movieola. They were all broken down. They were all on film so they were in little spools how we used to do it. And I had all the stuff. They had shipped all the stuff from France I think is where the original production was and I was just going through boxes and I found these boxes of scenes. And they were actually the plot points. So there were scenes that described what was happening, and then you understood what the next couple of scenes were about. And I was like "Wow! Check it out!!" So I cut those scenes, put it in the movie, and then did some other tightening and everything like that, and then we screened it for Roger. And it was a funny story; I'll just relate the story... Roger came in, and I told him the whole story about how when we got the movie: I cut it way down, I tightened it up, I got rid of all this stuff. And then I found these other scenes and put them in, and then I gave him the running time. Then I remember he goes like this, he stops and he goes, "Let me get this straight. It was 92 minutes when we bought it, you took out 12, and you added 6?" So basically we had an 86-minute movie, and we needed to get more time in it, because I had cut so much stuff out, even though I added scenes back. So I think he went back, and I went on to another movie, and then they figured out what they wanted to do, and they shot some new scenes. So another editor came on after me to edit the new scenes into the movie to give it some length.

**Stephen:** So that would account for the three names on the credits.

**Kevin:** Yeah, that's the three. So that's a very long story to get to why there were three editors. But that's what the story was.

**Stephen:** That leads right into the next question; can you describe the very first time you met Roger Corman?

**Kevin:** I can't remember the exact time I met him. It was at one of the meetings for one of the screenings. It might have been that screening for EMMANUELLE 5. He at that point was not as hands on as he had been previously with his other editors. That's what I've been told. Because he wasn't in the cutting room all the time like he used to be back a few years earlier before I started down there. He was being a little more broad-strokes kind of running his company. And he was very busy at that time. He was doing a movie a month, so he couldn't really get engaged in all the movies that were going on down there. So I think it was probably at one of those screenings, and so I would see him at the screenings. You would show him the movie, and then you would go back to his office, and he would tell you what he thought and give you ideas for things. And he'd perhaps say, "Lose a scene," or "I don't get why you have to have that..." and so he'd give you your notes and you would go make your cuts and then show it to him again in a few days and have him see it. He came down to the cutting room a couple of times, but for the most part when I was working down there he didn't

|||
|---|---|
| | really come to my cutting room too often. I think once or twice, that was it. |
| Stephen: | Did you work closely with Roger Corman when you were editing NOT OF THIS EARTH (1988) by Jim Wynorski? |
| Kevin: | Nope I did not work closely with him at all. Jim had a very good relationship with Roger, and Roger trusted Jim. That movie, Jim shot it in 10 days. We showed Roger a cut a few days after we were done shooting. Roger was really happy. He thought it needed to be punched up. We had an action scene that was pretty lame. And Roger thought it should be punched up, so he gave us an extra day or two days to shoot a car chase scene. So we added that. I think what we tried to do originally was use the car chase scene from the original version of NOT OF THIS EARTH and that wasn't really going to cut it. I think because it was in black and white. We were trying all sorts of things. And that movie was also short. So we wound up stealing a scene from another movie. Which was so hilarious. That was where I first got really used to stealing scenes from other movies and putting them into other Roger movies. And we did that quite often. And I became sort of the expert on that. We had a scene where a girl was creeping around the house thinking there were noises, she pulls out a knife, she's like walking through the kitchen, it's all scary...it's like a four-minute scene. And then at the very end she turns around and we just shot our girl turning around really fast and then we had our Alien Guy shoot her with his lightning eyes and kill her. So you didn't actually see it was a different girl right when she turned around. So all we shot was two shots and we stole a whole four-minute scene from another movie – it actually worked great. No one would ever know. |
| Stephen: | How many times did you work on Roger Corman films? |
| Kevin: | I worked on a lot. I don't have them all on my resume because there were so many. I don't know. I worked consistently there but then I would go back and work on things in between other jobs. |
| Stephen: | If you had to estimate a number how many would you say? |
| Kevin: | Probably about 7 or 10 feature films. |
| Stephen: | Would you call Roger Corman a mentor? |
| Kevin: | Absolutely. Yeah I would. His whole system was a really good place to be an editor. I think you learned a lot. Because you had to be ahead of him. He was ruthless. So if you really cared about what you were doing. If you really cared about a storyline or an actor or a performance or something like that, you better have it in very tight shape before he got to it. Because he had no patience for anything 'milking it' or anything that he didn't buy. He would just say "Cut it out." So if you wanted to keep a scene, if you were smart you would figure out a way to make it work for his eyes and make it work for the story. He would often just say, "Cut that scene out." And you'd be like, "Well, yeah but you can't do that because—" and he would be like, "Cut it out." So I got to the |

**point where I was going to try to have it where it didn't bother him. So you would cut it really tight, make it work and skate it by him. So yes, because of that, and a lot of editors took advantage of that, and you learned a lot. And it was a good place to learn. So yes I'd absolutely consider him a mentor.**

**Stephen:** Did you ever develop anything that you might describe as a personal relationship with him?

**Kevin:** Not really with Roger. He had a lot of people coming and going. There was a movie a month. But I felt I did, and I did talk to him a couple of years ago, which was very nice. He said he remembers me. I ran into him when he got his Academy Award, which was a great thing, and I was so happy he got it, and I got a chance to just talk to him and it was really sweet. He was like, "Oh Kevin I hear you are doing very well." Which I don't know if that really is true but that's what he said which was nice.

**Stephen:** Certainly nice to hear that from him huh?

**Kevin:** Yeah it was really great. But you know he had his own life going on and he was busy and running his company so... there were a lot of people there, it wasn't a small company. He probably had forty or fifty people on staff and then every movie he had a whole crew so you didn't really get a chance to know him. But I did a little bit. And I always got a kick out of him. Smart man.

**Stephen:** Are you in touch with anyone else from the days when you worked for Roger?

**Kevin:** Yeah. There are a few people that I still see once in a while and run into and I'm still friends with from my Roger Corman days. And some are Phedon Papamichael is this big huge DP these days and I wound up working with him on Alexander Payne's movies. And Janusz Kaminski sometimes, he was a DP down there then. Mike Elliot who is a producer. Jonathan Winfrey who is a director/producer. I see Jonathan all the time. Yeah, so we do keep in touch. There was a reunion a couple of years ago, which was a lot of fun. And that was really fun to see everybody who was down there when we were down there in the 80's.

**Stephen:** Did you have it down in the lumberyard where the company used to be?

**Kevin:** What's that?

**Stephen:** Remember the company used to right next to the lumberyard, or in the lumberyard?

**Kevin:** Yeah it was the lumberyard it was crazy.

**Stephen:** They don't still have the space right? I'm sure that's all gone right?

**Kevin:** No, there's all these really fancy lofts there now. Beautiful high-tech fancy looking lofts. I think that's been there for years. I think he sold that. He's still making movies though. Every once in a while someone will say, "Oh I cut a movie for Roger Corman." And I'm like, "Oh wow, that's fantastic."

**Stephen:** So after NOT OF THIS EARTH you worked on a film that was produced by Shapiro Glickenhaus Entertainment. How did that

Kevin: come about? And how do you remember the making of MOONTRAP?

Kevin: Well what happened was somewhere in that timeframe, I had known Kirk Ellis. I don't remember how it all happened. I think Kirk called up and said, "I need somebody to cut a trailer." I think it was for the AFM, or, I can't remember what it was exactly. But I said, "Sure!" I think I was still working at Roger's then. Yeah, of course I was.

Stephen: Actually I can give you a little inside information to help the story.

Kevin: Okay.

Stephen: Because I was the one... at the time I was cutting a fair number of the promos.

Kevin: Right. You were getting overwhelmed.

Stephen: And I just couldn't get it all done. And as much as I wanted to cut them and bill it. I also had my day job which was working for Alan and so on. And so I couldn't do it, and so I asked Kirk. Kirk and I went to USC together and knew one another, and I introduced Kirk to the company. And I said, "Do you know anyone who is good, fast and cheap?"

Kevin: Good, fast and cheap, that's me.

Stephen: That's right. Usually you only get to pick two of those things.

Kevin: But with me you got all three.

Stephen: At least then! And Kirk says, you know Kirk always had the answer, and he goes, "Sure, you know, there's this guy Kevin Tent he'll do it. I'll tell him to do it!"

Kevin: Oh that's funny.

Stephen: So anyway that's how he called you. So you pick it up from there.

Kevin: Yeah, I think maybe he saw NOT OF THIS EARTH. I think I invited him to a screening, and probably that was just perfect timing, and you had asked him for somebody, and I had done my first feature. So anyways, to make a long story short, I wound up cutting a couple of trailers for you guys. And then you guys were in production for MOONTRAP, and you needed a promo for AFM, and we cut one together. I think we used some Tangerine Dream music or something, I don't know, but it worked pretty great. I remember you, Steve, being really happy. And then I think it played very well at AFM, and then what happened was you guys had a cut of the movie, and you weren't completely happy with it. And I think you, Steve, because you were a Producer on it too, finagled me in to do an edit on it. So I wound up working on recutting it. Another one of my recuts that I did, which I've done a lot of and still do. It's something that I started doing at Roger's, and I did it with you guys on MOONTRAP. I think we wound up screening it for you guys, and then I think you screened it for Bob [Director/Producer Robert Dyke] and Mary [Post-Production Supervisor Mary Petryshyn]. And then we sort of all sat down and went into a room with different cuts and we came out with a sort of hybrid version of the final film. I mean they were pretty similar, if I remember correctly. Just some different performances, probably tighter, that kind of stuff. And that was my first substantial recut for you guys, for SGE. And then I wound up doing lots of promos.

**Stephen:** The SGE features BASKET CASE 2 & 3, since they were shot back-to-back, how come you only edited BASKET CASE 2 and not 3? Was there a separation between the postproduction of those films?

**Kevin:** Actually the question is not correct. FRANKENHOOKER and BASKET CASE 2 were shot back-to-back. BASKET CASE 3 was shot a few years later – I think a year later or two years later even. So I wound up cutting FRANKENHOOKER and then BASKET CASE 2. We shot FRANKENHOOKER first, and then they took two weeks off, had the same crew and everything, and went right into BASKET CASE 2. So I wound up cutting both those back-to-back, and that was a lot of fun.

**Stephen:** That absolutely answers the question. Hey why don't you tell that story about why, to this day, FRANKENHOOKER is still on your resume, and what happens when people see that?

**Kevin:** Yeah, I still have it on my resume and it's been there forever because, I'm proud of all the films I've worked on. So I keep FRANKENHOOKER on my resume for one specific reason. I get a big kick out of watching people see it on there. So what happens is, and what's happened in the past is, you go in for a meeting with the producer or the director, and you're sitting there, and they're looking at your credits and they go, "Oh you cut that oh, that's good, oh yeah you did a good job on that I saw that movie, oh yeah, yeah." And then their eyes go down to the bottom of the page and they see FRANKENHOOKER and they go, "Oh! You cut FRANKENHOOKER!" and I go, "Yeah, yeah, yeah." So many people saw that movie, and so many 'film' people saw that movie, and they always recognize it, and it's always kinda hilarious as I watch their expression as they see it. So that's why I keep it on there. And it's a good credit to have on there, you know? Some people might take it off, but not me, I'm proud of it.

**Stephen:** You're a trooper!

**Kevin:** I am! That's a good movie.

**Stephen:** Let me ask you about Frank Henenlotter, since he was the director of both BASKET CASE 2 and FRANKENHOOKER. When you think of Frank, what's the first thing that comes to your mind?

**Kevin:** He's a sweet guy and a little bit nervous. You know I haven't talked to him for years. But you know of course he would be nervous; he's directing a couple of big movies. He had only done a couple of really small independent movies, so this was a fairly good-sized budget this time for him. And I was, I guess you could say, forced upon him by SGE. Which, you know, that happens all the time. But I certainly enjoyed working on the movie with him, and I think we wound up having a good experience all in all by the end. You know it's always a little hard, I think he had wanted to edit it himself, and because of the schedule and because, of course, the studio doesn't want to necessarily hand over the reins to everything to a filmmaker that they don't really know that well at that time. But it was fun to work with him, and I think he's a real talent, and I think he's a very unique person and filmmaker.

**Stephen:** The last time you worked with SGE was on SLAUGHTER OF THE INNOCENTS which was written and directed by James Glickenhaus, is that correct?

**Kevin:** Yeah.

**Stephen:** Tell me a little bit about your working relationship with Jim Glickenhaus, and then after that just a little bit about your overall working relationship with SGE. You've already touched on that a little bit. What was it like working with Jim?

**Kevin:** It was great. I really liked it a lot. I totally loved it. He was a generous man, and his footage was all really good – it was all good solid stuff. It wasn't a difficult movie to cut. He's a very average guy. Very kind of casual and likeable. He was calm, which always is nice in the cutting room when there's not a lot of tension so you're feeling relaxed and you're doing good work. He was supportive, and we worked well together. It was a very very nice experience. Yeah, it was great. And I think we did a good job on the movie. You know we didn't have a lot of time, and we didn't have a lot of money and all that. It was a good experience and I think he was happy too.

**Stephen:** And how would you describe your overall working relationship with Shapiro Glickenhaus? You did do a lot of work there so—

**Kevin:** I did, I did. I mean if you count all the trailers and the promos and the recuts, and I did do a lot. You know it was a really fun place to work. It was a small company, all the people were young, well, not everyone was young... Alan and Lenny were a little older. You know you, and Kirk and all the Shapiro Glickenhaus girls—they were all adorable, it was a fun place, a fun experience. And it was moving quickly; you guys were doing a lot of stuff, so it was definitely a fun experience. And then to go work with Jim in New York, because you guys had the West Coast offices, and that was cool. Jim was in the Brill Building, and I had never been in the Brill Building before so working with him there was great.

**Stephen:** And you're an East Coast native right?

**Kevin:** I am yeah. And really because of Shapiro Glickenhaus, I really became sort of a bi-coastal editor because I work back there often. And I think a lot of it has to do with me establishing roots there as an editor back in day.

**Stephen:** Have you worked in New York City recently?

**Kevin:** I was there working for, uh... I told you that? Didn't I tell you that for the Scorsese thing?

**Stephen:** Can you talk a little bit about that?

**Kevin:** Yeah, it's that commercial. It's a short film and a series of commercials for casinos that are being built in Asia. So I wound up doing that for Marty. I wound up doing a couple of things... I thought I told you about that. I'm sure I did.

**Stephen:** Well you did but not in an interview.

**Kevin:** Ok, now I get it. Sorry, I forgot I was being interviewed for a second.

**Stephen:** Oh no! *(joking)* The man behind the curtain was not hidden for a moment!

**Kevin:** Yeah, they're a series of commercials. And the way Marty likes to do it is, he likes to shoot a short film and treat it like a little movie. So that's how we cut it. Then we kind of figure out how to cut a commercial out of it when we're done with the short film.

**Stephen:** So basically you get to cut your own trailer, is that a fair assessment of that...

**Kevin:** Yeah kinda. One of the things was to actually cut a trailer for it, which is pretty hilarious. And that leaked out on the internet for like two days, and then they pulled it. Somebody leaked it. But the short film will screen at opening of the Macao Casino in December of this year, I think, 2015.

**Stephen:** Was this the first time you ever worked with Martin Scorsese?

**Kevin:** No I worked with him the year before for a commercial campaign for Dolce & Gabana. And that was the first time I ever worked for him. And that was a lot of fun too. Again he made like a short film; it was like a four-minute short film, or three, I can't remember. And then we wound up having to cut like, oh I don't know, so many different commercials, versions of it for various markets, and various timeframes. One leaning towards women, one leaning towards men, you know. It was kind of crazy. But it was fun, and it was a great thrill to work with him. I only bring that up, and I only mention that because, really, working for Shapiro Glickenhaus in those early years sort of established me. There are so many people I know still from that time that are in New York, and I run into again while working there, so it's kind of been great to be part of the community there.

**Stephen:** When you were working either on one of Jim's films or one of the Henenlotter films wasn't your cutting room very nearby something that Martin Scorsese was cutting at the time?

**Kevin:** They were cutting GOODFELLAS. We were cutting FRANKENHOOKER and BASKET CASE 2 on the third floor of The Brill Building, and that's where Jim's office was; which is this amazing building. Marty was just down the hall, like right around the corner from Jim's office cutting GOODFELLAS. We would see him almost every day. He would be there cutting away. And also a movie called SHOCK TO THE SYSTEM was on our floor. And then SHE DEVIL and SILENCE OF THE LAMBS moved onto our floor. That was the same editor and the same cutting crew and they started cutting SILENCE OF THE LAMBS there. We were wrapping up then. But it was a star-studded floor. These great heavyweight films, and then FRANKENHOOKER.

**Stephen:** That's a cool story Kevin.

**Kevin:** Yeah, it was weird and funny.

**Stephen:** All right, let's get back on the script here okay? The first phase of your career is full of exploitation films with differing production values. Now you're working on huge studio movies, projects, how important was it for your development as an editor to learn about filmmaking on independent productions?

**Kevin:** I can't speak for other people, but I can just speak for myself, but I think it was enormously helpful, because I think you had to improvise a lot; you had to work fast, you had to gain confidence in your decision-making and move quickly. On independent films you don't have a lot of time; there's a lot of pressure. But for me, it was enormously beneficial. And I imagine it would be for other people too, but I can't really speak for them. But for me personally, it was a great way to learn and fine-tune my craft.

**Stephen:** Would it be fair to stay that perhaps that was your film school?

**Kevin:** Yeah absolutely. You know people often talk, if you want to go back to Roger Corman, people often say that that was like a film school there. And I would have to agree although, maybe not really a film school, but, if you were a person open to learning from the experience, which I was...I gained a lot from that. And it was fun, you know, I was also enjoying myself—

**Stephen:** And they paid you something right?

**Kevin:** They did. They didn't pay you a lot but, if you didn't have a lot of overhead, which I didn't, you were able to survive. So it wasn't so bad. I'm glad I don't work there anymore and make that much money anymore, but for that time in my life it was actually a very good place to learn, and I could absolutely say it was my film school.

**Stephen:** Let's talk a little bit about editing theory and practice, especially in kinematic moments, all the tempo and rhythm of an action scene depends on inventive editing, would you agree with that statement?

**Kevin:** Yeah. I would agree.

**Stephen:** So in this connection do you ever go on location to get the 'mood' of the film or do you strictly work with what you see on the editing table?

**Kevin:** I don't think it's necessary for an editor to be on the location to get the feeling of a film. I mean it's nice to go on location, but really you're dealing with the footage itself, and that's the important thing.

**Stephen:** Were you ever on any of the locations on any of the Glickenhaus movies?

**Kevin:** We went to Utah for Jim's movie [SLAUGHTER OF THE INNOCENTS] so while we were shooting in Salt Lake City, and they were shooting in Moab. We didn't go to Moab. They went for like two or three weeks down to Moab to shoot down there, and that was too far. You know we were on film then, too, so we had an entire editing room full of equipment:

KEMs and boxes of film and everything like that. So we didn't go to Moab. It might have been less, you could ask Jim; I think it was a couple of weeks they were in Moab, which is about 4 hours from Salt Lake. But we did spend the whole shoot in Salt Lake while we were shooting, and that was good we were there. We had dailies. Jim would come into the cutting room on the weekends, and I would show him the cuts. And then we packed up everything, and we moved to New York and finished the film in New York.

**Stephen:** Do you ever go to the set? I don't mean a distant location necessarily, but for any of the Shapiro Glickenhaus movies did you ever go on any of the sets?

**Kevin:** I went to the sets for FRANKENHOOKER and maybe BASKET CASE 2, or maybe just FRANKENHOOKER. But not a lot. Usually what happens is you can go to the set but you wind up standing around a lot. I think I went to set maybe once with Jim's movie, once or twice. But you have so much work to do that, at least for me, when I'm visiting the set I love saying hello to everybody and meeting all the players and meeting the cast and everything like that. I love that, that's fun. But after you're there, for an hour or so, at least me, you're like, "Oh my God I have so much work to do. I better get back to the cutting room and get going." You know it's a big job. You have a lot you have to keep up with. The camera notes and logs. You're supposed to have to cuts done by the end when they're done shooting. So it's a lot of work. So yes, I go to the set to visit, but I don't spend a lot of time there. Unless they call me. Sometimes they'll call me and want me on the set to look at stuff. And then fine, I'm glad to do that, but usually while I'm there I'm just thinking, "Oh my God there's just footage piling up back at the cutting room. I gotta get back there."

**Stephen:** How much of your personal fingerprints would you say are on the films that you work on? Does it vary according to the circumstances and the personalities of a specific project?

**Kevin:** Yeah, I would say it varies depending on the personalities. I think you like to think that you have absolutely have some influence on what's going on, with what the finished cut will be. But some directors are more collaborative than others. But I don't know even if you have a director who says that they're not collaborative, they are still [collaborative] to a certain extent I would imagine.

**Stephen:** Do you feel comfortable naming perhaps the most collaborative director you have worked with?

**Kevin:** Yeah, there are a bunch. Alexander Payne is very collaborative. Very respectful and very... treats editing as a real craft and understands it very well. Jim Mangold, I worked with him, he also is very collaborative. Barry Sonnenfeld, I've worked with him a bunch. And he too, Barry's pretty funny because Barry pretends he doesn't like to be in the cutting room, [and] I think he actually doesn't, but, I always made him come and sit there. And he would be annoyed, but I think he was happy because he actually was helping make decisions that make the cut better. I've always said that I find it's better to have the director there to make decisions together so that they don't later go, "Why'd you do that?" So at least they understand why we did something. We can always change it if it's not working for them anymore. But at least they'll know why something's done. So I prefer to have them there.

**Stephen**: Okay, we're going to go back to the beginning of your career now. You were twice credited as a director in the beginning of your career. What's the connection between BLACK BELT II from 1989 and THE SPYDER in 1988? Did you get to meet the original director, Joe Maria Avellana?

**Kevin**: Okay, so this goes back to Roger Corman. So what wound up happening is that Roger was not only making twelve films a year down in Venice, California, he was making four or five or six films in Peru or elsewhere around the world; he was making other movies. And so some of these came back, and they were in such bad shape that they really couldn't do anything with them. They were actually sort of dead in the water. Because I knew the film library really well because I'd done a movie called BACK TO HOLLYWOOD BOULEVARD where we stole scenes, we stole footage for all these other different movies. I knew Roger's library better than anybody. They would come to me and they'd say, "What can we do with this movie? We don't -- it's terrible! Can you recut it and figure out some stuff?" And I'd go, "Sure!" So I would recut the movies and sometimes I would add space wars from other movies and then figure out how to work it into the story.

One of the meetings, I think it was for ULTRA WARRIOR, this was hilarious — because I knew the library of Roger Corman movies so well, I found actors that were in other Peru movies, who were in the same movie that I was recutting, which was ULTRA WARRIOR. And so I took their footage and reused it in our movie and just made up bogus storylines to use it. But it wound up kind of working. At least I remember it kind of working. We have to see if, you know we weren't totally smoking crack! And it doesn't work at all...! So that is why I got those directing credits. They're not really technically directing credits, I don't think, but that's how they came about.

**Stephen**: So those three movies were all sort of back-to-back films then: SPYDER, BLACKBELT II and ULTRA WARRIOR, and because they were all shot in the same location and same country anyway and used a lot of the same actors, you were able to interchange the footage and cross-pollinate storylines.

**Kevin**: Yeah. That's kinda what I did. I didn't even know I had credit [on three], I thought there were just two of them. But I guess maybe there's three. I don't know. Yeah, that's how they came about.

**Stephen**: Maybe Roger still owes you a paycheck on a movie or two huh?

**Kevin**: Yeah. Maybe. It was just really fun to recut those too, they were in very rough shape. So it was a 'win-win' for me because they were only going to get better. I remember the one meeting I went into I go, sort of as a joke, but sort of serious I said, "You know what this movie needs?" And they were like, "What?!" And I go, "It needs a space war." And they're like, "Yes! A space war!! That's a great idea!!!"

**Stephen:** Oh God.

**Kevin:** So we added a space war. Started the movie with a big, huge space war.

**Stephen:** Incredible.

**Kevin:** Which works because it was a post-apocalyptic movie anyways. So it works perfectly. Started with a space war.

**Stephen:** Hilarious.

**Kevin:** Yeah it was very funny.

**Stephen:** Ok a general question, what do you think about martial arts, and fight scenes just in general in films? Do you find that there's any special challenges in editing sequences of that sort?

**Kevin:** Well it's been a while since I worked on martial arts films. I did a bunch for you guys. And I enjoyed doing them, and those were fun ones to do. I mean there's tricks of the trade that you use to make your fight scenes a little stronger, and of course sound is huge – a big player in it and music and everything like that. You know people that are really skilled at that... I wouldn't say I'm like super-skilled at cutting fight scenes, because I haven't done a lot of them lately. But it's definitely a talent, you know. And I think that people that do big action sequences, they become very good at cutting those. It's interesting.

**Stephen:** You've already answered this other question about whether you were on location in Peru for ULTRA WARRIOR you were not, is that correct?

**Kevin:** No, no they didn't give me that movie until months after it was done. I think they couldn't sell it; they couldn't do anything with it so they were like desperate for somebody to do something with it.

**Stephen:** Have you ever edited on location in a foreign country?

**Kevin:** Yes. I worked on a movie called THE GOLDEN COMPASS, and we shot a new ending to the movie, and we had to go to Bulgaria. And I cut on the set, and then cut on the plane coming back because we had a big hard release date. And we had to shoot the scene and get it cut into the movie, and we were mixing, and everything was happening all at once. And so I did, I cut in Bulgaria for like a weekend where we shot. I think we shot one day. And Canada, if you count that. That doesn't really count probably.

**Stephen:** Another general question about some of your earlier work, how do you feel about the movies, SPYDER, BLACKBELT II and ULTRA WARRIOR nowadays? When you look back at those films, what is the first thing that you think about?

**Kevin:** I think about laughing because I was making stuff up and finding actors in

|          | other movies and going: "How hilarious that this guy's in a submarine movie that now I'm going to use this same actor in this movie, and he's going to have a flashback?!" So I think it makes me laugh in a lot of ways. But I haven't seen those movies in so long. I mean we're talking twenty years ago, or maybe even longer, I don't know, a long time ago. I don't even think; I don't even know if you can find them. I don't know. |
|----------|---|
| Stephen: | Believe me if they can be found, Marco Siedelmann will find them. |
| Kevin:   | Ok. If he can find them, I would love to see them. Maybe they weren't as funny as I thought they were. They're probably terrible. But it was fun to do them. |
| Stephen: | Do you have a personal connection to science fiction, action or horror those genres at all? |
| Kevin:   | No. I love watching science fiction movies, I love science fiction. But like horror movies, I love a good scary movie, but it's not like I seek them out or anything like that. If you're talking about me editing them... I like them, but, I don't like really violent things too much. I mean fight scenes are fine and that kind of stuff. But gratuitous killing of people and stuff like that, it's hard for me a little bit so I don't really like to do that as much. |
| Stephen: | Let's shift gears for a second into some of your contemporary work, films like NEBRASKA, ABOUT SCHMIDT and SHANGHAI. They're more laconic and slow and steady, and steady in their editing pace. So what would you say that the main difference is between your work on films like that and just wild crazy exploitation pictures? |
| Kevin:   | If you look at Alexander Payne's films let's say, his are sort of more character developed, character driven -- they're funny but they're dramas. I've done a lot more of those. But I've also done comedies, but yeah I probably haven't done too many actiony things lately. I'm trying to think; I don't think I have. Or even a horror film in a long time. Yeah, it's a different style, and Alexander has grown as a filmmaker if you look at his earlier films. If you look at ELECTION, that movie is really well cut and fast and funny and wacky and all that stuff, but I think he's sort of grown as a filmmaker and become more sophisticated. We definitely, when we were working out ABOUT SCHMIDT, we said we want to cut less. And we've been doing that ever since. Less cutting but getting the same feel and getting all the same emotion at the same time without cutting as much is what we strive for. That's what we've been doing with his movies. |
| Stephen: | Would you say generally speaking that you will have more footage to work with when you cut a more laconic, slower moving drama than you would with an action film or vice versa? |
| Kevin:   | You mean like in your dailies, what would you have more of? |
| Stephen: | Yeah, like actually more material to go through and catalogue and consider. I know you said that you haven't done an action film in recent years, but, do you |

**Kevin:** have more dailies to deal with in a dramatic slower moving film then you would in a film with a lot of action in it?

**Kevin:** That's a good question. I don't know it's probably maybe about the same. But if it's a <u>big</u> action movie, they're going to have bazillions of footage. But you know some dramas have lots and lots of footage too, or comedies. I recently worked on a Nancy Meyers film, and she shoots a lot. She just keeps trying stuff, tries different takes. Tries this, tries that...

**Stephen:** Can you mention the name of the name of the Nancy Meyers film?

**Kevin:** Yeah it's called THE INTERN, it's coming out in September I believe. It's really adorable it's going to be a huge hit, I'm sure. And I was an extra hand, because they had so much footage to get through. So they needed help just wrestling the thing to the ground, so that's what I was there for. A really fun film.

**Stephen:** Well let's shift gears for a second out of movies into TV. You've worked on a number of high-class television programs, pilot episodes of NOTES FROM THE UNDERBELLY and HUNG for two examples.

**Kevin:** Yeah.

**Stephen:** Was this a personal choice at the time to edit TV versus films, and did you enjoy the process of working on a TV series?

**Kevin:** Yeah. I really did just the pilots, and I don't have anything against working on TV, you know, a lot of high end TV seems pretty good. It's just that I wind up working on, my niche that I've sort of fallen into, has been features so that's what I primarily do.

**Stephen:** What would you say the difference in the process of editing is between a TV series and a feature film? I know you just cut pilots as you say, have you ever cut series television, Kevin?

**Kevin:** I have not. And I know that's completely different. When you're doing a pilot, the pilot is treated a lot like a movie. So the director is still making a lot of the calls. At least in the instances that I was working. So it wasn't really like a TV series, where the show runners have come in yet, because these were pilots. They didn't know if they were going to get picked up or not. So it was really the director's decision; so you work for the director.

**Stephen:** So then is it fair to say in your experience working on pilots that it's very similar to a motion picture?

**Kevin:** Yeah, it was the director's call. And I did both with established directors, so the directors were the ones that were in charge basically of the whole thing. We definitely had to answer to the studios and networks and stuff, but it wasn't like there were show runners in the editing room; it was still the director.

**Stephen:** Got it.

**Kevin:** You know we did have show runners come in, but it's like the big decisions were still being guided by the director and his vision.

**Stephen:** Your work has been recognized with the prestigious Eddie Award, and you were nominated for an Academy Award® as well.

**Kevin:** Yeah.

**Stephen:** Also in 2014 you joined the Board of Directors of the American Cinema Editors, ACE. Can you tell us something about the value and meaning of this society of film editors, and then also can you talk a little bit about the experience of winning your Eddie and then being nominated for an Oscar®, what's all that like?

**Kevin:** It was really thrilling, and a little nerve-wracking. Nerve-wracking only in the sense that I was petrified about getting up in front of people and speaking. But besides that, it was a lot of fun. It's really an honor, what they say is true. It's really an honor to be nominated by your peers – they think that you did something of value. It's really flattering and moving, and it's great. I was thrilled – I couldn't believe it. It was fantastic. And it was also an honor to be nominated and then elected to the Board of ACE. It's a great organization. And really our goal is so simply stated: we just want to promote editing and promote the craft and promote who the editors are and make sure that they get the recognition for the hard work they do and the creative input they have on films and television. That's our stated goal, and I think it's great, and we really try hard to do it. In fact, some people work really hard to do it and it's great to be in their aura when they are working so hard to help do that. I wish I could do more, but I get so busy working; but I try, I try. Also we have a lot of educational programs. We try to promote young editors. We have an internship program. We do a lot. We try to do a lot. Considering it is all volunteer, and people are working. Film editors work long hours, and it's a hard job sometimes. But still these people on the Board and in all of ACE are always volunteering, and that's a beautiful thing.

**Stephen:** If you look back all those years ago, twenty-five years or whatever it is – crazy figure, maybe it's thirty years almost -- at the time that you spent at Shapiro Glickenhaus, if you had to pick one or two things, about that time - you look back on it and you think about how it affected who you are as an editing professional today, as someone who creates films, what would you say that one thing is?

**Kevin:** That's a hard question. I mean, I gained so much. First of all, you guys entrusted me with cutting your films, and that was an enormous boost to my confidence to do that. And when Jim asked me to do his movie; that was a very big movie for me. And that was enormously flattering and also just nice to know that he believed I could do it. I think that was a big thing. He trusted me when, you know all these movies, you know we didn't even talk about TC 2000 and those movies up in Toronto, but, he trusted me and that was really an honor and a flattering thing that he felt I was ready to cut his movie. For me, at that time, that was a very big movie. I can't remember what the budget was, but it was big. I have very fond memories of the whole time that I was working with you guys and working at

SGE. Lenny was great, a total sweetheart. It was a great time for those genres of movies too, and the movies you guys were making the markets were exploding. There was VHS and DVDs coming out. It was really an exciting time.

**Stephen:** Absolutely. I happen to agree with everything you just said.

**Kevin:** Yeah it was a lot of fun. You know I sometimes feel bad for young editors now or young filmmakers now, because, well, I guess it's kind of the same in some ways but it doesn't seem like it is as freewheeling as it was then.

**Stephen:** Yeah. It was the Wild West.

**Kevin:** It seemed that way!

---

By Stephen A. Roberts, via telephone
from Los Angeles
06May, 2015

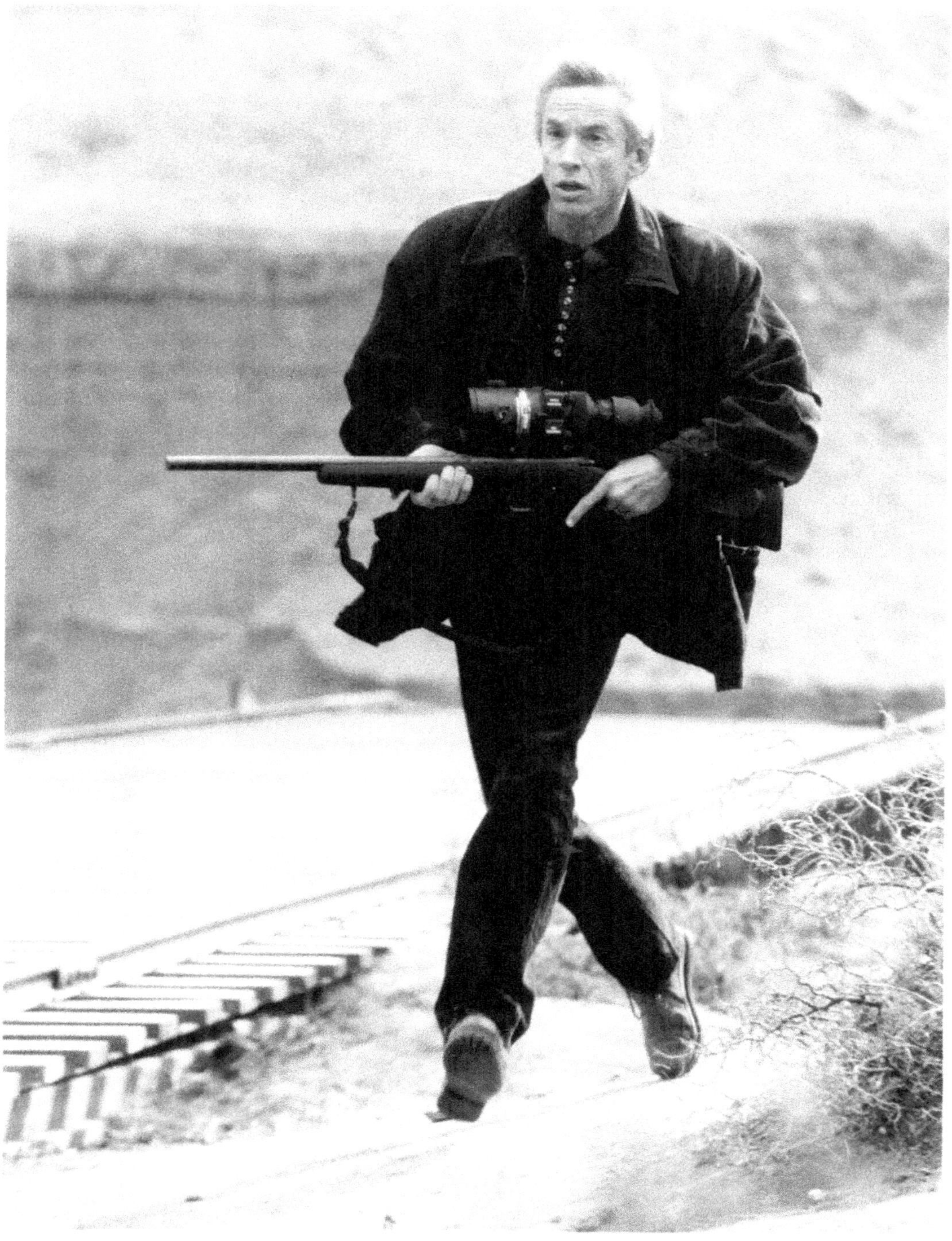

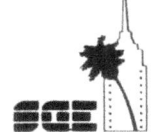

Copyright © 1993 SGE Entertainment Corporation
All rights reserved.
Permission is hereby granted to newspapers and other periodicals to reproduce this photograph for publicity or advertising except for the endorsement of products. This must not be sold, leased or given away.
Printed in U.S.A.

**SLAUGHTER OF THE INNOCENTS**

SOTI-1 SCOTT GLENN stars as FBI Special Agent Stephen Broderick in "SLAUGHTER OF THE INNOCENTS," a suspense thriller produced by Frank K. Isaac and written and directed by James Glickenhaus.

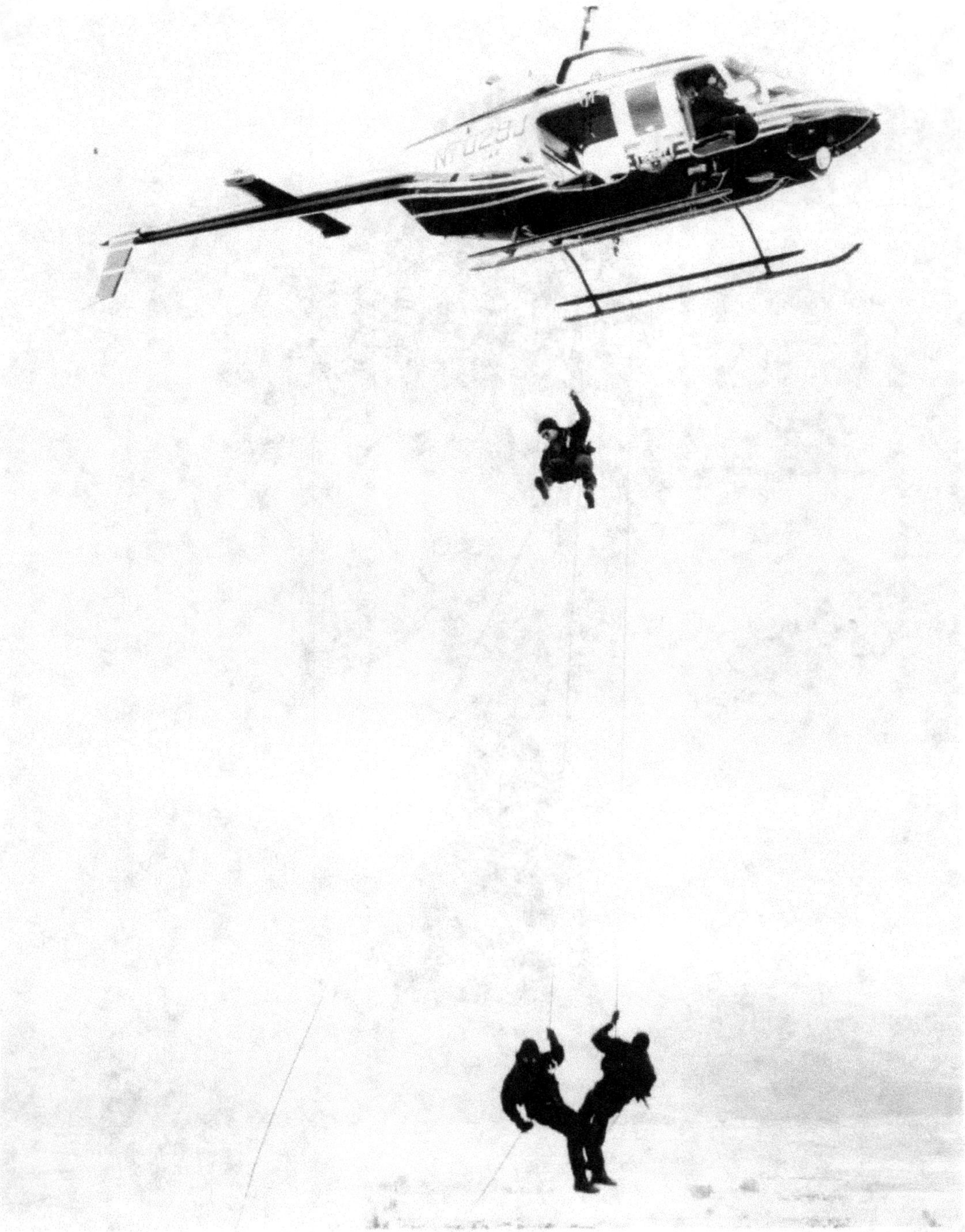

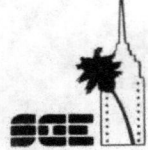

SLAUGHTER OF THE INNOCENTS

SOTI-5 Dramatic action scene from "SLAUGHTER OF THE INNOCENTS," a suspense thriller produced by Frank K. Isaac and written and directed by James Glickenhaus.

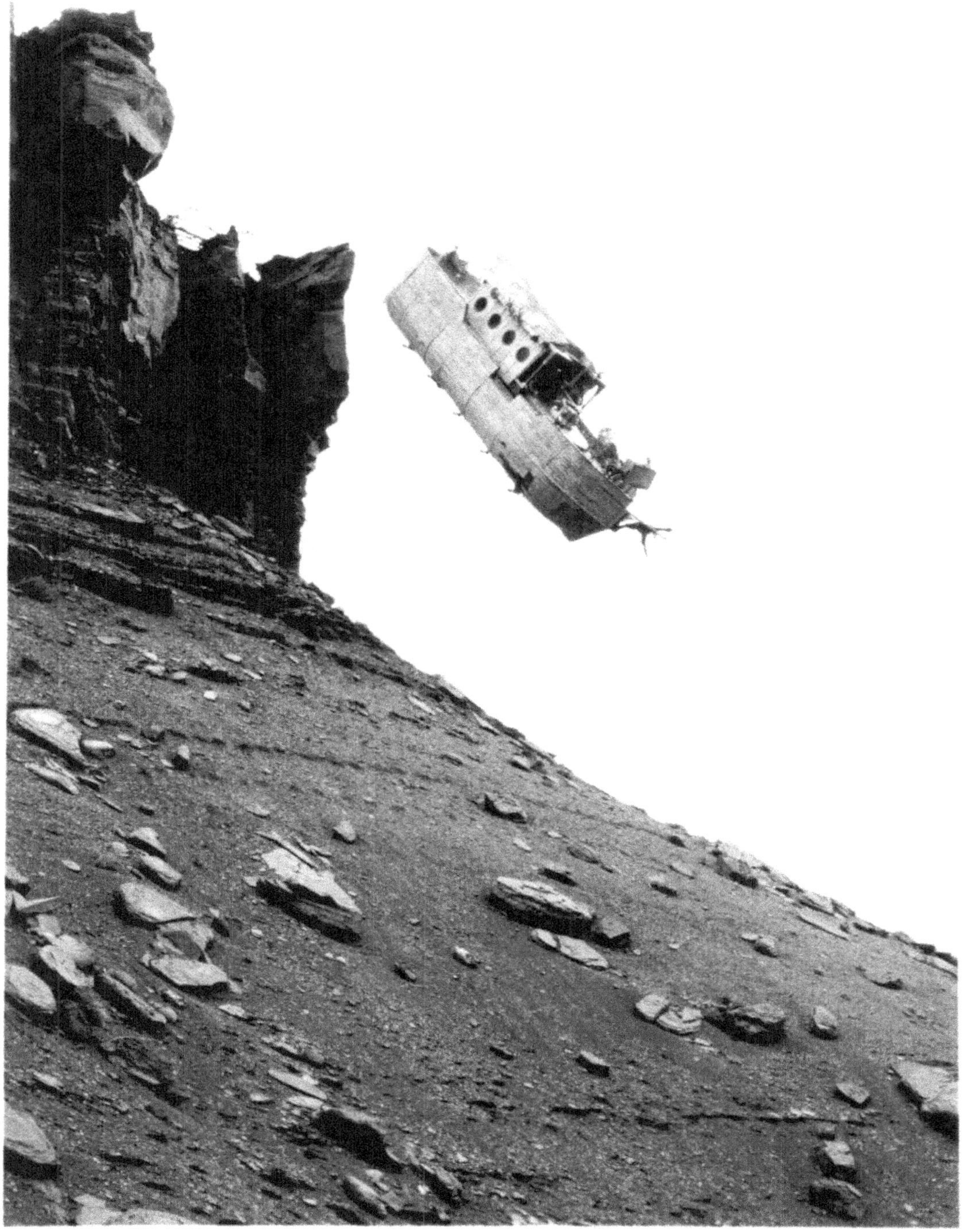

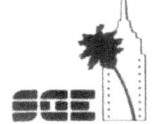

**SLAUGHTER OF THE INNOCENTS**

Copyright © 1993 SGE Entertainment Corporation
All rights reserved.
Permission is hereby granted to newspapers and other periodicals to reproduce this photograph for publicity or advertising except for the endorsement of products. This must not be sold, leased or given away.
Printed in U.S.A.

SOTI-4  Dramatic action scene from "SLAUGHTER OF THE INNOCENTS," a suspense thriller produced by Frank K. Isaac and written and directed by James Glickenhaus.

# Jefferson Richard

Jefferson Richard started a career as a blues musician in the early 60s before earning his degree at the Cambridge School Of Broadcasting and graduating from the American Academy Of Dramatic Arts in New York. At that time Jefferson got into directing stage plays, touring the whole country. Later, working side-by-side with veteran director Matt Cimber, Jefferson Richard became a well-known name in the business. In 1982, Cimber and Richard even got to work with Hollywood Legend Orson Welles, who made one of his very last screen performances in the crime thriller BUTTERFLY. Arriving at SGE in the mid-80s, Richard was responsible for some of the key pictures produced by the company, among them MANIAC COP, ONE MAN FORCE, SLAUGHTER OF THE INNOCENTS, RING OF STEEL & the very last SGE Picture, TIMEMASTER. In the 2000s, he produced films like GET CARTER, DRIVEN and CRIME IS KING, also a handful of direct-to-dvd horror sequels such as URBAN LEGENDS: BLOODY MARY.

**Marco:** Mr. Richard, you are recognized as a true pioneer of the independent film movement. What about your origins, how did you get into the film business? Was this always your plan or did it happen randomly?

**Jefferson:** I always wanted to be in film. My Grandfather won a wind-up 8mm Kodak camera when I was 16, and I started making music videos (about 18 years before MTV existed). I started out in broadcasting, music, and theater. But movies were my goal. Matt Cimber gave me my first big break becoming his assistant director and production manager. I ended up producing over a dozen films with him.

**Marco:** Which films or filmmakers would you name as an influence? Any favorites? Do you still go often to the movies and what kind of film do you prefer nowadays?

**Jefferson:** I would have to cite Orson Welles and Peter Bogdanovich as my biggest influences. I had the great fortune to work with Orson on BUTTERFLY and Peter on TEXASVILLE. I watch movies everyday in my home theater and try to see at least one film a month at the cinema. Oddly enough, the only type of films I don't like to watch are horror flicks. I love big action pictures and small foreign films. My personal taste is extremely eclectic.

**Marco:** The chance of becoming a midnight movie or video store cult favorite may be the reason for many independent filmmakers start the career with a horror movie. Some of them are doomed to stay at the horror genre forever. So, is it some kind of risky doing some grindhouse stuff if you want to develop a "serious" career in the business?

**Jefferson:** I think it is extremely risky to make a little horror film with no money. Although there are more content distribution outlets now, the quality of the material is much higher that in the golden years of VHS. Some guys get lucky, most get to rent their local theater and throw a viewing party for their family and friends.

**Marco:** If you have a small budget but desperately want to make a movie - Is it easier than making a horror film compared to other kinds of movies?

**Jefferson:** The easiest film to make is two guys on a porch playing checkers. But not many folks want to watch that for 90 minutes. So you add a monster or a bear or a naked girl. It goes from there. Oh, who am I kidding? No film is easy to make.

**Marco:** IN SEARCH OF A GOLDEN SKY is the one and only film you are credited officially as the director. Was it a bad experience? Why did you skip directing after this one?

**Jefferson:** I previously directed THE EXECUTIONER, which Tarantino cites as his influence for PULP FICTION. I loved shooting GOLDEN SKY. We had some differences in post production but for the most part it was a great expeience. I wrote and directed BERSERKER as well, and directed RIGGED.

**Marco:** According to the IMDB database you only directed parts of RIGGED in 1986. What happened, did the director get fired and you had to finish the film?

**Jefferson:** Yes. It was an unfortunate event. Very uncomfortable experience.

**Marco:** Over the decades you worked with a lot of companies and distribution houses. Please describe your impression of SGE.

**Jefferson:** SGE was one of the few companies around that wanted to raise the bar on the product they produced. I was always given a reasonable budget for each film I did with them. I consider Lenny Shapiro and Jim Glickenhaus to be a couple of the nicest, fairest bosses I ever had. They pretty much left me alone when it came to the production of the films, and I must have delivered as they kept asking me back.

**Marco:** You are credited as a producer of TIMEMASTER, which was the last film made by SGE. How do you remember working with James Glickenhaus? Were you on set a lot? Do you think it turned out well?

**Jefferson:** I was and am a hands-on producer. I am the first guy on the set and the last to leave. Working directly with Jim on SLAUGHTER OF THE INNOCENTS and TIMEMASTER were both invigorating experiences. Shooting the ski chase in the Swiss Alps was amazing. TIMEMASTER was also interesting because of all the CGI shots, which was fairly new tecnologhy at the time.

**Marco:** You are also credited as co-producer for at least two films by William Lustig. MANIAC COP (1988) was produced by SGE, and HIT LIST (1989) by Cinetel. How can you describe the difference, working for these two very different companies?

**Jefferson:** I enjoyed working with both companies equally. Cinetel let me do my thing as well.

**Marco:** Do you remember the exact number of films produced by SGE that you participated on?

**Jefferson:** I think five, six if you count BERSERKER which was independently produced.

**Marco:** Both films have a lot of scenes shot on location, MANIAC COP even more than HIT LIST. Is it nightmarish or joyful, shooting on the streets, all night, preparing difficult

|           | stunt scenes? And what exactly was your job during the making of these two films? |
|-----------|---|
| **Jefferson**: | My specialty has always been shooting on locations throughout the world. For me it's the way to go. |
| **Marco**: | Have you travelled a lot for shooting and presenting your films? |
| **Jefferson**: | I have traveled all over the world making pictures. |
| **Marco**: | In 1987 you scripted and directed BERSERKER, a slasher movie. Are you unhappy with this one? Why did you use an alias? What was your view on the slasher movie hype these days? |
| **Jefferson**: | I used an alias? If you mean Jef instead of Jefferson that was merely a choice at the time. I did quite a few second unit directing under that spelling. I think my agent at the time suggested it. I started to make BERSERKER as a serious slasher film but I kept thinking how silly those films were, so I guess I decided to go the camp route. It paid off. I am in negotiations to do a Blu ray special edition in the UK and the US. |
| **Marco**: | Do you have personal favorites among the films you worked at? Which one you like most? Any regrets? |
| **Jefferson**: | No regrets, except telling my investors to pass on THE KARATE KID. I like BUTTERFLY and the Mario Puzo film A TIME TO DIE. My all time favorite is THREE THOUSAND MILES TO GRACELAND. |
| **Marco**: | In the 2005/06 you produced sequels for two younger cult horror films. Why did you choose getting into URBAN LEGENDS 3 and I'LL ALWAYS KNOW WHAT YOU DID LAST SUMMER? Did both turn out as a success? |
| **Jefferson**: | Both pictures were successful. I was contacted by the studio as they wanted to shoot in Utah. I thought the material was tasteful good fun and signed on. |
| **Marco**: | There's still a market for horror, there always has been. Why do you think it's especially the horror movie which generates sequel after remake after prequel? |
| **Jefferson**: | I have no idea what the lure is. But there is an audience. I have always tried to make tasteful, scary films in that genre, although BERSERKER was initially banned in Germany. Go figure! |
| **Marco**: | So much has changed since you started in the movie business. Simply everything, the filmmaking, the distributing, the archiving, the piracy. Some things went better, others worse. All in all, what do you think about the brave new film world with streaming, bloggings, downloading, filesharing? |
| **Jefferson**: | I think it is wonderful. And TV has become more and more like movies. Although technically everything has changed, it still comes down to effectively tell a story! |
| **Marco**: | 35mm is dying. Do you miss celluloid? |
| **Jefferson**: | YES. Although the young audiences seem to prefer the crispness of digital, I do miss being able to work with a more textured palate. Digital projection, on the other hand is far better. Gone are the days of having to watch a scratchy, torn up print. |

**Marco:** You were on location while William Lustig shot MANIAC COP in Los Angeles. Taking this picture as an example, how much difference is there between shooting films on location in the USA on the West Coast as compared to the East Coast?

**Jefferson:** We shot most of the film in Los Angeles. We shot in New York on two separate occasions. L.A. was and is very easy to film in. That's what the city is about. New York, on the other hand, has its own unique set of logistics. For instance in L.A. we employed make up and wardrobe trailers. In NY we rented rooms for this purpose. In L.A. we paid police officers $35 to $50 an hour. In NY the city provided police gratis. Moving the company around in NY was much more difficult and we had several locations to shoot each night. But the crews there are used to it and did a bang up job. All in all it was a pleasure to shoot there.

**Marco:** Do you have any interesting anecdotes about the production of the Jim Glickenhaus directed SLAUGHTER OF THE INNOCENTS? There was a spectacular climactic stunt of an ark careening off a cliff for example. How do you remember the shoot in general?

**Jefferson:** SLAUGHTER OF THE INNOCENTS was an extremely challenging show. We started by shooting in Cleveland, then Salt Lake City and Kamas UT, Salina, UT, and finally in Moab, UT. All the action in the picture (as well as the special effects) is practical. There are no CGI shots. We really shot on Castle Rock and threw the ark off of it. The ark was constructed in a warehouse in Salt Lake, then cut into several interlocking pieces. It was then transported to Salina and locked together in a salt mine. It was then placed on a track in the mine and dressed. It had a hydraulic pulley device to make it travel back and forth. We shot the cave interiors there. Then the ark was disassembled once again and traveled to Moab where the guys had built an exterior cave that was also constructed in pieces. All the pieces were then airlifted via helicopter to the top of Castle Rock and assembled. The same hydraulic system was employed. It was like a carnival ride. The crew would hike up the trail every morning to shoot. We had three helicopters that airlifted equipment and some personnel. When you see the cast and/or stunt people riding on the ark right up to the edge, that is all real. Then in the final shot of the sequence we had several cameras covering the sendoff. To say the least it is a spectacular and exciting scene!

**Marco:** Is it much more stressful shooting stunts and action scenes on location or is it more or less the same as shooting a dialogue scene somewhere outside? Can you describe the differences and challenges of both?

**Jefferson:** Obviously a dialogue scene is easier. The logistics are much more controllable. This is a tough question for me to answer because I built a forty + year career on shooting difficult rough terrain sequences and formidable action/stunt scenes. For me the more the challenge the more exciting it is to shoot!

**Marco:** Do you like shooting scenes outdoors more than shooting scenes in a studio?

**Jefferson:** Absolutely!

**Marco:** Very few films nowadays are working with handcrafted, "real" practical action scenes like James Glickenhaus and other directors did for many SGE films. Do you miss this handmade filmmaking style?

**Jefferson:** I do in many respects, but on the other hand CG can be useful as a way to enhance a sequence, like in DRIVEN. The FAST & FURIOUS films use a combination of real action and CG. The trend now is to do more practical stunts and effects.

**Marco:** BERSERKER was distributed by SGE - has it made its money?

**Jefferson:** It did very well and is now considered a camp classic.

**Marco:** General question: have you shot literally all over the world?

**Jefferson:** Have not shot on every continent, but then again I'm not done yet!

**Marco:** What's a more challenging condition to work in: extreme heat or extreme cold? In the middle of a huge city or somewhere out in the nature?

**Jefferson:** All the conditions have their challenges. It's important to keep people warm in the cold and cool in the heat. It's also important to to hire the right crews for the right scenario. I am fortunate to have a core crew that has worked with me for years that love shooting in tough situations.

**Marco:** Have you ever met Quentin Tarantino in person? If yes, did you and he chat about THE EXECUTIONER? Are you flattered because he has named it as a personal influence?

**Jefferson:** Years ago he worked in a video store I went to. And yes, I was very flattered when he acknowledged THE EXECUTIONER on some of the talk shows. I had a possibility to work with him a few times but was not available.

**Marco:** Since TIMEMASTER, CGI had developed big time. Do you like it when films are partly done with digital effects and backgrounds?

**Jefferson:** If an effect works you shouldn't notice it. I don't much care for shooting a scene that takes place in Rome against a green screen on a stage in Culver City. But for films like AVATAR or THE HOBBIT it's the only way to go.

**Marco:** What do you think about the renaissance of 3D?

**Jefferson:** I love it!

**Marco:** Let's talk about ONE MAN FORCE. Where was the film shot?

**Jefferson:** The picture was filmed in Los Angeles.

**Marco:** And how often were you on set?

**Jefferson:** I was on set at all times. I set up an office in my van and work out of there. That way I can keep track of the day's work and give my input as well as get my office duties accomplished. I had one of those brick cell phones.

**Marco:** You are also credited as a second unit director on this film. What kind of additional footage was shot under your direction?

**Jefferson:** I would very often take a splinter unit out to film action shots with stunt doubles as well as insert shots the editor may want. We also shot a number of establishing shots and beauty shots. In this way we can shoot the film in less time and ensure great production value.

**Marco:** How did you get along with director Dale Trevillion? Did you know him or his work before the film was made?

**Jefferson:** I was not aware of his work before this project. He was a very organized director who allowed his staff to help execute his concepts and ideas. We remained friends for years.

**Marco:** How much was the budget?

**Jefferson:** The picture was financed by SGE. I don't recall the budget but I would guess in the 2-3 million dollar range.

**Marco:** Which budgetary items were the most expensive?

**Jefferson:** Stunts and special FX. That was always the key to success on these types of pictures.

**Marco:** The cast is excellent, especially in the case of supporting actors. Were you involved in the casting process?

**Jefferson:** Yes, I had quite a lot of input.

**Marco:** How do you remember ex-football pro John Matuszak? Had he not passed so early in his lifetime, do you think he would have had the chance to become an action film star? Was he easy-going on set?

**Jefferson:** "Tooze" was a big, friendly, lovable guy. He called me "Coach". I had a lot of experience working with NFL players in action movies (Mean Joe Greene, Gene Washington, Mercury Morris, etc.) so we got along real well. I'm a big guy too, so we had a lot of fun hanging out socially. I think he could have had a nice career in action, also in comedy as he was funny as hell.

**Marco:** The veteran stunt coordinator Spiro Razatos was in charge for the fight choreography. Since it was a key element in the film, did you work closely with Mr. Razatos?

**Jefferson:** Spiro and I have worked closely together on many films since the 1980s. He is one of the greatest Stunt Co-ordinators and 2nd Unit Directors in the business.

**Marco:** Like many of the action films of the 80s and 90s, ONE MAN FORCE was shot on 35mm but never given a theatrical release, is this correct?

**Jefferson:** We did shoot on 35mm. As far as theatrical release, that is a question for the distribution guys. I think it did play in a limited release but I can't be sure.

**Marco:** Do you think it's a shame that the film was never seen on the big screen?

**Jefferson:** Yes..I always like to see a theatrical release but in the video mania of the 80s and 90s that was not always the case.

**Marco:** Now on to RING OF STEEL. Did you get the impression it's even more Mr. Chapin's film compared to co-writer and director David Frost, who never directed another feature film?

**Jefferson:** Bob did have a lot of input during filming. David was more than open to ideas from everyone, but in the long run it was his picture. I don't know why he never directed another feature. He certainly was capable.

**Marco:** Some have said that the swordplay is ranked among the best of its kind in American action movies. Was this one of the most exciting parts in the production process?

**Jefferson:** Each sword fight sequence was meticulously choreographed. It was very exciting to see them come together. Again, that's where the money went.

**Marco:** Do you remember that the script had to be changed, especially the ending?

**Jefferson:** I don't recall but of course there are always suggestions and changes.

**Marco:** Would you say that RING OF STEEL was in any way neglected due to SGE being shut down not long after the film's completion?

**Jefferson:** I don't feel it was neglected. It had a nice home video release.

**Marco:** Which details do you remember most fondly about this project? Would you agree that it's very dark in tone and the swordplay focus is what makes it stand apart of other more run-of-the-mill subjects for action films?

**Jefferson:** The sword fight sequences are amazing. This is also a love story as well as dark action thriller. The production team was a great working unit. We all pretty much got along most of the time. If we did encounter any tension we would go to dinner and work things out.

**Marco:** How did the audience react? Do you know if it sold well internationally? Do you know any other details of distribution for this title?

**Jefferson:** Once again that would be a question for Lenny Shapiro. I make 'em. Other guys sell 'em!

By Marco Siedelmann, in writing
from Park City, Utah, 25May, 23April and 24Aug15

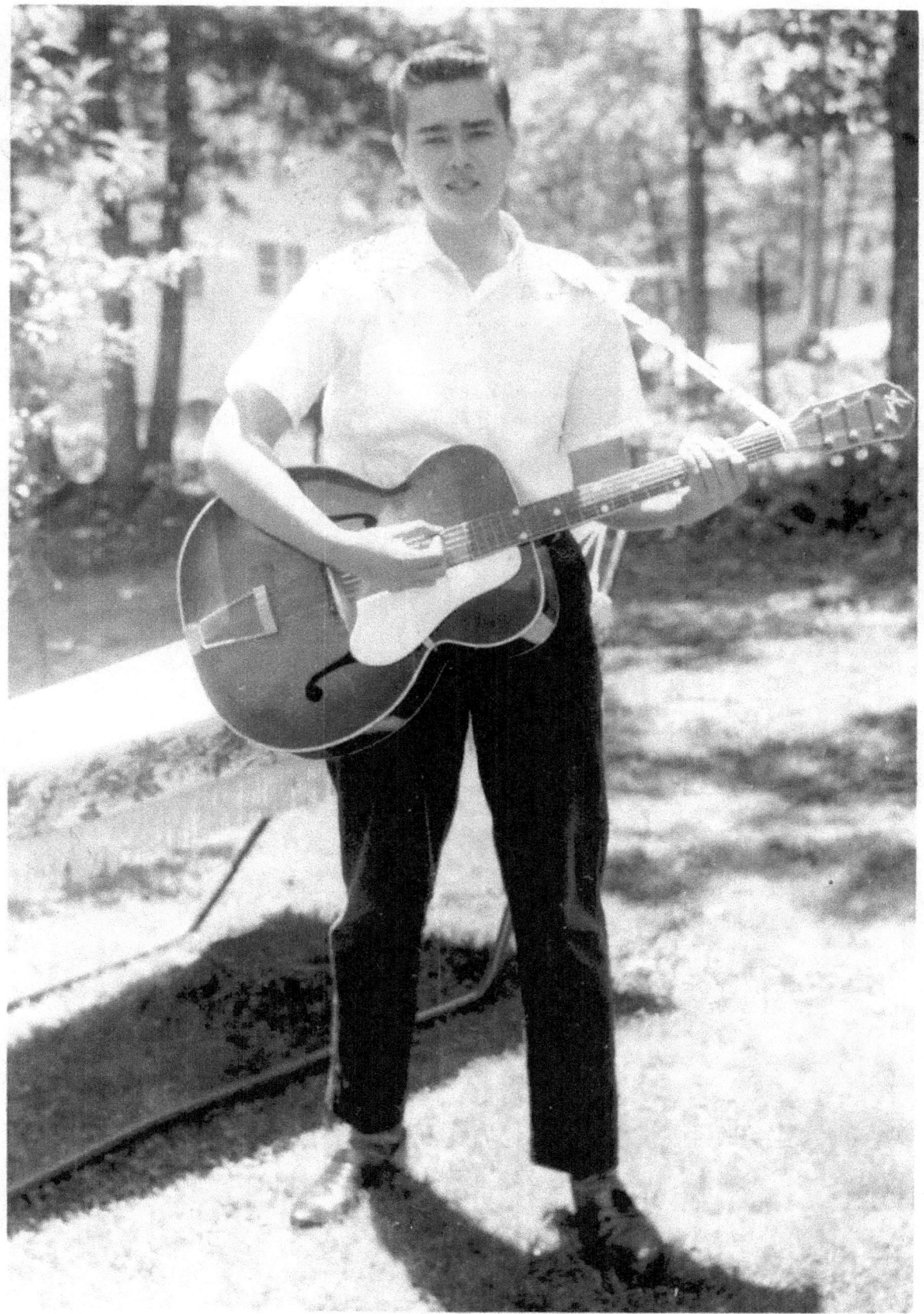

# SLAUGHTER OF THE INNOCENTS

Special Agent Stephen Broderick's uncanny ability in solving crimes brings him from Ohio to Utah to head up a state-wide investigation of the mysterious murders of two young children. Unknown to his colleagues, the celebrated detective often utilizes his son Jesse's computer talents in aiding him with his research. Broderick and his whiz-kid son soon connect the murders with a series of brutal killings that have occurred around Monument Valley.

But when a proud father's encouragement of innocent enthusiasm leads Jesse into the lair of a religious fanatic, Broderick's pursuit of the slayer immediately turns into an explosive battle as he tries to save his young son from the clutches of the deranged serial killer.

A terrifying spine-tingling thriller, "SLAUGHTER OF THE INNOCENTS" teams internationally acclaimed actor Scott Glenn ("The Silence of the Lambs," "The Hunt for Red October," "Backdraft") with newcomer Jesse Cameron-Glickenhaus in the roles of father and son. Sheila Tousey ("Thunderheart," "The Silent Tongue") and Darlanne Fluegel ("To Live and Die in L.A.," "Once Upon a Time in America") also star.

Directing from his original screenplay is noted director James Glickenhaus, who has thrilled audiences around the world with exciting action adventure films including "The Exterminator," "The Protector," "The Soldier," "Shakedown" and "McBain."

## CAST AND CREDITS

CAST:
Scott Glenn
Jesse Cameron-Glickenhaus
Sheila Tousey
Darlanne Fluegel
Zitto Kazann

MUSIC:
Joe Renzetti

EDITOR:
Kevin Tent

COSTUME DESIGNER:
Shawna Leavell

PRODUCTION DESIGNER:
Nicholas T. Preovolos

DIRECTOR OF PHOTOGRAPHY:
Mark Irwin, CSC

LINE PRODUCER:
Jefferson Richard

EXECUTIVE PRODUCERS:
Leonard Shapiro
Alan M. Solomon

PRODUCER:
Frank K. Isaac

WRITTEN AND DIRECTED BY:
James Glickenhaus

TYPE: Suspense/Thriller
RUNNING TIME: 104 minutes
FORMAT: Color

© 1993 SGE Entertainment Corp.
All Rights Reserved

Contact: Alan Solomon, Executive V.P.
12001 Ventura Place·Fourth Floor·Studio City, CA 91604·(818)766-8500
FAX (818)766-7873

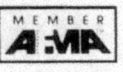
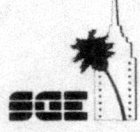

# SHAPIRO GLICKENHAUS
## ENTERTAINMENT

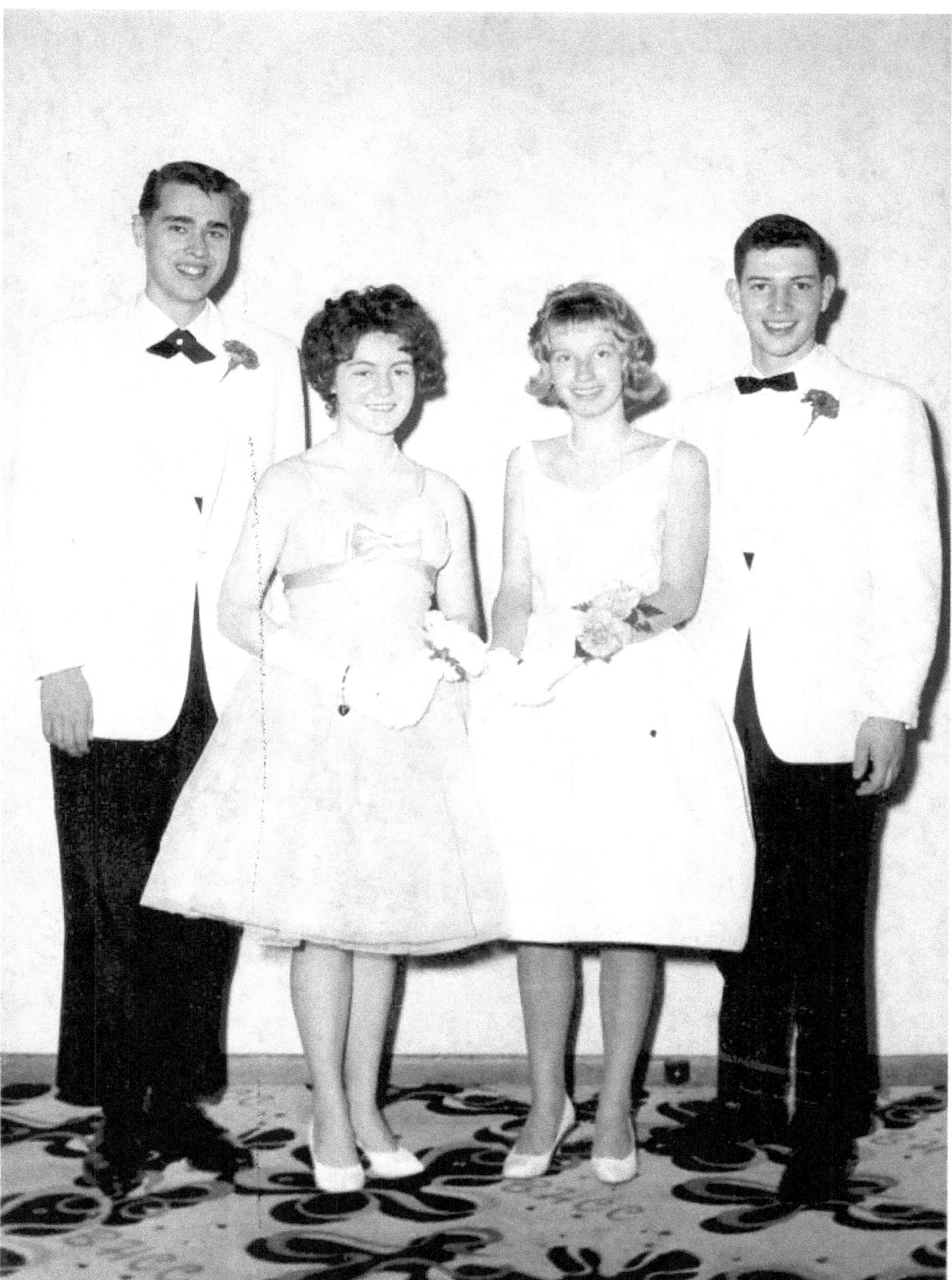

IT'S TOO LATE
TO RUN.
THERE'S NO TIME
TO SCREAM.
JUST CLOSE YOUR EYES
AND PRAY TO DIE.

# BERSERKER

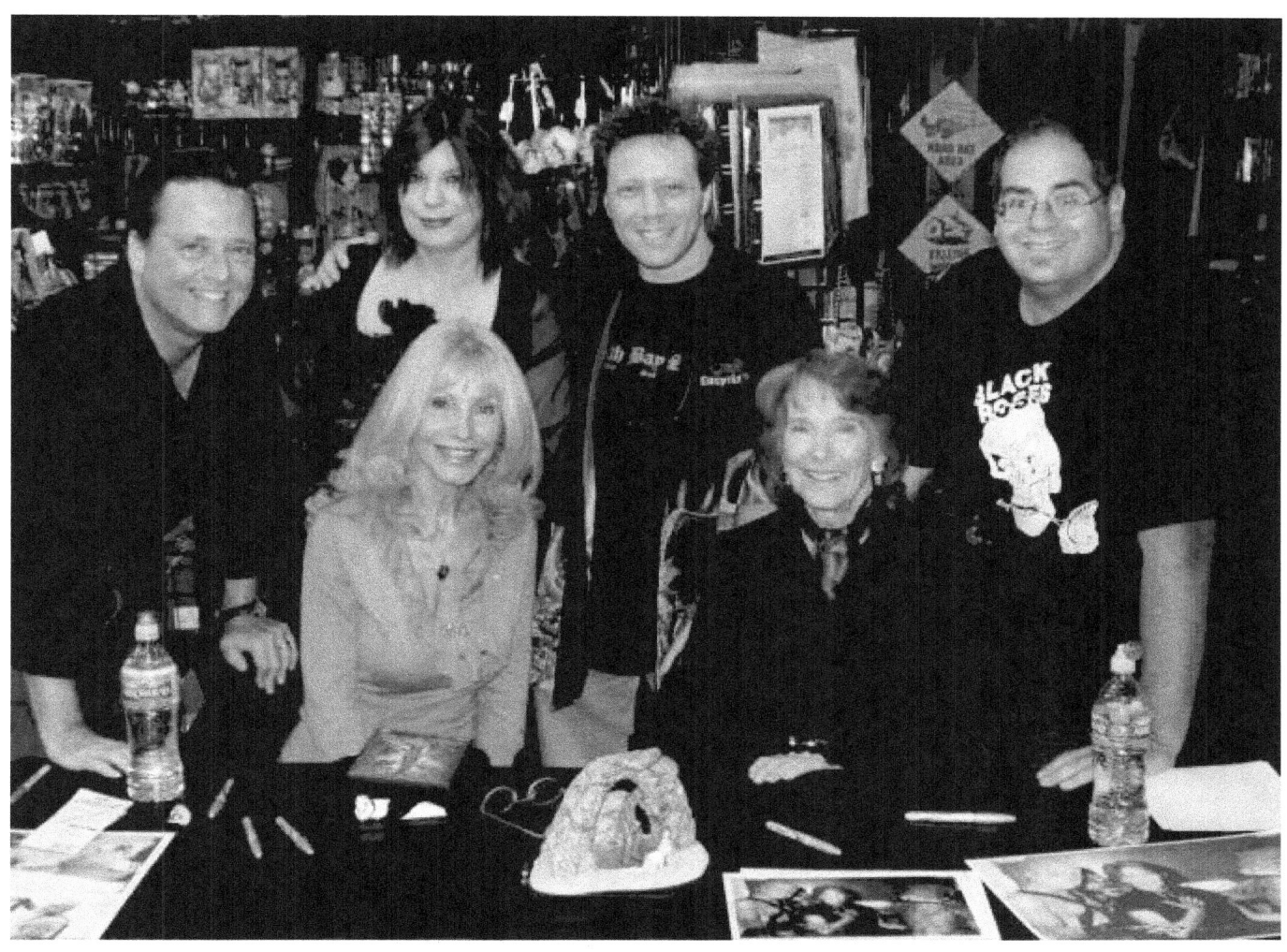

## Show Cue Sheet Report

**Series Name:** Not available or a standalone Program
**Program Title:** BLACK ROSES (1988)
**Program Number:** 0000
**Expected Air Date:** 1900-01-01
**Program Duration:** 002:00:00

**Printed:** September 29, 2010

### Usage Code Description:
V V: Visual Vocal   V I: Visual Instrumental   B V: Background Vocal   B I: Background Instrumental

| Cue # | Title | Time | Usage | Entitled Party Type | Entitled Party Name | O. Shares | C. Shares | Member Society |
|---|---|---|---|---|---|---|---|---|
| 0001 | BACKGROUND MUSIC | 000:05:33 | BI | COMPOSER/ | CONNELLY ROBERT | 50.00 | 50.00 | |
| | | | BI | ORIGINAL P | NAPOLIS MUSIC CORPORATION | 50.00 | 50.00 | BMI |
| 0002 | ME AGAINST THE WORLD | 000:00:21 | BV | COMPOSER/ | SCHACHTER GENE | 25.00 | 25.00 | BMI |
| | | | BV | COMPOSER/ | HARGES GREGORY | 25.00 | 25.00 | BMI |
| | | | BV | ORIGINAL P | FORTY WHACKS MUSIC | 50.00 | 50.00 | |
| 0003 | BACKGROUND MUSIC | 000:39:04 | BI | COMPOSER/ | SOLOMON ELLIOT | 50.00 | 50.00 | BMI |
| | | | BI | ORIGINAL P | NAPOLIS MUSIC CORPORATION | 50.00 | 50.00 | BMI |
| 0004 | KING OF KOOL | 000:01:10 | BV | COMPOSER/ | HENZERLING DAVID | 50.00 | 50.00 | ASCAP |

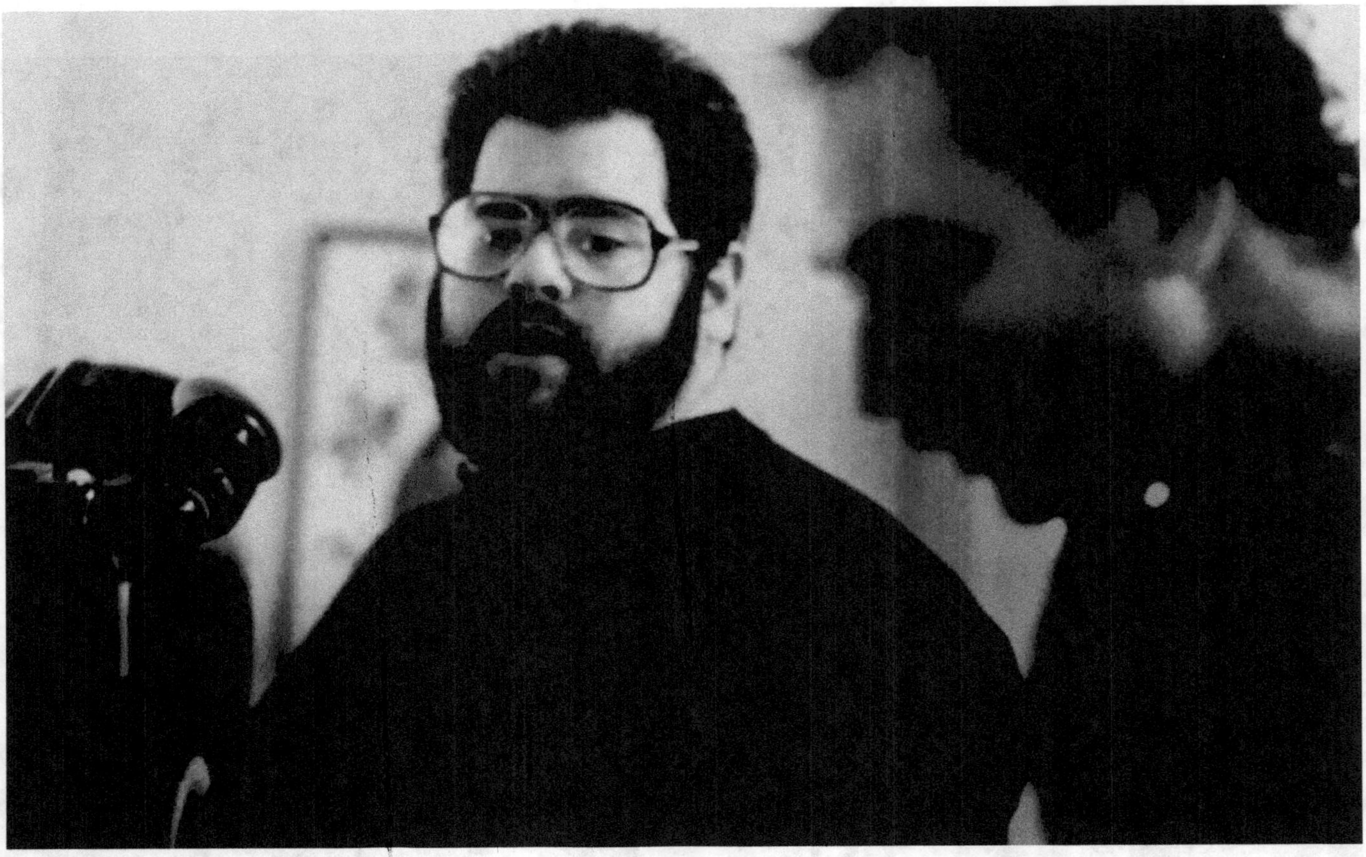

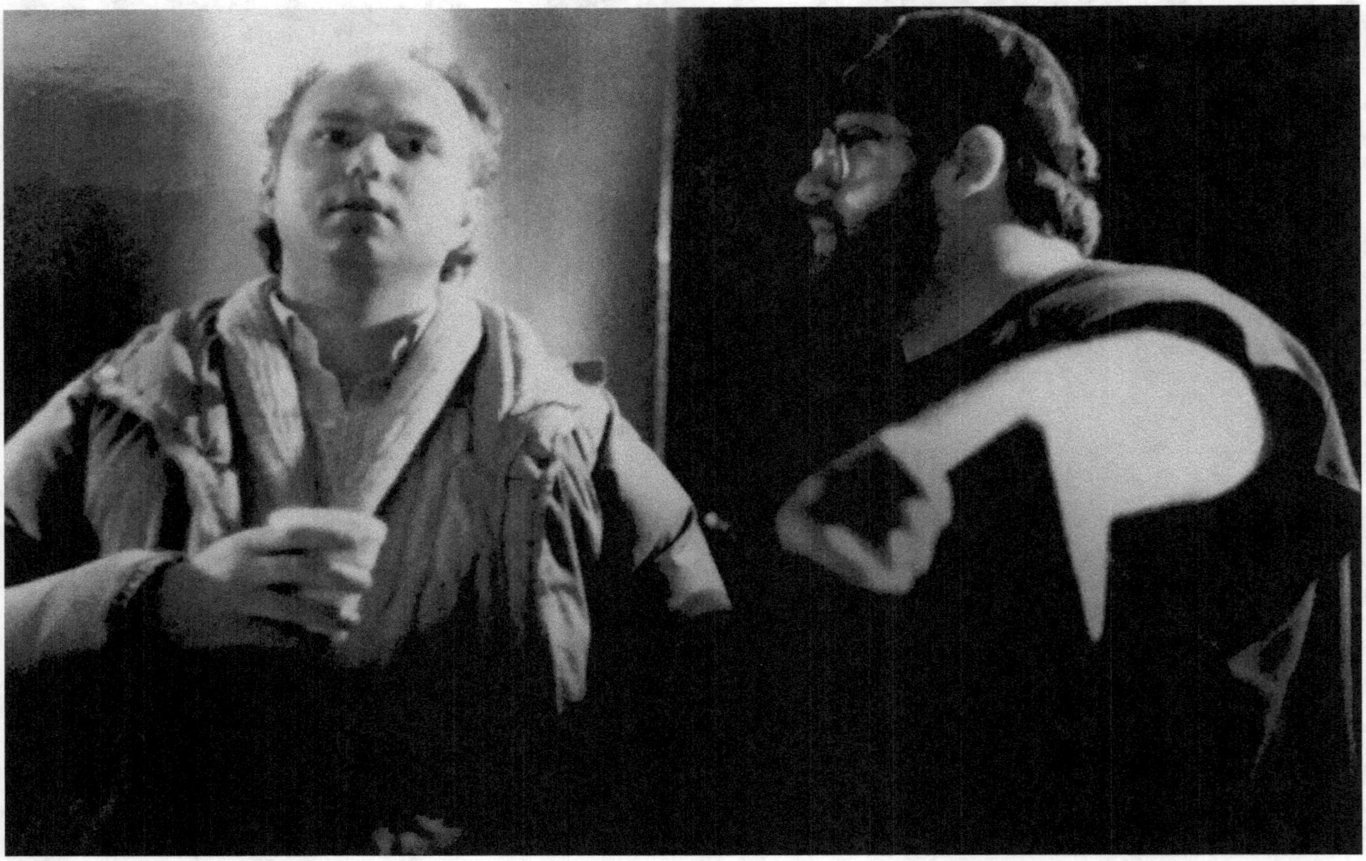

# Black Roses

*Turn up the volume
Turn down the lights...
But don't watch it alone.*

You are about to find out that everything your mother told you about Rock & Roll is true. When the sleepy town of Mill Basin is invaded by a sleazy band of hard rockers, the self-righteous townspeople try to stop their concert series. When the band finally overcomes parental objections, a town full of normal mid-western kids begins to turn bad. BLOODSHED, RIOTS and horrible MASS MURDERS assail defenseless Mill Basin. These kids turn into monsters right before your very eyes. *THE SPECIAL EFFECTS ARE FANTASTIC.*

**Color Approx 90 min.**

IMPERIAL ENTERTAINMENT CORP
6430 Sunset Blvd. Suite 1500 Hollywood, CA 90028

**WARNING:** Licensed only for non-commercial private exhibition in homes. Any public performance, other use, or copying is strictly prohibited and may subject the offender to civil liability and severe criminal penalties. (Title 17, United States Code, Sections 501 and 506.)

© 1988 Imperial Entertainment Corp All Rights Reserved

2238-92002-3

2002

VHS hi-fi

**BLACK ROSES**

**CONTINUITY/DIALOGUE LIST**

JR Media Services, Inc.
2501 W. Burbank Blvd.    Suite 200    Burbank, CA 91505
Ph: 818-557-0200    Fax: 818-557-0201
www.jrmediaservices.com

**BLACK ROSES**

| # | TIME CODE | CONTINUITY | DIALOGUE |
|---|---|---|---|
| 1. | 01:00:00 | Establishing - City skyline, night. | |
| 2. | 01:00:07 | Establishing - City sidewalks, night. Young people walk, congregate. | |
| 3. | 01:0019 | Establishing - Signs on venue entrance advertise all night show. | |
| 4. | 01:00:23 | Int. - Concert Venue - Night. BLACK ROSES BAND MEMBERS dressed as demons play rock music on stage. AUDIENCE cheers. | AUDIENCE: [cheering] |
| 5. | 01:00:28 | DAMIAN with demon face sings into microphone. | DAMIAN: [sings] *It's just me.* |
| 6. | 01:00:34 | AUDIENCE leaps to feet. DAMIAN tosses his cape to the crowd. | [rock music begins] |
| 7. | 01:00:49 | DAMIAN with demonic face sings into microphone to crowd. BLACK ROSES BAND MEMBERS play instruments. Audience dances, enjoying the show, cheering, pumping their arms. | DAMIAN: [sings] *Leave me alone* *I'm on the fence* *I'm not made of stone* *Why doesn't it ever make sense?* *I'm sick of all this indecision* *You're messing with my mind* *This ain't no false façade* *And this ain't no freak disguise* *'Cause I am for real* *You don't know what I feel* *Must treat this in my [wheel]* *I cannot wait* *I won't be second rate* *In for the kill* |

# Cynthia Cirile

Cynthia Cirile entered the film industry in a very unusual way: starting as a writer for numerous magazines, she became the muse of adult film veteran director Henri Pachard. In the mid-eighties she was well-known as one of the very few female creatives behind the camera within the New Yorker porn film industry. Under the alias Joyce James, she directed the cult-favorite DRILLER. On the set of that movie she met John Fasano - the unconventional beginning of a love story and also a creative relationship. Together they made the low-budget horror films ROCK N ROLL NIGHTMARE, BLACK ROSES (one of the very first In-house-productions by SGE) and THE JITTERS. John Fasano developed a terrific career as a writer and producer, and for many years Cynthia Cirile and Fasano teamed up for movies like RAPID FIRE (starring Brandon Lee) or GINOSTRA (starring Harvey Keitel).

**Marco:** John Fasano's first feature film ROCK 'N' ROLL NIGHTMARE was made for around 40,000 dollars, is this correct? Who financed the project?

**Cynthia:** I believe the total was more like $45 grand. John was a new 24 year-old filmmaker. Sometimes he used the psuedonym, Awesome Welles! John and I both had written some prior low-budget flicks, but he was really anxious to do a friendly horror film for as close to a zero budget as possible. We lived in NY then, in the early 80's, but somehow John had a connection with Lenny Shapiro. John made Lenny an offer he couldn't refuse to make a full-length feature film for under $50 grand. No one thought we could do it - but we did! As far as I know, Lenny Shapiro and Alan Solomon financed the film.

**Marco:** Was it planned as kind of a blueprint for the bigger movie BLACK ROSES? Was SGE, or Leonard Shapiro already involved in your first film? Any intersections in the productions?

**Cynthia:** No - not at all. John Fasano and Jon-Mikl Thor had struck up a friendship around 1982. I was good friends with Thor's wife at the time, Rusty Hamilton, who makes a cameo in ROCK 'N' ROLL NIGHTMARE. It was Rusty who told me to find a nice big boy like my Jon! It was hilarious when I did, and "our Johns/Jon's" got along like gang busters. Thor had an idea for something based roughly on his Thor stage act. These guys loved each other and trusted each other implicitly, and were forever friends. John Fasano was sort of dedicated to fulfilling Jon Thor's dream, and vice versa. But no - there was no connection whatsoever between ROCK 'N' ROLL NIGHTMARE and BLACK ROSES. The only connection was that Lenny Shapiro and Alan Solomon insisted on having a good soundtrack for our next film so it made sense to have the next film - BLACK ROSES - be based around a rock band.

**Marco:** Right after ROCK 'N' ROLL NIGHTMARE - it was your second film mixing the main topics of hard rock music and freaky horror elements. Were you and John Fasano very into that kind of music?

**Cynthia:** Not at all!!! All of the music in ROCK 'N' ROLL NIGHTMARE is Thor's. We liked his sound, and indeed - his music, not just from ROCK 'N' ROLL NIGHTMARE, has stood up! But for BLACK ROSES? The music was very carefully planned out - helmed by Alan Solomon - and executed by his brilliant son, Elliot Solomon. Elliot wrote My Home Town, BLACK ROSES opener. He sang it, too. Elliot is a terrific talent, and he also got us all the other hip bands that appear on the groovy soundtrack. While Elliot did an amazing job this was our first main problem with SGE. I had cast Broadway musical star Sal Viviano as Damian. Not only because he was ideal for the part, and the nicest person in the world - but also because he was a brilliant singer and showman! Sal took the part primarily so he could show off his pipes! He ended up having to lip sync to the BLACK ROSES songs. John and I were devastated. John's musical tastes ran to whatever was on the radio at the time. He liked show tunes mostly, and was a terrific singer himself. He had appeared in musical theater since he was a teen. My taste has always run to folk rock - like Crosby,Stills, Nash and Young - Poco, Pete Seeger….The Band! Clearly the music of BLACK ROSES was not the kind of music that either John or I would listen to at home. But - as a family, all of us sang along with the soundtracks to both ROCK 'N' ROLL NIGHTMARE and BLACK ROSES all the time!

**Marco:** BLACK ROSES was the first Fasano film featuring the cinematography of Paul Mitchnick. He became an important creative partner, right? How did you find him?

**Cynthia:** How did we find him?? HA!!! "Paul was a pathetic orphan on the streets of Toronto! We gave him a bowl of gruel, and he was forever indebted to us!" Honestly, I haven't a clue how we found Mitchnick! Ask him! I think Mitchnick (everyone calls him Mitchnick. He hates it - and says, "Can't you just call me Paul?") John didn't get along with our hippyish DP on ROCK 'N' ROLL NIGHTMARE - Mark McCay (I think?). Mitchnick was very zen - and if you worked with John Fasano you needed to be zen, or you'd lose your mind! Mitchnick offered a place of peace for John who called him handsome. I think Mitchnick calls everyone handsome, but it was adorable, and a great way to diffuse John's anger or frustration! Fasano: Loud, booming, He Who Must Be Obeyed. Mitchnick: He who will willingly Obey, and call you Handsome, besides! They were a perfect working team. And close friends. John and I were all about helping our friends and family get work. We would go the extra mile, and I think this is one reason why we have so many wonderful friends now. And Paul Mitchnick is at the top of that list!

**Marco:** The young Elliot Solomon – the eldest son of SGE key figure Alan Solomon - made the score for BLACK ROSES, and he did a good job. Was there some kind of private connection?

**Cynthia:** As I inferred—none whatsoever! Elliot was thrust upon us, quite literally, and we were very upset! I was upset that Sal Viviano wouldn't be singing the songs, but I was also furious that as the screenwriter and producer of the film I had almost no say in the lyrical content of the songs! This seemed insane to me! How did I know that the songs the BLACK ROSES would sing would have the message or impact I wanted them to? I most certainly let these feelings be known! I was permitted to write an annotated list of the messages/key phrases that I needed Damian to say or sing. Frankly - I thought I would be completely ignored, and that the songs would be godawful. When I first heard My Hometown edited into the first cut of the film - I was so grateful to Elliot Solomon - I can't tell you! He so clearly understood exactly what I wanted and needed for Damian/BLACK ROSES to convey. And then when the parents leave - and Damian tears into Rock Invasion? "The time has come to get together - we're gonna rock this town tonight!" Seeing and hearing that transition - the most important (to me!) in the film - was one of the greatest thrills of my life. Elliot had ingested the story of BLACK ROSES, and in those songs he brought Black Roses to life! With a lot of help from Sal Viviano!!!

**Marco:** Looking back on BLACK ROSES, what comes to your mind first? Did you work closely with many people from SGE? Did you enjoy the atmosphere, was it friendly and private?

**Cynthia:** First? Truly the scene I just described. When Damian gets rid of the parents, and shows himself for who he really is. Being there, organizing and recruiting all those frigging extras! The monster-making and co-ordination of that scene! Wow! Toughest scene I ever produced. So - being there, in Hamilton, Ontario - and then seeing it all cut together so beautifully? I can truly say that my favorite scenes in BLACK ROSES, the ones that most fulfilled my vision for the film are of Sal Viviano on stage as Damian, and the kids going nuttier and nuttier! I think those scenes hold up today beautifully, and to do it on an almost non-existent budget! Whew. It's a thrill to have all the money you want to make a film! And you can be proud when it's over. Or not! I was involved in big budget studio films later on that I have almost nothing to be proud of at all!

**Marco:** Was working with SGE friendly and private?

**Cynthia:** Hmmm! Yes! No! Well - friendly, sure. Private in the context of filmmakers (John and I) vs our financiers?? Well…SGE wanted a lot for their half-million bucks. Not only did they insist, and get their way, on controlling all the music/lyrics/subsequent album. But they also had requisite amounts of blood that needed to be shed, and bras that needed to be shed! Making blood and monsters is nothing compared to supplying an adequate number of breasts for an SGE film! Basically - we were told that there must be a breast every 7 minutes of film! Since I had the joy of casting both ROCK 'N' ROLL NIGHTMARE and BLACK ROSES in my basement in Yonkers, NY, by the way - I had the joyful privilege of informing every female actor that she would have to show, if not her breasts - then, at the very least: one breast! For some bizarre reason, a lot of these female actors weren't all that keen to bare themselves on screen! In these cases I was forced to hire stunt breasts! If you think I'm kidding...I most certainly am not! The best case of stunt breasts is in BLACK ROSES - just prior to the scene where Julie goes to Matt Moorhouse's house to seduce him. Just prior to that is a ludicrous insert show of a tall, skinny woman with tiny breasts - and one of her arms inexplicably reptilian. She's massaging her boobs as she looks into my antique oak dresser with mirror! Meaning: the scene was with some unknown actress, shot in my basement - with the use of my personal furniture. Most of the furniture like the scene where the Soprano's star Big Pussy (Vicent Pastore) gets sucked into the stereo? My living room. My couch. My stereo!

**Marco:** Carla Ferrigno stars in a supporting role. Did you try to get her husband Lou on camera as well?

**Cynthia:** I didn't. John didn't know Lou Ferrigno well at this point. They had met, but after BLACK ROSES Lou and John became extremely close friends. They had a great deal in common. Italian American men of similar backgrounds, both of whom felt handicapped in various ways - I know John was always thinking about Lou. I think maybe they were too similar.

**Marco:** The early films directed by John Fasano are – literally – family movies. What was the difference between ROCK 'N' ROLL NIGHTMARE, and BLACK ROSES?

**Cynthia:** Budget!!! And - a script by me! I had only written a few scripts before writing BLACK ROSES - and if I had a do-over, I am quite confident that with an additional 25 years practice as a writer - I could write a far better BLACK ROSES now than then. But that being said - it is what it is. What just kills me is when I read - or people ask me, whether I actually believe that rock 'n roll is the devil. Oh, dear!!! Talk about missing the point! On the other hand - maybe I needed to be even more sardonic to get across the point that in my view - it's the goody-two shoes parents' committee who are evil - not the kids. I was poking fun at the parents' groups that have censured rock since it's inception. My hero is Patti Smith: "Baby, Baby, baby is a rock 'n roll nigger!" That's my kind of rock music! Shake it up! I think the most important function of rock is precisely that—to say blam! To blow things up. To make people sit up and pay attention. The irony in BLACK ROSES is that in this case—the annoying parents group is right! It is supposed to be ironic that they are right. I'm off point! ROCK 'N' ROLL NIGHTMARE was a "family film" because we love working with family and friends—and because only family and friends will work for free plus McDonald's! For RRNM—John and I gathered all our friends and family who in any way wanted to work on the film. This would be a very long list, but I'll cite these people as "genuine family." The film opens with me, making scrambled eggs in the kitchen! My son, Jesse D'Angelo—answers me from the top of the steps! My brother, Jim Cirile, plays the Triton's famous Stig—known for his deliberate vacillating Aussie accent! Jim Cirile also made many of the gags for ROCK 'N' ROLL NIGHTMARE. Behind the scenes is John's little sister, Felicia Fasano who did the hair and make-up on both ROCK 'N' ROLL NIGHTMARE and BLACK ROSES. But in addition Felicia also helped cast BLACK ROSES! She is now one of the most in demand casting directors in America casting CALIFORNICATION, HOUSE OF LIES, and you name it. That's family. Friends? Everyone but the Canadians! Jon Thor, his wife, Rusty Hamilton, were my close friends. Frank Dietz and his wife were friends of John's from high school. So was Dee Dee O'Malley who plays the keyboard player in the Tritonz. We would've brought all our friends to Canada, but the film was made under strict Canadian context guidelines. It helped a lot that John Thor was Canadian! We were forced to cast Canadians to fulfill these laws, and this didn't work out too well, especially in BLACK ROSES. It was also a Canadian content film. I had to give up my producer's credit or my screenwriter credit which was a tough choice! I choice to give up my producer credit, but I did not like it! Who would? BLACK ROSES was as much a family and friend film as ROCK 'N' ROLL NIGHTMARE. The difference was that now we could actually pay people! Not a lot - but something is better than nothing! So, family: John makes a quick cameo in BLACK ROSES! He can be seen in a street scene kicking someone! My son, Jesse D'Angelo had his hair platinum blonde, and has his innocence destroyed by BLACK ROSES! Friends abound in BLACK ROSES! Frank Dietz reappears from ROCK 'N' ROLL NIGHTMARE as Johnny, and he's in full make-up as a member of the band, BLACK ROSES, as well which very few people know. John's friend Chet Nakelski is also behind makeup as a member of BLACK ROSES, and we scored Vanilla Fudge's iconic Carmine Appice for the drummer of BLACK ROSES. Cool! John's parents Mary and John Fasano, Sr., attend the parents' meeting! Anthony C. Bua, who gives a riveting performance as Tony was a brilliant young sculptor working out of our basement!

**Marco:** You were in charge of the film, mainly as a producer and also as a scriptwriter. Was it your first script for a feature film? Did it change much during the production?

**Cynthia:** I had written a few other low budget scripts in another genre, and had even directed a full-length feature by this time. But I was not an experienced screenwriter. I was a literary scholar, a college professor of English and American literature, and I had zero interest in horror films. In fact, the closest to horror films I'd ever seen were Hitchcock films and Universal monsters. My voice in the film is Matt Moorhouse. I am, or was - Matt Moorhouse. The name is an actual literary reference. I was the teacher with a room full of kids who didn't know who Ralph Waldo Emerson was! I adored Walt Whitman, and I could not get my kids interested! I was a very unusual kind of college teacher - to say the least! I considered it my job to get kids to learn to think and to question. I did it in some very strange ways! Theatrical ways. For some reason I didn't want my protagonist to be more than progressive, and genuinely trying to make a connection with his kids. For me - to make an English teacher the guy who saves the kids was very fulfilling! As for the monsters? I could've cared less! That was all John Fasano! He was obsessed with monsters, especially the CREATURE FROM THE BLACK LAGOON, and THE WOLF MAN, since he was a kid. It meant a great, great deal that he could hire Julie Adams for BLACK ROSES. That was a wonderful moment for him! I honestly can't recall the actual script, the words of BLACK ROSES, changing in the slightest! Certainly not the classroom scenes! In that regard SGE left us alone! They didn't give a crap about the script - as long as there was bloodshed, some monsters, and gratuitous tits every 7 minutes!

**Marco:** For a while you lived in the same neighborhood as Jim Glickenhaus. When you first met him there were a lot of movie-like vibrations around, do you agree?

**Cynthia:** John and I lived in Westchester County, New York - a suburb of Manhattan. Jim Glickenhaus lived in a glamorous mansion in Rye. Close, but hardly the same neighborhood! Our sons were the same age, and both named Jesse! They got along very well, and so did John and Jim. John spent a lot of time on the set of Jim G's movie, SHAKEDOWN, and he met Sam Elliot there. To say that Mr. Elliot was rude would be...accurate! The two Jesses were given cameos in the big denouement - on a roller coaster together, I think. Rather oddly, you can't even see the kids in SHAKEDOWN. When John and I made a movie we made sure you could see our kids' faces! I don't remember Jim's personal or professional involvement with BLACK ROSES - other than he was part of SGE. SGE knew I wasn't thrilled about the necessity of our re-shooting footage of random, unconnected tits. This was after we had wrapped BLACK ROSES, and had a first cut. SGE demanded more tits, and more monsters! Sheesh! John was hardly pleased, either since anyone with half a brain could see that these inserts didn't match. Not in lighting, set, or - most importantly - body types! I read a thread recently about BLACK ROSES where someone described the random tits scene as "really hot!" I found that utterly hilarious!

**Marco:** Who created the monster design, and how much of the budget had to be spent on the great make-up and mechanical creature effects?

**Cynthia:** Which monster design? There are so many! There are all the facial designs for the band - the face of Damian, the Julie monster, and the Damian monster, I guess it's called - who Matt must fight at the very end. So many geniuses here. Anthony C. Bua sculpted the Julie monster in our basement. The Damian monster was designed by Richie Alonzo, and worn in the film by Dan Platt. So many people dedicated themselves to the monster designs and make-up in BLACK ROSES that I just hate to leave people out!

I'm not the best person to ask about the FX.

**Marco:** Nowadays BLACK ROSES is kind of a cult favorite. What kind of reactions did the film get at the time? And did it find a huge audience internationally?

**Cynthia:** BLACK ROSES was kind of a cult favorite from the minute it was released on video. The box cover design, with the bas relief of a guitar, sold like mad! And the soundtrack album, with music by so many hot bands? Oh, yes. Alan Solomon and Elliot Solomon knew what they were doing on that score! People who love monsters were intrigued by our Julie monster, and the Damian monster. The transformed BLACK ROSES band itself got a lot of attention from magazines like Fangoria. But none of us ever imagined that BLACK ROSES would become the international cult hit it is today!

**Marco:** Do you think the tragic dimension of your original script had been transported in the movie?

**Cynthia:** Yes, I do. John took it very seriously, indeed! I mean the idea of teenagers being brainwashed to kill their parents? It was a pretty queasy subject! It was made even weirder by having so many real people in the film. For example Keith Miller is the high school adviser who gets flung out the window by a turned Black Roses fanatic. In real life Keith Miller had been the director of the playhouse where John and Frank Dietz had done tons of plays on L.I. Tony Bua, who sets himself on fire is our pal! But maybe worst was Frank Dietz/Johnny who brought a framed photo of himself as a baby to the set. In the scene where evil Johnny shoots his father in the head - John cuts away to the photo of Frank/Johnny as a baby, with blood streaked across it! That gave me the willies! Too real for my taste! But you ask if the deeper, more twisted messages of my script come across? I think so - in a scene like Johnny's face streaked with blood - it becomes far more real—for the people on the set, and therefore-to the audience at large.

**Marco:** Was there a theatrical release anywhere, was BLACK ROSES at least shown at a few festivals from an original celluloid copy?

**Cynthia:** Not that I know of, no!

**Marco:** Sonoko Sakai was involved in the financing/licencing/production of John Fasanos third film THE JITTERS, which wasn't distributed by SGE. Did you get in touch with Ms. Sakai during the production process of BLACK ROSES?

**Cynthia:** Yes - Sonoko was very much involved in the production, the financing, and most certainly the subject matter of our film THE JITTERS - also starring Sal Viviano from BLACK ROSES! I don't recall that John or I knew Sonoko prior to making THE JITTERS. She was great to work with.

**Marco:** Who made the artwork for BLACK ROSES, for example the original poster design? Were you and John Fasano involved in that, was it an important aspect for you?

**Cynthia:** It was very important to us! We had some input. basically, that the box needed to convey that this film contained rock music, monsters, and an assortment of mis-matched tits! I wasn't crazy about the box cover which shows what I know! It was a huge hit!

**Marco:** What was attractive about shooting low-budget independent horror movies when both you and John Fasano were involved in much bigger films and projects?

**Cynthia:** When John and I partnered to make a string of low budget indy films, we thought of it as a way to satisfy our creative needs, and put food on our table, too! We didn't think of it as a jumping board to bigger and better things, though going from a budget of $45 grand on ROCK 'N' ROLL NIGHTMARE to a budget of nearly half a million on BLACK ROSES was nice! Mostly - and this was most important to us both - we used that difference in budget to pay all our wonderful actors, FX people, and growing team! There was huge pleasure in seeing your friend make something - act something, write something - and be able to give them actual dollars for doing it! There was also the thrill of telling these people, and telling ourselves, too. That we had no limits on what we could say or do or create! I mean SGE, clearly would have their say! But ultimately, they really did leave us alone to do what we wanted. And how do I know this? I only know this because we soon loaded up the truck and moved to Beverly. Hills, that is. Swimming pools, movie stars. 'cept we moved to Pacific Palisades which is the Beverly Hills of now. When we were living in NY as indie filmmakers, well, life was simpler, to say the least. When we made our early horror flicks like ROCK 'N' ROLL NIGHTMARE and BLACK ROSES, we imagined that we were somewhat put upon by our executive producers/financiers/SGE. Haaaaaaa!!! If only we'd known how good we had it back in the good old days working for SGE! The fantasy of becoming Hollywood hyphenates lured John before it did me. Why? Because John started making films on Super 8 film, usually blowing things up since he was eight! When I was eight, I was reading the Brontes and writing poetry! My ambition was to be an English teacher, duh! But once John got the Hollywood bug, I got it, too. After working for both indie and the fun, fabulous lots of Paramount and Sony (formerly MGM) and feeling part of history - you soon learn that as a writer, you are little more than a toady, an errand boy. And if you're a girl - well, you're not really welcome at all. Neither John nor I ever got over the desire, the need, to somehow go back in time and be indie filmmakers again. We were always disappointed, disgusted - and in general - learned the hard way that the film SUNSET BOULEVARD is no fantasy. So! You indie filmmakers out there that want to make it big time? My advice? Stay where you are! Make movies or books or igloos and show them to your friends, your community - post them on You-Tube. Do not become part of this machine. This is an evil, awful, despicable town, and I am not lying when I say that anytime my children have appeared in a film or television show, they have been surrounded at all times by multiple escorts! Hollywood Babylon is not just a metaphor! John always fantasized about making films for fun. I'm surprised he never did. He was always working on five scripts at once! But I think he got the biggest kick out of making little films with our kids in them. Our kids' school projects were almost always these crazy little movies!

**Marco:** What would you say, how much personal ambition did you spend on the writing of that script? Did you and John Fasano work very closely? Meaning, in the writing- and pre-production-phase, and also at the actual shoot, and the final editing?

**Cynthia:** In retrospect - if I'd had any idea of the kind of impact BLACK ROSES would have, and over so many decades, I would've spent far more time on the script. I was pretty much a snob about horror/monster movies. I tried to convince myself that BLACK ROSES was about a terrific English teacher who somehow manages to get his classes to read Emerson and Whitman! For me, the monsters and tits were just thrown in to sell the thing! John knew how much this particular subject meant to me personally so he wouldn't have dared to touch a word. On the other hand he was, and rightly so, adamant about the monster/blood or tit every seven minute rule! I took things way more seriously than John, always. He could always see the way to make pretty much anything work whereas I always stuck to my guns. Perhaps because both my parents were detectives! The editing was a different story. One thing you need to learn, and fast if you want to make movies, is that you are not alone! This is a collaborative art form, and you'd better like that, or not get involved in film at all. Naturally, I wanted more classroom scenes, and less people setting themselves on fire! Fewer boob-switches and more quotes from obscure writers! Strangely, though? Of all the produced films I have made, I am the most proud of the script of BLACK ROSES. I have plenty of scripts in my closet that are far better. But on screen, no! Because once studios become involved—there are studio executives. And everyone must have their say. Before you know it - only one gag of yours remains in a film that you initially pitched to the studio! But that's a story for another book.

---

By Marco Siedelmann, in writing,
from Los Angeles
27July, 2015

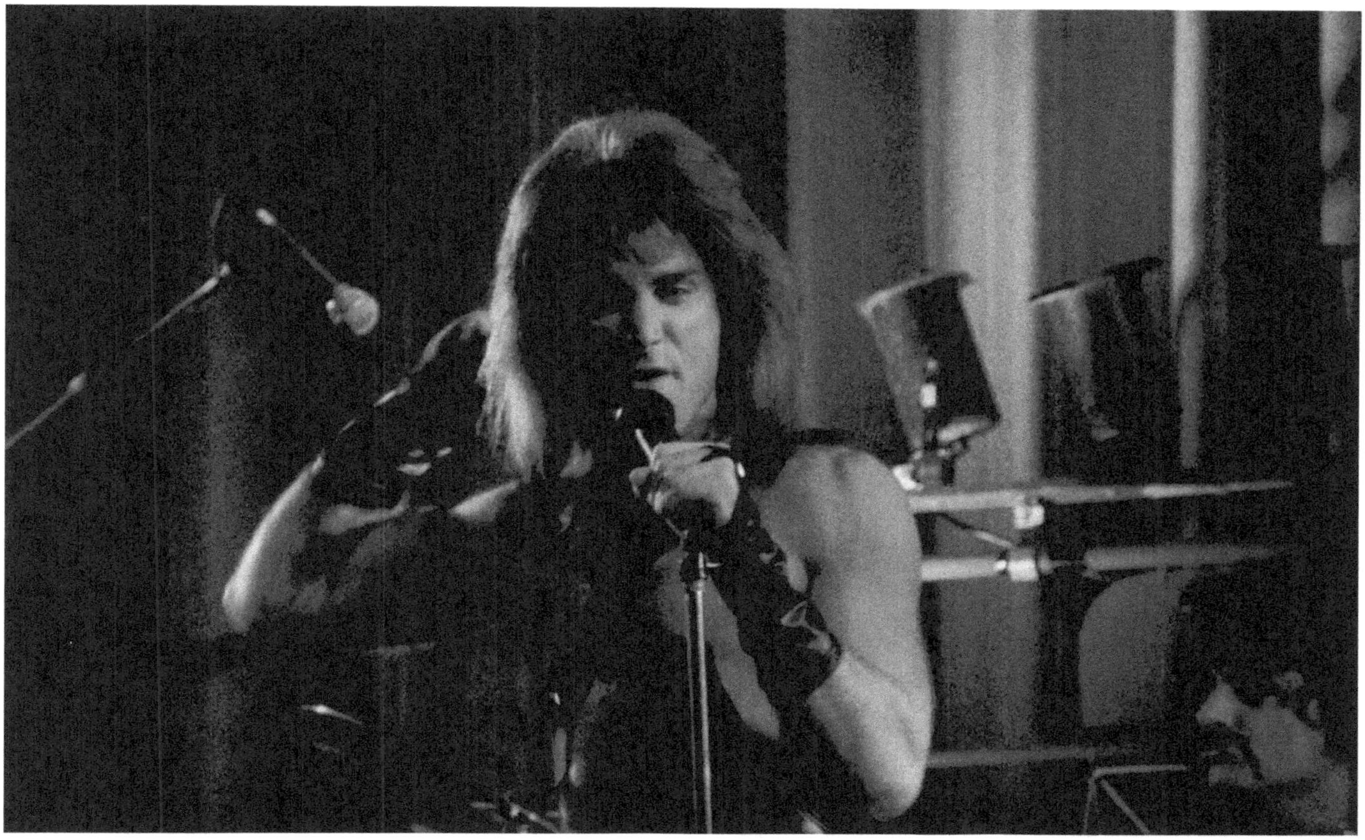

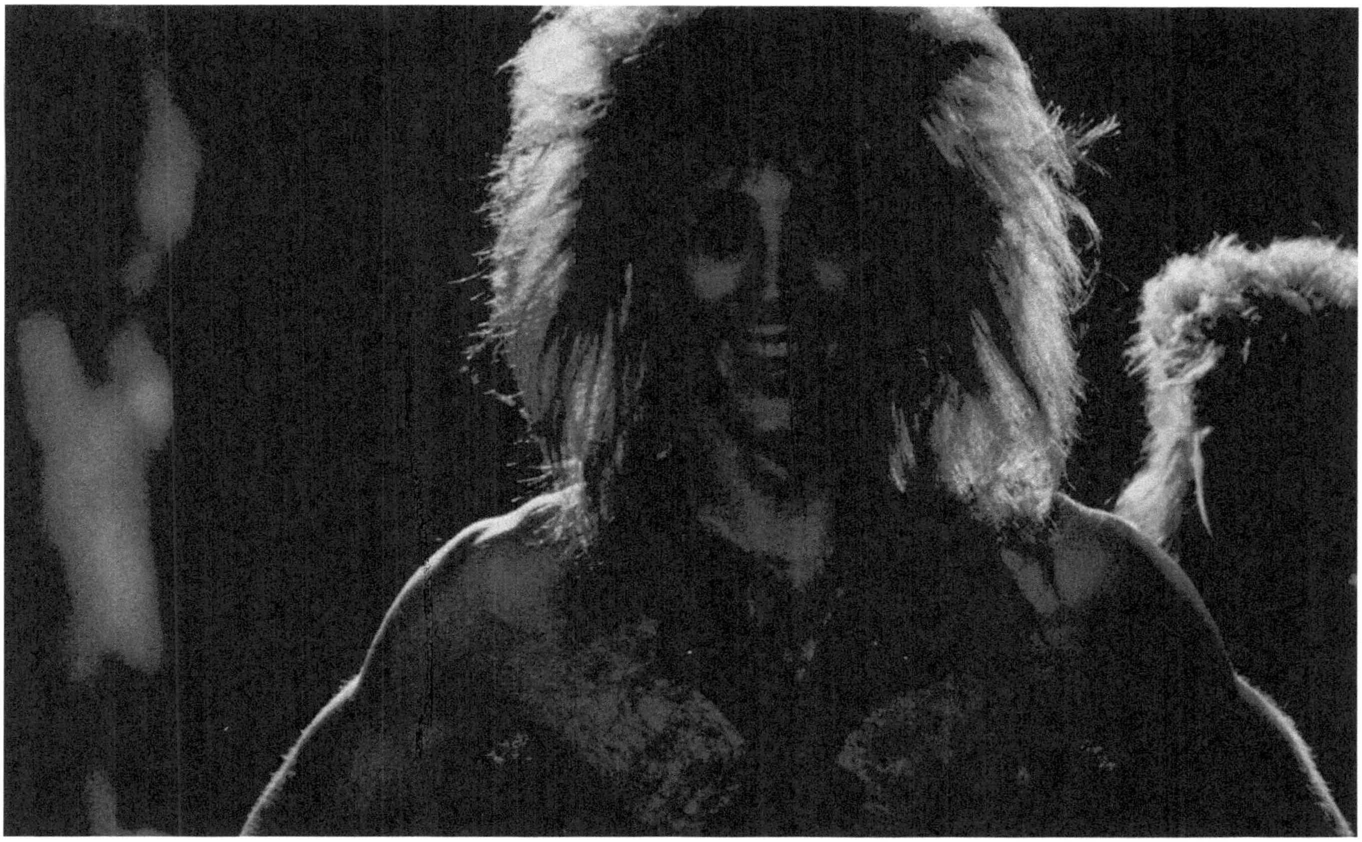

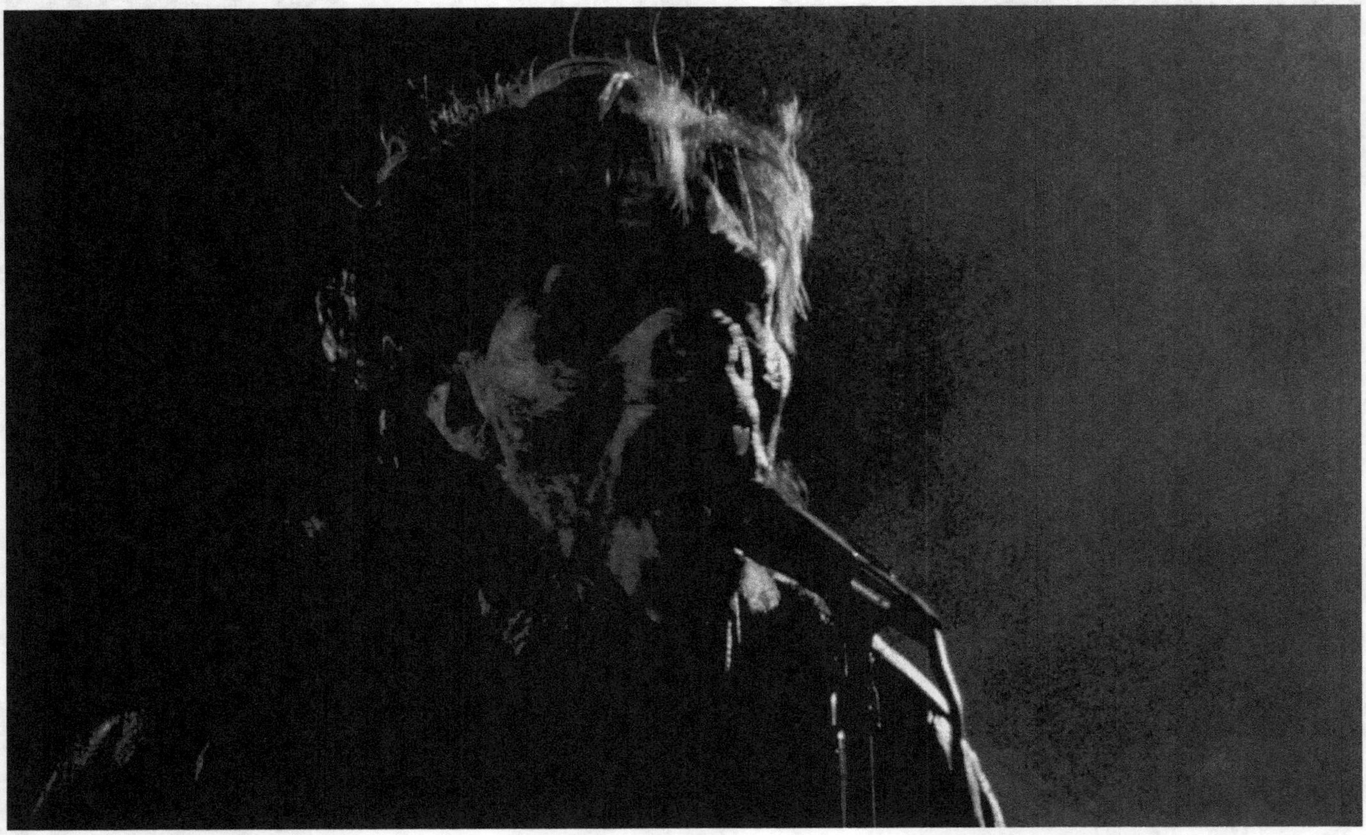

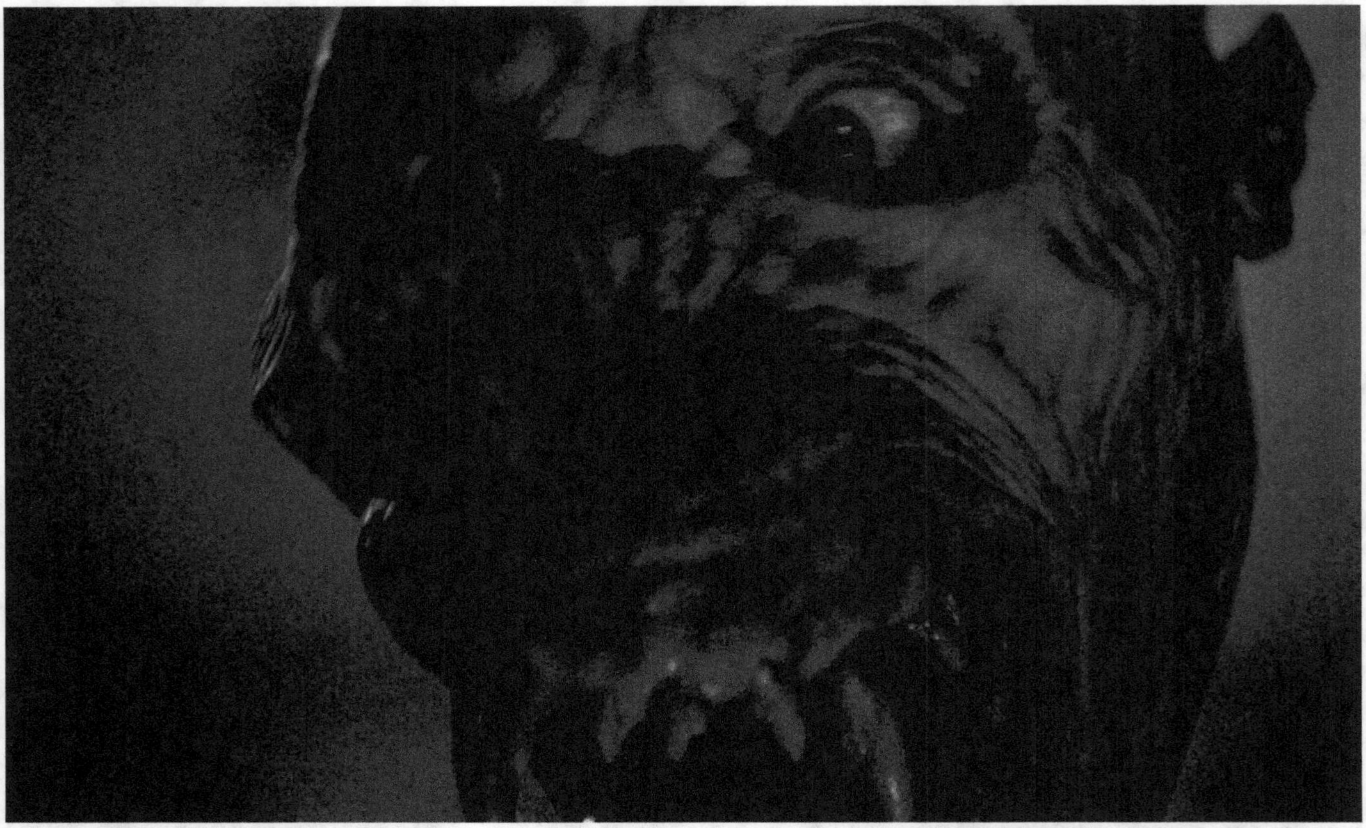

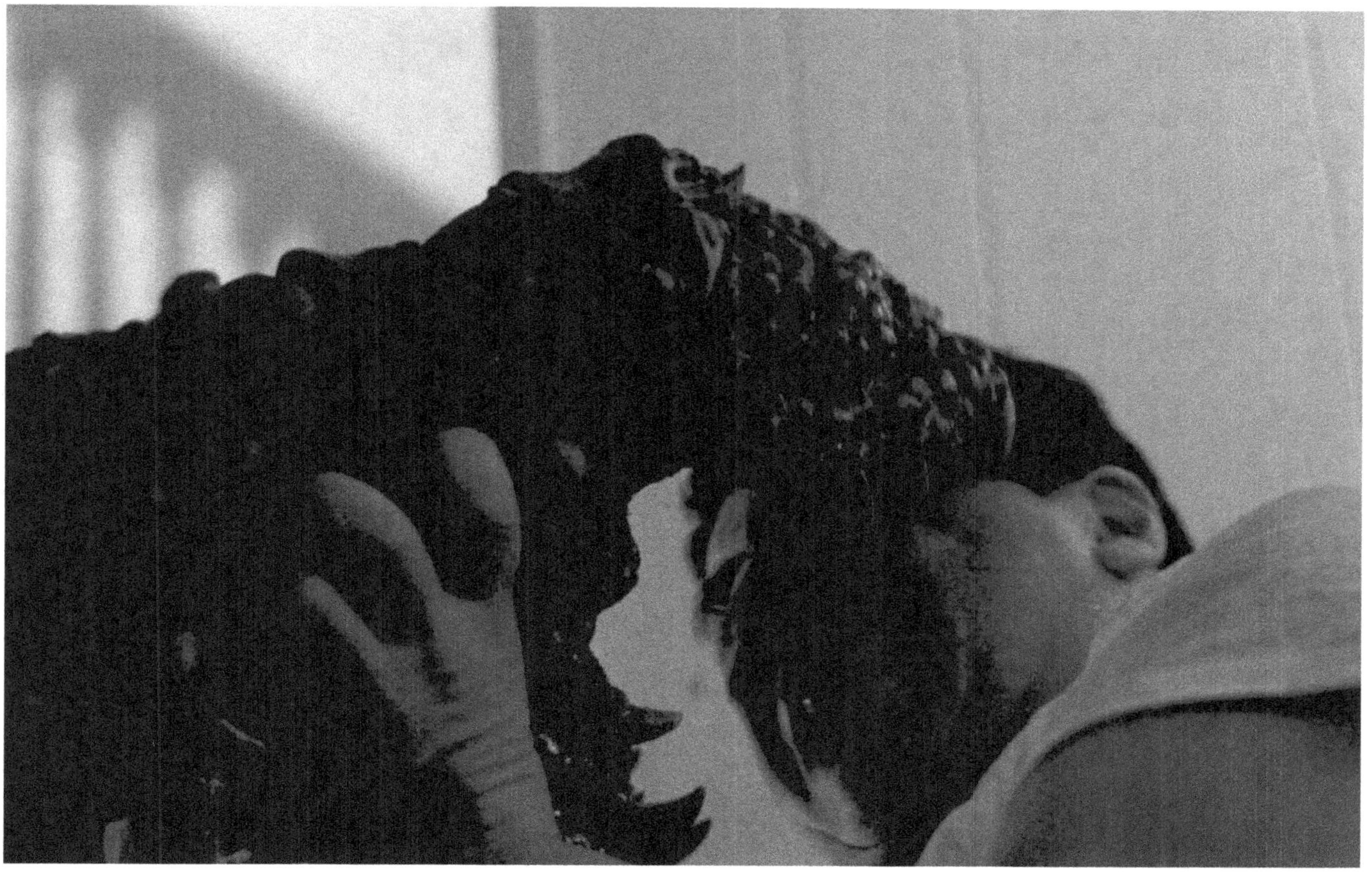

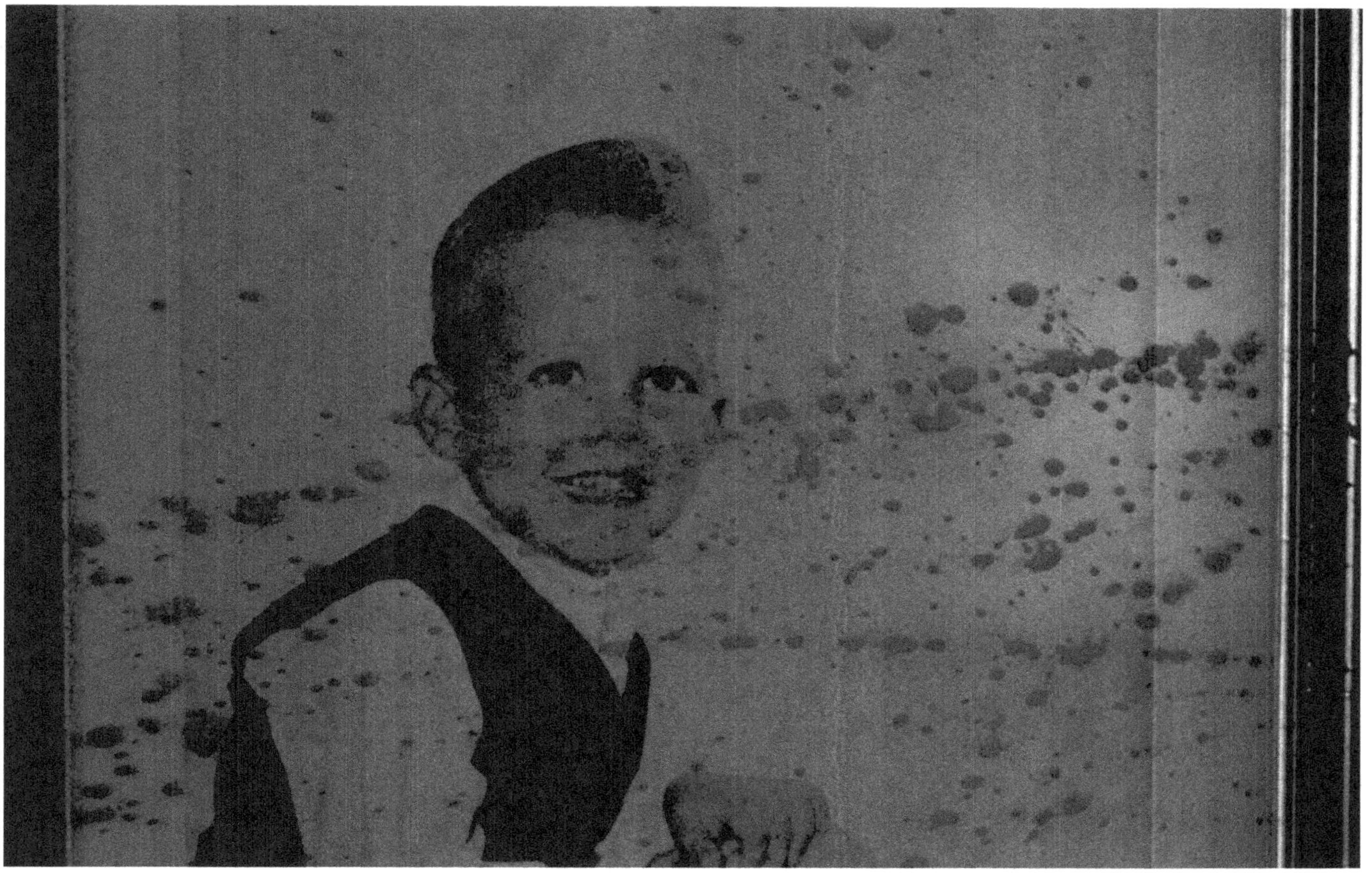

LIVE FOR ONE NIGHT ONLY...

THAT'S ALL THEY'LL EVER NEED.

# Black Roses

SHAPIRO ENTERTAINMENT PRESENTS "BLACK ROSES"
STARRING JOHN MARTIN • KEN SWOFFORD • JULIE ADAMS • CARMINE APPICE AND SAL VIVIANO
MUSIC BY MASI AND ELLIOT SOLOMON  PHOTOGRAPHY BY PAUL MITCHNICK
SCREENPLAY BY CINDY SORRELL  PRODUCED BY RAY VAN DOORN AND JOHN FASANO
EXECUTIVE PRODUCER LEONARD SHAPIRO  ASSOCIATE PRODUCER JERRY LANDESMAN  EXECUTIVE IN CHARGE OF PRODUCTION FRANK ISAAC  DIRECTED BY JOHN FASANO
©1987 SHAPIRO ENTERTAINMENT

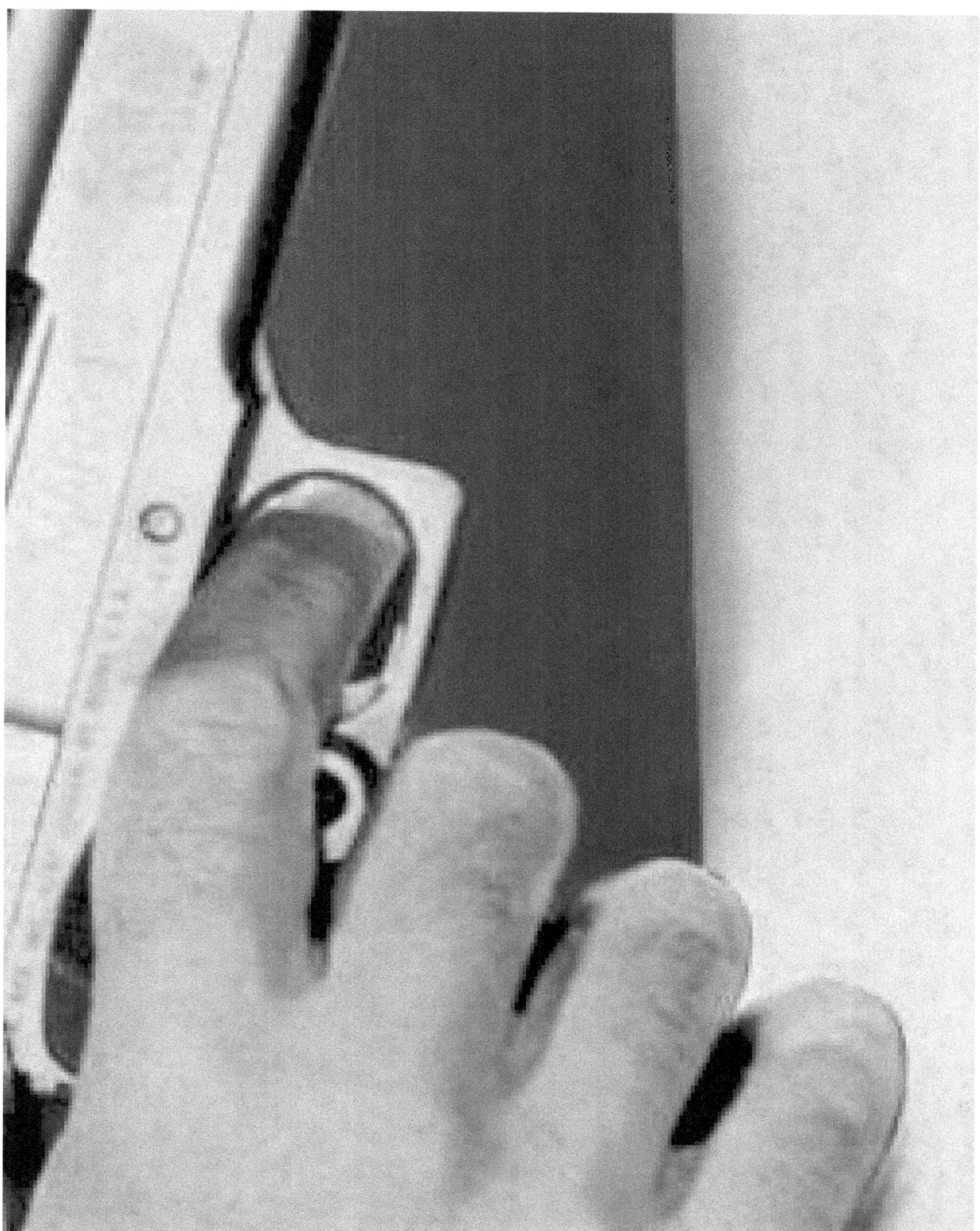

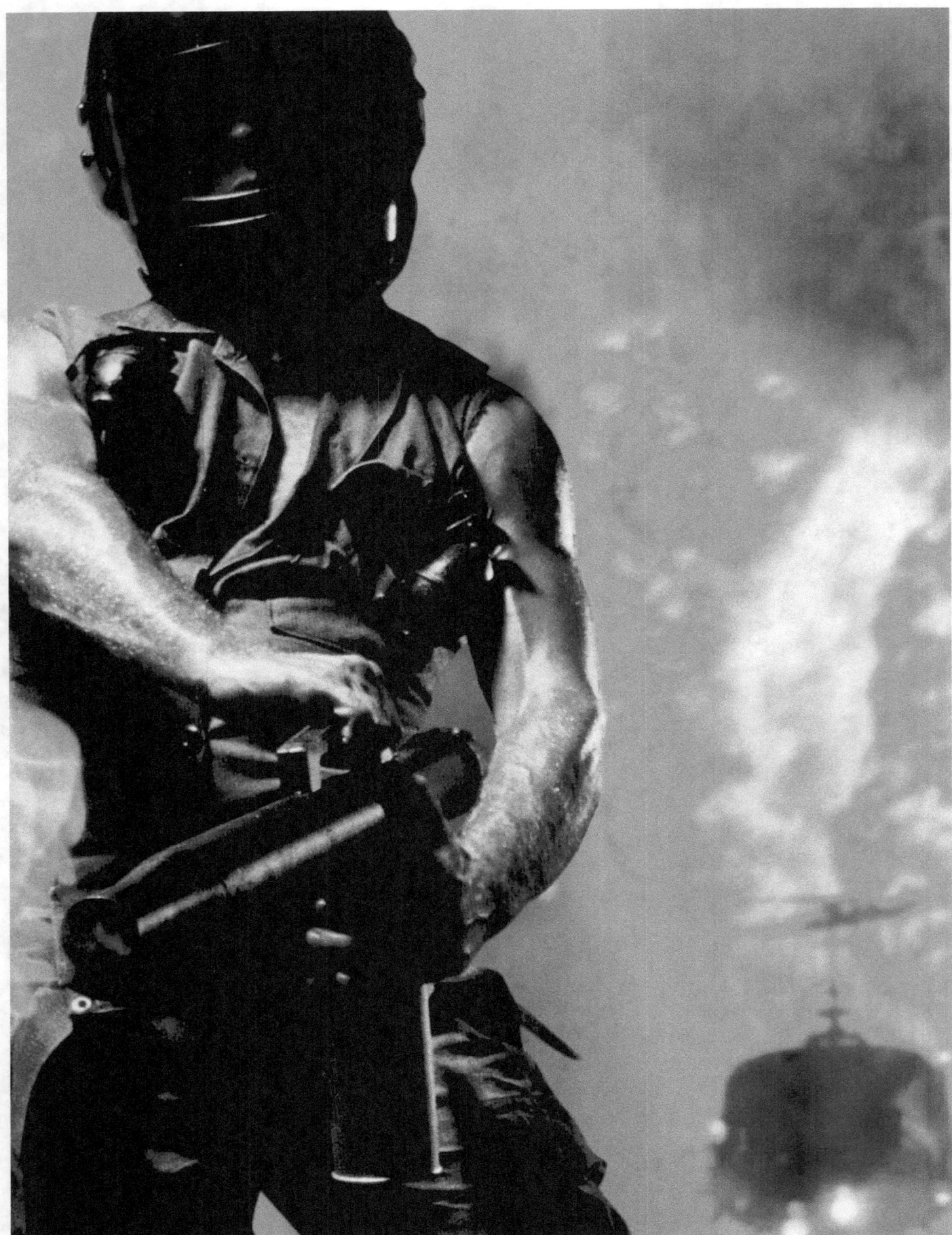

# III. The VHS Explosion: SGE Goes Nuclear in Home Video

*"The audience is always right."*

– Cecil B. DeMille

# James Glickenhaus (Part I)

James Glickenhaus entered the film scene early in the hey-day of exploitations films. He comes from a well-known New Yorker business dynasty, and the money he put into the company made it possible for SGE to hit the industry on a very high level - not only as a distributor but also as a production company financing their own titles. He met co-founder Leonard Shapiro when he directed the films THE EXTERMINATOR and THE SOLDIER. He then created THE PROTECTOR, Jackie Chan's entry to the American market. Right after SGE was founded, Jim Glickenhaus directed the cop film masterpiece SHAKEDOWN, starring Peter Weller and Sam Elliot. He continued with movies like MCBAIN and SLAUGHTER OF THE INNOCENTS, and he also directed SGE's very last production TIMEMASTER, starring the filmmaker's son Jesse Glickenhaus in the leading role.

**Nadia:** Do you remember a key moment in your life, kind of an awakening of the love for cinema?

**James:** Yeah, I used to like movies when I was a kid. I lived kind of in a suburb but it was pretty rural, so my mom could take a few dollars and I could take a bus to White Plains and buy a ticket for 25 cents, and buy a ticket for the movie for 50 cents and you know, a cheeseburger and a milkshake at the place next door, and still have enough money to come home. And I remember going to the RKO in White Plains. It just showed endless double features, I mean I saw films and I didn't know who made them at that time. Like Sergio Leone's COLOSSUS OF RHODES, some of the early horror films like FALL OF THE HOUSE OF USHER, and then they had shows I remember. The "twist" was really hot then, and they had a movie, ROCK AROUND THE CLOCK and DON'T KNOCK THE TWIST and Chubbie Checker came and, like put on a show half time...

**Nadia:** Cool!

**James:** Yeah, it was very cool. And I like westerns, and all kinds of movies. So I started watching them pretty young when I was able to do it. And as I grew up, you know the 60s were kind of magic. Some of the French New Wave films, American filmmakers, films like EASY RIDER, FIVE EASY PIECES - which were sort of very different to the pictures you could make today but in that early time you could do a film like FIVE EASY PIECES with Nicholson. He just walks out on his life, puts his jacket, gets into a truck, heading to Canada in the middle of winter. Or in EASY RIDER where the guys get killed in the end, shot up by rednecks. And sort of the intersection of film and music, too - where I think EASY RIDER was one of the first rock themed scored films. You know?

**Nadia:** Yeah!

**James:** Even Dylan wrote the ballad on EASY RIDER...he didn't put his name on it because there was some sort of dispute with the record company. So I really liked that. It also was magical times, meaning sort of what it is today. You could make films with very little money in those days. But we shot film, it was a little different to what happened with film now, the video. It was all on film, super 16, blown up to

35mm. But these were magic times, guys like Martin Scorsese, and Brian De Palma, De Niro, movies like TAXI DRIVER, or HI MOM!, or JOE (1970, John Avildsen). You know, some of the early films like that. And I just loved them all.

**Nadia:** That's great. So when did you decide to becoming a filmmaker? Or was it always your dream?

**James:** Well, I always liked films, and I always wanted to make them. One of the colleges I went to, Antioch, was a work-study college, so it got me into an apprenticeship with an industrial filmmaker, and I got a lot of experience making industrial films at the time. It was the beginning of film schools, MIT had a film school, but they were sort of documentary based. They had made some great documentaries up there. I sort of audited some classes in film, but I was interested in stories. For me, my filmmaking was sort of an outgrowth of campfires where you sit around the campfire and tell tales, ghost tales. And I like action films, visual things. I mean, I was really amazed by Spaghetti Westerns which were sort of iconic westerns, but they were shot in Spain by Italian guys. Sergio Leone, he really started Eastwood. And anti-heroes, The Man with No Name, and just guys who didn't always get the babe. They sort of left town after doing what they did. Yet again, alone. That kind of interested me, and the 60s were a time you could make anti-hero movies, and everything didn't have to have a happy ending. Things could be more complex. But if you, you had to do them, you did special effects, there really weren't too many. You know, fade-in, fade-out, double exposure but certainly not the computer generated effects which you have today.

**Nadia:** About THE ASTROLOGER: It's very rarely seen today, and often overlooked as your debut as a director.

**James:** You know, Meg's father wrote the book THE ASTROLOGER, and it was published by Random House, and it did very well. At first my idea was to produce it, so I tried to get in touch with, actually some producers. I drove up to Martha's Vineyard, meeting David Brown, who was producing JAWS at that time. They went back and forth, and then I kinda got a Hollywood agent who was interested in it and Rod Sterling was willing to write the screenplay, which I thought was amazing, after THE TWILIGHT ZONE. But oddly, there was no one in Hollywood who seemed to care about that at that time, which I thought was kind of crazy. And then I got in touch with William Friedkin, he had just finished THE EXORCIST, and I tried to get him, and he sort of half-assed was, and then wasn't. I finally realized, that route - the traditional Hollywood route - was long and fraught with peril. So I just figured what if we could raise a small amount of money. Like, let's go out and make a movie. It certainly was pretty amateurish, none of us really knew what we're doing. But we finished it. And those were times when people were willing to help. We made this incredible deal, and shot the film in 35mm Panavision. I mean I thought we were going to shoot in Super

16, but a movie lab gave us a great price to develop, and we got a good price to mix and make the sound effects on the film. You know they did it for a piece of backend. They were just helping filmmakers. So we made it, and when it was done we found some distributors. Distribution was much, much different in those days. There were local distributors, who really connected with the theaters - well, this is for independent films, not for Hollywood films. There were no national releases [for independent films]. At the time of THE EXTERMINATOR, the company American Cinema Releasing was the first one that really went wide with 800 prints. Before that they made around 50 prints. I mean THE GRADUATE, they stuck in 50 cities, [it] just went on week after week, after week. The films played for years. Because there was no video and television for films like that. So I worked on that because I wanted to learn about that part of the business. So I sort of put the cans of film in the back of a rental car, drove all over the South where they had drive-ins, of all the things, and they did come in and do promotions. Actually, we made money. People went to the movies, every Friday night. They just went.

**Nadia:** Yeah!

**James:** And if you could cut together a cool trailer, and if you showed up in a little town, they were delighted to put you on the radio, and promote it. Or a local TV reporter would come out, and meet with you. It wasn't quite four-walling, but you could make a deal, and you got paid after that, and went to the next one. So we did that, and then one of the distributors in Texas looked at it. He said, "Look: The only part of this movie that's watchable is all the action stuff. Maybe you should make an action film." And so I set off, actually, to make a silent action film. My goal was what Leone had done in THE GOOD, THE BAD, AND THE UGLY. You know, 14 minutes of film before anyone's saying anything. Actually the first draft of THE EXTERMINATOR was silent. There was very, very little dialogue. And I realized that that wasn't going to work, I needed more dialogue in it. But that was a time you could experiment. As you know, you were involved with it. You could go to Cannes at the Marché du Film, you could make sales, and if you made a decent film, you could cover the budget - with the foreign markets. And then you could come to the United States, and if you could find some distribution, you could make some more money with it.

**Nadia:** THE EXTERMINATOR, THE SOLDIER, THE PROTECTOR - they were all made before you teamed up with Leonard Shapiro to found SGE.

**James:** Yes, although I met Lenny when I did THE EXTERMINATOR, he was at Avco Embassy with Bob Rehme, and they wound up distributing the film. That was the first time that I met Lenny, and so I met him as a distributor. He and I worked out a deal, and THE EXTERMINATOR was a very, very successful film for them. Lenny was so naive he forgot to include video rights for them, but we sorted that out.

**Nadia:** *(laughing)*

**James:** It was a lucrative film for me, and then they said: "Ok, let's make another movie.", which would be the second movie, THE SOLDIER, which Lenny was involved in, and helped get financed. Then Avco Embassy basically was sold, and the company completely changed. They had a totally different idea, and they let go of Lenny. He went off on his own and formed Shapiro Entertainment, in the beginning as a producer's rep. I was his first client as a producer's rep, although I'm not sure exactly what he did for me. *(laughing)*

**Nadia:** And there was THE PROTECTOR, with Golden Harvest.

**James:** Yeah. What happened with that was, I got a call from Golden Harvest. They said: "Look, we have this huge Asian star - Jackie Chan, he makes this Hong Kong chop-sockey films." I mean, they were kind of cold about it actually, they said to keep him happy we need to make an American film. They were like, "We'll give you total carte blanche, you can do whatever you like when you make a film with him." I said, "Yeah!" I had never been to Hong Kong, so they flew me there. I went on a tour, and I came up with some script ideas. That's how THE PROTECTOR happened, but it was financed entirely by Golden Harvest, and picked up by Warner Brothers.

**Nadia:** So why eventually did you choose to work with Leonard Shapiro and Alan Solomon? Was it sometimes difficult separating personal friendship and business?

**James:** I don't know, there were different times back then. I certainly knew Lenny less. And with Alan, we always stayed in touch, we were always friendly. They were kind of making the go, and it was their pick-ups and producing. These films, although the one film Lenny produced almost killed the company before I got involved, MUGSY'S GIRLS. But my idea was, distribution work was sort of a base. If I could establish a base that kept the doors open and paid the bills, I maybe could use that for making bigger and better films. There was never the idea that all the films I was going to make would go through SGE. I was still able to direct films on my own. In retrospect, and this is looking back, I sort of had a choice to make. I could move to L.A., I had a big agent. I could have just done Hollywood films, it would have been a better thing to do, but on the other hand I did like Lenny, I did like Alan, and I enjoyed our time together. So I look back on it. They certainly didn't mind when I wanted to do my own thing, so it wasn't them. I think I had a hope that I could stay in New York, and have the base of the company cover expenses, and introduce us to filmmakers. And there were some filmmakers I kinda liked and wanted to work with. Like Frank Henenlotter. I like him, I mean I still work with him. I was in his film CHASING BANKSY, which is opened in New York on Thursday.

**Nadia:** Oh really? Cool. How does the job of being an Executive Producer differ from being the on-set producer?

**James:** The only films that I really was an Executive Producer for, that I had hands on production, was with Frank. I liked working with him. So basically, FRANKENHOOKER and BASKET CASE 2 & 3. The Lustig film (MANIAC COP) was going on its own, and I was making SHAKEDOWN at that time, so I really didn't have much time to put in any input on that. I guess my sort of brief to Lenny and Alan was, as long as they made money I was fine with it. To pay the bills, and keep the thing going. And if you were a company, you had to make 10 or 12 films a year, B-Movies, just to keep the doors open. In fairness to those guys, they were pretty good for a while, picking films that did well. I don't know that they lost that ability or that the market just changed, and it became sort of impossible to keep the whole thing going. A little of both I mean, you were there, I mean you could probably answer this better than me.

**Nadia:** Yeah, I was the one that picked DR. , which lost the video company, I don't know, hundreds of thousands of dollars, I don't know how much. That was my fault.

**James:** Right, it wasn't only that. It was that, the world changed, and quite frankly, there are guys who are huge in Hollywood today who would sit down and tell you that they're geniuses but they just got lucky. I mean the Weinstein brothers, if they hadn't had THE CRYING GAME, that would have been it. So there's a lot of that in Hollywood. And I think that makes a lot of people bitter, too. People who had been talented, and smart, better than these people look at it, why does it happened to them and did not happened to me? Have you seen LOVE AND MERCY, the Brian Wilson film?

**Nadia:** No, I haven't yet...

**James:** It's worth seeing, because it's sort of that. It goes in the whole music business, and it's the same thing. Artistic talent is a blessing and a curse. And it doesn't always end happily. This is a lot different then business. I mean when Brian made the album that was really from his heart, it did very poorly. You know, there's always that. Later on people come to understand how good it is, and what's involved, and how it works out.

**Nadia:** You come from a business family, has this aspect influenced your work as a producer?

**James:** I was always thoughtful, you can't run a company, and have employees, and be reckless. Otherwise it would go down very quickly. I think that the truth of it was in fairness Lenny and Alan, they ran a tight ship, they weren't reckless, or impulsive. They made mistakes, we all made mistakes. But we got too big and geared up for stuff that would have worked if the films had worked like RED SCORPION. So we had to cut back. it wasn't like we were losing tons of money, it was just something that there was no future. And the time did come to move on.
One important thing was we didn't go bankrupt. There just was a certain point where was no future. So I closed the doors. But it wasn't like some of the other guys, like Cannon or someone who lost big money.

**Nadia:** So SGE did pick up more than a hundred titles. How were the decisions about a particular film made? All three together - Lenny, Alan, and you? I remember it that way, right?

**James:** Yeah, that's a fair statement. We all decided together, once again with a caveat - there's sort of a saying on Wall Street: There is fish for eating, and there is fish for buying. So there were fish we were eating, and there were fish we were buying, but never would be eating. There were certainly some deals, how should I say ... that were only for financial reasons. We made money with it. By and large we did. Also being a distributor was really not a bad gig, because sometimes the producers spend their life savings on films starring, you know, bimbos who couldn't act their way out of a paper bag. And you can get a film you had spent $4 million on for nothing. Being in first position, you can make some sales. You always made your 20 percent or whatever you did. So it wasn't the worst thing for you.

**Nadia:** Chris Ingvordsen did the biggest number of SGE distributed productions. Was there some kind of close connection to him or his work?

**James:** Well, I think Chris really was really self-sustaining, he came to us with finished films, and that he believed in. We distributed them. We sometimes put up money for ad campaigns, or posters, or taking him to Cannes. But since we were in first position, we gave him total latitude, because he was really the one taking the financial risk. Even if we put out some money, we were always in first position, and I don't think we ever lost money on Chris Ingvordsen. He may or may not, have it's what I don't know. But I like Chris, he was a genuine guy who made films and they delivered, as you know they had found customers. But I just think the thing with us was, we never produced a piece of crap, and sold it to someone. No one ever was unhappy with the films we delivered.

**Nadia:** Why did SGE not produce the sequels to MANIAC COP?

**James:** I just didn't like Lustig. I did not want to work with him again. *(laughter)*

**Nadia:** SHAKEDOWN is one of the best films of its decade - What changed for you as a filmmaker, when you did SHAKEDOWN - produced by your very own company?

**James:** I think SHAKEDOWN really did work. I think I got a little screwed, but I don't blame anyone for this but myself. I made a deal with Universal, and they had a hole in their schedule, and they had to have a film for a certain day in May, for some bizarre reasons I forgot about. And I didn't have time to finally fine-tune it. If I had, I would have done the ending a little more believable, which I think would have helped it, but the film worked. I mean it was about something important, and it did well. It made millions of dollars. It still does, it's still playing. It was actually on July 5th playing at the Castro Theater, with ROBOCOP. Someone called me up from the theater, and said they're all watching. It was funny. But, look: it started, I had a lot of freedom. No distributor, and we had the foreign sales, and really developed it. We sort of got together with Dino De Laurentiis but then he went bankrupt. He had some wacky crazy deals, that would have been interesting, had he not gone bankrupt. It was basically that he could put up $5 million, and he just had theatrical and HBO rights. We would have video. So it actually would have been very lucrative for us, when it would have worked. But it didn't. Then Universal came in. And listen, Universal liked the film, and they did well, whatever. They were a machine, and I think we got caught up when they needed a film for that date. But things at the end, so they got a little bit ... wack. Life is like that.

**Nadia:** What about Frank Henenlotter, did you see the original BASKET CASE at that time?

**James:** I met Frank in Cannes when I had THE EXTERMINATOR, and I saw BASKET CASE. And I really liked it. And it was from an era that SHAKEDOWN sort of was set in, when 42nd Street just had those grindhouses, double features, and stuff like that. I liked Frank, I liked BASKET CASE, it was a quite powerful film, I thought 42nd Street, the seamy side of it was an amazing thing that was going to disappear, and it has. It became Disneyland. And SHAKEDOWN, which was really shot on 42nd Street - we shot down there for two nights in a row, midnight til six in the morning. Real stunts and stuff. You really can't do anything like that anymore. Those grindhouses, they all became Disney palaces. I think that was my attraction to Frank. He's really an artist. Perhaps he's not the most commercial person in the world, sometimes he needs ten years to make a film. The last one he did was CHASING BANKSY. But he's certainly fun to work with. I enjoyed it. And there always was a bunch of young people working with him.

**Nadia:** I love BASKET CASE 2, I think it's one of the best films ever, it still really holds up.

**James:** Yes, he made some good stuff. I like FRANKENHOOKER!

**Nadia:** Yeah, me too!
So, although it's one of the best pictures of its kind, MCBAIN did not well at the theatrical box office. Did it make its money afterwards - with home video, television, and international sales?

**James:** You know, the problem with MCBAIN at the box office was, in those days it was very tough - unless you had the money - to go out in a massive release. It didn't do terribly in New York, it didn't do well. But had we gone national with it, I think we could even have sold more videos we did, and some more television deals then we made. As it was, we lost money on MCBAIN. But it wasn't a disaster. We got big foreign sales out of it.

**Nadia:** Yeah, that's what I remember. Do you agree that the film came too late since action movies had become more and more family entertainment? Was it important to you making it rather dark and gritty?

**James:** Yeah, I think for whatever the reasons dark action films were more interesting, probably because of my roots in the 60s films we talked about earlier. Look at TAXI DRIVER, I mean that was a dark film. I don't know if that would play today. I also think that by then action films become like comic book characters, like Batman. And they didn't care if the villians were stupid. The stuff that I did was a nuance darker, and everybody wanted heroes, no more anti-heroes. And I think politically there was something that ran into censorship problems in some countries because no one wanted to face the fact there were countries who are just taken over by narcos. Whole countries.

**Nadia:** Yeah, especially at that time, it was awful.

**James:** I mean an interesting thing was years later - maybe it was in Santa Monica, or something - I ran into a guy - and I believed him – he purported to know Escobar in Columbia. He was sort of a rich jet setter, but it had a ring the truth. He said, Pablo loved that film! You come down and meet them! You know, you meet some strange people at 3 in the morning. But this wasn't like the guy was making this up. He believed this was true. There's great parties, and you'll love it! So we could fly down there!

**Nadia:** When you agreed with a director about a particular film, did you leave him alone during the production process?

**James:** Oh yeah, I interfered very little, I think even William Lustig would say that. I did make some cuts with Frank's films, 'cause he was obsessed about some things. Just like, enough is enough. The bizarre foot fetishes. These long scenes in FRANKENHOOKER with Patty Mullen's toes, which you know after awhile... But yeah, I left people alone.

**Nadia:** Is it very important for you to see a film on the big screen, and what do you think about VHS, and how your films looked on video?

**James:** Yeah, I remember going to 42nd Street, and seeing four movies at a time. On the big screen, on huge screens. And then screens got smaller ... I don't want to sound like DeMille in SUNSET BOULEVARD - but they did! They changed. The only difference I think is, that I never took it personally. I had a great time, a big time, you know?

**Nadia:** You are considered being absolutely not an enthusiast when it comes to CGI effects. But TIMEMASTER contains lots of early CGI stuff. How do you feel about the film today?

**James:** The film was made at the very beginning of CGI, but I think at TIMEMASTER there was a reason for it. Because of the images you couldn't photograph. What it became was in a disaster movie, they said, ok let's write a thing with buildings split in half and a hero like Tom Cruise jumps from one roof to another skyscraper. There were others that fail. Stuff like that just bores the hell out of me.

**Nadia:** You did not like the sequel of THE EXTERMINATOR at all, true?

**James:** I had nothing to do with it. Mark was a childhood friend, I think we had grown apart by the end of THE EXTERMINATOR. It was a way to let him go on and see what

**he** could do. So I had let him do it. The real sequel to THE EXTERMINATOR was FIRST BLOOD. I actually spoke to Sylvester Stallone and those guys. It was the way it was, sort of like: Get your gun off, walk north, and bring in the first blood. I don't mean literally, or that they ripped it off. I just mean the story of it.

**Nadia:** Your films starred people like Michael Ironside, Pat Morita, Klaus Kinski, Christopher Walken, Michael Ginty, Jackie Chan, and lots more. Although you never worked with a particular actor again. How important was it for SGE to cover such star names in the films?

**James:** We needed stars to sell, we definitely did. There are ones I would have loved working with again. But they died. Christopher George - liked him, would have worked with him again. he died shortly there after. Samantha I liked a lot, and I thought she was a very good actress. I did not make a film where she would fit again. I mean she was really British. Casting in THE EXTERMINATOR kinda worked but it wasn't her fault, but it was a little strange. But I certainly would have worked with her. Chris Walken I liked, and we stayed in touch.

**Nadia:** Ironside...

**James:** I mean, Ironside - I didn't have another role for him, so it wasn't that I wound up hating all of them! A lot of them I never wanted to see again! But that said, they were very important. You have to remove THE SOLDIER and THE PROTECTOR because those were studio films. And the studio really had a lot of say, that's how i got Ken Wahl, and I got Klaus Kinski because Kinski liked my movies. He was a great guy on the set for one day. Making a movie with Klaus would have been impossible.

**Nadia:** Right! What was he like?

**James:** I knew him. He was a fierce talent, but with everything, with all the baggage that it brought. He was like, he did everything to excess. His acting, his womanizing, his behavior on the set. And he liked to come across as a complete lunatic. However, if you told him to fuck off he understood. He didn't take that personally. And I was totally happy, and willing to do that. And I think his most successful films were amazing films. I'm thinking about the ones he did with Werner Herzog. FITZCARRALDO, for example. He also died, I would have used him again.

**Nadia:** Why did you shut down SGE?

**James:** It stopped being fun. It was just too much. The world changed on us. People always ask, why did you leave the film business? You can give a glib, stupid answer, but there's some truth in it. Dino de Laurentiis said to me: "Jim, by the time you can get into the parties, you won't want to go." There was a lot of truth to that. And then the thing I always said, when people have asked for sound bites for tv etc., that it's a lot more fun getting coked up with actresses out of Winnebegos in their twenties than in their forties. That's true, and I don't mean it any actress or actor in particular! There were just people who destroying themselves in front of you.

**Nadia:** And it just became unpleasant and sad to see.

That's great! – so let's go back THE EXTERMINATOR and how you worked for the first time with composer Joe Renzetti on this production. Was he your number one choice for the score? What was interesting about him?

**James:** I was working with a music guy, Murray Barber, who had been a promoter and producer and had toured, you know with Black groups, like the Four whatevers, and you know, really at a time when those guys were getting screwed, sort of in the shadow of Motown – they'd have a concert with say The Drifters, and if the Drifters wanted too much money, they'd just get four other guys that looked kind of like them, and say they were The Drifters. And I remember Murray saying that one venue that they'd agreed to go to, that when they showed up just changed the terms of the deal, just because they could. They'd driven all night...

Anyway, he knew Renzetti and hooked me up with him. He also hooked me up with a lot of musicians in your town, in Nashville, that wrote songs like later, on THE SOLDIER, George Strait, and on THE EXTERMINATOR, Chip Taylor who was Jon Voight's brother, wrote 'Angel of the Morning', he wrote the Theme for an American Hero the main song. And Roger Bowling was a really famous guy, wrote a bunch of Kenny Roger's songs. Unfortunately he had brain cancer and killed himself shortly thereafter. But he wrote 'Heal It', the title song in THE EXTERMINATOR. And Renzetti did the music, and I think he did a very good job. You know, we had things like 'Disco Inferno' from The Tramps, and the original music – I like the music a lot.

**Nadia:** There were some differences between you and main actor Robert Ginty, correct? Was it about the character development?

**James:** Oh there really weren't differences. You know, Ginty, as some actors are, was very full of himself, and was a bit of a pain in the ass, but there weren't differences. I would say no differences though, artistically or creatively, at all – we were completely on the same page. I just wasn't in the mood to put up with his crap. And you know years later he apologized for his behavior, and actually wanted to do more stuff with me, but I just wasn't that interested at that point. You know, Ginty's an interesting guy. He had tremendous promise, he was in COMING HOME, he was in that tv series BAA BAA BLACK SHEEP, and after THE EXTERMINATOR, he was huge. But he just got into a "take-a-check" mode and he just took a lot of really terrible low-budget crap. He had a big agent, as I remember it, at the time, Jack Gillardi, who was married to Annette Funicello, but I don't know...he went on his way. And then I think he did EXTERMINATOR 2 and that really didn't help him that much. He became sort of an artist in his own way, he directed and wrote some films, and wrote some poetry and such. We stayed in touch over the years. But he just wasn't someone I enjoyed working with that much, not as an actor but just as a

**Nadia:** person on the set. But no, there were no major differences, no artistic differences.

**Nadia:** It's obviously not the typical action film - what were you going for when conceiving and writing THE EXTERMINATOR?

**James:** I think it was a sort of a cautionary tale, that if the criminal justice system broke down, and there was just this wave of crimes – which seemed to be happening in New York City at this time. I mean there was crack cocaine and just a lot of senseless crazy killings – that vigilantism was going to be a reality. It was a theme others had expressed – DIRTY HARRY, DEATH WISH, things like that, rage, to some extent TAXI DRIVER was about revenge, and that kind of stuff. But having said that it was more film noire to me, you know – NY City, the dark underbelly, based on incidents that did in fact happen. The term I used at the time was "faction" – it wasn't true but it could have beent true. The other thing was looking at someone like Ginty, who wasn't an ultra-macho, terminating, like Schwarzenegger type, he was just a common person who got pushed too far, and snapped, and went and did his thing.

**Nadia:** Please describe your work with cinematographer Robert M. Baldwin. Later MCBAIN was his very last feature film. Was it important to get a veteran behind the camera?

**James:** Yeah, Baldwin was a real veteran, a real professional, and I think he gave a real great visual look to the film. I enjoyed working with him. As often happens, you're on a set, you're thrown into these incredibly intense relationships, both the best and worst of everybody comes out, and you need a little time between working with them again, if ever.

**Nadia:** Did you want to neutralize the glory of revenge that's been often praised in vigilante films?

**James:** No, I think people look for simple sound bites – I was just making movies...

**Nadia:** The music by Tangerine Dream created a very dark atmosphere right from the beginning. Did you get what you needed from the score?

**James:** I liked them, they were friends of mine. I went to concerts of theirs in Berlin where they turned the amplifiers toward East Berlin, it was an interesting time. I first came across them on the William Friedkin film, THE SORCERER, which everybody thought was a sequel to THE EXORCIST, but it was really a remake of THE TREASURE OF SIERRA MADRE, a film about greed. But they had a terrific score, and I wanted to work with them. And Chris Franke actually became a friend, I spent time with him in Berlin, and he scored also the film MCBAIN, which I enjoyed.

**Nadia:** Would you agree THE SOLDIER is like an antithesis of the Bond films?

**James:** I think the Bond films are a great genre, escapist entertainment is what they are. I think THE SOLDIER was really more about the real world, the laxity of security on plutonium, which is still really shocking and lax, and could really come home to roost some day. And the idea that the

Russians really were bad guys, and often a lot of events that happened in the real world were manipulated by people behind the scenes to cull advantage. And that was the point of THE SOLDIER – that something that on face value was fanatical terrorists was really the Russians pretending to be terrorists that would precipitate a crisis that would destroy the United States. It was a bit more complex. At the time I was reading a lot of John LeCarré, who I think has written the best spy novels, like THE NIGHT PORTER, LITTLE DRUMMER GIRL. I think you must have met him, because a lot of his female characters are like you, a lot *(laughter)*. But I think that he wrote very interesting female characters, and I was trying to do that with the Israeli agent in THE SOLDIER, Alberta Watson, who I think...the Israelis really were on their own planet. They thought the whole world was going to try to take them out, as they had once, and that was how they saw the whole world. I think the Ken Wahl character was trying to see the whole world and deal with it. But that was sort of my attempt at LeCarré.

**Nadia:** Many directors had problems with Klaus Kinski. How did he come into the production, how many days did he stay and was he difficult on set?

**James:** I think Klaus was one of those guys who actually was a legend in a way. I think that he tried to be an incredible asshole, but if you stood up to him and said, you know, "Stop it!", he did stop! I remember Boyce's girlfriend at the time picking him up at the airport and having him move to front seat so she wouldn't get physically assaulted. I mean, he was unabashed, only in a sort of fantasy, trashy movies do guys, you know...say to waitresses "You're very beautiful, do you want to go upstairs and fuck? " He actually did stuff like that, and shockingly it actually worked sometimes (laughter)! In the middle of dinner, you'd suddenly be like, where'd Klaus go? *(laughter)* But having said that, it does take two people to engage in behavior like that. And he also was oblivious if someone slammed him in the head and said "Fuck you." you know, he didn't take it personally. But with me...oddly, I think that we played a bit of guts poker, in the sense that we were under-budget, I had some extra money, I said hey let's get Klaus Kinski. So I made him an offer, and his agent called, and said "Klaus is an artist, and this is a very small role, and you're not offering him anything" . And I said, "OK no problem, don't do it." And he said, "Well, I didn't say that!" And he showed it to Kinski and Kinski said he'd do it. I remember Boyce asking the agent, well, why did he decide to do it, and he said... "Artists, you never know!" *(laughter)* He was an artist, but on the other hand, would I have wanted to make FITZCARRALDO with him, for 3 months in the Amazon, no. But for one day in St. Anton, where I controlled everything, sure. And he was very friendly and nice to me, and over the years was very respectful, and you know actually in a news conference with Herzog, where he went berserk, in Cannes, he noticed me and said "There's a real director." which of course was crazy. No, I liked him. He had a strange relationship with his daughter...

**Nadia:** Where did the production take place?

**James:** Oh, all over. We shot in East Berlin, West Berlin, Israel, Egypt, Washington, Philly, NY, a lot of locations. It came about because there was a producer who'd seen THE EXTERMINATOR and said, "Look I'll do your next film, I don't care what it is, but you have to shoot some scenes in Berlin because I have subsidies and money tied up there." I'd never been there. So he flew me to Berlin, I walked around and thought, this is very cool visually, and wrote the script. And then of course he crapped out, and I wound up having to get the financing from Avco Embassy. So it was kind of...I decided to shoot there because I thought it was cool!

**Nadia:** There's a director's cut, which is runs a few minutes shorter than the regular version, is this true? And how did it come about?

**James:** Yes, no mystery to that – it was because in Japan, they have to have a minimum time for a theatrical release, so I put back about a minute and a half to give them the time that they needed. I think the stuff I put back, was stuff I had cut just to make it a bit more fast paced, but it wasn't like there was any great meaning to that.

**Nadia:** Jackie Chan was not a popular star in the US when you cast him for the role - he even did not speak English at the time, is this correct?

**James:** The problem was this. You know, Jackie was basically like a cash machine to Golden Harvest, they just wanted him to make these chop-sockey, Asian films and comedies and he'd shoot three at a time, and they'd ship him off to Japan where he was allegedly a pop star, this whole life they made for him that was ridiculous, you know he's looking for the right girl....hell he was married and had a kid at the time. It was just awful. And then Chan came up with me, because evidently when he released his first breakout in the U.S., THE BIG BRAWL, which didn't do that well, it came out the weekend THE EXTERMINATOR came out, and it creamed his film. So he wanted to work with me. And here's the thing, I think Jackie just assumed I was going to be just like everyone else in his life, which was, Yes Sir, what do you want done, you're the best, let's all go out and party. Which I had no interest in, and I had no interest in making another Hong Kong Jackie Chan film. So I told them that, and they said no problem, he wants to make a U.S. film that will work in the U.S., and I got total creative control, final cut, wrote the script, everything. They paid for it all. It did become obvious that they had misled me on how much English he spoke, he really did not speak much English. He could kind of understand you, but he could not act with an English speaking actor, ad lib off them, anything. So that was very tough for Danny Aiello, he sort of had to parrot some stuff. And also they were doing all these promotions with him, to promote his Chinese films, they were sending him to Japan to sing pop

**Nadia:** songs while we were shooting, we had to flip the schedule so we were actually shooting day for night, it was a bit of a pain in the ass! But I didn't take it personally, and it was really interesting shooting and working in Hong Kong. And I had a really great relationship with Golden Harvest, they actually gave me a pretty big bonus when we were done with the film, they were pretty happy with it, and for putting up with them and everything.

**Nadia:** Many fans criticise the use of his martial arts skills in this movie. Why did you not use more fighting scenes for this one?

**James:** There was a lot of martial arts, I just got bored with how much there was and so, and I also wanted to make martial arts sequences that I frankly thought were realistic, not this Hong Kong opera/ballet stuff that had been around. I enjoyed martial arts, but you know I was really a fan of Bruce Lee, you know who was really different from Jackie. Bruce Lee was a real martial artist, Jackie Chan was not a martial artist, he could not do martial arts. I mean he needed a body guard, not to really protect him but because every martial artist in the world wanted to pick a fight with him to show him they could beat him...which they could do! His idea of martial arts, I just thought was stupid, a joke. When the film was done, for the Asian audience who obviously wanted more fights, more martial arts scenes, Golden Harvest came to me and said, we're really sorry, but he wants to expand the fight scenes, do you want to come expand them? I had final cut, final decision on the film, and I said, look knock yourselves out for the Asian audiences, but it can't be shown anywhere else, and they agreed. They actually shot some additional footage, Chan directed, and sent me a copy of it, and I was like, hey if that's what they want....good luck.

**Nadia:** The film was shot in Hong Kong and in New York. Did you direct the production on both sides? How was it to work in Hong Kong?

**James:** I loved Hong Kong, I mean, I almost got off the bus there. It was visually incredible – you remember, the sights, the food, the sweating, the architecture, and you know, you go outside to a sweat bath, and the food, and the weather, and the hotels had rooms that overlooked the airport runway, shook the building. So it was a trip. But having said that, I didn't mind going home...

**Nadia:** I always think of a pure hard boiled detective story when it comes to THE PROTECTOR. Why did you choose not to cast Jackie Chan in a humorous role?

**James:** I just didn't want to make another ha-ha, chop-sockey, Jackie Chan film. And if you really want to see, left to his own devices, how silly his films can be, I mean look at the last extravaganza, ZODIAC, or something, I don't think it was distributed in the U.S., he spent millions and the film's fucking unwatchable...

**Nadia:** For many of your films Donna DeSeta managed the casting. Did she handle most of the SGE productions? Please explain the relevance of a regular casting department.

**James:** Donna was the wife of Bill Deseta who was an art director who did MCBAIN, and was on THE SOLDIER and THE PROTECTOR, she is Bernadette Peter's sister, and really looks like her, and she is a great Casting Director, one of the best working, knew all the Broadway actors, and really brought some great actors to my films. She was great, I used her even after I stopped using her husband. She did all my films.

**Nadia:** Why are there two titles, and which do you prefer personally?

**James:** It started as BLUE JEAN COP, I always liked BLUE JEAN COP. SHAKEDOWN was Universal's title, in their infinite stupidity, they chose it, and I didn't fight them on it.

**Nadia:** You mentioned the shoot-out in SHAKEDOWN was your most complicated action scene ever. Please paint us a picture.

**James:** It was pretty amazing to sit in a director's chair on 42nd street, at Broadway and 7th, at 2 in the morning, and call "Action", having shut the whole place down! We used a lot of real things, that was the hyper-center of AIDS, and there were all of those, you know, little cubicle hook-up places for gay guys down there, and it was scary, to go through those places. A lot of people had died, and they'd been shut down by the board of health, but they were still there, and you just saw all this stuff, then you saw really sad things in these rooms, you know, like a tooth-brush, like in the middle of all this, people were trying to take care of themselves, very sad stuff. Very interesting. And you know, I always thought that was visually interesting. And to go into the New Amsterdam, which was changing, it had just been bought by Disney and was going to be made into this Disney thing. And so we put all these porno movie titles on the the theatres, and there'd be guys going, wow, is this playing!? And we'd say no, it's a movie set... *(laughter)*. But it was the end of The Deuce, they called it The Deuce. There were the double houses where back-to-back features showed – people used to live in those theatres, which was what I was kinda showing with the scene with Sam Elliot, people live there, and would bring their whole families there. You'd see babes in arms watching Machete Girl Cannibals or something. Strange times, never probably to be duplicated. And that was when those theatres grossed incredible amounts of money, when we opened THE EXTERMINATOR, we were on 42nd St., and around the corner in a legitimate theatre, both grossed over $100k the first weekend, it was incredible!

**Nadia:** Did you get along with Peter Weller? Was ROBOCOP the reason you wanted him for the main role?

**James:** You know we needed some stars, and ROBOCOP gave him some cred, but I think – I didn't want him for the Sam Elliott role. The problem that I had with Weller was that he still saw himself as an action hero, so there was a little bit of that. But it worked out, I liked him, I kept in touch, he was always very friendly. I didn't have any problem with him. Elliott, actually, even though I had a bit of a blow up with him because Weller wanted to do some action shit, he also interestingly enough, asked me to direct a film with him years later. It was a western, that he had bought the rights to – Louis L'Amour. He was going to do it with his wife...but that never happened and life went on.

**Nadia:** It got good reviews, even Ebert loved it.

**James:** I think a lot of my films got good reviews, THE SOLDIER got a great review from the LA Times, and THE EXTERMINATOR got some good reviews. I mean listen, there were a lot of crap reviews and people that thought it was junk, but by and large, I got some fairly prestigious reviews, and the films made money which was all that really mattered.

**Nadia:** How much importance did the love story subplot have for you?

**James:** It was sort of a dual thing. I think with action films at the time, there were women in them but they were the bims you'd fuck and die. And I was just trying to make female characters that were a little more fleshed out and real. I don't know if I succeeded or not, she was kinda sardonic in the courtroom scenes with him. It was funny that they went from the bedroom to then sparring with each other in court. I liked her, I liked that part. And I did try to get female characters that had a reason to be, as opposed to just the obligatory scene where they take their shirt off.

**Nadia:** As in SHAKEDOWN, you worked several times with co-producer J. Boyce Harman Jr. - even before SGE. Talk a bit about your friendship and partnership.

**James:** Boyce was Boyce...they broke the mold when they made him. He was very smart, a literary guy, he indulged in wretched excess in his personal life, which killed him at a young age – his eating food that was extremely unhealthy. Not exercising, and his relationships with women were certainly entertaining. *(both laugh)*

**Nadia:** I remember that one....in Cannes, at Hotel du Cap?

**James:** - Lisa...yeah the hooker. And then he got married eventually, to Leslie. They never lived together, she went to Columbia and studied linguistics, and I believe works for the CIA translating code and stuff now. Look, Boyce was a friend, and I liked him a lot. I think that he had a expensive lifestyle – dinner every night for 200 bucks easily, and he needed to work and make money. And I think he kind of resented that I would make a film and then sort of disappear for 9 months. And he got involved with other people, and then he got a little strange, and became somewhat reclusive, and I sort of dropped out of touch with him – though I thought I was still friendly with him, but you can think that and the other side doesn't, you know. I think my sister ran into him on the Upper West Side, and said he looked very disheveled and went into this loud rant about how "Your brother never calls me, and he's just abandoned me!" which of course was not true, but anyway, that was Boyce. I do miss him. He is the only one – Boyce had a story about the naked girl who he found in his apartment who had discovered that her husband was having an affair with her brother, and then she had eaten all the pills in his house and drank all the wine, and broke the sink off the wall *(laughing)* and it just kept going on and on and then she said, "And I never understood why he didn't want anal sex.", and Boyce said, "Well he was getting it somewhere else!" *(both laughing)* – but he was the only one in the world who could tell this story in a loud voice in a restaurant and get away with it! *(both laughing long)*

**Nadia:** I loved Boyce, he made me laugh so hard all the time!

**James:** Yeah, right, who else could tell such a story, and he'd get all ....shit. You couldn't stand up, you were laughing so hard. Aw Boyce, rest in peace.

**Nadia:** How long did you shoot in the Philippines? How was that, what comes to mind first?

**James:** Well, the Philippines was an amazing place, I mean, you remember it. I think in retrospect it was a great thing to take Jesse there, because he was around 11, and from this very privileged background, and I think when he saw 12,000 homeless kids under the age of 12 on the streets, it really changed him, for the good. I think that was good. I think you saw a society where anything was for sale, which was a little sad, but it was a society where we could rent all those things, the aircraft, the rebels, the generals, the machetes, you remember those – passage for the people. It was cool.

**Nadia:** How much money was spent on MCBAIN, and what part of the production process was most expensive?

**James:** The actors got a lot of money – the budget was like $6-7 million, because you could get extras for a dollar a day.

**Nadia:** Remember that village we blew up, that everyone had moved in to, so we had a to build another one for them to live in?

**James:** Yeah...exactly. They were living in it.

**Nadia:** Margaret Shan Jensen worked on several SGE productions, among them MANIAC COP and SHAKEDOWN. MCBAIN was her debut as a costume designer, which must have been a huge job. Do you remember working with her?

**James:** She was from Boyce, a lot of the crew came from Boyce, and I deferred to him, like Bill Deseta and Bob Baldwin, and Margaret. They were really good. Boyce was a very good line-producer. He couldn't go on like he did, abusing his body and such, but he had a certain je ne sais quoi!

**Nadia:** Would you say that MCBAIN includes more political implications compared to your other work?

**James:** I think it is, I think it's really saying that if you allow drug lords or religious fanatics, or whatever to take over a country, that a lot of bad stuff happens, and I think we're seeing it in the world today.

**Nadia:** Years after THE SOLDIER you worked again with Christopher Franke from Tangerine Dream. What was different compared to working with him as a member of a band?

**James:** He was really Tangerine Dream, the others kind of came and went, so I really enjoyed working with him.

**Nadia:** After the results of MCBAIN, were you fed up with pure action movies? What made you switch to a much more suspense based movie?

**James:** I just had never done one and wanted to. I kind of had a fascination with what made people crazy — had read too much, staring into the abyss, meeting those guys from the FBI, the profilers and that sort of thing. But also the idea, in the case of this serial killer — yeah, what he was doing was bad stuff, but it also was sort of inevitable if you abuse children, it's not going to turn out well. Sort of the contrast between good parents, Scott Glenn, and Mordecai's parents in the film and the way he was abused. If you do that, it's inevitable.

**Nadia:** Any main reason that made you choose Utah for the key locations?

**James:** It is such an incredible place, and I wanted also to cut the budget, and Utah was a right-to-work state, so I knew we could film there for less money. So I went there and said, "I'm going to write a script that takes place here." A great back-drop.

**Nadia:** While scripting the movie, what kind of research did you do about the investigative work, which is a main topic in SLAUGHTER OF THE INNOCENTS?

**James:** I sent an early draft of the script to the FBI, asking if they'd help us, and they said "It's an interesting thing, we will help you." There are certain procedures and stuff, that you've written that obviously could never happen. So I said, "What if I did a disclaimer in the beginning thanking the FBI, saying that it is a work of fiction, and a lot of things depicted would not happen in real life." And they said "Great!" They were very helpful, they took me and introduced me to a lot of FBI agents that gave me access to a lot of profiling that they did, and the stuff that John Douglas did. Although John, who was sort of the archetypal guy in SILENCE OF THE LAMBS, and he wrote a book on this, he kind of went crazy. He got too close to these people. One of the problems of it is that in a movie, you film the scene and then the people, the serrated bodies, get up and sit and have craft-services. You know, in real life that doesn't happen. I think the guys that were really there, day to day, connected to it and the gore, and the ultra sexual violence, it screwed them up. Both men and women. But they were very helpful. A lot of FBI folk were in the film, actually, they liked it and would show up on location. A lot of the raids were real FBI guys.

**Nadia:** Nicholas T. Preovolos was in charge of the production design for SLAUGHTER OF THE INNOCENTS and TIMEMASTER — I think he did a magnificent job, do you agree?

**James:** He was an artist and had a lot of really interesting visual ideas. He did a great job. He was a person where I could mention, you know this scene is a Hieronymus Bosch painting, and he'd get it. And understood what that was. The boy-toys of the world may not know who that was.

**Nadia:** Frank K. Isaac was co-producer on this movie - he was a key member in the days of SGE, correct? Can you talk a bit about him?

**James:** Frank was very business like, an organized guy. He worked with Lenny before he worked with me, but I didn't see any reason why he couldn't be a line-producer, and he was very good.

**Nadia:** Your son Jesse Cameron-Glickenhaus appeared in a few supporting roles and in a very important one in SLAUGHTER OF THE INNOCENTS. When did you decide to give him the lead role in a movie?

**James:** He was 12 I think, and I wanted – sort of thinking this might be my last film – for many years I'd been writing a script that was originally called ROOM AT THE END OF THE UNIVERSE, and it was a sci-fi, very dark, film that I was never able to get off the ground. Though at one point Tom Cruise was interested in it, and at one time Meryl Streep was interested in it, so it went back and forth and to the studios, but it never happened. So I just said, I re-wrote it and and made it more of a kids film, and that was TIMEMASTER.

**Nadia:** He has chosen another career - but at that point, did he want to become an actor?

**James:** He was just a kid, he liked acting – he could have been one, he was good, but the thing is, if you really, really want to succeed in Hollywood, it's like that line in the Dylan song. *"How much abuse will you be able to take? Well, there's no way to tell by that first kiss What's a sweet heart like you do in' in a dump like this?"*

I think that's true – you just have to be able to take a lot of pain and personal rejection, having your life get totally fucked up, and really kissing a lot of dramatic failure, and just wanting to succeed so much that you're willing to do it. And I think some people are, and some people who are, and it doesn't work, and some people who just say I have other things to do!

**Nadia:** When you started the production of TIMEMASTER, did you already know it would be your last film?

**James:** Yeah, I did sort of. I always was going to have to deal with Wall Street and my family's business, and I thought that sooner rather than later was the right time to do it, when I could understand it, and that turned out to be true. And the other thing was the business was changing. I think the only way I could have gone on was move to LA, cultivate this agent thing, and have a studio deal for films, and I just didn't have it in me. I remember Steven Seagal sent me a script he wanted me to do for Warner, and I just couldn't. For better or worse.

**Nadia:** Since the film is packed with pop-cultural references: Did you cast Pat Morita because of his iconic role from the KARATE KID series?

**James:** Yeah, of course, there was a lot – Michael Dorn from STAR TREK, etc.

**Nadia:** The film has some western elements. Did you choose some locations that were used in classic western movies?

**James:** Well I had always wanted to make a western, from when I was a little kid and saw Leone's ONCE UPON A TIME IN THE WEST, so I did actually go look where that was shot, in Spain, but that was no longer really viable. But I did want to do the classic locations. TIMEMASTER was a time-travel film, which are very hard to do and to make work, and make coherent, and the film had all of those problems, but it was fun.

**Nadia:** While developing the script and the main character, how much was Jesse involved? Was it kind of a family movie throughout all steps of production?

**James:** Oh he was involved, not really in the script, but in his acting and realizing the role.

**Nadia:** Any particular memories on TOUGH AND DEADLY?

**James:** I don't really know. I wasn't involved in those films, Lenny said they'd make money, I said whatever. I'm not putting them down, and they were fine. But Lenny had this thing with Billy Blanks, and you know, Alan had his deals, etc, Jalal...etc...

---

By Marco Siedelmann & Nadia Bruce-Rawlings, in writing and via telephone
from Rye, New York
July 2015

An overworked lawyer.
An undercover cop.
In a city where everyone is for sale...
They're the best
money can't buy.

# PETER WELLER SAM ELLIOTT
# SHAKEDOWN
*Whatever you do... don't call the cops.*

SHAPIRO/GLICKENHAUS ENTERTAINMENT PRESENTS A JAMES GLICKENHAUS FILM PETER WELLER SAM ELLIOTT "SHAKEDOWN"
PATRICIA CHARBONNEAU, ANTONIO FARGAS AND BLANCHE BAKER EDITED BY PAUL FRIED DIRECTOR OF PHOTOGRAPHY JOHN LINDLEY EXECUTIVE PRODUCERS LEONARD SHAPIRO AND
ALAN M. SOLOMON PRODUCED BY J. BOYCE HARMAN, JR. WRITTEN AND DIRECTED BY JAMES GLICKENHAUS A UNIVERSAL PICTURE

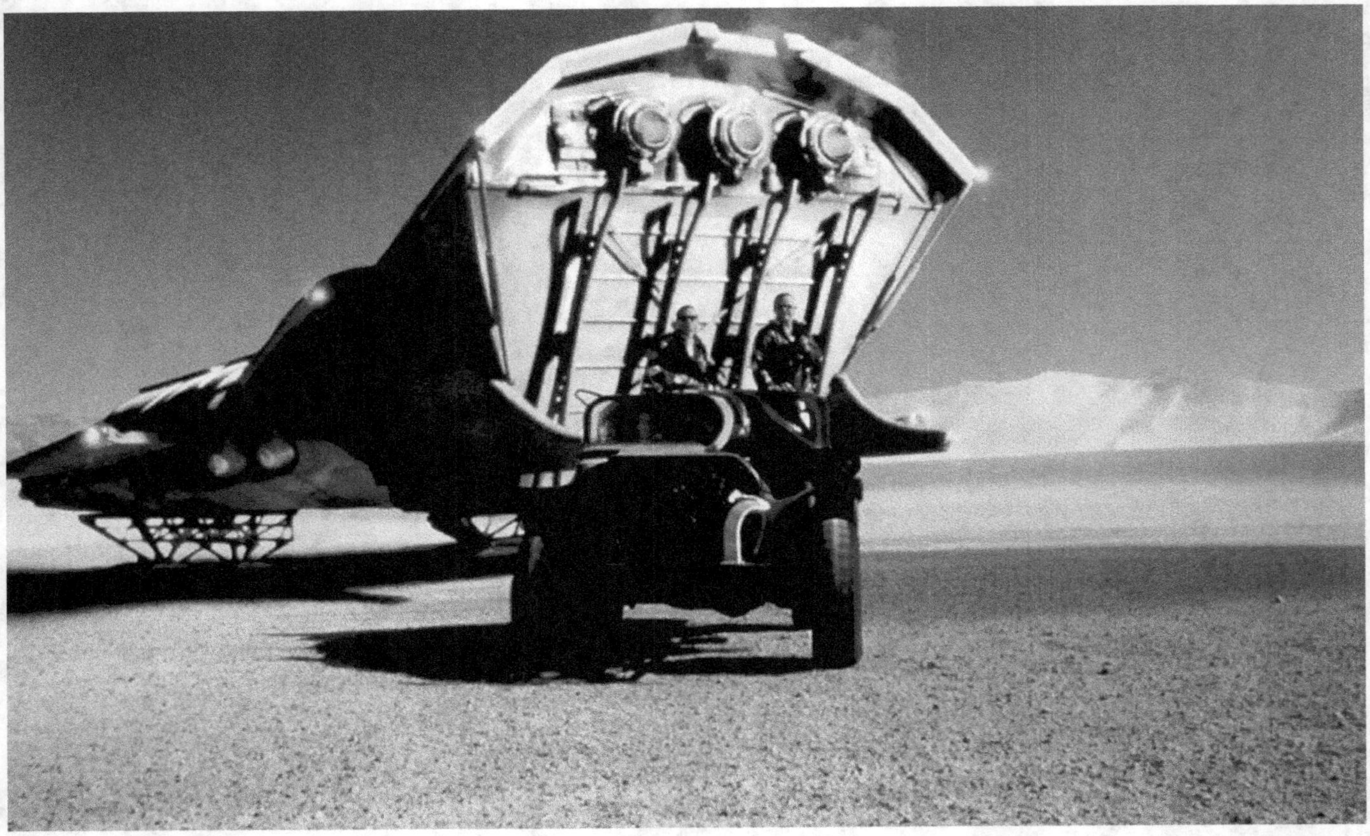

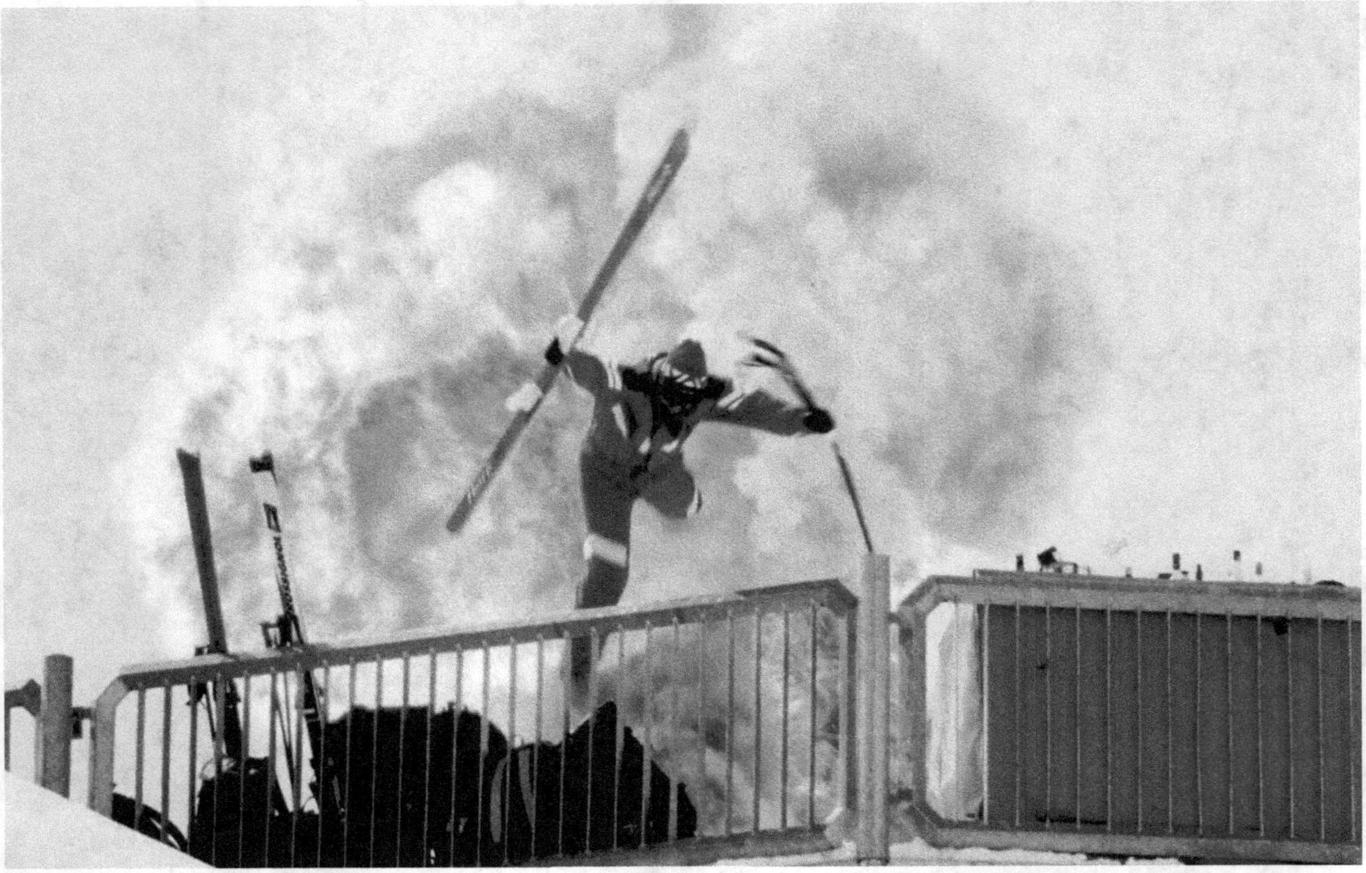

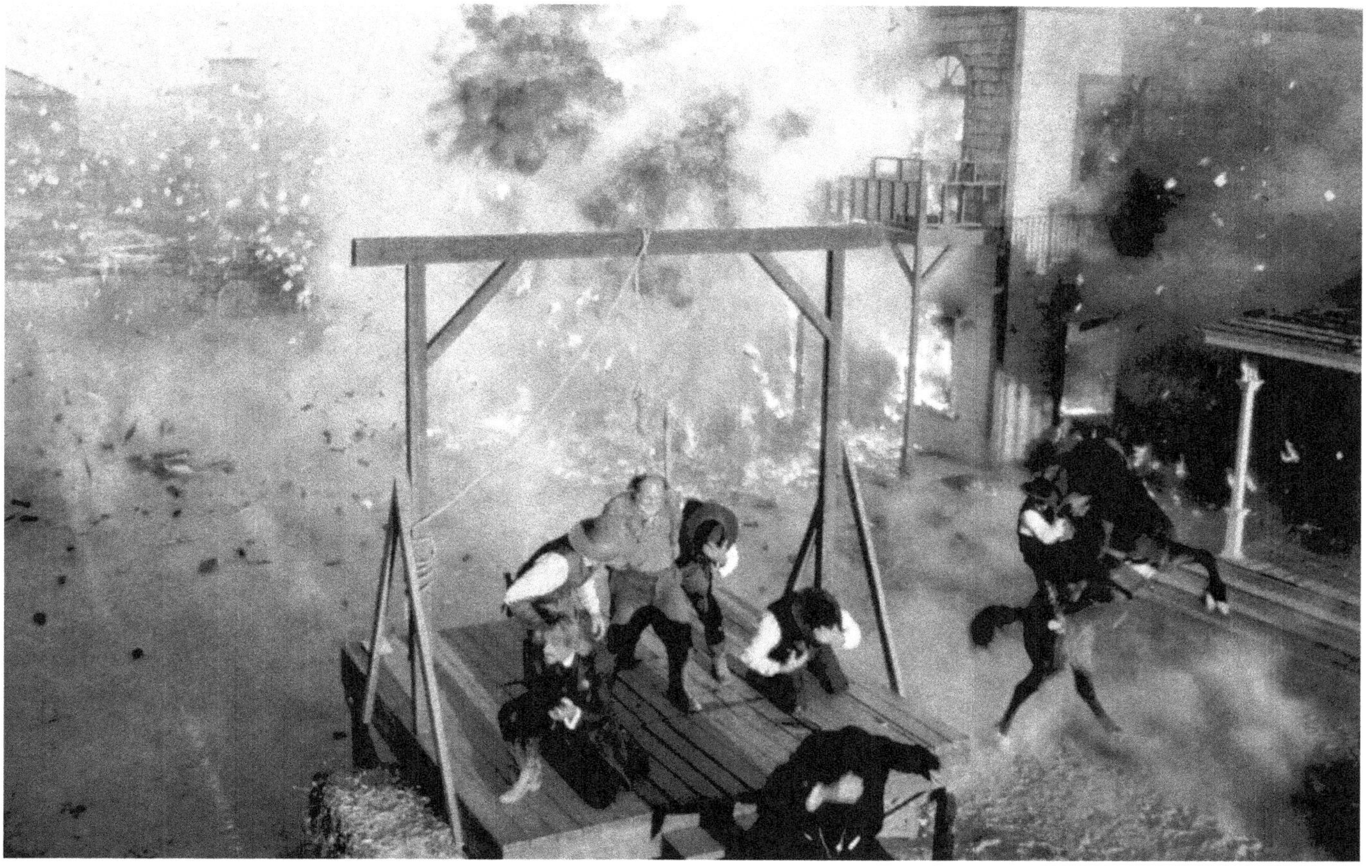

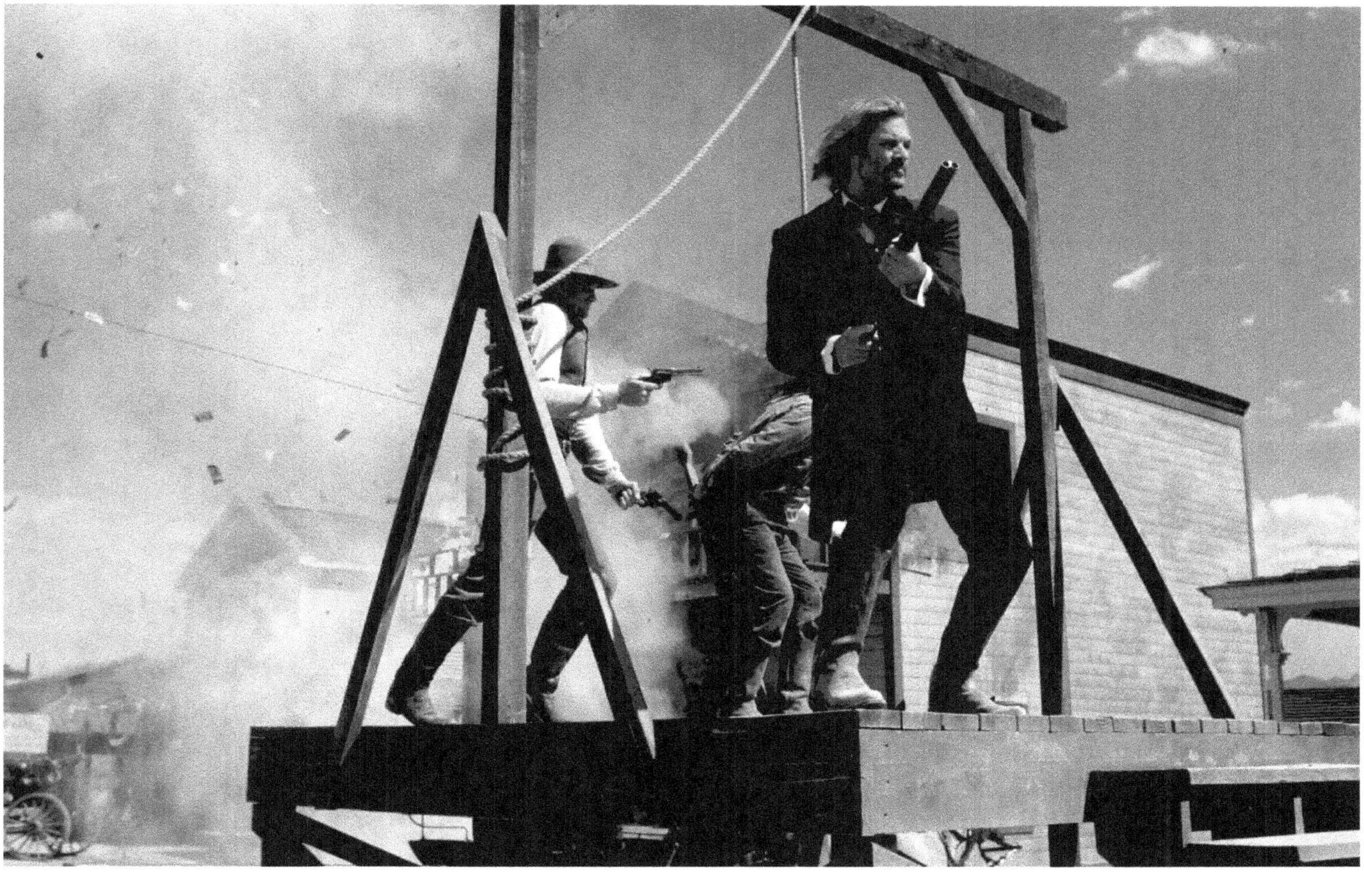

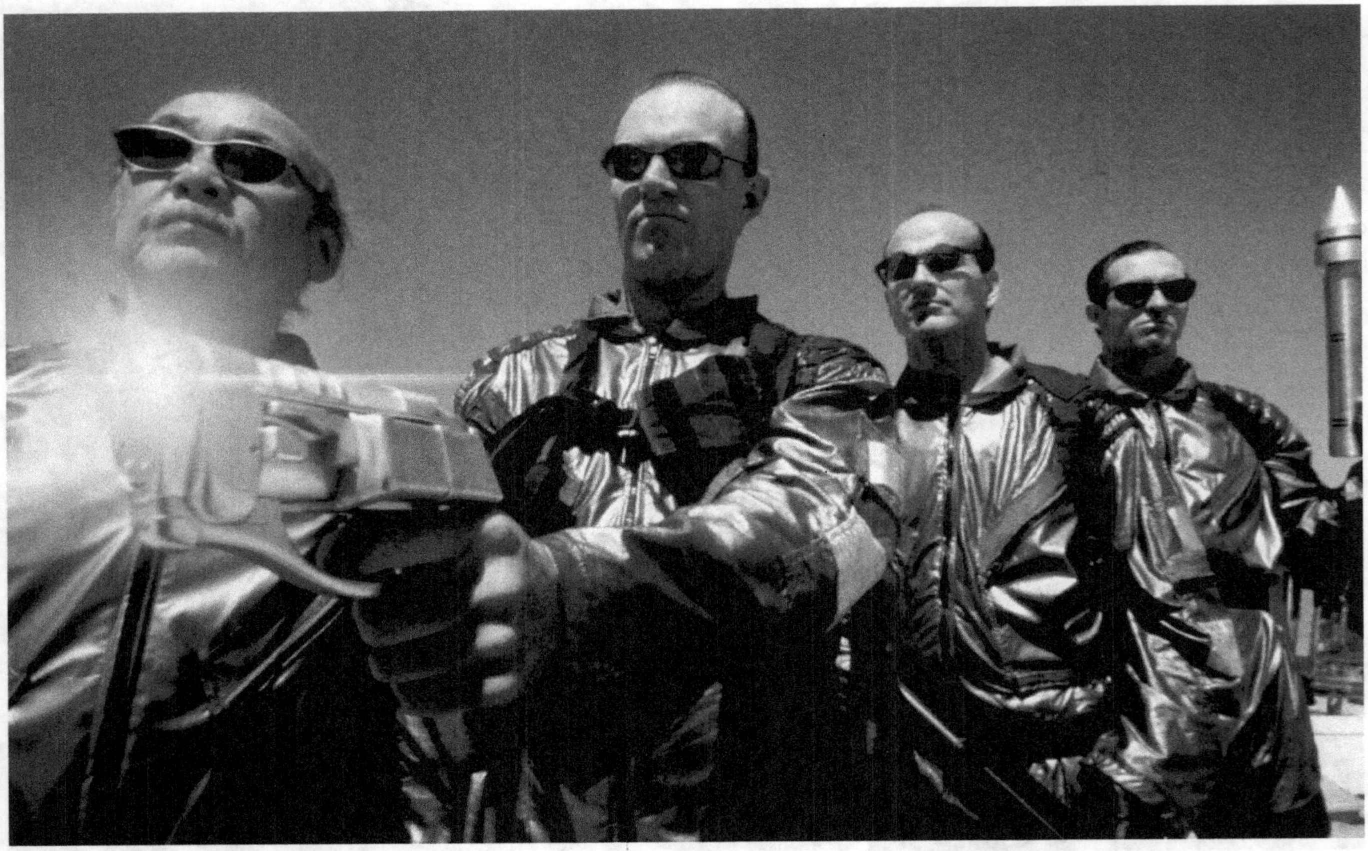

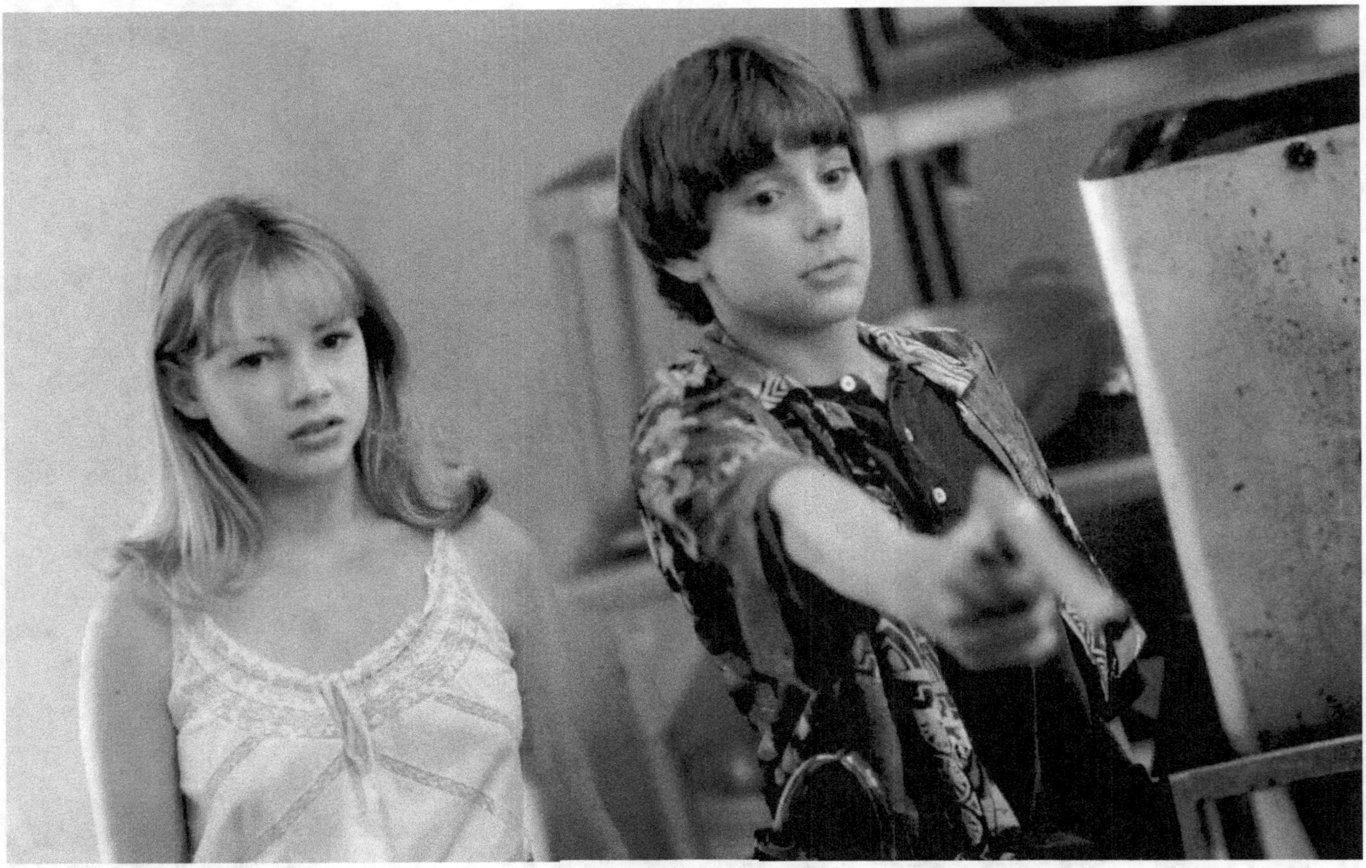

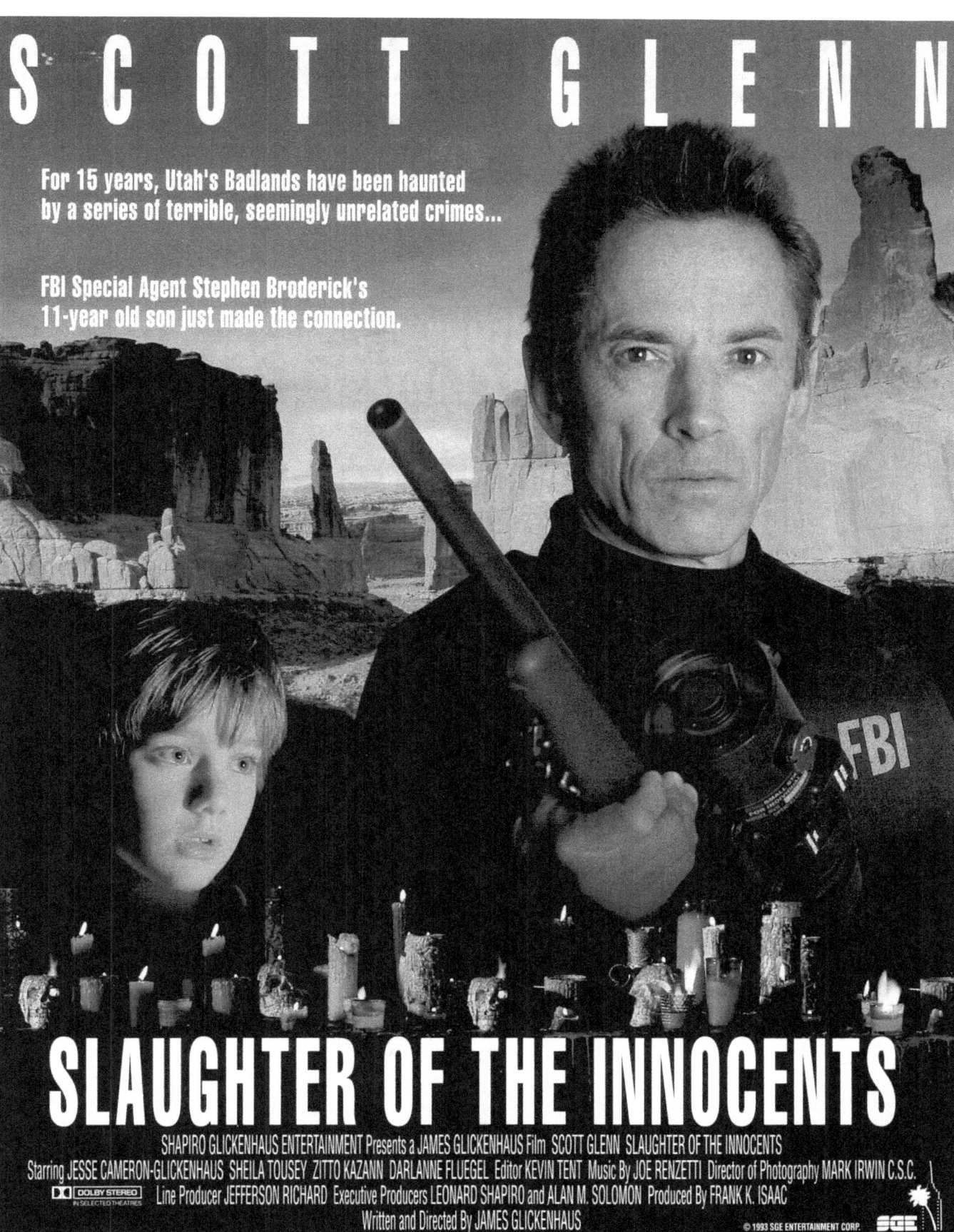

## APPEALING CAST!

Starring **Pat Morita**. This popular, highly recognizable star portrays a character reminiscent of his Academy Award®-nominated role in *The Karate Kid*. Also starring **Michael Dorn** ("Worf" in *Star Trek: Generations*), **Michelle Williams** (*Species*), **Joanna Pacula** (*Tombstone*) and **Jesse Cameron-Glickenhaus** (*Slaughter of the Innocents*).

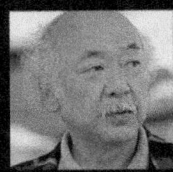 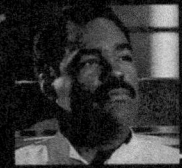 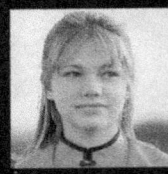 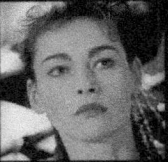 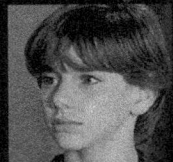

## COMBINES SCI-FI ADVENTURE—A KID'S FAVORITE— AND FAMILY FANTASY!

This winning mix equals fun family viewing which makes for surefire rentals!

## TIMED FOR SUCCESS!

The December 27 release of *Timemaster* has been strategically timed to coincide with peak rental periods. It's a perfect opportunity to have fresh product in your store when demand is at its highest.

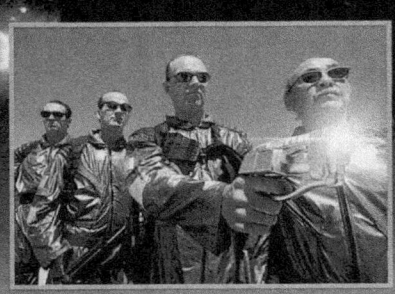 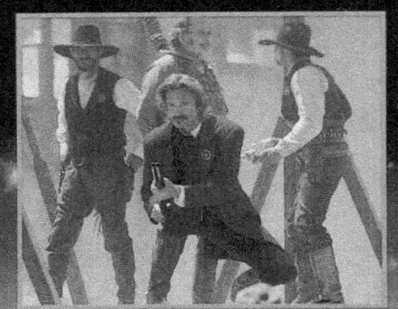 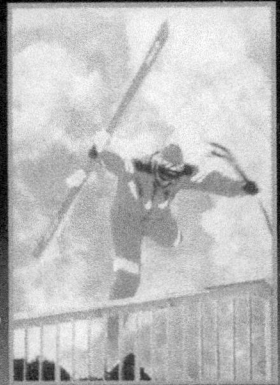

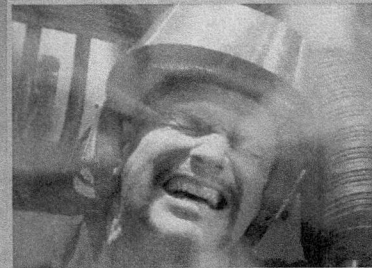 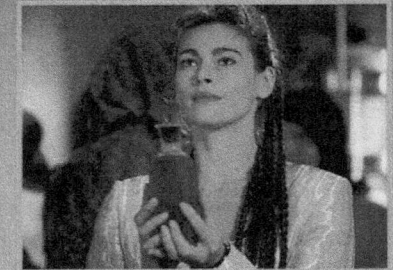

## STREET DATE: DECEMBER 27, 1995

Call Your Sales Representative and Order Today!

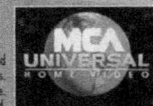

"Academy Awards®" and "Oscars®" are the registered trademarks and service marks of the Academy of Motion Picture Arts and Sciences.
Advertising and promotional details subject to change without notice.
©1995 SGE Entertainment Corporation. All Rights Reserved.

# GET THE *TIMEMASTER* PRE-PACK, AND YOUR RENTAL PROFITS WILL ADD UP IN NO TIME AT ALL!

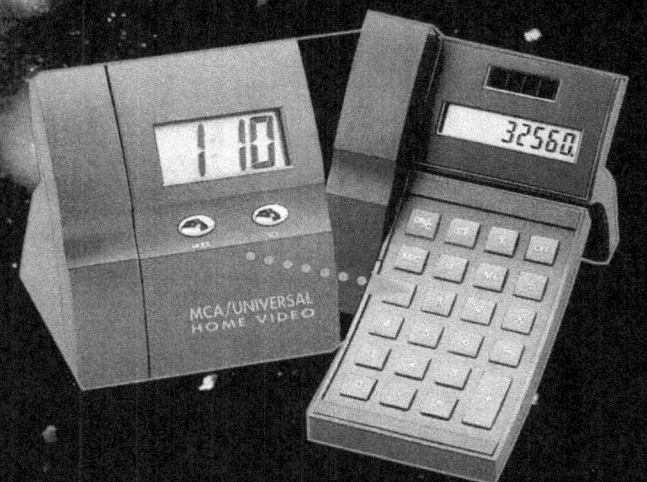

Purchase 3 units of *TIMEMASTER* and receive a space-age desk clock that *transforms* into a full-function, 8-digit, dual-power calculator. Easy time set. Lifetime warranty against mechanical failure. Includes one AAA battery.

## • • • PLUS! • • •

Cash in on another film for the whole family! Get an attractive baseball jersey with a picture of *"Babe"* on the left front chest.

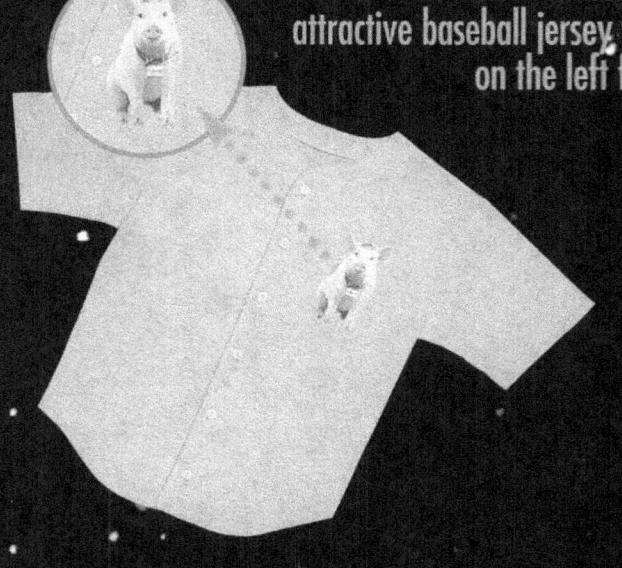

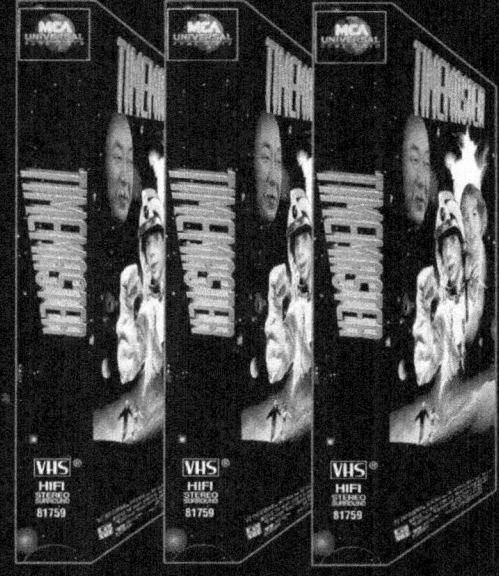

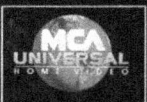
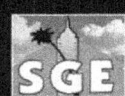

Pre-Pack Sel. #82625 • Total Estimated Value: $65.00
(Details on items may change slightly)

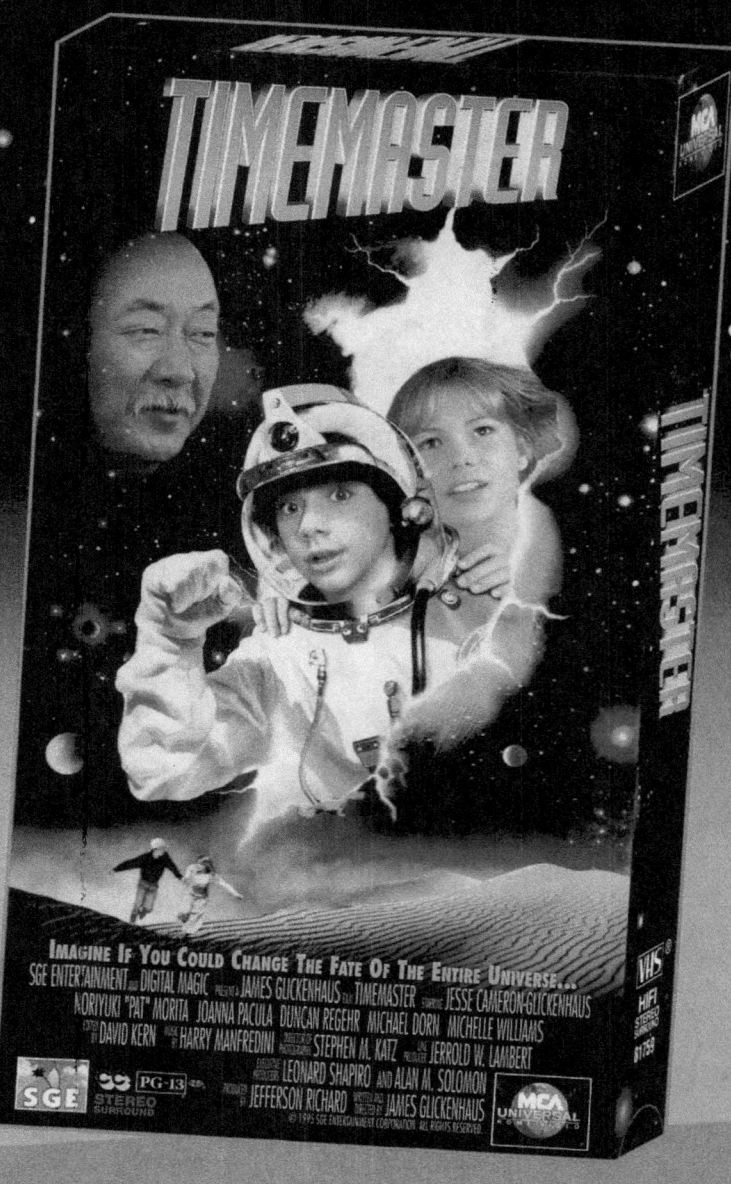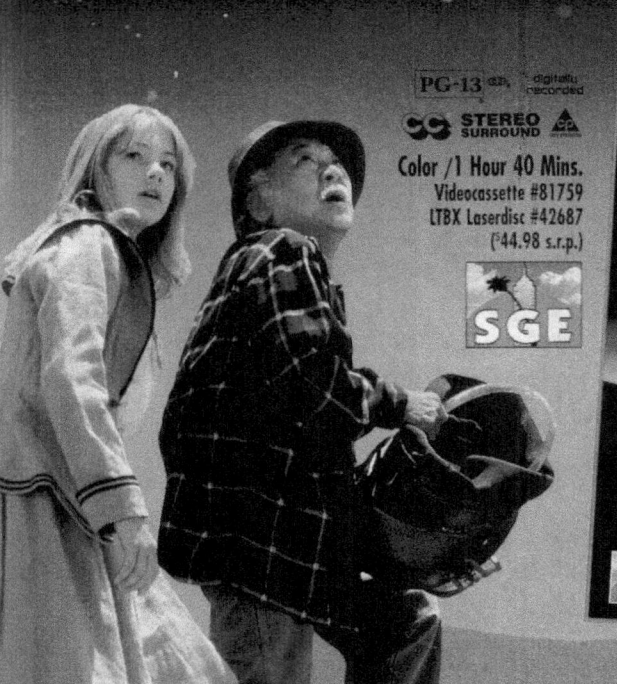

# COMING IN THE FUTURE

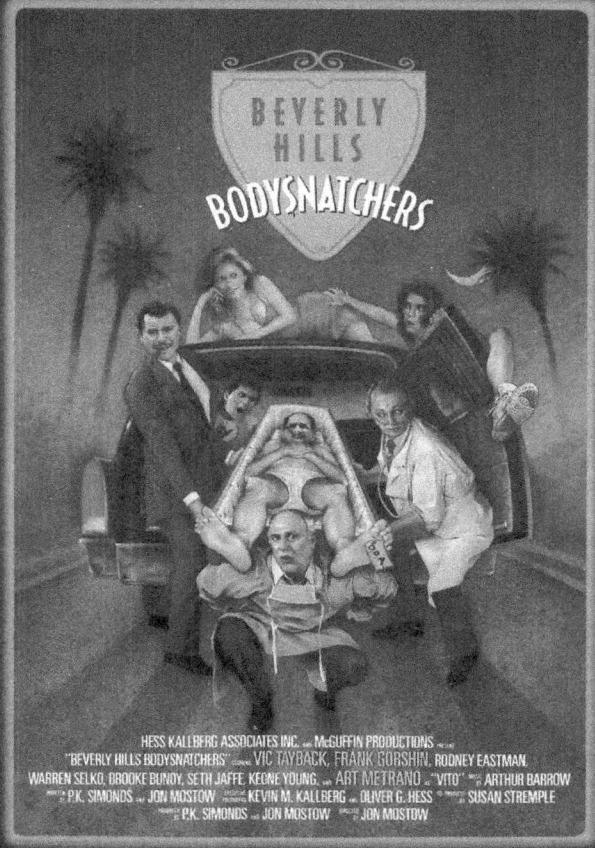

# THIS OCTOBER FROM
# SGE HOME VIDEO

DON SPIELVOGEL  Western Regional Manager  (818) 882-1851
HAROLD KOMISAR  Eastern Regional Manager  (203) 259-9703
LARRY COULTER  Central Regional Manager  (317) 248-1116
SCOTT STEVENS  Southern Regional Manager  (817) 860-0531

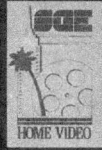

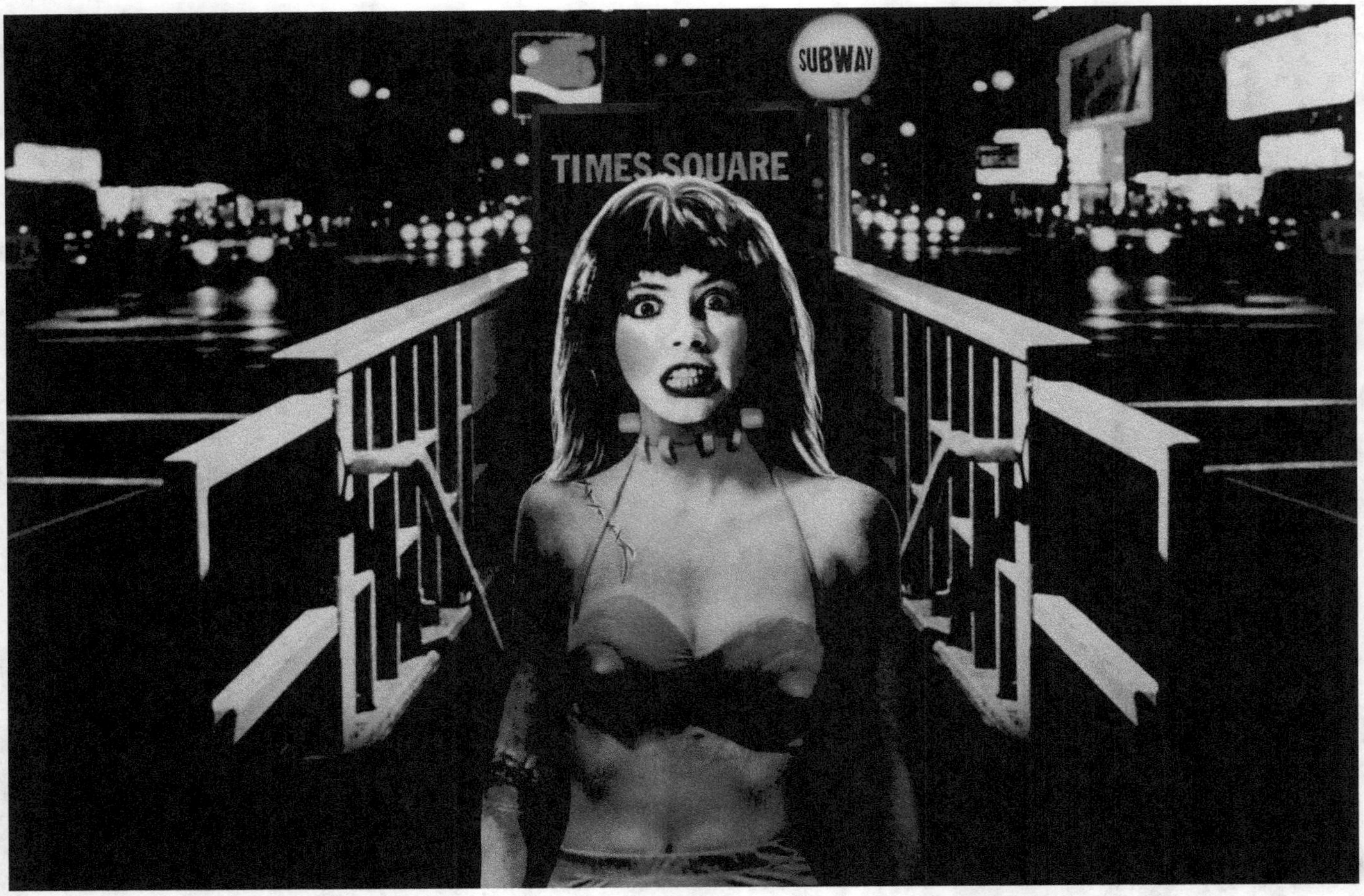

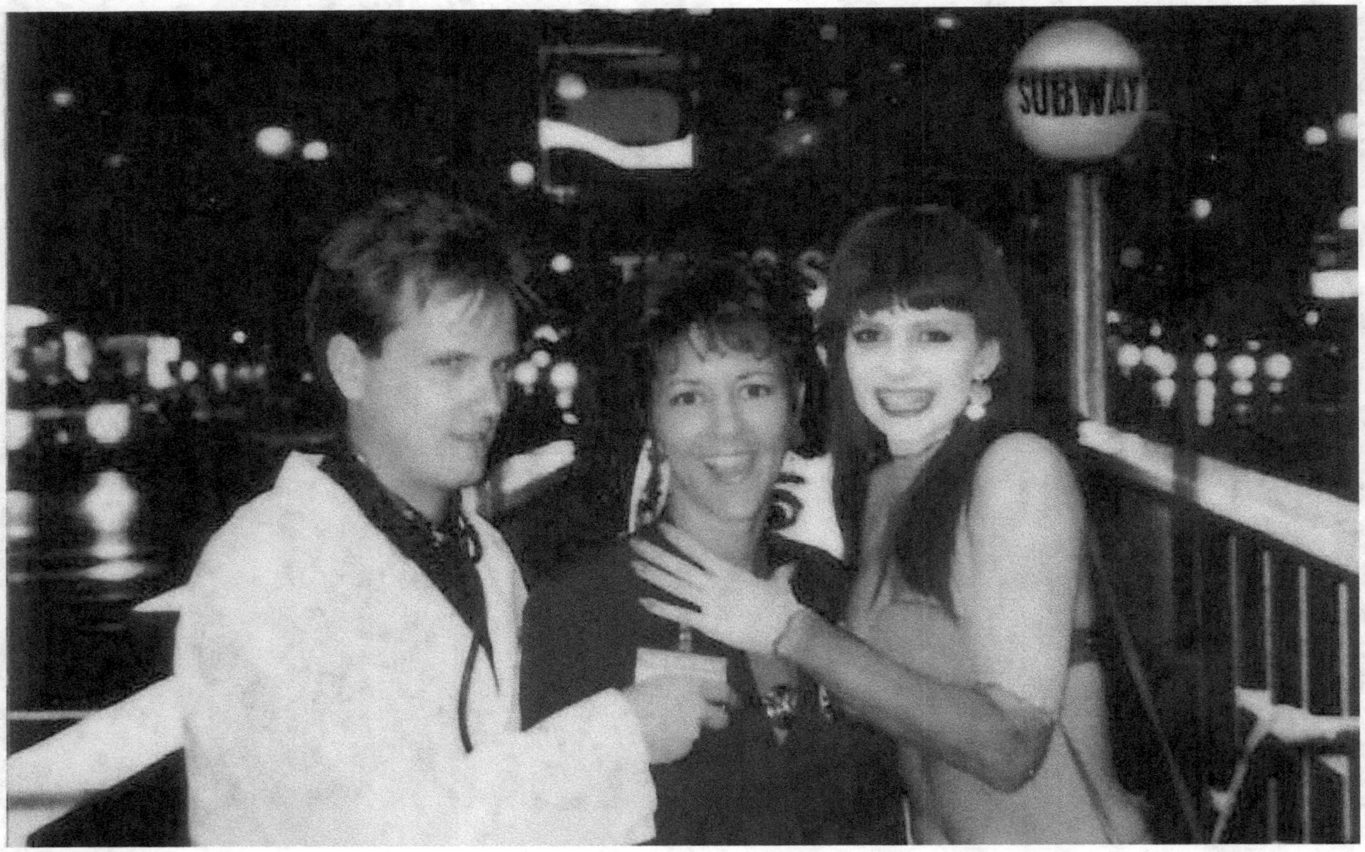

# Andi Elliott

A graduate of Loyola Marymount University, Andi Elliot here represents the SGE Home Video Division, where she worked closely with Peter Pidutti as well as Jacqueline Palmiere. Andi worked on the marketing of some of the most famous SGE titles, including the first ever Talking Box, used to market FRANKENHOOKER. Ms. Elliott went on to work at Warner Home Video for several years, and continued her successful career at Variety, where she is currently Account Manager for Variety Events. Andi is married and lives in the Washington DC metro area.

**Marco:** Please tell me about your origins. Where were you born and raised, and what kind of education led you into movie business?

**Andi:** I was born in Baltimore, Maryland but moved frequently as a child to such states as Connecticut and Florida, finally ending up in California in 1973. I received a BA in Communication Arts from Loyola Marymount University in Los Angeles. My C. A. major covered film, television, scriptwriting, and media studies. I've always been a big movie fan, so I was thrilled to get a job working in the home entertainment division of 20th Century Fox upon graduating in 1982.

**Marco:** When did you start at SGE, and how long did you stay there?

**Andi:** I was hired at the start of the home video division – I believe 1988, and stayed until it was turned over to MCA/Universal – I think it was 1992.

**Marco:** Did you train your professional skills in this era?

**Andi:** Yes, I have been in the home video industry since 1982 in various roles as customer service rep, sales administration, and marketing services.

**Marco:** As a sales person, how much are you involved and interested in the creative part of filmmaking?

**Andi:** I haven't made a film since my senior short film project in college. In my home video industry career, I've been involved in marketing and promoting finished films, but never actually creating films.

**Marco:** Are you a cinematic person in general, and what kind of films do you prefer as a part of the audience?

**Andi:** I've always been a big movie fan – ever since I was a kid. I like all genres of film, as long as they are well made. My favorite films are THE GODFATHER and THE GODFATHER II. If I am flipping channels on the television and come across either one, I will watch them.

**Marco:** Please describe how did it come about, when SGE formed a video distribution wing.

**Andi:** When my good friend, the late Pete Pidutti, was hired to run the home video division of SGE in 1988, he asked me to come work with him and run sales administration and marketing. Pete and I had been working together in home video for several years, first at Media Home

Entertainment and then Celebrity Home Entertainment.

**Marco:** What was your exact function there, and who were the people you worked the closest with at the company?

**Andi:** In my role at SGE, I worked most closely with Pete Pidutti as I managed the various stages of our video releases. I dealt with designers who created packaging and key art, and printers for the packaging and marketing collateral, duplicators of our videotapes, as well as trade publications, etc. I also dealt with our sales representatives (Harold Komisar, Don Spielvogel, Ann Everett and Larry Coulter), providing them with sales materials, and our home video clients, processing their orders. I also managed our trade show presence at the annual VSDA (Video Software Dealers Association) convention in Las Vegas.

**Marco:** How did a normal day look like for you? Did you always deal with a bunch of titles at the same time?

**Andi:** We really only released 1-2 titles per month, but I did all of the life-cycle tasks described above for each one.

**Marco:** What's the most exciting part of your work? Did you travel a lot or was the biggest part of the work done strictly in the office?

**Andi:** Because most of my work was done in the office, the most exciting part for me was when I could occasionally go out on the road, sometimes with the film's stars, to promote the video release. I also always loved the VSDA convention because it was an opportunity to see so many people in the industry that I knew.

**Marco:** Many of the SGE productions were not screened in theatres, a huge part were distributed on VHS exclusively. So I assume, it was a very important Division for SGE?

**Andi:** For those titles with no theatrical release, the home video release, international distribution and tv rights were the only revenue streams. I was not privy to the revenue numbers that each of these divisions represented.

**Marco:** How many video tapes were manufactured for a common film release by SGE?

**Andi:** Depended on the title..a successful release like RED SCORPION or BASKET CASE 2 would sell 80,000 to 120,000 copies.

**Marco:** How much did the company spend on this, and what was the regular price for a particular film copy on VHS?

**Andi:** I don't remember our cost of goods at the time, but our suggested list price was based on the fact that the titles were to be rented by retailers to the public. So the suggested list was $79.98, for example, and we sold it to the video wholesalers for probably about $54, then they in turn sold it to the retailers. Retailers probably paid about $65 and then put it on the shelf and rented it for $4-5 a night.

**Marco:** Was it always risky, calculating the numbers for that?

Andi: No.

Marco: Is there one deal you remember very well? What was the most successful SGE movie, you participated on the distribution for?

Andi: The big tentpole title was RED SCORPION, starring Dolph Lundgren, which was the first title released by the home video division. There was some controversy with the theatrical release, so Len and Jim wanted and needed us to ship a lot of video units. I think we sold 120,000 copies, but I can't remember exactly. We also did well with BASKET CASE 2 because horror is popular on video and BASKET CASE was a known entity. Were some films huge flops as well? Yes – too many!

Marco: A key aspect for video distribution was always the front cover design. Were you in charge of the artwork as well, did you pick artists and final design?

Andi: Yes, I was responsible for providing outside designers with our theatrical key art and directing them on the VHS box design. Was there one or another example for the right cover which sold the film (more or less) on its own? We had the first talking video box in the industry – for FRANKENHOOKER. You pushed the box and it said, "Want a date?" I believe this title performed better than it would have without the special box.

Marco: What's the formula for a good cover artwork?

Andi: Video boxes need to feature the key stars prominently and be compelling so they stand out on the shelf in the video store.

Marco: Thinking back, was the time at SGE a key part of your career?

Andi: My time at SGE was important because I learned more skills – specifically with marketing – that I hadn't done at previous jobs.

Marco: After SGE was shut down, what happened in your life?

Andi: I went to work at Warner Home Video doing promotions for the western region, then left to sell advertising for Video Business magazine – the leading trade publication for the industry.

Marco: And did you stay in touch with some of the colleagues?

Andi: Pete and I were always close until he died suddenly in 2005. I still remain friends with the sales representatives as well. Lenny and I kept in touch and would see each other at events like VSDA.

Marco: Since the heyday of video distribution, nearly everything has changed in distribution, filmmaking, piracy. Simply everything. Do you think about the 80s and 90s as the good old days or do you think movie industry has evolved in a good way?

Andi: I think of it as the good old days for the home video industry, because everyone was making money and having a great time. As the industry evolved, and more and more of the business was concentrated at the big box stores and independent video retailers went out of business, it became tougher for independent films to do well.

**Marco:** Do you think screening and downloading-on-demand is the future for film distribution?

**Andi:** I think that the current forms of distribution give greater opportunities to independent filmmakers. They no longer have to pay big money for theatrical releases, which was cost prohibitive. Now they have many ways to find an audience and have their film seen. Social media provides a less expensive way to promote your film, as opposed to expensive newspaper advertising of the old days.

**Marco:** How would you describe the situation with DVD and BD nowadays, compared to the video distribution in the past?

**Andi:** Obviously the streaming video options mean that the physical disc business is dwindling. Special features and the opportunity to save a digital copy to your cloud à la UltraViolet are a boon to some titles. But as more younger generations grow up watching films on their tablets or cell phones, discs will no longer be produced.

**Marco:** Another general question: Did you have to deal with a lot of piracy in the video age? And what about contemporary piracy - who is more affected by it, the majors or the indies?

**Andi:** I did not have to deal with piracy issues. But nowadays the studios have to deal with more aggressive piracy because they release the bigger, more desireable films.

---

**By Marco Siedelmann & Nadia Bruce-Rawlings**
in writing from Washington, D.C.
24Aug, 2015

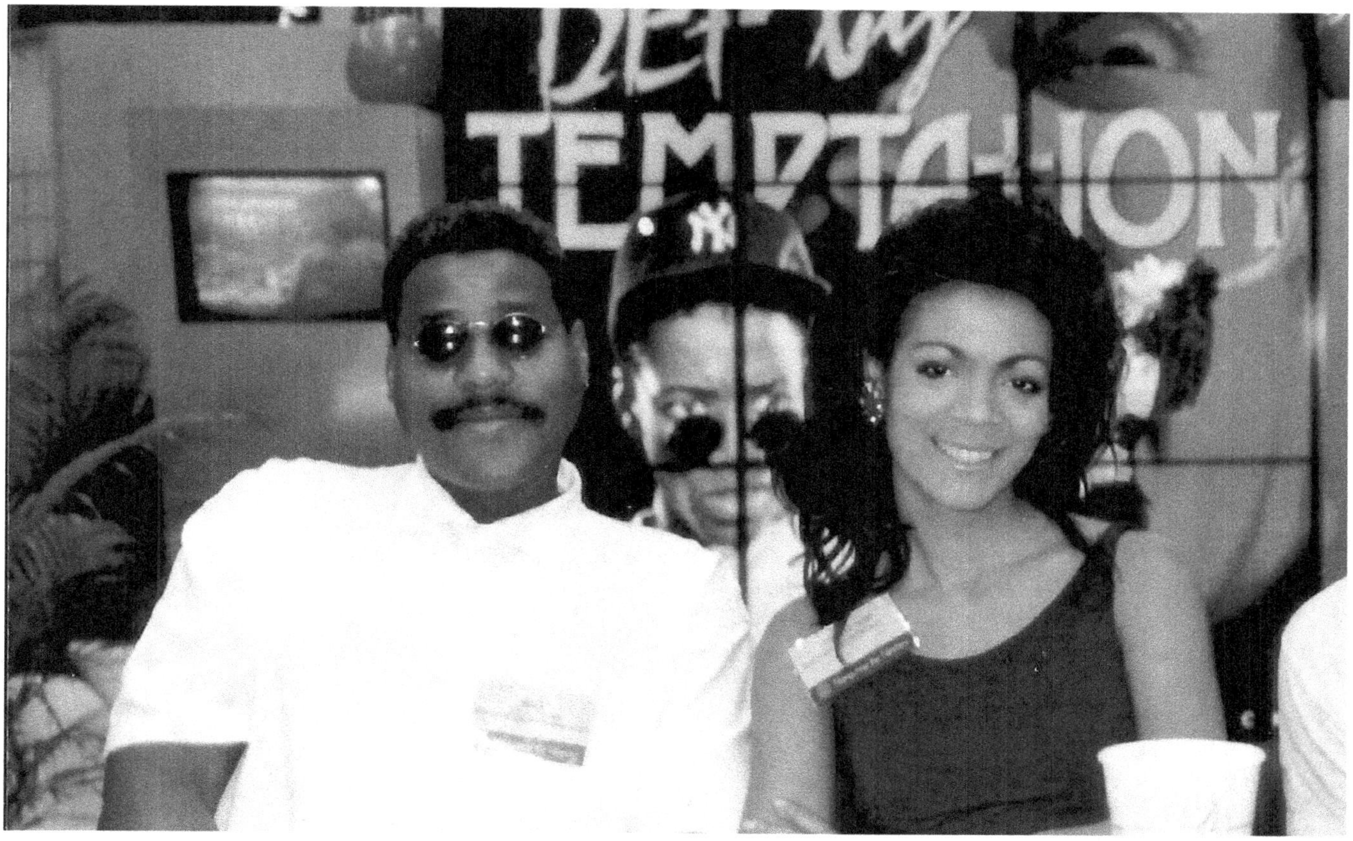

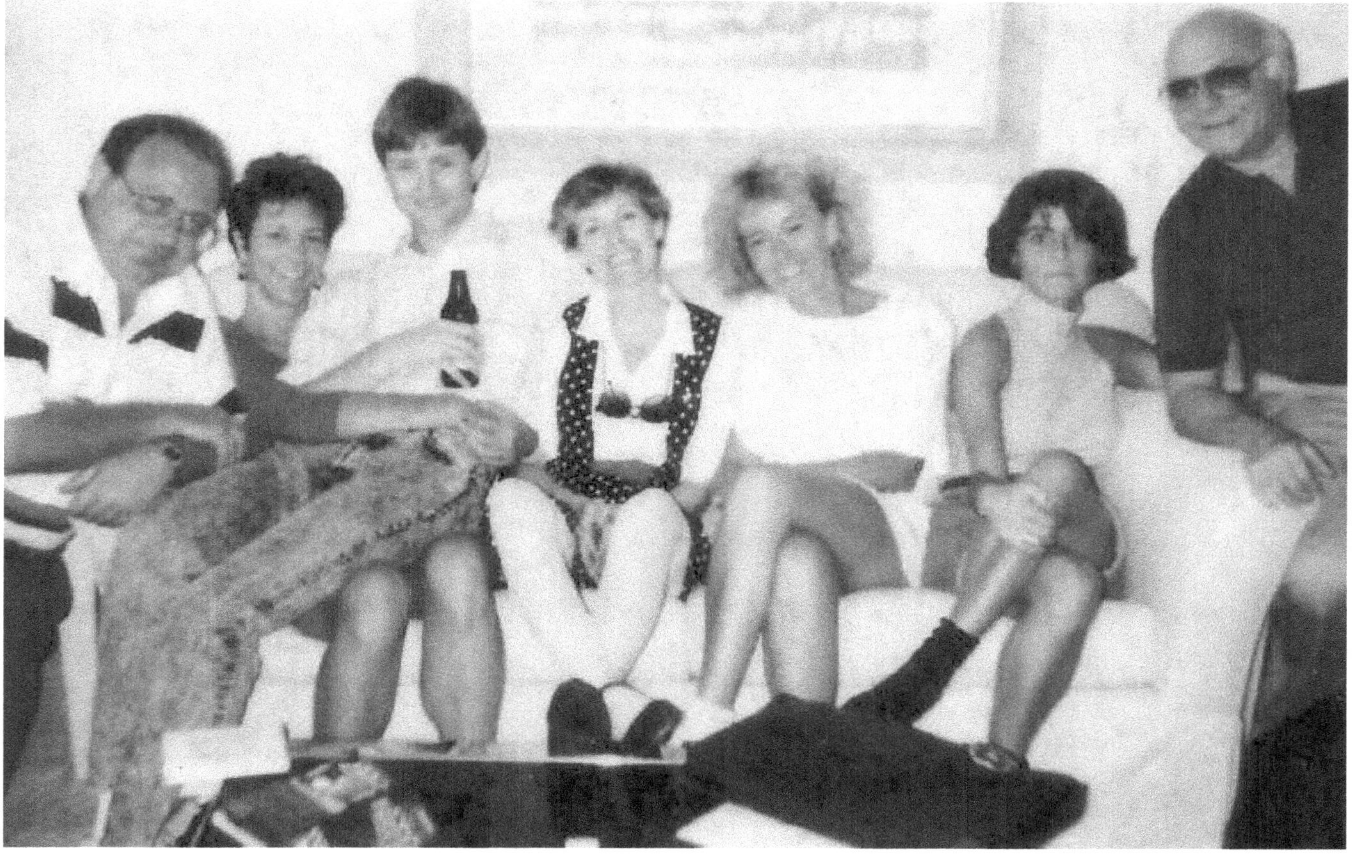

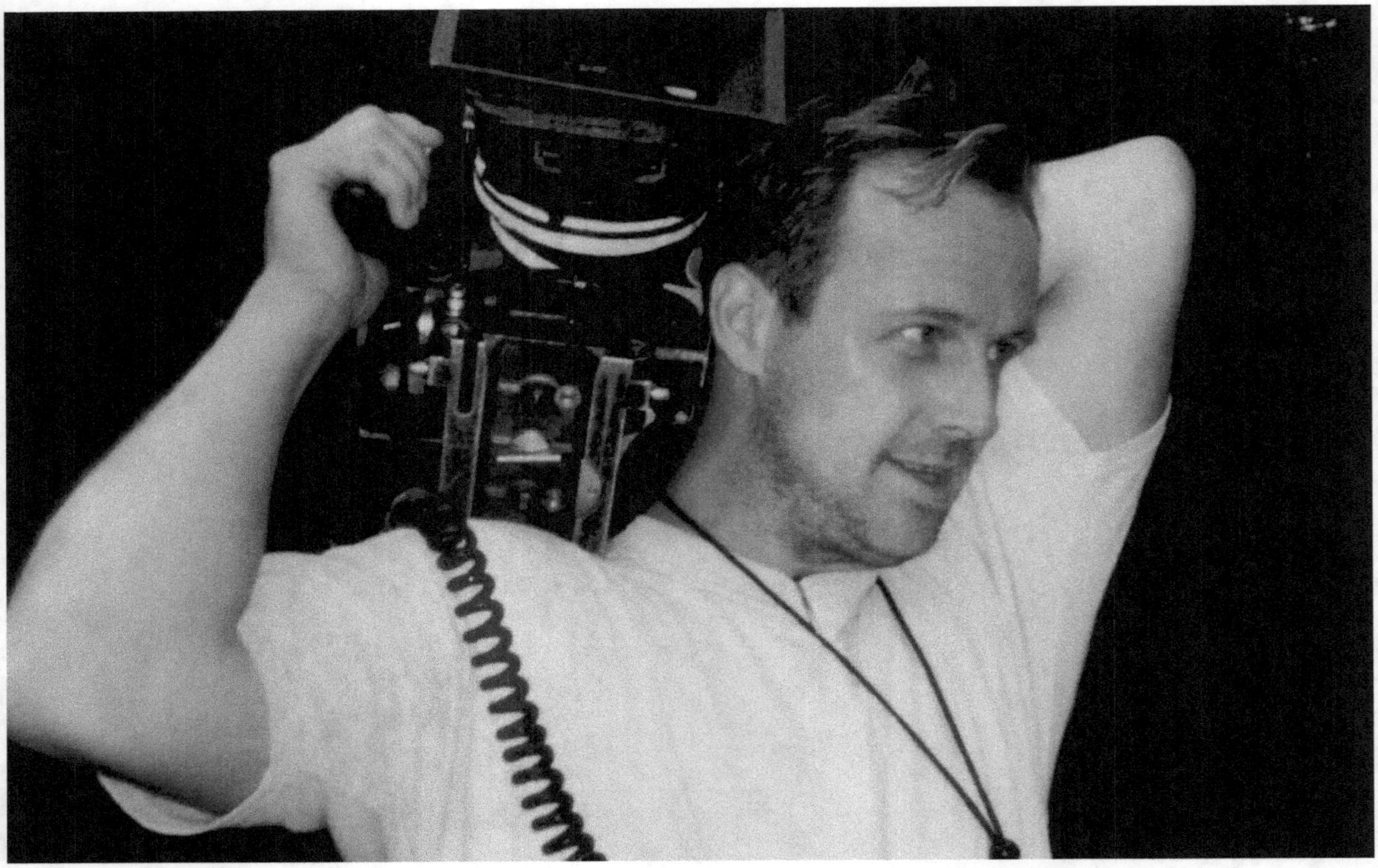

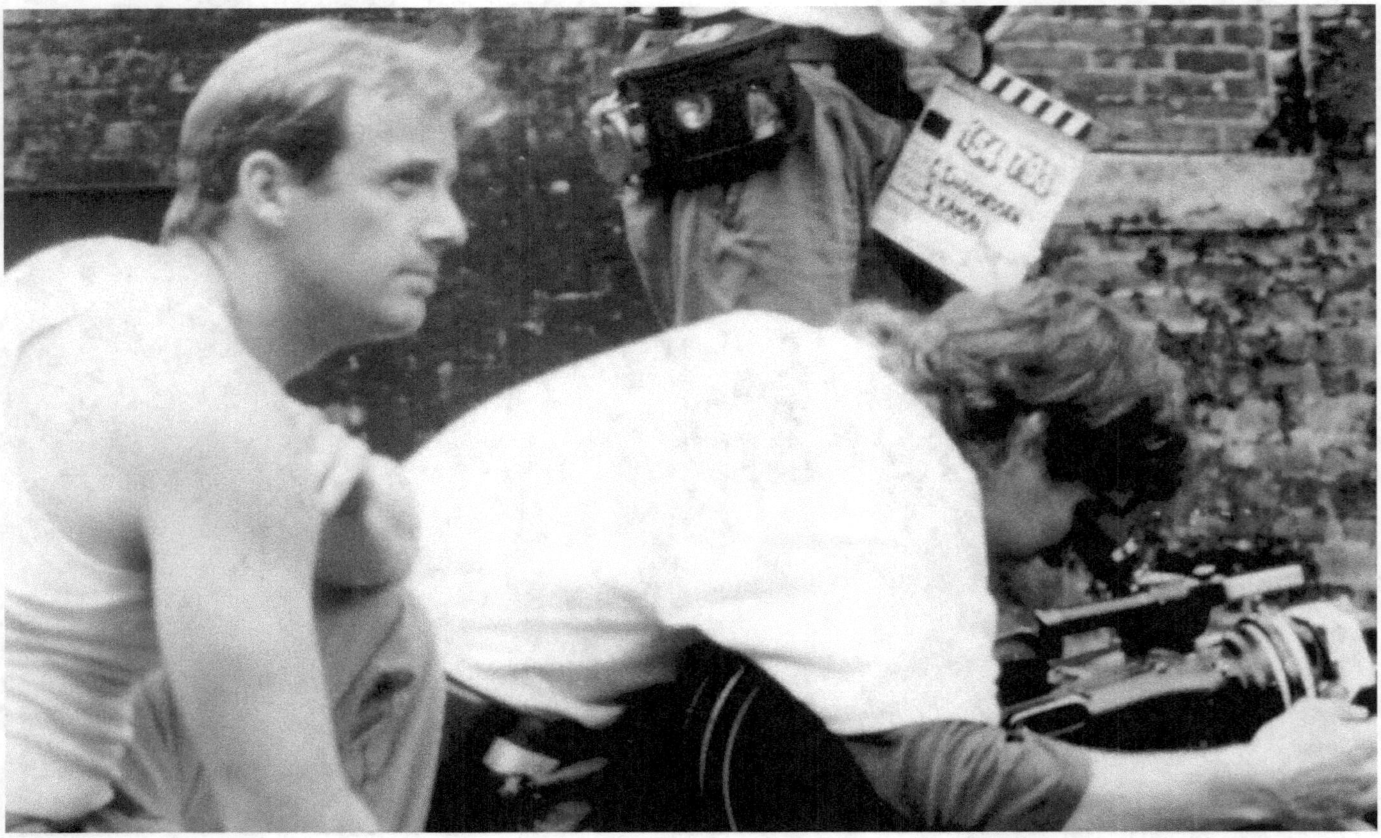

R2.45K
A63.3

Once Enemies, Now They're Forced To Be...

# COMRADES IN ARMS

It's VERY Personal.

**PROMARK ENTERTAINMENT GROUP** Presents a **CINEMA SCIENCES** Production **COMRADES IN ARMS**
Starring **LYLE ALZADO**, **RICK WASHBURN**, **JOHN CHRISTIAN** and **LANCE HENRIKSEN** as Rob Reed Director of Photography **STEVEN KAMAN**
Music by **PAUL AVGERINOS** Executive Producer **MARC L. BAILIN** Written and Produced by **J. CHRISTIAN INGVORDSEN**, **STEVE KAMAN** and **JOHN WEINER**
© 1991 Cinema Sciences Corp. Directed by **J. CHRISTIAN INGVORDSEN**

**PROMARK**
ENTERTAINMENT GROUP

# LYLE ALZADO  RICK WASHBURN  LANCE HENRIKSEN

Unlikely allies.
Unbeatable force.

# COMRADES IN ARMS

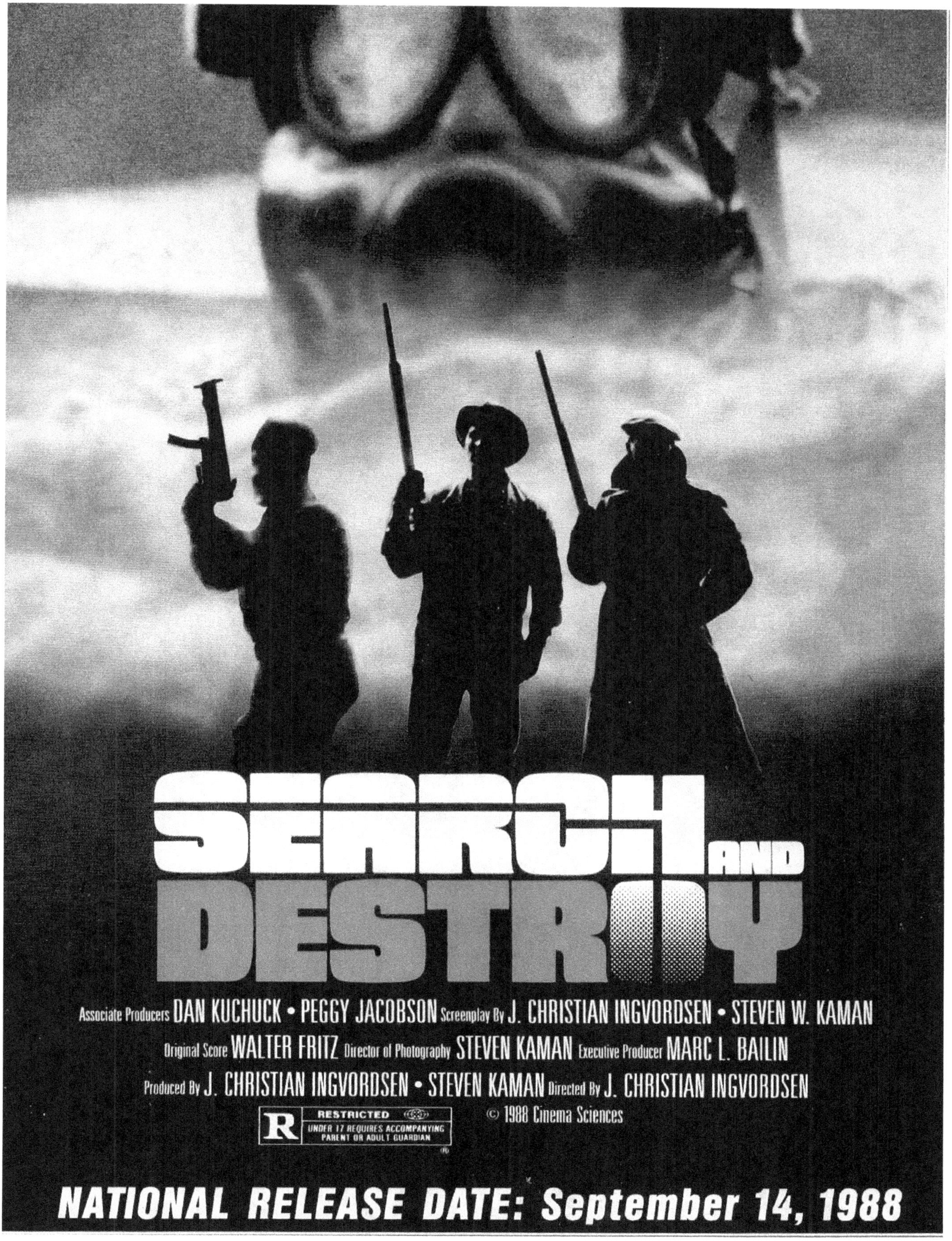

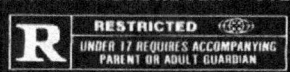

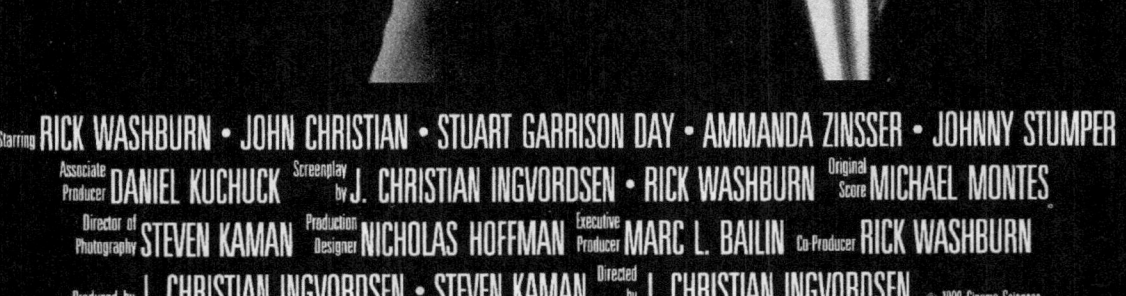

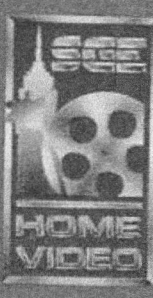

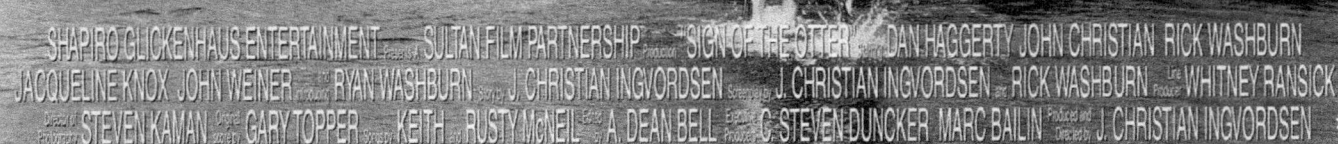

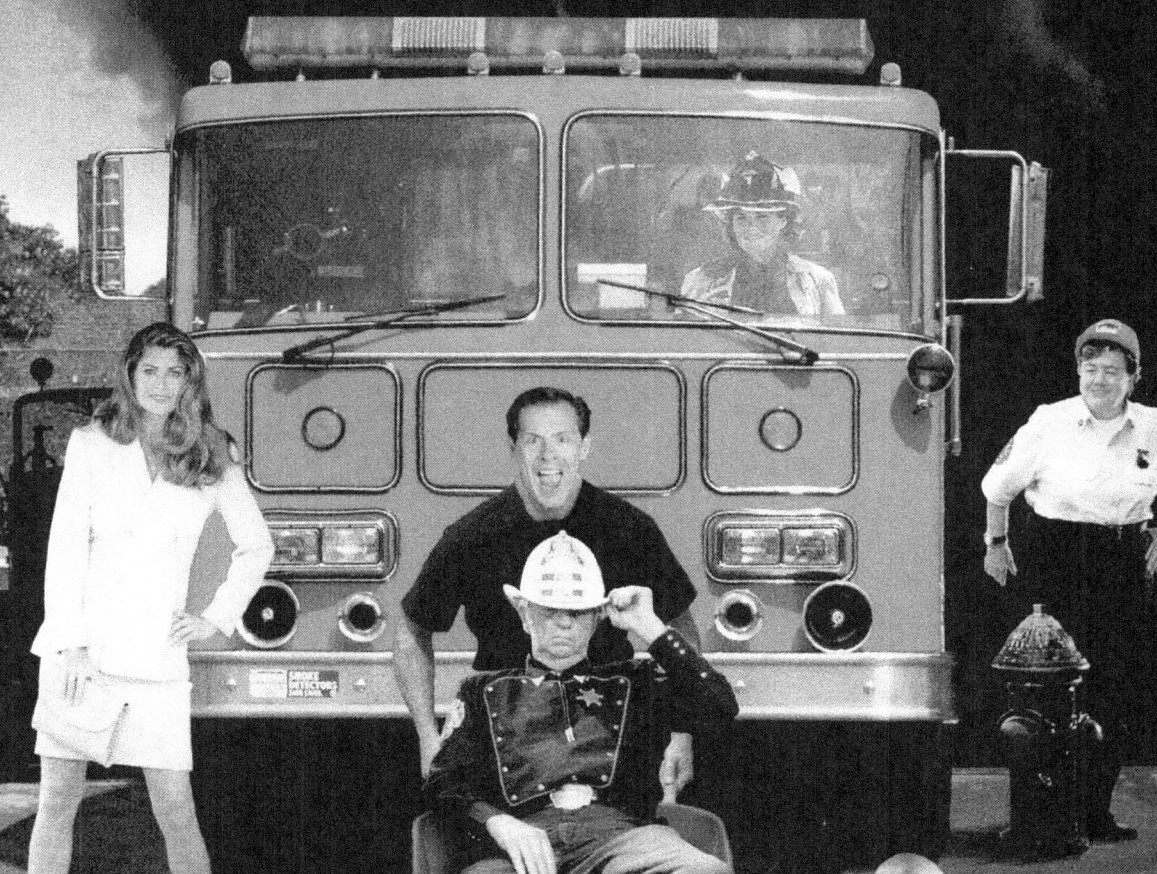

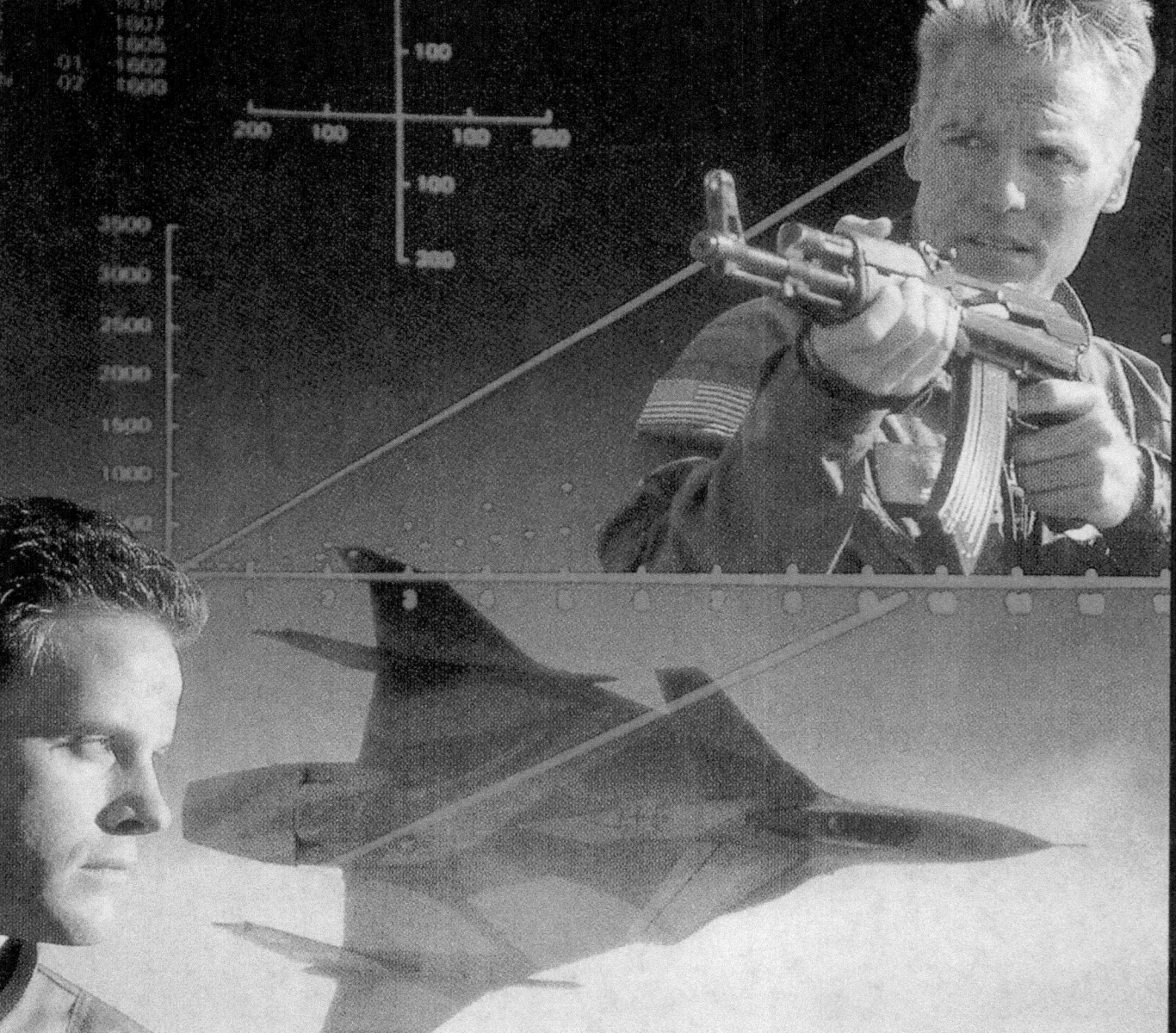

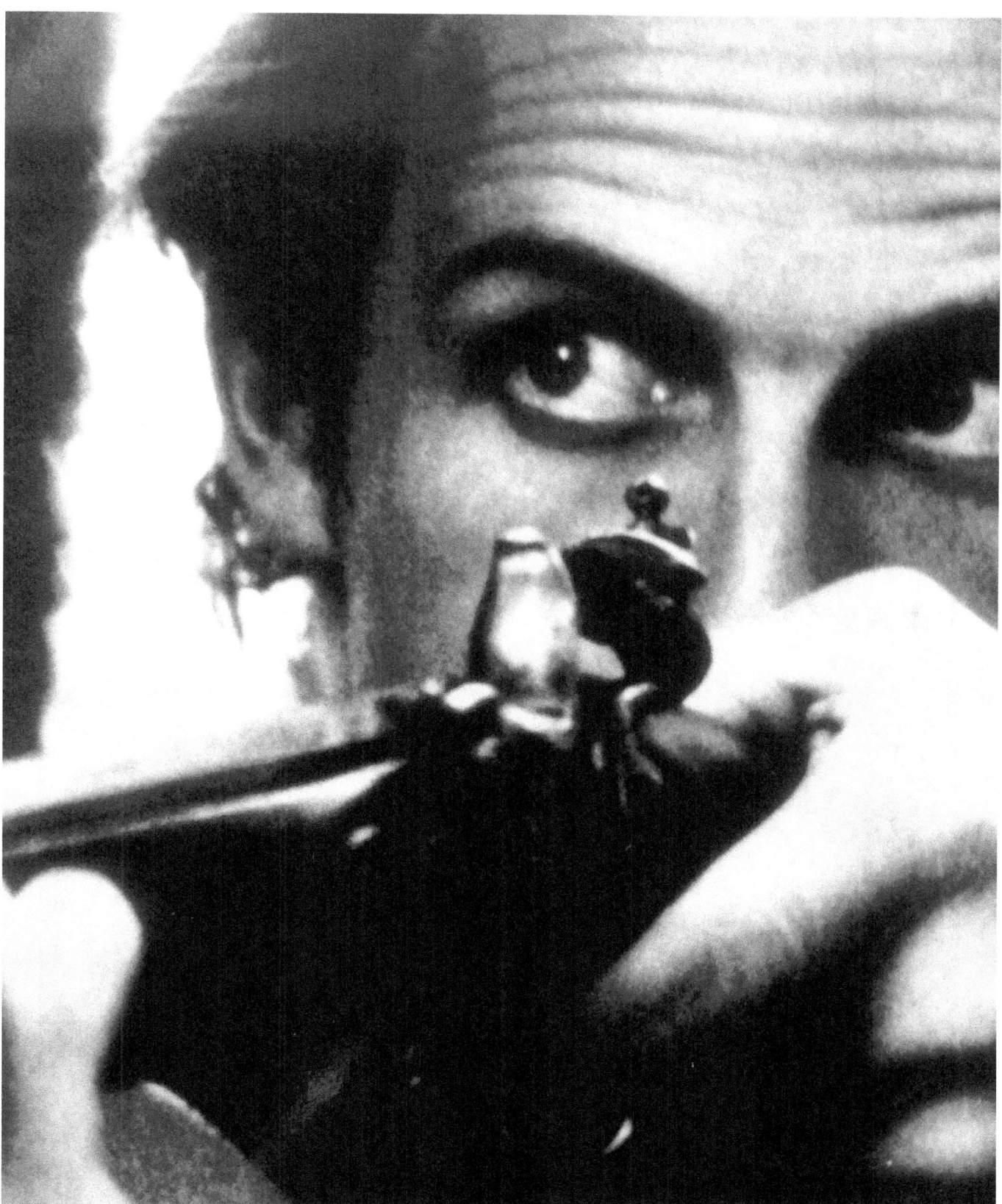

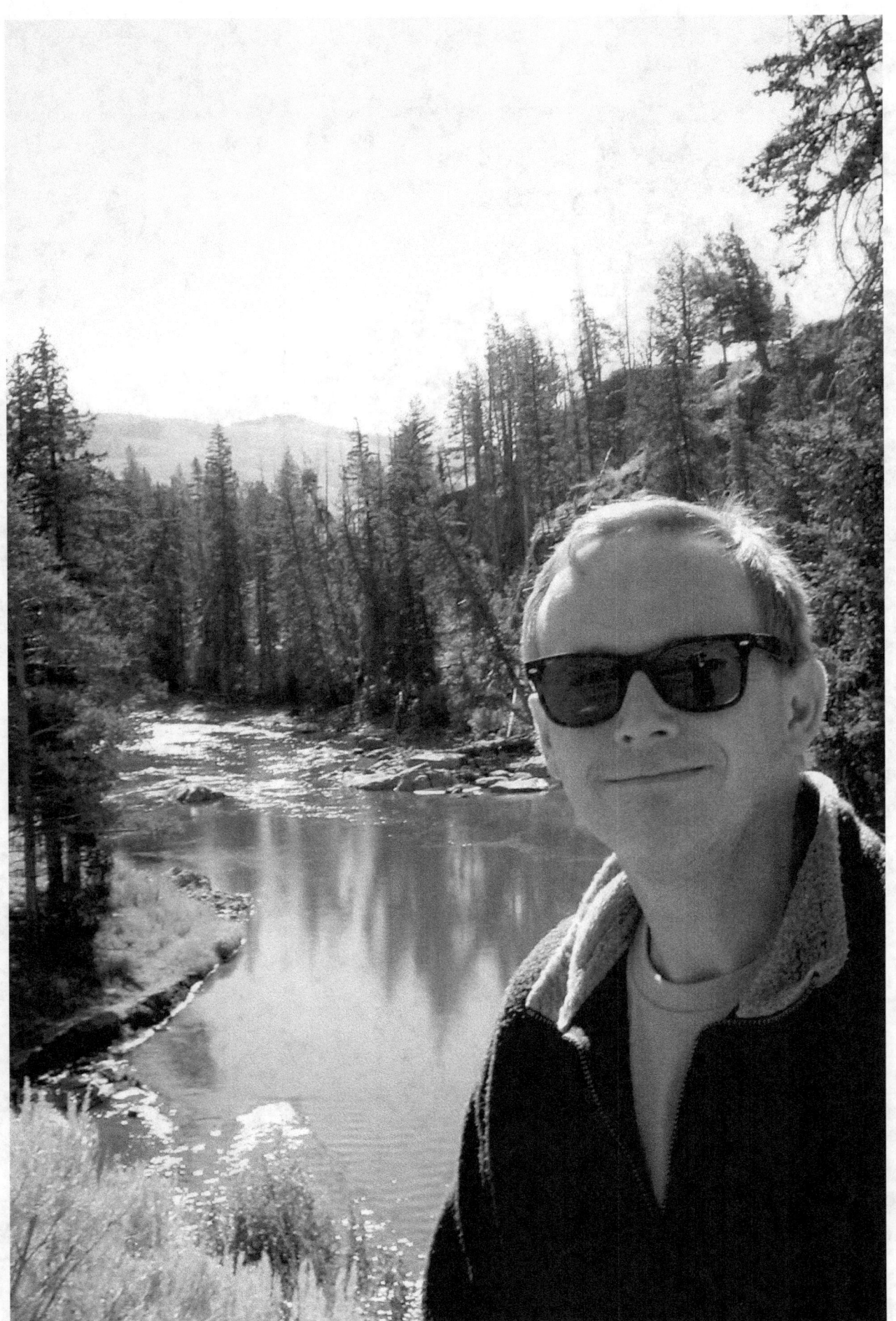

# J. Christian Ingvordsen

Among the huge catalogue of titles SGE distributed, Chris Ingvordsen's movies mark the most considerable number of pick-ups from one director. As of today Ingvordsen has released more than 20 feature films. Often military-themed, most of his movies are devoted to the action genre. Nearly ten titles of his most prolific career phase were handled by SGE, among them gangster films like MOB WAR (1988) starring Jake LaMotta, and THE OUTFIT (1994), including Billy Drago and Lance Henriksen. After SGE was closed down, Chris continued business relationships with Alan Solomon. Probably the most popular title with Alan was AIRBOSS in 1997. After directing the horror movie BLOOD RELIC in 2005, Chris Ingvordsen took a break from filmmaking for ten years until TAR PIT was released early in 2015.

**Nadia:** You were born in Copenhagen. How long did you spend in Denmark? Did you move to the USA to attend the well-known Duke University or did you live there already?

**Christian:** Yeah, I was born in Copenhagen, but I only lived there less than a year. So I really grew up in the US. I went to Duke University.

**Nadia:** So you grew up in North Carolina, right?

**Christian:** Yes.

**Nadia:** Tell me something about the awakening of your love for cinema. Which films and screenings can be marked as key moments in your life? Have you always been fascinated by action and movement?

**Christian:** I kind of grew up in the golden age of 70's movies. It was a great time to grow up. THE FRENCH CONNECTION and THE GODFATHER, those sort of films. They had a lot to do with what my love for cinema came from. And there was an awakening too at that time of film making that led to studio films - I don't mean major studio, I mean shot in-studio like a Cassavette-verité style, gritty New York cop movies. I sort of grew up with that. In a way I think it really did influence my later style.

**Nadia:** You might be influenced by Pakula, Sydney Pollack and Walter Hill.

**Christian:** Indeed, that nails a couple of influences. Certainly for HANGMEN. From Pakula, I liked THE PARALLAX VIEW, which is a great film of his, a better example is Pollack. I met Pakula with HANGMEN, he did a lot of tense conspiracy type of films. And that's a very good influence. Pollack probably more, I love Pollack. He did fantastic movies like THREE DAYS OF THE CONDOR, very much like HANGMEN. A very good example, I remember seeing this in the theatre and loving it....the CIA trying to kill his own agents. And a great movie called THE YAKUZA, I love this. Also JEREMIAH JOHNSON, CASTLE KEEP - I mean, I love Pollack. And actually right, I love Walter Hill, a big big influence. I love SOUTHERN COMFORT, DRIVER and THE LONG RIDERS, I think he did one of the best western of all time. JOHNNY HANDSOME, also with Lance Henriksen. Another name you can put in there is George Roy Hill, he did BUTCH CASSIDY AND SUNDANCE KID. But I also love Peckinpah and Clint Eastwood. I like the Coen Brothers, NO COUNTRY FOR

OLD MEN. I love Scorsese, Sydney Lumet, John Ford. A lot of influences like that.

**Nadia:** Talk about the connection between Sultan Films and SGE.

**Christian:** My very first company was actually called Cinema Sciences. It was a production company, I was making feature films. And my connection to Shapiro Glickenhaus was basically just as a distributor. The first film where I met them with was called FIREHOUSE. I think that was 1985, if I remember correctly. I shot that in New York, made a print and schlepped it out to L.A. and screened it for people. One of the companies I screened it for was SGE. That's where the relationship really started, with that film, FIREHOUSE. So, HANGMEN was the following year after FIREHOUSE. That was the second film that SGE was sales agent/distributor for.

**Nadia:** Right.

**Christian:** They were really a distributor, they were also sales agents for domestic deals. In that case video.

**Nadia:** So you met Lenny with FIREHOUSE?

**Christian:** Yes, it was FIREHOUSE. You know, the first partner or principal at SGE I met was a woman named Kelly Ross. I guess she was the acquisitions person?

**Nadia:** She was.

**Christian:** I remember meeting her at the screening; she rented some screening room somewhere in L.A. She was there and liked the film, and then after that I met the other people, which were Lenny and Jim and Alan Solomon.

**Nadia:** That was actually before Jim, because Jim didn't come till ... probably 1987.

**Christian:** So it was still Shapiro Entertainment then?

**Nadia:** Yes

**Christian:** So, that's a little context there, it was even earlier than the partnership between Jim and Lenny, which turned into SGE. That's how far back that goes. I think it was 1985 when I first went out there with FIREHOUSE.

**Nadia:** That was before me even. *(laughing)* - Let's talk about Lenny. We love Lenny, do you love him?

**Christian:** He is just a very affable, warm, nice person; you can't help but like Lenny. It was always really fun to see him. I'm based in New York City, so I would only see those guys from SGE - or Lenny, for instance - at the American Film Market, which, back in the day - wasn't it in the fall?

**Nadia:** It was in February, I think.

**Christian:** Also, usually I remember at the Cannes Film Market a bunch of times. Also MIFED. So, that's really where I'd seen Lenny, but a few times I did part of the filming of my features in L.A. for various reasons. For locations or name actors or some other reasons, that was a reason I did see Lenny as well.

**Nadia:** You probably worked more with Alan Solomon, right?

**Christian:** It's hard to say, I think after SGE closed, Alan Solomon who was the acquisition/sales guy at SGE went on to start his own company called Amsell. So I kept doing business with him. But you know, I'd still would run into Lenny here and there. It was kind of a long distance relationship. My recollection of Lenny is just he is just a warm, likeable person, just a mensch, you know? Just running into him somewhere was so great. And SGE, especially at Cannes, they were always throwing a great party. Like a theme kind of party. One year in Cannes, it was a for probably SPIRIT OF THE EAGLE, it was a western, sort of kids' movie starring Dan Haggerty. So, I remember this great kind of cowboys and indian party in some hotel in Cannes.

**Nadia:** I threw one, I think it was for BLUE JEAN COP. We had a BBQ and I hired a band from England. And it was all red, white, and blue kind of thing. Pretty funny. It was like an All American Party.

**Christian:** Back in the day, that was part of the hoopla you did for these foreign film markets. Throwing a party was a big part of your marketing, so that was fun. A couple of times, I remember running into Alan, Lenny and Jim. Jim was shooting BLUE JEAN COP, which ended up becoming SHAKEDOWN. So that was shot in New York City, kind of a higher budget version of that kind of movie I was doing there. So I was on the set couple of times. And that was kind of fun. Those are my memories of that.

**Nadia:** SGE was your sales agent and distributor; you were not an in-house producer, though you were very prolific with SGE.

**Christian:** I did a lot of films that were released or distributed through SGE, and before that Shapiro Entertainment, but it was more of an arms-length agreement because I always did my own financing out of New York. So when the films were done, and it was time to sell them -- back in the day - actually it's still true - you really needed a sales agent, some one who went to all the foreign markets, some one who knew the buyers, who knew how to market to the foreign territories. You needed a distributor/sales agent. And I had this ongoing relationship with Lenny, with Alan, with Jim. Let's face it, this is a really tough business. There are silly bad actors and lot of bad business practices. So when you have a comfort level with people that you trust and like, and have done business with, it makes sense to continue with that. So I always trusted them and liked them, that's why I released all my films with them. So basically I would do a film; shoot it, produce it, and they would do the sales on that. Each of us had our own company, and it was just a long business relationship, based on mutual trust and friendship. I really liked those guys..

**Nadia:** Yes, you were the most prolific director I think. We had most of your films.

**Christian:** I kind of hit... just to get into a little film history here: There was a golden moment of opportunity in the 80s. So starting from the mid-80s to almost the mid-90s, or really the early 90s - especially the home video boom. In the US and also foreign, there was an incessant need for product. I think the American major studios got into it a little late, they were worried about copyright infringement. They didn't quite understand how VHS worked in those days. They thought, "people are gonna pirate everything!". They really got into the game late, so it was a golden opportunity for entrepeneurs, people like myself, to actually make product and to make, you know, things with fairly big themes. Exploitation movies, action movies, whatever, were being done by independents and real independents like me. So I took advantage of that golden opportunity, and I did so many films in those days. Because they were making money. I really pushed myself very hard, I was making two films, at least, a year. Sometimes three. So that was kind of the most prolific part of my career, in the 80s and early 90s.

**Nadia:** HANGMEN, compared to the lighter entertainment style of action films of that time, it seemed much darker, almost horror if you will, if not to say nihilistic.

**Christian:** Here's a quick evolution of my career: I got out of college and always wanted to be a filmmaker and a lot of these guys, friends from college went on to real jobs, most of them on Wall Street, most of them working in NY. I actually had pretty easy access to capital early on. I did my first film, which was actually called MODEL BEHAVIOR, when I was 21 or 22, my first feature film. For the time it was a pretty big budget disaster. It was under a million bucks but back in 1982 that was like 5 or 10 million.

**Nadia:** Right!

**Christian:** I did everything the right way, all the unions and lots of crew, vehicles, and all that stuff and it was a complete and utter disaster. It was not a *(laughing)* ... really good film. And actually, it lost a lot of money. What I learned from that experience was, there was another way to approach film making, more organic hands-on level. I was the producer on that, but what I learned from that experience was that I should learn all the other aspects of filmmaking. Me and my first partner, Steve Kaman, after that learning experience - it really was a commercial disaster for us and of course all the people put up the money for it; everybody lost money. There was no way we would going to raise a big budget for another film. We did crew work. I worked as a key-grip on a lot of movies. I really learned filmmaking from the ground up. I learned how to shoot as a cameraman, how to do light, sound, and grip. I learned every aspect of filmmaking. The next chance we had, we wanted to do another feature, Steve Kaman and I. We decided to do the most commercial film we could possibly do. We thought of T&A exploitation. We came up with the idea for FIREHOUSE, about three woman trying to join the all-male fire department. It was a gender-bending T&A romantic comedy thing. You know, very, very tame. And a lot of stuff going on. Firemen - very visual! Firetrucks, and flashing lights, fire, and beautiful girls. And it actually was a cute little movie. Speaking of which, it was one of Alan Solomon's favorite films, probably his favorite film I ever did. He liked it, and also it kept making money. And it had a fairly big release domestically. On video and also USA, Cable bought it, one of the first big cable buys. It just was a movie that really clicked. However, it wasn't really the genre that I liked to do, and it wasn't what Steve liked to do. We really wanted to do gritty, action movies.

So after FIREHOUSE, which was kind of a success, the next movie we wanted to do was an action movie. This is more of the style I liked going to see as a fan. HANGMEN, it's definitely gritty and kind of realistic. With the bad CIA and a lot of conspiracy theories. But we really had a fun time doing it, and I don't think it's a dark part of my personality, it's more that I just love movies like that. It wasn't intentionally gritty and dark but it just turned out that way, and it was also a very big success for us. That was really the type of movie I wanted to do: action movies. That was successful again, had a very big domestic video release and foreign did fine as well. The next film we were able to do was a straight out action movie. SEARCH & DESTROY, things like that. Because in the 80s there was an insatiable need for product internationally and domestically. These type of low budget action movies, there really was a way that true independents like I could into that. So that's what happened.

**Nadia:** Your partner, Steve Kaman, did you guys meet in college?

**Christian:** I met Steve after college. He was a graduate of the very prestigious NYU film school; he learned film in college. I met him after college, when I came back to New York City where my family lived. I think I met him the summer after graduating. We were both entrepreneurial, we wanted to start a company, a production company and make movies ultimately. We tried to begin with commercials, and things like that. But as young whipper-snappers, we didn't get really far with that. Through the connections that I had, to capital, to people I could raise money from...it was really my friends of the same age, early twenties. But they were working at the Wall Street, making money. And we were able to make our own features, so that was the connection. Steve and I clicked on a very entrepreneurial level. And also, we kind of liked the same type of movies.

**Nadia:** Well, please let me know about Danny Kutchuck. In BLUE VENGEANCE he even served as the co-director. What's the significance of him as a creative partner? And what about BLUE VENGEANCE - was it easier, or even more complicated with a co-director?

**Christian:** It was the first horror film I did, and I think we shot it in 1989. I saw in a lot of databases like IMDB that it is co-directed by Danny Kuchuck who worked with us for many years. What actually happened, it wasn't a co-director thing. We had Danny, he was going to shoot a film for us.

I think we did a trailer or promo for that, I think it was called ADRENIACS. It was another horror movie. Like organ-harvesting It was about the classic organ thing: People wake up one morning, and one of their kidneys is gone. In this case it was the adrenal gland taken from live people to make this crazy drug Adreniacs. So I think Danny shot probably a promo for us. We were doing this a lot of times with this three markets going on, and gave it to Lenny and Alan, to see if we get some pre-sale, and then we would shoot the movie. It was crazy, but it was something we did in the 80s. Just to see if that movie would work. I think we probably didn't get a good reaction for it. I'm not sure, but maybe this test, we called BLUE VENGEANCE. But when it came to the actual BLUE VENGEANCE Danny had moved on to L.A. - He was a guy who worked for us for many years. Also very talented. On MODEL BEHAVIOR I was the producer, and I needed a production assistant. I didn't hire him, I have no idea where he came from. These two young guys Danny Kuchuck, and John Weiner. At that point, I think they were still in high school. They were just fun, and wonderful kids. Everybody loved them on set so they kind of worked with me for years. They moved to LA, and became writers. They actually did very well as punch-up writers, and script doctors. They actually made a film together called CRYPTIC. A Sci-Fi-Movie that I highly recommend, it's one of the best low budget science fiction film I've ever seen. But back to the question: Danny Kuchuck wasn't the co-director, I directed and produced it myself.

**Nadia:** Are you personally fascinated by the serial killer phenomonen?

**Christian:** BLUE VENGEANCE was shot in 1989 with a really good cinematographer called Michael Spiller. He was the Director of Photography there, and he turned it into a great career, directing SEX AND THE CITY, he won an Emmy, and so on. So he was my DP on that, and I wanted to do a gritty New York City based movie, and at the time it was kind of like a horror-slasher film seemed to be good commercially. But it's very NY also: I play a New York Cop in it, we have a serial killer, there's a kind of rock and roll comic-book obsessed guy. It was just a lot of fun doing that. Am I obsessed with serial killers...?

**Nadia:** *(laughing)*

**Christian:** ... probably not, but maybe we all are! But it's just a very good dramatic theme for a film. Because... I think we all are obsessed with it, so that's the answer. Yes, probably I am, but so is the audience. And that was another weird film, as far as distribution. That still hasn't been released domestically or in the US DVD market, it was just a foreign release. It's a film I'm very proud of, I think it really holds up. A really good film. We shot in CBGBs of all places, the iconic punk club in NYC. Once in a while on youtube I see a clip from it, but more because of the CBGB connection.

**Nadia:** The cinematography is excellent! Steve Kaman was not the cinematographer for BLUE VENGEANCE?

**Christian:** Also, wrong credits in databases. Steve Kaman wasn't the DP on that, he had actually moved to L.A. as well at that point. A lot of my players who had worked with me for a long time had made their way to Los Angeles which is of course really where the film business is. There's a small industry in New York. I always stayed there because I was one of the few guys making films there. So Steve didn't shoot that, it was Michael "Mike" Spiller. He worked with me for years, doing things like the key grip on my early movies. I met him in the early 80s, and he was a assistant cameraman. He went on to be a Director of Photography, a fantastic one. So he shot BLUE VENGEANCE, and he did a really good job. It was a lot of fun working with him. He went on to be a pretty big name in the business. He shot many seasons of SEX AND THE CITY. Actually he directed some episodes, and he's a television director now. He just won an Emmy last year.

**Nadia:** If you had a bigger budget that time, shooting BLUE VENGEANCE, do you think you had made it a gory and gruesome serial killer film like William Lustig's MANIAC?

**Christian:** BLUE VENGEANCE - just like the rest of my films from that era - was made very inexpensively. One thing I point out to people that are making this type of film would be: The only way you can survive, make it sustainable, and actually make a living out of it, is <u>not</u> spending a lot of money. You always run out of money. You have to use your innovation, your creativity, your drive. That's what you have. What you don't have is money. I think the idea for BLUE VENGEANCE is sort of a good one. It's about that kid that's obsessed with heavy metal bands, and comic books, and fantasy. But at the same time he's psychotic, he's a serial killer who's obsessed with that kind of pop culture. I think it's an interesting idea which really would have worked better with a lot of money. Unfortunately when you don't have money ... you know, it is what it is. We did it fairly cheaply, and fairly quickly. You can say that on every film you do. I'm sure every filmmaker could say that for every film, if I just had more money it would have been a great movie...!

**Nadia:** So then, we get to Sandra Bullock and Julia Roberts...

**Christian:** Here's the thing about that. It's often been said about me, how did he cast those people? I picked them out of nowhere, and in case for both of them it's sort of true. Sandra Bullock had just graduated from college. She had come to New York, trying to make it as an actress. Absolutely like the 100.000 other actors who shot up to NYC that summer. She found an agent somehow, she came to a casting call of ours, and I literally could see the talent instantly. There are a lot of people that try acting, but you know a very real small percentage is really talented, and I could see that right away. I don't think it's any talent I have, it's just part of my job. Casting is such a major part of making a film. Your film really is your script and your actors. So you better be good at casting, take as much time you can and take it very serious, obviously. That was the deal with Sandra Bullock. Julia Roberts is actually an interesting story: The lead actress in FIREHOUSE - Julia was her room-mate. She came as a walk-on. So that really doesn't count but she was a wonderful person. Here's the Sandra Bullock story: She was so cool and such a true gal, just one of the crew. The end of the day she was collecting garbage or loading the grip truck. I often used her story to problematic actors. Sandra Bullock, what was she like? I tell the truth, she was pitching in with us. We were a small film company, we all gave it our all, and she was literally loading the grip truck with us. It was part of her success, pitching in like that.

**Nadia:** There were plans in the early 90s for a sequel of FIREHOUSE?

**Christian:** Yeah, they wanted to do FIREHOUSE 2. For some reason - I kind of persued it with Alan Solomon. Alan did some artwork. It was going to be a light T&A type FIREHOUSE, but it actually morphed into another big budget disaster for me, which was BACKFIRE. We did it with a lot of money, to do it with the full deal and union and everything. We had names, we had Robert Mitchum in it, Telly Savalas, Shelly Winters. We had multiple Oscar-winners in this movie. Mary McCormick - another casting thing. We found her out of the blue but she went on doing WEST WING and lots of other big films like ARMAGEDDON. A great actress. And also Kristen Johnson went on to do THIRD ROCK FROM THE SUN. So a lof of interesting people — Edie Falco, of course from THE SOPRANOS. So FIREHOUSE 2, what should have been another nice low budget movie morphed into a bigger budget movie. It would have been much nicer to do FIREHOUSE 2, but...

**Nadia:** Your films clearly express personal trademarks. You are involved in all the key functions behind the camera. Would you call yourself an auteur?

**Christian:** The auteur in a strict sense, kind of in the French new wave - this one person who is kind of responsible creatively, and it's a very pretentious concept. I don't think that exists in filmmaking now, because it's a product of so many different creative people: Actors, the cinematographer, the director, the production designer. There's so many people, making a film – it's such a collaborative and complex thing, so I think the auteur-thing is pretentious. But I would say that, um, in a small sense, I mean in the sense that I'm usually the person that comes up with the idea or the story, write it or co-write it, at least in the old days you always be on the writing team, come up with the financing, produce it, direct it, act in it. So in kind of a small way, maybe I'm an auteur, but I don't want to go with the pretentiousness of that. I would say that I always had one key creative partner. Steve Kaman in the early days as a collaborator, a co-producer. He would be the director of photography, and usually the editor. You can't do it by yourself, it's impossible. But I always had sort of a collaborator. Starting in the mid 90s, Matthew Howe has been my collaborator. Very much the

| | |
|---|---|
| | same as Steve Kaman was. Matt Howe is a writer, a co-producer, director of photography, editor. These missing parts of the puzzle that I generally don't do or, you know, there's someone better at it. I think you need one partner. I think that's the answer. But back to what I said before, I think as a filmmaker you have got to learn every single job on the set. I really can do anything, from shooting to sound, to acting, whatever. In the old days, I think a lot of us thought that was what you had to do. It's probably a very good place to be as a filmmaker. You need to do everything so you know what the gaffer's job is, and what it takes to be an actor, what they are going through. I think it's a very important part of the process, though. So that's a long answer about being a hybrid-auteur. |
| **Nadia:** | Almost every director has experienced it, sadly: Despite your best intentions a film turns out badly. So, you talked about BACKFIRE and MODEL BEHAVIOR. |
| **Christian:** | The truth is, that always happens. I think it's because, as an artist or a creative person, it's so complicated to do a film, there are so many elements. If you're looking at a blank sheet of paper or a canvas, you want to paint a painting. That's an easy path of expressing yourself, but it's so complicated to do a film. So many things can go wrong. So many other elements to it. Actors that seemed good but are not. All kinds of other complications. Unfortunately it happens all the time, but that's the good thing about having such a large body of work! *(laughing)* - You love all your movies, but you go out and do the next one if the one you just did is disappointing, and sometimes they are, no doubt about it. |
| **Nadia:** | Why do you prefer serious, kind of dark, action films? |
| **Christian:** | Yeah, I think that's just a personal preference. I do like those type of films, and I think the comedy thing is very tough to do, and I doubt that I have a good.... - I just think I'm not very good at that. The action stuff and the drama, I think I'm actually much better at drama and suspense. I'm better at drama than comedy, I think. Comedy takes a certain sensibility, and I don't think I have it. |
| **Nadia:** | Let's talk about SHOCKTROOP. It has an extended running time. That sounds like box-office poison for a small action film. Do you agree or was it exactly what you wanted to get out of this project? |
| **Christian:** | It had a long running time, which is two hours. Maybe we were thinking we're making an epic or something. Looking back this wasn't a very good decision. *(laughing)* It wasn't anything I did on purpose, it just ended up that way. A mistake probably, a B-movie action film really shouldn't be more than 90 minutes, it just doesn't work. Anyway, a good example of that is THE OUTFIT. Back in those days Lenny had a deal with Universal/MCA for home video. So actually THE OUTFIT was released by a studio for home video. I think it was kind of long, too. But they did their own cut, and got 90 minutes. And honestly they did a pretty good job, you know. |

*(laughing)* Sometimes directors really grouse about others cutting their films but at least in that case they did get a much better pace of a film. So that probably should have happened to SHOCKTROOP, but it was sort of this epic. But it was also one of the most fun films to do. It was about the Russian-Afghan war, and very few people had done that. RAMBO III I think is about that...

**Nadia:** Right.

**Christian:** Kevin Reynolds made a movie called THE BEAST OF WAR in 1988 which was about a Russian tank crew, and there were maybe two or three others. But that's it, no one was doing that, so we thought this would be a good idea for a film. It's about an American soldier who gets captured by the Russians, he's thrown in a Gulag, and he can escape with the help of an Afghani prisoner. They make it to Afghanistan, and so on. It's really kind of a big movie, although it was actually one of the most simple movies I ever did. We shot it all in Colorado, of all places. I took a long road trip and shot the Mesa Verde cliff dwellings from thousands of years ago, which was worked very well for the peasant huts of the Afghanis. I remember just doing this road trip, and I went to a national park. I think we had a station wagon, we had a small crew, and we were doubling as the actors. Even talked the park rangers into putting on Russian uniforms, and a bunch of tourists. We had bags of peasant rag-type stuff. We conned like 20 tourists into being Afghani soldiers. Back in the day that kind of filmmaking was tremendously fun, sort of balls-out filmmaking. It was a lot of fun doing a movie like that.

**Nadia:** Danny Aiello is featured in SHOCKTROOP. So did you need a huge part of the budget just for him? Was he the most expensive actor you ever hired? How many days did he spend on the set, and was it a nice experience?

**Christian:** One of the things about SHOCKTROOP was the star. I think it was 1988, at least the end of the 80s. The home video boom which had sort of fueled a lot of my filmmaking in the 80s was kind of slowing down when Alan mentioned to us we needed some name actors at that point. We've always done movies with no name actors, and obviously they are so much easier to do. Not paying big fees, not dealing with egos, no catering to demanding big actors. But those days were over, so in SHOCKTROOP, Alan gave us the heads up that we needed an actor that had a name, and he suggested Danny Aiello. He knew him because Jim Glickenhaus had done a film with him called THE PROTECTOR. It starred Danny Aiello and Jackie Chan. I think Jim Glickenhaus was one of the people who really discovered Jackie Chan, he was just sort of doing Hong Kong Films. Jim may have been the person who brought him to an American audience. So Alan actually had Danny Aiello's home number, so we were able to get around his agent, and get right to him. We were able to do what I call "money-whip" him. We wrote a part for him in which he played the CIA director which we could shoot in a very small amount of time, but it was in six or seven scenes in the movie. That was the way we could put his name on the movie, without doing a kind of a big star type movie. I met Danny Aiello, and we offered him 50.000 dollars. For doing one day on the movie. I mean, he was great. Completely professional, just a regular guy. I was very lucky with a lot of actors like that. Lance Henriksen, Billy Drago, and others - they were really just good guys to work with. And they go from A movies to B movies, constantly. They saw we had a really small crew, very small production, but we were good guys, and we knew what we were doing. It was actually a fun day with Danny Aiello. We shot 3 or 4 scenes, kind of in offices in New York City, in a limo, things like that. We had taken out this house, which was a mansion. So we were driving out in a limo, and he said, "First I did not want to do your little movie, but then I said to myself: 50 grand! Danny, what are you, an asshole?" So that's the story. He decided to do it for the money, which was great. We had our star without a lot of hassle, and made SHOCKTROOP a better film to sell because it had a name in it.

**Nadia:** The SHOCKTROOP score is unliked by many action fans, mostly because it appears very pushy and bothersome. Also very repetitive – there has to be a conception about this very cold and unfriendly and not-at-all-heroic scoring? How do you remember working with Chris Burke?

**Christian:** He was great! The way it sort of worked in the lower budget levels. You can find people that are very talented, and want to do their first films. Didn't have a chance before, so you would trade that for the fact that you wouldn't be paying them much. That's a staple in the film business. Since forever. They are getting a chance to start a career, and you are not paying a lot of money to get a talented person. Chris Burke did a few films for us, and he was extremely talented. As his career takes off you are able to pay him less, and you have to say goodbye to all these talented people. They're moving up the ladder. That's the story about Chris Burke, and the score - it worked for me, but some people have their problems with it. It's just one of those things when you're making a film, and it doesn't matter if it's low budget, or if it's a 200 million dollar project. You always wish something could be better, there are always compromises. There's always something that doesn't work. Hopefully it's nothing super-important like the actors are bad, or there's a disaster like your set is washed away from a typhoon. Maybe in this case the score doesn't work for a lot of fans, but that's just one of the things that happens. Our low budget films have always been done very cheaply, and very quickly. So something has to give.

**Nadia:** SHOCKTROOP is among your films that are not available internationally at the moment. Why not? Has it ever been released on DVD? If not, where's the problem, what's happened?

**Christian:** A lot of these international sales deals are usually for 7-10 years. So once that time elapses, unless you can find a new distributor, theyre probably not available. Although for SHOCKTROOP I sold the DVD rights to Echo Bridge Entertainment. What they are doing now is, they make DVDs with multiple films - you know, just like 5 movies on a DVD. So SHOCKTROOP is actually available on such an Echo Bridge compilation-DVD, and it's on the cover. That's an example of kinda recycling these films, and finding new markets for them. The licence deal was done a couple of years ago, some of my movies are actually available on DVD. I don't know about internationally, but certainly in this country.

**Nadia:** Your most unlikely film was THE LITTLE PATRIOT, which was very ambitious with the epic landscapes. How long was the shoot, how many different locations?

**Christian:** My company was based in New York City, but I live in upstate New York which is a very rural landscape. I came up with the idea. Actually I think Lenny or Alan suggested doing it, because they have had such a big success with their Dan Haggerty little kids' movie which was called SPIRIT OF THE EAGLE. So I think they suggested doing that. I live in an area in upstate NY that has a lot of history about the [American] Revolutionary War. The story itself was based on actual historical events. It was shot basically in upstate New York and various Revolutionary War forts in New York state,. It was a lot of fun doing it, but unfortunately I couldn't help myself from making it more of an action film. It's so hard for a kids movie. But anyway, it didn't do very well initially, because maybe the market moved on. That wasn't a very good tip from *(laughing)* the guys of SGE. It sat on the shelf for a while but we finally got a release for it. I really enjoyed doing it though. It should have been a kids' movie but it's really more of an action movie. Also, it was the same year that THE LAST OF THE MOHICANS came out. I remember screening our dailies at a lab in NY City, I think it was Technicolor or something. And screening, and they'd say, "Ok here are your dailies." and it was THE LAST OF THE MOHICANS dailies! And we'd laugh and say, "No, we don't have Daniel-Day Lewis in our movie..."

**Nadia:** What do you think in general about the political agenda in your movies?

**Christian:** That's a good question because in a way I think they do have a political agenda. The answer is that I think, as a person you are expressing yourself creatively through your art or in this case with filmmaking. You definately put that out there. I don't know where to go with it, you could say I really do have a political agenda. That's a completely valid argument.

**Nadia:** To me, COMRADES IN ARMS is among your best films. A reviewer once called it "ahead of it's time" because it's one of the very first films about the war against terror. Do you agree?

**Christian:** Well, I guess I would agree, in the sense that I've always been interested in both history and kind of international affairs. It just seemed to me that a movie about former enemies having to collaborate against a really greater threat, which in this case is terrorism, seemed just like a natural theme for a movie. In a way that was very pressing at the time. An even greater example that is the movie AIRBOSS, which I did in the late 90s. Actually it was AIRBOSS III, thematically. That was about Osama Bin Laden and the Taliban, and we wrote that movie three years before 9/11. All the information was out there, just no one realized it to put it together. So in a way, another example of that - what did you say, "being ahead of its time".. So, COMRADES IN ARMS, that's a good example, I would agree with that. But certainly AIRBOSS even more so.

**Nadia:** Ok, there were four AIRBOSSES. Are these your most successful works?

**Christian:** Yeah, they did very well on the foreign market. It was the late 90s when foreign markets like Germany and Japan were paying pretty good money. They probably were the most successful of all the films. They were just the right approach to doing an action film. We were trying to do TOP GUN on a low budget. It's not as easy as it sounds, but we managed to make them fairly good films. With a real dog-fight sequence and things like that, we managed to do that with radio control planes and stuff like that.

**Nadia:** Did you go in to the first one thinking there'd be sequels?

**Christian:** No, probably not. No, actually. It's an Alan Solomon story. ABSOLUTE AGGRESSION which was the sequel to CYBER VENGEANCE: virtual reality science fiction movies where the characters are forced to go back to historical scenarios and battle it out for sort of, for the pleasure of rich patrons. Hard to get into the whole story of CYBER VENGEANCE, but basically it's THE MOST DANGEROUS GAME, where a rich guy is so jaded, the only thing that gets him excited is actually hunting actual other people. So he hunts these prisoners in a virtual reality, that's the story. And CYBER VENGEANCE and ABSOLUTE AGGRESSION, which was the sequel to that, there was a sequence in that, a jet dog-fighting sequence. One of the characters in the cockpit, doing a TOP GUN style fight. The buyers loved that so much that at AFM or one of the markets, Alan Solomon suggested, "Why not to do a straight-out jet fighter movie. I do think that could really work because the buyers went crazy over that. " And sure, why not? That was on Alan's suggestion so, spot on. We ended up doing AIRBOSS, and that went so well that we wound up doing four of them.

**Nadia:** Frank Zagarino is a cult favorite actor for many action fans. What made you choose him for AIRBOSS, and what do you like about his acting?

**Christian:** Here's the thing, this is a good question because it's an example of the symbiotic relationship I had with Alan Solomon and AMSELL Entertainment, who became my new distributor after SGE. We were talking about doing this jet action film, which was his suggestion because the buyer liked the jet sequence in ABSOLUTE AGGRESSION. As he often did, he suggested actors, and Frank Zagarino had been in one of his films, and he had his number. I met Frank, he was coming to New York. I think he was coming back from one of these movies shot in South

Africa, he did a bunch of movies there, he was staying for a day or so. You know, Frank is a great action star, great actor and a really good guy. We just hit it off. I could tell that he would be an easy person to work with. When you're doing a low budget movie it's kind of important. You don't have time and money and certainly have no time to deal with actors that would be a problem on set. After I met Frank I gave him the part in AIRBOSS and we worked together for four more movies. He became a friend, as has been the case a couple of times. I became good friends with Billy Drago and Lance Henriksen. These are guys I used in a bunch of movies, same with Frank.

**Nadia:** You mentioned ABSOLUTE AGGRESSION — Is it true it was made in the 90s but first released in 2004?

**Christian:** Yes, I think that is true. You know the reason those type of things happened is because the domestic DVD market had kind of fallen out in the late 90s. The foreign market was still doing very well but the domestic video market had really dried up for true independents like that. I think what probably happened was I was not able to get a domestic dvd deal until 2004. So that's probably true. It had been released overseas, in Japan and South Korea, Taiwan and Germany, but probably not domestically in the US so maybe it's not appearing on imdb or something. When you're doing these movies you are kind of at the mercy of the marketplace. One year foreign is good and domestic isn't, and it flip flops. You just have to keep trying to fill all your stuff in various markets. It's just the best you can do. Depending on when new markets open up - not just markets but new technology also. VHS turned into DVD which turned into streaming or video on demand. You just have to keep trying to get them out there. Well, it's probably true.

**Nadia:** What feedback do you receive, what titles are remembered most by your fans?

**Christian:** Some of the earlier ones. HANGMEN I think is being remembered. I think AIRBOSS is fairly well reviewed. THE OUTFIT...which was...

**Nadia:** Yeah, THE OUTFIT. That was fantastic!

**Christian:** The gangster film I did, which had a great cast. Lance Henriksen, Billy Drago, Martin Kove, a really good cast. People seemed to like that. THE LITTLE PATRIOT, the kids' colonial-era thing, has some fans. The comedies not so much, I think I've never been so good at those. Those are some examples. And about feedback from audience, I do get letters and emails once in a while. People reviewing on different internet sides or even just on Amazon. You can tell that people actually have seen your body of work or reference it, and that's kinda cool to see.

**Nadia:** You mentioned that SGE was not involved in the financing of your films. Was there any difference with THE OUTFIT? Alan Solomon has a producer credit, so was this the beginning of a closer partnership with him?

**Christian:** So I had an interesting relationship with Shapiro Entertainment, and with SGE. They were not involved in the production of my films, or the financing. They were distributors, and sales agents. We had a close relationship, but they weren't actually financiers on that. Even THE OUTFIT. Alan Solomon actually has an executive producer credit in a number of my movies. But executive producer often is kind of a honorary credit that people get. So that was the deal with that. Some of our main investors and backers got this credit as well. That's pretty typical in the business. The relationship I did have, especially with Alan: Alan went to all the international sales markets and back in the day that was the way you sold films. Physically went to the MIFED in Milan, and AFM, which was in the American Film Market in Los Angeles, or the Cannes Marche, which coincided with the Cannes Film Festival. He actually went there, rented a suite in one of the hotels, and that was kind of your office. Buyers walked in and out all day long, you ran an endless vhs tape of promos and trailers. There were one-sheets handed out, and that's how the business worked. So Alan went to all of those, and he really had his finger on the pulse of what was selling. So, about THE OUTFIT, the thing is: I was talking to Alan a lot of time, maybe ten, twelve times a year. Maybe more, almost every month. Alan said, there was a film he saw at the last market that worked really well. It was the Cannes market or something, and it was a '30s gangster movie, with tommy guns, old cars, things like that. Menahem Golan did that, and it was called KILL THE DUTCHMAN. It did very well, and Alan said, that's something you guys could do. I thought about it, and it sounded like a lot of fun, so I came up with a story idea for THE OUTFIT. The film was originally called THE RACKET, or PIECE OF THE ACTION, or something. It was about the Leggs Diamond / Dutch Schultz rivalry in New York in the 20s. So that was kind of the origin of THE OUTFIT.

**Nadia:** When you had the idea for the film, were you worried about the immense effort you would have to bring into a Period Piece? (The cars, clothing, locations, etc) – Was it one of your most expensive films?

**Christian:** It was a lot of fun to do, and at that point the most money I ever spent on a film, it was my biggest production, because it was a period piece. The costumes have to be correct, the locations have to be correct. The period cars, we had actually bought. Four cars Model A fords, two trucks for the bootleggers filled with cases of booze, the other one was something like a police car. It was just a challenge, I really love doing that type of period piece. It's a challenge all the way around, the set design, and the wardrobe has to be correct, but you also can't see anything modern. So if you're shooting in a city street just like we found in upstate New York which looked very 30s, obviously you have to hide parking signs, and other cars, and things like that. It's a challenge, but it's also fun. So that's that. But I also did a lot of historical stuff. In SIGN OF THE OTTER **aka** THE LITTLE PATRIOT, which takes place in the American

Revolutionary War. CYBER VENGEANCE, which was kind of a virtual reality game that takes place in historical periods. That's something I've always been drawn to. The challenge is the fun of it.

**Nadia:** I'm fascinated about the fact that you bought the cars. What did you do with them after?

**Christian:** Well, you obviously can rent some vehicles for any movie you're doing. 50s, 60s, 70s, early cars. You can rent them, but it's kind of expensive to do that. I figured it would make more sense to own the cars. So we wouldn't always worry about how much it cost, and that gave us a lot of production freedom. At the end of the movie the cars were still valuable, so we actually sold them. I kept one a long time. It was very cool and I kinda miss it. But it's amazing, these old Fords from the 20s, a lot of them are still running now. And it's a testimony to what great cars they were, because they are not that rare, so they weren't that expensive. And they still ain't.

**Nadia:** Can you tell something about budgets and box office responses to your films?

**Christian:** It's going to be hard to answer in short. Biggest and most complicated question, because I've done movies basically in three different decades. Oh god, actually four. It has changed so much, you know. In the eighties it was with home video and in foreign markets you could do really well. Some of these films brought a lot of returns. In the ninetees it became a little bit harder. I think the taste, especially overseas, became a little more sophisticated; you had to put names in it. Back in the eighties you could really make any kind of movies. Now you had to find actors with big names. We had Danny Aiello in SHOCKTROOP. My partner and I really tried to find good actors with good names. That, obviously, made the budgets go up. Frank Zagarino is another example for that. All my films I did, up until FORT DOOM, were shot on 35mm film which is a sheer expense. Something you couldn't get around, you had the lab cost and making the print. It was hundreds of thousands of dollars, even though it was a low budget movie, you couldn't get away with that. That's one of the reasons until high def digital video came out, it really shut down a lot of lower budget filmmakers. You couldn't afford to do anymore because the market didn't support it. I hope this answers the question but I can go on and on with that. The answer in a quick way, budgets went up and down. I had budgets in the million dollar range for some films, for instance BACKFIRE. That might be five or six million dollars today. And there were other films for virtually nothing. I've done every size budget.

**Nadia:** Sometimes you edited scenes from earlier films. Did you make that as some kind of self references?

**Christian:** I'm trying to figure how to answer this. We never edited scenes from other films but since we're doing action movies we used shots like an explosion, a gunfight, pieces of action scenes. We were always trying to recycle those because we owned that footage. Whenever I did something like a big explosion sequence shot with multiple cameras, I always made sure to duplicate that negative so they could be used again. You know, that's what low budget filmmakers are doing since the beginning. Roger Corman was very smart and inventive doing that. It's a good business decision doing it, because back in the day we worked with a big budget, we could do a big explosion, that's one thing. We had an explosion in HANGMEN shot with multiple cameras. Obviously I used that again in MOB WAR. It took tens of thousands dollars to shoot that, why not try to re-purpose that on something else? In TAR PIT I used something from MOB WAR. We had a great miniature street scene in MOB WAR, miniature buildings and we had this big explosion, we save it even today. When you had the budgets, in this age you don't have those budgets and then the special effects were very particulary done. Hundreds of buildings exploding, and people building models and things like that. And we shot that with four or five cameras. It's just smart business to recycle shots. I did a lot of military themed action films. Matthew Howe, my partner on those films, and I were able to get permission from the US Navy to shoot on many occasions. We shot on four different US aircraft carriers which kind of hadn't been done since TOP GUN. We were absolutely low budget, but we made very good contacts in the US military, and they let us shoot that stuff. Obviously we have a tremendous amount of footage of jet fighters, submarines and aircraft carriers. We're gonna recycle those any chance we can. And that's an example.

**Nadia:** Are you still shooting on 35mm film? Was TAR PIT shot on HD?

**Christian:** Yeah, high def, digital. The last movie that I shot on film was THE BOG CREATURES, which was in 2001. It just became impossible to shoot on film, and we were aware of high def video, it was really just beginning to come in, in the early 2000s. Especially for foreign buyers, it hadn't reached acceptance then. So, we been wanting to make a switch-over to that but we weren't able to until there was a critical mass of acceptance. Especially German buyers, in fact, they just wouldn't accept it. So it was a really tough decision, we weren't getting the returns for that budget and it was too expensive, shooting on 35 anymore. When high def video came in, it'd make things a lot easier. In terms of what you actually spending on it, it's maybe ten percent of what 35mm film was. That made it possible to shoot movies again. So TAR PIT was shot digitally.

**Nadia:** Let's talk about the last ten years. Why did you take such a long break? And what happened with TAR PIT, how did that come about?

**Christian:** Well, the reason I took the break was really kind of a business decision. It became almost impossible for lower budget filmmakers to work after 2005, because the business got so bad, the foreign sales were almost completely very tough to get. You can't get name actors without paying a lot of money, it became impossible at that point. So I went out and did other business interests for ten years, although I did some documentaries during those years. I did a documentary about the time I spent down at the World Trade Center (after 9/11). I took some footage there as a rescue worker. But I didn't do a feature film. As a filmmaker and as an artist that was something completely missing in my life. The need to express yourself, something I wanted to do. My partner Matt Howe and I, we have developed probably three or four different scripts. We were raising money for them and doing pre-production. But nothing really happened, it's the same old story. You can hear it from a thousand other filmmakers. It became tougher and tougher to make a movie but you were still trying to get something off the ground. But finally, a lot of things that happened in the film business, for example digital. The videocameras became very inexpensive, the post production technology can all be done on a laptop now. I remember having an Avid back in the late ninetees, like a $50,000 Avid. Now with a $300 FinalCut program Sound edit can be made very simply on the laptop, too. It became much easier to do a film again. I think that long ten years was mostly because of the business. We'll see what happens on TAR PIT on digital streaming and things like that. You have a filmmaker with a lot of experience like me or Matt Howe, who have the skills and hopefully the talent to do it but the business is almost completely gone away. I think a lot of people are facing the same issue, how to get back into business. Hopefully with TAR PIT, I think it is absolutely the best film I've ever done. Great actors and script, a really gritty, solid film. If that's the comeback-film, I'm very proud of it.

**Nadia:** I can attest that the market is still hell right now and that's so sad.

**Christian:** You wanna keep on going, it's in your blood. You can't stop, you have to figure out a way about the commercial part. You gave to be able to at least get your money back, otherwise you can't do films. It's the old story, everybody is facing that right now. And your clients as well, for sure.

**Nadia:** Oh, they all hate me right now. *(laughing)*

---

**By Nadia Bruce-Rawlings via telephone from New York**

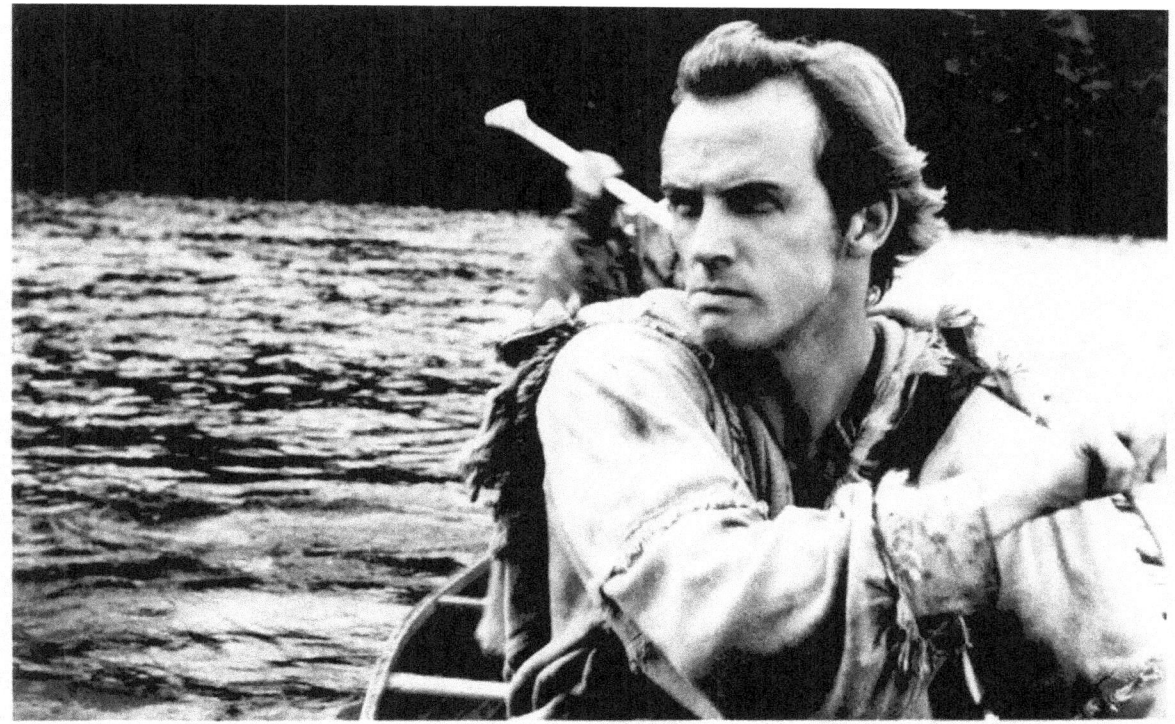

**SIGN OF THE OTTER**

Starring: Dan Haggerty, John Christian, Rick Washburn,
Jaqueline Knox and introducing Ryan Washburn
Produced & Directed by J. Christian Ingvordsen
Written by J. Christian Ingvordsen and Rick Washburn
© Copyright 1992 SGE Entertainment Corp.

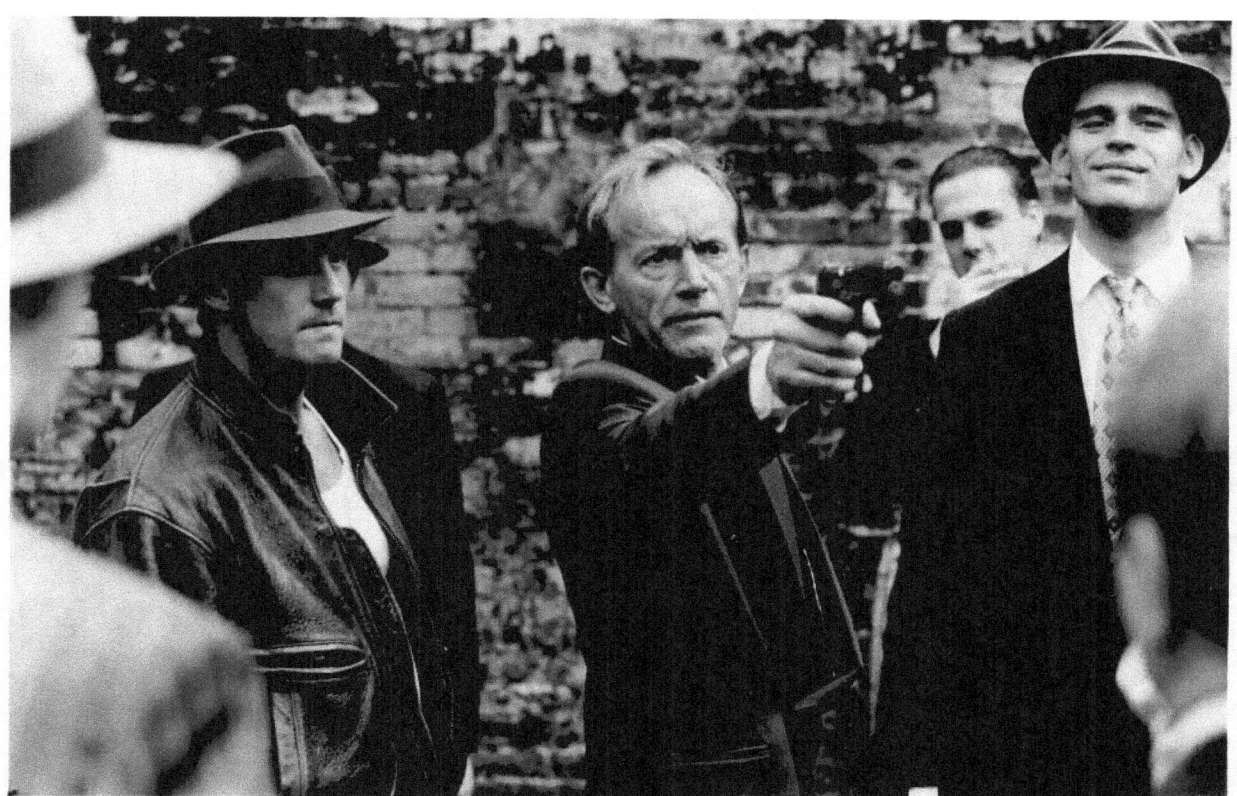

THE OUTFIT
Starring Lance Henriksen and Billy Drago

Written and Directed by J. Christian Ingvordsen
© Copyright 1992 Cinema Sciences

# AIRBOSS IV
## ECO WARRIOR

**FRANK ZAGARINO**

AMSELL ENTERTAINMENT PRESENTS AIRBOSS IV - ECO WARRIOR
STARRING: FRANK ZAGARINO  JOHN CHRISTIAN  JERRY KOKICH  KELLY GLEESON  LARA THEODOS
SCREENPLAY BY: MATTHEW M. HOWE & J. CHRISTIAN INGVORDSEN
EXECUTIVE PRODUCERS: C. STEVEN DUNCKER  GARY L. ZWERLING & ALAN M. SOLOMON
PRODUCED BY: DANIEL YAWITZ & ALAN W. SINSHEIMER
DIRECTED BY: J. CHRISTIAN INGVORDSEN
©1999 COVERT JUSTICE LP. ALL RIGHTS RESERVED.

AMSELL ENTERTAINMENT INC

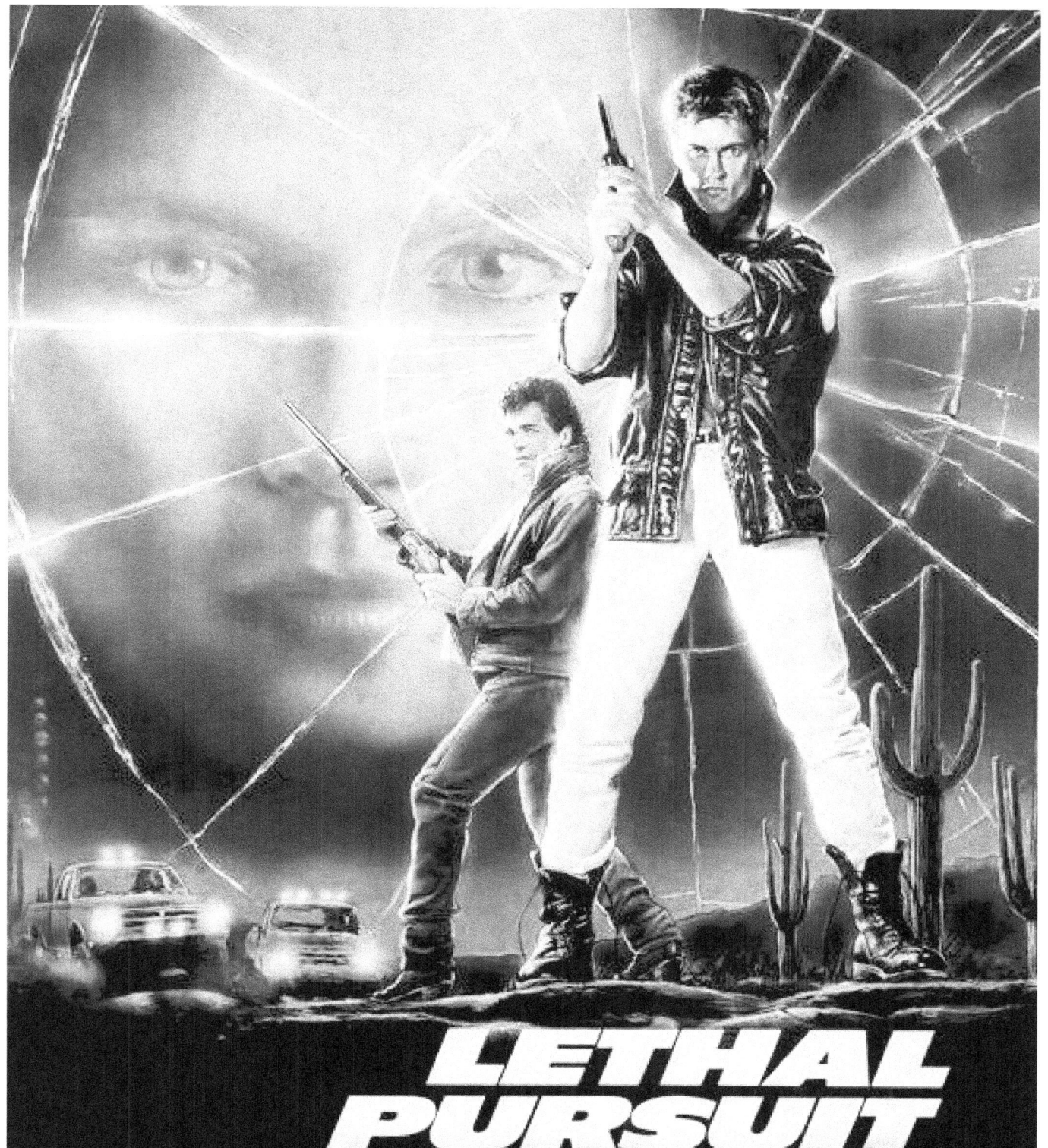

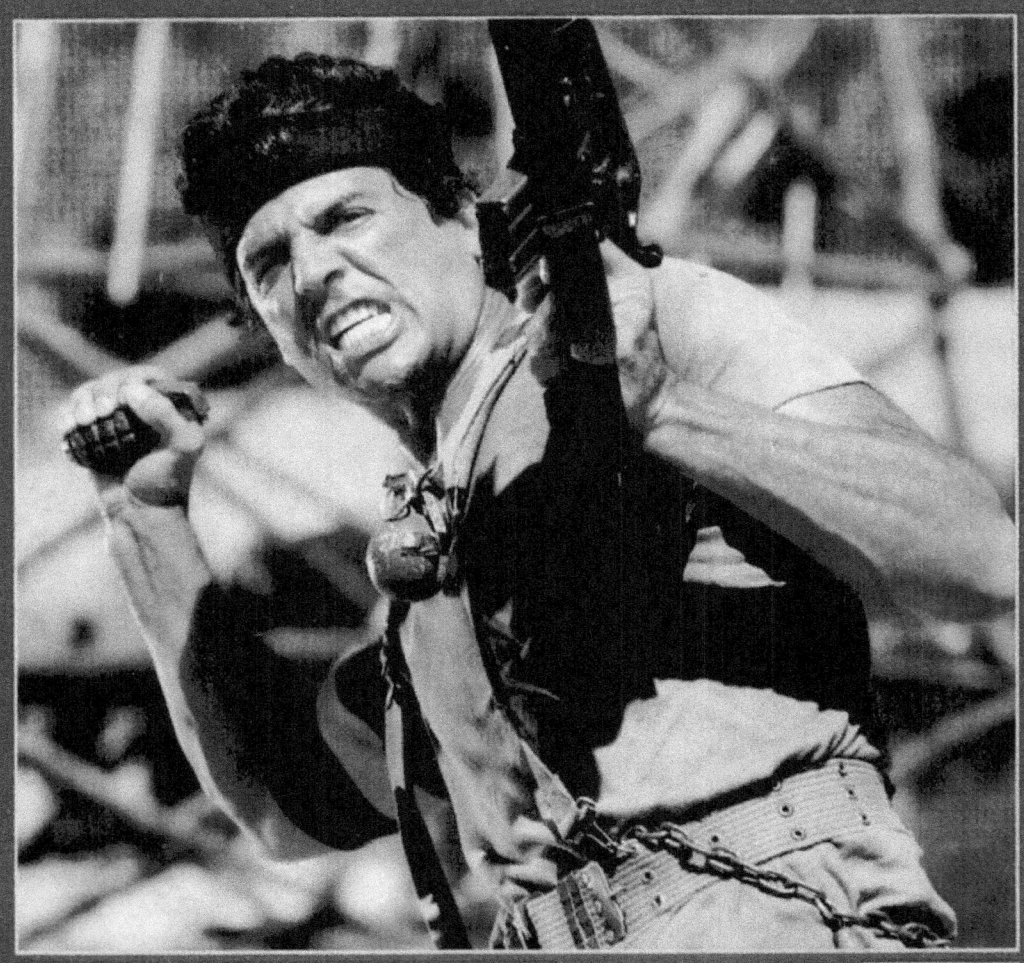

# TC 2000

The year is 2020.
He's mostly human,
and totally invincible...
Until now.

SHAPIRO GLICKENHAUS ENTERTAINMENT PRESENTS A FILM ONE PRODUCTION
BOLO YEUNG  JALAL MERHI  BILLY BLANKS  "TC 2000" STARRING BOBBIE PHILLIPS
MATTHIAS HUES  HARRY MOK  KELLY GALLANT  DIRECTOR OF PHOTOGRAPHY CURTIS PETERSEN
PRODUCTION DESIGNER JASNA STEFANOVIC  ASSOCIATE PRODUCERS J. STEPHEN MAUNDER & KEVIN WARD  CO-PRODUCER DALE HILDEBRAND
EDITOR REID DENNISON  MUSIC BY V. ROUJE  STORY BY J. STEPHEN MAUNDER AND RICHARD M. SAMUELS
PRODUCED BY JALAL MERHI  WRITTEN AND DIRECTED BY T.J. SCOTT
© 1993 TC 2000 PRODUCTIONS. ALL RIGHTS RESERVED.

13123

GLICKENHAUS
HOME VIDEO

# DR CALIGARI

CULT COMEDY
VIDEOCASSETTE
VHS
STEREO
HI-FI
SGE
2018

From the creators of "Cafe Flesh"... "the cult film of the eighties."

# DR CALIGARI

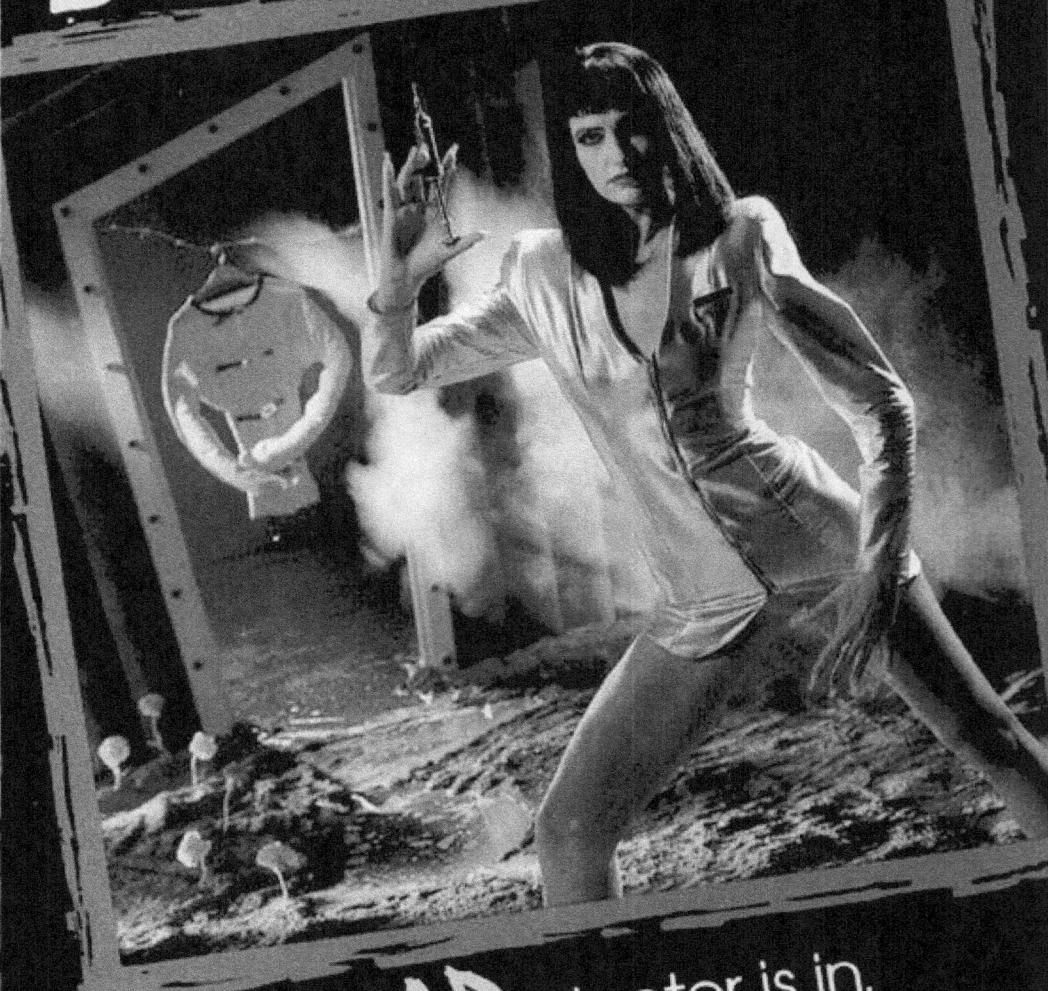

the MAD doctor is in.

"A twisted, skewed, day-glo world...A visual explosion reflecting a mad world!" — VARIETY

"...consistently outrageous and imaginative" — KEVIN THOMAS, LOS ANGELES TIMES

## SHAPIRO GLICKENHAUS HOME VIDEO

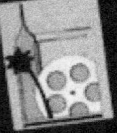

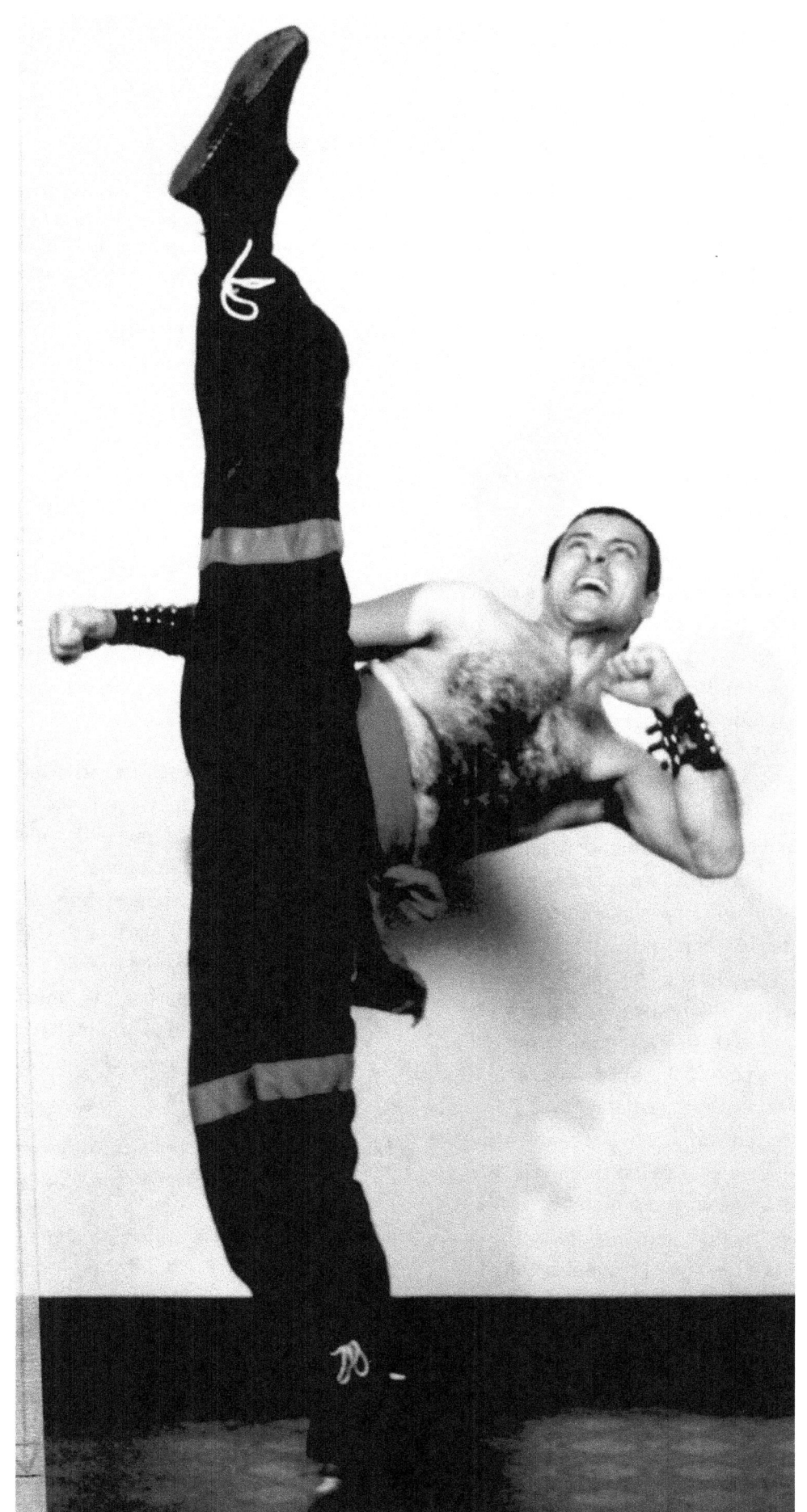

# Jalal Merhi

Jalal Merhi founded the production company Film One in 1989 and started with a series of successful action films which were sold internationally. Merhi is often called "Beirut's Steven Seagal" because of the skillfull fighting techniques he's shown on the silver screen. More than 20 feature films have been made by Film One, and seven of these films were directed by the him, including the CIRCUIT Trilogy, starring Olivier Gruner. Jalal Merhi always prefered working with actual real-life martial artists like Billy Blanks, Cynthia Rothrock, Bolo Yeung, Loren Avedon and many more. SGE had a business relationship with Jalal Merhi in the very early years of his filmmaking, starting with the 1991 TIGER CLAWS, and continuing with TALONS OF THE EAGLE, directed by Michael Kennedy. The third and last collaboration was the over-the-top sci-fi-action film TC 2000 (T.J. Scott, 1993).

**Marco:** Let's start at the beginning; where were you born and raised?

**Jalal:** I was born in Brazil, then I went as a kid to Lebanon for few years. At 20 years old, I moved to Canada in order to learn English, but I enjoyed the freedom of living alone and being self-sufficient. In addition, I found a great kung fu school in Toronto, so I stayed. My love of martial arts started at the age of 11, I found my grandfather's gloves and fitness books from when he lived in Ohio, USA, and was an amateur boxer, so I worked on getting fit first. My grandfather immigrated to the US at 16 years old with his dad in 1896. They worked in the mines of Pennsylvania, then moved to Ohio, after serving in the US Army, but my father did not like the cold of the North so as a teen he moved to Brazil, where I was born. Then I started with taekwondo, and after that I joined a club called the Benzi Club in Beirut. The club was a member of JKA, I still have my first membership card, and T shirt. As a teenager I moved to Canada and started with Choy Lay Fut and Hung Gar, then continued with Shotokan because it was close to my JKA style too, and got 2nd Dan in that. I did compete in approximately 150 tournaments, placing in the top 3 in 90% of them; this is how I met Billy Blanks, Cynthia [Rothrock] and most of the other martial artists I used in my films.

**Marco:** Has cinema always been important to you? And if so, since what age?

**Jalal:** I was a cinema fan all my life. As a teen I would save my transportation money and lunch money, and after school two to three times a week I would go to movies that showed 2 films - one drama and one either cowboy or horror. I think I have seen every black and white Dracula film ever made, and then in the late 60s when Chinese martial arts films started to take over, I used to dream that one day I would go to Hollywood and someone would discover me.

**Marco:** FEARLESS TIGER took a few years before it was released in the USA.

**Jalal:** FEARLESS TIGER originally was named BLACK PEARLS, it was shot over two years, 1989 to 1990, and it was what Alan Solomon and Lenny Shapiro liked, but they asked me if I can do something more hardcore with a better budget.

**Marco:** Was TIGER CLAWS your first international success?

**Jalal:** TIGER CLAWS was my first success, it was released theatrically in over 20 markets. The way the script came to mind is interesting, the writer Steven Maunder was a kung fu student of mine.

**Marco:** How did your partnership with SGE come about? Can you share the background story of that with us?

**Jalal:** Jeff Sackman, who was the person I was dealing with at Cineplex [in Canada], and who had purchased my film BLACK PEARLS, suggested I go to the 1990 Cannes Film market. That was the last year Cineplex had its own international distribution operation. So they helped me and provided me with a badge. Also Jeff at that market introduced me to Bob Weinstein. He and I spent most of the market together, and he introduced me to Iggy Pop who starred, and I think did some music for his film HARDWARE. I sat next to Iggy in the screening, and I remember it was very loud. Jeff also took me to the SGE office and introduced me to Lenny and Alan, and told them that I could be the next big thing to come out of Canada. He gave them a VHS Copy of the BLACK PEARLS film. I was invited to the SGE party at Cannes. At the party I met a young pretty girl that worked for SGE, and we danced the whole night. Alan knew as he watched BLACK PEARLS that I could do more, so he asked if I had other bigger ideas. So I told him about TIGER CLAWS, but I did not have a full script, but he said if I could shoot something and show him, they might come in on it as partners.

**Marco:** The directing style of FEARLESS TIGER seems not as professional as TIGER CLAWS, for example. Who was Ron Hulme, why did you choose him as a director and can you tell us what happened to him?

**Jalal:** Ron Hulme was a friend of Steve Maunder, they both went to the same college, and we were initially thinking small. Ron hadn't directed any action before.

**Marco:** It seems like you are influenced by the Asian style of action filmmaking, would you agree with that?

**Jalal:** Film One's style was developed due the fact that martial arts was my door into film making. I studied film in college, but my professor told me not to waste my time and go do other jobs, because no one would hire me, with my accent, and other things he said. But my chance came in a martial art tournament where a producer (Jim J Ross) was looking for talent for his upcoming film. At that event, I won the grand championship in weapons and open hand forms, so he picked me and few others.

**Marco:** What kind of movies did you prefer to watch before starting your producing career?

**Jalal:** I have watched all, from THE GODFATHER to SATURDAY NIGHT FEVER, but since I am not a good dancer or a great actor, I made films that reflect the talent I have.

**Marco:** Kelly Makin did quite a great job on TIGER CLAWS. How do you remember working with him? Were you on set for all the shooting?

**Jalal:** Kelly was hired after the first promo shoot in October, It was refreshing to work with Kelly, he knew what he was doing, he was a more experienced director, and did not have personal issues with me, he allowed me to keep the martial arts part and cover it, while he told the story. We tried to hire him for TALONS, but he was on another film, and we had to deliver a 1-2 punch fast while buyers were still interested. But I was on set for all aspects; we used also the footage from the October shoot also.

**Marco:** About Michael Kennedy, who also did a fine directing job on TALONS OF THE EAGLE, how familiar with his previous work were you before hiring him for TALONS...? How did you and he first meet?

**Jalal:** When we did not get Kelly, we looked for other directors, we set up auditions at my Film One studio. After meeting a few, I was impressed with Michael's calm demeanor and knowledge of martial arts films. We sent the info to SGE, and SGE approved him. He was great to work with.

**Marco:** TIGER CLAWS was your first film featuring the iconic female action star Cynthia Rothrock. Since action films are dominated by male stars, how important was it at the time for you to balance male dominance with female fighters? Was casting Ms. Rothrock a conscious choice by you to 'buck the trend' or was it just a chance factor of the deal at the time?

**Jalal:** I knew Cynthia from competition days then she went to Hong Kong and became an action star, but in the 1990 Cannes Festival we reconnected, and spent some time together, went around to the French country side - there was a Cherry Festival, and we had a chance to talk about TIGER CLAWS. She liked the idea. So we stayed in contact, and four months later in early October, I flew her to Toronto, and we shot part one of the film, including the alley fight, as a sample to show Alan and to Universal. It took few months to edit, and Alan had it to show at the American Film Market in February 1991. They liked it, and two months later we had a deal. We supplied 55% (which 25 % of it was Canadian Government grants), of the budget, and SGE gave us an advance of 45%.

**Marco:** The whole TIGER CLAWS budget, purported to be around USD$2.5 million, came from your private money, is that correct? How was the funding of the film originally planned, and did anything change during production and/or post production to alter the original plan?

**Jalal:** The real Budget was an audited cost of $1,240,043 but SGE taught me never to show the real budget! It was a miracle, to achieve what we did with that budget.

**Marco:** All in all, you worked on three film projects with SGE, is that correct? Was SGE involved in any way in the financing of the movies themselves, or was it only a marketing and distribution deal?

**Jalal:** We started as a distribution deal with advances but TIGER CLAWS was so successful that SGE wanted to be part of the production. SGE and I worked on four films. I signed a contract with Billy Blanks to do TALONS OF THE EAGLE 2 (aka BACK IN ACTION), but due to a disagreement SGE signed my attorney George Flack as a producer, and he had access to my well trained crew, and did 2 films. They did come up with bigger budget looking films, but they did go over our usual budget on both.

**Marco:** Let's take the three SGE films as an example, have there ever been 35mm celluloid hard copies of these films? Are they archived at all?

**Jalal:** We have all original footage and masters in 35MM, including a lot of props used in the films.

**Marco:** When you started filmmaking in the early 1990's, the video boom was at its peak, especially for the kinds of action films you were producing. Did you release all your movies as video premieres only, or, did you try theatrical releases as well? Was the big screen not an option for low budget indie action movies at the time?

**Jalal:** We did release all of my films theatrically in Canada, the Middle East, Brazil, Spanish-Speaking South America, Philippines, and many other territories, I remember Jeff Sackman, after coming back from a trip in Mexico, telling me about a TIGER CLAWS poster being two stories high over the theater. Another fun story: two of my crew went on a backpacking trip in Africa, and they said that they were in Madagascar, and they saw in a small village an open-air cinema, with the poster of TALONS OF THE EAGLE, saying "Airing Tonight" posted on a tree.

**Marco:** The dystopian sci-fi movie TC 2000 was your final collaboration with SGE. Compared to other marketing and distribution companies you worked with, how do you remember the SGE partnership?

**Jalal:** It was great, until it wasn't. TC 2000 was a difficult film to make work, someone wanted many "names" in the film, and we wrote a script around the names, so I feel it was very formulated. The original cut was different, but Jim wanted more opening action between Matthias and Billy, so we cut a section and replaced it with the gym fight. The budget was more then I wanted to spend on such a film, approximately $1.7 Million, a lot more then TALONS OF THE EAGLE.

**Marco:** Can you give us an impression of how business with SGE worked in general? Was it mostly on the phone or in written form? Which SGE people do you remember most from this era? Was Alan Solomon a key collaborator with you? How do you remember working with Leonard Shapiro? Did you interact directly with James Glickenhaus?

**Jalal:** We had SGE representatives on set at Film One office. Alan was straightforward with what he wanted; he changed the title of EAGLE CLAWS into TALONS OF THE EAGLE. Also he changed TIGER CLAWS 2 to TC 2000, and I think Jim decided to make it more of a sci-fi film, and suggested I either not be in the film or be a bad guy. Lenny was the politician, he would smoothen things when things get tough. Jim was way above my pay grade.

**Marco:** Did you work with any people from the SGE circle after the company was closed down? Can you describe how networking worked in those SGE days?

**Jalal:** Yes I did work with Alan and Lenny, but mostly Alan, although the deal was different. He was straight forward a distributor with no advance, and we did our own delivery to clients in most cases.

**Marco:** When it comes to visualizing martial arts and fight scene choreography, what's your formula?

**Jalal:** Firstly we check what the talent can do.

**Marco:** For example, can you name a few personal no-no's?

**Jalal:** I do not like to show super human, unbelievable feats, or to show a non-martial artist with cinema tricks doing what would have taken martial artist years to learn.

**Marco:** What defines a great fight scene in your opinion?

**Jalal:** It has to flow and have equal opponents in talent and ability. I do not like to over-cut a fight where we do not see what is really happening. That's the problem with new TV's and the ability to stop and pause - what worked in cinema and a lot of older films does not work as well now.

**Marco:** You established your own production company, Film One, in the early 1990's.

**Jalal:** Film One was established and is still active today, one of the longest running production companies.

**Marco:** What can you say about the American independent action films released in that particular era?

**Jalal:** To me, that was the opportue time, the old gold rush of film making. I felt dreams could come true, what I dreamed about as a child riding a donkey and selling grapes from my parents' orchard to tourists.

**Marco:** Did you have a fair number of personal friendships or/and business intersections? Was there some kind of a "scene" would you say?

**Jalal:** My company Film One did cause a shake up in Canada, as so many were wondering, where did this guy come from? I was not the average filmmaker going through the ranks, because I left film school as soon as my professor told me that I am wasting my time, so I did not have many friends. Looking back now, all that were on my payroll, the person that I could credit into breaking into the Canadian market, is Jeff Sackman. He helped and gave me a domestic deal for Canada, and introduced me to the international market.

**Marco:** There are a lot of films you produced with Stephen Maunder as a crew-member. For example all three SGE related films were scripted by him. Can you share some memories about this creative partnership? Would you say many details of the films reflect the participation of Mr. Maunder?

**Jalal:** Stephen Maunder was my kung fu student, and he was a fan of Hong Kong films, so I hired him full time to write. He introduced me to a lot of York University students, as crew, so I was overwhelmed with beginners on BLACK PEARS. They did their best, but looking back I should have hired a few professionals, since I wasn't one.

**Marco:** Were you in charge of the fight choreography for all of your films? And if not, who was? As a producer, were you on the set all of the time? Would you say you preferred to control all details and aspects of the moviemaking process on the films you produced then?

**Jalal:** I was always hands-on. When I started these films, we had no one in Canada that had done this before, so we were learning as we went, and BLACK PEARLS was our school. I never had time off, I was there with the first person on set, and left with the last person, and signed the checks, and it did show and effect my performance often. But I did bring in, as we grew bigger, others that helped with the choreography.

**Marco:** There was a noticeable drop in low-budget/independent action films at the end of the 1990s. After a few years, a new wave of action was established via direct-to-DVD. As a consequence, Van Damme, Lundgren and other icons of the genre won back a lot of their status. What's your opinion of the contemporary market situation of these types of movies, meaning low budget action films? How has VOD (video-on-demand) changed the market, if at all?

**Jalal:** The VHS market with mom-and-pop stores was great for us, because the decision was made on a micro level. They were more in touch with their customers, the big box stores were good to me, but if they did not take the film, you were left with no one else. The VOD market is ok, but it is tough. Too much work for little return due to distribution cost, and piracy, so you see all involved, except for the few you mentioned, are actually living day-to-day. I have three kids that needed to go to University, so I moved to TV too, and combining both I managed to keep the dream alive.

**Marco:** What about the importance of martial arts, especially, and sports in general in your personal life nowadays? Can you describe your day-to-day life for us?

**Jalal:** I'm still keeping fit, and martial arts is a huge part of my life, but I am more of a producer-director now.

**Marco:** Are there any anecdotal stories that we haven't touched on that you'd like to share about your SGE days, whether they be meaningful to your career as a producer, or the enrichment of yourself as a person, or just something fun? What is something you can remember that happened back then that you think is worth mentioning?

**Jalal:** SGE thought of a lot of me, I had passion and knew a lot of martial artists, from competition days: Billy Blanks and I met in

Buffalo, at the Golden Dragon Kung Fu Tournament in 1987, I believe. At the time I had a deal for Billy to star in BLACK PEARLS as Bo, but he got an offer for a small role in LOCK UP, with Sylvester Stallone, so I let him out of the contract with no penalty. Two years later I proposed him to Alan and Lenny, and they loved the idea, for TALONS OF THE EAGLE, this was the first starring good-guy role for Billy. During the first film market screening of TIGER CLAWS, Alan asked me to go to the screening. The theater filled up fast, and the screening started, but 10 minutes into the film, people clutching bags started to leave, and my heart was sinking, by the end of the film not many were left. I was sick in my stomach, so I went to the office. Alan was very busy, but the sales office was in a good mood, when Alan finished he congratulated me and said that buyers rushed in order to get the film for their territory! One of the controllers that SGE sent to keep an eye on the production was Frank Isaac. Since I came from a jewelry background, and I still had that connection, he asked if I can get him a good deal on a diamond because he was getting married, so I did. On TC 2000, we were asked to take the cutting copy to NY and screen for Jim. I said, "It is better if Jim flies in." but he wanted to screen on his flat bed editing suit, so my editor and I did. Jim was not pleased and felt it needed more action, and less Jalal. I got back to the Film One office and found out Jim had contacted Deluxe Labs in order to remove the negatives and move it to his lab in NY. I could not do that because I would have lost the government of Ontario grant, which demands the post-production is done in Canada. I had borrowed against it from the Royal Bank, over $400,000.00, with my studio and my home as a collateral. I was sent all kinds of legal notices, so I took the negatives out of the Lab and kept them in a safe place, until the legality of ownership was cleared through legal means, and I was the legal owner. That is when we did a re-shoot, the opening fight at the gym. I had to change attorneys, because my attorney at the time was more on the side of SGE, and he became their Canadian producer on BACK IN ACTION.

**By Marco Siedelmann, in writing
from Toronto, Ontario, Canada
22July, 2015**

EXHIBIT "B"

SHORT FORM ASSIGNMENT

Reference is hereby made to the Agreement dated this 15th day of October, 1992, by and between 826579 Ontario Inc., D.B.A. Film One Productions, Inc., and MCA Home Video, Inc., (the "Agreement").

For good and valuable consideration, receipt of which is hereby acknowledged, the undersigned, 826579 Ontario Inc., D.B.A. Film One Productions, Inc., (hereinafter "Assignor"), hereby assigns to MCA Home Video, Inc. (hereinafter "Assignee"), its successors and assigns, the sole and exclusive right and license to distribute, exploit, market, issue, reissue and otherwise dispose of and use the Picture produced, acquired or co-produced by Assignor, in the home video medium in the Distribution Territory during the Distribution Term as more fully set forth in the Agreement.

Assignor also hereby assigns to Assignee all existing and future claims and causes of actions relating to any infringement or violation of any of the rights in and to the Picture assigned to Assignee hereunder during the Term of distribution granted to Assignee by Assignor as provided for in the Agreement.

IN WITNESS WHEREOF, the undersigned has executed this Agreement on this 16th day of October, 1992, at 397 DONLANDS AVE. TORONTO, ONTARIO

826579 Ontario Inc.,
D.B.A. Film One Productions, Inc.,
RE: TALONS OF THE EAGLE

By _____

Exhibit "B"

## DISTRIBUTION ACQUISITION AGREEMENT

THIS AGREEMENT dated this 15th day of October, 1992, by and between 826579 ONTARIO INC., D.B.A. FILM ONE PRODUCTIONS, INC., ("Licensor"), 397 Donlands Avenue, Toronto, Ontario Canada M4J 3S2, and MCA HOME VIDEO, INC., (hereinafter "MCA"), 70 Universal City Plaza, Suite 435, Universal City, California 91608.

Subject to and as modified by all the terms, provisions and conditions of this Agreement, the parties hereby agree to the following:

1. **THE PICTURE:** The terms and conditions of this Agreement shall govern MCA's exclusive right to distribute the film "TALONS OF THE EAGLE".

2. **TERRITORY:** The distribution territory ("Distribution Territory") for the Picture shall consist of the United States and its territories and possessions.

3. **TERM:**

    (a) **Distribution Term:** The distribution term ("Distribution Term") for the Picture shall be for a period of five (5) years, commencing on the home video release date of the Picture.

    (b) MCA may during the six (6) month period following the conclusion of the Distribution Term (the "Sell-Off Period") for the Picture continue to exploit all Home Video Devices made prior to the end of the Distribution Term, in all manners allowed during the Distribution Term, but MCA may not produce or manufacture Home Video Devices during the Sell-Off Period except as necessary to fulfill orders received prior to the commencement of the Sell-Off Period. Following the conclusion of the Distribution Term, if Licensor continues to retain distribution rights to the Picture, Licensor shall notify MCA thereof, and the parties hereto shall negotiate in good faith for a period of thirty (30) days with regard to the extension of the Distribution Term of this Agreement. If the parties cannot agree on such terms, the Licensor shall be free to grant such rights to any third party.

4. **DELIVERY:** Licensor shall deliver the Picture to MCA by making complete delivery of the items set forth herein, including any applicable exhibits hereof during the Agreement Term hereof in a timely manner in order to provide MCA with a sufficient amount of time in which to market and distribute such Picture.

5. **Intentionally Omitted.**

6. **GRANT OF RIGHTS:** Licensor hereby grants to MCA the sole and exclusive right and license to distribute the Picture during the Distribution Term in the Distribution Territory in the home video medium. As used in this Agreement, "Home Video" means the distribution of prerecorded videocassettes, discs or other devices for home use, whether now known or hereinafter devised (and such devices are sometimes referred to herein as "Home Video Devices").

Licensor shall deliver the following materials:

1. All black-and-white still photographs and negatives (30 minimum) and color transparencies (50 minimum of 35mm, 2¼ x 2¼, or 4 x 5) of production stills suitable for publicity and advertising (at least one-third to include principal players). Titled and captioned with all persons identified. Written clearances where a player has still approval.

2. One detailed story synopsis of the Picture.

3. Four (4) copies of music cue sheets (listing all music in order of appearance in the Picture, including reel, cue sequence, duration of cue, title of each musical composition, composer, publisher, and usage rights; also indicate whether instrumental, instrumental visual, vocal, vocal visual or other.

4. Composer agreements, synchronization licenses, master recording licenses and artists' licenses.

5. Two (2) copies of final main and end title credits.

6. One biography of each principal player, producer, director and writers (1-3 typewritten pages).

7. One copy of all advertising artwork if prepared by Licensor.

8. Copy of the copyright certificate for the Picture.

9. One billing block to be utilized on the Videocassette sleeves and in advertising of the Picture.

10. A written list of any restrictions (advertising, credit or editing) contained in agreements under which any services or rights were acquired or used in connection with the Picture.

11. A copy of the MPAA rating certificate.

MCA/UNIVERSAL HOME VIDEO, INC., 70 UNIVERSAL CITY PLAZA, UNIVERSAL CITY, CALIFORNIA 91608, FAX: (818) 777

Direct Dial Number

September 20, 1992

Mr. Jalal Merhi
c/o Shapiro Glickenhaus Entertainment
12001 Ventura Place, 4th Floor
Studio City, CA 91604

Dear Jalal,

Enclosed are some souvenir shots of you from the 1992 VSDA Convention in Las Vegas. It was nice meeting you at the MCA/Universal Booth and seeing you recently at the screenin "Talons of the Eagle" at Universal. We look forward to wor with you in the future.

Sincerely,

Evan Fong
Publicity Manager

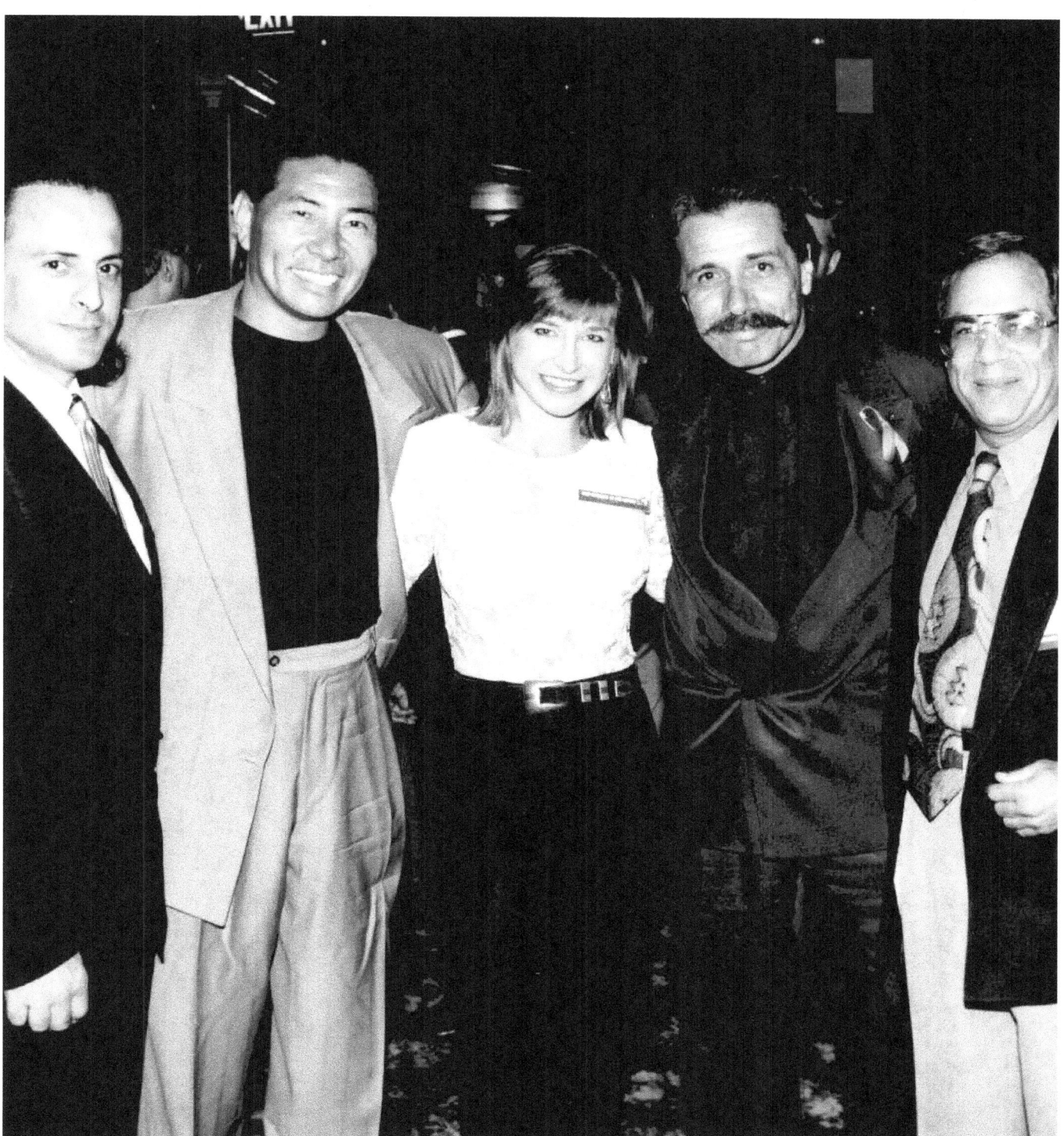

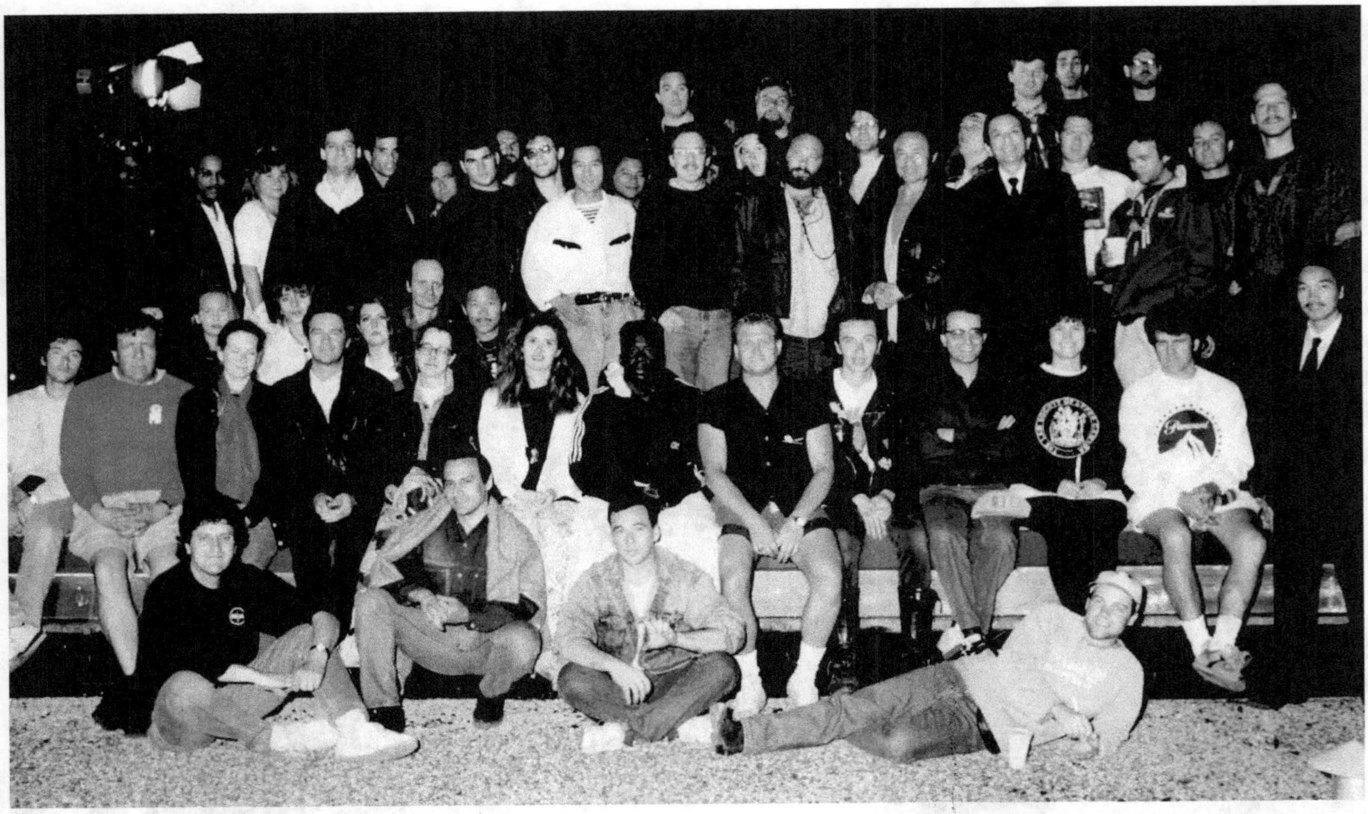

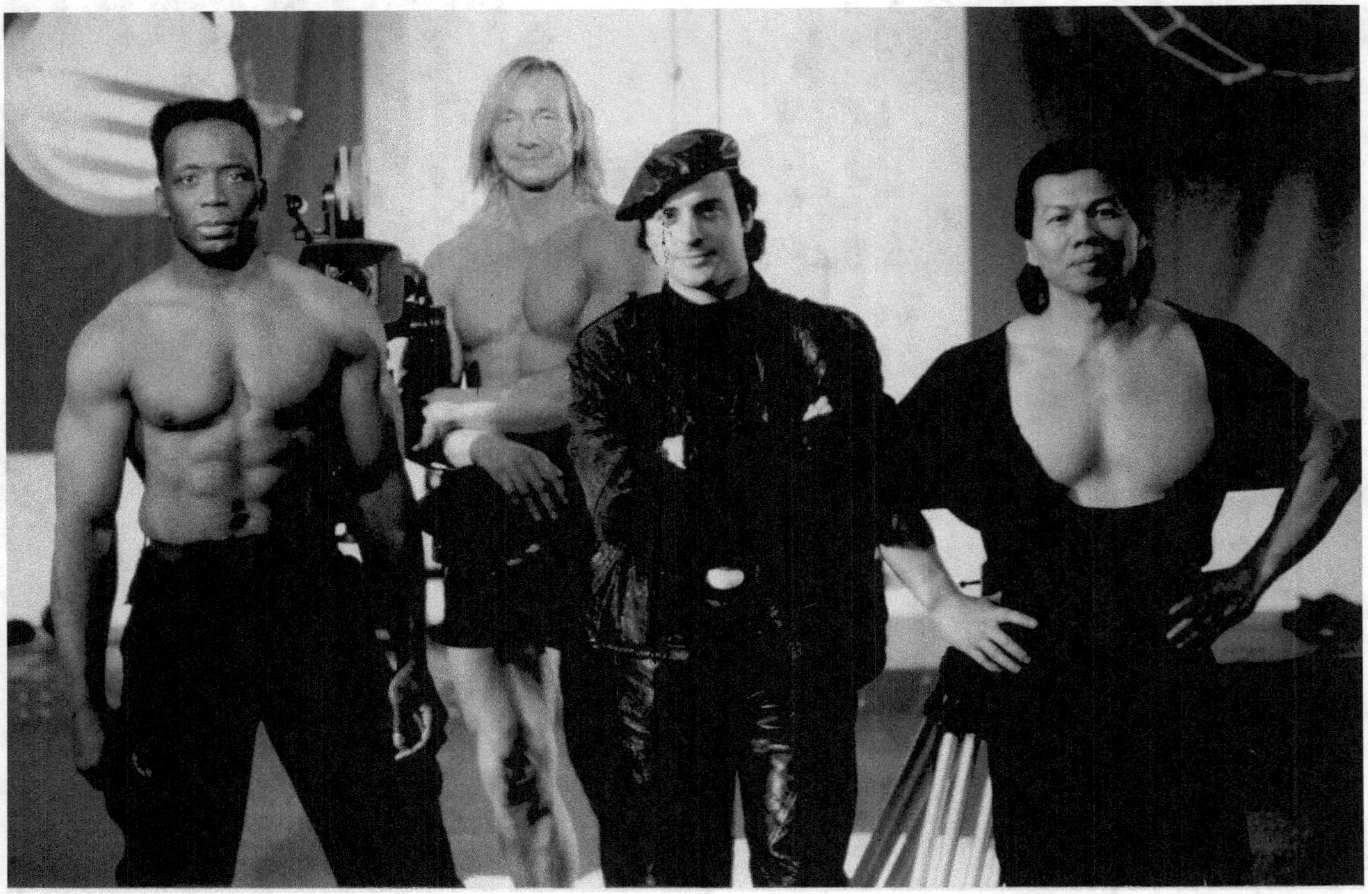

# Jacqueline Palmiere

Starting in the early years of the company history as a receptionist, Jacqueline Palmiere was born in Rochester, NY and moved to Los Angeles in the late 1980's. For our Interview she kindly shared some loving memories about the atmosphere within the company, and how she was trained in several sections by Alan Solomon, Jim Glickenhaus and Leonard Shapiro. She participated in the SGE Home Video Division and worked closely with Andi Elliot and other SGE regulars. She has her own business now, back in her hometown of Rochester.

**Marco:** When did you join SGE? How long did you stay at the company, and what jobs have you been working in?

**Jacqueline:** I joined the SGE Family in 1988ish. I am from Rochester, New York, it was a cold March winter in Rochester, and my best friend Charlie LaLoggia called. He was in Los Angeles for the opening of LADY IN WHITE (he was the executive producer and his cousin Frank was the director). Charlie asked me to fly to Los Angeles for the weekend to get warm and meet some of his friends. I went to L.A., and the first day I was there, I met Lenny Shapiro. I told him I wanted to move to Los Angeles, Lenny immediately took Charlie and myself to see SGE in Studio City. Lenny introduced me to Nadia Bruce and Alan Solomon, and then offered me a receptionist position...I said YES, and moved there two weeks later. I owe moving to L.A. and having the greatest experience for 12 years to Lenny and my friend Charlie (who has passed away).

**Marco:** Do you have any favorites among the films produced by SGE?

**Jacqueline:** Absolutely...FRANKENHOOKER and BASKET CASE.

**Marco:** SGE set the focus on action and horror films, which were very popular in the 1980s. As part of the audience, do you like those kind of movies in general?

**Jacqueline:** I did at that time when I worked at SGE, but not so much anymore.

**Marco:** When SGE started the Video Division, you transferred over there. How was the transition, and which did you prefer?

**Jacqueline:** The transition was very smooth and easy because of the great crew SGE hired to run the division. Peter and Andi were truly good people and really knew the video business. I learned everything there was about video because they took me under their wings and mentored me just like Lenny, Alan and Jim did. As far as what division I preferred, it would be SGE because my best friends were all there, and I spent more time with Lenny and Alan.

**Marco:** Thinking of your time at SGE, what comes to your mind first? Was it a time of apprenticeship for you?

**Jacqueline:** Family and loyalty are the first words that come to mind. We sincerely cared about one another, we were a family. Lenny, Alan and Jim were great mentors and really made SGE the greatest place to work. Lenny made sure we all had gym memberships to keep us healthy, and

Lenny and I would schedule an after-work party once a month down stairs in the restaurant. Lenny, Alan and Jim were business partners but they were great friends that respected one another.

**Marco:** Have you remained friends with a number of your colleagues at SGE?

**Jacqueline:** The Girls: Nadia, Stephanie, Darby, Marilyn and myself were best friends and sisters...we still are in touch and care about one another. I would drop everything if any of the SGE Team needed me.

**Marco:** How was it to work at SGE? Was there a strict hierachy within the company or was it merely casual?

**Jacqueline:** My finest working memories are with SGE, and the greatest friends I have ever had in my life. There was definitely a chain of command, but everyone treated each other with love and respect not matter what position you held there.

**Marco:** After SGE, have you been active constantly in the movie business?

**Jacqueline:** After I left SGE, I worked casting commercials and then became the match-maker on LOVE CONNECTION, until it was canceled. I moved back to Rochester 12 years later and have been self employed ever since. SGE taught me so much about business and how to treat your employees...I owe my work ethics to Lenny, Alan and Jim.

---

By Marco Siedelmann, in writing
from Rochester, New York
30April, 2015

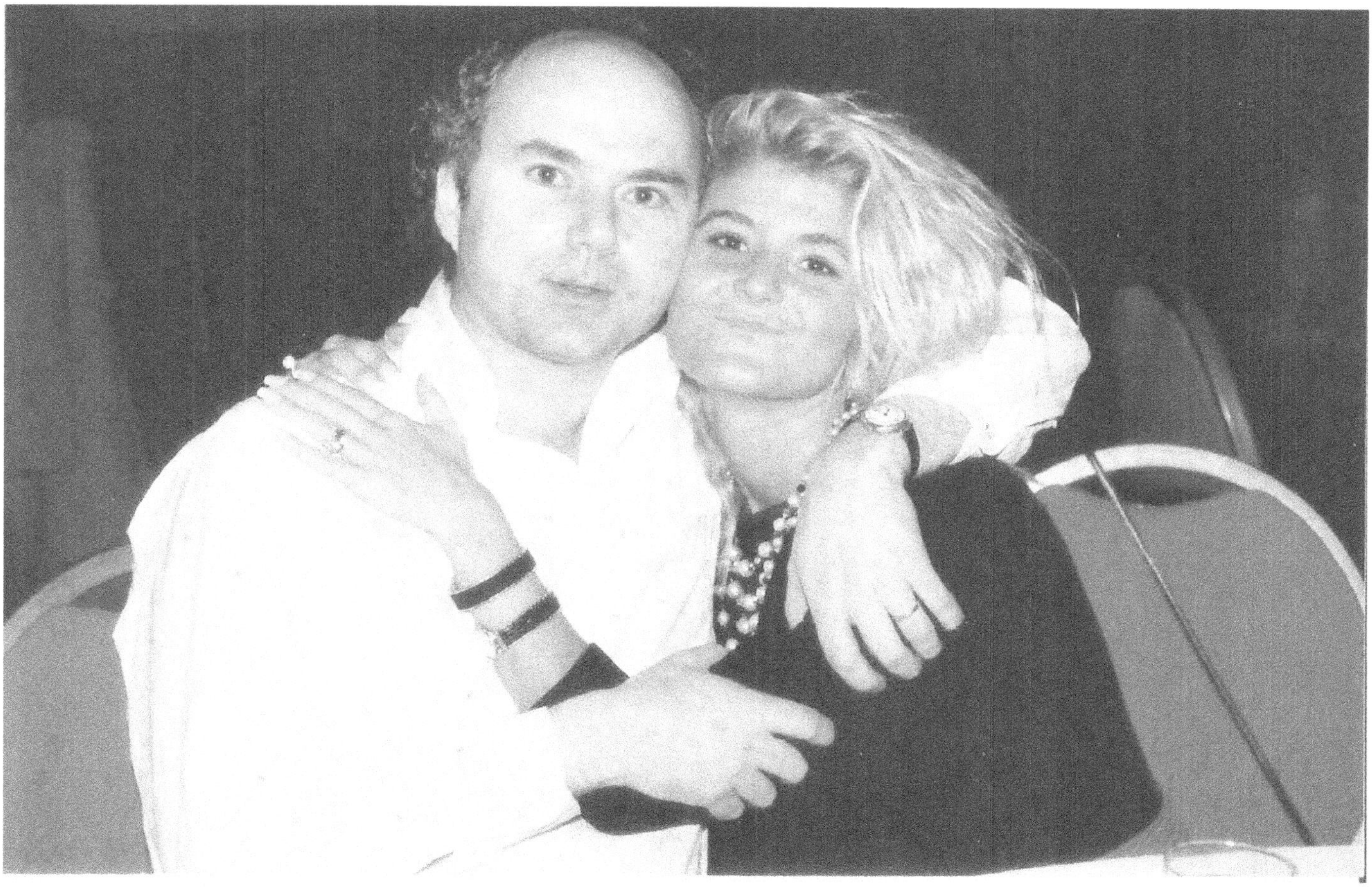

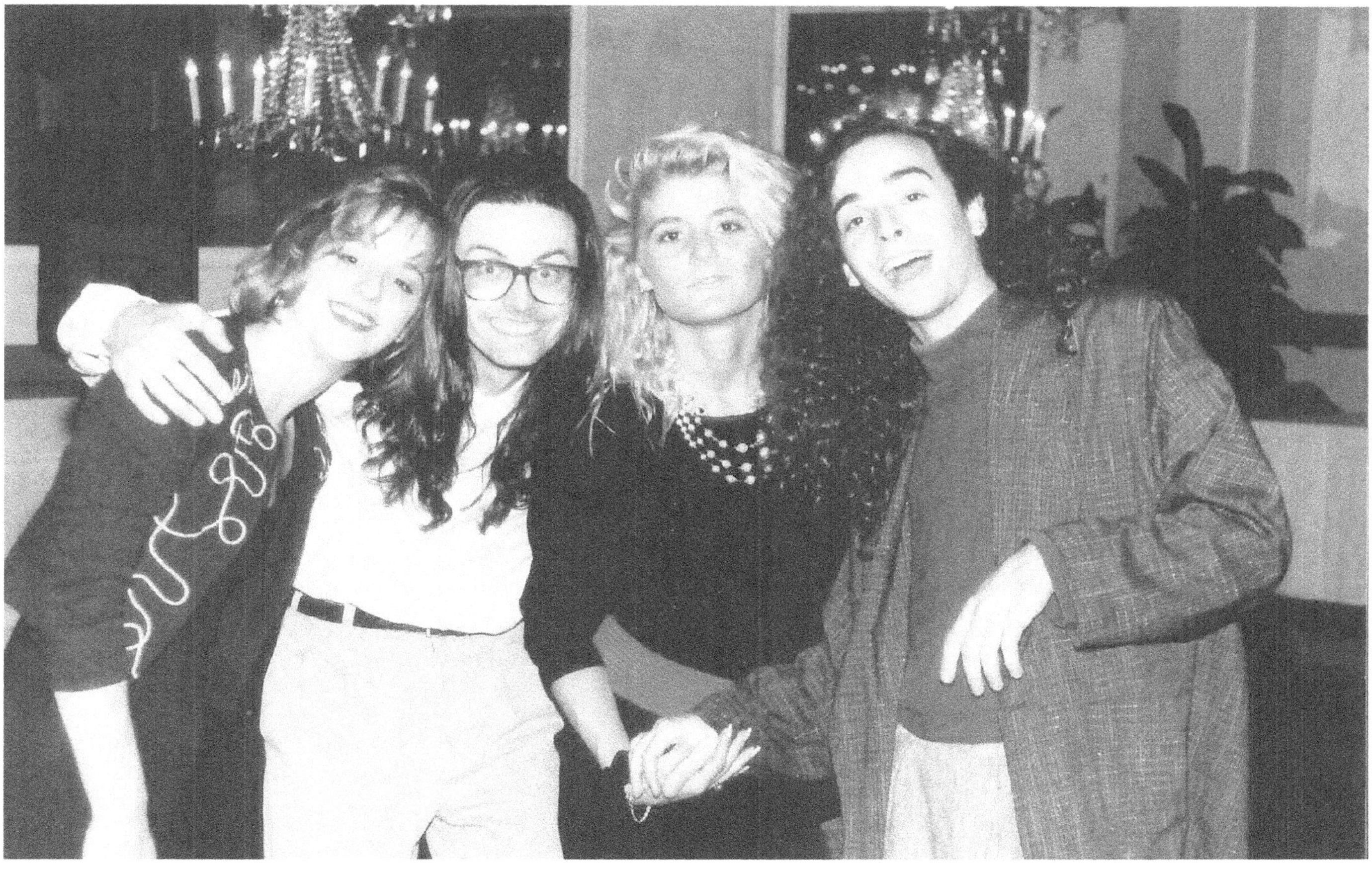

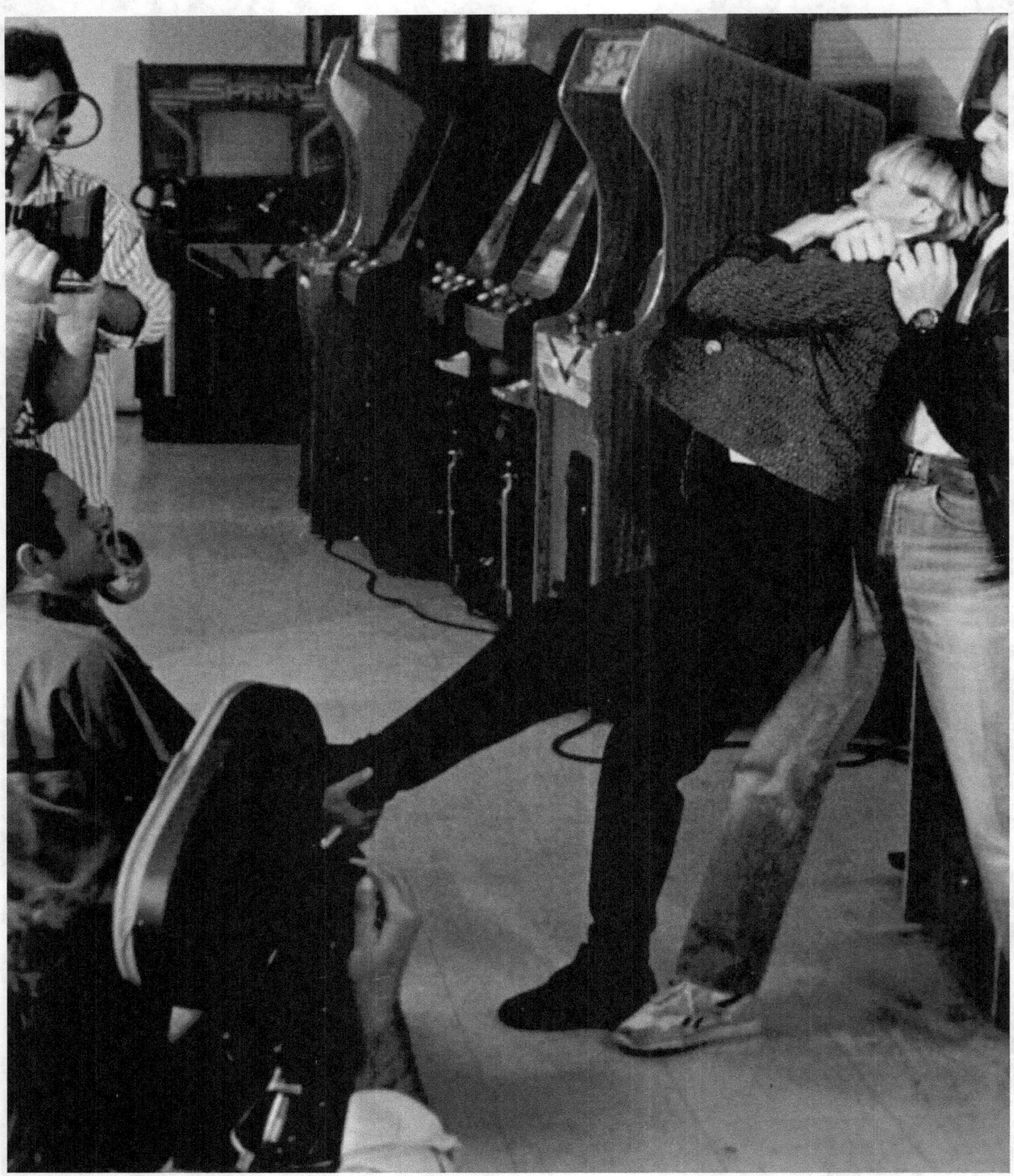

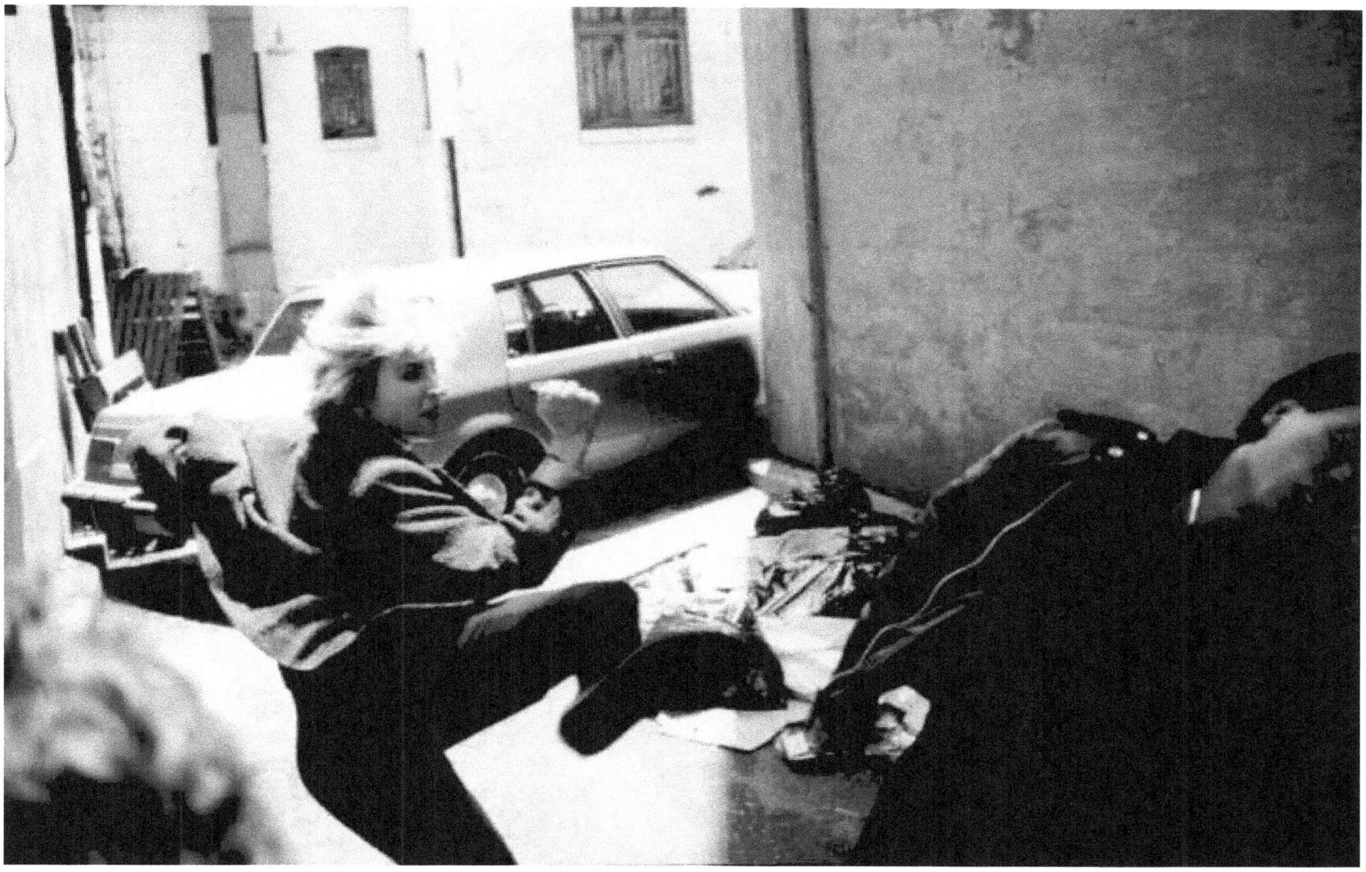

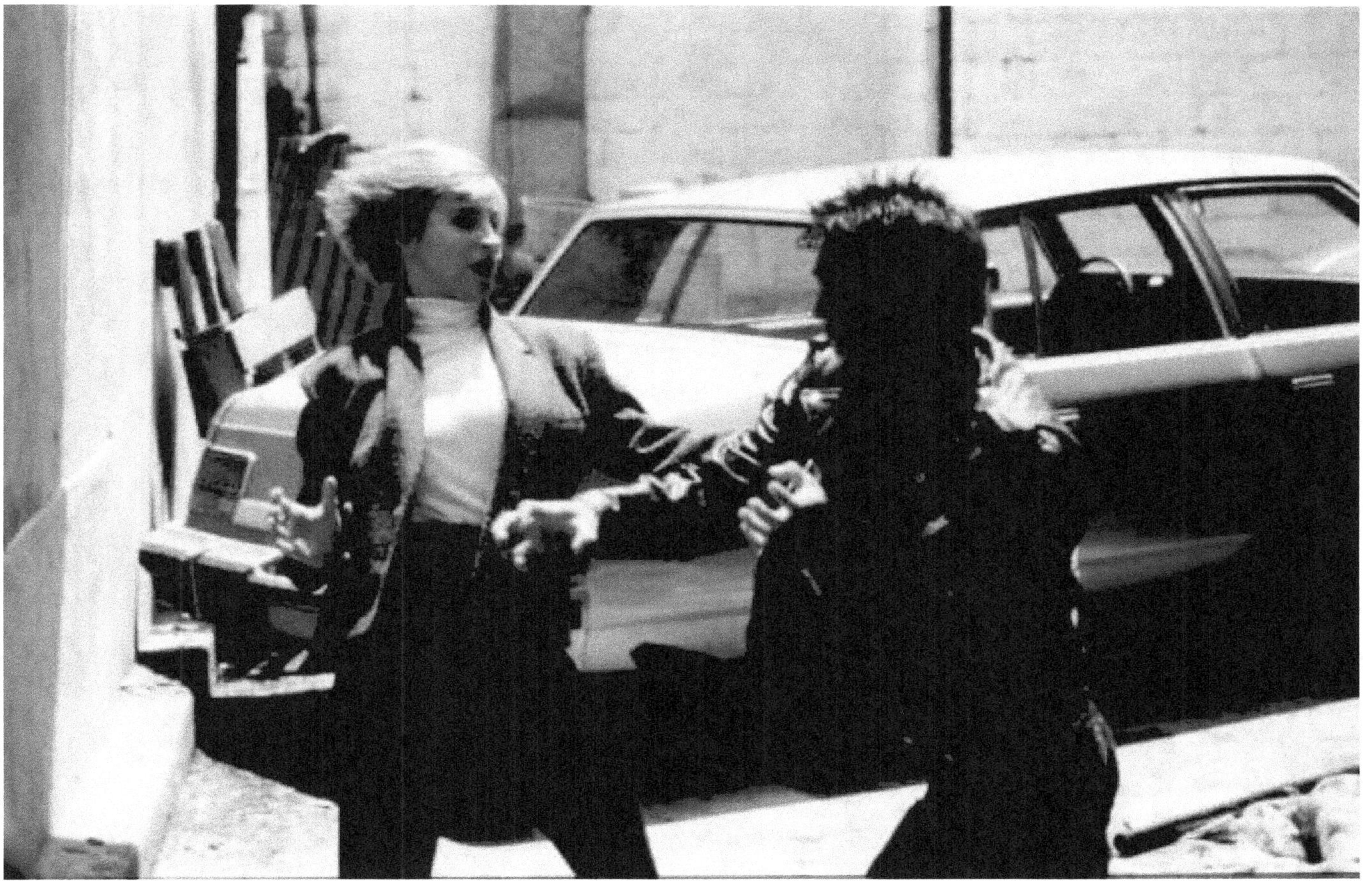

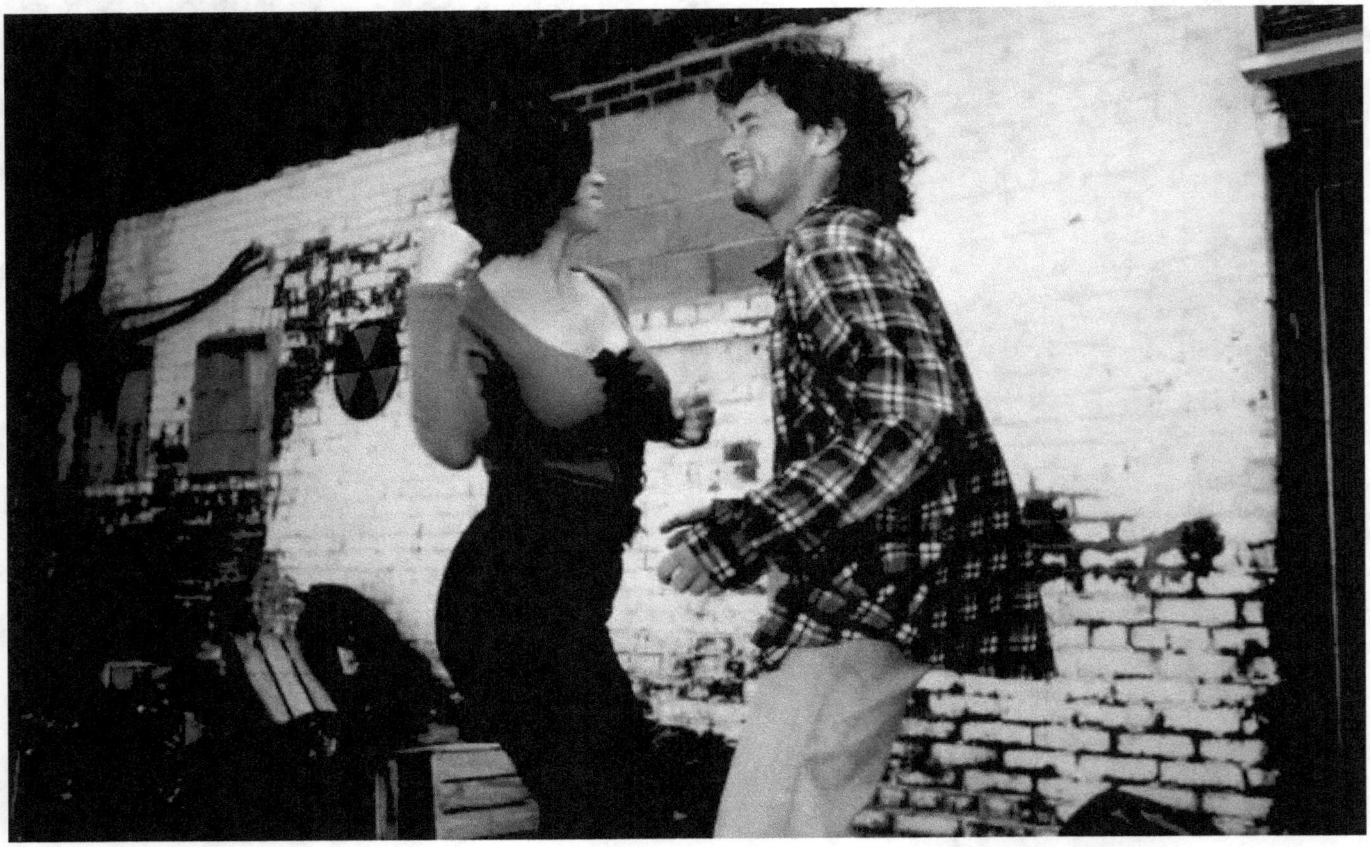

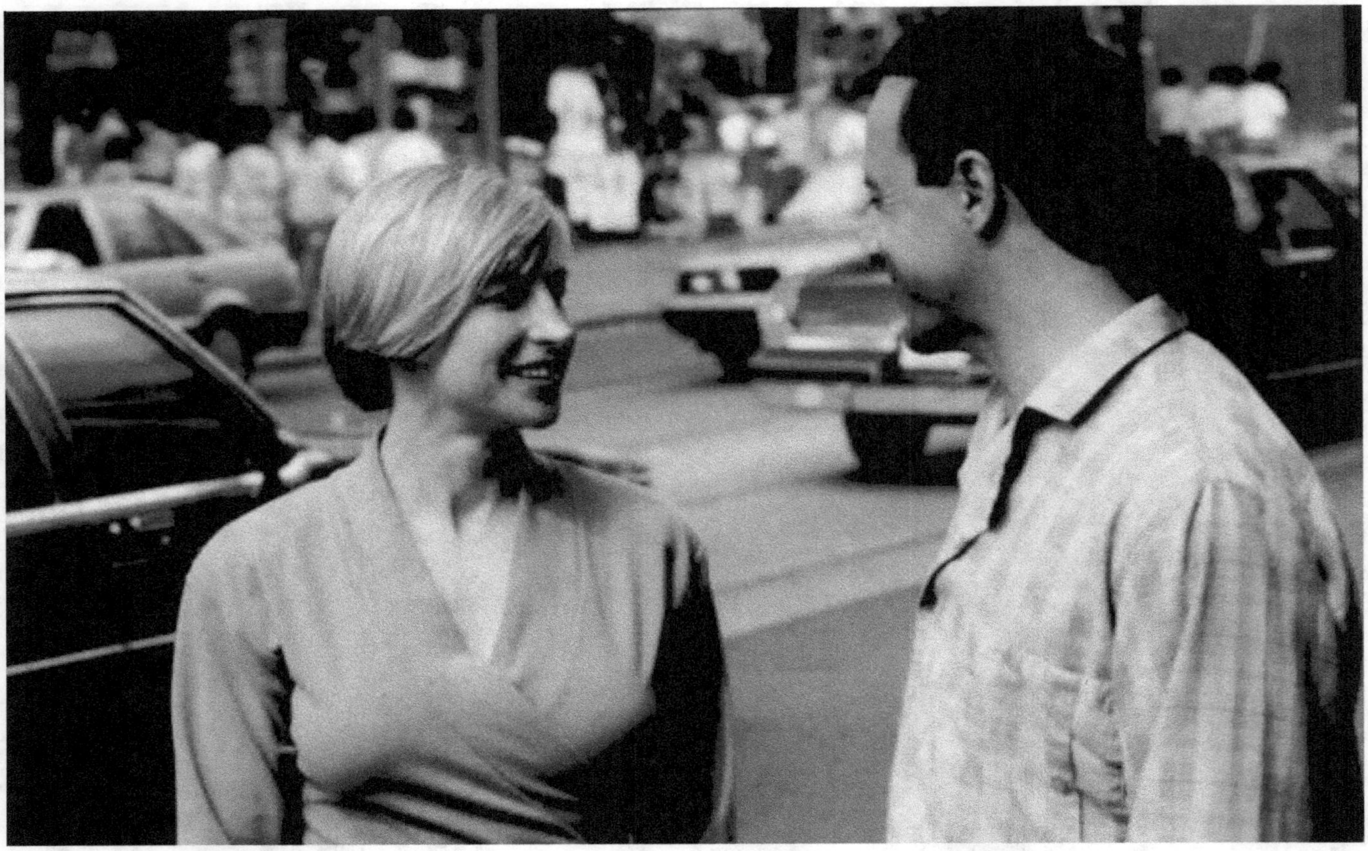

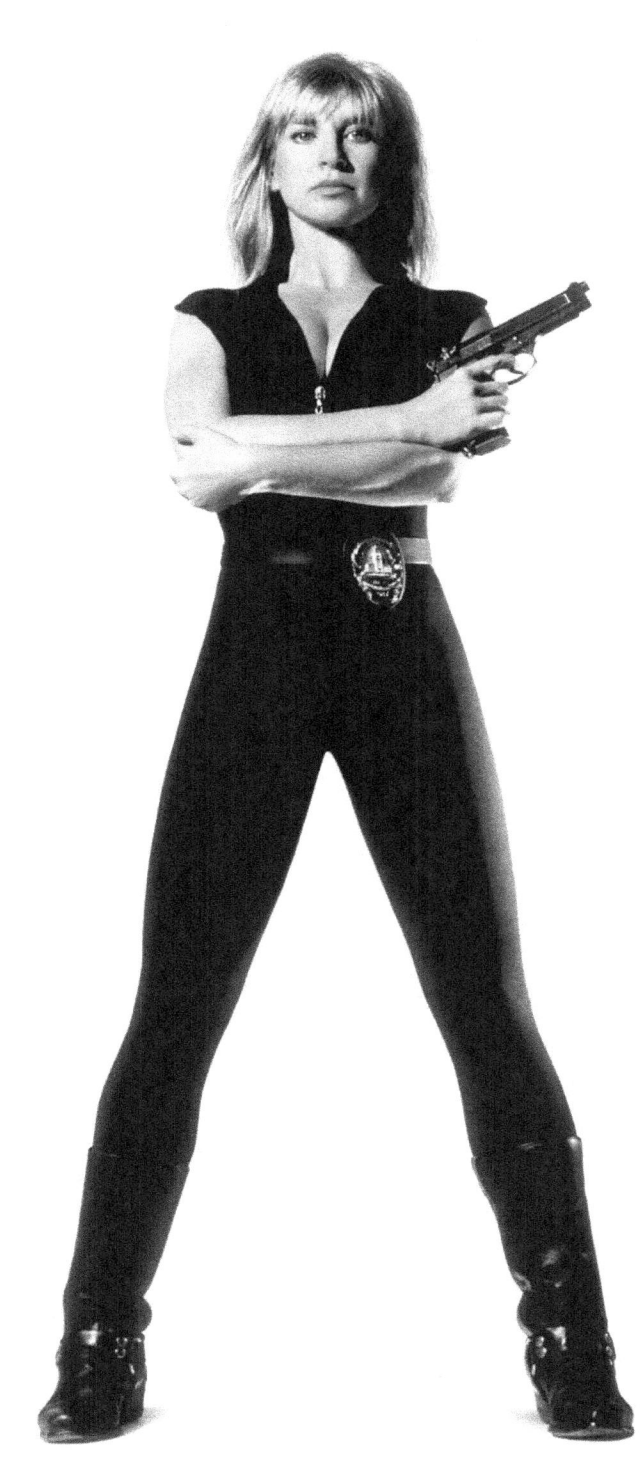

# Cynthia Rothrock

Cynthia Rothrock is both an actress and a skilled martial arts fighter. For five straight years she was the undisputed world karate champion in both forms. Rothrock has also been inducted into the Black Belt Hall of Fame and Inside Kung-Fu Hall of Fame. She was discovered for the movie business while starring in a television commercial spot for Kentucky Fried Chicken, and she starred in numerous action films produced in Hong Kong, where she spent five years of her life. "Lady Dragon" rose quickly to stardom in Asia before switching to the US Market. A fair number of solid direct-to-video productions featured her in the leading role, among them RAGE AND HONOR 1 & 2, SWORN TO JUSTICE, FAST GETAWAY, MARTIAL LAW 1 & 2. She starred in two films which were picked up for distribution by SGE: the 1987 release, NO RETREAT NO SURRENDER II (directed by Corey Yuen) introduced her in a remarkable supporting role to the American audience; and TIGER CLAWS (followed by two sequels) which remains a fan favorite even today. When action films and the home video business declined, she took a break from acting and concentrated on giving instruction seminars in several martial arts clubs all over the world. Recently she came back to the silver screen, starring in the upcoming all-star-films THE MARTIAL ARTS KID and SHOWDOWN IN MANILA.

**Marco:** When you worked in Hong Kong in your early career, you moved there for a while, correct?

**Cynthia:** Yeah, I lived there three years.

**Marco:** Ok, how was that? Did you learn the language or was it all in English?

**Cynthia:** No one spoke English, nobody on the set. So I started learning Mandarin because they told me to learn the language - but nobody spoke Mandarin! *(laughs)* They said it would be easier to learn but everybody on the set was speaking Cantonese. When I began to learn Cantonese, I came to a point, at least sometimes, to understand what people were saying. It was almost a combination of sign language and what they were saying - they didn't understand me because I was often putting the wrong accent on it, but I got to a point where I could pretty much translate for Corey Yuen when he was talking to the actors. I could order in restaurants, I knew how to get a taxi cab. So I got to a point where I could get around. But I couldn't speak fluently.

**Marco:** And about your private life, did you make many friends there, or did you fly to the US on regular basis?

**Cynthia:** No I didn't. Well, the first year I was still competing. I needed to finish off the year Number One because my goal was to be undefeated for five years in a row. I had to fly three times to the States so I would fly, get there on Friday, compete on Saturday, fly back Sunday and then be on the set as soon as I could. It was pretty rough, but I did that. Then after that, I just pretty much stayed there; I made friends. I had a couple of really good friends, and you know everytime I did a movie I made a few more friends. Most of the times I guess I made friends with people that could speak English as well.

**Marco:** What about Richard Norten, he appeared in a number of your early films.

**Cynthia:** The first one we did together was SHANGHAI EXPRESS.

**Marco:** Did he live in Hong Kong as well?

**Cynthia:** He just lived there for that film, and I'm not sure how long that took. Two and a half months or so. That one was a quick one. *(laughs)*

**Marco:** Did you become personal friends?

**Cynthia:** Yeah, right away we hit it off. First of all I was, " Uuuhhh, someone I can talk to. " So we hung out, we laughed at all that silly stuff that was going on and you know, to this day we are best of friends.

**Marco:** When it came to NO RETREAT NO SURRENDER 2, was it co-produced by US producers?

**Cynthia:** Well, the funny thing was it was a very unusual shoot. It was the after the second film I did for Corey Yuen, and it was a huge success. Yuen said, let's use her for a movie. And so we did NO RETREAT NO SURRENDER 2. We had an American crew, we had a Chinese crew - with Corey Yuen directing - and we also had a Thai crew because we were shooting in Thailand. It was kinda interesting because no one was able to communicate, and everybody had his own ideas. I think the intent was, they did NO RETREAT NO SURRENDER, and they made a lot of money worldwide, especially the US market. So it was made more to be like an US production.

**Marco:** In Germany it was also a huge success, it was titled KARATE TIGER. Had you actually seen the original movie before you shot this sequel?

**Cynthia:** No, I didn't see the first one, and the second one actually was quite funny. I was over in Thailand. Corey Yuen was directing, and I knew him because of YES MADAM. And they didn't tell me that Kurt McKinney and Jean-Claude van Damme were not in the movie. We didn't know that, we thought they were. What happened was, Jean-Claude van Damme got BLOODSPORT, and he picked this bigger production.

**Marco:** So, at first he should have appeared in the sequel?

**Cynthia:** He was supposed to be, and so should Kurt McKinney. What happened was, Jean-Claude van Damme talked Kurt McKinney out of this. Because the film was going to be shot in Thailand, and that would be dangerous. So Kurt backed, out which probably was a big mistake for him, and Jean-Claude went on to do bigger films. So what happened with Loren Avedon, they gave him a call, and Loren answers the phone. They said, they're looking for a guy that could kick and who is ready to leave tomorrow. To go to Thailand. And he was like, That's me! I can do it. They said he shall come over to the office now, he showed some kicks. He was a great martial artist so they hired him. So when he got to Thailand, they did not tell Corey Yuen that it wasn't Kurt McKinney.

**Marco:** *(laughing)*

**Cynthia:** I didn't know! When they introduced me to Loren they introduced him as his character name. I thought it was Kurt McKinney!

**Marco**: Brilliant!

**Cynthia**: I thought: Wow! I had seen movies with Kurt McKinney, and I was like, you look so different than on film! *(giggling)* And then Matthias Hues was playing the van Damme part, and Matthias Hues wasn't really a martial artist at this point, and Corey Yuen was really upset. Matthias played a great part and he was good at it, but he wasn't really a fighter.

**Marco**: So he developed his martial arts skills later?

**Cynthia**: Yes, exactly!

**Marco**: I think in Hong Kong that was something that didn't happen to a director - doing martial arts with people not skilled in martial arts?

**Cynthia**: Yeah, pretty much.

**Marco**: But when you were shooting NO RETREAT NO SURRENDER 2 it was clear for you, that you would be starring in a supporting role?

**Cynthia**: You know what, actually I did know. Loren Avedon was the lead, and then Max Thayer. I don't know if I was third billing, or something like that. I liked that film, I still like it today. It still was a good premise, a good story, the action was really good. So that one I actually liked and I did like the part of the character.

**Marco**: It was the film that introduced you to a wider audience?

**Cynthia**: The American market, yeah. Because it was an English speaking film.

**Marco**: And the European market as well?

**Cynthia**: Yeah! And I think other than Bruce Lee's films, this was the first attempt using American actors in a somewhat-kind-of Hong Kong production.

**Marco**: Did all the shooting take place in Thailand, or was there footage shot in the US or in Hong Kong?

**Cynthia**: No, everything was shot in Thailand.

**Marco**: And how do you remember that?

**Cynthia**: *(laughing)* I remember all the crew was not getting along. The Chinese against the Thai, the Thai against the Americans. I remember one day there almost going to be a big fight between the Thai stuntmen and the Chinese stuntmen. It was pretty bizarre, we were there four months. About halfway through the filming, Max Thayer got in an argument with Corey Yuen, and he said, "I'm quitting." And we were all like, "No! We are more than two months into this shoot, you can't quit. If we had to re-film his stuff with someone else, we would have to stay there longer." We were living in pretty primitive conditions. We didn't have rooms with air conditioners, very little beds, no tv, nothing to do. I mean, it was pretty primitive.

**Marco**: This was in Bangkok?

**Cynthia**: No, we didn't shoot in Bangkok. We shot a little bit, but not much. It was all shot in the outskirts of Thailand, in the countryside and stuff. Yeah, I just remember that Max and Corey Yuen got into that, and Max was going to quit. And

| | |
|---|---|
| | I think Max said that word to Corey Yuen, and he was like, hey - I know that word! |
| **Marco:** | *(laughing)* |
| **Cynthia:** | ...but in the end everybody was kind of ok. It was just kinda crazy. After that film, Max and I had become very good friends, too - until today. I like it when you're doing a movie, and there are very strange conditions, everybody bonds. You keep this bond forever, about all the strange stuff that kind of went on. |
| **Marco:** | Fun fact from the German version: In the final scene your dead body is carried. In German they added an off-commentary, and you can her the thinking of the main character going something like: "She'll make it!" |
| **Cynthia:** | *(laughing hard)* That's very funny, I'm dead but I'll make it. |
| **Marco:** | There was a Hong Kong film where you died at the end and they shot another ending because of that? |
| **Cynthia:** | Yeah, yeah, that was RIGHTING WRONGS! In the original movie Yuen and I both die. And, people didn't like it. They hated it! Even in Taiwan, people didn't want to go and see it. They were like, we're not going to see that movie because Cynthia and Yuen are dead. So I was shooting CHINA O'BRIAN, and Corey Yuen called. He said, we need to change the scene, she's not going to be dead. I can't remember if they flew me back to Hong Kong. I think they did. They flew me back to change the scene, and also Yuen Biao. So there's two versions out there: one we die, and one we don't. And we showed the one we did not die, and everybody loved it. |
| **Marco:** | But you can find both versions out there? |
| **Cynthia:** | Yes, you can. I prefer the one that we die. Because, it was a shock. You know what I mean, I get brutally stabbed in the throat. And Yuen Biao jumps off a helicopter, and he dies in the water. Uh yeah, I did go back to Hong Kong because we shot the scene were I'm in a sling on the boat, and I stick him up in the water. That's how it ends. *(laughing)* But yeah, it's very funny because the people did not want to accept the fact that we died. |
| **Marco:** | Maybe people like to see the hero die in a military situation, in a heroic act but they don't want to see the martial arts hero die. |
| **Cynthia:** | Yeah! But in that case I was kind of the hero because I ran in front of Loren Avedon and saved his life. So instead of him getting shot I took the bullet. So it was a little bit different. It's not like a fight scene, and the bad guy stabs me in the throat, and I'm stuck on the wall with a spear in my neck! It was very gruesome. |
| **Marco:** | It's very hard to get a proper overlook with all the different versions, cuts, and the many titles. |
| **Cynthia:** | Yeah, they change them lots of times. |
| **Marco:** | Also the international titles. In Germany they made a series of around 10 films with the KARATE TIGER title. |
| **Cynthia:** | *(laughing)* Yes, I think back then they tried to capitalize on everything that was |

|        |                                                                                                                                                                                                                                                                                                                                 |
|--------|---|
| | successful, even if it had nothing to do with the film. They would just say, "This is part three!" |
| Marco: | Also included in this "series" was THE KING OF THE KICKBOXERS from 1990. |
| Cynthia: | Oh, the one with Loren. |
| Marco: | Exactly. So you already were shooting CHINA O'BRIAN when you got to Hong Kong for the alternative end shootings of RIGHTING WRONGS. Was this your first appearance as a leading actress in American movies? |
| Cynthia: | Yeah, although it was still a Hong Kong production. |
| Marco: | Oh, ok. So it was Golden Harvest? |
| Cynthia: | Yes, exactly. After I did YES MADAM I signed a three-picture-deal with Golden Harvest. I was supposed to do a film with Jackie Chan, and that's when he got hurt. I was supposed to be the bad guy in that film (ARMOR OF GODS). So they put me in RIGHTING WRONGS instead. And then I had two more pictures and they said, do you want to shoot two American pictures? You know, and we'll finish up your three-picture-deal. And I was like, yeah. It was all with American crew, except they brought the stunt/fight coordinators from Hong Kong. It was merely an American production and crew. |
| Marco: | And Robert Clouse, he was a veteran behind the camera. |
| Cynthia: | Yeah, because he did ENTER THE DRAGON, which was a huge success. |
| Marco: | Indeed, a legendary film. Was he an American director? |
| Cynthia: | Yes, he was from the US. |
| Marco: | Did he know much about the actual sport? |
| Cynthia: | I think, obviously when he did ENTER THE DRAGON, I'm pretty sure Bruce Lee was in control of everything. How to shoot it, what he wanted to do. Honestly, the fighting was left pretty much to the choreographers, he just like shot it. His shooting was different, actually I said there were two parts shot in six weeks. In Hong Kong it would took probably a year to shoot the two of them. We really had to get it done fast, which I wasn't used to. He wanted to shoot everything all in one shot. Without taking cuts and doing inserts like Hong Kong was really famous for because if you get hit in the head, they come in for a close up and show that foot hitting the head. Robert wanted everything to be just one long shot. And to me, I prefer the filming of the Hong Kong style. How they do the master and then do a lot of close ups. I like that, it was more powerful and looked better. I think Robert didn't like that style. So there were a little bit of confrontation between the fight choreographers, how to shoot it. And in the end it kind of was what Robert wanted. He was the director. |
| Marco: | There's another picture, which was actually never shot. The producers wanted to get you on the top of a high building for that, is this true? |

**Cynthia**: Yes, yes. Actually before I was shooting CHINA O'BRIAN they were thinking about the next Hong Kong movie. And the director wanted me to jump off a gigantic high rise. One of those big Hong Kong highrises. On a wire, just jump down, with no net! I was like, that's scary for me without a net, and it was so high. I mean, when I did the jump in BLONDE FURY aka LADY REPORTER I just jumped from a building. But this was a thousand feet, without safety net, going all the way down. And you know what the crazy thing is? I would have done it. I would have been scared out of my mind to do it, but luckily that's when they said I could do the CHINA O'BRIAN instead. And I was like, yeah, yeah, yeah. I don't have to do this jump.

**Marco**: Yeah, of course!

**Cynthia**: And that's one of the differences between the American and the Hong Kong film industry: A lot of the stunts are very dangerous. And very easy to get hurt.

**Marco**: Did stunt people often get hurt seriously, or even die?

**Cynthia**: We had some injuries on LADY REPORTER. We were doing a fight scene on a net. I don't know what happened, something happened to the guy on the net. He fell to the ground and he got paralyzed for life from that stunt. Actually at CHINA O'BRIAN someone died, but it wasn't a stunt accident - he was the pyro technics guy, something went very wrong.

**Marco**: So some very dangerous situations came up.

**Cynthia**: The funny thing is in American films they wouldn't even let me do stunt scenes like that. Even in CHINA O'BRIAN when I wanted to drive the car they said, no you can't. They are actually afraid that you will get hurt, and in Hong Kong they want to see the actor physically do that stunt. It's much more impressive. To me, it was always worth the injuries because the filming was just brilliant.

**Marco**: Jackie Chan - who is famous for his many stunt injuries - he was the producer on TOP SQUAD.

**Cynthia**: Yes, this was a funny one. Because I wasn't originally supposed to be in that film. They had a bunch of girls fighting, and they were almost done with it, and it wasn't looking good. And Golden Harvest said, "We need to get Cynthia for a couple of fight scenes and make it better!" So that's what happened on that movie, it was almost finished when they called me in. A couple of fight scenes, being the head of the inspectors, and they could make a lot more money out of this. *(laughing)*

**Marco**: This is the one with three leading female fighters, correct?

**Cynthia**: There were quite a few girls, I don't remember. The police force was all girls and I was the Captain.

**Marco**: I think there was a girl from Hong Kong, and you were from Scotland Yard in the film?

**Cynthia:** Yeah, probably that's true. And they didn't like me, because they were not doing well, and I had to get them in shape, or something. *(laughing)*

**Marco:** So THE MILLIONAIRE EXPRESS - directed by Sammo Hung - was not a Golden Harvest production, correct?

**Cynthia:** I'm not sure what company produced it, it might have been DNB. I only worked with Golden Harvest and DNB Films.

**Marco:** So you wasn't under contract at Golden Harvest as an exclusive?

**Cynthia:** No, actually I did the first movie with DNB Films, it wasn't Golden Harvest. It was YES MADAM. And then Golden Harvest signed me for that 3-picture-deal, and I did RIGHTING WRONGS and both CHINA O'BRIAN 1 & 2. At the time I was shooting it, INSPECTORS WEAR SKIRTS came along and it was kind of an interesting thing because there was another company that asked me to shoot a film. And they wanted to pay me a lot of money for one week. Golden Harvest wouldn't let me do it. They said, no, your contract says you can't do it. But then this other company - and I think it was with THE MAGIC CRYSTAL - they wanted me to do it, but I couldn't because Golden Harvest was not going to let me do it. So the next day Corey Yuen calls me at the office and we went to a restaurant, and he said you have to do the film! I said, I would like to do it, it's more money for me. I think what happened was, they were a pretty powerful company and they said to Raymond Chow, you've got to let her do this. So I was ending up doing that while I was shooting RIGHTING WRONGS.

They waited for me to get back and shoot that film.

**Marco:** Was PRINCE OF THE SUN your last Hong Kong movie?

**Cynthia:** Yeah, I think it was my last production in Hong Kong, correct.

**Marco:** Is it true that it has a multi-million-dollar budget?

**Cynthia:** Well, *(laughing)* that were not US dollars. It mean it was a bigger production, we went to Nepal and we had all the monks, the scenery, and all this - but no, it wasn't that kind of blockbuster money.

**Marco:** But it was a hig-class production in Hong Kong?

**Cynthia:** Yes.

**Marco:** I think it's impressive. But not better than the early ones, because it's kind of ... differing in style and quality.

**Cynthia:** Yes, it was kind of a copy of THE GOLDEN CHILD. *(laughing)*

**Marco:** Yeah, the one with Eddie Murphy. - And what about Leo Fong?

**Cynthia:** What happened with that one, I was shooting CHINA O'BRIAN, and he hired me to do three days of shooting on his film, it should be only a small part. I got to the set to do it, and the first two days he didn't use me. And only the third day he did. I thought, Jeez, I will be for less than three minutes in this movie. But it wasn't my fault, because for whatever reasons he only used the third day. And I had to leave. What ended up with that movie, it was like horrible. They actually got a guy - Berney Pock - and he played me as a ninja. And it was a guy the whole film, so my body type changed. And that was horrible, I mean the movie - actually they had a woman take her top off, showing her boobs and pretending it was me. And it wasn't! I was technically not longer than five minutes in that movie, but I was billed as a lead in it. I actually thought, can I sue them for this? The producer was from Singapore, and they said I had to go to Singapore and sue there, so I just said forget about it. That's the deal about this one, that totally isn't me - the ninja is a guy.

**Marco:** The same old exploitation tricks.

**Cynthia:** Yes, exploitation for sure.

**Marco:** It also happened to numerous actresses that starred in exploitation cinema, if they had showed her boobs, the director afterwards cut in hardcore sex scenes, or something. Not the nicest thing to do.

**Cynthia:** Well, one rule is: If you don't see the face, it's not the person.

**Marco:** So, TIGER CLAWS. Was it right after you did CHINA O'BRIAN?

**Cynthia:** After CHINA O'BRIAN I did the MARTIAL LAW films, and then I got to TIGER CLAWS.

**Marco:** This was your first American highlight as a lead actress, would you agree on that?

**Cynthia:** I think it was still a supporting role. It wasn't until I did SWORN TO JUSTICE, I really think this was the first movie I did the lead for. In MARTIAL LAW I did the supporting role, in FAST GETAWAY and I think I did also in TIGER CLAWS.

**Marco:** Maybe it wasn't intended but you became the star in the TIGER CLAWS series, correct?

**Cynthia:** Exactly. Jalal had it because he was the star. He produced it, he put a lot of his own money into the film. That was his vehicle for success. I was a partner but still, I was a supporting actress. You know, we had fun. It was great. Jalal was smart, he was able to do his own movie, and put himself in the leading role. And make a success out of this.

**Marco:** Do you remember when you met him for the very first time?

**Cynthia:** I think I might have met him at the SGE office, he wanted to do this picture. It's been a long time and I don't remember that much. But I think he simply came down to L.A., and he said he wanted to use me in TIGER CLAWS.

**Marco:** Jalal Merhi was very skilled in martial arts, correct?

**Cynthia:** Yes, very much.

**Marco:** And was he also into competitions?

**Cynthia:** No, I don't think so. He's a martial artist, but I think he had a jewely business and that's what his main thing was. I don't know. He wasn't in the competetive circles that I was in. He might have competed in Canada. He just was a martial arts teacher.

**Marco:** Were there problems during the shootings of TIGER CLAWS?

**Cynthia:** I don't remember that. I know there were some problems with Bolo Yeung. Because Jalal Merhi was the star and the producer, he had so much going on. A lot of hats to wear. There might have been some issues. I remember Bolo wasn't coming to the set because he didn't get paid. And I remember telling him to come, to trust Jalal. I think there some money issues but I said, he'll pay you, he'll not rip you off.

**Marco:** You worked on several more movies with Jalal.

**Cynthia:** Well, just the TIGER CLAWS series.

**Marco:** Comparing the different studios you worked with - just like P.M. Entertainment and several others - what was it like with SGE?

**Cynthia:** You know I felt comfortable with all of them, really. The difference is: P.M. was more involved. They were on the set every day. At NO RETREAT NO SURRENDER 2 and TIGER CLAWS, we never saw anybody from SGE on the set. They let Jalal take charge, they let Corey Yuen take charge. P.M. were in charge of everything. I think with NO RETREAT NO SURRENDER 2 they bought it from Seasonal Films, and distributed it, so it became their film. I think Jalal Merhi financed the whole first TIGER CLAWS. I remember Jalal had to blow up a car on set, and he never got a car for that. So he blew up his own Porsche. And we're all going, oh my gosh! That's dedication. He really wanted to have a good movie. *(laughing)*

**Marco:** You mentioned SWORN TO JUSTICE, it's one of the films you also produced. When did you decide to produce it and why was that?

**Cynthia:** Technically on SWORN TO JUSTICE my part as a producer wasn't really like quote the producer. I just had a say in some of the things I wanted. So I wouldn't say I was really the producer. The producer would say, this is my film. Basically all I did was to say who I wanted for the choreography, who I wanted for make-up, the director, the lead guy. But that was about the extent of it. I didn't get paid as a producer, or anything. I've been Associate Producer on a few films, and really it was just a title. It's not really doing anything. I would say, honestly I haven't really been involved in the producing aspect, as of yet.

**Marco:** But these films are a little more crafted by your ideas?

**Cynthia:** No, I think the thing with the label "Associate Producer", it just looked good. I really don't think I had any other job than if I wasn't being the associate, just being the actress.

**Marco:** How much does it mean to you when shooting a martial arts film, that what you bring on the screen is realistic, as far as the sports/action scenes?

**Cynthia:** In my action scenes I'm trying to make it all realistic. Even if it's something in the Jackie Chan style. I always try to be realistic. As far as real-life action and movie action, it's different. In movies you're stopping, you would give around

30 or 40 percent compared to what you would give on the street. You don't hit them that hard. When you train traditional martial arts you learn how to do that. You learn to be able to focus, to stop where you want. So you are totally in control what you are doing. In that aspect, it's similiar. In a real situation you would not stop, you would go right through.

**Marco:** Do you prefer fighting men or women?

**Cynthia:** I prefer fighting men, although I do fight women, and that's not bad. When I fight men I'm not afraid to kick a little harder. When I'm fighting women, maybe I could hurt them. I'm not saying that women are not tough, because they really are. But you just have a little bit more feeling that if you hit a guy very hard he can take it. I don't know but I guess it's because of the women I have fought in the past. I'm sure they are out there and they could do it, but I haven't really experienced that yet. I think my best fights were probably with men.

**Marco:** Do you see yourself as a representing women in martial arts films? Or have you never thought about this gender stuff?

**Cynthia:** Well, obviously I have thought about it, because when I started martial arts there were not many women doing it. So I came up in a field that was dominated by men, and there even were fallacies that if you were a women, you couldn't do it. Which is totally wrong, because it's all about technique and power. Actually women can be smaller and faster, and get in deeper. I have gender movies because they didn't want a woman as a lead, because it might not sell, or whatever. And I think it's the same in Hollywood now, not even only with action pictures. I think the best roles go to males, and I guess it's the same when I was doing films with all the guys. All the guys went on to bigger A-movies, and I stayed at the same thing. And it's not like they were all better then me, I think it's just a gender thing.

**Marco:** Do you think martial arts films have some kind of role model function when it comes to the moral or philosophy of the sports? Is it important to you?

**Cynthia:** It is. One of the best things someone said to me is, I want you in my movie because I want you to be a role model to my daughter. Basically, what it does, it teaches people, I think everybody should do martial arts. Because you never know when you will need to defend yourself, or defend someone else. It makes you stronger, it makes you confident, and it keeps you in good shape. So why not? It doesn't matter, men, or woman, or children. Everybody should do it, and I think a lot of times, especially for me, woman go see my films and they're like: wow, if she could do it, I could do it because she's not that big, and she's tough. And I love that. Even guys emailed me, I saw your movies and started with martial arts. That, to me, is a good legacy to have. People saw my films, and it brought them into learning how to defend themselves and be better people.

**Marco:** You have already appeared in the Hollywood movie EYE FOR AN EYE as a martial arts instructor. This is what you're going if you are not making movies, correct?

**Cynthia:** Yes, movies are my first love and what I want to do. But I also love teaching. You know, I've been doing it for such a long time. I like helping people to learn techniques, and defend themselves. Because I have known people that have been attacked, or raped, or whatever, and it would have been so easy in such situations to turn out. Some people think I'm just an action star and not that I'm really a teacher in martial arts sports. I teach quite well, I've had schools. I see myself doing the rest of my life one or the other, or both.

**Marco:** What significance does it have for an action star to have a franchise like you had with MARTIAL LAW, or the TIGER CLAWS movies? Is it important to come back with the same character?

**Cynthia:** I think if you do a film, and you're an actor, and they bring you back for a second one it says you did a good job. The movie was successful, so everybody would love that. Not every movie has a sequel but I'm proud that a lot of mine have. A lot of movies don't have a sequel so you just try to get out of it the best you can. But I think any actor would love to came back when there's a second one.

**Marco:** You mostly played the good/positive part but you also played bad girl roles. What do you prefer? What's great about being a hero, and what's great about being an anti-hero?

**Cynthia:** I like playing both! I think I like playing the hero a little bit better, because I guess I can relate to it more. I'm not really like a mean, bad person, but it's fun to play one sometimes. *(laughing)* In most of my films I have been the good guy but if someone would come to me and offer me such a role in an A-movie it would be great. Sometimes the bad guys are interesting characters as well. As an actor, I don't think it really matters which role you do if the role is good.

**Marco:** One negative thing in playing the bad part might be you have to lose at the end?

**Cynthia:** *(laughing)* True. Or get killed. I guess in a perfect world you could be the bad guy and not get killed. You can have the upperhand.

By Marco Siedelmann, in person
in Munich, Germany
13June, 2015

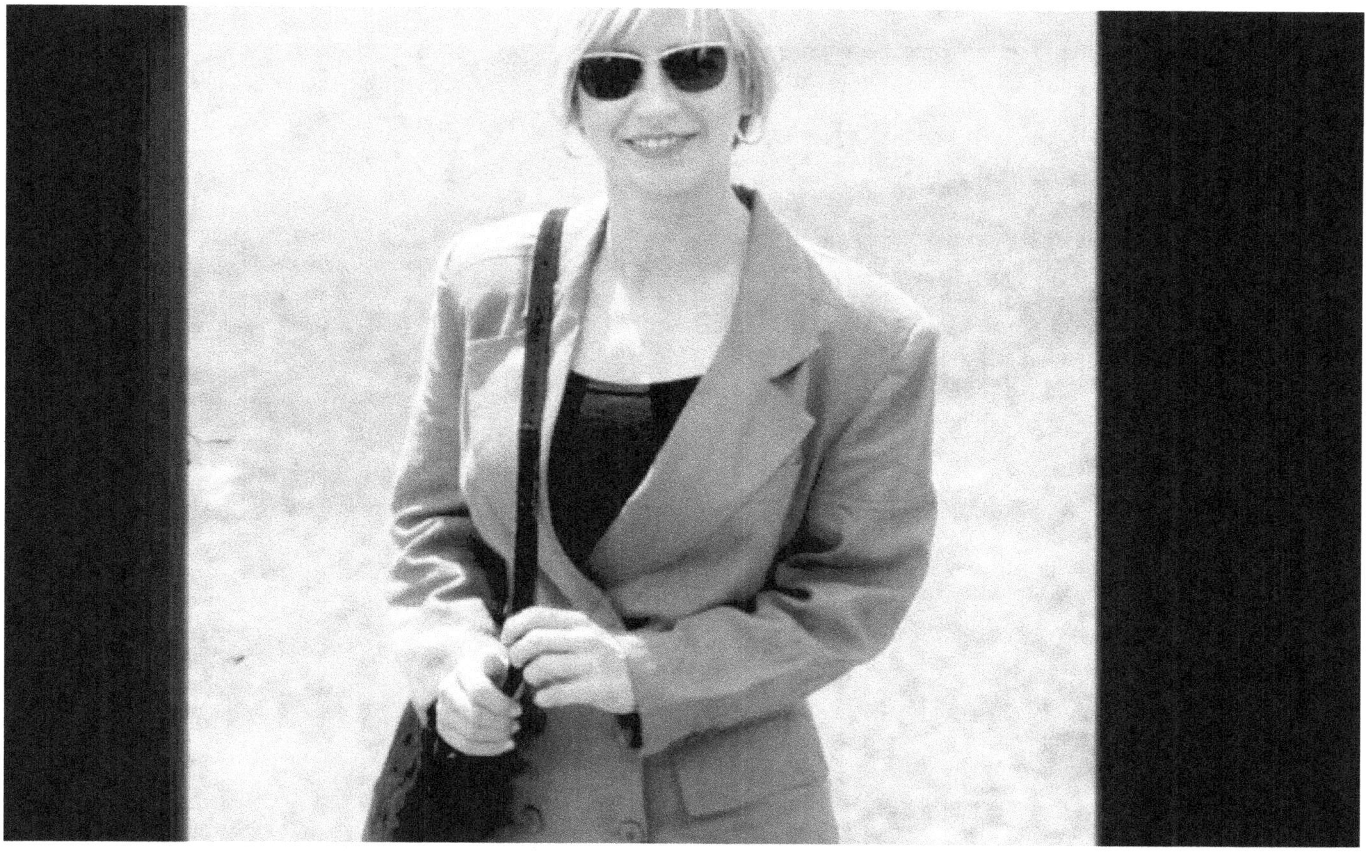

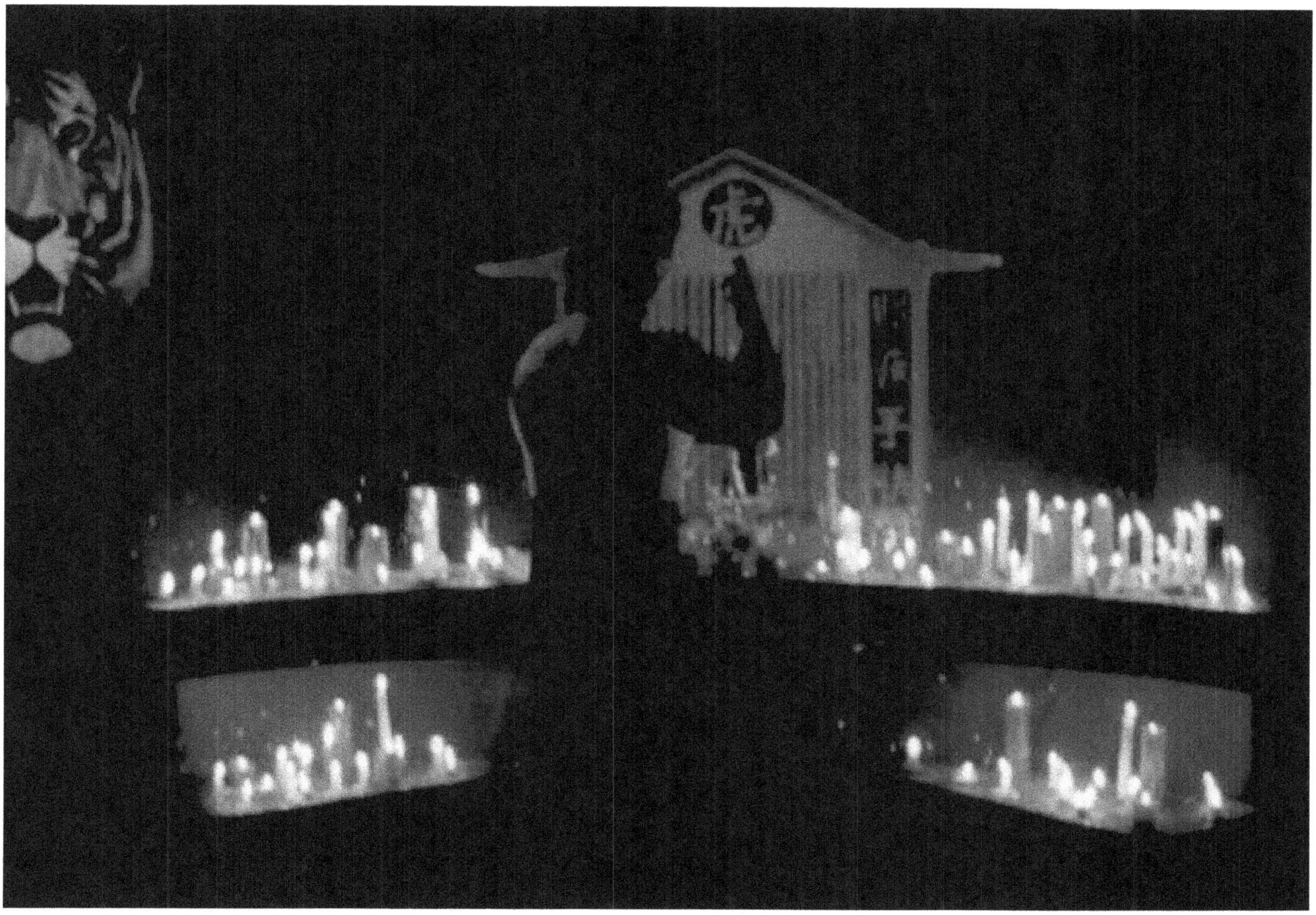

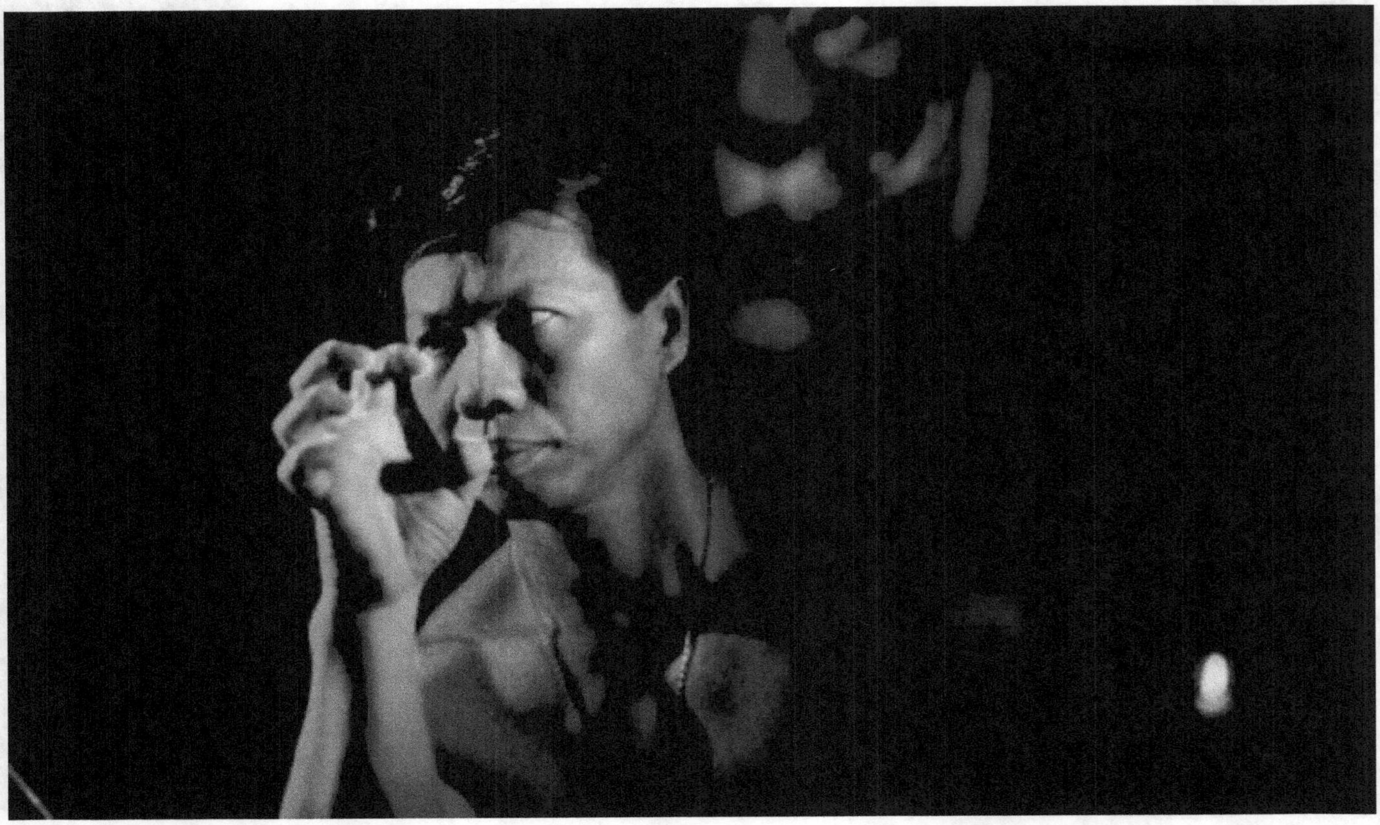

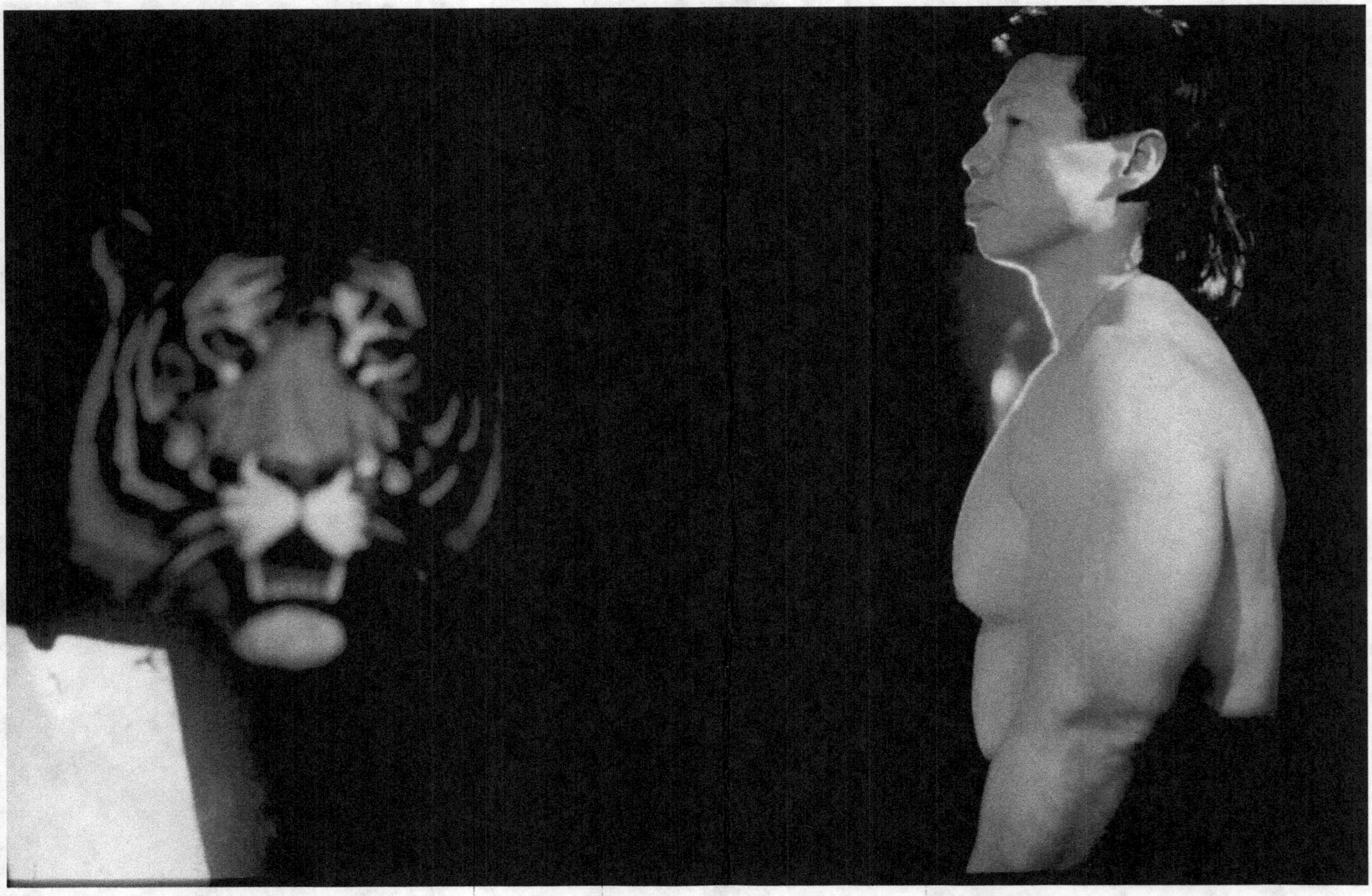

# IV. Expansion and The Red Scorpion Experiment

*"You have to think anyway, so why not think big?"*

– Donald Trump

They think they control him.
Think again.

**DOLPH LUNDGREN**

# RED SCORPION

# Joseph Zito

Director/producer Joseph Zito was born in New York City. He began his cinematic career in film distribution. Zito made his debut picture in the mid 70s with the Patty Hearst-inspired exploitation feature ABDUCTION, then BLOODRAGE, the brutal slasher item THE PROWLER, and the superior slice'n'dice sequel FRIDAY THE 13TH: THE LAST CHAPTER. Zito twice worked with the legendary Chuck Norris, directing the Cannon Films' INVASION USA and MISSING IN ACTION. With SGE, Zito created one particular movie: RED SCORPION. RED SCORPION had by far the biggest theatrical release SGE ever handled, and even today it remains a bestseller in the international market. Joseph returned one decade later with DELTA FORCE: THE LOST PATROL (1999) and POWER PLAY (2002). Zito is a frequent lecturer at universities and colleges around the country including USC, University of Ohio at Bowling Green and UCLA. He currently divides his time between the US and working in the Middle East as producer of a large-scale hospital drama television series.

**Marco:** You worked one time with Shapiro Glickenhaus Entertainment - the company was the distributor for RED SCORPION, is this correct?

**Joe:** Yes. SGE was the distributor of RED SCORPION. They didn't have anything to do with the production but when it was completed, and they saw a product reel we had made, SGE stepped up with the highest bid and they got worldwide distribution rights.

**Marco:** How did the cooperation come about, and what comes first to your mind, thinking of SGE? Did they do a good job on RED SCORPION?

**Joe:** Let me answer the second part first: What's the first thing that comes to mind when I think of SGE? Lenny's psychotic laugh. I think anyone who knows him would probably agree. As to how the cooperation came about, it was because of a chance meeting at the American Film Market in Santa Monica. I made a long product reel of what I thought were the best complete scenes in the movie because we hadn't completed all the editing at that time. We rented a tiny room (the cheapest they had) at the AFM and screened the reel for a few buyers at a time. Luckily, international distributors who had bought my earlier action films, MISSING IN ACTION and INVASION USA, wanted to see the new one. We'd let a few in, lock the door and screen the reel. There was always a "screening in progress" sign on the locked door, which only made more buyers want to see it. We didn't even tell people the price but just said we were accepting bids. This drove them all crazy and speaking of crazy, who came along, Jim and Lenny, who had an office nearby. After being turned away a few times they finally saw the reel and said, "How can we get it?" - In the end, they got the rights because they offered the most, but in fact no company would have put more effort into distributing the film. They built an entire distribution and marketing team to launch RED SCORPION, which no other independent distributor would have done.

**Marco:** Compared to other distribution or production companies you worked with, what was the difference with SGE?

**Joe:** Other distributors ran a business and that was it. SGE was a business, but felt like a family first. There was a lot of fun and laughing (often at Lenny's expense) mixed in with the hard work.

**Marco:** Do you remember which key people from SGE you worked with on the distribution of RED SCORPION?

**Joe:** The great thing about the RED SCORPION experience at SGE was that they allowed a director (in this case, me---thanks, Len) to get involved in every aspect of the distribution and marketing. In the end it was their call, as it should be, but they always heard the director's thoughts. This is kind of rare at the big studios in Hollywood where the director is usually thought of as an annoyance whose work is finished, so who cares what they think?

**Marco:** Were you familiar with James Glickenhaus, Leonard Shapiro or Alan Solomon at the time?

**Joe:** I knew Jim and Len a little and had seen Alan around at the markets, but I only got to spend a lot of time with them all when they showed an interest in RED SCORPION. After that I saw them every day for months and I've continued the friendship with Len to this day. Maybe that's because we haven't worked together again.

**Marco:** RED SCORPION had a huge impact in media and film criticism worldwide. How do you remember the reputation of the movie at the time of its theatrical release?

**Joe:** I know there has been a lot written about RED SCORPION but most of it has been done long after the film's initial release. I've seen many great things said about the film from fans and bloggers but at the time of the U.S. theatrical release critics pretty much didn't get it, didn't like it or just ignored it and wrote mostly about South Africa since the film was shot in Namibia which was in the process of becoming the separate country it is today, but then was controlled by South Africa which was getting lots of bad press in the US at that time because of Apartheid. Also, Dolph was playing a Russian soldier and the Soviet Union basically collapsed just before the film was released. So I'd say politics was discussed more than the movie itself, which is just a simple bad guy becomes good guy action film. I guess you could say I went on a few promotion tours sponsored by SGE to promote the film. They mostly consisted of flying to Cannes and Milan (which at the time also hosted a huge film market) and eating and drinking in good restaurants. As I recall, SGE did all the promoting and I handled most of the eating and drinking.

**Marco:** Had you seen the films produced by SGE before you worked with them?

**Joe:** I had only seen Jim's films, and the ones I saw weren't SGE releases. I had never seen an SGE produced or distributed film - other than Jim's - and I don't believe that has changed to this day.

**Marco:** From when RED SCORPION was released until SGE was shut down, you did not direct another film. If you had directed another one, would SGE have been your choice for producing and/or distributing?

**Joe:** I never worked with SGE again though I remain great friends with Len as I've said and I was very close to Alan Solomon for many years. I lost touch with Jim after SGE was over but I read about him all the time and hope I get to see him again sometime.

---

**By Marco Siedelmann in writing**
**Cairo, Egypt**
**May 2015**

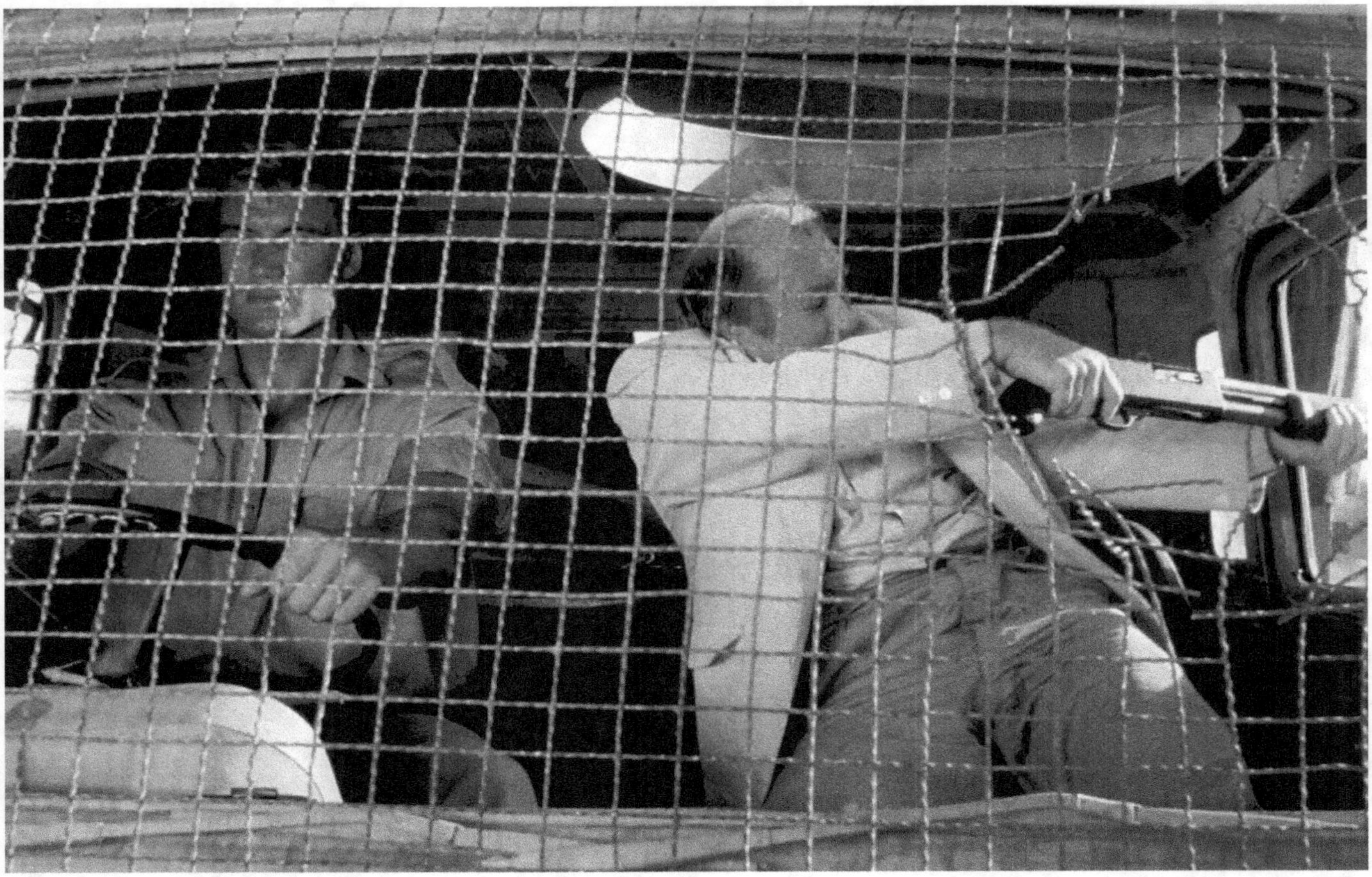

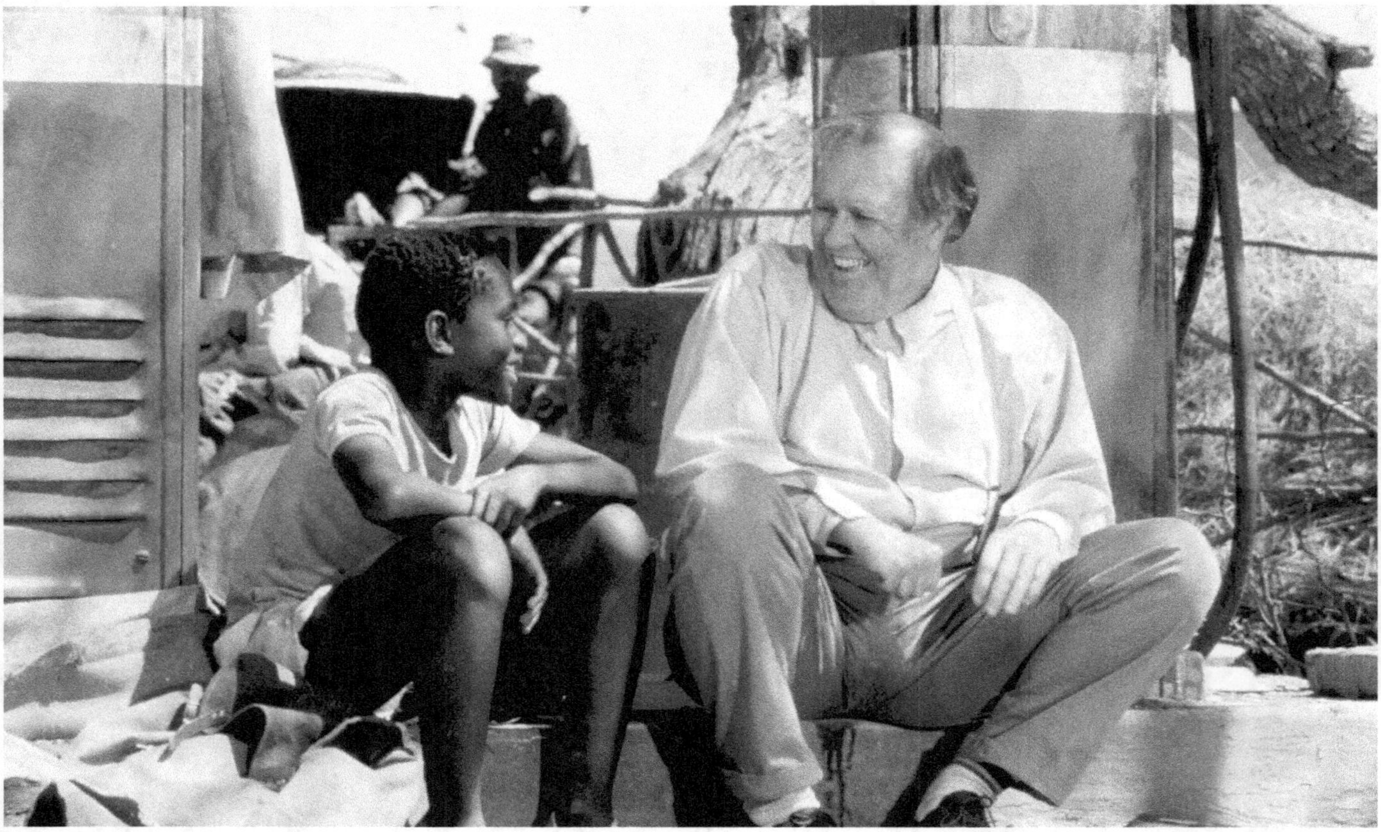

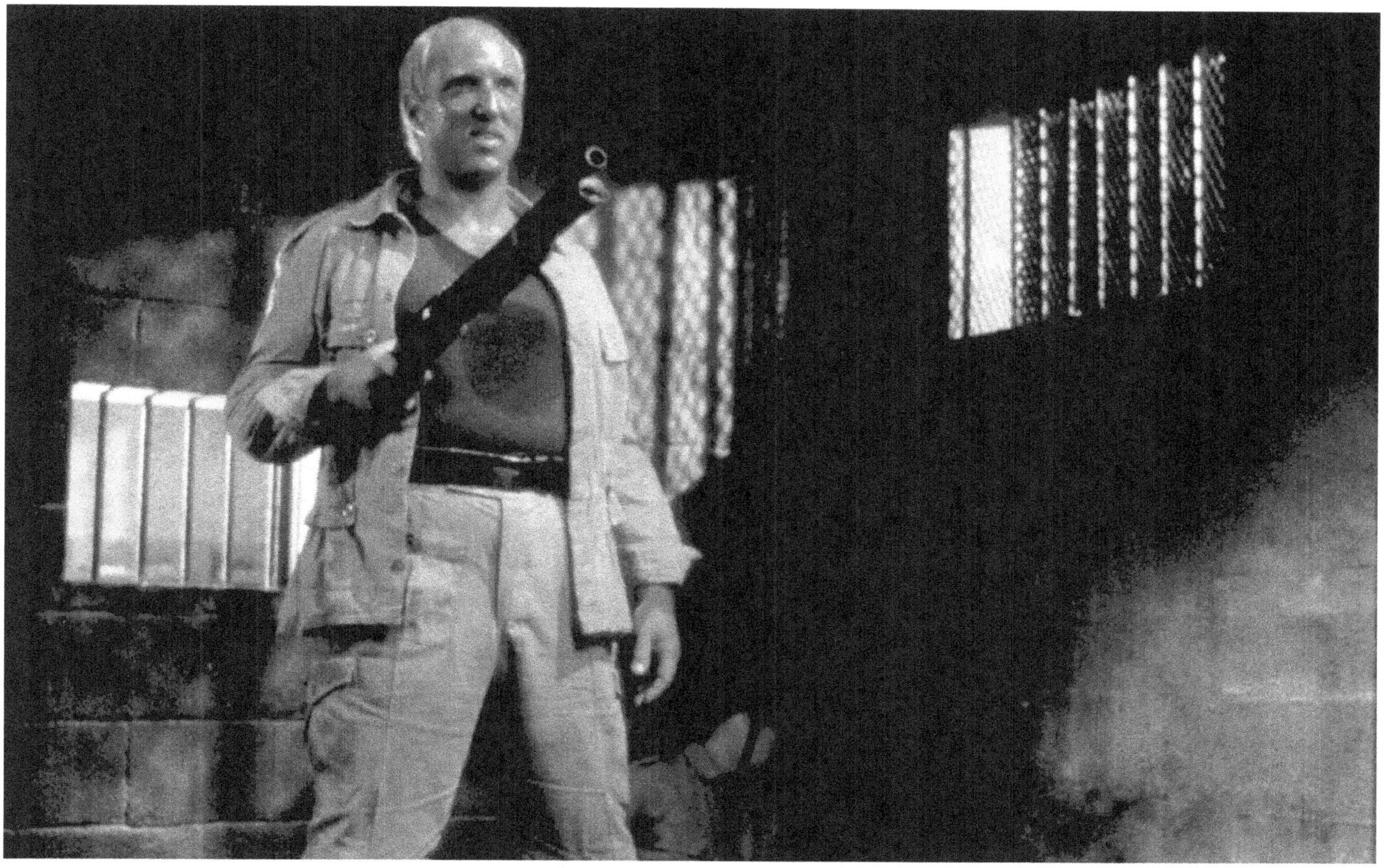

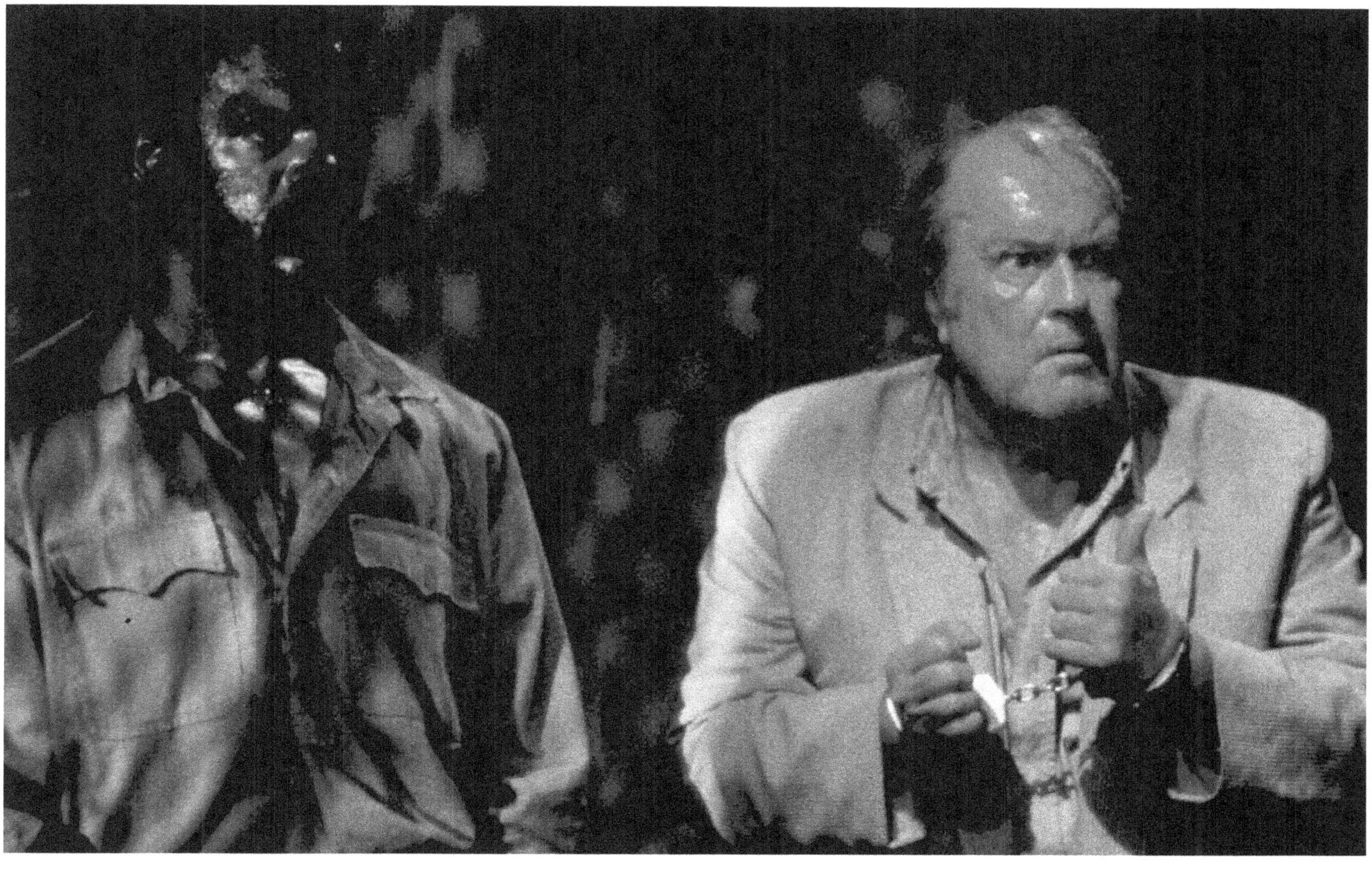

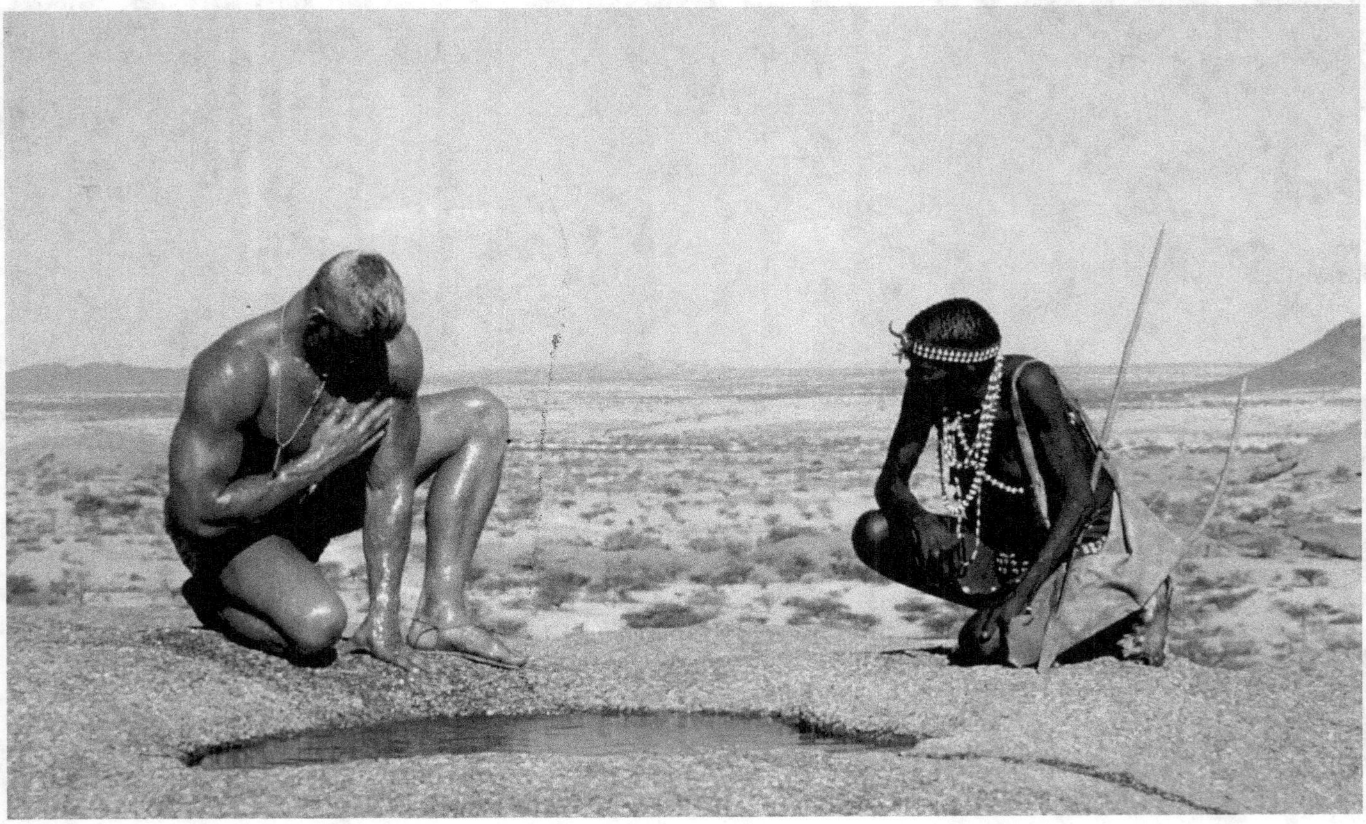

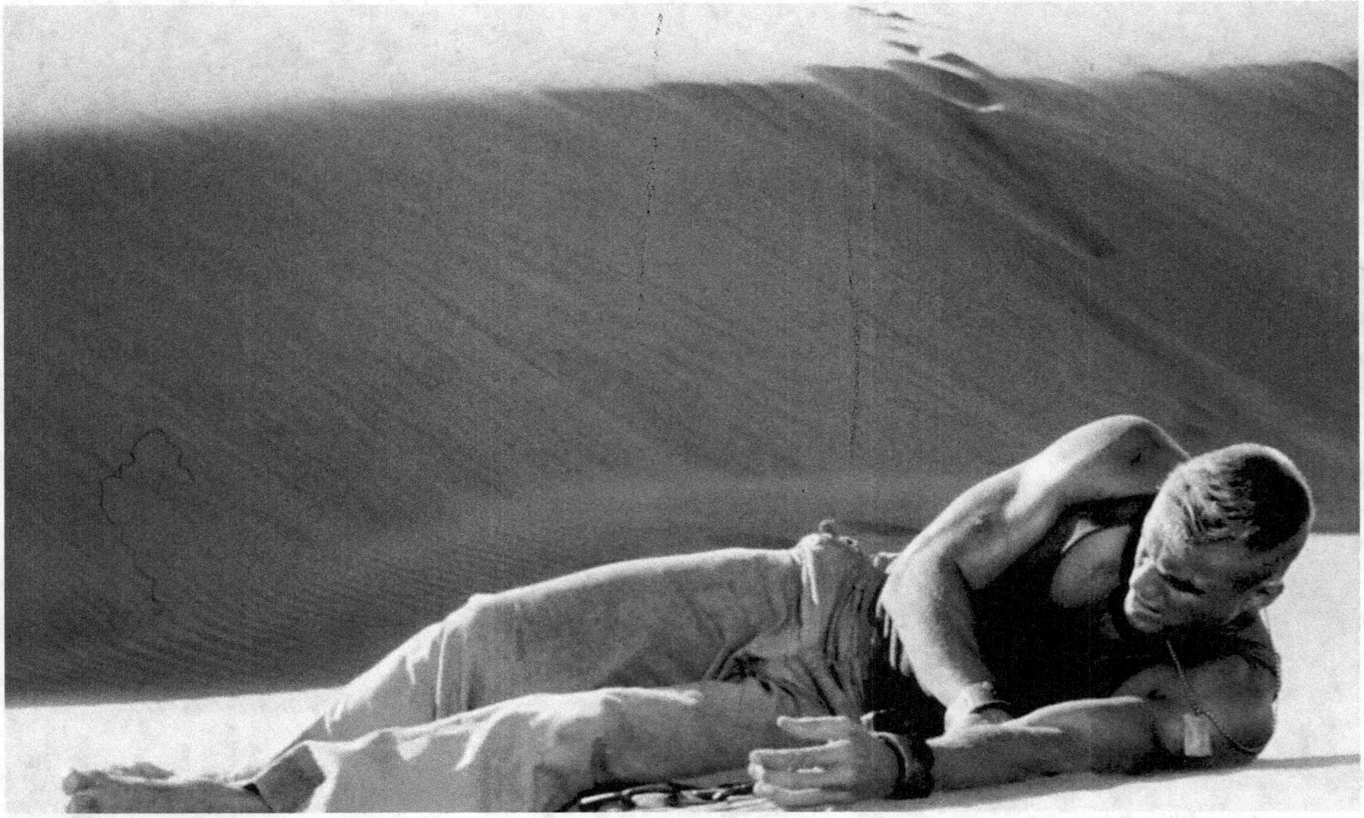

# Stephanie Denton

Stephanie Denton started her sales career at SGE, working closely with Alan Solomon, and quickly became very successful. Her years at SGE trained her well, and she moved on to become President of International Sales at such companies as Lakeshore Entertainment, Initial Entertainment, and Lions Gate International. Among many other deals, she was highly involved in distributing the notorious SAW franchise, which gained a cult-following worldwide. Currently she is president of New Cadence Entertainment.

**Nadia:** Ms. Denton, how did you join the movie industry, was it a particular thing that lead you into it, or was it always your plan? Where were you born and raised?

**Stephanie:** I didn't really think about being in the "film business" when I was a kid. I was definitely passionate about movies, but when I left my home in Las Vegas, Nevada in 1986 to move to L.A., it was because there was an amazing music scene here at the time, and I hoped to find a way into the music industry. I spent my first few years in L.A. working odds and end jobs and seeing different bands almost every night, but didn't find any long term employment opportunities in music. On a bit of a fluke, one day I went in to interview for a temp job at a production/distribution company called I.R.C., and I've been in the business ever since.

**Nadia:** When did you decide that becoming a sales person would be your thing? Did you have artistic ambitions as well; directing, shooting or writing films on your own?

**Stephanie:** I had an amazing experience at IRC and moved up from answering phones and doing script coverage, into assisting the sales department and then doing my own smaller territory sales. It was a quick trajectory, but my boss at the time, Sandy Cobe, told me once that he knew the minute he saw me close my first deal that I would be hooked, and he was right.

**Nadia:** When did you join SGE and how long did you stay there? How much importance has the SGE era had in your personal career? Did you learn about the business there?

**Stephanie:** SGE was my second job in the business, and the two years I spent there working under Alan Solomon in International Sales, played an integral part in my growth in the business. Alan wasn't always "easy", but he had a big heart and was one of the smartest people I have ever worked for. He was meticulous in the way he handled his deals and, coming from a legal background, he taught all of us to be incredibly "buttoned up" in our dealings. I think this gave us all a real leg up as it provided us with an in depth understanding of the deals themselves.

**Nadia:** Please describe your work at SGE, what did a regular day look like? Did you work mostly at the company itself or were you on location of the shoots as well?

**Stephanie:** The days at SGE were really amazing for me personally, as I made several close friends that I still keep in touch with to this day. I wasn't on any of the sets for production, so my day to day was really more about finishing up the deals we had closed at the markets and then turning around and prepping for the next one (market) a month later. We had a lot of films, and we sold strongly into all of the markets, so there was a huge amount of time spent keeping all of that paperwork organized.

**Nadia:** Did you travel a lot for SGE business?

**Stephanie:** My role in sales kept me on the road, going to festivals and markets, 6-8 times a year. It was an incredibly busy time, and SGE had some very strong action titles that buyers would line up to come in and buy. The market was incredibly buoyant at that time. We used to joke that you could sell your own home movies to the video distributors if you had a good editor and a car chase.

**Nadia:** Do you have a favorite film, produced by SGE? Were you in close contact with the creative people like directors and writers at all?

**Stephanie:** We sold a lot of fun titles. I guess MANIAC COP would be my favorite of the more popular titles SGE produced, but my all-time favorite was definitely FRANKENHOOKER. Talk about a tagline… 'A terrifying tale of sluts and bolts' HAHAHAHAHA! Which leads to my anecdote below…

**Nadia:** Any anecdotes, you like to share about the SGE era?

**Stephanie:** I have two - The first would have to be when I walked into the Principe bar during MIFED and 30+ drunken buyers, all wearing their light up FRANKENHOOKER pins, got up and yelled "WANNA DATE, GOING OUT, GOT ANY MONEY??" (which was a famous quote from the film). It was epic.
The second was when Alan Solomon bought me 4th row tickets to go to La Scala. Of course it was the day after he threatened to send me home from Italy in the middle of the market because I was having too much FUN, but nevertheless, it was a grand and very memorable gesture that I will never forget.

**Nadia:** What happened after SGE was shut down? What was the next career step?

**Stephanie:** I left prior to SGE closing, and went to work for my old boss from IRC, Steven Karash, at his new sales company, ULYSSE Entertainment.

**Nadia:** You were involved in the worldwide marketing of the notorious SAW series. How did that come about, are you still working with Lions Gate Entertainment?

**Stephanie:** I haven't worked at LGE since 2007, but was definitely fortunate to sell the SAW franchise. The producers of the film made something really special when they came up with the concept of SAW (1), and it was great to see a truly "indie" low budget film, turn into the behemoth franchise that it's become. It was my first time working on a franchise of that level and the marketing tie-ins were just amazing.

**Nadia:** As a producer you participated at films like MADHOUSE and SKINWALKERS. Are you personally into horror films, do you like to watch them?

**Stephanie:** Although I'm not much for the slasher "torture porn" horror that's been popular over the last few years, I love the horror/thriller genre and have always really enjoyed putting those films together. I'm a total nerd/fan of both visual and practical effects so I love that piece of it, but I also really enjoy working with a lot of the writers and directors in this space. Whether they're putting together the rules and building a "world" or just finding creative ways to scare the hell out of the audience, they're a pretty interesting group.

**Nadia:** How much has changed in your job, comparing nowadays to the days of SGE?

**Stephanie:** The simple answer would be to say that the "boom" days of the video markets are long since gone, so it's much harder to do the kind of numbers we used to back in those days. There is no longer the same need for "product" that there was then, and the buyers are much more selective. It's harder. Period. There's less demand and the margins are lower so if you don't have the right script and the right package, you're not going to make any of the overflow sales that we used to be able to pull off back in the SGE days. That said, I believe that, in the end, this business is all about relationships and content. If you have those two things, it's still a great business to be in.

**Nadia:** Do you care about critics and film journalism? Do you read about the films you are working with? And do you think there is still some importance of film criticism, is it influencing the economic success of a picture?

**Stephanie:** I think critics will always matter to more to the independent film companies, than they will to the studios. Of course no one wants a bad review, but I think it doesn't have quite the same effect when you're dealing with films that have studio releases in the US. I've seen a lot of films with awful reviews, still make a boat load of money because the studio backed the release with P+A.

**Nadia:** You worked a lot of times with Darren Lynn Bousman. Are you still in contact?

**Stephanie:** I worked on a few films with Darren and definitely had a great experience. We're not in touch really, but I think he is a good filmmaker and a really good guy.

**Nadia:** Are there many intersections of private life and work life, did you became friends with a lot of people from the business?

**Stephanie:** Absolutely. I practically grew up in this business so there are people that I've known for 30 years at this point, some that I still see when I go to markets. In that respect, I feel really fortunate because I've made real friends, all over the world. Some of my best friends today are people I met through this business. How cool is that?

**Nadia:** There's No Business Like Show Business - except the film business. What do you love most, and what do you hate most about your job?

**Stephanie:** I love the people I've been fortunate enough to meet, and all of the wonderful places I've been, and helping people I believe in get their films made. I hate the fact that there never seem to be enough hours in the day to spend time with, go to, or do all of the things that I love.

By Nadia Bruce-Rawlings, in writing
in Los Angeles, California
19July, 2015

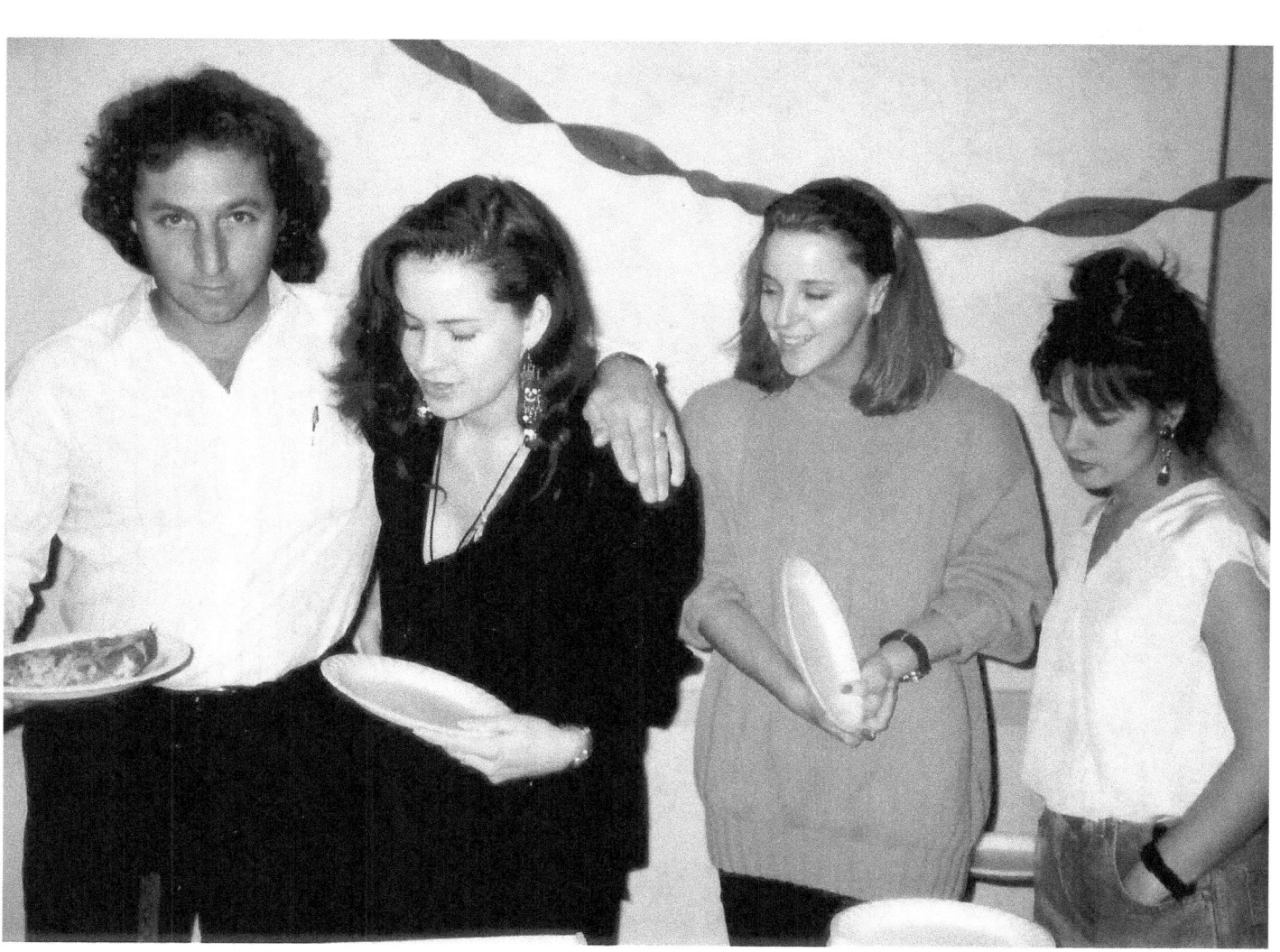

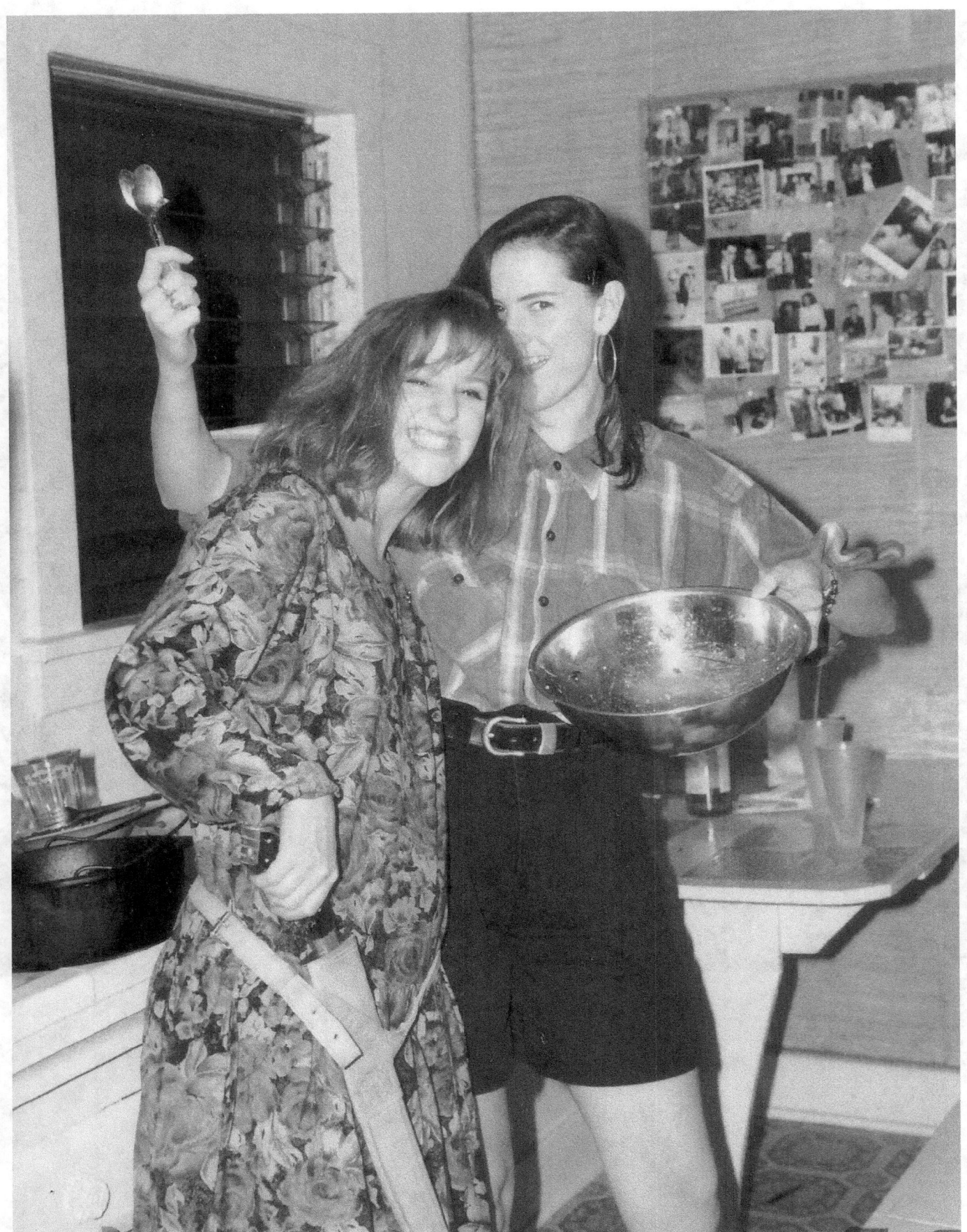

# Bob Berney

Bob Berney was in charge of marketing and publicity for SGE's US domestic theatrical division that operated in the late 80s. The division's biggest and premier title was RED SCORPION, which had a national release of approximately 1200 prints. Berney also oversaw a number of domestic regional theatrical releases including MOONTRAP, THE WIZARD OF SPEED AND TIME and others. After SGE, Berney continued an enormously successful career. His work includes some of the biggest American independent films in history, among them THE PASSION OF CHRIST, MY BIG FAT GREEK WEDDING, PAN'S LABYRINTH, LA VIE EN ROSE, DRIVE and many more. He headed the internationally acclaimed distribution company Picturehouse in 2005, founded as a joint venture between HBO and New Line Cinema. Picturehouse was shut down in 2008 but was revived by Bob Berney in 2013, including a partnership with Netflix. He has most recently been appointed head of movie marketing and distribution by Amazon Studios.

**Marco:** Prior to working with SGE in the 1980s, how would you describe your career at that juncture? Where, and how, did you learn your skills? Did you have a formal education in the movie business (for example, university) or did you learn by doing?

**Bob:** I went to University of Texas at Austin and studied film production and history with a B.S. degree in Radio-Television-Film. During college I was also a projectionist and theatre manager and went on to manage movie theatres for AMC Theatres. I moved to Dallas and managed and programmed the Inwood Theatre, an art house theatre that was one of the first movie theatres with a bar and restaurant. (The Inwood is currently owned by Marc Cuban's Landmark Theatre Chain). We hosted many film festivals and community events at the theatre including The USA Film Festival and Joe Bob Brigg's Drive-In Film Festival. I was recruited to join FilmDallas, a local production company that also moved into distribution. New World Pictures ended up buying the company and we moved to Los Angeles but as soon as we arrived, New World exited the film business to focus on Television and I began looking for new opportunities in distribution and marketing in Los Angeles.

**Marco:** You were in charge of marketing and publicity for SGE's short-lived US domestic theatrical division that existed in the late-1980s. What's the story on how you became employed at SGE?

**Bob:** I was working with several sub-distributors (independent theatrical sales teams) around the country at FilmDallas and in those discussions I heard that Lenny Shapiro was considering gearing up for RED SCORPION. Lenny called and we started discussing the plans for the film and the SGE operation.

**Marco:** SGE's theatrical division's best known, and biggest title (in fact perhaps the purpose for its founding) was the feature RED SCORPION (1989). This film had a US domestic release of approximately 1200 prints, a sizable theatrical release for the time. Do you remember what your impression was when you screened the movie for the very first time?

**Bob:** The film had a big look for indie films at the time and featured Dolph Lundgren, who was valuable in the international market, and he had many fans in the U.S. market as well. Also featured in the film was the iconic Soviet "Hind" attack helicopter that I thought gave the film its key image. At that time, there were few films available for independent distribution that could actually hold up to a wide release, and I thought this one had a shot.

**Marco:** RED SCORPION was discussed widely in the media at the time of its release. Were you aware of this controversy? And if so, were you fearful in any way, in terms of the release's business success potential, because of the movie's perceived political implications?

**Bob:** I wasn't too worried about the implications on the release because by the time the film came to SGE, it has already gone through the controversy and had fallen out of the Warner Bros release schedule. The action movie fans responding to the explosions in the trailer for the film were not discussing the behind the scenes politics of the production.

**Marco:** You are close friends with Leonard Shapiro for a long time, is this correct? How did you and he meet for the first time? Are you and Mr. Shapiro still in close touch?

**Bob:** I've known Lenny since the late 80s. Although we probably met at Cannes and AFM previously, I met with him in 1988-89 as we discussed RED SCORPION and also the on-going theatrical distribution operation that he and Jim were planning.

**Marco:** Can you describe what it was like working with Leonard Shapiro at SGE?

**Bob:** It was like being in one of the FAST & FURIOUS movies. I met lots of characters and things were changing rapidly as we worked against the clock to pull a team together and get the movie ready for a wide release. In the middle of it all, though, Lenny was calm and decisive. He was the ultimate optimist and believer in the film and the independent business. On a personal level, he was and is a wonderful guy, a true mensch that really cared about his employees and friends in the business.

**Marco:** At what point did you begin to work with your wife Jeanne? Did the two of you meet in connection with work-related circumstances?

**Bob:** Jeanne and I met in Dallas when I operated the Inwood Theatre. She managed a band and rented the theatre for a performance and fashion event. Later when she ran the Film & Digital Entertainment Group of Rogers & Cowan Public Relations, she worked on several film projects that I distributed over the years. In recent years, we worked together at FilmDistrict and the new Picturehouse, and that has been a fantastic experience.

**Marco:** Before you moved to Los Angeles to work with SGE, among other things, you were an art house theater manager and programmer. So, is it a safe assumption

|   |   |
|---|---|
| | that you have a lifelong connection to motion pictures in general? |
| **Bob:** | Yes, I can never escape! |
| **Marco:** | What happened after SGE? What was your next career step? |
| **Bob:** | I joined TRITON films with Jonathan Dana, Bobby Rock and Jeff Ivers. We handled some beautiful art films including A BRIEF HISTORY OF TIME where we had Stephen Hawking come to Los Angeles for a premiere at the Academy. |
| **Marco:** | Have you moved a lot over the years? Did you spend time outside of the USA or have you always lived in America? |
| **Bob:** | In 2001, I was hired to start IFC Films distribution and the company moved our family from Los Angeles to New York, and I've lived there since then. At IFC Films, we distributed some amazing films including Y TU MAMÁ TAMBIÉN and MY BIG FAT GREEK WEDDING. |
| **Marco:** | In 2005 you and some partners founded the company Picturehouse. The movies distributed there enjoyed significant financial and critical success. At the time of Picturehouse's founding did you feel like you were realizing your very own 'dream' company? |
| **Bob:** | Prior to Picturehouse, I formed Newmarket Films with two other partners. At Newmarket Films, we released THE PASSION OF THE CHRIST, which is still the highest grossing independently released film of all time. Other titles included WHALE RIDER and MONSTER (Charlize Theron won the Best Actress Academy Award for MONSTER). Later the Newmarket Films distribution team in NY was sold to New Line Films and HBO Films and re-named Picturehouse. |
| **Marco:** | It seems like the business philosophy of the company was highly focused on presenting a tasteful catalogue of high-class films, would you say this is accurate? |
| **Bob:** | The idea behind Newmarket Films and Picturehouse was to find quality films with substantial audiences not being served by the larger studios. |
| **Marco:** | Please tell me about your time with Newmarket Films. There you were a partner and served as President, is this correct? Were you in charge of the deals for THE PASSION OF THE CHRIST, MY BIG FAT GREEK WEDDING, MEMENTO and the other independent super hits that went through Newmarket? |
| **Bob:** | I was a partner/founder and President of Newmarket Films. We released PASSION OF THE CHRIST, WHALE RIDER, MONSTER, REAL WOMAN HAVE CURVES, and many other titles. We did not release GREEK WEDDING, that was when I was with IFC Films. MEMENTO was released by Newmarket Films but before we actually formed the company. It was done as a "one-off" project when I was still starting IFC Films. |
| **Marco:** | In 2013 Picturehouse was revived by you -- for this comeback, a partnership with Netflix was secured. Was the Netflix deal the reason for setting up the company again? |

**Bob:** Netflix was certainly one of the key reasons but I wanted to work with Jeanne and have our own company. Netflix and Universal Studios Home Entertainment have been great partners for Picturehouse.

**Marco:** Do you prefer working with a number of partners on a long-term basis? Are you still in business with people you met during your SGE time for example? If so, can you describe the nature of that cooperation?

**Bob:** Yes, I prefer to keep the team together as much as possible. For example, John and Lange have worked with me for many years. John worked on RED SCORPION and Dan joined around the release of THE PASSION OF THE CHRIST.

**Marco:** Would you say that Video-On-Demand (VOD) is an emerging dominant main distribution method for movies?

**Bob:** There is a trend to "day & date" releases with minimal theatrical on the same day as VOD and digital release. It's been growing in the indie sector but seems still to be a way off for the studio films; however, the changes and trends are clear.

**Marco:** Are there more risks for piracy in the present times than before?

**Bob:** Absolutely, larger companies are going in all markets globally to try to counter piracy, it's a huge issue.

**Marco:** Over your career, you have worked with so many different films of almost every kind. In your opinion, what's the difference between selling an action or horror movie, meaning 'genre films', compared to those from well-known auteurs like Robert Altman?

**Bob:** It's all about connecting the film with the audience and targeting the marketing rather than using a shotgun approach and buying everything. The genre films we have worked on were much bigger releases (MONGOL, INSIDIOUS, DON'T BE AFRAID OF THE DARK, DRIVE) than some of the platform releases but also were very director driven. The filmmaker focus at Picturehouse is what connects the genre films to the auteur directors, they are all strong storytellers.

**Marco:** Picturehouse is distributing documentaries, besides its features, are documentaries more easy to sell internationally?

**Bob:** We are really not doing that many documentaries yet. We did release METALLICA - THROUGH THE NEVER, but that film was really a hybrid feature; a concert with narrative story and not a traditional music documentary.

**Marco:** Can you talk a little bit about which projects you have finalized recently? What's your main focus at the moment?

**Bob:** We are working on GLORIA, a Mexican production directed by Christian Keller. It's a biopic about Gloria Trevi, one of the biggest pop/rock icons in Latin America. Her story is very controversial and dramatic and the actress, Sofia Espinosa, is garnering great reviews for her portrayal of "the Mexican Madonna."

Picturehouse is also releasing BIG STONE GAP by writer/director Adriani Tagliani. She based the film on her best-selling series of books about life in the small Virginia town of Big Stone Gap. The film stars Ashley Judd, Patrick Wilson and Whoopi Goldberg.

**Marco:** Looking back the 25 or so years to your time at SGE, if you had to pick one main thing, how would you say the independent movie business changed?

**Bob:** In those early SGE days, the "indie" business was still really considered to be on the fringes of Hollywood. Only brave executives like Lenny Shapiro and Jim Glickenhaus would take on wide release films that really competed with the studios. They both had had success and beat the system before and were up for the challenge. Over the years, the independent sector has really become a key factor in the worldwide film business. There is no ceiling and audiences around the world don't really differentiate between studio or indie films. Good movies of any budget or scope can really connect with audiences worldwide. I believe that one of the key moments in the indie history was when I was at Newmarket Films and we released THE PASSION OF THE CHRIST on close to 4000 screens and broke box office records.

**Marco:** Do you have any anecdotal stories you'd like to share about your SGE days?

**Bob:** One of my favorite memories was going to New York to the set of FRANKENHOOKER, a film that Jim was producing for Frank Henenlotter, a local NY filmmaker proud to be called an "exploitation director." It was chaotic fun, and they were also making a sequel to his earlier film BASKET CASE that I had played back in the day at the midnight shows at the Inwood Theatre. Lenny was such a force and a believer in any project he was behind. His enthusiasm was both crazy and infectious. He really made you want to do everything for the films, they had to work! Jim was a truly unique character in the NY films scene with offices in the Brill building, and he often came down the Hudson River in a classic cigar boat to work. Together, he and Lenny were a power team. When we first moved to Los Angeles, and I began working at SGE, Jeanne was pregnant with Sean. I'll never forget being in Cedars-Sinai hospital and seeing this huge plant with flowers and balloons delivered to the room from Lenny and all the gang at SGE. It made us really feel welcome to the city and to a great group of friends and colleagues. We kept that plant in our house for a long time and it grew into a beautiful tree, a great reminder of my time with Lenny and friends at SGE.

By Marco Siedelmann, in writing
from New York, New York
20May, 2015

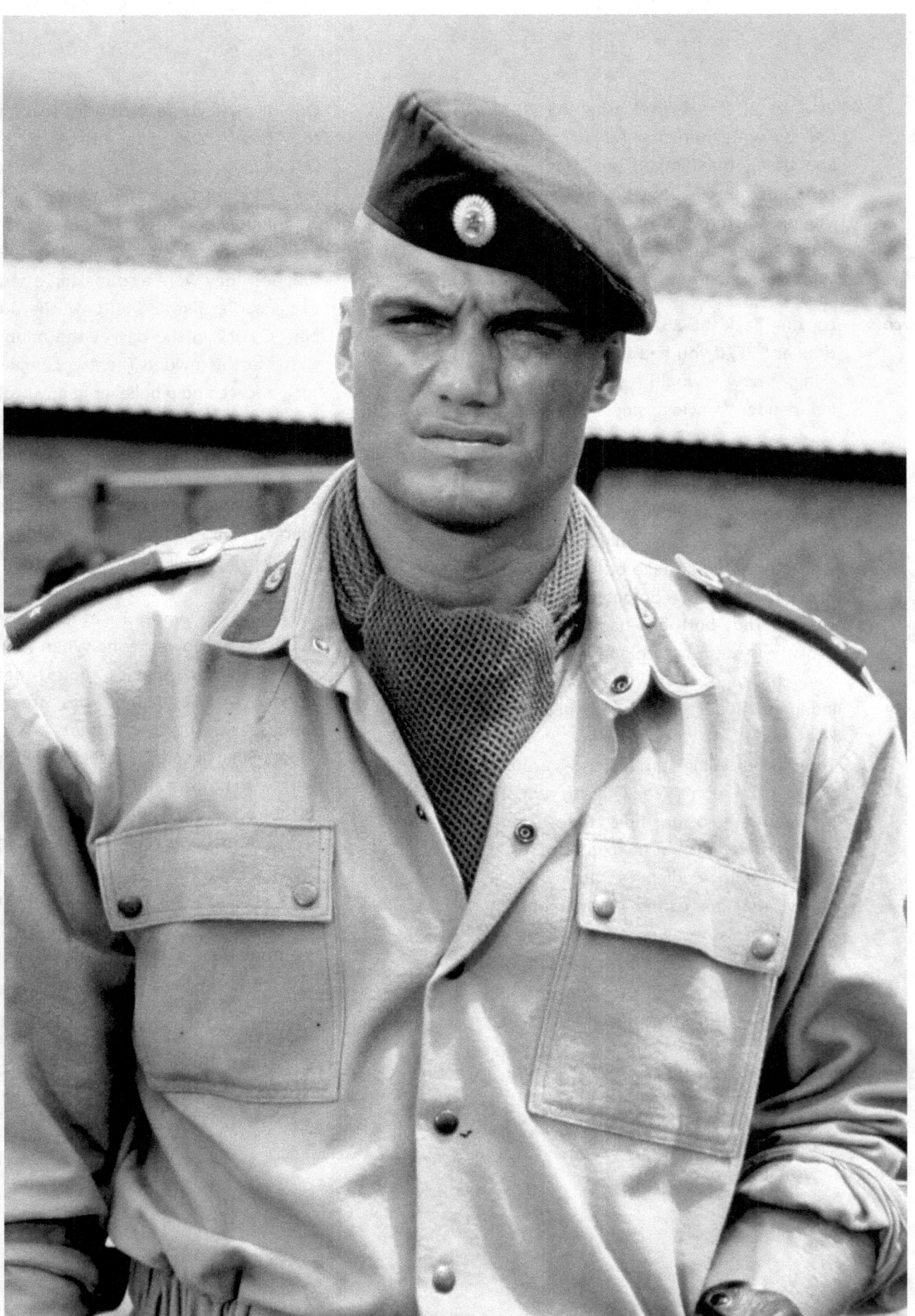

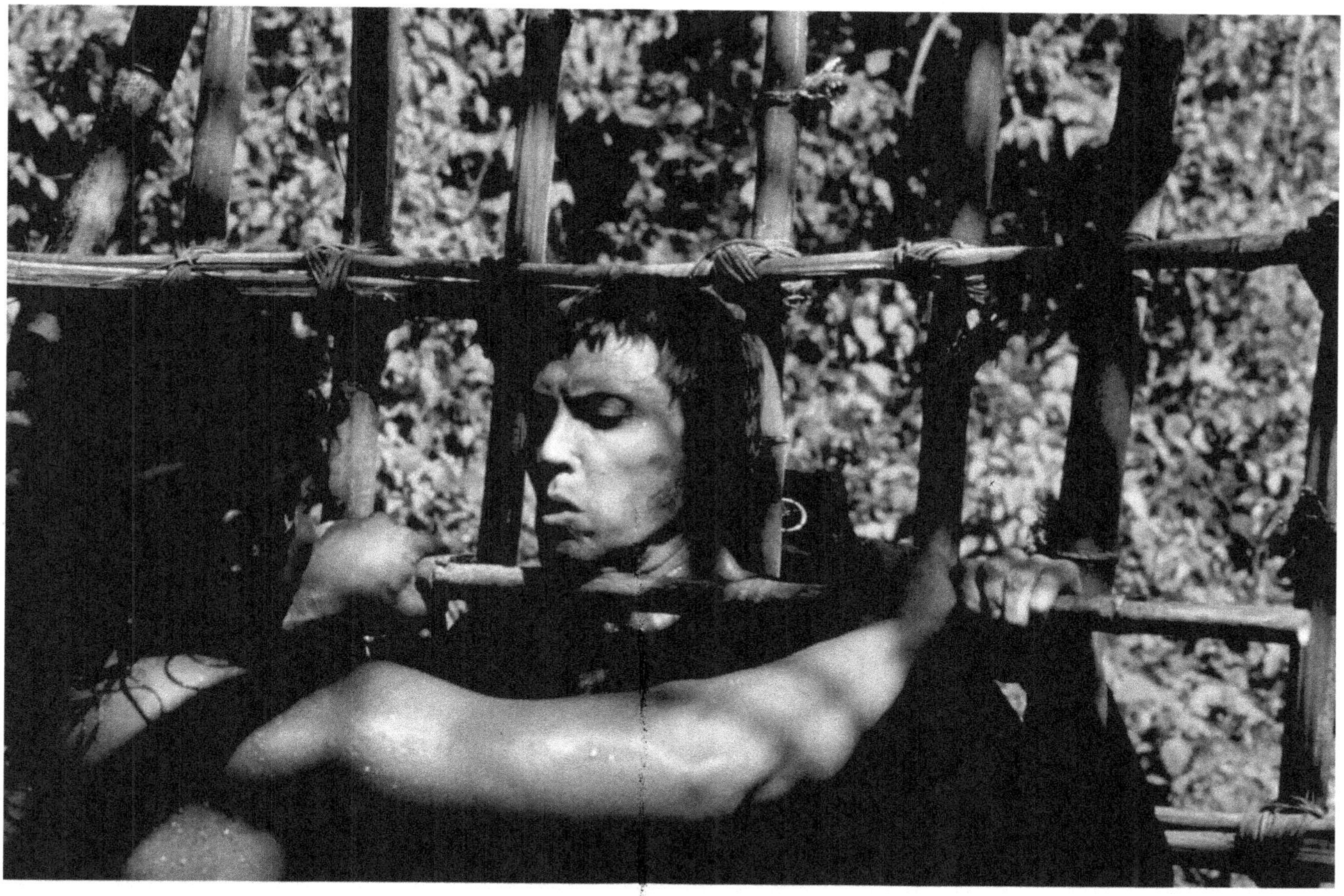

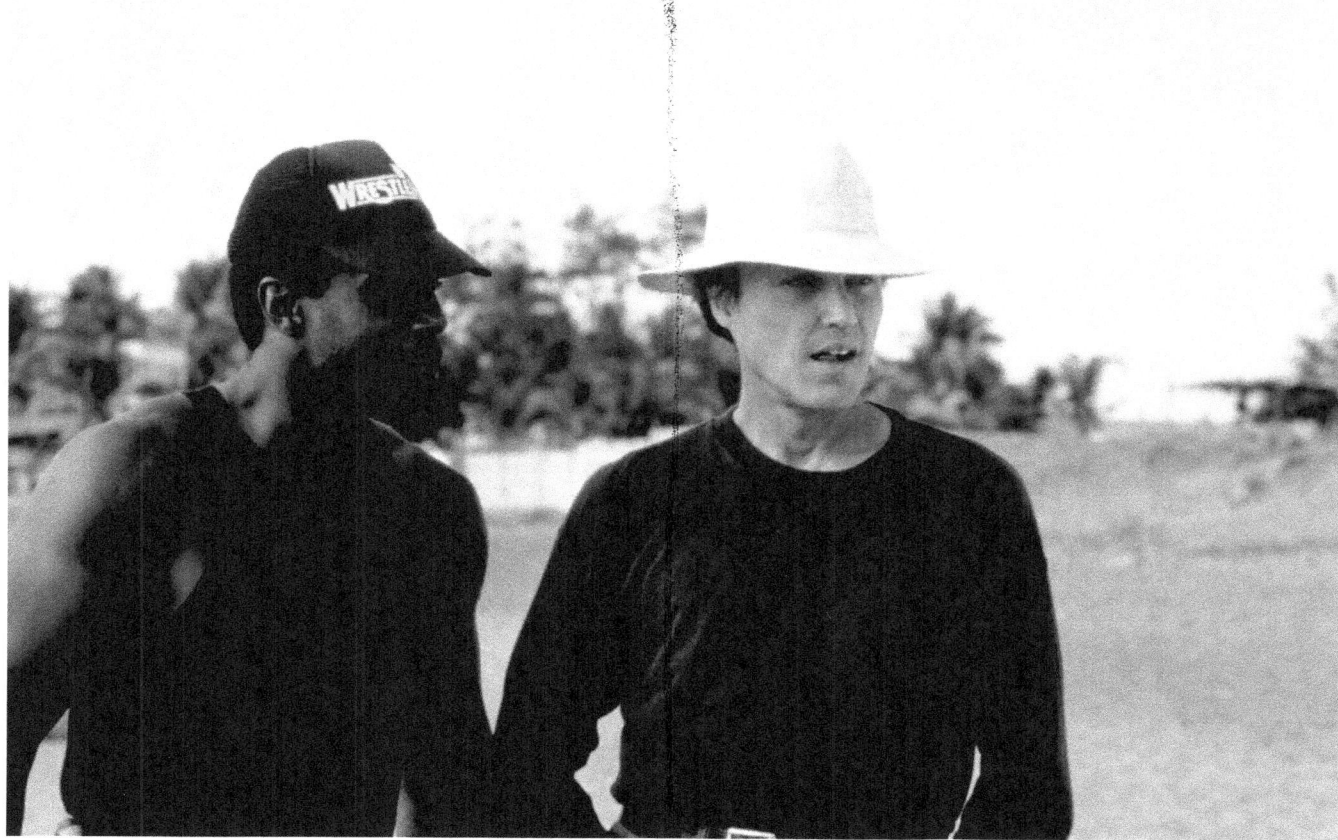

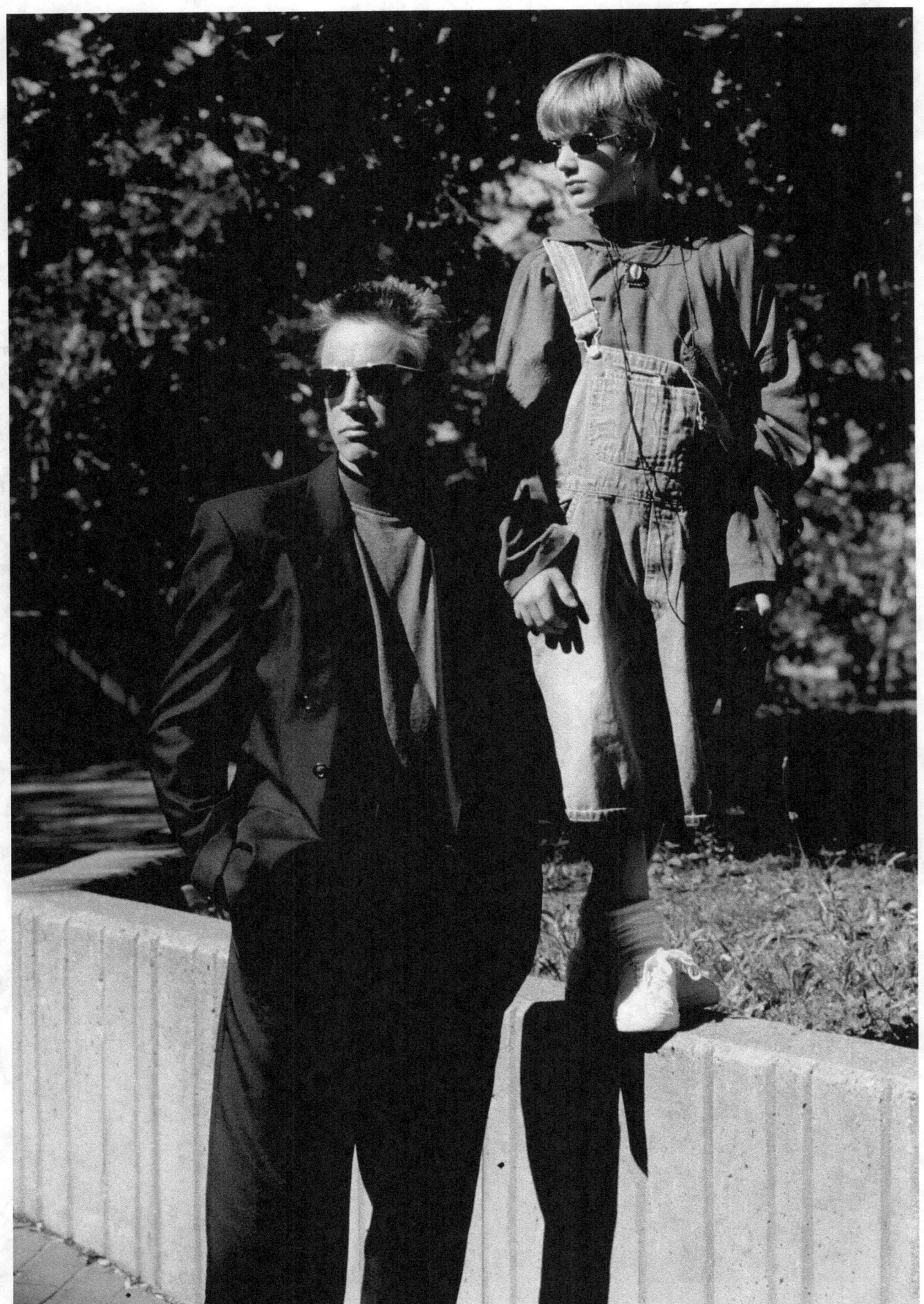

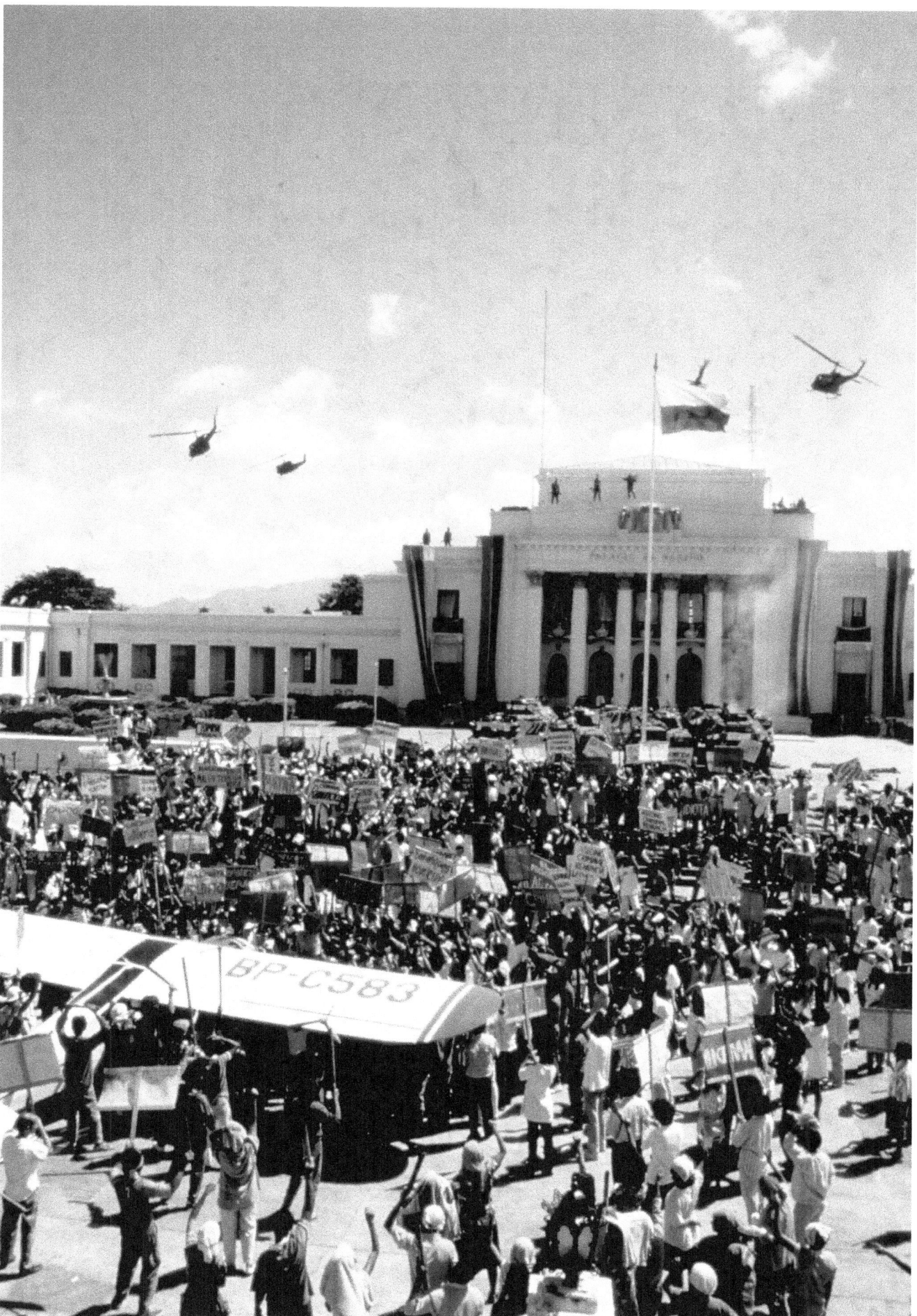

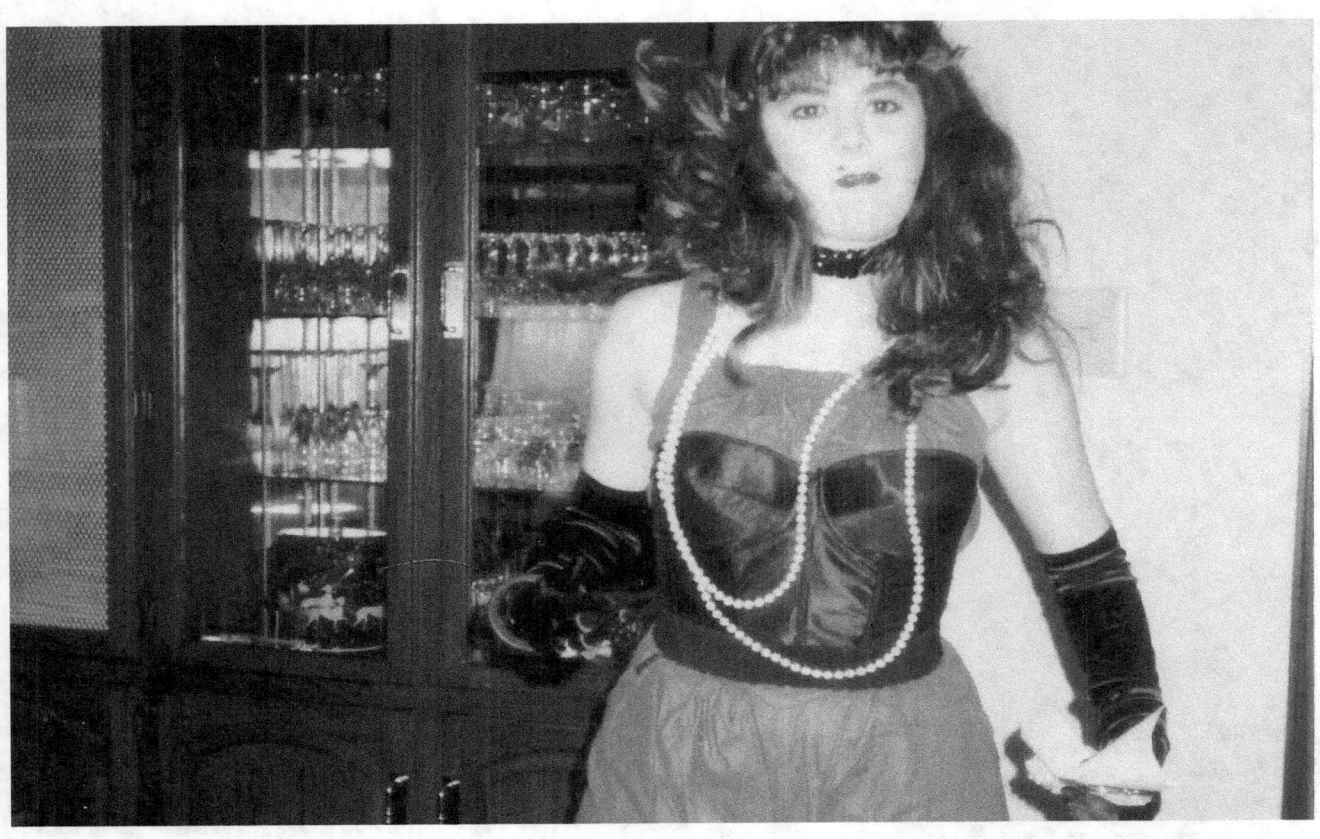

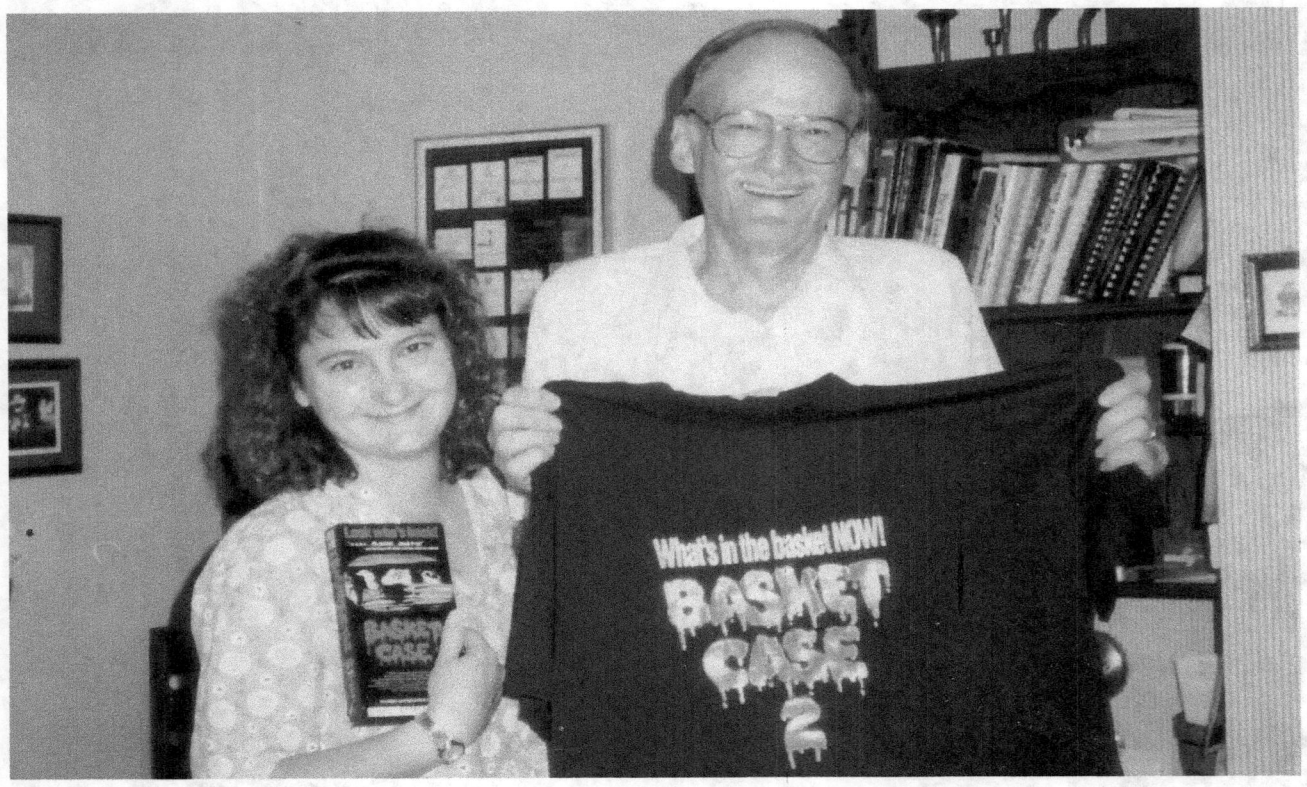

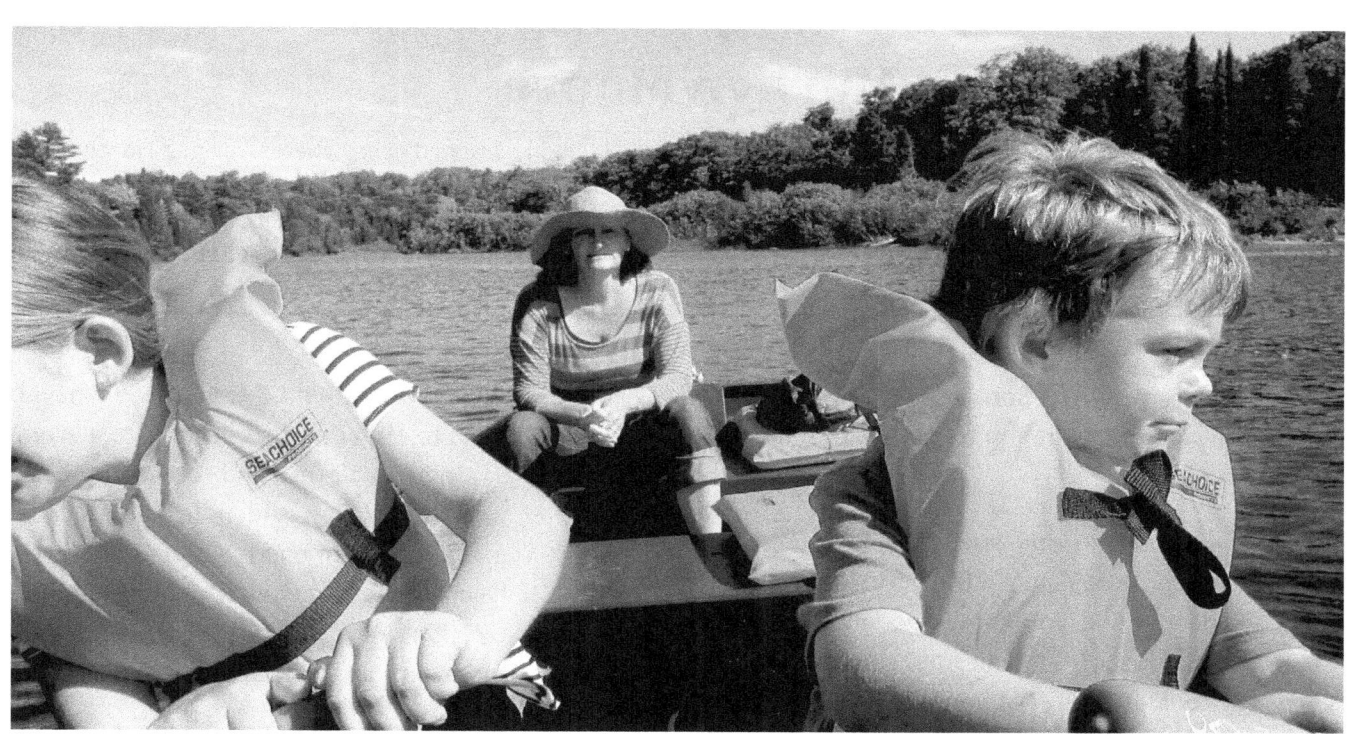

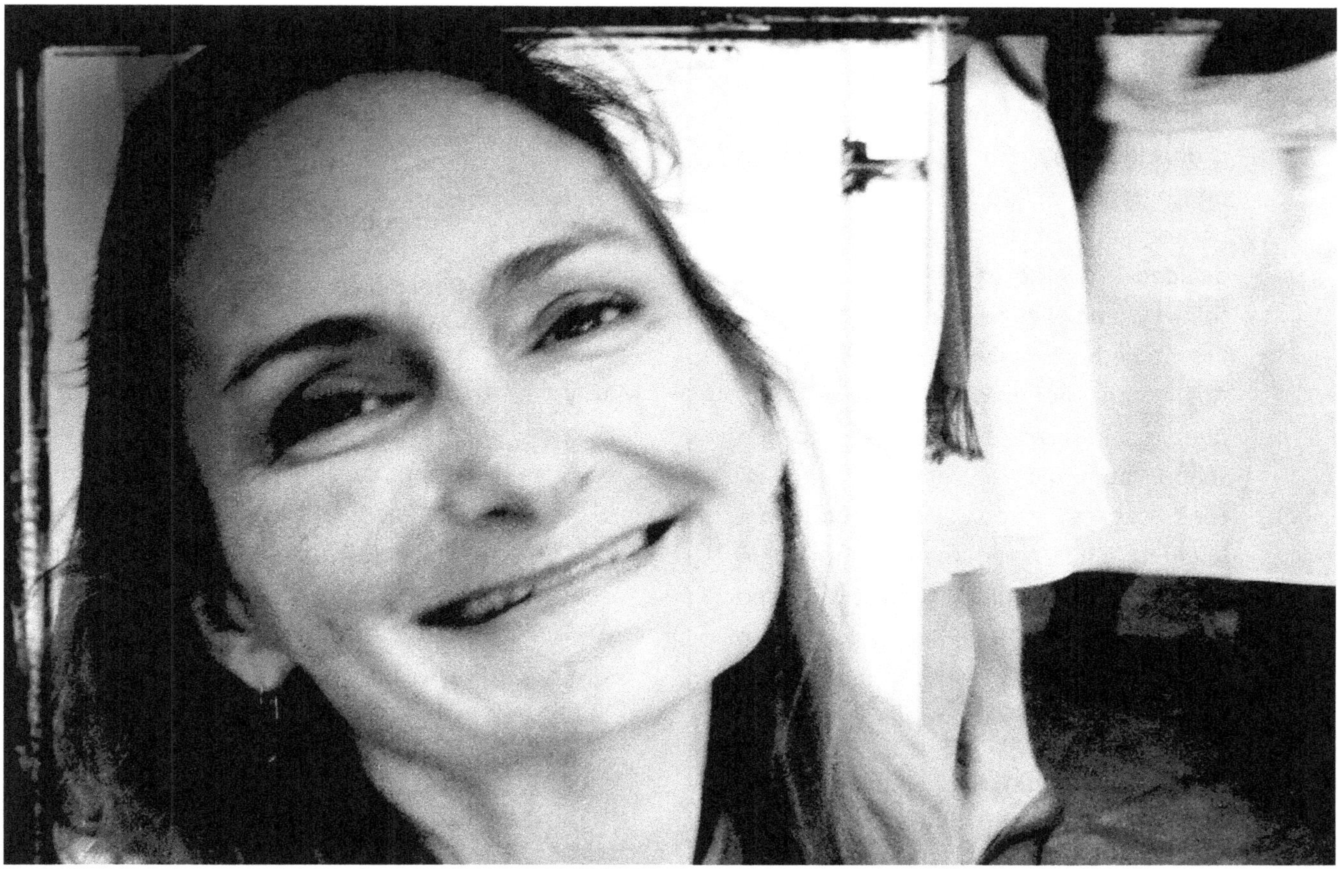

# Marilyn Moore

Marilyn Moore was trained at SGE as Acquisitions Director, but she actually assisted everywhere, working closely with Frank K. Isaac and with the heads of the company. She graduated from film school with an emphasis in Editing, and after leaving SGE, Marilyn was an assistant editor on many feature films, as well as on many television series - among them the THE X-FILES. Later on she was editor on AMERICA'S NEXT TOP MODEL for more than 12 years. Married with two children, Marilyn recently moved to Lansing, Michigan.

**Nadia:** Where were you born and raised? Was it always your dream to be in the film industry?

**Marilyn:** I was born in Houston TX, and raised in southern Lousiana, in Lafayette and New Orleans. And you know, working in the film industry --- it didn't occur to me that it could actually happen, that my dream could come true! It was just something I loved, going to the movies. The impact of films in my life. Like THE DEER HUNTER, had a huge impact, witnessing this history. I just could never get enough movies. And then I did photography in high school, and I decided maybe I wanted to go to photography school. I started out in photography at Texas A&M, and then decided I wanted to study film. I didn't think I would ever be able to work in film! I switched to University of Texas, in Austin, and got into film school there. People said it was hard to get into film school, but I did it! I fortunately got in, took lots of Theory, Film Production, loved it all! Started making movies in college, but still, I didn't think it would go anywhere. I mean, what you take in college hardly ever turns into a career, right? Yes...so my dreams came true!

**Nadia:** So why/how did you move to Los Angeles?

**Marilyn:** Well, it was either LA or NY, and I'd never been to either place. I decided to start in Southern California, and I drove out there with a fellow film student from UT, a class mate, so we moved out without ever having visited, moved in with some other UT film makers, you know...renting a room without a job, and there I was.

**Nadia:** That's how I actually got to LA...drove out there, without a job and no idea what I was going to do there, with like 25 bucks to my name! Funny...

**Marilyn:** Yeah! You have no idea, you have to be young and stupid to be able to make that dream happen! And to you know, realize your dreams on very little!

**Nadia:** So how did you start at SGE? Weren't you interning somewhere?

**Marilyn:** Actually no! After UT I went for six months to London and worked there at a greeting cards company, lived there, struggling financially, and I knew after that I would go back to Lafayette and then drive to LA. So there I was in LA, and I looked through Variety and the Hollywood Reporter, through the classifieds, and I saw an ad for an International Sales Assistant at a company but it didn't say SGE on it. I thought Ah! International! I just came back from living abroad, maybe I can do this! It's perfect. Ha. I knew nothing about International Sales, but I applied for the job and sure enough got a call from Shapiro Glickenhaus, for an interview, and I remember writing down the name of the company...I had the interview on a Monday. And over that weekend, I remembered the name, and I went to a movie and a trailer came on for RED SCORPION, oh wow...yeah. I was like, haha, look at this movie, action/adventure. Not the type of movie I was drawn to, just not my kind of thing. And at the end of the trailer, there was the company name...Shapiro Glickenhaus Entertainment! And I said, wow, that's where I'm interviewing on Monday. RED SCORPION. So that's how that job came up. The interview was with Alan Solomon.

**Nadia:** I remember you coming in, actually, we were all talking about you. Ha.

**Marilyn:** You were?! Oh gosh, one came in through those glass doors and that marble desk, and that round couch, in the reception area! The beautiful 4th floor, suite 404! So I interviewed with Alan, and you know, I had no experience. He knew I was not the right person at all, but he wanted to meet me because I had just lived in London, and he was from Great Britain, and he wanted to talk with me about it and see what I was all about. Fortunately he was curious! He said, you know what, this job is not right for you, but...we have another job available. Assistant to Acquisitions, to Frank Isaac, and you can interview with him, for that position. And I was like "Wow! Sure!" So it just worked out, just because Alan was curious to meet this person who had lived in his country. *[laughs]* He knew I knew nothing other than having a film degree. He wanted to know if I had any typing skills I think.

**Nadia:** That's so funny. I remember because I think at the time I was Frank's assistant.

**Marilyn:** That's right! That's how that worked out. You got moved up to the International Sales position, and I got your job! I remember you training me, in that little room.

**Nadia:** What was your main job during that period? How long did you work there?

**Marilyn:** So yes, I worked there from 1989 to 1991, for about 2.5 years. The beginning of the RED SCORPION release, until the end of 1991. My job the whole time was working in Acquisitions. That entailed working with Frank Isaac. Doing contracts, putting in percentages – he would stand over my shoulder and tell me exactly what to type for the domestic deals. And then reading scripts, lots of scripts. Going to the American Film Market as a presence, basically, to teach me about it, which I'm so grateful for. I would go to the Market, go to the screenings for the films that were for sale for foreign. And ...we never bought anything. We were just present – "Hi, we're still here, Shapiro Glickenhaus". And it kept us active, and me active. I read scripts, and I would write a summary, and if anything really stood out I would talk with Frank about it. Kind of

|          | fielding his phone calls, etc. It was a perfectly good entry level job! |
|---|---|
| **Nadia**: | According to the regular databases, your first film credit was on the cult-favorite sci-fi-action film, INTERCEPTOR. Did you work closely with director Michael Cohn? |
| **Marilyn**: | Michael Cohn was coincidentally an instructor of mine at UT in Austin, TX. Yes, he taught directing. So I knew him from UT, however it was just a coincidence that I got hired on as an assistant editor. That was 1992. What happened, is that these two producers bought all this fighter footage, airplane footage, and decided to make a movie where they could use this plane fighter footage, you know!? So, Michael Cohn was the director, and that was my very first...oh yes, the editor was Glenn Morgan, and I was his assistant. That was my first paid assistant job. I ended up working with him on at least 4 more movies. He became, certainly, an editing mentor of mine. That was the beginning of a long relationship with him. |
| **Nadia**: | You worked very closely with Frank Isaac at SGE. Did you become personal friends, or is he something like a mentor for you? |
| **Marilyn**: | We did not become friends, really – he was all business. He wasn't really a mentor, he didn't really share that much of his knowledge. I didn't inquire that much. He was very kind, and very good at what he did. I didn't get the benefits of his knowledge. But I trusted him! That was one thing, that Lenny and Alan did very well – they hired great people to work in their office, and created a very symbiotic relationship with their employees, and they – we cared about them! It was a great environment to work in. Lenny always was kind and included me in meetings, like pre-production meetings and he was so generous to invite us in to his office and his meetings. I mean, I had nothing to contribute, but I learned so much. It was for my benefit, he was so gracious. Also Len taught classes at UCLA Extension, and he allowed us to go to his classes for free that he taught. He was a wonderful instructor for UCLA Extension, and he did that out of the goodness of his heart as well. So many students came into his class. He didn't have time! But he did it! It was certainly all for our benefit, which benefitted our company. |
| **Nadia**: | Were you in touch with SGE people, on a business level, until SGE was shut down in 1995? What did you learn working there? |
| **Marilyn**: | On a business level, no, but friends...we bloomed into life-long friends. And the beginning of a life-long career in film. I worked in production and I got a taste of the business aspect, of contracts and such, while at SGE, and I decided I wanted to venture into editing. I had done some in college, but I wanted to really do it seriously. I made some phone calls, interviewing some editors that we had used on SGE films, and one of them was Kevin Tent. I gave him a call and asked him about his career and any advice he could give me. I knew I would begin as an apprentice, I was willing to do anything to learn editing. So he was so generous and talked to me for at least an hour. I think at that time he had already edited ELECTION, and he'd done several of |

SGE's films. He was always very approachable, and I admired his work. So anyway, I started a non-paying job as an apprentice editor on a film and then that's when my editing career started!

**Nadia:** You worked as an assistant director and editor to some of the most popular high quality TV series of the late 90s and early 2000s. You worked on X FILES…

**Marilyn:** I started out on sitcoms, and actually on features. I enjoyed that, however it's very laborious — lots of editing changes, the same movie for 7-9 months, and if it's a bad movie, it's rough! You're, you know, you're polishing shit! And you do it for 9 months. And I was always the assistant on the features. And honestly I worked on some amazing features, I loved the ones like THE CRYING GAME, and getting to meet Forrest Whitaker — I got to work on the first feature he directed, which was in 1993, STRAPPED, where I was with Glenn Morgan again. And then some other ones — PANTHER, with Mario and Melvin Van Peebles. They are fabulous. Melvin was an amazing, renessaince man to work with. He actually came over to my house, and he insisted I make him gumbo, because he knew I was from Louisiana. So he was like, "Enough of this, I'm coming over!" He came over with his wife, and I was like, "Yes Sir!" Thank God it turned out really, really, good, the best chicken and sausage gumbo I've ever made. It was so good. So yes, the highlights of assisting in features. But then I wanted to head into higher turn-over, and work in TV, and so I worked on episodes for like two months, then the next one. I worked on sitcoms, then tv hour-long dramas, the most high-profile one was THE X-FILES. A couple of seasons of THE X-FILES. And then I moved into editing, and started on THE INVISIBLE MAN, which was also on the SyFy Network, so that was my first series of editing. Remember? I was out in Burbank working my tail off; I mean, I never saw my son. And then from there I edited on several other shows till they got cancelled. And then AMERICA'S NEXT TOPMODEL came along, and I did that for the next 7 years! And I loved it.

**Nadia:** So that was what you stayed on till you moved out of California.

**Marilyn:** I did, I stayed on it in part because it was Union. I had a goal in mind, I wanted to be vested, which required I think 25,000 hours in 20 years or 15 years in the union, so I wanted to make that my goal. Plus I was having children, I got married, and working on TOP MODEL, I had established a relationship of trust, so I could kind of get there when I got there in the morning, after taking care of my family, and they knew I would get my work done. So it was just a really great job. It is a fun show! Talk of action-adventure! From RED SCORPION to TOP MODEL, I mean I ended up in action-adventure after all! We did not keep you waiting there, it was always something. We wrapped up every episode with lots of entertainment!

**Nadia:** Did you interact with Tyra Banks?

**Marilyn:** I did a little bit, more at the beginning with her coming into the edit room. I worked on the final episode, in Season One. A friend brought me in, because

**they** were crunched for time, and we were working weekends, and Tyra would come in and look at different scenes and such. So yes, I worked with her then, and then she was always very involved. Not so much in the room, she ended up giving us email notes and stuff.

**Nadia:** Nerd question: Isn't it a shame that SERENITY was turned down?

**Marilyn:** Hahahahaa OK. I think that was FIREFLY which was a TV show created by Joss Whedon, I think they changed the name. So it lasted 6 episodes, and I was the assistant editor on that, and it has a huge cult following. Yes, it is a shame! He was an amazing...I didn't realize the cult following he had until then. That was a great six months working with him and the other editors he hired.

**Nadia:** As part of the audience, what kind of movies do you enjoy most? Do you watch a lot of movies and television stuff in private?

**Marilyn:** That question's really hard. I would say, I tend to really like satirical, dark humor films, more along those lines. Go back to BLOOD SIMPLE and the Coen Brothers, FARGO, some of my favorite movies actually are ones that Kevin Tent has edited, Alexander Payne films, um, CITIZEN RUTH, ELECTION, FIVE WAYS, LOST IN TRANSLATION. That's kinda where I can count on being entertained.

**Nadia:** Yes...you and I are not the blockbuster movie audience.

**Marilyn:** *(laughs)* Totally not running out to see...I don't even know what's out there right now! I will watch HARRY POTTER films because of my kids, they read those. We saw, the other day, the George Clooney kids' movie....what's it called... TOMORROW LAND – it was so nonsensical! I liked the message but the execution of the story was so bad. I get so critical of story – with the editing I can sort of play along, but if the story drags, I am like, "Snap to it!" even if someone's talking to me! I want to edit them! Get to the point....! I just get really critical of the story line.

**Nadia:** The final question would be how important was the SGE era to you:

**Marilyn:** It really cemented my time in LA. It was my first paying job, I believe it was $325 a week *(laughs)*. It was the growing of relationships, the feeling like I actually was learning, I was taking everything in, nice families around me. Len and Alan sharing their lives with their employees. It really just had everything to with why I stayed in LA, it just really grounded me.

---

By Nadia Bruce-Rawlings, via telephone
from Lansing, Michigan
20June, 2015

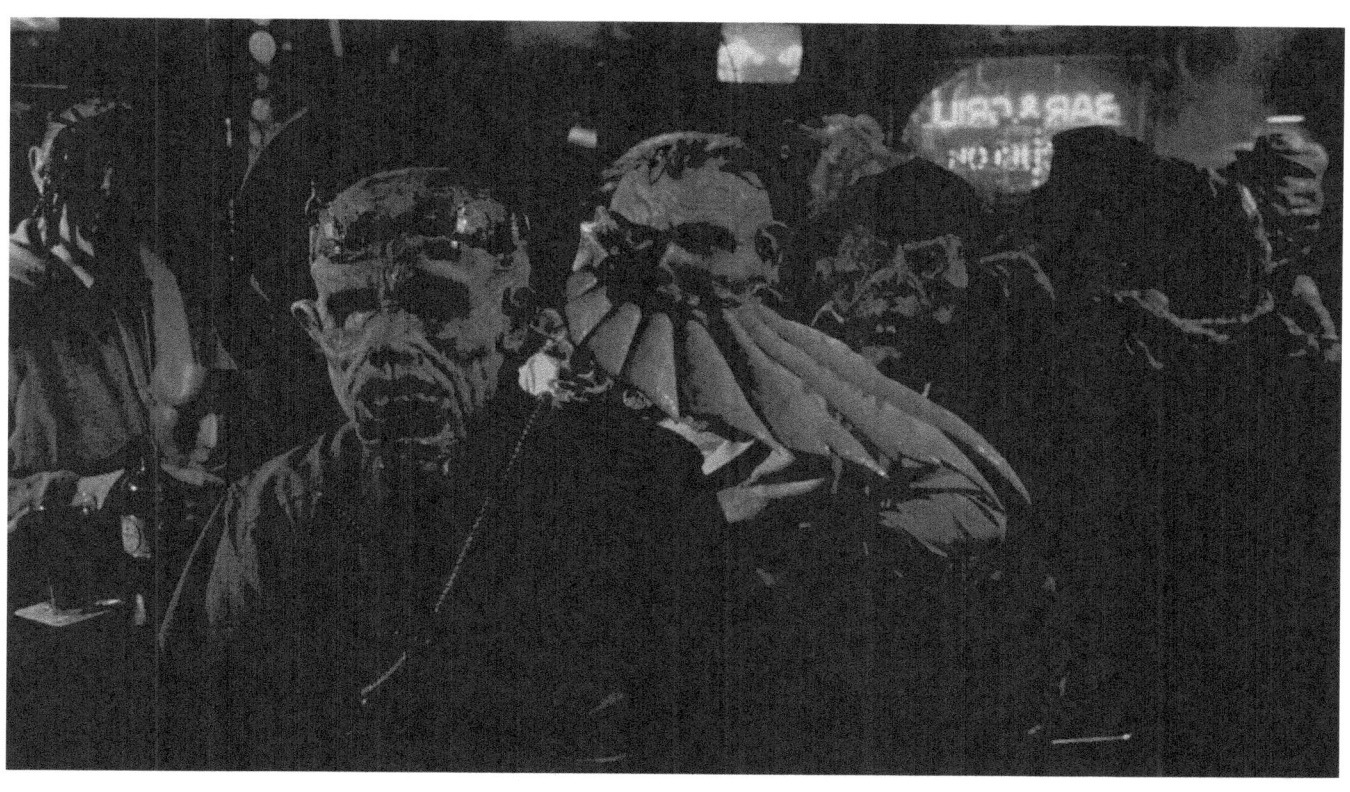

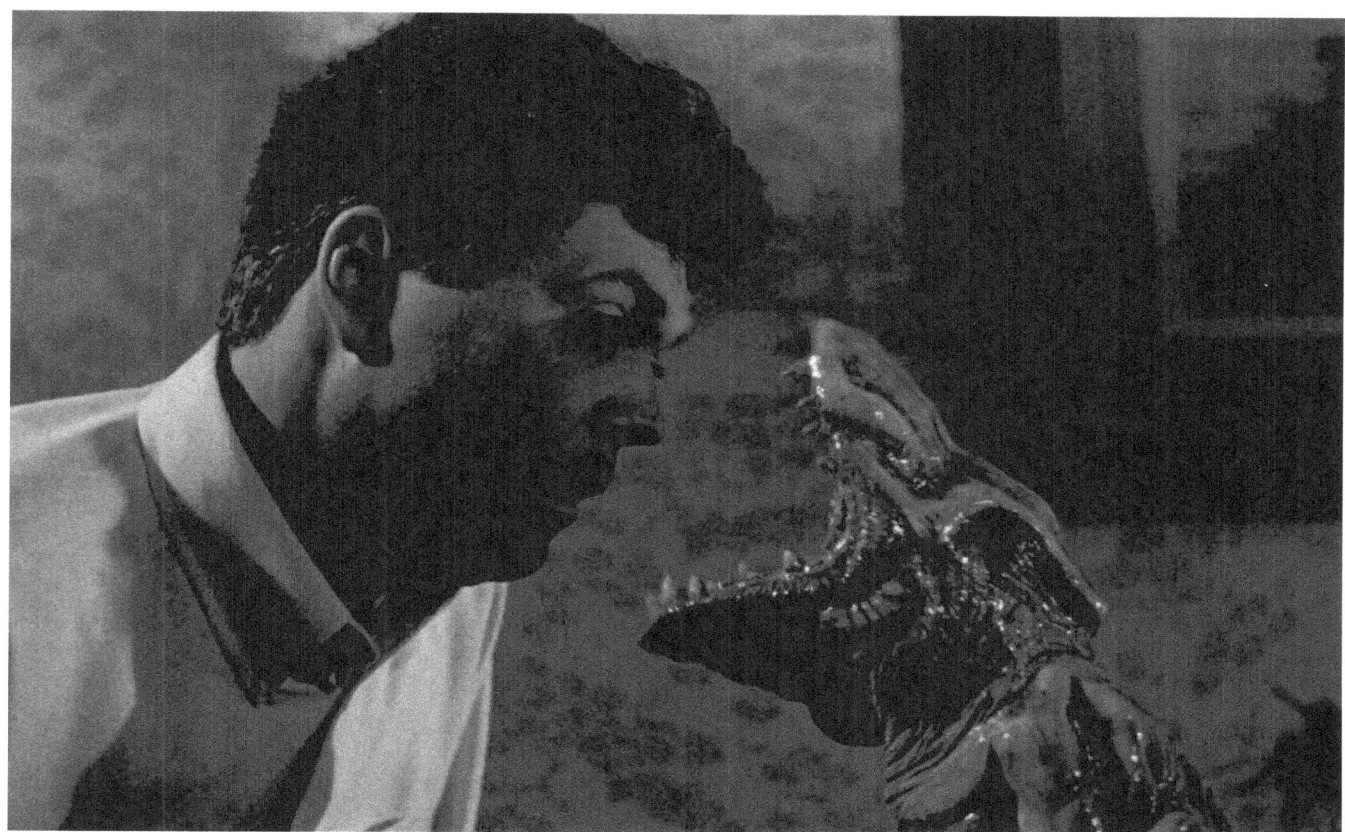

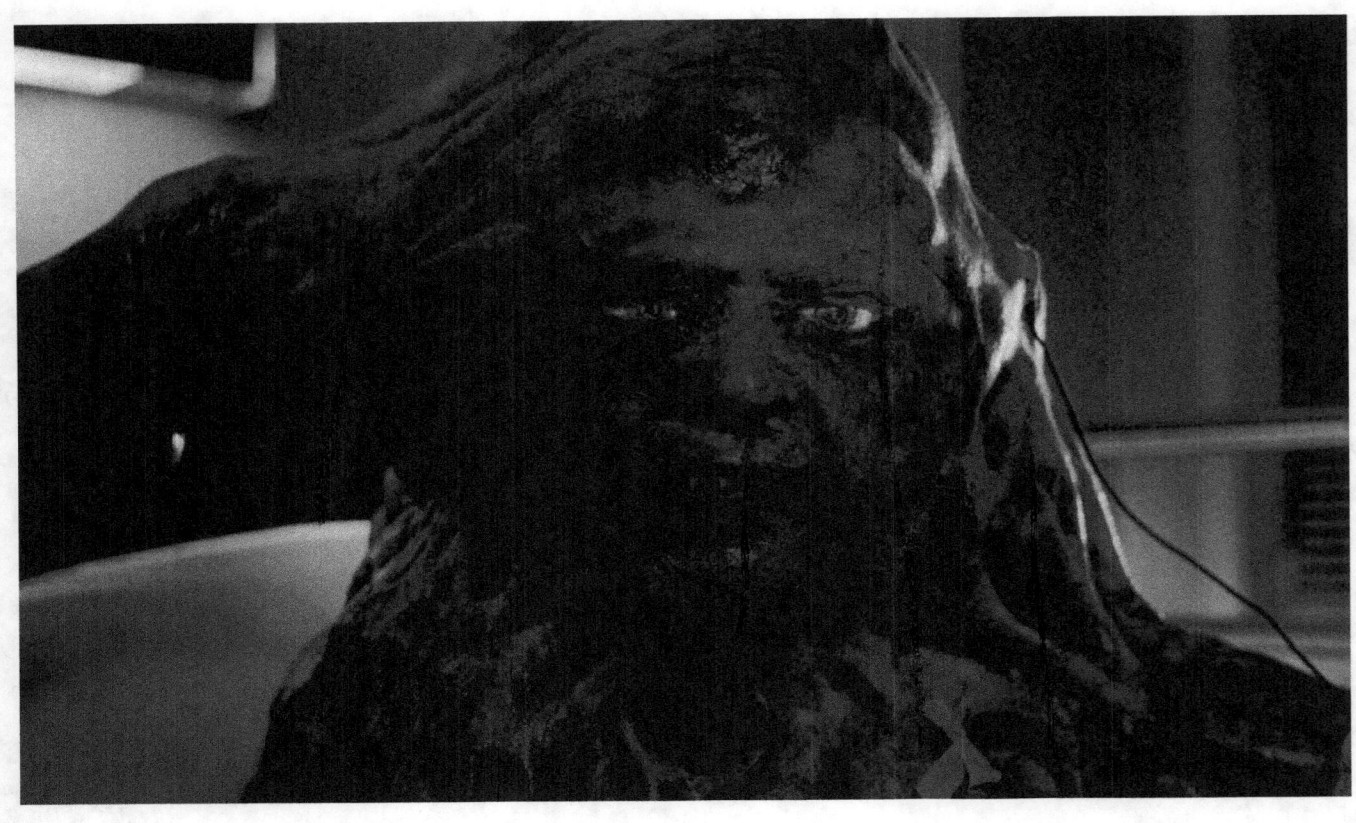
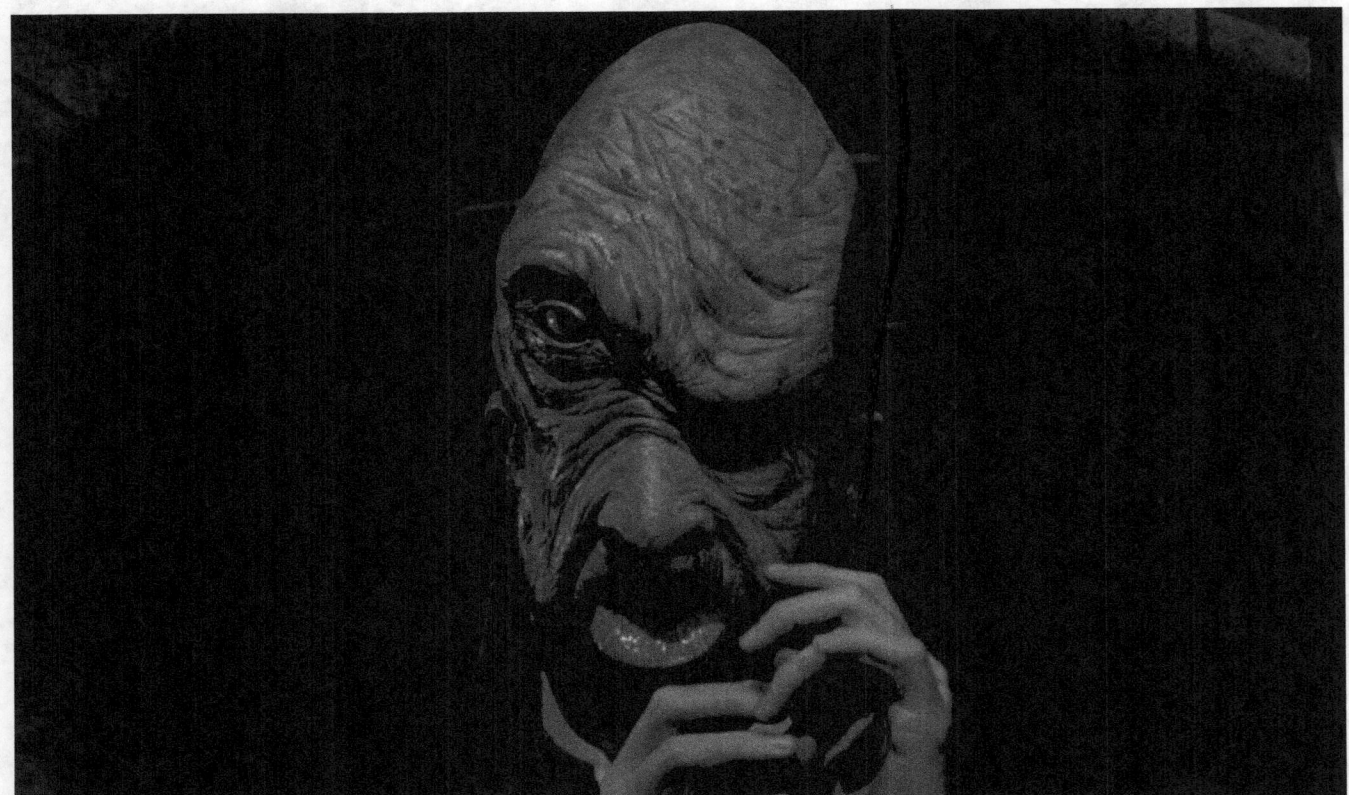

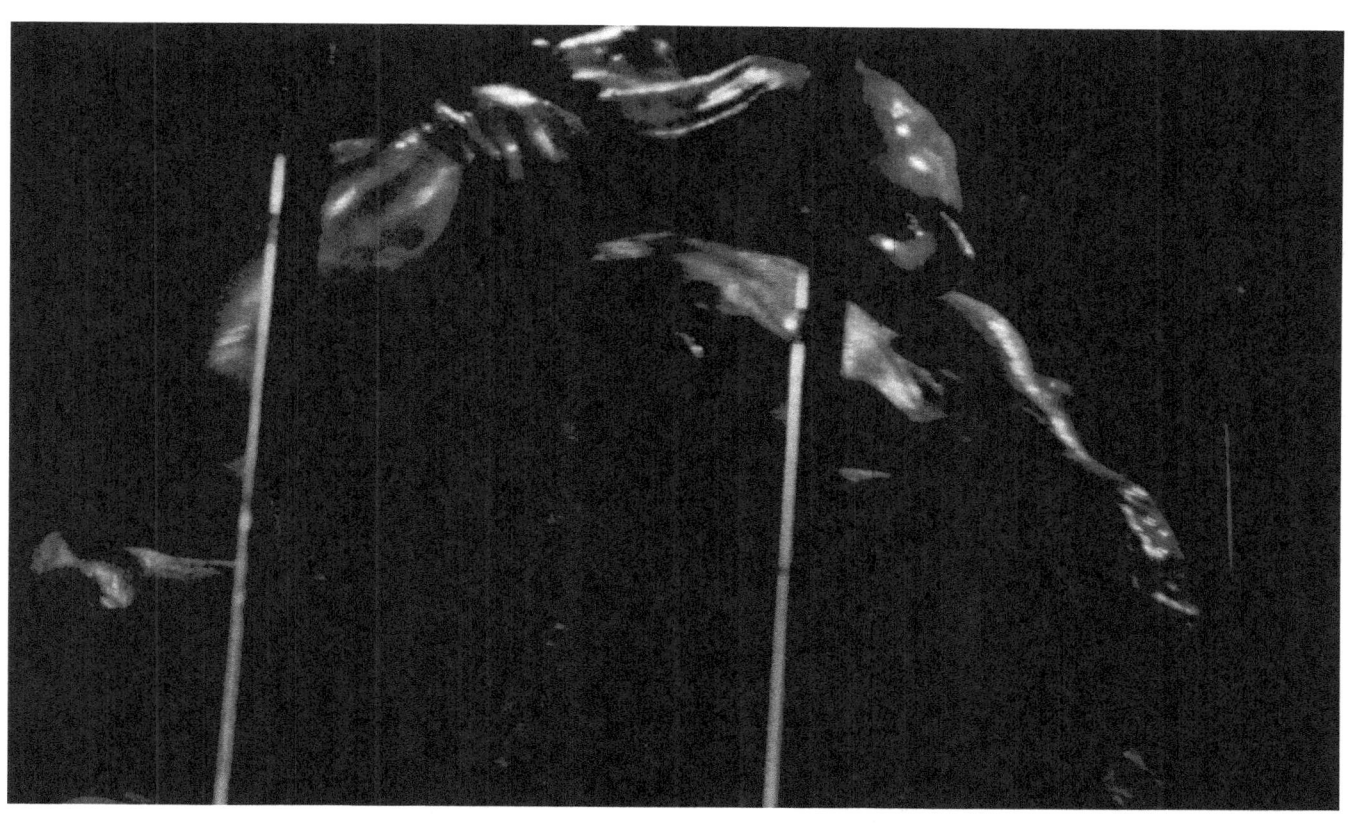
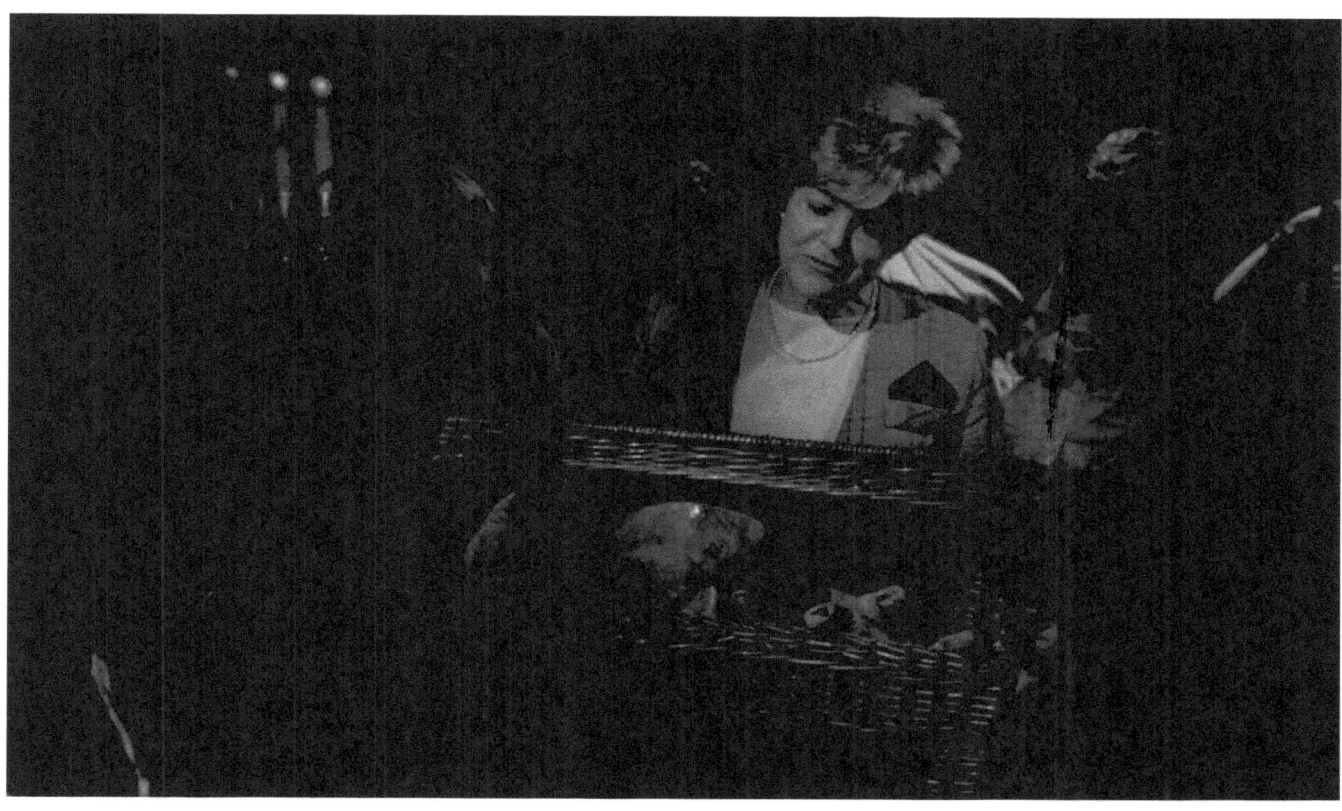

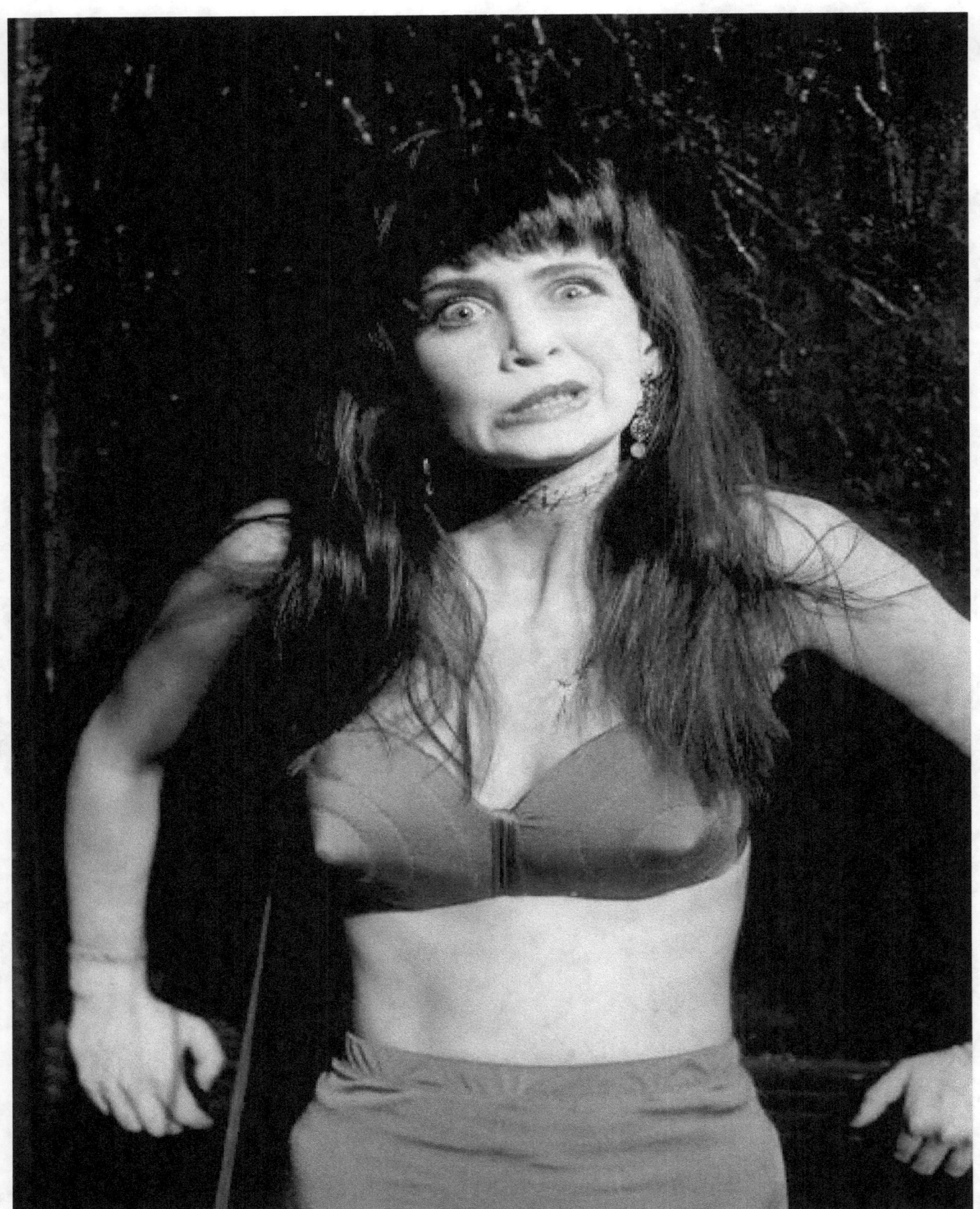

# RING OF STEEL

**JOE DON BAKER · CAROL ALT · ROBERT CHAPIN**

ACTION-ADVENTURE

DEATH HAS JUST BECOME A SPECTATOR SPORT

R — RESTRICTED

STEREO

---

**RING OF STEEL**

With the fatal flash of a broken blade, a young man finds himself trapped in an obsessive world of swordfighting-for-profit where victory is bought with blood, and death is the only escape. **Joe Don Baker** stars with Carol Alt, Robert Chapin, Gary Kasper and Darlene Vogel in this riveting action-thriller.

After accidentally killing an opponent in a fencing match, one-time Olympic hopeful Alex Frayer (Chapin) is an outcast, shunned by all except his girlfriend Elena. Enter the mysterious Man In Black (Baker), owner of a decadent nightclub where the rich and powerful come to watch and wager as modern-day gladiators fight in the *Ring of Steel* for fabulous rewards...and their lives. Unaware of the deadly stakes, Alex wins a duel and is showered with money — and the attention of Tanya (Alt), the club's sultry manager. When he discovers the club's dark secret, he refuses to fight, but blackmail draws him deeper into the sadistic ring and he is forced to confront the Ring's psychotic champion (Kasper) in mortal combat.

Blazing with spectacular swordplay, this action-packed adventure pits man against man in the ultimate clash for survival where the only weapons are strength, cunning, and cold steel.

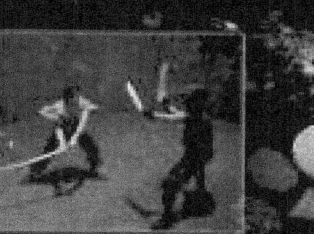

VHS
HI FI STEREO
81757

Color/1 Hr. 34 Mins.

## FROM THE DIRECTOR OF "DARKMAN"

Trapped in time.
Surrounded by evil.
Low on gas.

# ARMY OF DARKNESS

DINO DE LAURENTIIS COMMUNICATIONS PRESENTS A RENAISSANCE PICTURES PRODUCTION BRUCE CAMPBELL "ARMY OF DARKNESS" EMBETH DAVIDTZ "MARCH OF THE DEAD" THEME BY DANNY ELFMAN MUSIC BY JOSEPH LODUCA EDITED BY BOB MURAWSKI PRODUCTION DESIGN BY TONY TREMBLAY DIRECTOR OF PHOTOGRAPHY BILL POPE CO-PRODUCER BRUCE CAMPBELL WRITTEN BY SAM RAIMI & IVAN RAIMI PRODUCED BY ROBERT TAPERT DIRECTED BY SAM RAIMI A UNIVERSAL RELEASE

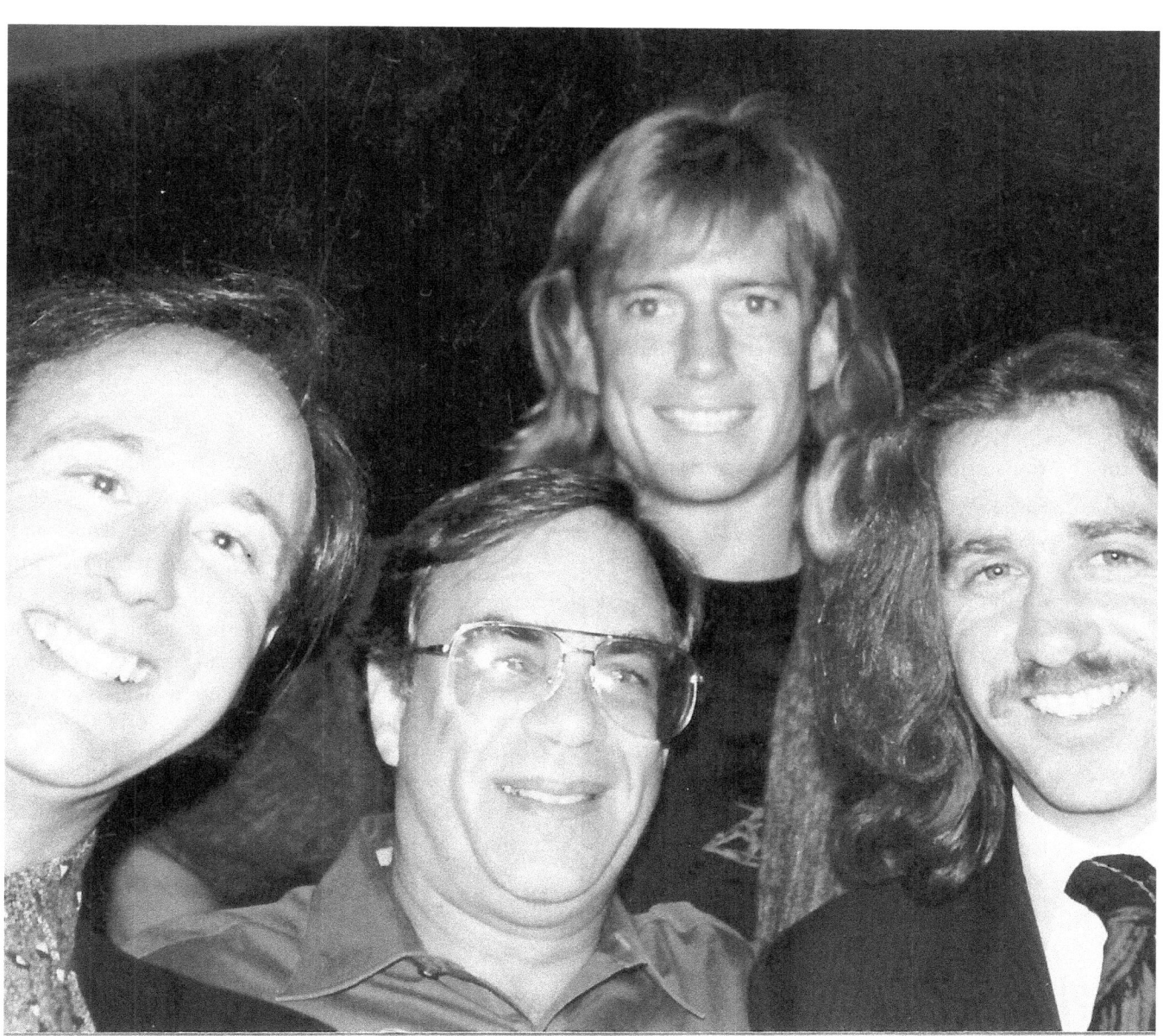

# Robert Chapin

Robert Chapin began in the film industry as a visual effect artist and stunt specialist, working behind the camera on major productions like THE BABE, ROBOCOP 3, HOOK, and ARMY OF DARKNESS. His one and only SGE production, RING OF STEEL, is devoted to one of his personal passions, sword-fighting. Chapin trained in the sport for years before he started a film career. Chapin debuted onscreen in one of the leading roles in RING OF STEEL. Afterwards he quickly evolved as a digital artist and fight/stunt choreographer and served on dozens of Hollywood blockbusters. Films like ARMAGEDDON, THE MAD PROFESSOR, and ALMOST FAMOUS are included in his work, but an even more personal project would be THE HUNTED, a web series running since 2001 - again including extended sword play, which is clearly still a passion for Robert Chapin, who directs the series. In 2015, a successful crowdfunding effort was initiated for an upcoming feature film based on the series.

**Marco:** You started with several sports at a young age - not only martial arts, one of your biggest passions seems to be the art of swordplay. Tell me about your fascination for this kind of combat.

**Robert:** Never really had a fascination for swordplay until after high school. I was actually a music major, and I happened to be performing at a renaissance fair in Miami when I saw a living chessgame. Played on a huge 40ft square chessboard, the pieces would fight to the death to win their square. Now this was awesome, and way cooler than being a wandering minstrel. I joined the Royal Chessmen in '82, and within three months I learned how to swordfight, and I was performing in my first show. It was just fun, and I never really thought of making a career of it, but I found myself taking martial arts and gymnastic classes to make myself a better swordsman.

**Marco:** According to our information, you joined a group of swordplay performers called RING OF STEEL in the 80s. I assume the title and the script is based on that part of your life. How personal is this script and when did the idea come up for the story?

**Robert:** Robert Dawson was the director of the stage combat group RING OF STEEL in Miami. It was a great experience, and I went from working heavy weapons in the Chessmen to rapiers - light, fast and flashy. The group actually had nothing to do with the movie, other than some of the names and characters that were taken from a few of my fight buddies.

**Marco:** Before RING OF STEEL, you had already entered the film business and contributed to a fair number of big productions like ARMY OF DARKNESS and ROBOCOP 3. Was it always the plan, writing and/or directing on your own?

**Robert:** When I came to LA, I had no idea what I was going to do. Swordfighting was still a hobby. That is, until I got my first big gig on HOOK. I spent six months on that show, getting paid to swordfight, which was awesome. I also got to meet practically everyone in the business - Spielberg, Robin Williams, Dustin Hoffman, and pretty much every stuntman in LA. It was a fantastic experience! I even worked six weeks on ARMY OF DARKNESS at the same time. We'd spend all day shooting HOOK and then drive out to the desert to shoot ARMY OF DARKNESS all night, sleeping between takes.

It was on ARMY OF DARKNESS that I got the idea for RING OF STEEL from a buddy of mine. I asked him if I could develop it into a script, and he said sure. Yea, he was cool with it until he sued me three years later when the film came out. You're not anything in LA until someone sues you. The original script I came up with for RING OF STEEL was very dark - more like DEER HUNTER. My character starts on death row for murder. In flashback, we learn he was forced to fight in the ring to save his girlfriend, but then he actually starts enjoying it - blinded by the drugs and the money. By the time his girlfriend is finally set free, he doesn't even recognize her. The opening of the film is also based on a true event where a fencer was killed in the 1982 world championships.

**Marco:** How did things come up, what's the background story behind the production of RING OF STEEL? Did SGE finance the film? Did they leave you alone with the film, or was there discussions about the conception?

**Robert:** I knew the script was marketable, but I was a first-time writer who had never starred in a film before. I teamed up with David Speaker, who was interested in producing a film, but had never done so. He then introduced me to our director, David Frost, and our lead bad guy, Gary Kasper. So we had the beginnings of a cast and crew, but we still had no idea what we were doing. We tried dozens of crazy ideas to sell the film, and at one point we tried cold-calling a list of name actors to be in it. Yea, that didn't work. I finally realized the best way to sell the film was to put together a kickass fight scene and shoot a trailer for the American Film Market. We would invite production companies to watch us shoot the trailer - most of whom had never seen a live swordfight before. It was a risky gamble, but we pooled together $10k to shoot it. Our pitch was simple. It's BLOODSPORT with swords. Among the production companies we invited to the filming was SGE, who already had a distribution deal through MCA/Universal. They were blown away by what they saw. We already had partial financing through an independent investor, but SGE bought them out, choosing to fund the film completely. We were assigned Jef Richardson as our line producer, but otherwise we were allowed to keep our entire cast and crew. They had some doubts about me in the leading role, so I actually had to audition for Lenny, Jim and a room full of producers and casting directors. I also had to let Lenny win a racquetball game, but that's another story. The biggest difficulty, however, was deciding on our star cameo to play the Man in Black. I imagined him to be a distinguished older Englishman who could use a sword. I suggested Christopher Lee, who had done swordplay years ago in THE THREE MUSKETEEERS (this was before he was to star in LORD OF THE RINGS and STAR WARS). But all Jim and Lenny said was, "Who's that?" We bounced around a bunch of names including Billy Blanks and David Hasselhoff (who I had doubled on BAYWATCH), but we finally decided on Joe Don Baker, who did a great job. Side note - he was convinced to take the job by a Vegas stripper.

**Marco:** Composer Jeff Beal did an awesome job on the score of the film, don't you agree?

**Robert:** I love his score. And RING OF STEEL was his first foray into soundtracks. This is before his amazing career doing soundtracks on shows like ROME. SGE takes credit for finding him. I should also note that our art director, my buddy Matt Gratzner (also his first movie) went on to create one of the biggest model shops in LA, New Deal Studios, which has worked on films like INTERSTELLAR.

**Marco:** Can you give me some numbers and info about the production? What kind of budget did you have, how many crew members, how many shooting days?

**Robert:** We had a budget of 1.5 million dollars with a 14 day shoot schedule - pretty tight for most films, but fairly standard for SGE from what I understand. And even though we had a fairly decent budget, it was pretty tight for what we were trying to do. We didn't even have money to buy t-shirts for the cast and crew. I had to dig into my own savings (of which I had none) to buy shirts. And I'm glad I did. After the first week, the crew was grumbling and getting ready to walk. It was then I learned the power of "schwag". I pulled out the shirts and the crew was so thrilled, they pulled extra hours to finish the show. Not a bad deal for $10 a shirt.

**Marco:** The swordplay is one of the very best ever seen in American action films. Were you in charge of parts of the fight choreography?

**Robert:** My biggest contribution to the swordplay is that I insisted we had a month of rehearsals, which is unusual for most action films. I also insisted that everyone choreograph their own fights, which gave them all a unique feel. We had some of the best fighters in the biz such as James Lew from BIG TROUBLE IN LITTLE CHINA. And who better to know the fighters' capabilities than the fighters themselves.

**Marco:** How did you shoot 21 fight scenes in one day?

**Robert:** Rehearsal! Everyone knew their choreography so well, we could do the fight from top to bottom with no stops. We also knew exactly how we wanted to shoot them.

**Marco:** The film was directed and co-written by David Frost. How do you remember your creative partnership on RING OF STEEL? Did you get along?

**Robert:** David was with us from the very beginning - helping to create the trailer that eventually sold the show. More than anything, David was a fantastic producer and salesman. He was the one who really sold the show to SGE. He also did a great job directing the show even though it was his second gig after BARBARIAN QUEEN 2. We did have our differences, however, which had to do with radical changes to my original script.

**Marco:** Let's get a little bit into private anecdotes. You made out with Carol Alt during shooting, correct? Were you a couple for some time?

**Robert:** Nice. Carol and I met on the show and I was a bit intimidated. Her character was supposed to involve a steamy sex sequence in the shower, but Carol wasn't up to that and we swapped the love scene to my character's girlfriend, played by Darlene Vogel (from PACIFIC BLUE). Still, Carol and I were supposed to kiss, and I wanted us to be comfortable with that. I wasn't sure how to go about that, and David Frost suggested I take her and/or Darlene out to dinner. I figured I'd just have a chat with them on set, but Carol was being all mysterious. I figured out later that she was trying to be in character, all the time. When I saw her one day out of makeup and out of character, I almost didn't recognize her. Darlene and I broke the ice immediately when I walked in on her accidentally while she was dressing. She simply said "Well, you're gonna see it anyway. " I had never done a love scene before, but I heard it was very technical. The set was cleared, but there were still at least a dozen crew members hanging around. David Frost certainly tried to direct the scene, but he was a bit sheepish - especially since Darlene and I didn't seem to need any direction.

**Marco:** The original script had to be changed since its tone was too dark, is this true? When did this happen and how much of your intention is still in there?

**Robert:** This is a sore spot for me, as is with most first time screenwriters. The original script had been through a year of four drafts, and everyone loved it. Our producer and director loved it enough to spend a year trying to sell the film, and SGE loved it enough to invest $1.5 million. It wasn't until our first big script meeting with SGE where Jim mentioned he didn't believe the aforementioned sex scene in the shower where Carol Alt's character says "Tie me up." Jim commented "That stuff just doesn't happen... Does it?" Silence. Apparently, it had never happened for Jim, and that moment led to a comment that the script needed a revision. Suddenly everyone was on board that the script was flawed. My producer, director, everyone bailed on me, and they wouldn't even let me attempt a rewrite. Instead they paid some other writer $20k to rewrite the script (I was only paid $2k), and they wouldn't even let me be a part of the story sessions. I was definitely not a happy camper, but whatever it took to get the film done. Unfortunately, the new script was atrocious. Fortunately, SGE realized it was crap, and went back to my original script, allowing David Frost to do the rewrite with my input. I still wasn't happy, and I didn't even want credit, but David convinced me otherwise. The hardest part was trying to play a character that was nowhere as cool as my original script. We did manage to save a few of my fave scenes though - mostly comical. A certain fight with a chicken, being forced to fight my buddy in the ring, and a scene that has a Dungeons and Dragons geek audition to be a fighter. Looking back on it now, the film is nowhere as cool as it could've been, but it's still not bad. Joe Don Baker thought the film was awesome and was ready to bust out his checkbook to make sure it had a theatrical release (the film was cut on 35mm with surround sound). Lenny said not to worry about it, and he promised we'd get a theatrical release, which of course never happened. As far as a I could tell, they never even advertised for the film. I took it upon myself to grab a huge roll of posters and run around LA trying to put them up. It was ridiculous - the star of the film running around LA trying to put up his own posters. I got caught a few times, and I was forced to either take 'em down or run. SGE did, however, send us on a cross country tour to promote the film. They wanted to send someone along with me, so they asked me about the show's bad guy, Gary Kasper. "Is he stable?" Yes, he's just a great actor and a big ol puppy dog. But I wanted to do something different to promote the film, so Gary and I brought swords along and did live swordfights for every big video convention and every mom and pop video store in North America. We had a blast!

**Marco:** Nowadays you work regularly on acclaimed Hollywood productions. How do you make your living, and what kind of projects do you do only out of passion? Mainly you are a visual effects designer, correct?

**Robert:** Among other things, I'm a VFX artist and have a fairly extensive resume working on films such as X-MEN and AVENGERS. I'm still very much involved in acting and stunts, however, and now finally pushing my way into the world of directing.

**Marco:** Your web series THE HUNTED seems to be your most personal project since RING OF STEEL, would you agree on that? How was the series financed in its early days?

**Robert:** I've developed a bunch of films in the years after RING OF STEEL, but financing is always an issue. Even though RING OF STEEL was a success in home video, SGE claimed they never made any money, and we never saw a dime, even though we were promised 30% of the worldwide gross. They claimed they were broke, even though their next film SLAUGHTER OF THE INNOCENTS was made for at least $10 million. Not sure where they got that money. After RING OF STEEL, I teamed up with David Frost and David Speaker again, to produce a video game version of the show. The design was revolutionary, and all we needed was for SGE to allow us to use the name RING OF STEEL. They said no, even though we offered them 50% of the profits just to use the name of our own film. Seriously? That was pretty much the end of our dealings with SGE. Too bad since I've got a great idea for the sequel to RING OF STEEL, but I have no idea who owns it now that the company is dissolved. But I wasn't about to give up after the video game fiasco. I wrote several films, including a pirate film called PIRATES BLOOD and tried to pitch it the same way I did RING OF STEEL, but that was the same year Renny Harlin released CUTTHROAT ISLAND, which was a colossal disaster. I was tired of begging for money, and I needed a project that required virtually no money. I was teaching a stage combat class at the time and I wanted my students to have some experience performing on film, so I came up with the idea of shooting a web series. THE HUNTED is a sword-slinging, vampire-slaying cross between BUFFY and COPS and is shot reality TV style, which allows for no-budget crappy video, lighting and sound. It was also one of the first web shows online and is still running 15 years later. What's unique about the show is that it's based on user content, meaning that virtually anyone, anywhere can shoot their own episode. We now have over 100 episodes online from all over the world.

**Marco:** And can you tell us something about the upcoming movie based on the series?

**Robert:** There was always an intention to take the show to the next level, which I assumed would be a TV show and then maybe a feature film. But why wait? I knew how to make a feature film. And there was now this wonderful thing called crowd funding through Kickstarter, and fans of the show came together to make it possible. We've since shot and finished post production on the film, and it looks pretty damn cool -

especially for the budget. We're now in the process of self-distribution and the whole landscape has changed completely since RING OF STEEL. It's all about online video on demand and which portal will give you the most viewers for the best return.

**Marco:** As a trainer you worked with lots of action-heroes like Olivier Gruner and even major stars like Robin Williams. Are you still into such jobs?

**Robert:** There's only a handful of sword guys in LA, so I still occasionally get occasion to work with celebs in strange venues such as the LA Opera punching out Placido Domingo. I've also had the pleasure to work with folks such as Marc Singer (BEASTMASTER), Karl Urban (LORD OF THE RINGS), and John Saxon (ENTER THE DRAGON) – the thing about wearing so many hats is that some people either see me as a sword guy or a VFX guy. As a VFX guy, I've worked with some amazing directors such as Ridley Scott (ALIENS), The Coen Brothers (BIG LEBOWSKI), and Bryan Singer (X MEN).

**Marco:** What do you enjoy most in giving fighting instructions?

**Robert:** I actually really enjoy teaching swordplay to folks who think they can't do it. It's really not as mysterious as some "experts" make it out to be, and it's not as physically demanding as doing like a standing backflip. It's mostly technical, and the basics are pretty darn simple. That being said, it can also be extremely dangerous if done incorrectly.

**Marco:** As a specialist in swordplay on screen, please name a few titles which set the standards for high class sword action? Any all-time-favorites?

**Robert:** The old days of Hollywood knew how to rehearse and shoot a swordfight. Actors trained and rehearsed for months to make things look perfect. I've been on film shoots where I've had 10 minutes to choreograph a swordfight with an actor who had never held sword before in their lives. Most folks would say Errol Flynn, but while he could put on a great show, he was not a great swordsman. Basil Rathbone, however, was the bomb! Check him out in a film called MARK OF ZORRO. A highly technical and brilliantly executed swordfight that's shot really well. Even better than Flynn was Danny Kaye in one of my fave films THE COURT JESTER, choreographed by Ralph Faulkner. Basil was quoted as saying that Kaye was better than Flynn ever was. Virtually any film choreographed by Bill Hobbs - DUELISTS, ROB ROY, and Richard Lester's THREE MUSKETEERS. Hobbs is one of the greats of his time. I'm also hopeful for a brilliant choreographer buddy of mine, Richard Ryan, who did some badass work on TROY. So what happens when you give people adequate rehearsal time and take the time to film it correctly? You get a film called PRINCESS BRIDE. Bob Anderson did a magnificent job on the choreography, and he's a great guy. I met him when I was being considered as a stunt double for one of the leads on THE MASK OF ZORRO.

**Marco:** Is RING OF STEEL still remembered by many action fans?

**Robert:** Apparently, the film has become required viewing for anyone who is into stage combat and swordplay. I was actually contacted recently by one group that had taken upon themselves to recreate all of the choreography. For a low-budget action film that was made in the early 90s, I'm amazed that anyone still remembers it. I still occasionally get recognized, and even though I made no money on the film, that first starring role opened the door to a whole new world of opportunities. It's helped to give me credibility, and I've starred in several films since then. Soon after RING OF STEEL, I was offered a starring role on another low budget film, but the script was terrible, so I passed on it. That show somehow got picked up and became HERCULES. I've come to learn that there's all sorts of missed opportunities in LA, but you can't just wait around for them. The only guarantee for success are the opportunities you make for yourself, which is what I did for RING OF STEEL and now THE HUNTED. I'm not sure what kind of staying power any of SGE's other films have experienced, but I know there's quite a fan following out there for RING OF STEEL, and I'm ready to shoot that sequel whenever they are. Ultimately, I'm grateful that SGE took a chance on us. Risking $1.5 million dollars is no small thing - especially when you're giving it to a first-time actor, producer and director. For that, I owe them a huge debt of gratitude.

---

**By Marco Siedelmann, in writing**
**from New York, New York**
**30May, 2015**

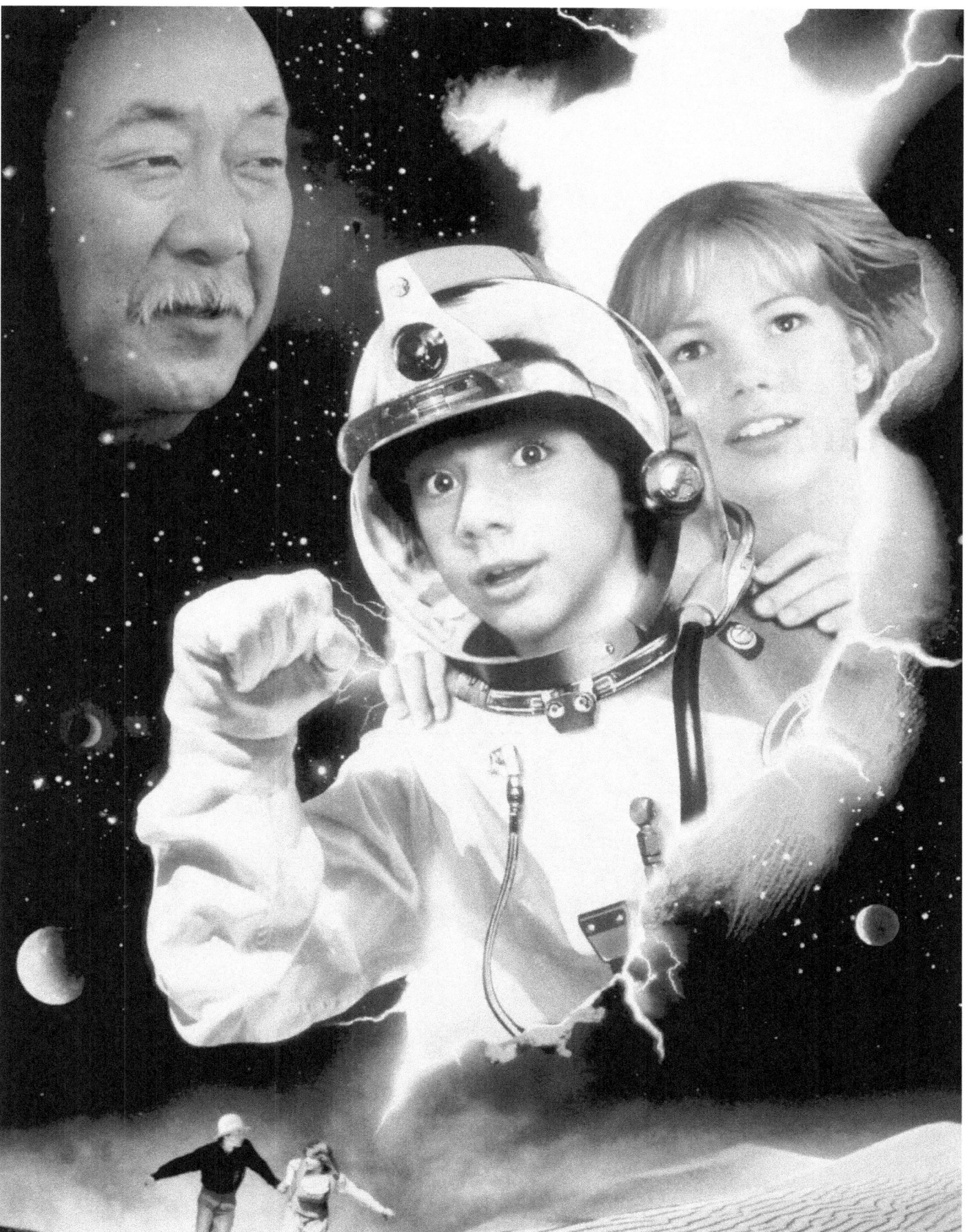

# V. The Remains of the Day: Life after SGE …

*"Every crowd has a silver lining."*
– P.T. Barnum

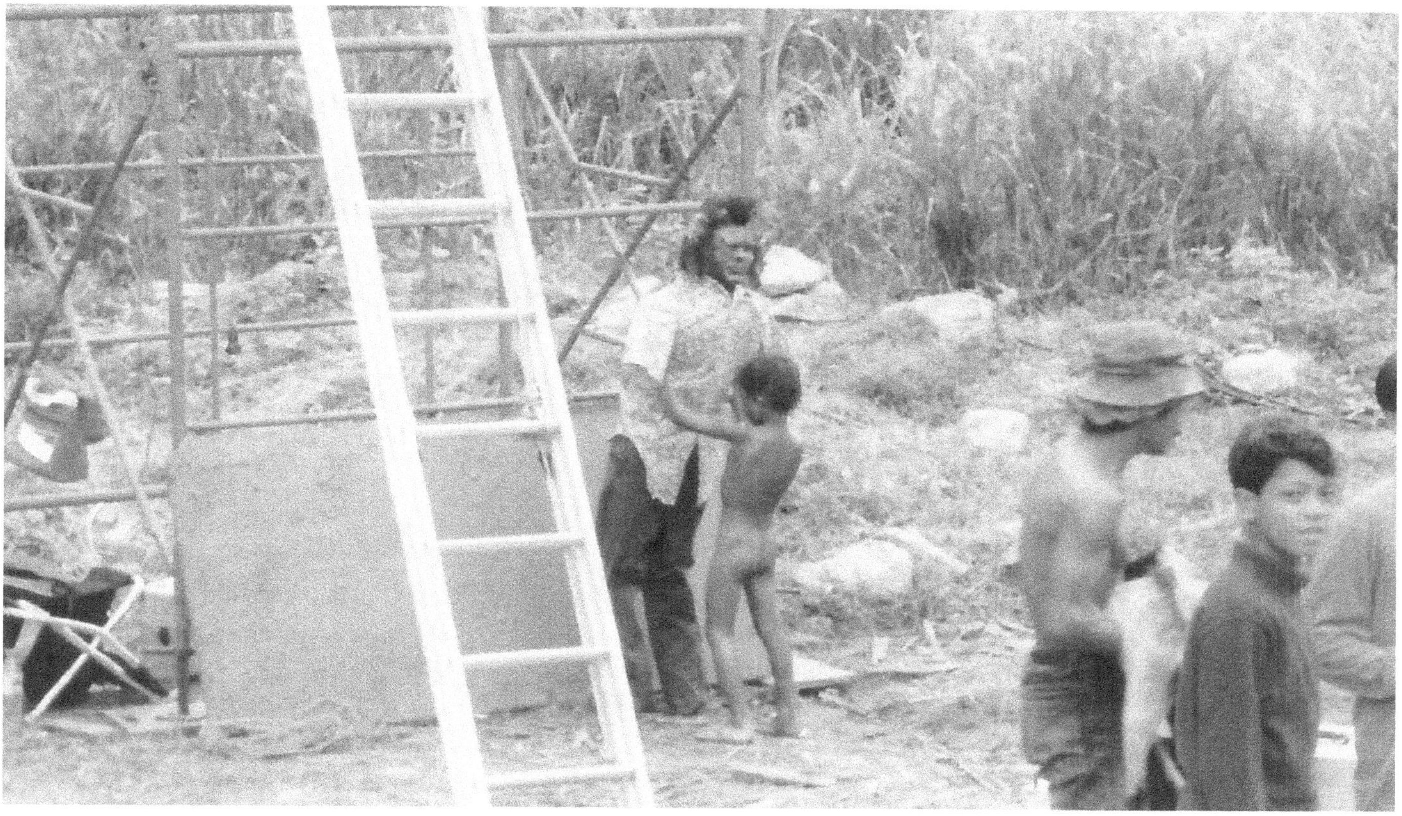

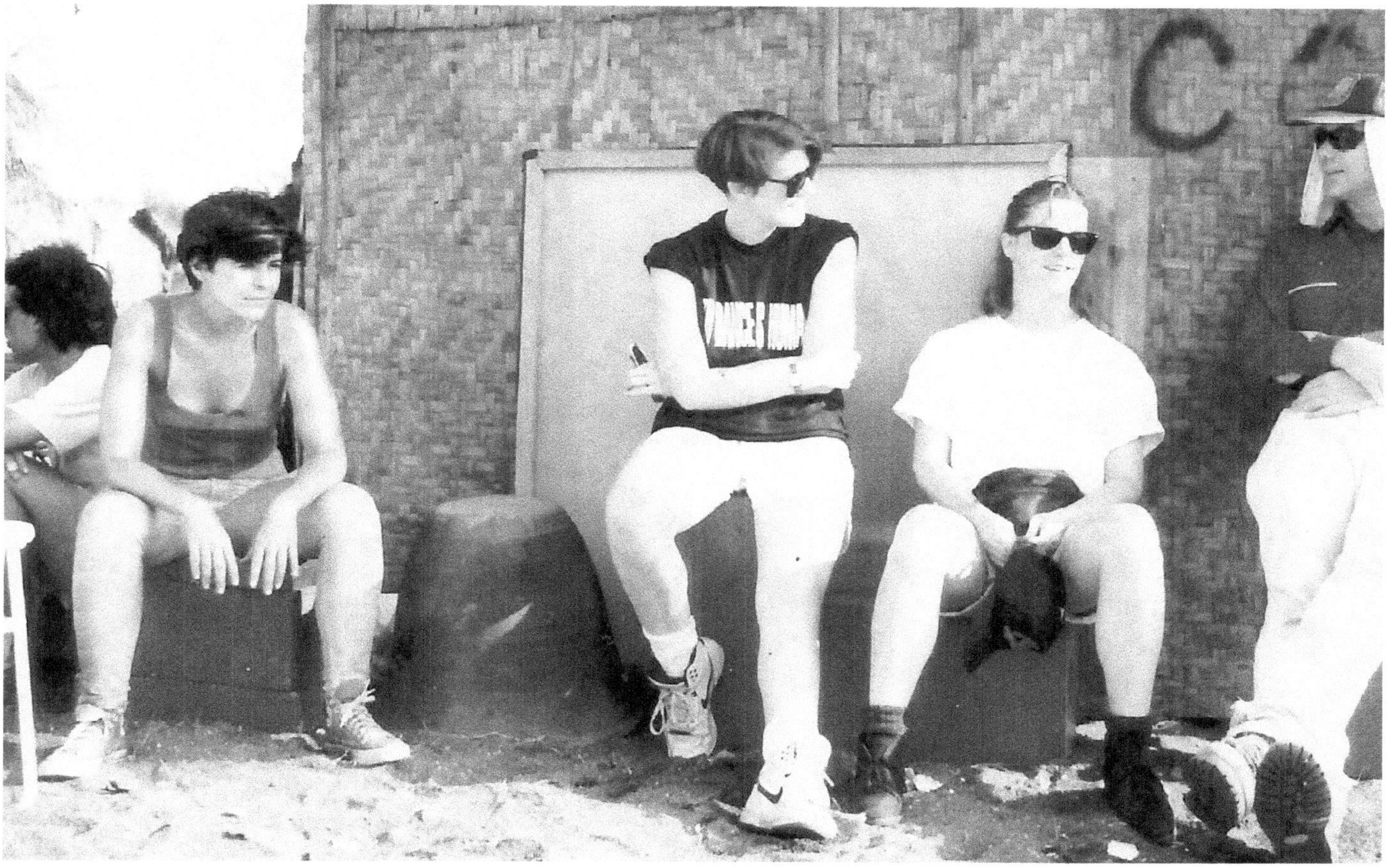

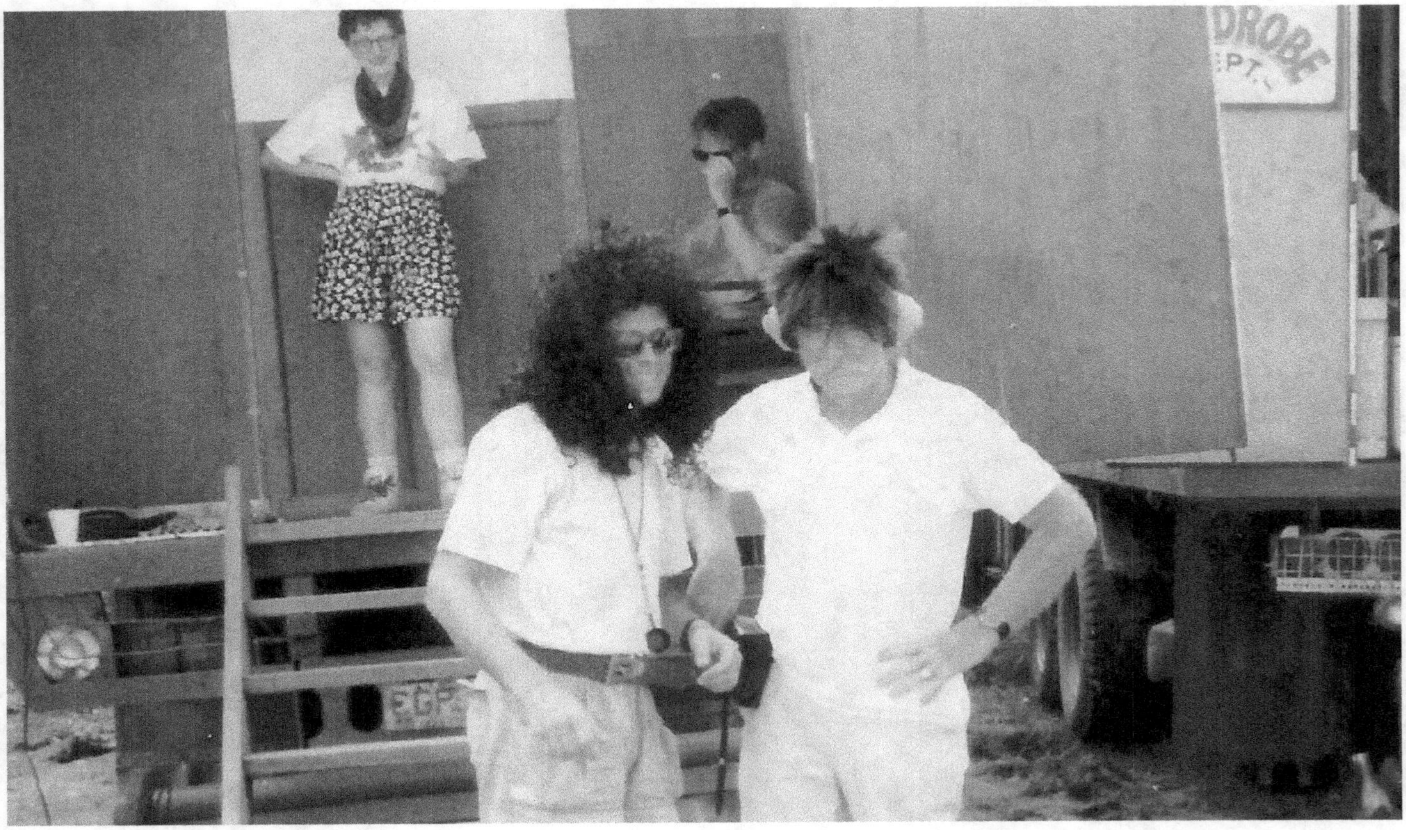

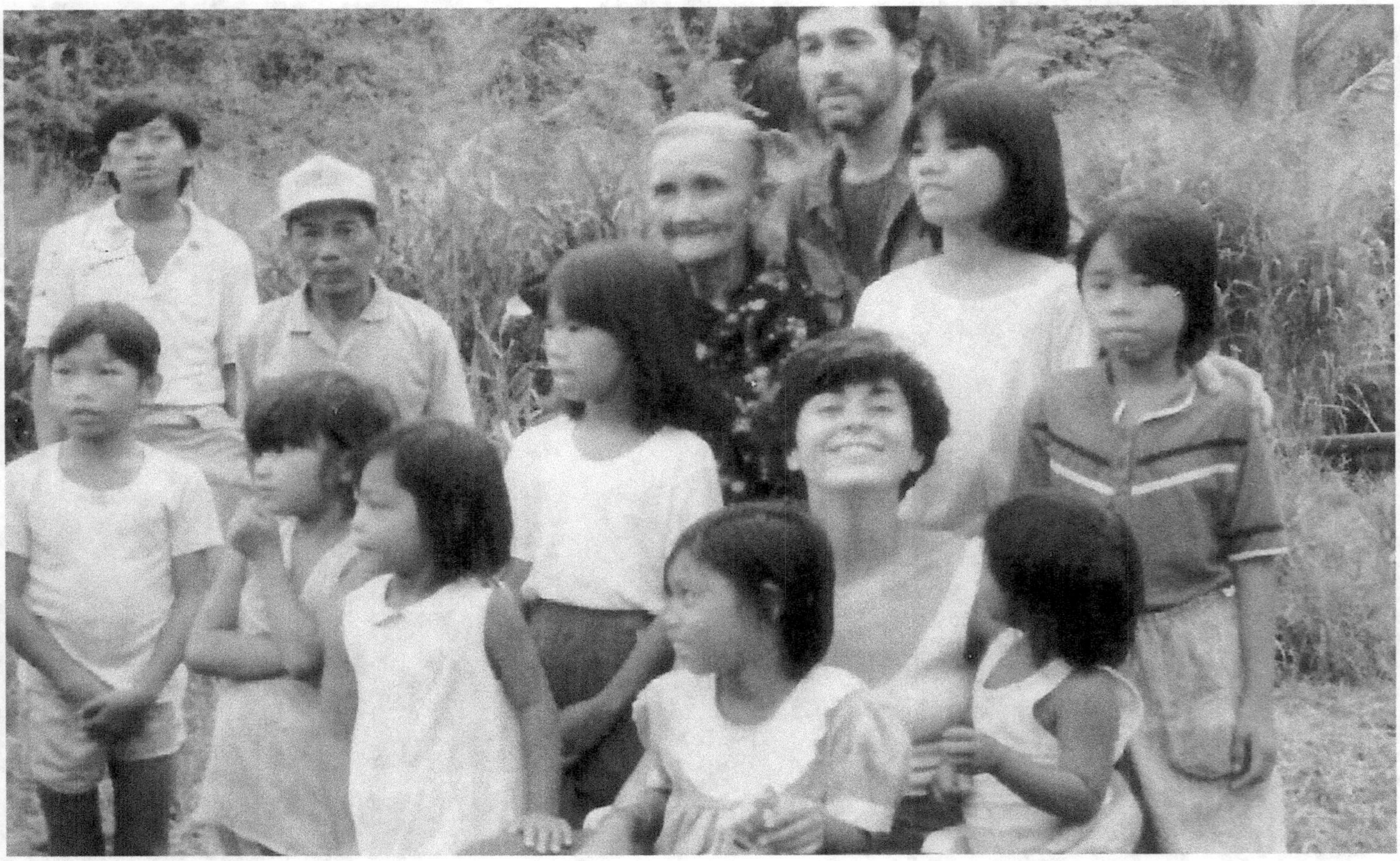

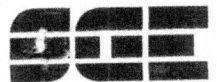

SHAPIRO GLICKENHAUS ENTERTAINMENT

# MCBAIN

## Production Notes

A large-scale, action-adventure motion picture, **MCBAIN** stars Academy Award winner Christopher Walken ("The Deer Hunter," "Biloxi Blues") in the title role and Maria Conchita Alonso ("Moscow On The Hudson," "Extreme Prejudice," "Predator II"). Directing from his original screenplay is noted action director James Glickenhaus ("The Exterminator," "The Soldier," "Shakedown/Blue Jean Cop").

**MCBAIN** begins at the end of the Vietnam War, when prisoner of war McBain is rescued in the jungles of North Vietnam by a group of seven Rangers as he is about to be killed by his captors. Afterwards, when McBain expresses his gratitude, the leader of the Rangers, Santos (Chick Vennera), takes out a hundred dollar bill, tears it in two, hands half to McBain, and says, "If the other half reaches you, you can pay me back."

Eighteen years later, Santos is killed in Colombia while leading the fight against drug lords and corrupt politicians. His sister, Christina (Maria Conchita Alonso), goes to New York with Santos' half of the hundred dollar bill to find McBain and enlist his help. McBain and four of the Rangers (Michael Ironside, Steve James, Jay Patterson, Thomas G. Waites) who served with Santos in Vietnam agree to go to Colombia to help Christina and the rebels overthrow the corrupt regime and break the power of the drug lords.

Shapiro Glickenhaus Entertainment presents a Boyce Harman Production of a James Glickenhaus Film, directed and written by James Glickenhaus. The film stars Christopher Walken, Maria Conchita Alonso, Michael Ironside, Steve James, Jay Patterson, Thomas G. Waites, Russell Dennis Baker, Hector Ubarry, Victor Argo and Chick Vennera. J. Boyce

LT. VARGAS:
Simon Escobar is here to see you.

EL PRESIDENTE:
Show him in. Gentlemen, what a pleasure to see you. What a pleasant surprise. He was the Commanding Officer in charge of guarding your factory at El Nigin. He failed. He claims he doesn't know who attacked him but I'm sure a few more moments with the Babe will refresh his memory.

HANS:
Ignorance is not a crime. Failure is a crime.

ESCOBAR:
Sit down El Presidente.

EL PRESIDENTE:
Surely the Americans do not want another hostage situation. I think I scared them pretty good no?

ESCOBAR:
No...the Americans are the most powerless powerful people in the world, until you give them a legitimate reason to intervene. Only an idiot would do that...no?

EL PRESIDENTE:
You cannot talk to me like that I control the army.

ESCOBAR:
The last president told me the same thing. I still send the flowers everyday. He lives in a big white house you can't miss it's right in the center of the cemetery. You are still the President but Hans is in charge. The rebel army must be wiped out and the peasants must be taught that the price for helping them is very dear. Sit down Presidente.

---

EXT. AIR ABOVE JUNGLE VILLAGE - DAY

HANS:
Let's go! Ready go!

---

EXT. JUNGLE VILLAGE - DAY

GILL:
What's the matter man what is it?

# SCARS

## PROSE AND POETRY

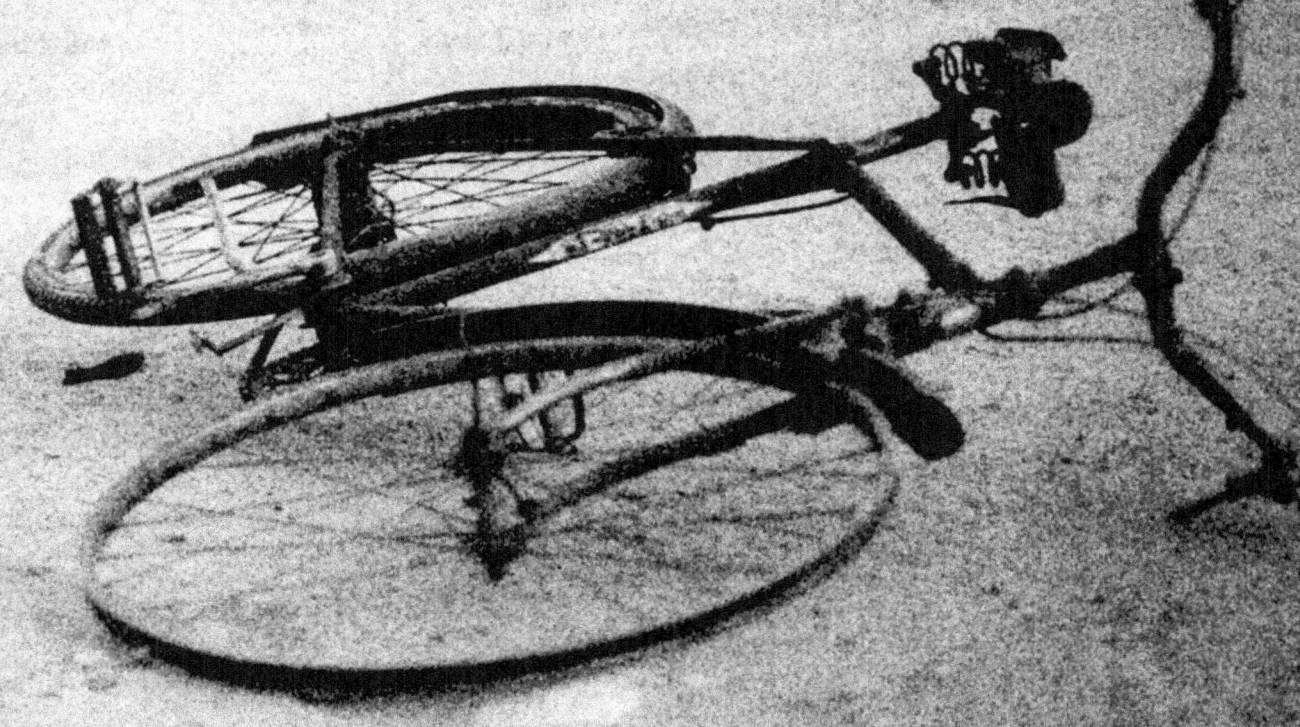

## BY NADIA BRUCE-RAWLINGS

# Nadia Bruce-Rawlings

Nadia Bruce-Rawlings grew up all over the world and started her career in the very early days of SGE. She worked at the company from 1987-1994, working very closely with Alan Solomon as well as the other partners. After SGE, her career in the movie industry grew as a business affairs executive at other independent film distributors such as the multiple Academy Award winning production company GK Film, as well as Franchise Pictures International, Gold Circle International, and Arclight International. In 2008, she founded NBR Media, which handles both the SGE library and the Chris Ingvordsen library. In addition, she acts as a sales agent on a select number of newly produced titles. Besides her regular business she writes short-stories, and her first collection, Scars, was published in fall 2014 by Punk Hostage Press. Nadia now lives in Nashville with her husband, five kids, and two dogs.

**Marco:** Nadia, you worked around eight years at Shapiro Glickenhaus Entertainment. Please tell me something about your background and what route took you there.

**Nadia:** I went to the University of Colorado as a Business Administration major and then moved to Los Angeles when I was 21. SGE was my first real job – I started as the receptionist, then became an acquisitions assistant, then worked with Alan Solomon as Director of International Sales. I worked there for eight years, learning essentially every aspect of the business, from reading scripts to production contracts to licensing contracts to marketing and PR.

**Marco:** Tell me something about your childhood first. For example, how did it come you spend some years of youth in Cairo, Egypt?

**Nadia:** My dad worked for an oil company, so we lived all over the world. I was born in Canada, my brother and sister were born in Libya, we lived in Cairo, Egypt for 4 years, and then in Stavanger, Norway for 4 years, where I went to high school. Then to Denver, and I ended up going to University of Colorado, in Boulder. Moving around was very fun and educational, the travel was amazing, but it was hard leaving friends so often.

**Marco:** What's the first title you were involved with? Were you ever on a film set?

**Nadia:** I joined SGE right before SHAKEDOWN was shot in New York, and then I was production secretary on MANIAC COP, but working out of the main SGE office. I was on the set of MCBAIN, in the Philippines, for about a month. That was really fun and different – they had great locations, in the jungle and on an army base. It's there that I met Michael Ironside, with whom I became close friends, along with his wife. It was a fun shoot, lots of action and explosions.

**Marco:** You must have been one of the very first regulars working at Shapiro Glickenhaus. With how many people did you work closely? Were you involved in all the film projects produced by SGE?

**Nadia:** When I first started, in April of 1987, it was actually still just Shapiro Entertainment. The company was very small, maybe 7-10 employees. Then it became Shapiro Glickenhaus Entertainment, and eventually formed its own Theatrical and Video department, to at least double or more that amount of people. It was very exciting. The late 80s and early 90s were exciting times in film sales – you would go to MIFED and sell a film based on a synopsis and artwork. People were bidding like crazy for these films that had no elements even attached yet. The foreign video market was booming, and they needed product, and companies like SGE knew exactly how to provide it.

**Marco:** What about your personal preferences when it comes to film: Were you always fascinated by action films or did the genre even hold a special appeal for you?

**Nadia:** I actually was always an art-film lover – the fact that I worked at SGE was a bit ironic, but I grew to love films such as BASKET CASE (1,2&3) and FRANKENHOOKER. They were my favorites. I also learned the economic value of exploitation films and action films. I am definitely not the target audience, but I can appreciate what other people want to see.

**Marco:** Maybe this sounds kind of naive but anyway: As a woman working mainly on tough action films, was it hard to stay in the business?

**Nadia:** I think the independent film industry has been actually quite kind to women – there are many powerful female sales execs in the indie biz these days. In the early years that I worked, some of the foreign distributors did not want to deal with women, but I believe that has changed to a great extent. I worked in the sales and distribution arena though, so I'm not sure what it's like to work in production on such films.

**Marco:** Please share some memories and tell me about the most stressful work.

**Nadia:** My stressful days were spent closing loans and deals in order to finance the projects. There were days that I would be on the phone with Japan at midnight and with Germany or the UK at 6 in the morning, trying to get signatures so the film would get financed in time.

**Marco:** In 1995, TIMEMASTER finished an era of crafted, handmade action film history that was written by SGE. How did you continue working in the film business?

**Nadia:** After SGE I worked at Franchise Films as VP of Business Affairs, and then on to Gold Circle, Regent International, Graham King's company IEG, and then Arclight International. In all of these places I was the VP of Business Affairs. I drafted and negotiated all the international and domestic distribution agreements, the Notices of Assignment to close loans on all the films, the Security Agreements, etc., etc. I grew a bit weary of all the legalese, to be honest. Jim Glickenhaus contacted me when Alan Solomon passed away, to close up the Amsell office (which was SGE's successor), and we decided to re-master many of the SGE library films into true HD. Don May Jr. of Synapse Films did amazing work on the remastering, and I was able to license the films quite successfully throughout the world. I formed my own company, NBR

Media, and picked up a few other new titles to license worldwide. The longevity of the SGE titles is truly amazing – I am still closing deals on RED SCORPION, THE EXTERMINATOR, MANIAC COP, as well as the Henenlotter titles.

**Marco:** After SGE you worked at a lot of well-known distributing and production companies. Most popular probably would be GK Films. How did it happen and how do you remember working for the enourmesly successfull Graham King. In which way the work for him was a different thing compared to SGE?

**Nadia:** I'd known Graham for years; he and Alan Solomon were buddies and he had actually tried to hire me years before when I was still working with Alan. But actually in this case, Stephanie Denton (also a former SGE employee) had just started working there, and she called me while I was grocery shopping to offer me a job there. I was blown away…here I was buying toilet paper and she was offering me a once-in-a-lifetime job! I worked there only about two years. We had far fewer titles than we did at SGE, but of course much bigger budget and of critical acclaim. I focused solely on contracts and collections. It was a small office, few staff, but we all worked hard of course. It was an honor to work for an Academy Award winning company.

**Marco:** Did it feel like a huge personal loss to leave the company, and have you remained friends with many of the people you worked with at SGE?

**Nadia:** My best friends were made at SGE. Truly! Two of my bridesmaids, my best friends in the world, were met there. The others; we have stayed in constant contact throughout the years. We have an SGE dinner every year at the AFM. I speak with Lenny Shapiro very often. He and Alan Solomon were truly my mentors and like fathers to me. I literally grew up there. When Alan Solomon passed away, his funeral was filled with former SGE employees, all of whom had lovely memories to share. One story I love is from when we were trying to get an MPAA rating for FRANKENHOOKER. We sent it to them, and Jack Valenti apparently said the film should be rated "S" for "Shit". We had a party for Lenny Shapiro's birthday that month, and we played Pin The Tail on the Donkey. However, we put a picture of Jack Valenti on the donkey's face, and turned it into Pin the Tail on Jack Valenti. I actually folded that up when we were finished (I believe Lenny won!) and mailed it anonymously to the MPAA. Let's just say that we had a lot of fun working at SGE, though we also worked very, very hard. We spent hours of overtime getting ready for the Film Markets such as the AFM, MIFED, Cannes, and the Tokyo Market. The entire office would pitch in making press kits and avail-lists for Alan. Lenny made sure we were properly fed all the time, and he paid for our gym memberships so we were healthy. It was a fantastic work environment. We were taught very well by Len, Alan and Jim as well. I honestly learned everything about foreign distribution from Alan.

**Marco:** During the late 80s the tendency of mainstream action films was to lighten up the conflicts with comedy elements and less graphic violence.

**Nadia:** We wanted, as Alan Solomon once famously said in a development meeting, lots of "People hitting people...and breasts." And then of course there were the Henenlotter titles, which added a lot of levity to our line-up. We just were really excellent at staying with what the marketplace wanted. MANIAC COP is one of the very few films, blending horror and action film trademarks directly.

**Marco:** How do you remember the work with cult director William Lustig and actor Bruce Campbell?

**Nadia:** I worked in the production office for MANIAC COP, in LA. Bill was a hoot – always very outgoing and loud and filled with laughter and life, though I never had to work with him on set. Sadly, because I am a huge fan, I didn't even get to meet Bruce Campbell, as far as I remember. But I met Robert Zdar who played the MANIAC COP – he was scary looking with the great big jaw, and he was very tall and intimidating, but as kind and nice as can be.

**Marco:** For how long was the crew abroad?

**Nadia:** On MANIAC COP I think they shot in NY and LA, not abroad. But for MCBAIN they shot in the Philippines for about 2 months I believe. I was on set for about a month. It was a great time. I met Michael Ironside on that film, and became great lifelong friends with him and his wife.

**Marco:** Talking about the artworks for SGE: Who was in charge of them?

**Nadia:** We used several great agencies in LA for our art. I seem to remember that the art was overseen by Len, Jim and Alan all equally, and then the rest of the staff would also weigh in with ideas and suggestions. I remember that we used David Kaiser a lot, as well as a gentlemen named Ken Goodman. The artwork for foreign was very, very important of course, and we sometimes used a couple of different options.

**Marco:** You learned about the artistic value of exploitation films, or do you mean economical aspects?

**Nadia:** I learned everything! While of course we tried to give the films as much artistic value as possible, clearly these were exploitation films. So the emphasis was on how to produce these films as economically as possible, with elements that would bring in the audience and the buyers. Alan Solomon and Lenny Shapiro both taught me everything I know about distribution. I learned about contracts and collections, I learned about all the deal points, I learned how to create a relationship with the important buyers, I learned how important artwork and trailers were, etc. I literally knew nothing about the film biz when I started there, and by the time I left I think I was very well versed in film distribution, in contract administration and negotiation, and in the marketing aspects as well.

**Marco:** Which films of SGE became the most popular cult favorites? What's the bestseller on DVD/BD?

**Nadia:** THE EXTERMINATOR has a huge following, as does RED SCORPION. The cult favorites are definitely MANIAC COP, the BASKET CASE trilogy, and FRANKENHOOKER. In fact, FRANKENHOOKER has a 35mm print that makes the rounds for midnight screenings throughout the US.

**Marco:** Have the films been remastered from original copies? Is there still an archive, covering the celluloid copies?

**Nadia:** Don May Jr., of Synapse Films (who released the BluRays of all our titles in the US recently) did all the remastering into true HD from the original materials. I have had tremendous compliments on the quality of the new masters; he is truly one of the best in the industry. It took quite some time after Alan passed away to find all the materials which were at various labs and in storage places. We now have all the materials that may be used in the near future at a lab in LA, and the archive materials are all in a storage facility in New York.

**Marco:** Tell me something about your writing. Was this always a passionate hobby for you or did you start late with this?

**Nadia:** Writing and reading have always been my passion, particularly short stories. My stories come to me in spurts – I don't write every day at all; there will be months with no writing. But then suddenly a story will come to me, and it just spills out. A lot of my stories are very personal and catharctic. I have submitted them to various literary magazines, and I have won some awards from Glimmer Train journal, of which I am quite proud. At some point in 2014, I sent a short story to Iris Berry, who is an editor at Punk Hostage Press, and an amazing writer and performance artist in Los Angeles. I knew her vaguely through my brother. I'm a huge fan of hers, and frankly did not expect her to even have time to read the story, much less comment on it. But she did read it, and she told me that I write "phenomonally" and that Punk Hostage Press wanted to publish a collection of my short stories! I was really overwhelmed, I have to say! We put together the collection, which includes 3 poems as well, and used a photo of my brother's (Geoffrey Cordner) for the cover, and the book Scars was published in November of 2014. It honestly has been a life-long dream to be published, so this has all been very exciting for me.

**Marco:** Is there any influence in Scars from your work in the movie business?

**Nadia:** Scars is a collection of very personal stories. Only two of them are fiction; the rest of the collection is all true. I went through a very tough time after my mother passed away of cancer in 1994. The stories are mostly about a descent into hell, recovery and redemption from that hell. I discuss physical abuse, drug and alcohol abuse, hate and love. The title story, Scars, is about my physical scars and the emotional scars behind them. Punk Hostage Press has placed many of the books in prisons, jails, rehab centers and women's shelters. My hope is that people who are going through a hard time, through physical or substance abuse of any kind, will read this book and find hope in it. I hope that my story will inspire others and help them to realize that there is always a way out. I now have almost 18 years sober and a fantastic life. As far as the movie business influencing the book: I think the main way I was influenced was by the love from the people I met at SGE. My best friends in the world were met there (Darby Walker and Marilyn Moore), and also I have remained close with Len, Jim, Stephen Roberts, and of course Alan before he passed away. They were all so supportive of me when I got sober and worked my way back into the Industry.

**Marco:** What kind of short stories do you prefer as a reader? Are there some influences that come to your mind? Do you rather prefer a hard boiled crime story?

**Nadia:** I'm more of a heavy duty literature person! I love Hemingway and Faulkner and Sandra Cisneros and Cormac McCarthy. I love words that paint a picture, that paint a feeling. All the old Beatnik writers of course, Kerouac in particular. He was my hero for a very long time, I love his style and what he and Bukowski brought to the literary world. Sandra Cisneros is a big influence – her book *The House On Mango Street* makes me sob every time I read it. She is brilliant with words, with an emotion.

**Marco:** Let's talk about NBR Media Inc. - it was established in 2008. What made you decide to form your very own company?

**Nadia:** I wanted to work my own hours and do my own thing – I was definitely overly stressed doing Business Affairs at such high profile companies. I wanted to spend time with my daughter and have time for myself. It initially began as a company that other indies could use to draft agreements and financing documents. Then when Alan passed away, Jim Glickenhaus asked me to take over handling the SGE library, and I became a Sales Agent.

**Marco:** Besides managing the film library by SGE, NBR Media specializes in international sales. Do you pick these films, for example Chris Ingvordsens TAR PIT or SEASON OF DARKNESS by Jay Woelfel? How close do you work with the filmmakers?

**Nadia:** Chris and Jay both picked me, I think – I'd been in touch over the years with Chris, and was handling his library as well. When he decided to shoot a new film, I was really excited at the opportunity to continue working with him. He's a great guy and a great filmmaker.

**Marco:** The famous Lloyd Kaufman is quoted on your website: "Movies are art, and the spirit of the movie depends on the creators." - Have you ever worked with Troma Studios? When did you hear Mr. Kaufman coming up with this saying - and did it become the main idea of your business philosophy?

**Nadia:** We worked with Troma actually at SGE – we released a film of theirs called DEF BY TEMPTATION. Lloyd is an amazing guy, brilliant, funny and fun. I remember when we were in discussions with them to handle DEF, at Cannes, Lloyd would send the Troma-ettes over to get Lenny to come to a meeting. These girls were something! And always accompanied by Toxie. As far as the quote, I just think it is so true – you can feel the creators of a film deep down.

**Marco:** So many things changed in filmmaking and distribution since the early days of your career until nowadays. For independently produced action and horror films, is there still a market?

**Nadia:** There is really not much of a market at all anymore. It's all VOD, all studio films, all big names and big money. I worry what film students have as far as a future. Yes it's easy to make a film now, digitally, but to find a release for it is next to impossible. The audience has become so discerning and mature, it's not like the old days. People don't want to give an indie film like SEX, LIES AND VIDEOTAPE a chance...there are a lot of those types of films being made, but no one wants to watch them. I have this brilliant film called WORM. It's received amazing reviews, festivals love it, everyone who watches it loves it. I did manage to get a US DVD release for it from Synapse, who are also trying to exploit it on VOD, but for foreign it is too difficult. There are no stars and there's no action, so no foreign deal. Sad...

**Marco:** Today you live in Tennessee. When you moved there, did you think it's a better place for raising kids and having a family?

**Nadia:** We left LA in 2011 or so. It's too expensive, too crowded, too materialistic, too "plastic". I miss the weather and my friends, but for the kids it's better to grow up in a more "realistic" environment.

**Marco:** You recently dealt with two films which were shot there, correct? Tell me about the films and do you have a special connection to these films.

**Nadia:** I picked up two Tennessee films, WORM, which I already mentioned, and FALLS THE SHADOW, which was released in the US as ZOMBIE WARZ. Both were made by local producer/directors, and both just really stood out to me. There is a small film-market here in Nashville called FilmCom where I found these two. I had a lot of luck both foreign and domestic with FALLS THE SHADOW, which was a post-apocalyptical movie with a real heart. It did very well. WORM is my favorite all time film, I swear. It just grabbed me. As I mentioned, it's a tough one to sell, but it deserves to be seen. The filmmakers are a very talented group, I hope they go on to make other films that really succeed financially as well as critically.

---

By Nadia Bruce-Rawlings in writing
from Old Hickory, Tennessee
26April, 2015

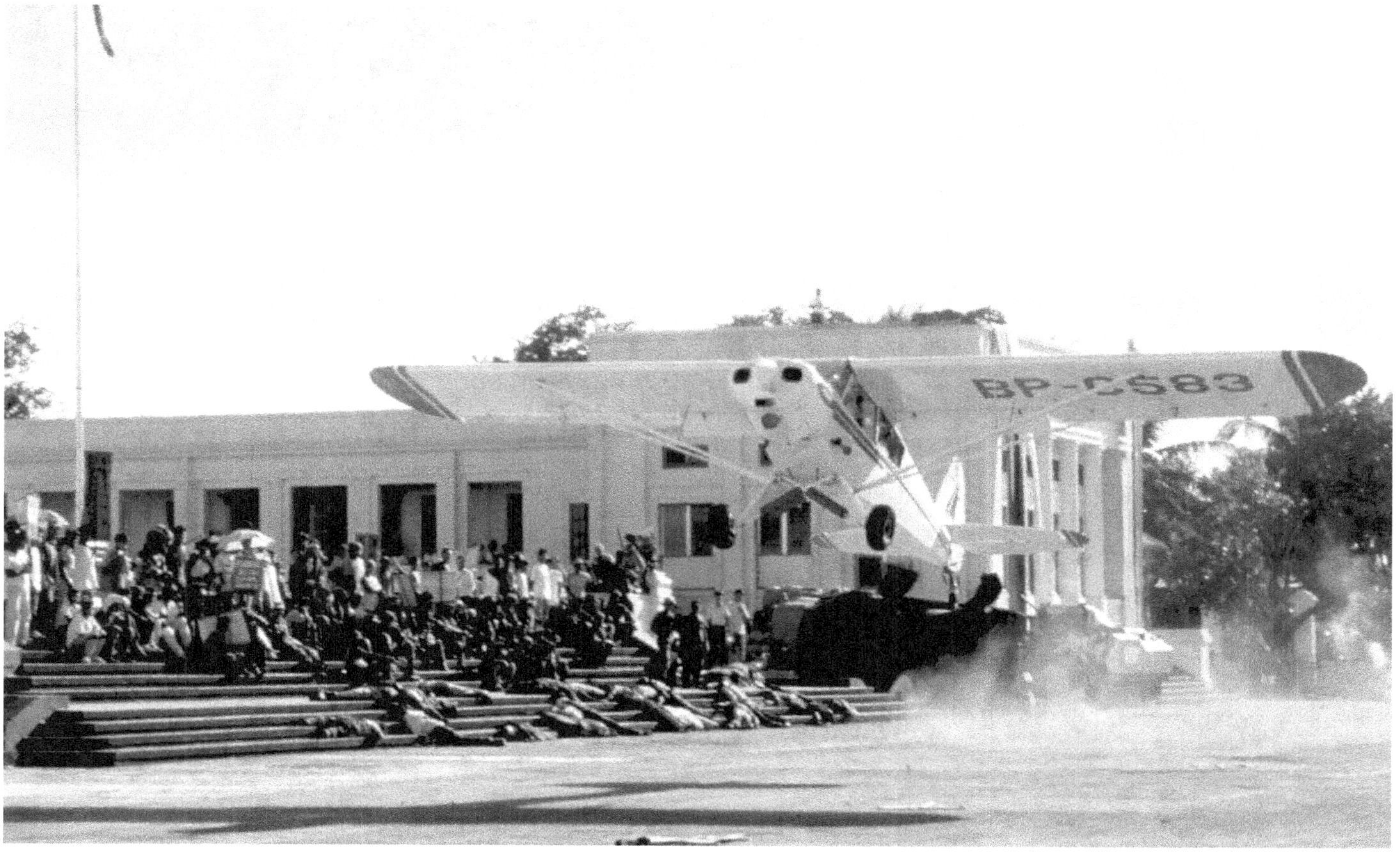

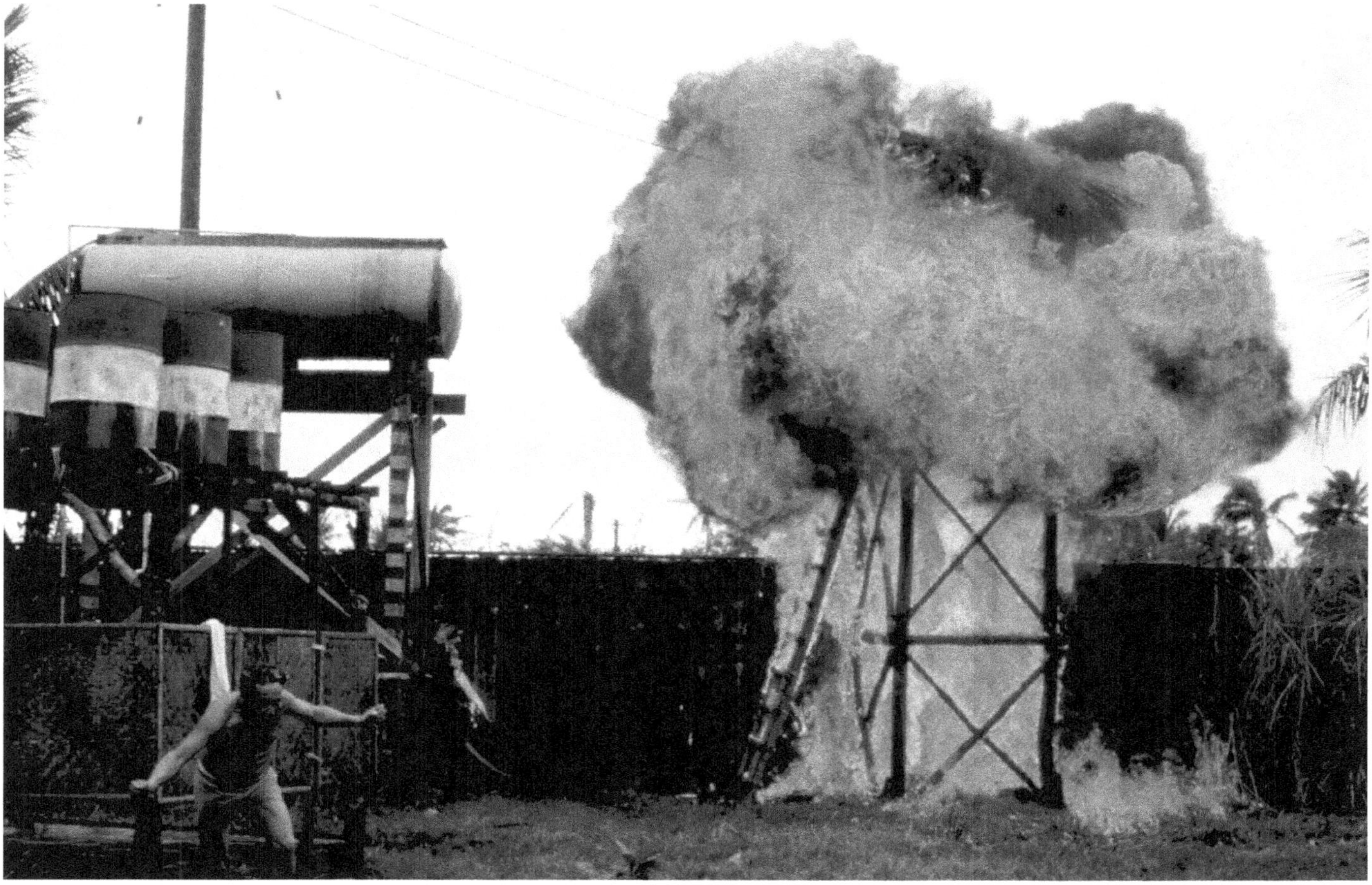

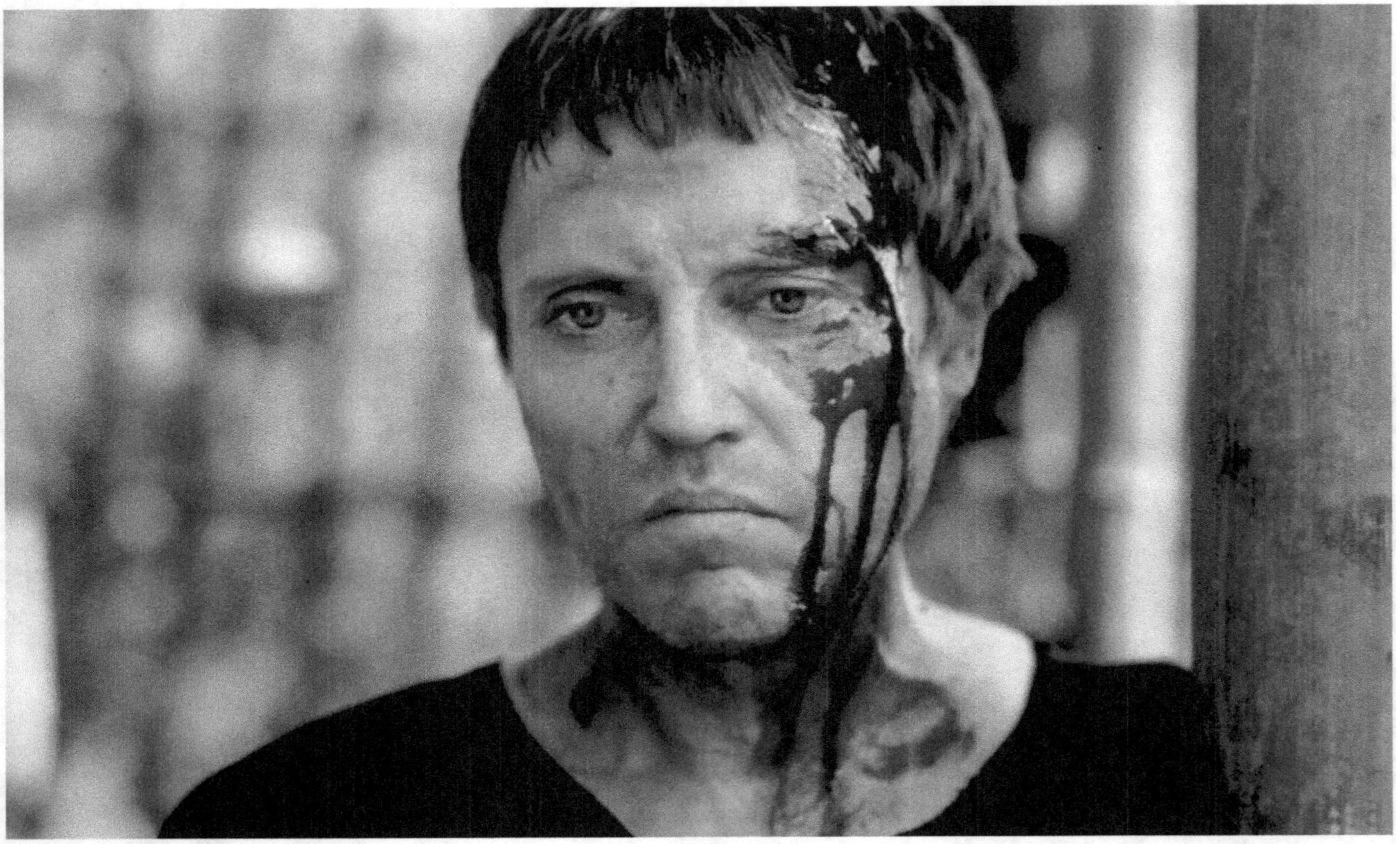

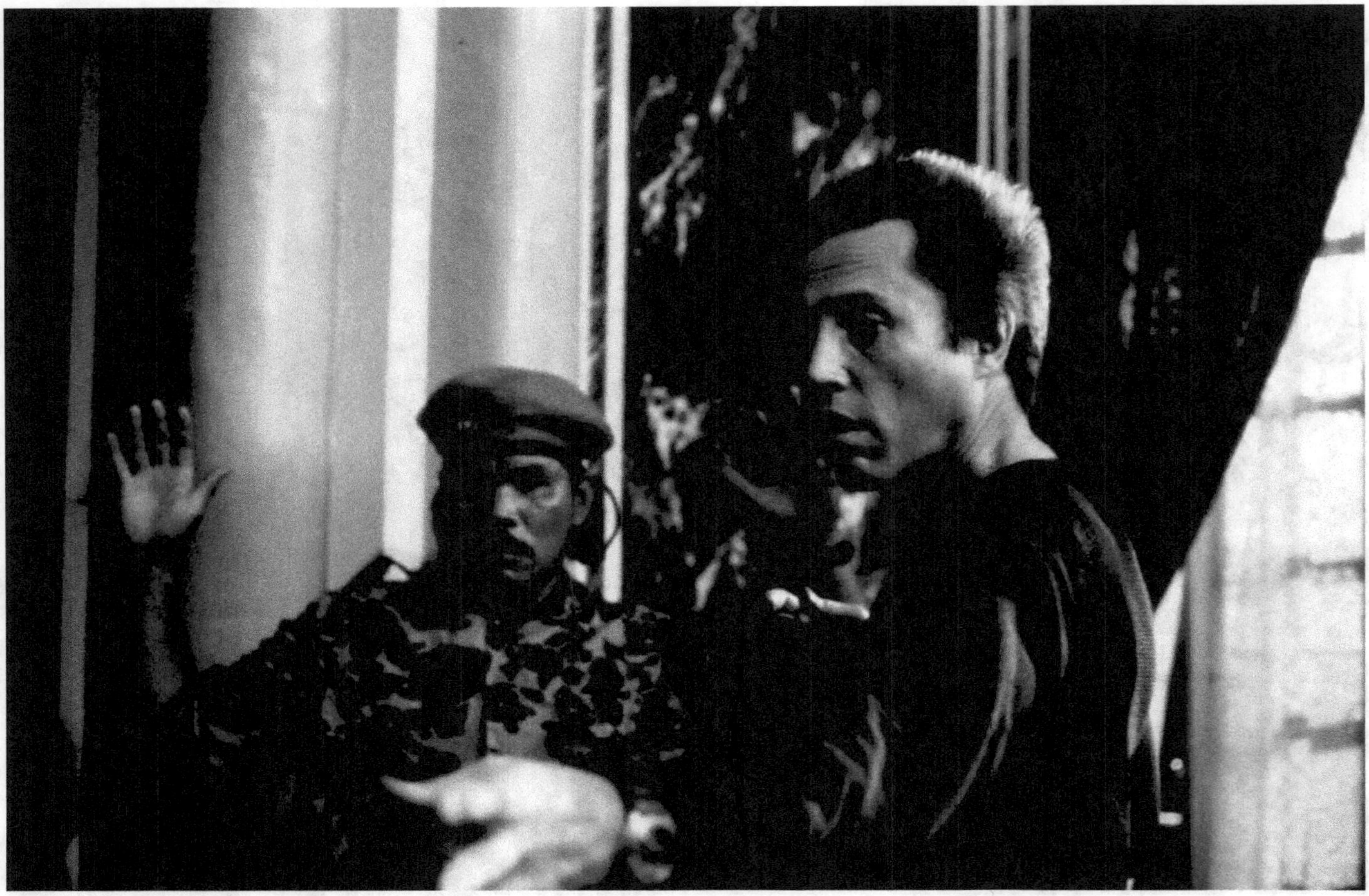

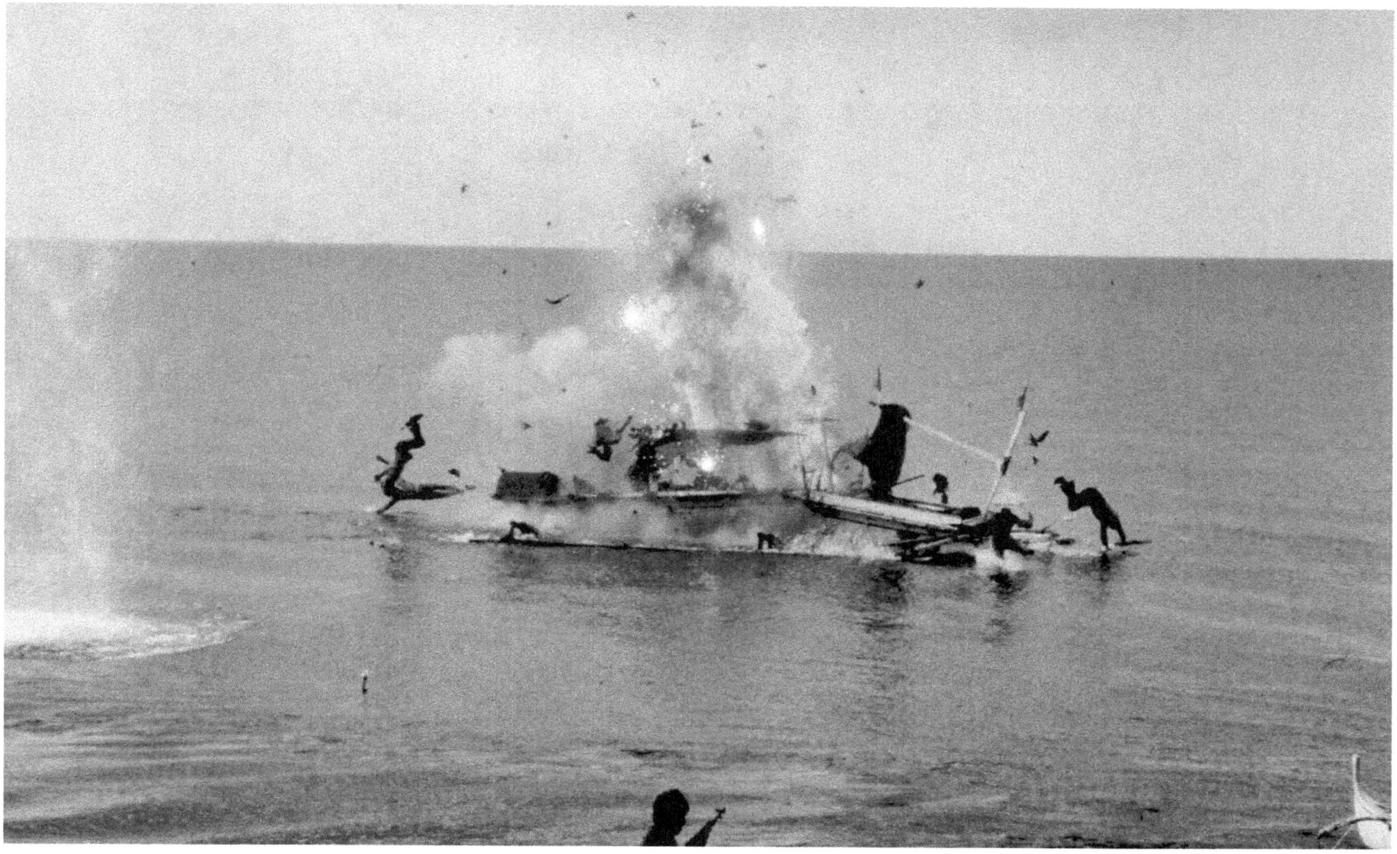

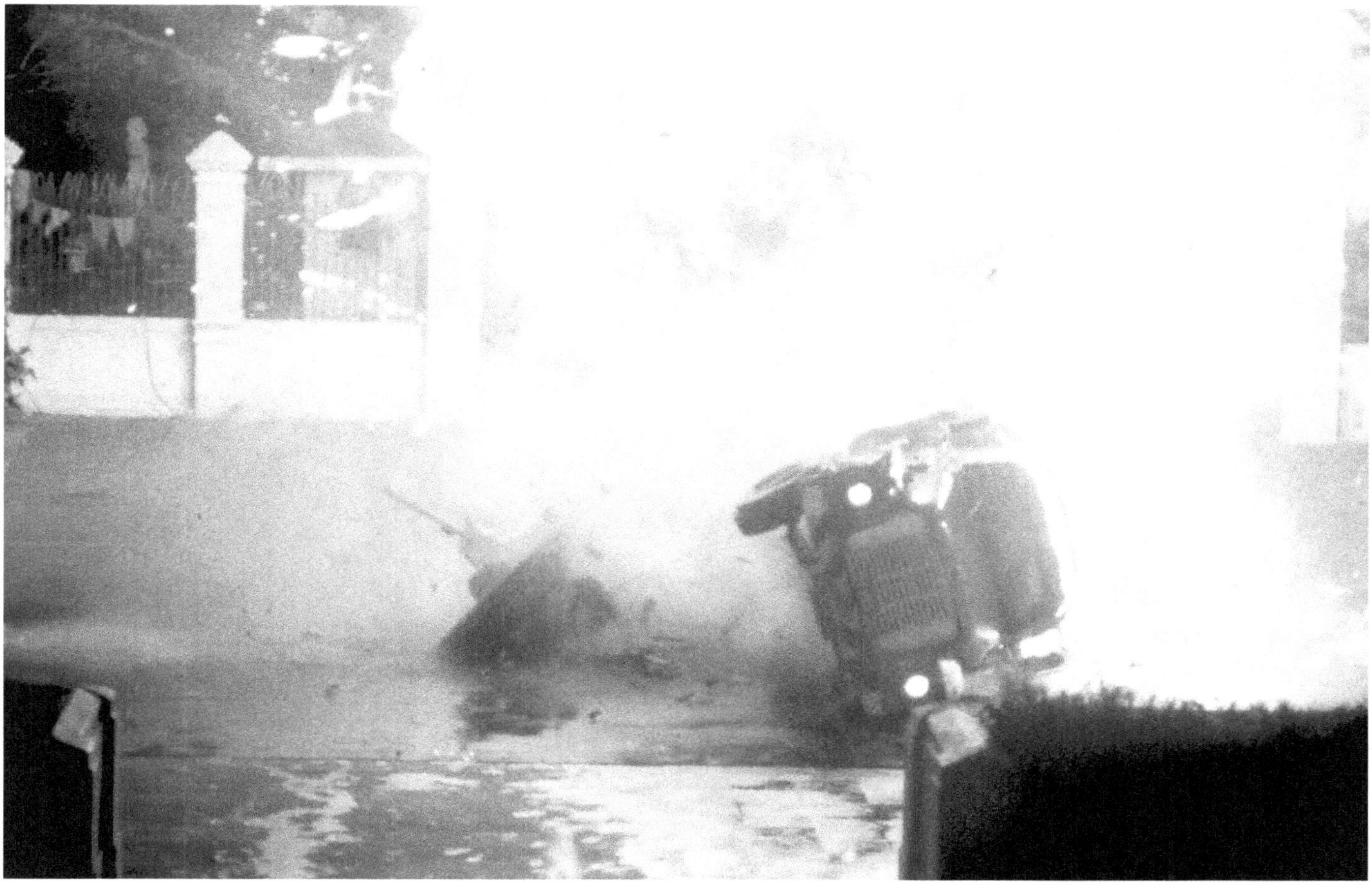

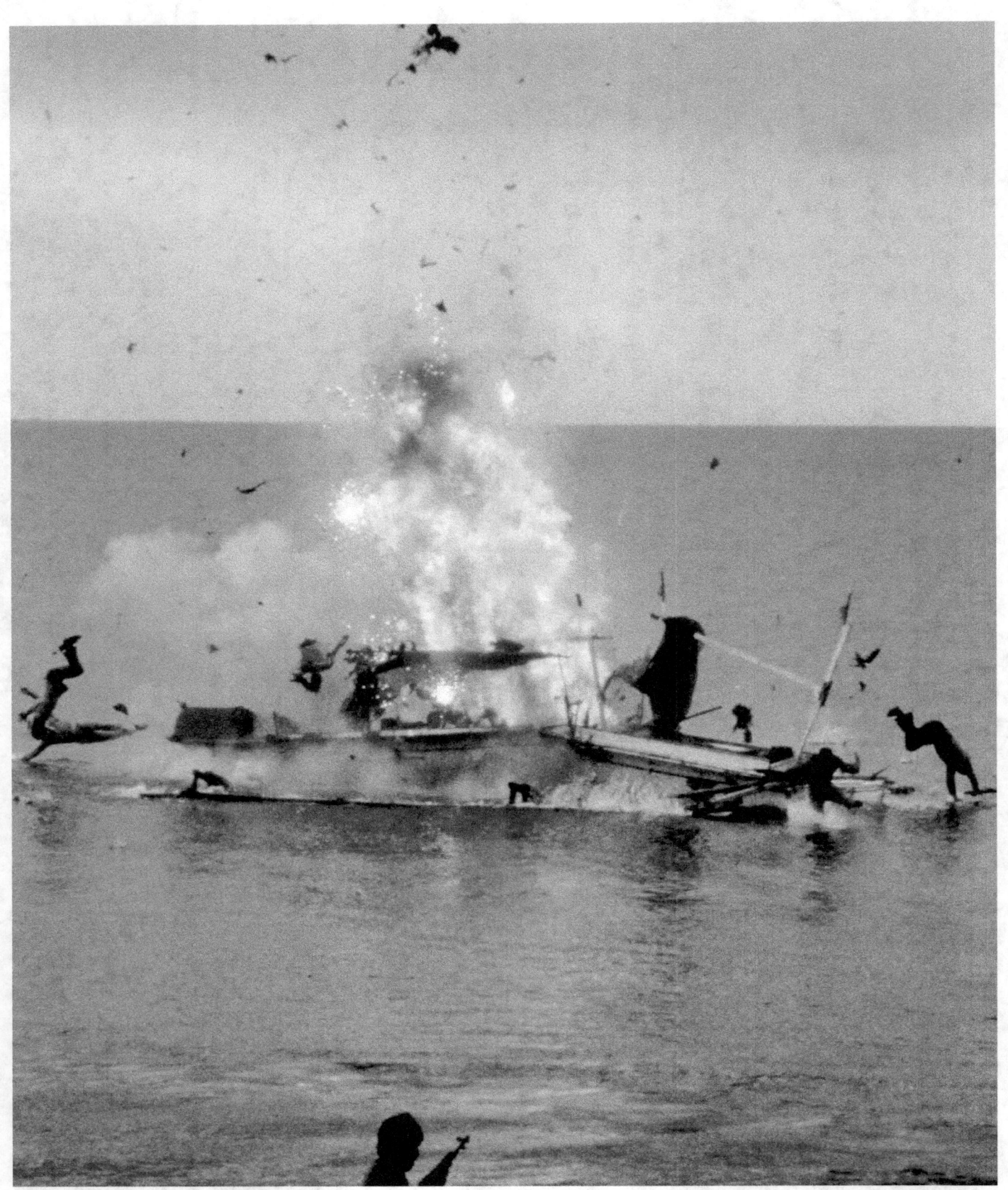

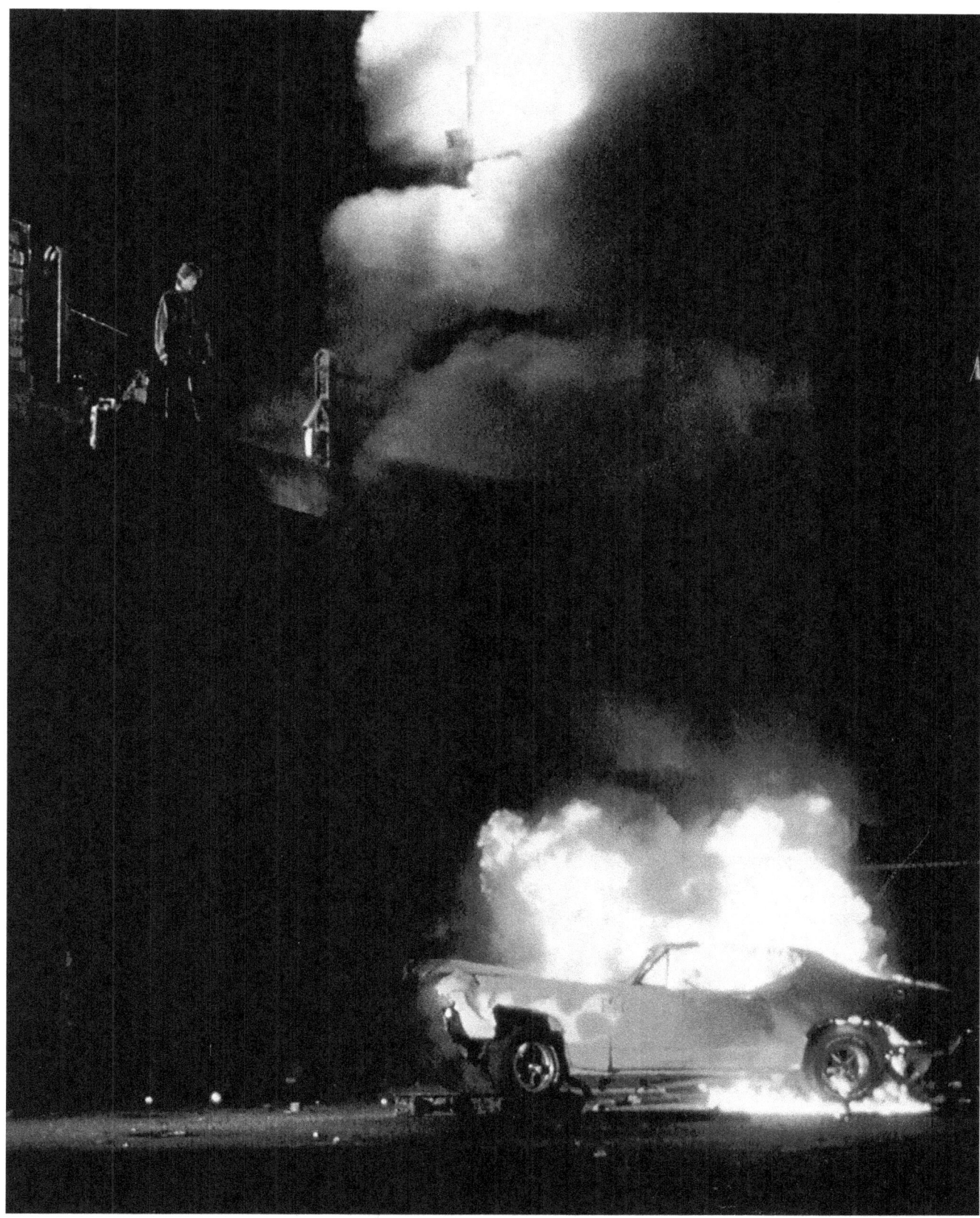

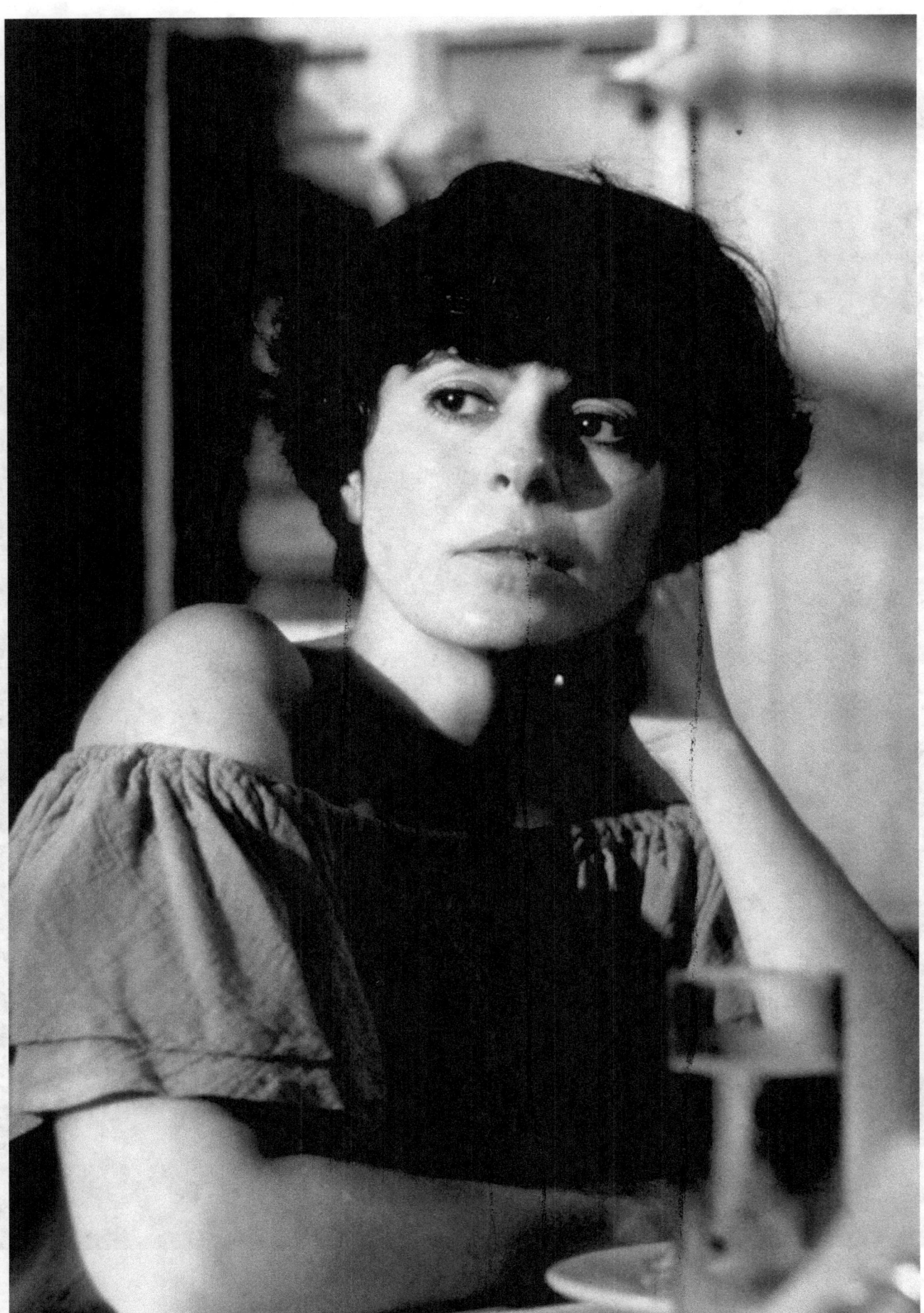

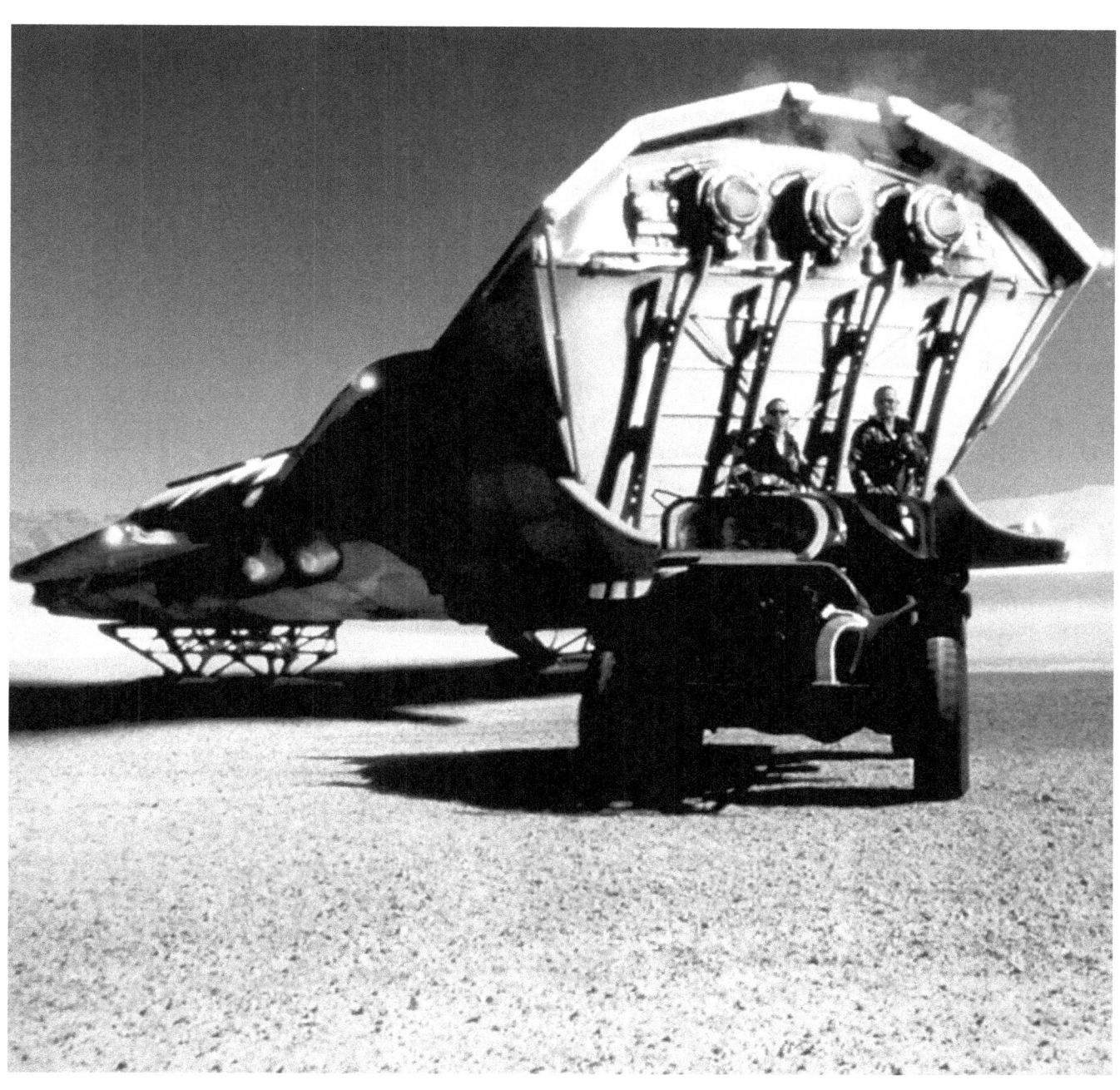

# James Glickenhaus (Part II)

Since SGE closed its doors, Jim Glickenhaus has not returned to filmmaking; instead he turned toward the family business. In addition, Mr. Glickenhaus is known for his passion for racing cars. He is not only a collector of rare and precious cars from different decades, but he is completely involved with the Scuderia Cameron Glickenhaus. The team around Jim Glickenhaus has the purpose of designing and engineering unique vehicles, including road and racing cars. The company is highly acclaimed among experts and won the Fia Alternative Energies Champion Award in 2012.

**Nadia:** When did you develop such an interest in sports cars?

**James:** Oh gosh, it was when I was 14, or 15, I would buy wrecked cars and learn how they worked, hot rod them and turn them into drag racers. I liked cars and mechanics for a long, long time.

**Nadia:** Do you remember the first car in your collection? And do you drive all the cars once in a while?

**James:** Yeah, I drive all of them once in a while, I'm not someone who just collects cars. But that being said, you know there's another problem with cars. They become taken up by people who buy them, and sell them for huge money. So some of these cars become somewhat valuable. It makes it harder to get more of them. And I really don't want to own a car that I don't have the time to drive. So my collection is full.

**Nadia:** Right.

**James:** And I also became a constructor. We now design, engineer, and build race cars, and sell them. I find it's a very interesting thing to do. So the first car I had, it was a 54-Studebaker without an engine, and I put in a Pontiac engine, a Corvette transmission, and turned it into drag racer.

**Nadia:** How do you shelter yourself from exorbitance...

**James:** I really haven't sold a collector car for 40 years. I have every car I bought. To me, I like stories. So the cars I own are sort of pieces of history, like I own the oldest Ferrari in existence. It was the first one Enzo Ferrari sold. It enabled him to start his company, and turn it into what he did. I own a very famous Ferrari Race Car, a P3-4, that finished first in Daytona in 1967. It then became the basis of the gigantic Ford-Ferrari wars between Enzo Ferrari and Henry II. And I own one of the Fords that raced against it. And I own Dusenbergs, which are sort of amazing things, built during the Depression, and they're very beautiful. So the cars I own are stories. I like stories, pieces of history. Also I like them as a bit of a time machine, so when you drive them it's like you squint your eyes, and you go back in time.

**Nadia:** You never placed one of them as a key element for a scene in your films?

**James:** My Lola was in THE ASTROLOGER, and we had a drag racing scene in SHAKEDOWN. It wasn't my car, but we had them. In THE EXTERMINATOR we had hot rods and car races, I did car chasing scenes. But no, I never really put any particular car in. I like the engineering, and oddly enough at this late stage in my life, in November I'm going to be titled by the government of Italy. They are giving me an engineering title. An honorary one, with a ceremony in Turin. That's what I'm doing. Figure out how to make them better, and preserving them. And where there's an intersection of art. The cars I have are really unique, one of a kind. Show cars that were important in their time. One car that I own really first appeared with a model in a Pucci dress holding onto an Afghan on the cover of Vogue. Another one was with André Courrèges and Twiggy and Mary Quant arguing about who invented the mini skirt. There were many mini skirted babes standing in front of the car, photographed with it. I like the intersection of art and cars, and I also collect art. It's been a passion for a long time.

**Nadia:** You have a special focus on the Ferrari brand. What's the special thing about their cars?

**James:** I think it's a very operatic story, Ferrari. You know, he's sitting on Christmas day in his factory, unable to pay the heat. And he's in his overcoat, instead of being home having Christmas dinner, and his friend Luigi Chinetti stops by and says, "If you build cars, I could sell 'em." What he wanted to do is race cars. He was an interesting guy, a bit of a dictator. Harsh guy, and a talented guy. Got into a huge pissing match with Ford, the Ford-Ferrari Wars, but they were stories. And I also think they are very beautiful. They sort of say form follows function, but when things became more efficient and they weren't as pretty - they stuck with being pretty for a while. Cars were very curvaceous. I mean, they claim that the P3/4 is Sophia Loren's ass, and it probably is! *(laughs)* Eventually before it changed, Enzo died, another guy named Luca Di Montezemolo took it over. We went through a few pissing matches, but it worked out. Then it was just time for me to go on my own. There's one thing to know about Enzo, he started with Alfa Romeo. When a Ferrari beat an Alfa Romeo, he said: "I feel like I've killed my mother." Our cars have beaten Ferrari's, but I don't feel like I've killed my mother. It has just been an interesting adventure. They started writing me letters, saying I was trading on their name. No one would let me drive their car, except for the badge. And I said: "Ok, I'll take the badge off on youtube." and millions of people watched it. But I've always been a bit of an asshole.

**Nadia:** What's the story behind founding the Scuderia Cameron-Glickenhaus?

**James:** Scuderia means racing stable. In older times knights were under scuderia. It's basically Meg is Cameron and I'm Glickenhaus. I had a badge that had the fit of a Ferrari – took that out. So to make sure I stood out, it is the torch of the Statue of Liberty. And the red white and blue is for America. So it's pretty simple. And the font of the SCG, is that of the Declaration of Independence. So that's sort of what it is.

**Nadia:** What kind of projects are realised? Is it about designing and engineering new models?

**James:** Yes, that's what we do, we're designing, and engineering, and racing, and selling cars. So we have race cars that we sell, and we have a road version of it, that we're going to be selling. And we actually have an alliance with a major manufacture who is going to be providing us engine, and other services. It's not going to be a thing that you are seeing many of them. They're sold for over a million dollars. But we do sell them. We've won an FI World Championship.

**Nadia:** What kind of work do you do exactly for SCG?

**James:** Well, I provide the overview of the company, and the financing, and ideas! But I think it's true, and like with the films. You don't make a movie by yourself. I mean there are some film makers who are very hands-on, but if you look at great movies, the score is what you might remember. Sergio Leone was a fantastic filmmaker, but was it Eastwood who made that movie work, or was it composer Enrico Morricone? It's among the best scores ever made. Same thing with JAWS, I mean Spielberg is a very talented guy, and the story was real good. But that music really got you. So it's a collaborative effort, and I realized that with any kind of company. And I think I did that with SGE, I never stood on your head while you did what you did. I try to get full freedom. And I certainly gave Lenny freedom, and Alan sometimes. Perhaps a little too much to those guys. It's just the way I am.

**Nadia:** The styling of your cars is influenced by the 60s and 70s.

**James:** It is a little bit. One of the hardest things with cars today is, what's aerodynamically efficient is not necessarily beautiful. So the hardest thing I do, and the most contribution I think I have to our cars, is making them very fast, very aerodynamically efficient, but still have a certain beauty to them. And the wow factor, I think. And even if you know nothing about cars you look at them, and just go: Wow! That's something that makes them worth driving 50 years down the road.

**Nadia:** What kinds of competitions do the cars appear in?

**James:** We're endurance sports cars, so we race in the 24 hours of the Nürburgring, and in the future we hope to race in LeMans. And other endurance races around the world.

**Nadia:** SCG won an award for alternative energy in 2012. What kind of importance has this aspect in general?

**James:** Well, it's the aspect that young people are looking at. The resources of the world are finite, and the idea was: Could we use a system that recaptured lost braking energy, and convert it into power. To

| | |
|---|---|
| | make the car go faster. And this says a lot about the applications for road cars, because it saves fuel. It's a hybrid. The one thing I think people are not realizing |
| | is that racing cars, which are put at the extreme test as they are, develop systems that are used by everybody. I mean, the rear view mirror, the automatic transmission, radial tires, hybrid technology. A lot of it comes out of racing. And if it wasn't for that it wouldn't be on the cars that we all drive. |
| **Nadia:** | You are probably envied by countless men all over the world for the founding of SCG. Would you say that this is the kind of work that fulfills you more than other projects you did in the past? |
| **James:** | Oh, no, no. It's all fun. I mean I enjoyed it all. Listen I enjoy being a sculptor, and I went back and sculpted. So I like it all, it's all cool stuff, and I think I am very lucky. I've been able to follow my dreams, and I do think that there are a lot of people who love cars. A lot of guys who love cars probably more than anything else. I've just been lucky to follow my dreams, nothing more, nothing less. |
| **Nadia:** | Do you miss filmmaking? |
| **James:** | At least I still act in them with Frank Henenlotter, I am writing a script. I have been very busy so I haven't gotten back to it for a while. And I do think I'll make another film, but I think if I do it's going to be like the old days. A very small crew, a very small film. And it will be about something. Having said that, I mean who knows? If anything you can answer that. Do you miss it? Your life changes all around you. You know what I'm saying? |
| **Nadia:** | It's funny. Sometimes I do a lot, but… |
| **James:** | I mean we all had some great times, some amazing times. However, there's also a lot of mishegosh, I think that comes with it. I saw Henenlotter's film last night, CHASING BANKSY, me and a million hipsters. It was sort of like a cross between EXIT THROUGH THE GIFT SHOP and FACTORY GIRL. They're talking with someone re a limited theatrical release, etc., it could do great in a limited release. I saw Gabe Bartalos, he's great. Frank's ok….there's just a whole group of young hipsters, music people, film people, that seem to just be in an interesting place. |

**By Nadia Bruce-Rawlings, in writing**
**from Los Angeles**
**27July, 2015**

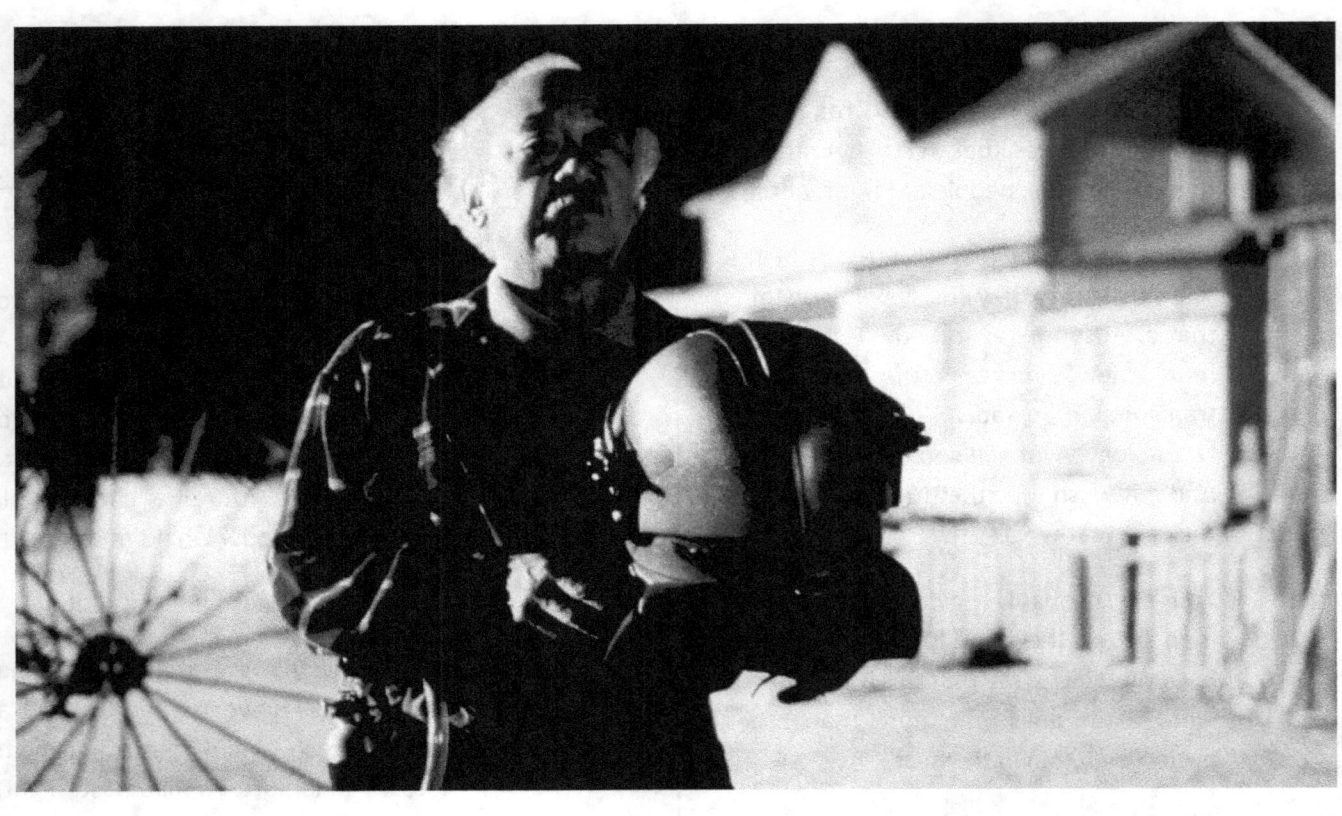

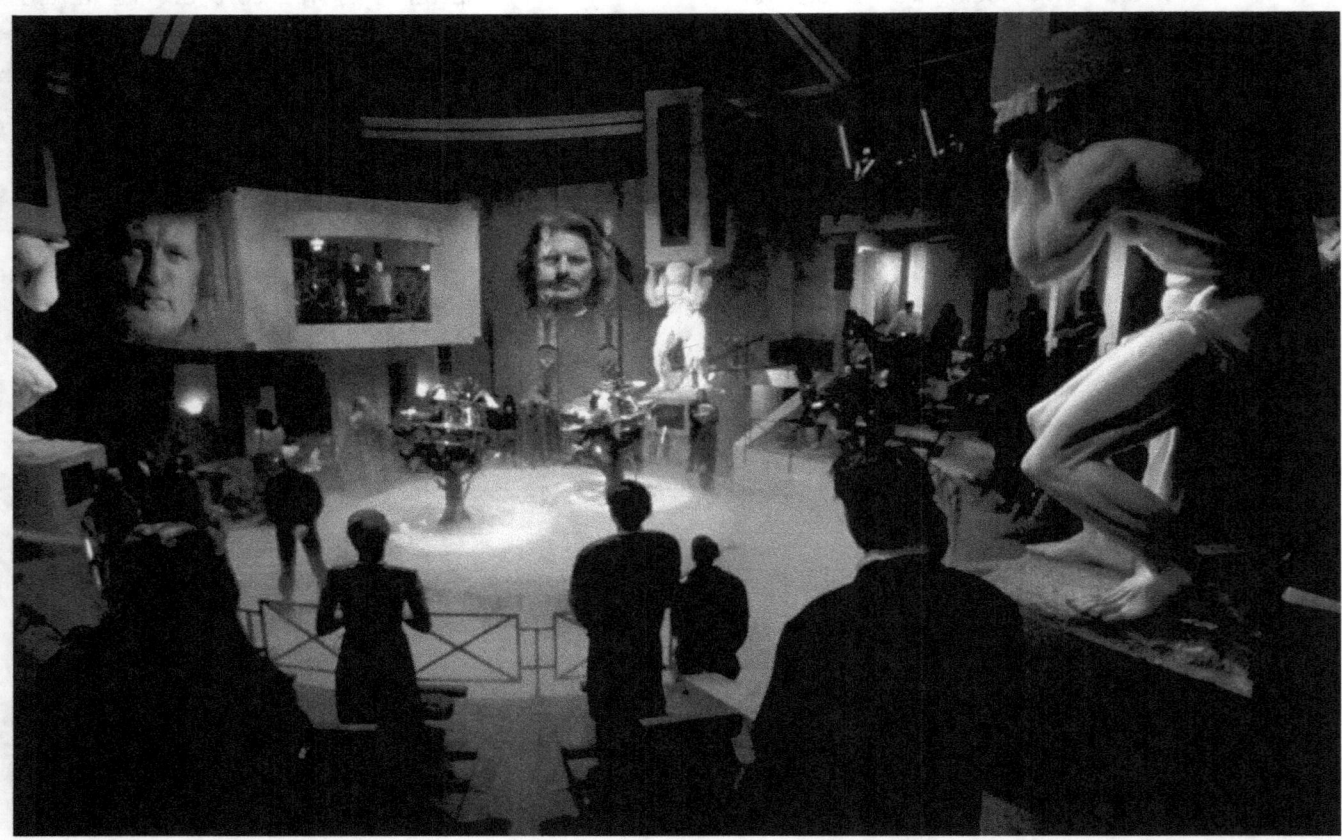

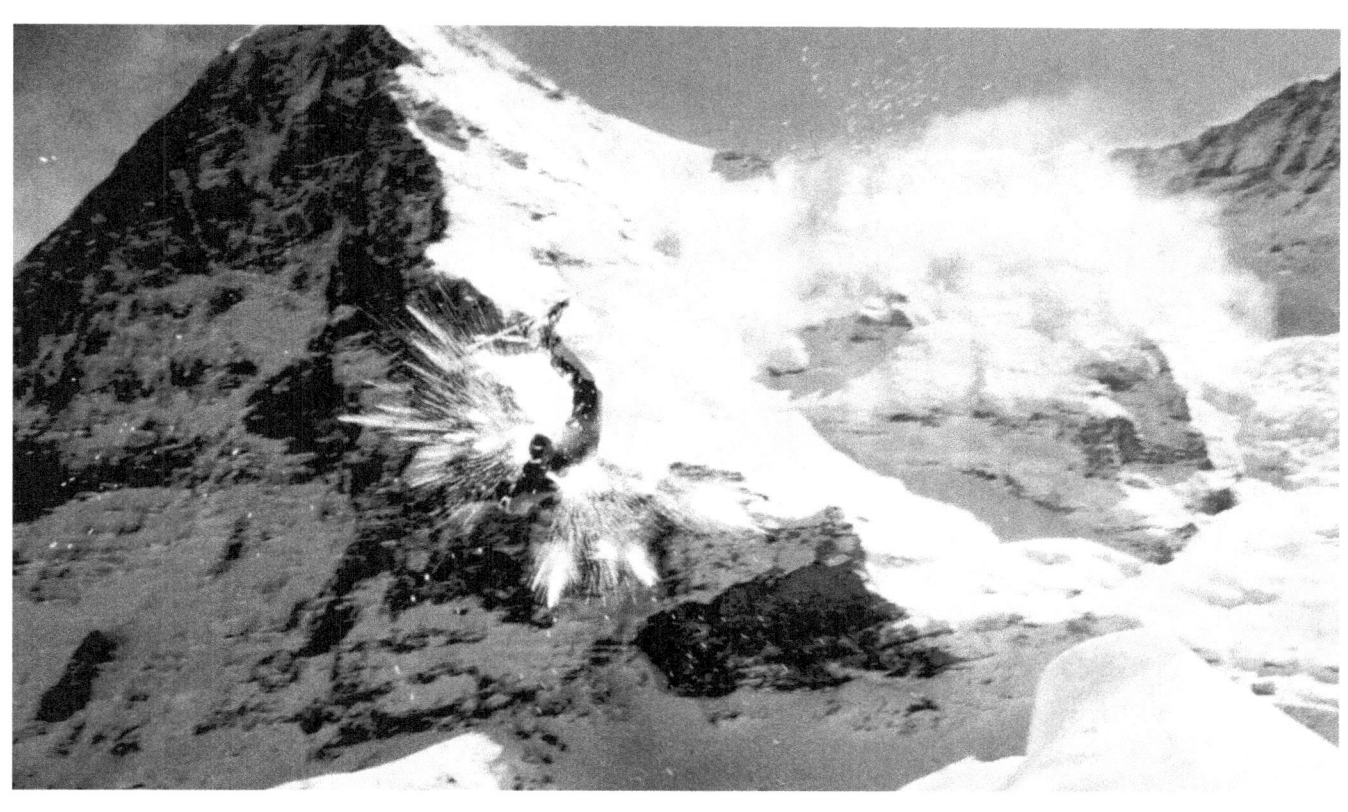

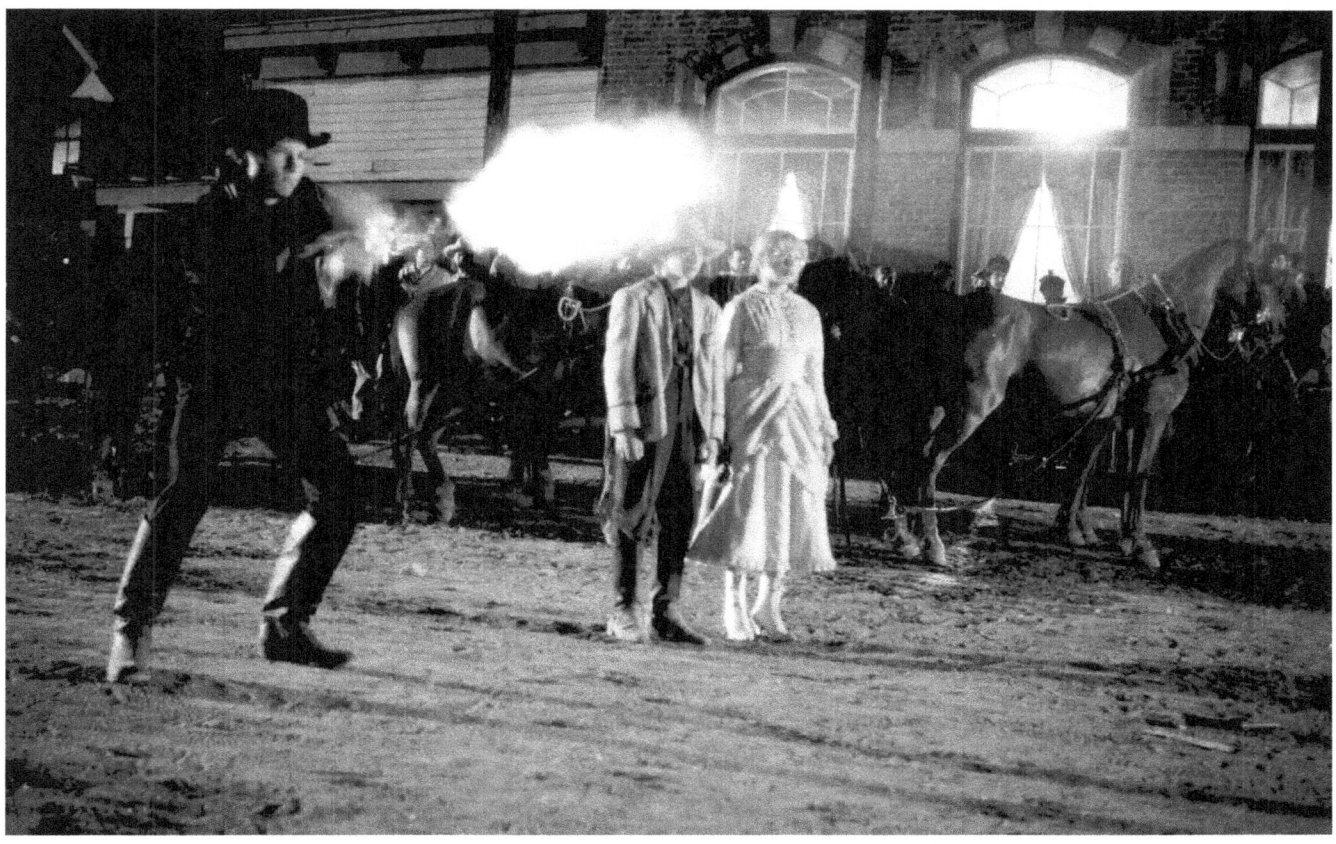

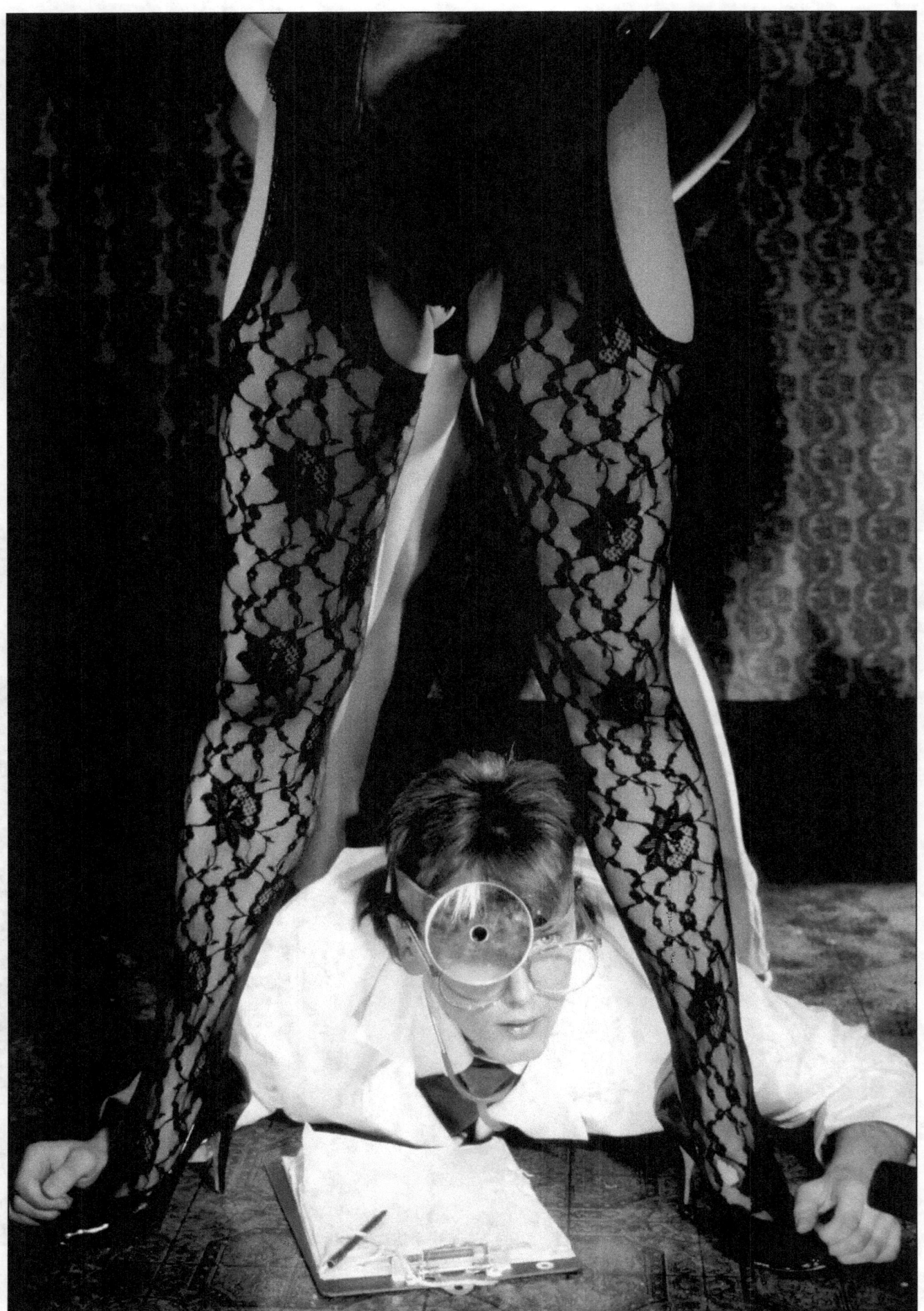

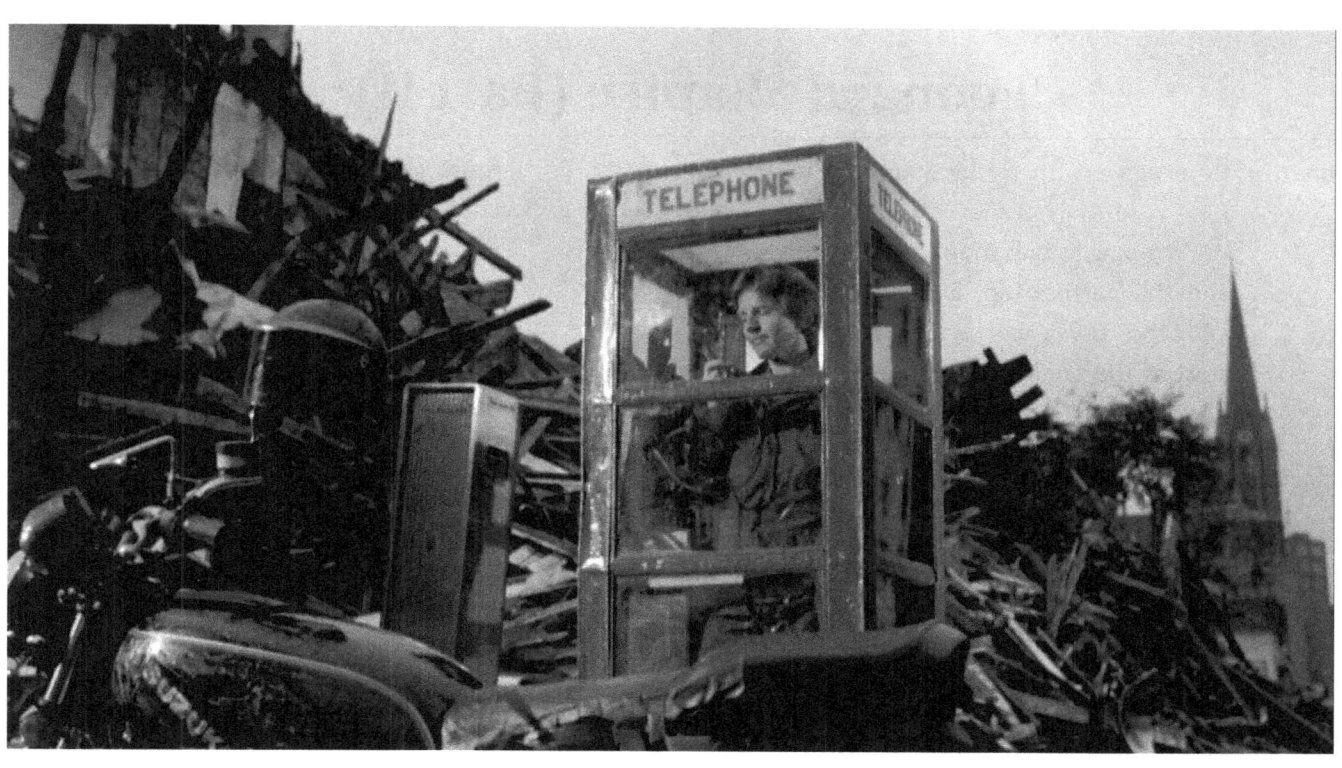

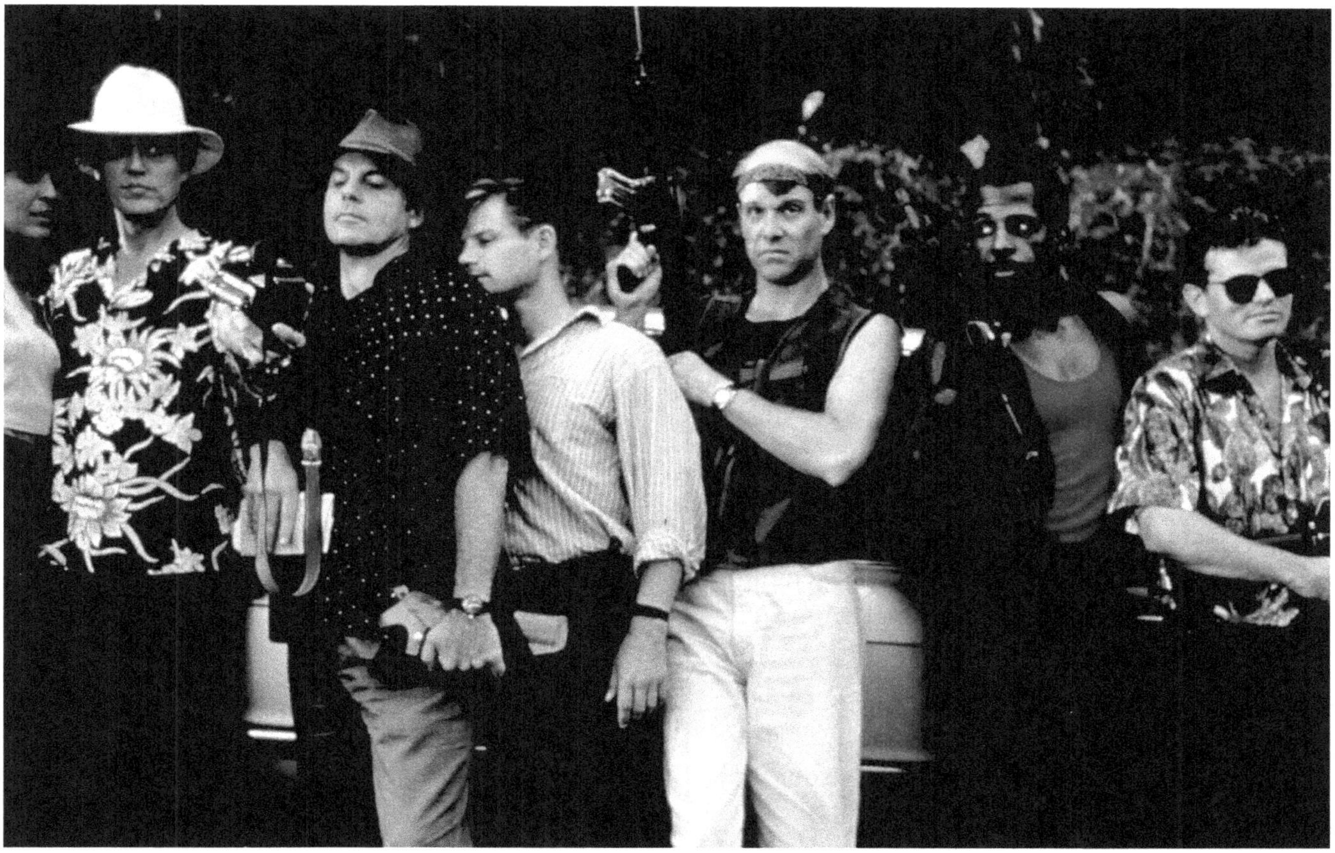

# Leonard Shapiro (Part II)

**Stephen:** Here again with Lenny Shapiro, Sunday June 7. At Marmalade Café with mojitos! We're going to talk about Jim Glickenhaus and the partnership, and how it began and the personal relationship. Lenny, start at the beginning, why do you think partnering with Jim was a good idea?

**Leonard:** Well, any indie company needs really top filmmakers to be part of what they're doing. I met Jim at Avco Embassy Pictures, when I screened THE EXTERMINATOR, which Avco Embassy picked up for US/Canada distribution. The commitment was pretty simple; we'd give the film a theatrical shot, and it started in NY. I must say because I was pretty aggressive in the acquisition area, and every deal was critical to us, so going theatrical was a very critical commitment. So we had to give it a theatrical in New York City as its first major release, which was what Jim wanted, a major part of what he wanted for his film. It ended up being the highlight, up to that point, of my career. Because we opened the film in about 91 theatres in a showcase multiple run, NY, Jersey, Connecticut, which is as many prints as you could get into that marketplace for an opening, the most that had ever been done before. The picture went through the roof, it was a million dollar gross the first weekend! If anything can start a good relationship it's a gross like that! And more importantly, I'll never forget that night. I was in LA, Jim was at the theatre, and I said "Jim, as soon as the film opens and as soon as there's a gross, please call me and let me know what the numbers are." He called me after the matinees, and they were ok, they were fair, we couldn't really tell what was going to happen. The National Theatre, it was a big single theatre, in NY on 43rd Street., a very popular house right near 42nd street, and we also had it at another theatre called The Lyric, that was right on 42nd street, that they didn't really advertise, but they ran it from midday all through the night on a continuous run, and you never really get grosses on that. But we were getting grosses on The National. However, when the picture started, the opening scene of THE EXTERMINATOR is a major action scene, a confrontation between the Viet Cong group and the American soldiers, and they basically behead some of THE SOLDIERs all in a line-up, right? And it was such a gruesome scene. There's a whole story about getting an R rating and such, that Avco Embassy got for the film, that whole process, that whole scene was a game changer in its own right on the way the MPAA looked at films. After this picture they never rated films the same way again!

**Stephen:** Did you break the MPAA system? *(laughs)*

**Leonard:** Yes! Because they let you bring film back, after they tell you what to do, the same day. So we were editing as they were telling us the changes to make, and if I remember correctly we brought the film back 4-5 times in the same day! And then they forgot what they were looking at, after a while, and we went back to our original cut! Now I don't know if this should be printed....but anyway! Nowadays you can't get another appointment for a conversation on a film for two weeks after the first change. You can't go back and make the change. Anyway, that scene was so impressive to action fans, that the audience at The National - sold out, 1100 seats - did not leave after the movie because they wanted to see the scene again! So you have another 1100 people outside the theatre trying to get in, you have 1100 inside the theatre, you have fights breaking out, chaos! So when I called Jim, "Hey what's our number, how are we doing?" He said, "I have no idea, there're fights all over the place, the audience won't leave, we can't get the people outside into the showing, and even though it's chaotic, it's certainly not bad for business!" *(laughter)*

**Stephen:** So that's how your relationship with Jim began. Where did it go from there, at what point did you decide to partner with him in the company, take me through the intervening 2-3 years.

**Leonard:** Well, through a series of decisions, Avco Embassy picked up Jim's next film, THE SOLDIER, which he was producing in Buffalo with another financier, and the financing fell out. So to make a long story short, Jim called me, said "Len I'm in preproduction, I have the sets built, I have the cast ready to go (Ken Wahl), ready to go…" I said "I'll pitch it to the head of the company, Frank Capra Jr., and if he's encouraged by the potential of this, since the company's up for sale, we'll bring you out, and we'll pitch it to Avco before they sell the company, and maybe there's a slight chance we can get it done." So sure enough, Frank loved the concept, Jim flew out with his producing partner Boyce Harman, and Roger Burlage, the head of finance, spoke to the Avco finance people, and in 24 hours we got the deal done and Jim was in pre-production with Avco Embassy.

**Stephen:** Then he shot the film and he put some footage together, but before he could get to his director's cut, they wanted to see the movie, right?

**Leonard:** Right, so the new principals of Embassy and their production staff wanted to see the film, but Jim had not done his director's cut yet, so through a lot of positioning and game playing Jim was able to get his director's cut ready for the Cannes Film Festival/Market, and it was shown there, and the owners of the company came to the screening. Alan Horn and his production staff, and maybe even Norman Lear, who were the new owners of Embassy Pictures. They went to the screening and it played phenomenally, it sold out in foreign, and they wanted Jim to come on board, and they offered Jim a 3 picture deal!

**Stephen:** He didn't end up making any more films for them?

**Leonard:** No he wanted to stay on his own, and produce and write and direct for other companies. The next film that I recall that Jim made was a film called THE PROTECTOR for Golden Harvest. I was already not working, I had already started my own company Shapiro Entertainment, and Jim made the film for Golden Harvest. I was building my company, Jim actually - that film was with Jackie Chan and Danny Aiello, it was a major hit, especially in the Asian areas. Warner bought the US, it was a major success for Jim.

**Stephen**: Alright. Well, let me ask you a question that has more to do with your personal relationship with Jim. Why do you think that - there are many reasons that partnerships come together, whether they be financial or just seem like a good idea at the time, or an opportunity, but there's also a personal relationship. There is also a human connection-- talk a little about your connection with Jim and why you think the two of you really got along so well and were able to be partners?

**Leonard**: During this period of THE EXTERMINATOR, THE SOLDIER, THE PROTECTOR — we were very close with each other regarding the marketing, the distribution of these films, and Jim had become a major creative writing directing force, in the indie business, he loved the independent business, and I was hoping at some point that with his creative talent, and with the distribution and marketing that I was setting up, over the 3-4 years that I had under my belt at Shapiro Entertainment - at some point that the stars would align and those two situations, distribution/marketing and what Jim had, would come together. He was working on a lot of scripts, on a lot of projects, he was getting a lot of offers, but I think he wanted to control the situation, be in charge of his own destiny, have a partner that he could rely on, and have the same vision with, and we had a couple of those discussions. The film he was working on was a picture called SHAKEDOWN aka BLUE JEAN COP, and I loved the project. He wanted to control all the elements, the production, the distribution and the only way he could do that was to find the right home for it, with somebody that he wanted to work with. I think we both came to the conclusion that we could be the right home, at Shapiro Entertainment. We made a production-distribution operation and called it Shapiro Glickenhaus Entertainment. We started out with the first picture being SHAKEDOWN, and hopefully to do a lot more and to build a long-term relationship.

**Stephen**: Now before SHAKEDOWN, there was MANIAC COP, right, that pre-dated it calendar-wise. That was a William Lustig film with some New York roots to it. And SHAKEDOWN happened after that. What would you say that it is about the way Jim makes his movies, what is it that you can't do?

**Leonard**: Well, first of all, I always considered myself a deal maker in the marketing/distribution arena, and I was also learning and growing in that area as Jim was making bigger and bigger films that were getting more and more successful in the marketplace. Since we both had the same goal, and since the friendship and the trust was so close, what we both wanted to do – those five years or so, from THE EXTERMINATOR through SHAKEDOWN, of collaboration, were great years of trying to build something and trying to run the place with the use of studios with a big level of support.

**Stephen:** On a human level, were you having fun? Was that a time that you look back on and think "Wow that was fun!"

**Leonard:** As far as the entertainment business goes, as far as building companies, and Jim building a really successful career, I would have to say that both Jim and I enjoyed those years in the film business together as our best years in the business.

**Stephen:** Looking back on it now all these years later, if you could name one moment, and you think: "that's one moment that really captures the spirit of Shapiro Glickenhaus Entertainment in a human way" -- the two of you together, whether it was Cannes, New York, Los Angeles, on set, wherever that might be, one moment that you think that was the one moment that defined the company what would that moment be?

**Leonard:** To be honest, on that question, I would have to say there was 100 moments, every day was a new beginning, you know? We were on the phone 2-3 times a day for like 8—10 years and it was all great. We really enjoyed, learned and accomplished something. Everything that we did was positive and enjoyable, and I can't think of any one moment that stands out, other than everything we did was on that level.

**Stephen:** This is a bit of a personal comment here, because I was there, but I can tell you that if I answered the phone at SGE, and it was Jim, I'd put him through to you, and you picked the phone up, for 8 years it was like just one long conversation. It really felt like a continuous connection. I don't know if that's a New York thing.

**Leonard:** I think if I can recall those conversations, and I can, it was because we knew what we were doing, we loved our business, we loved our challenges, we knew how tough the business was, we knew what it took to be successful on a film, in a company, in all the different divisions we were running. We had a deal with Universal; we had big foreign deals; big companies overseas were buying our films; we had a great foreign sales head; we had some great parties. We knew how to have fun; we knew how to try to be successful; and we gave it all we had, 24-7, because Jim was always there. He always wanted to make it work, was always being a creative force for the company on all levels. I mean, how could you not enjoy those times!? Shapiro Glickenhaus was successful, we were considered a leading independent, and we were always trying to make good films and to move forward and feel good.

By Stephen A. Roberts, in person
Calabasas, California at Marmalade Café
26April, 2015 - 07June, 2015 - 03July, 2015

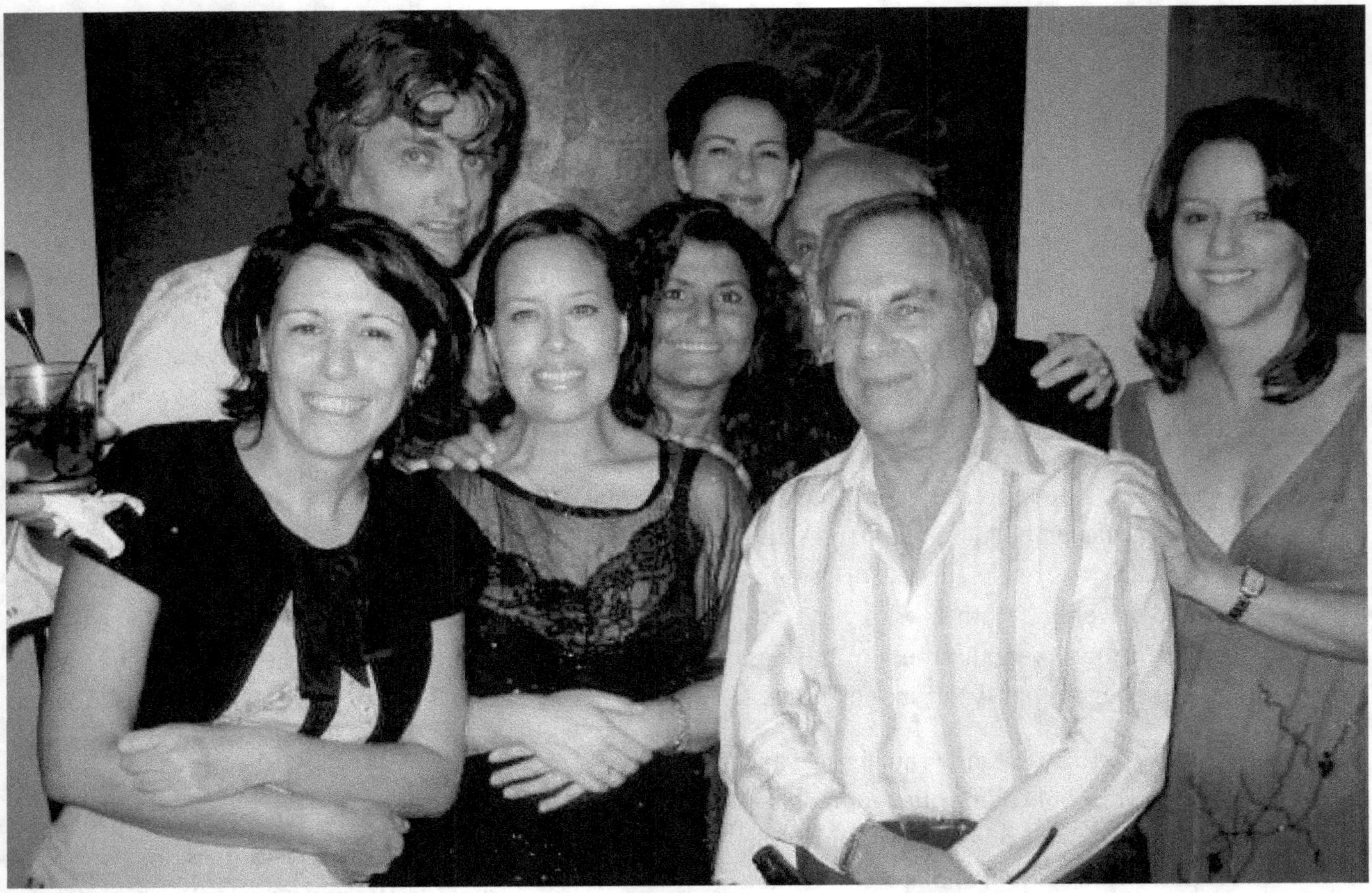

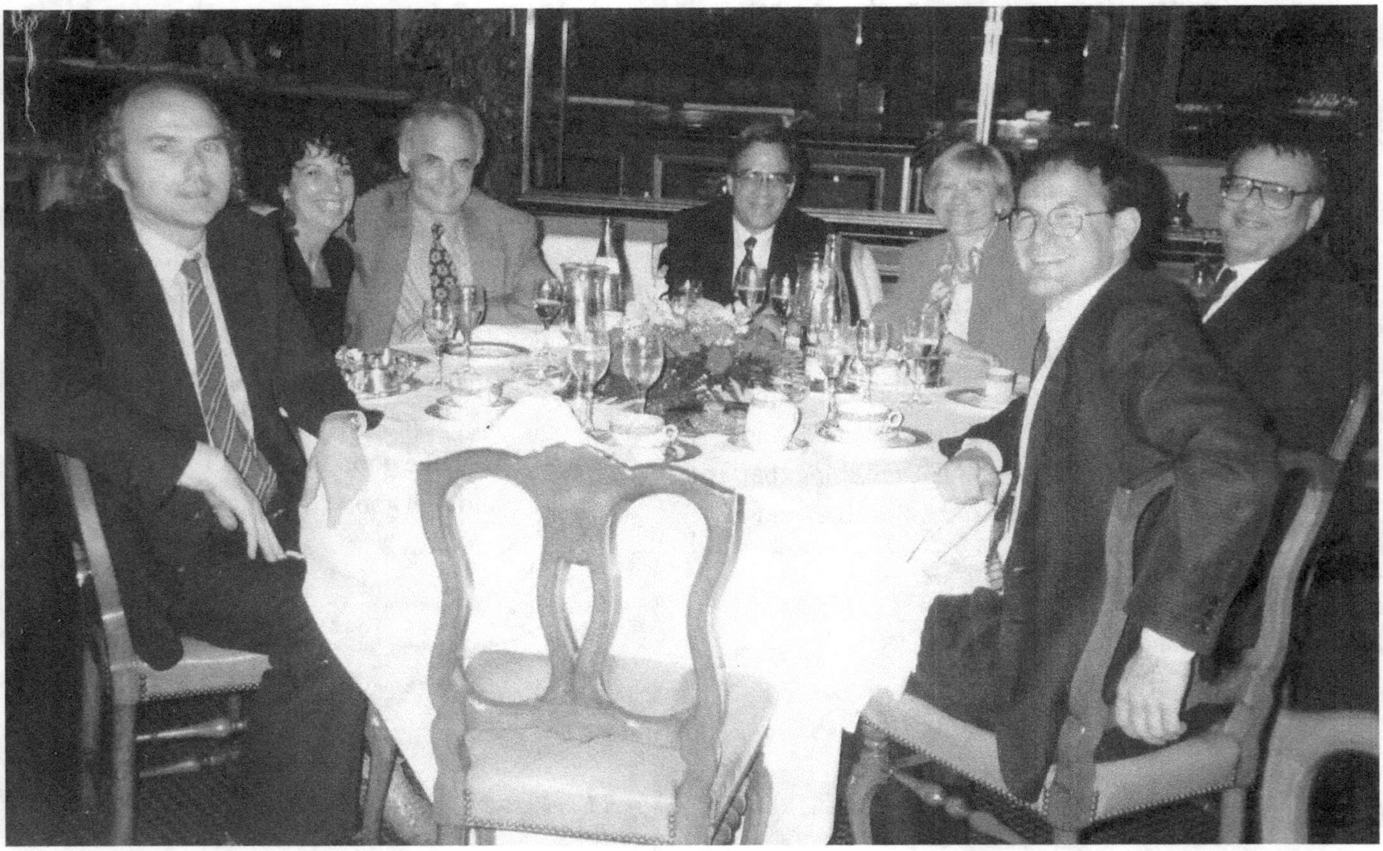

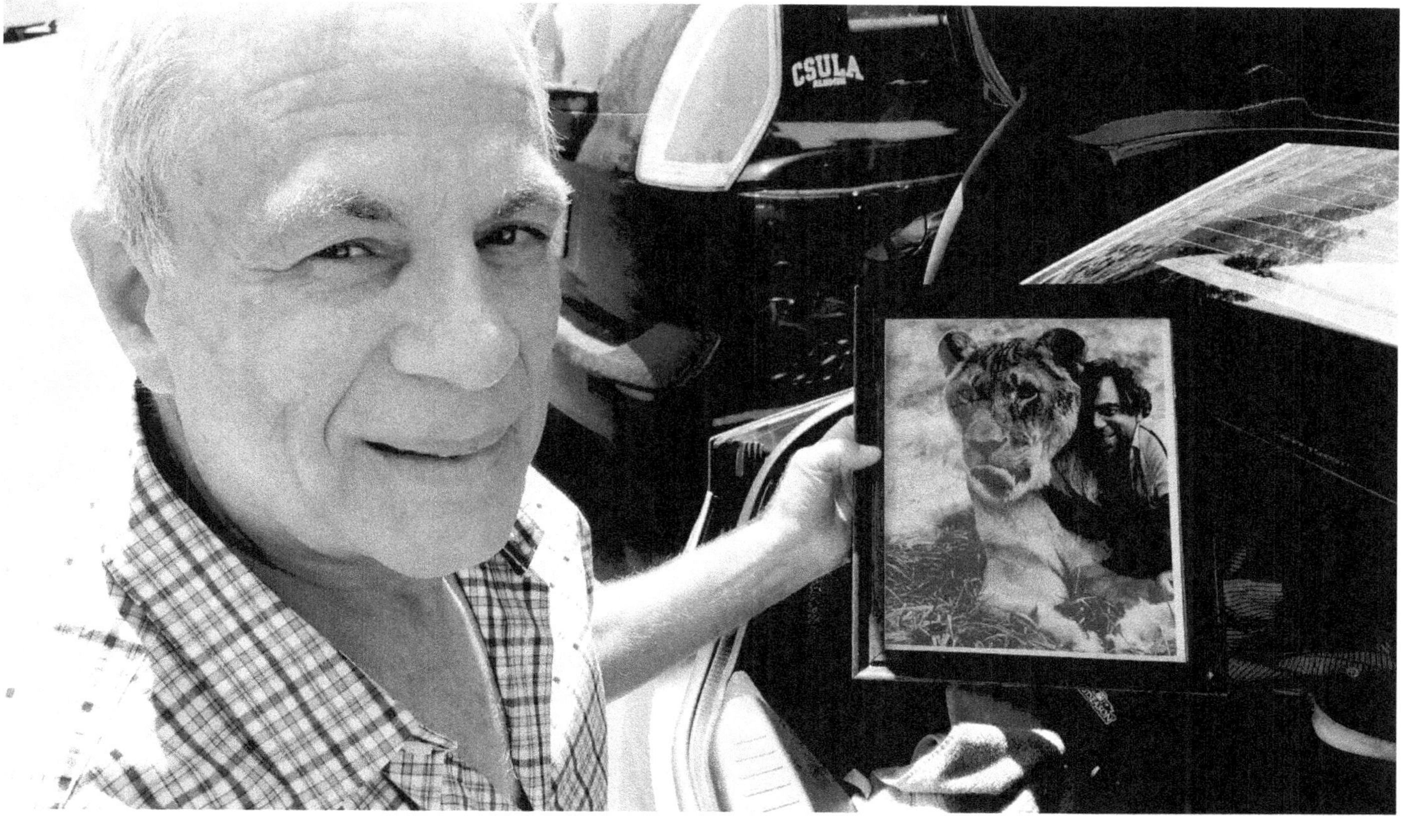

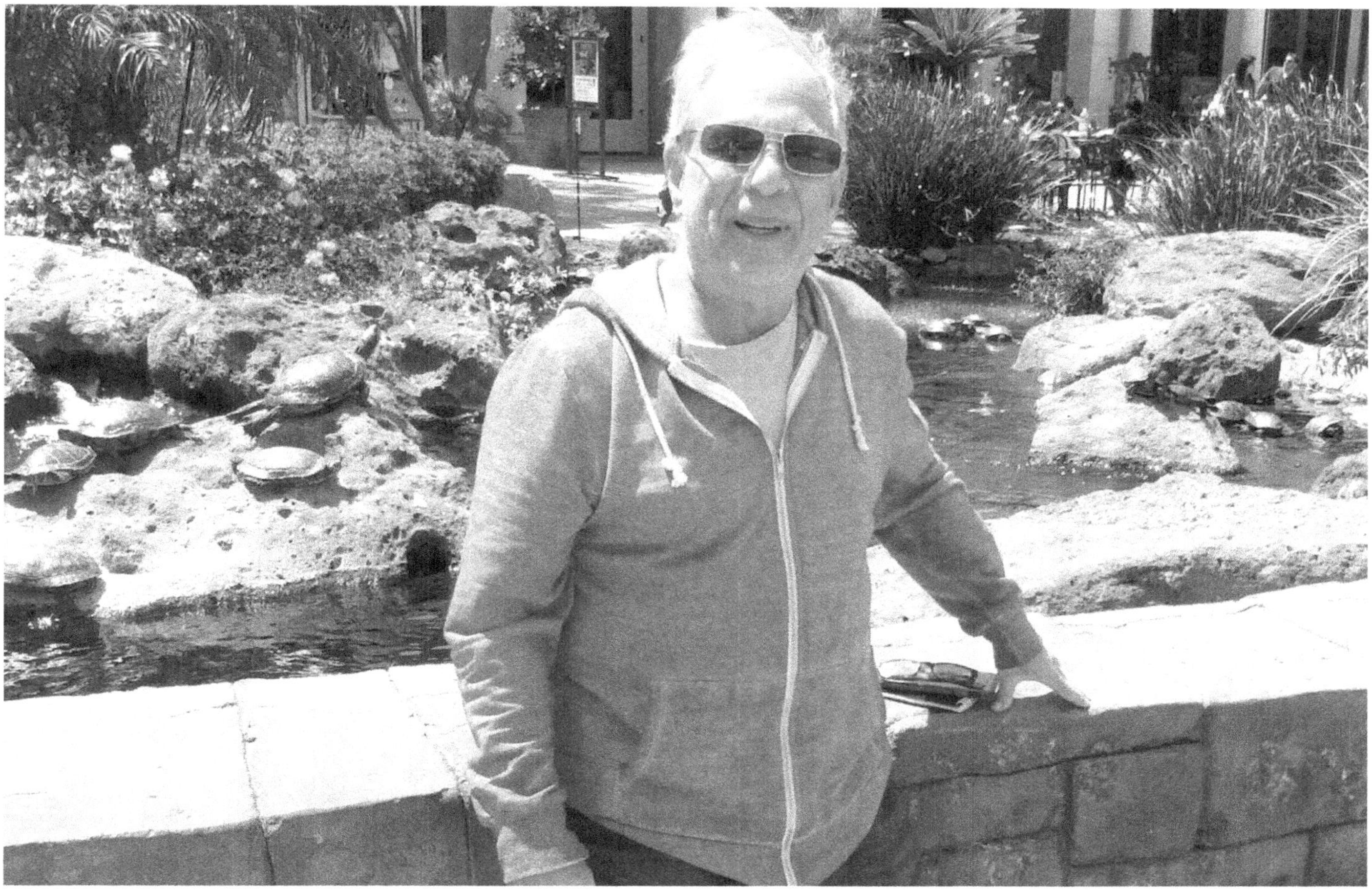

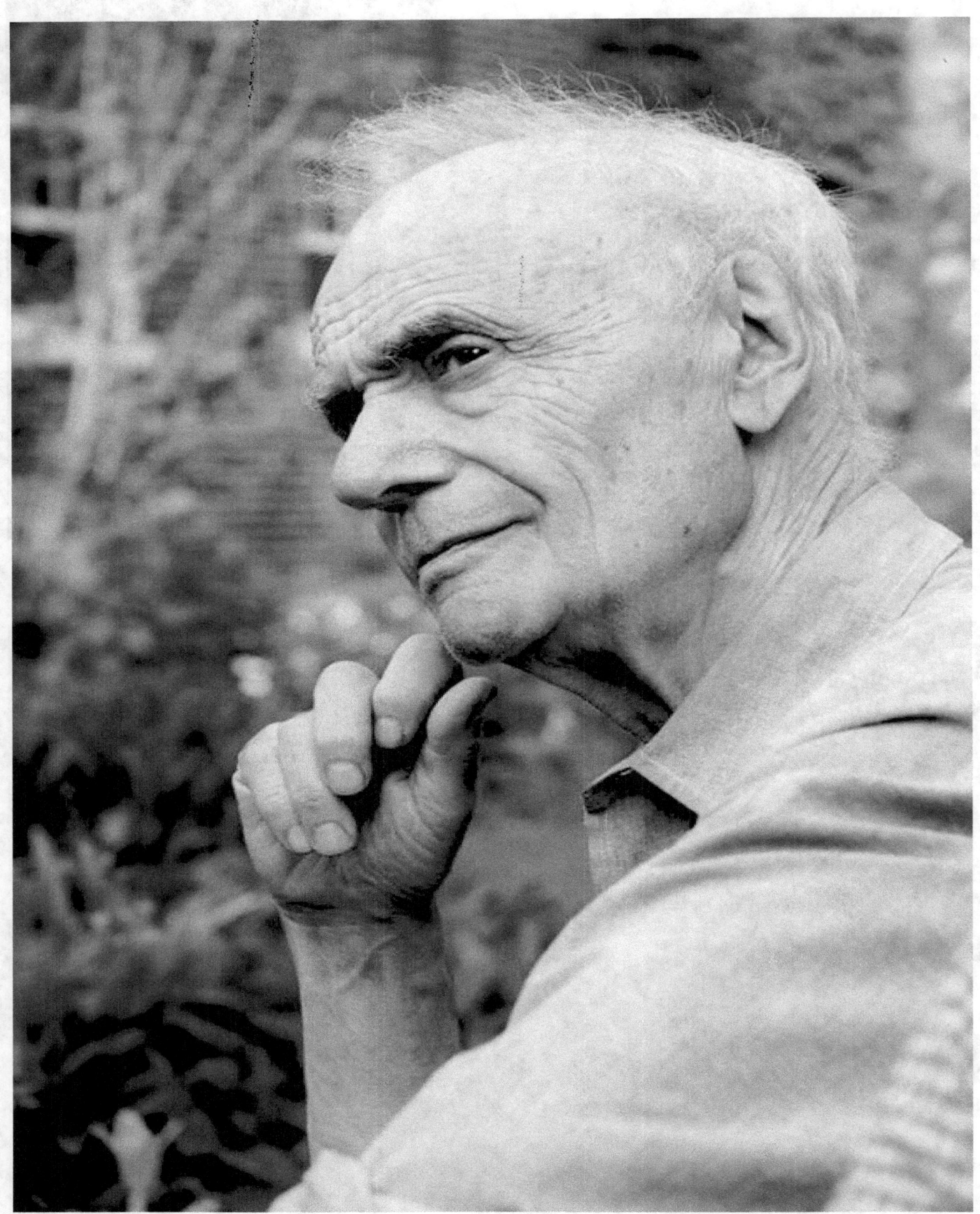

# Afterword: A Song of Solomon

Nadia & Stephen were both hired by Shapiro Entertainment Corp. (the precursor to SGE) on April Fool's Day, two years apart (Stephen in '85, Nadia in '87.) Both were young, beautiful and fearless (Stephen was 25 and married with children, Nadia was 21 and single and frisky.) Both worked at SEC/SGE mostly for the one-of-a-kind Alan Michael Solomon of England. Alan changed their professional and private lives in profound ways that still, now more than 30 years on, constantly remind them of him. Since he's not around to speak for himself (Alan passed in 2010), and his contribution to SGE was so significant, the Editors of this book thought it fitting that Alan get the Afterword – so that's what this is all about. What follows are highly personal, episodic reminiscences that attempt to capture Alan's essence (as Nadia & Stephen knew it) – his lightning in a bottle – the stuff that made him go; or at least the stuff he used on the two Co-Editors of this book, to make them go.

The Solomonster. Many claim to have coined that moniker. It's hard to say who actually did, though. But one thing is for sure: it stuck! Alan could be exceedingly cruel and uncommonly kind, sometimes in the same breath. He set the bar very high and wasn't shy about telling us when we'd met it with our foreheads instead of our brains. He made Nadia cry and Stephen mad. Often. But we respected him, and we learned from him, and most of all we loved him. And we miss him, a lot. What follows is an unrepentant tribute to him. So if you're curious about what made Alan Solomon tick, (and by extension, what made SGE tick) spend a little time here now. Alan could be bloody mysterious; and he knew it, and that was part of his charm.

*When I first started at Shapiro Entertainment Corporation, it wasn't even Shapiro Glickenhaus Entertainment yet. I'd just moved to LA from Colorado and was working in a vitamin factory as a secretary. John Alexander, my first boyfriend, had gotten me an interview as the receptionist/assistant to Lenny, who was warm and kind and funny. On the other hand, Alan Solomon scared the crap out of me! John worked with him, and everyone else seemed scared of him, except Lenny. I had to send international telexes for Alan, and he seemed impressed that I knew where various countries were... but was quick to anger if I messed up in any way. He would write notes on a million yellow legal pads and had number 2 pencils that he'd write with till there was just a fraction of an inch left to them. His office was a massive stack of papers, seemingly in no order whatsoever and definitely a fire-hazard. Yet still, he could find what he wanted in a New York minute.*

I was Alan's main whipping boy for nearly a decade; and to this day I wear those scars as badges of courage. I remember how he'd write cryptic pencil notes on everything from letters to contracts to telexes in that tortured, gnarled, spiderlike-script of his. Once deciphered, it all made perfect sense though. I remember him saying that the way Lenny worked utterly baffled him. He claimed he couldn't figure out how Len could run a meeting full of people, and speak in riddles so seductive, that everyone in the room would leave feeling as if they'd heard exactly what <u>they</u> wanted to hear, even if they had totally opposite impressions of what actually had happened in the meeting. Alan was in awe of that.

*The Solomonster was not happy when Len got the huge salt-water aquarium for his office. And yet, Alan was the first to stare at those fish, mesmerized and fascinated. He made sure we fed the fish on time and took care of the aquarium properly. Alan was the last one in the office every day, always dressed in a dapper vintage suit and tie. But he would call early every morning to be sure all the "SGE Girls" were on time. And he would often come to us at 6:45PM with a stack of telexes and mail to get out before we left. He stuttered and nervously rubbed his cauliflower ear, earned as a boxer in the British Navy. He expected us all to work ceaselessly, but when the World Cup was on he spent hours in the screening room, taping every game and re-watching every kick.*

Alan could be very mean. But could also be extremely tender. Like the time his sensitive teenage son Darren came to the office extremely upset, and Alan consoled him. The mercurial Persian Producer, Tony Zarindast, had gotten into a huge shouting match with his equally hot-blooded sister in front of Darren, and Tony Z literally threw a typewriter at her! Darren was in tears, and Alan was uncommonly compassionate to him. It was a sweet side I didn't know Alan had. I remember how proud Alan was when Darren got a gig playing bass in Ray Charles's touring band. And I also remember how proud he was of his eldest son Elliot when he produced the BLACK ROSES soundtrack album. He was a good dad. And in many ways a father figure to me. Since I was an Englishman-by-birth, I always felt a 'Brit Bond' with Alan. To describe Producers and Buyers he'd sometimes use phrases like, "He's a Jack-the-Lad that one," in reference to a particularly roguish character. And when I'd look at him confused, he'd say "Ask your Dad what that means." That was Alan.

*In Cannes one year, our whole office got a stomach virus. Very sexily, I vomited all over the front of the Carlton and in a taxi...lovely. But The Solomonster had no sympathy for any of it. I was expected to be in the office at the Marché first thing in the morning, greeting people and typing contracts. Speaking of contracts...he did not know how to use a computer. Instead, he would make photocopies of various contracts, cut them all up, and tape them back together to get the proper verbiage. None of these were saved in any computer at that point. So I spent countless hours, retyping legalese to his satisfaction. I learned an incredible amount. I honor him as my mentor, and I went on to become VP of Business Affairs for some leading indie studios. Without him, I would have known nothing. He never wanted to be on the company letterhead, but he was definitely an equal partner that helped to keep the SGE name and business running.*

At the end of a threatening letter to a Producer or Licensee, Alan would often write, "And cc (insert an actual lawyer's name here) but don't send it to him." He understood contract law enough to know how to wield it. He was sending 'a message'. I also remember how he'd smoke filter-less cigarettes ... just a few puffs, then put them out, saving the remnants to relight later. He also smoked cigarettes very, very short, so they almost burned his fingertips. This habit (hoarding partially-smoked cig butts and then 'savoring' them to their nubs) was hold-over behavior from his war-time childhood in London as the Germans relentlessly bombarded the city. Alan was evacuated to the English countryside at the age of 5 to escape the Nazi onslaught. When I discovered this (not from him mind you), it explained a lot.

*When Alan and I went to the Tokyo Festival and Market, we closed up the market office to spend hours combing the jazz record stores. It was then that I discovered he had edited books on jazz and was a huge aficionado. He took me to see McCoy Tyner at the Tokyo Blue Note. We rode the subway through Tokyo to do touristy things (did I mention we were supposedly there to work??), and he spent an hour or so telling me about his mother's death and how devastated he had been. A poignant memory that I shall never forget. Years later, I would take my daughter to see The Solomonster (now said with love) at his company AmSell, still housed in the old SGE Ventura Place office. He was like a grandfather to her, letting her play, giving her little gifts. Over the years, I always visited him at the AFM. Despite a drop in business, he always had loyal distributors who would come by, if not to buy, certainly to visit and pay their respects to him, still dressed in his dapper vintage suits and ties.*

*I remember how, during SGE days, at one point he was very serious about jogging and extremely proud of how much weight it helped him lose. I recall how he was always the last person to leave the office, but would usually arrive rather late, like an hour before lunch. Of course, by the time he got in, I'd barely scratched the surface of all the work he'd left for me the night before. He had a strong intellect and a dogged temperament. When he set his mind to something, whether it was losing weight or negotiating a deal, he usually prevailed. He taught me tenacity. And grit.*

*When he became ill, those of the SGE gang who still lived in LA rallied around to visit. I, amongst many others, went to see him in the hospital and held his hand while he told me he was just too tired to go on. His adoring wife Alix had passed some years before, and he told me how he missed her. She was his yin to his yang, a vibrant, artistic free spirit whom he loved beyond words. When he finally passed, the word went around the globe quickly. Buyers and producers paid their respects, speaking highly of the man we all loved despite his rough edges. The old employees of SGE flocked to the funeral and many of us spoke. It was a beautiful tribute to a man who gave so much behind the scenes to SGE.*

Like Nad, I also visited Alan at Cedars-Sinai Hospital in his final days. I knew he wasn't doing well because Len had called me to share that he'd seen him and encouraged me to see him as well. I wanted to catch Alan up on how my young children (whom he knew) had grown into fine young men and women, and also to brag a bit on my new family; so, I made a little photo slideshow for him to see – a 20-year montage. The plan was to meet some of the SGE girls at Cedars, and I got there a little early on purpose so I could spend some one-on-one time with Alan. He watched the slideshow and grinned that toothy Brit grin of his. We talked about boxing and football. It was very emotional. Once the girls showed up the room came to life. There was lots of yapping and occasionally Alan would doze off, but, out of respect - none of us openly recognized it. He even took a meal while we were there. He didn't eat much. Not even the ice cream, a treat I particularly remember him coveting. Before we left, I kissed his forehead. Eleven days later he was gone. I think of him often and value deeply the way he influenced me. Strange that they can touch us, but we can't touch them. Shame that's a one-way channel. Definitely a cruel quirk of the universe.

By *Nadia Bruce-Rawlings* & Stephen A. Roberts
July 2015

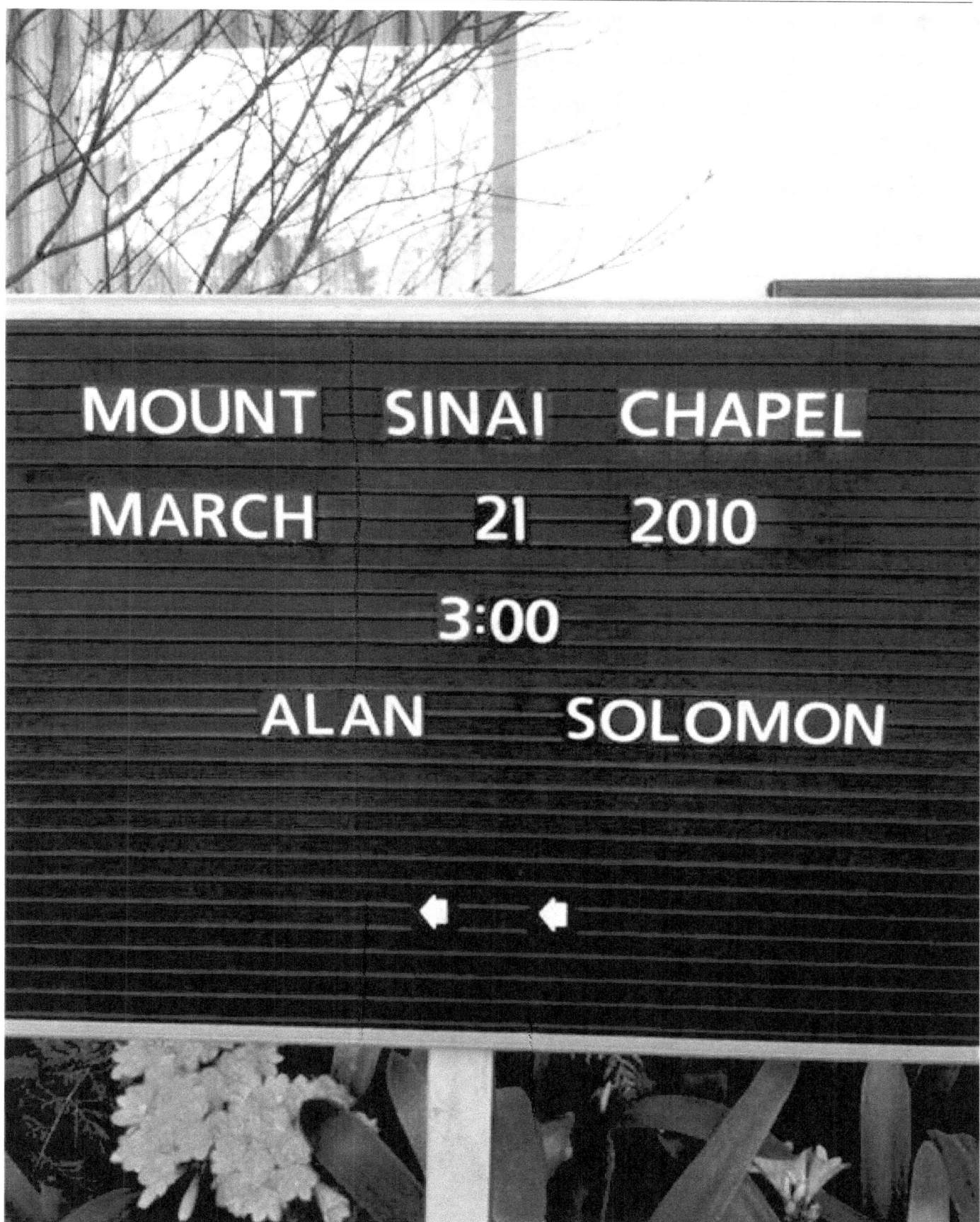

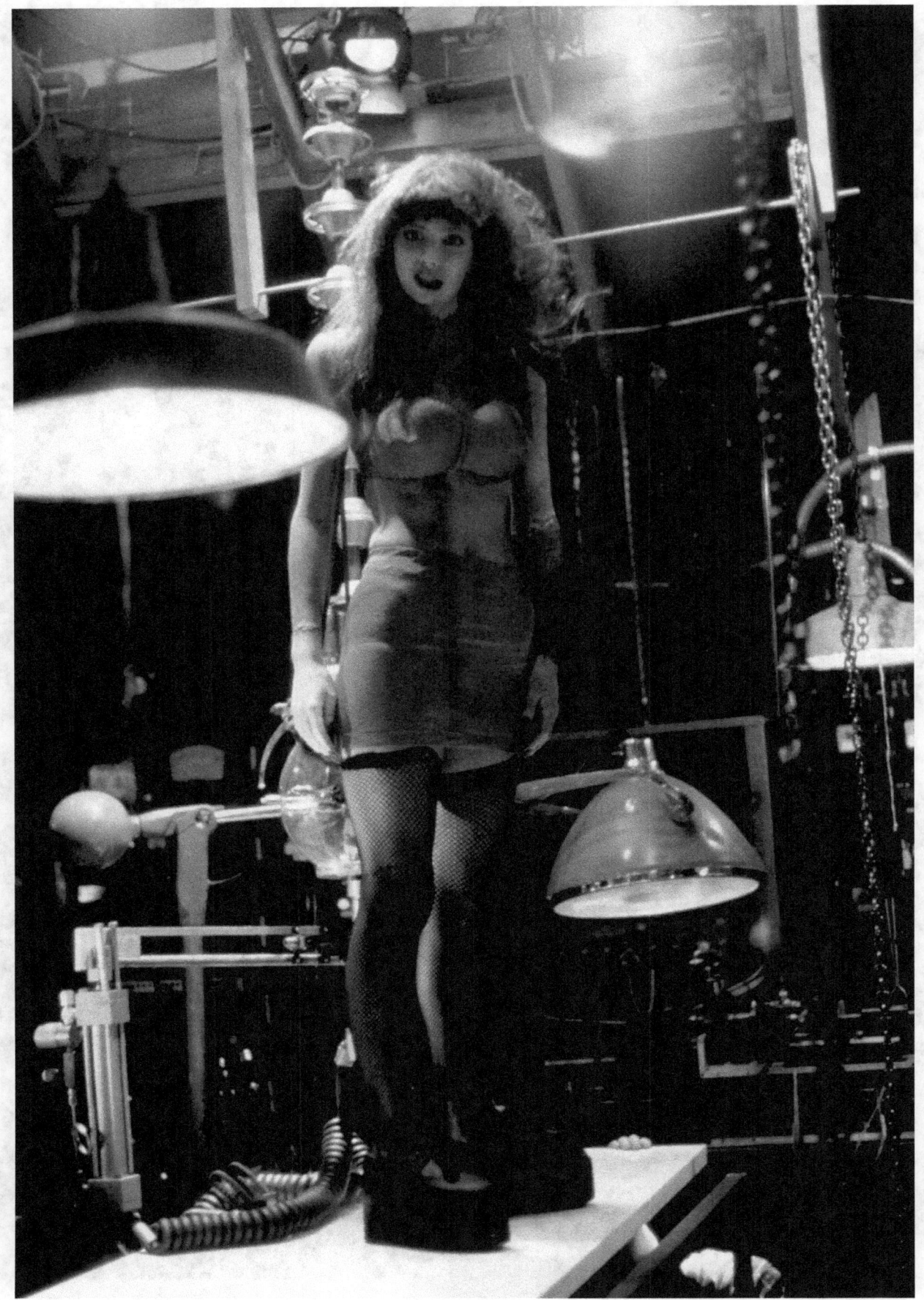

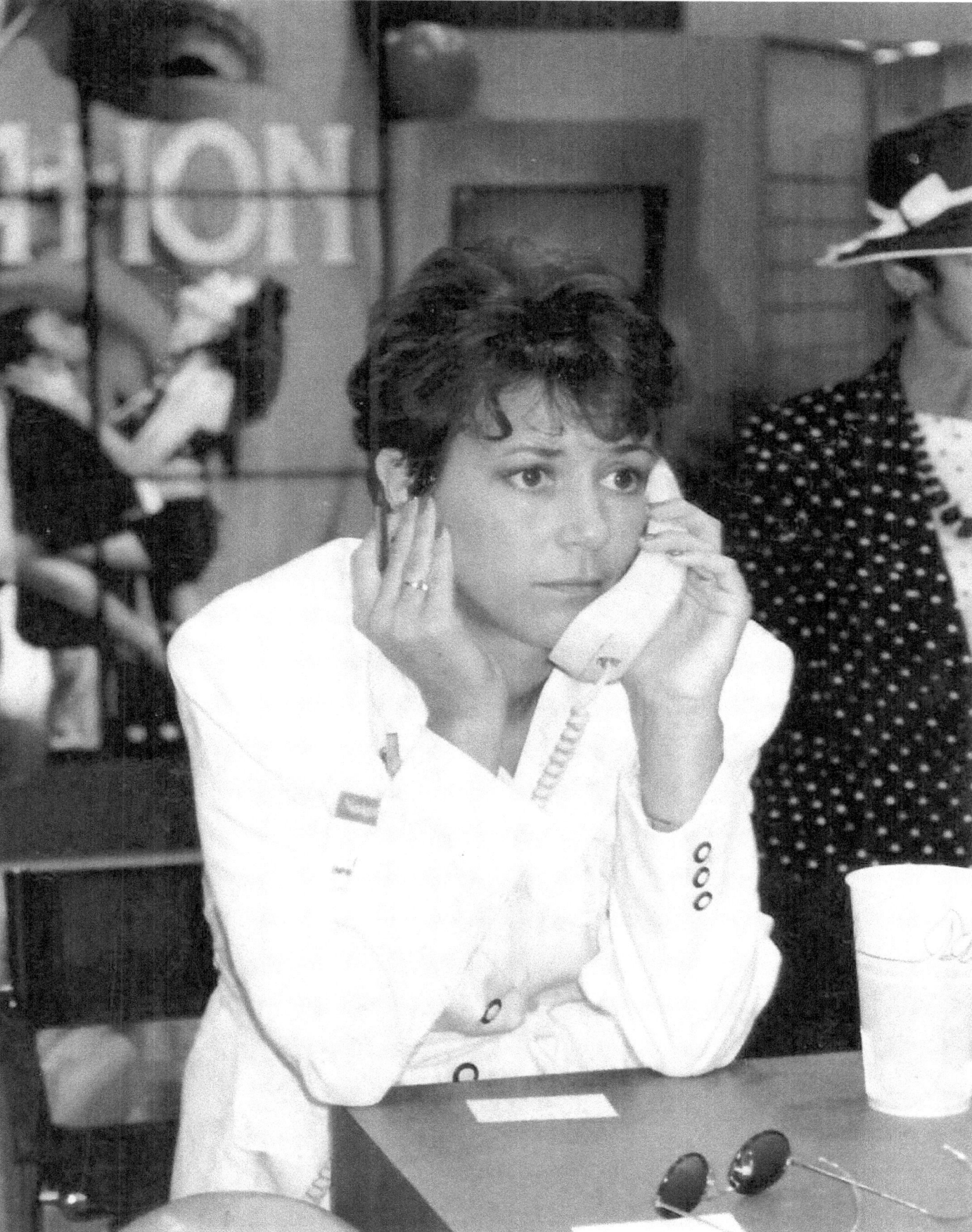

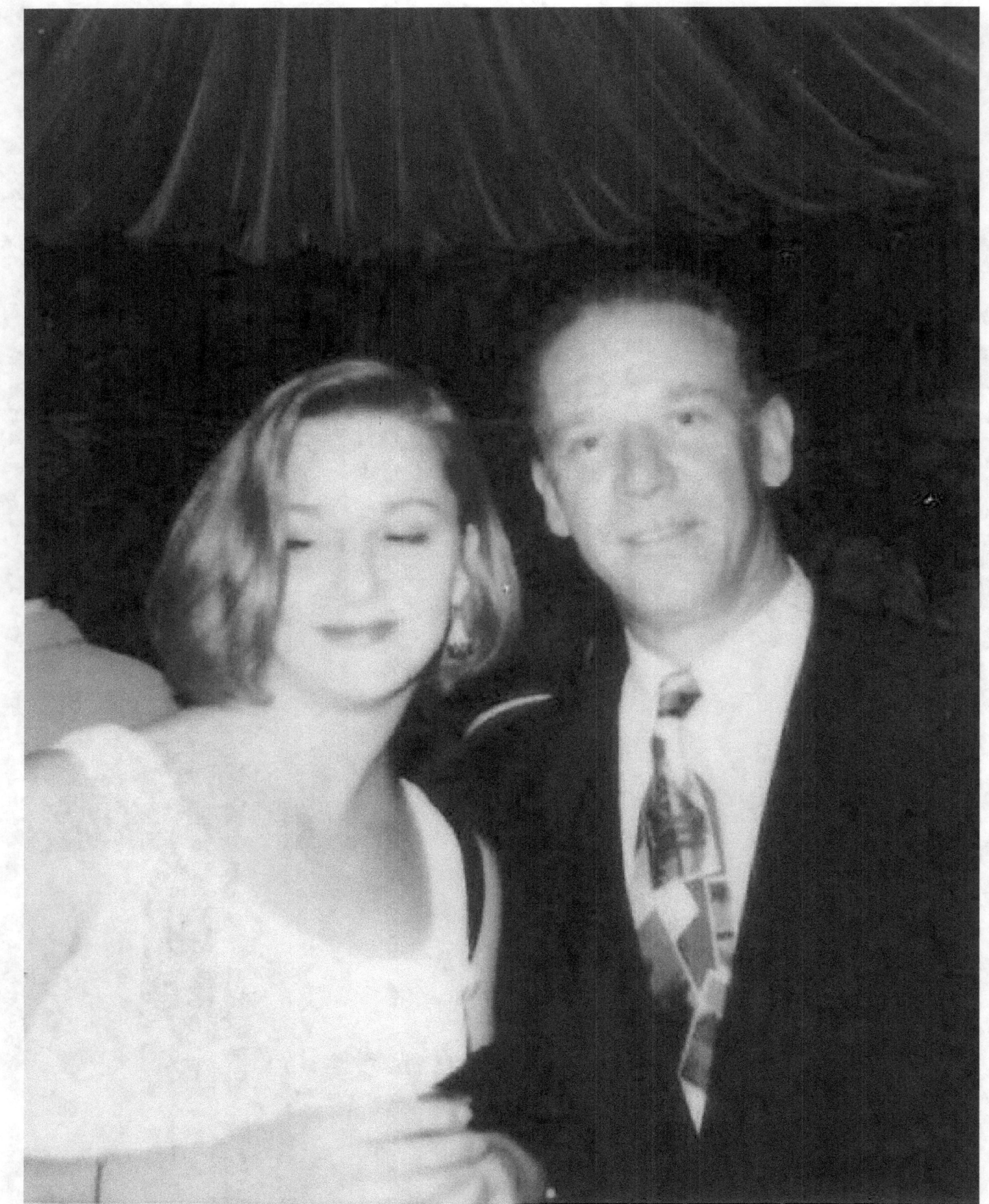

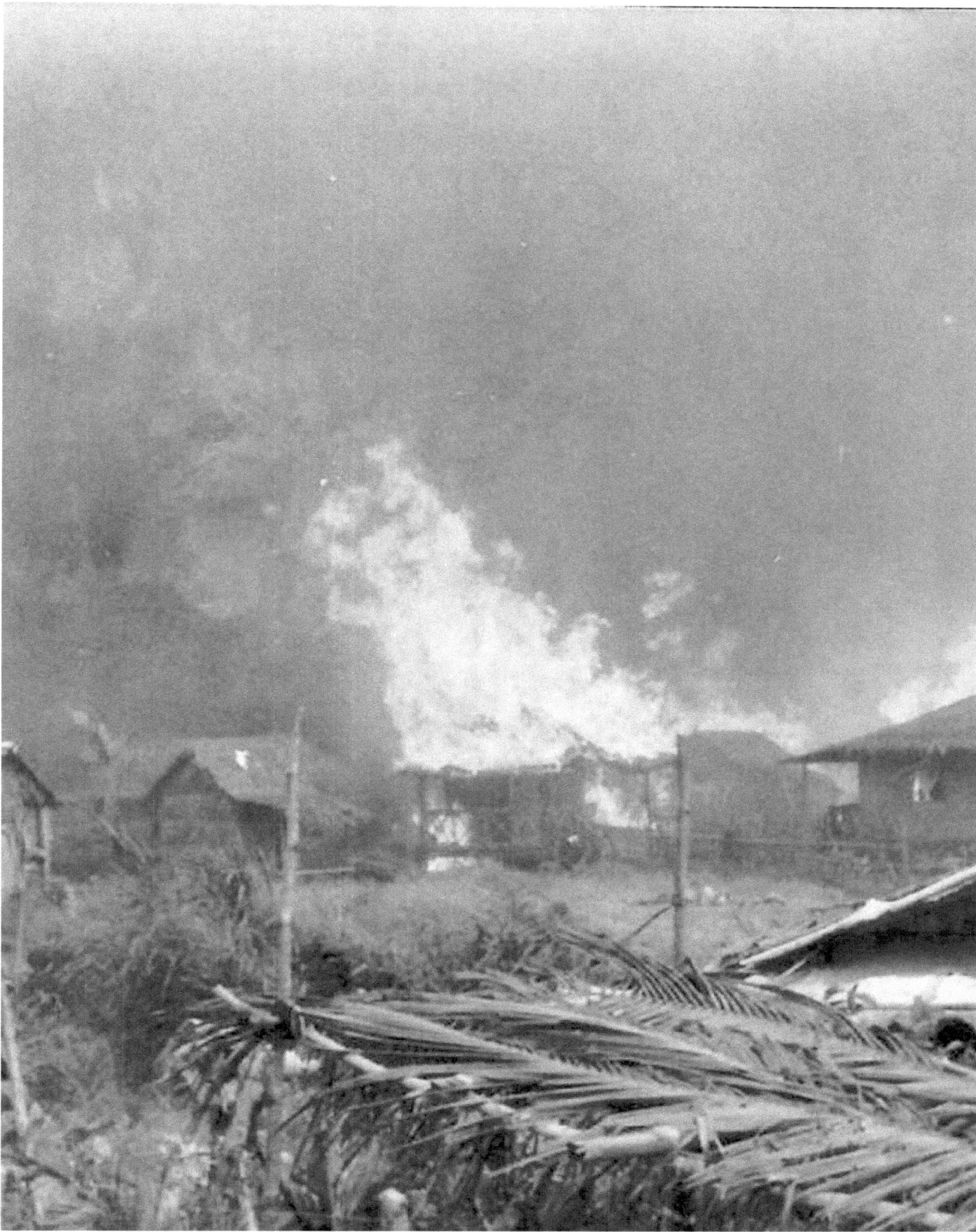

# MEET THE JUDGE... THE JURY... AND THE EXECUTIONER!

# ONE MAN FORCE

**JOHN MATUSZAK** (THE GOONIES) **CHARLES NAPIER** (RAMBO)
**SAM JONES** (FLASH GORDON) **RONNY COX** (BEVERLY HILLS COP)
**RICHARD LYNCH** (LITTLE NIKITA)

hifi

JESSE CAMERON - GLICKENHAUS

Imagina si pudieras viajar
a través del tiempo ...
Si pudieras cambiar el pasado ...
Si pudieras cambiar el futuro.

EL SEÑOR
DEL TIEMPO
**MASTER ME**

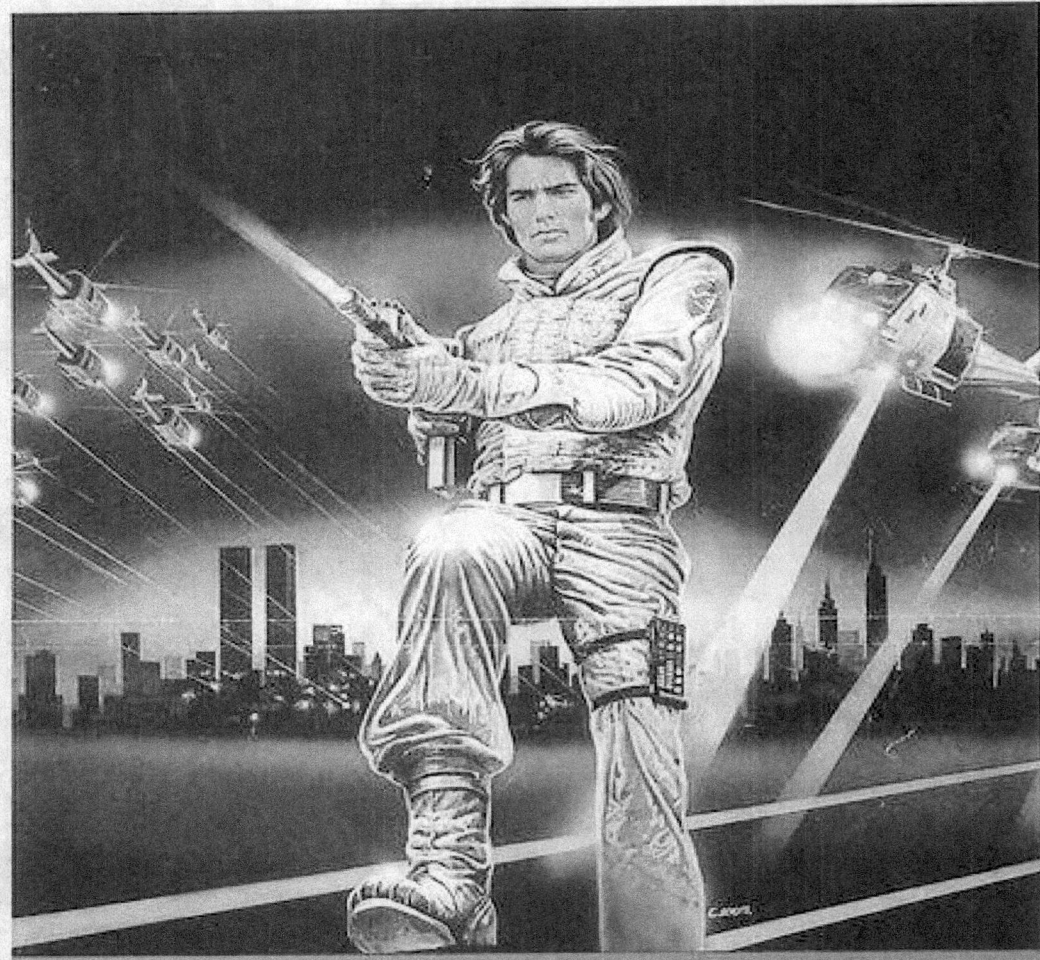

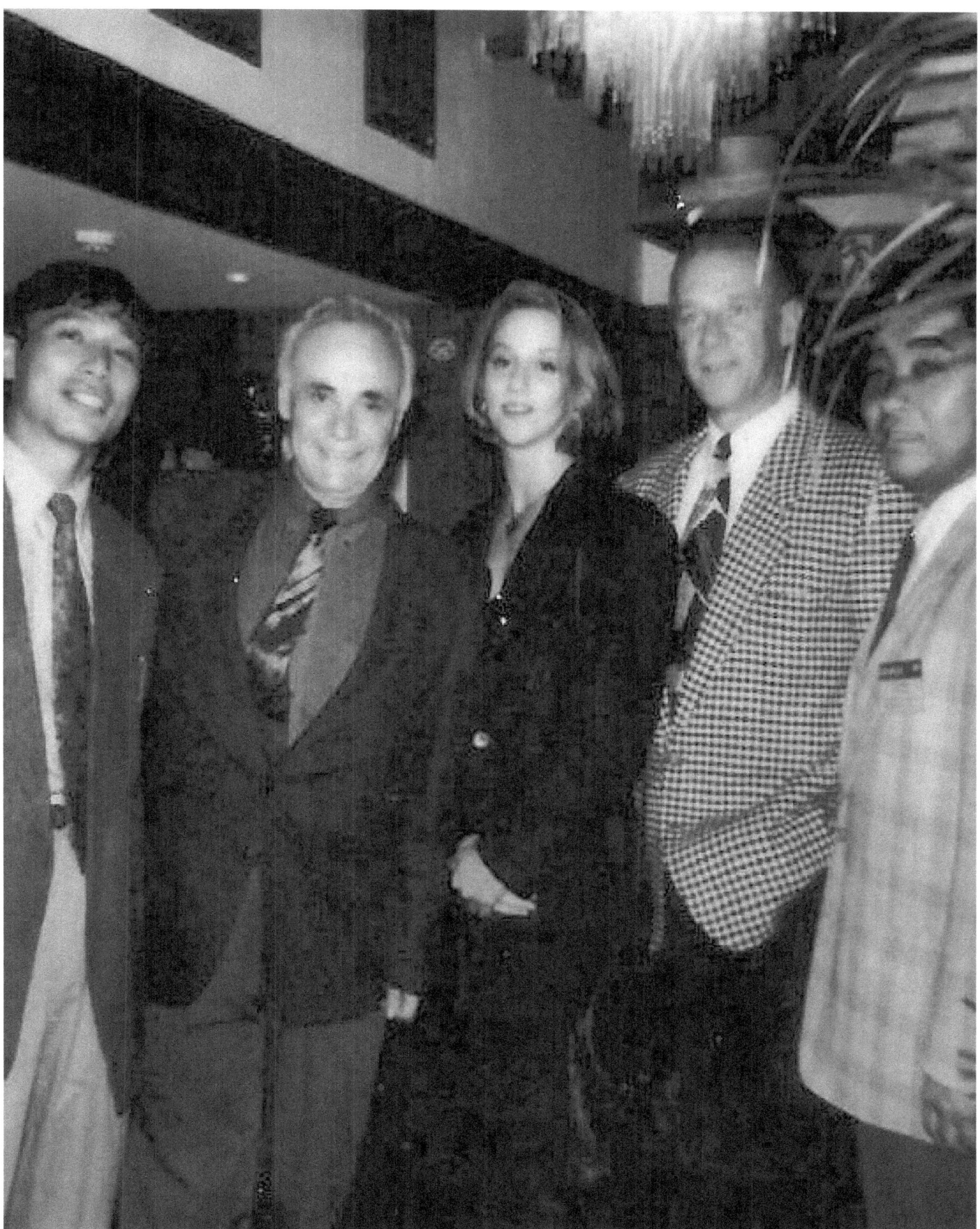

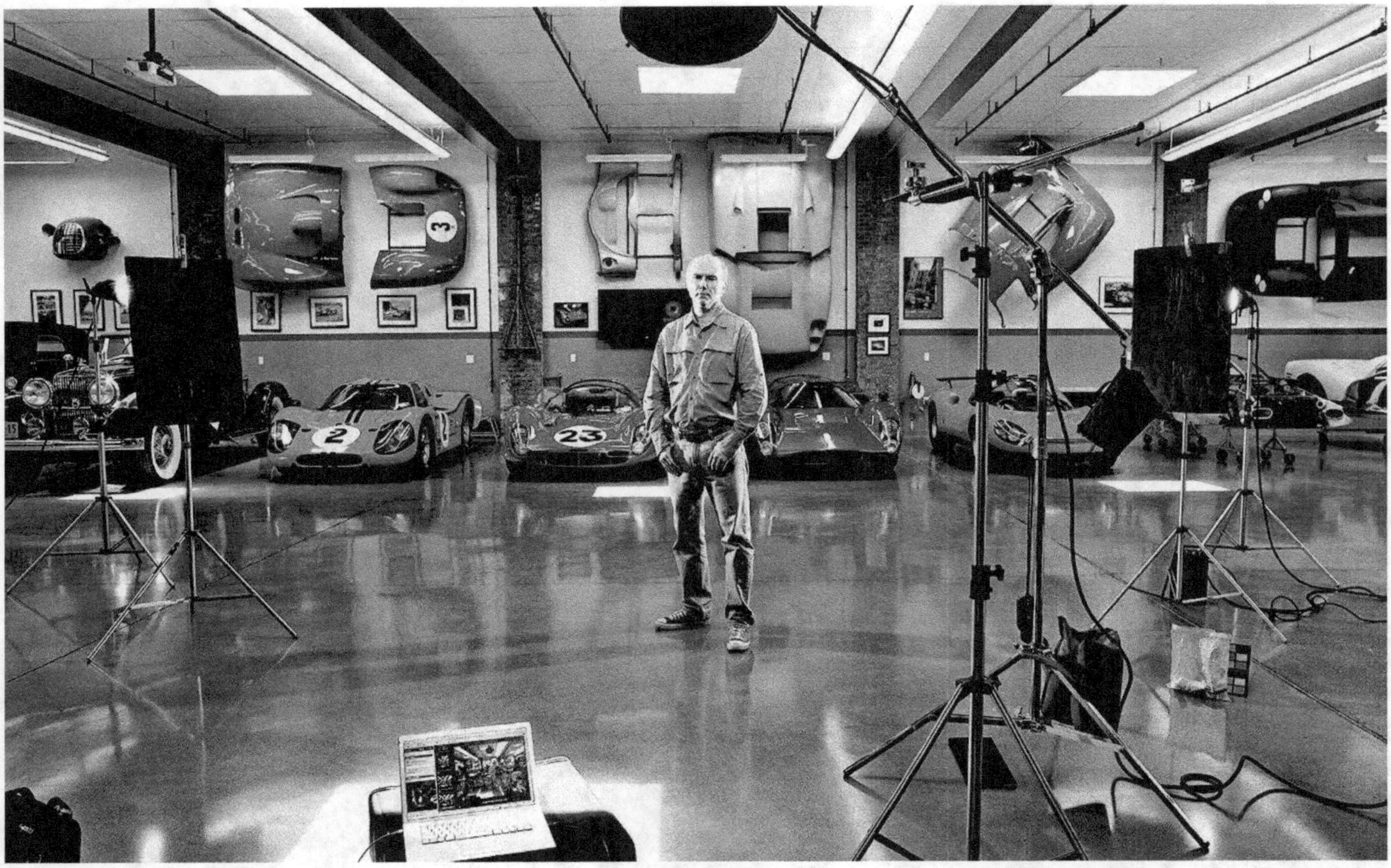

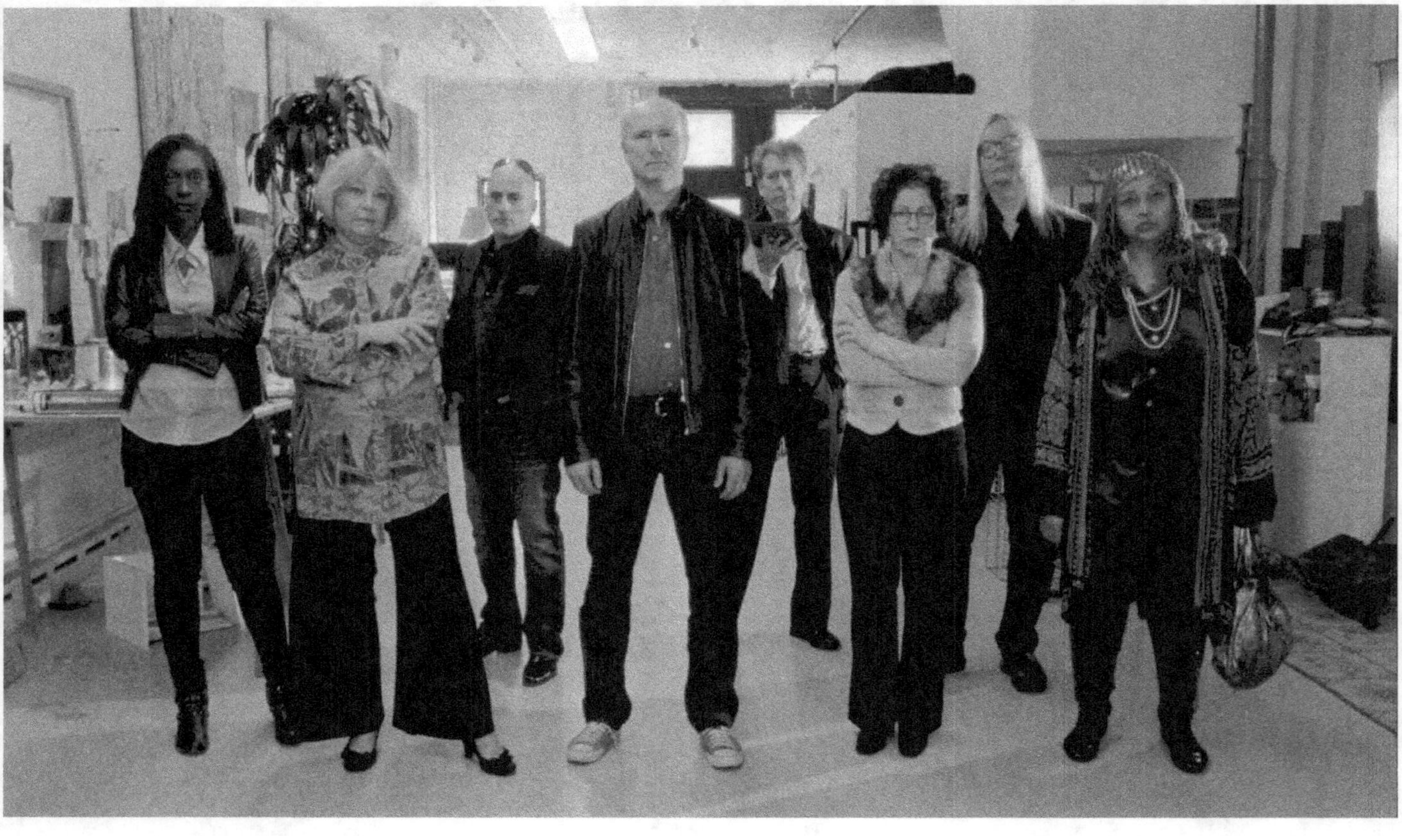

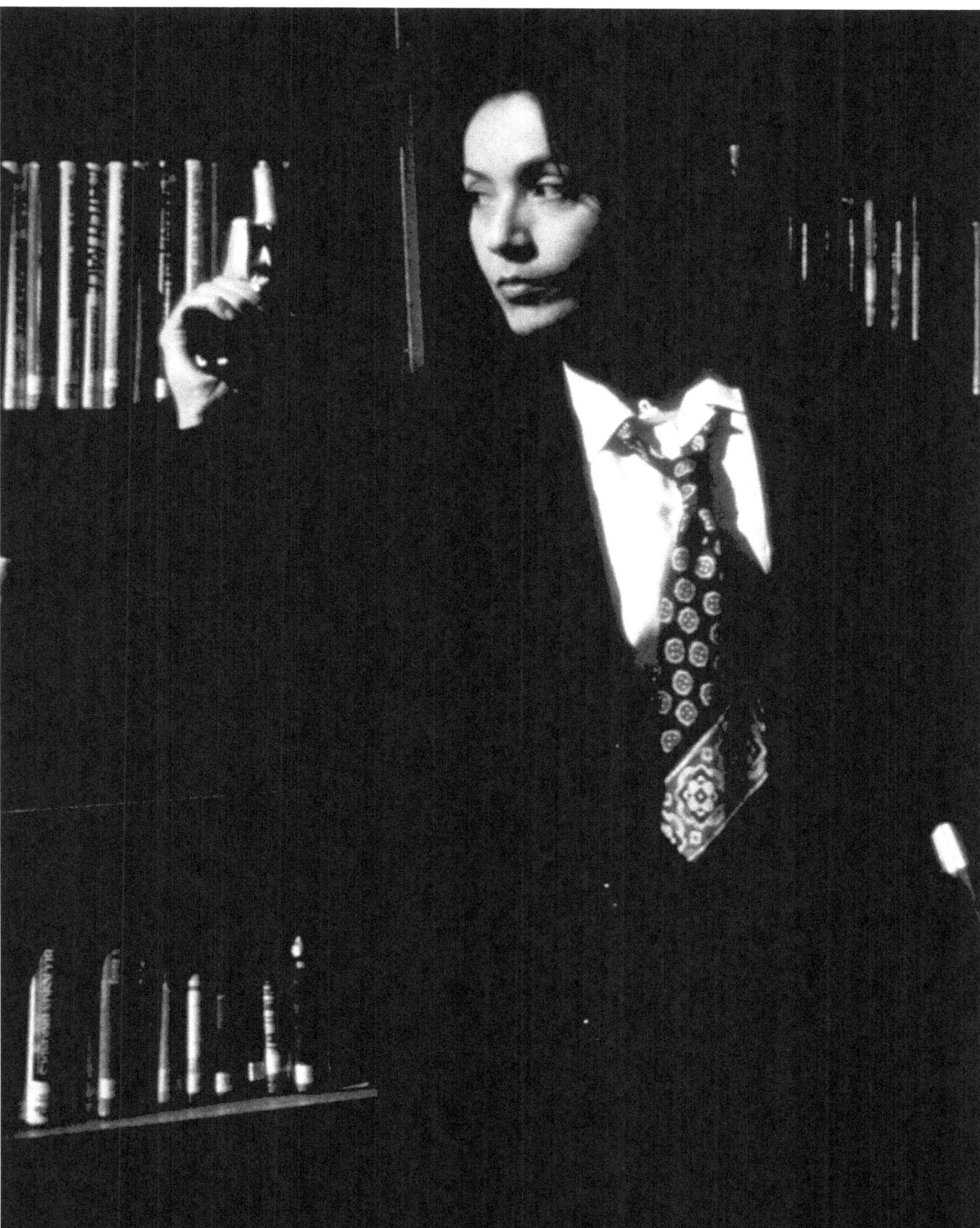

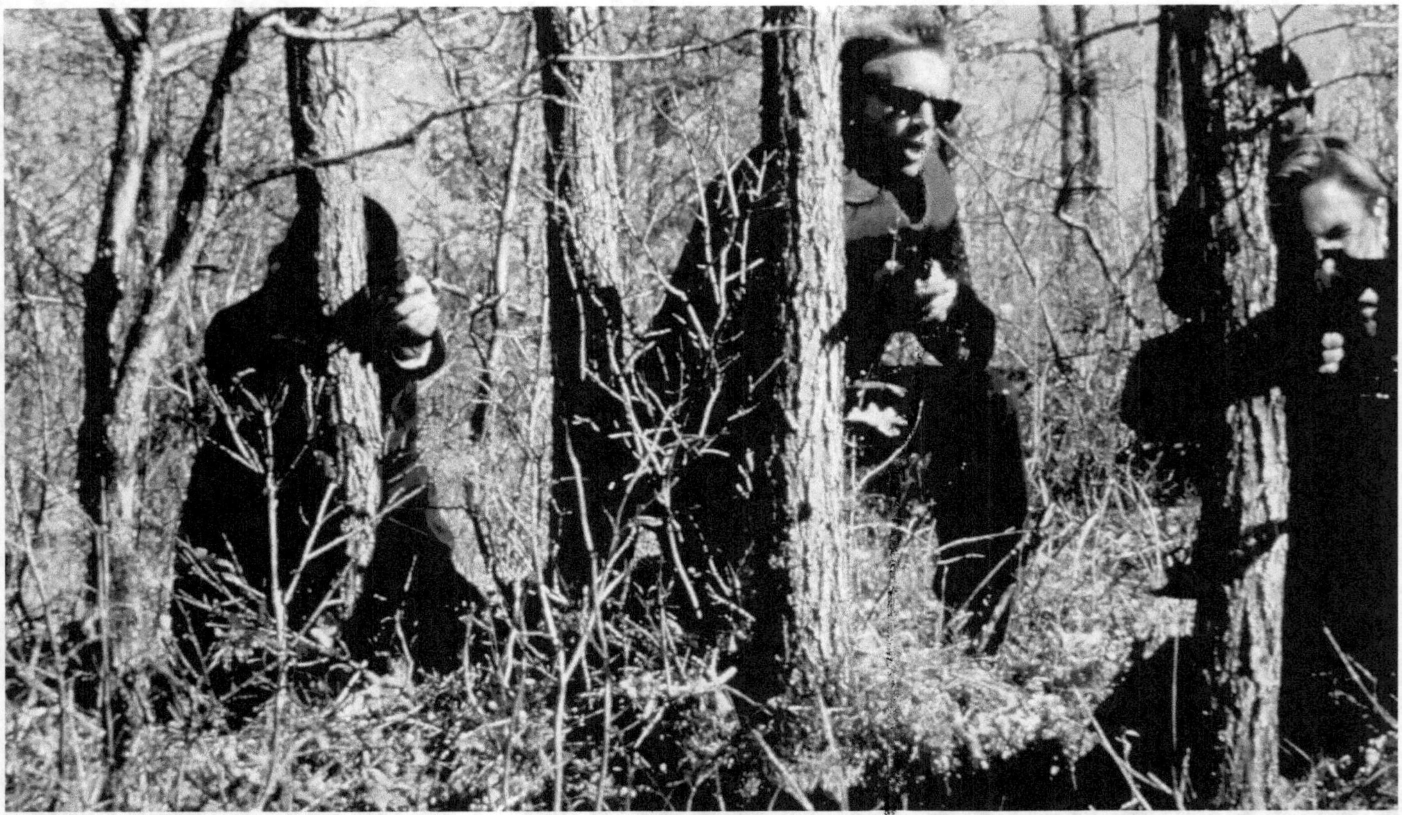

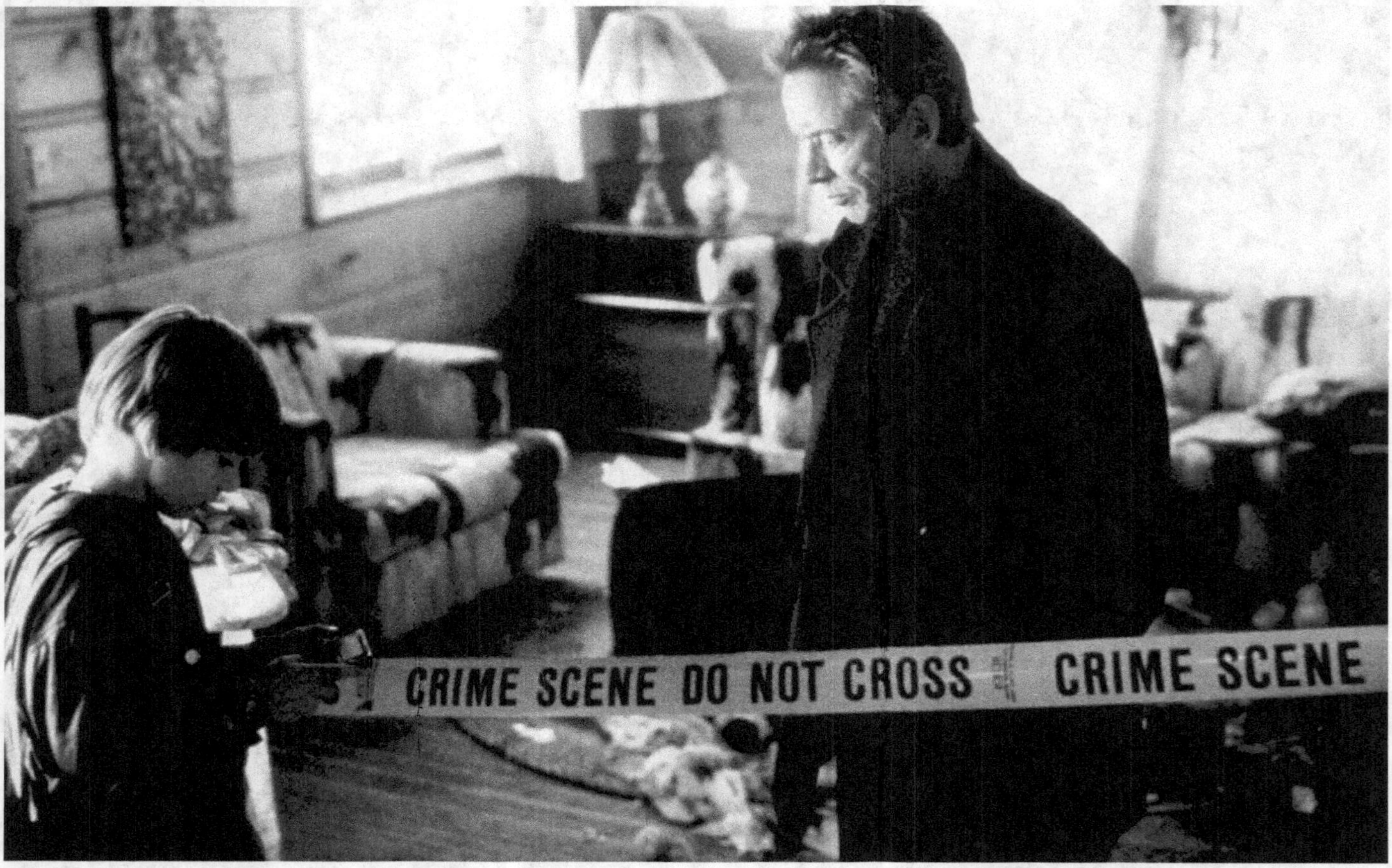

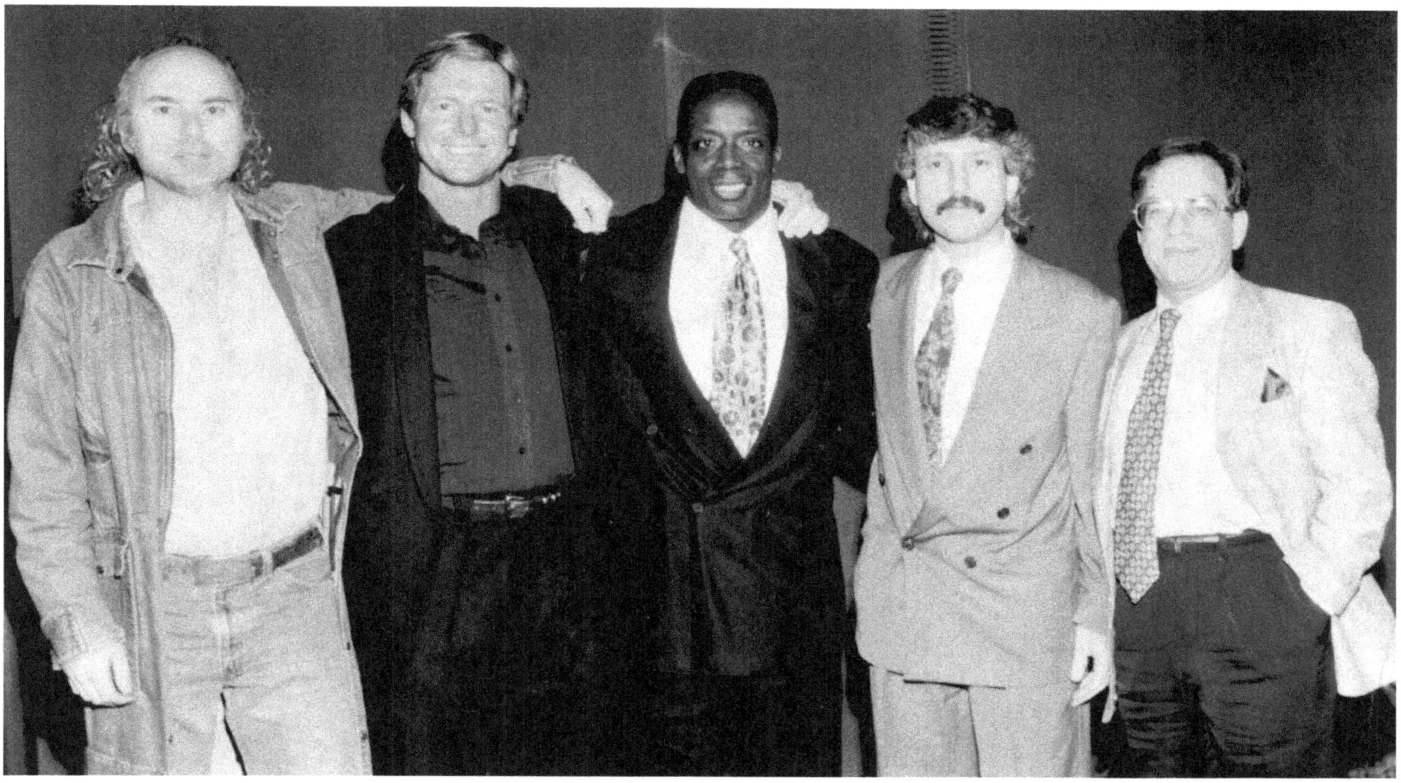

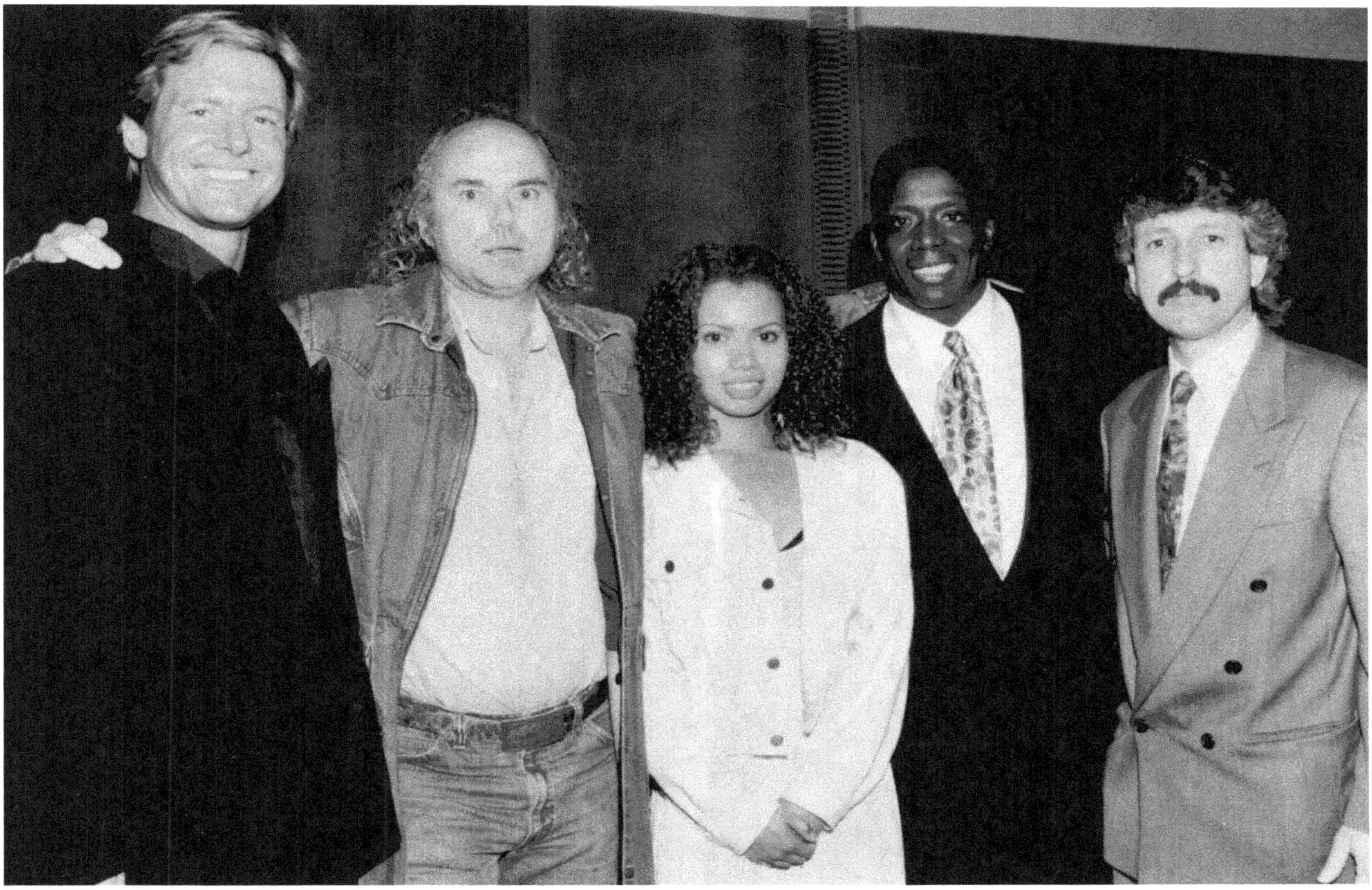

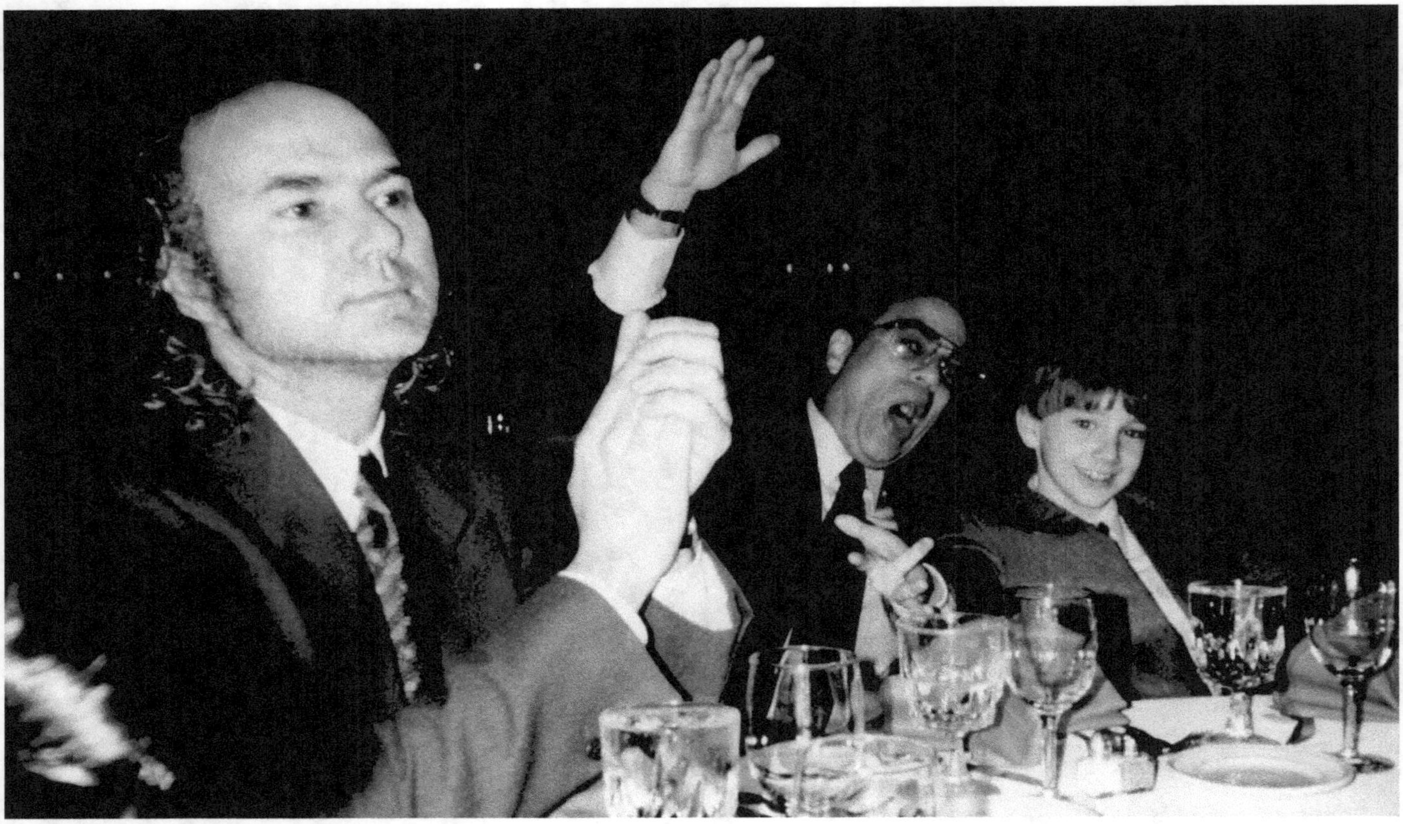

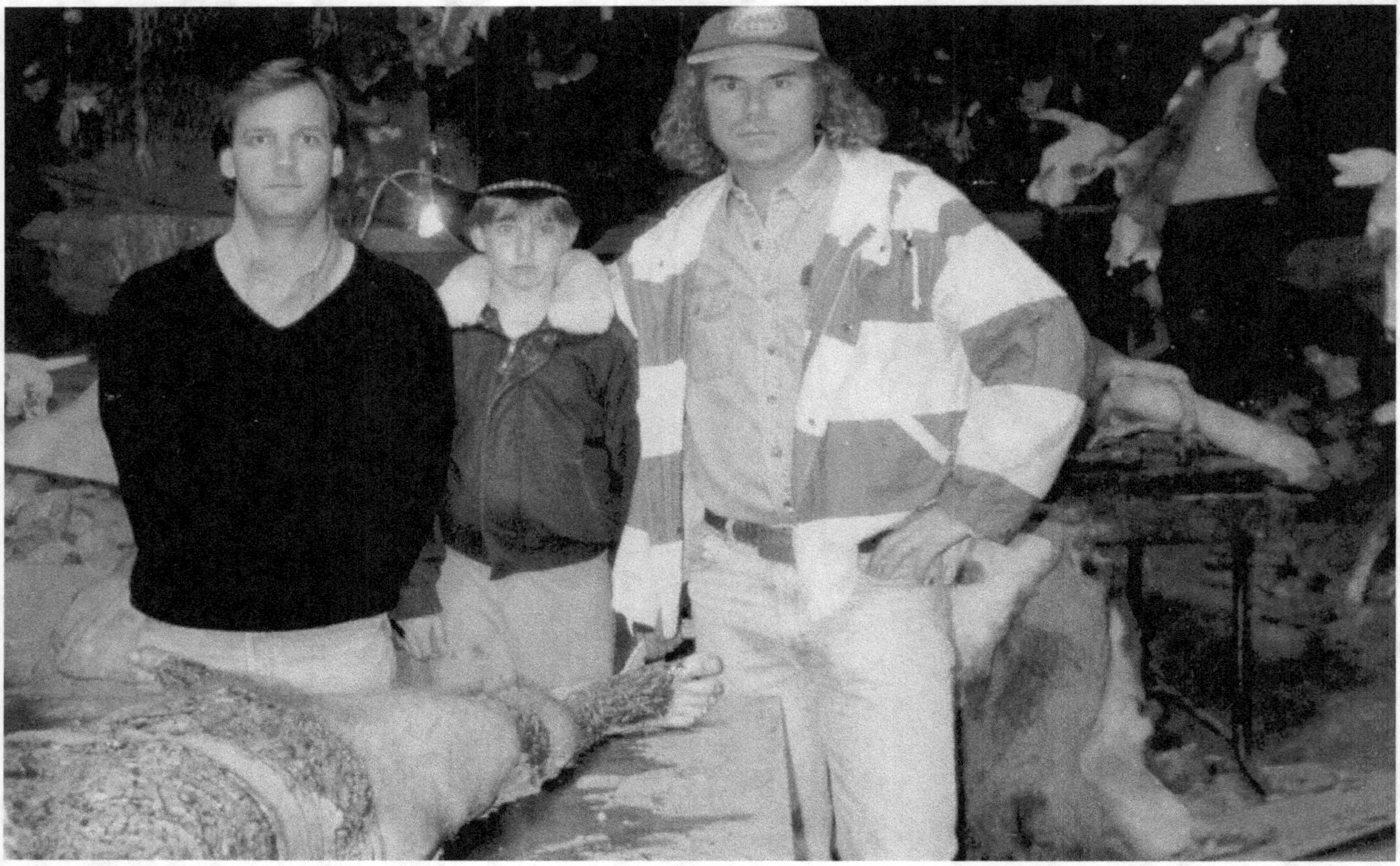

"THERE IS MORE HONESTY AND JOY IN ANY ONE MINUTE OF 'THE WIZARD OF SPEED AND TIME' THAN IN SAY, THE ENTIRE POLISHED, BUT ROBOTIC "STAR TREK" SERIES PUT TOGETHER."
—Nat Segaloff, BOSTON HERALD

"'THE WIZARD OF SPEED AND TIME' IS AN EXCITING AND HEARTFELT MOVIE ABOUT THE COMPULSION TO MAKE MOVIES."
—Betsy Sherman, BOSTON GLOBE

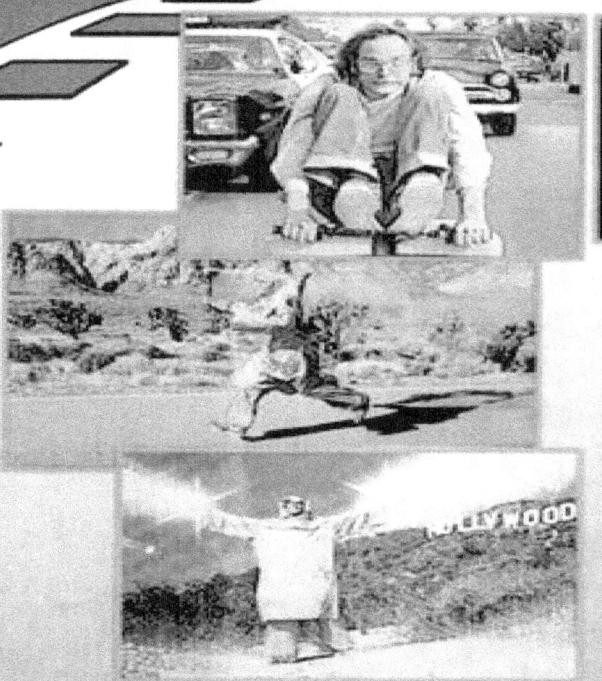
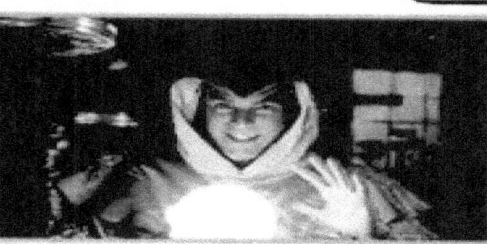

You're in for a wild and comic Hollywood adventure when the award-winning WIZARD OF SPEED AND TIME takes you on an incredible journey into the dazzling world of special effects. Filmmaker Mike Jittlov gets his "big break" in show business when two battling producers hire him to film a segment for their upcoming TV special. But what Mike doesn't know is that there's a $25,000 side bet that he won't deliver.

Now the race is on! With his small crew helping, Mike acts in the film as a magical wizard who brings an entire film studio to life via animation and a marathon of spectacular effects. Even though the crew struggles through many hardships, unexpected studio sabotage, and even a crazy car chase through Hollywood, the results are astounding.

It's fast and funny...wonderful and eye-boggling. Plan on having the best fun you've had in years when THE WIZARD OF SPEED AND TIME brings his amazing bag of tricks to your door.

1989, COLOR  PG
RUNNING TIME: 92 MIN.

© 1988 SHAPIRO GLICKENHAUS ENTERTAINMENT, CORP.

DOLBY STEREO

Closed captioned by the National Captioning Institute. Used with permission.

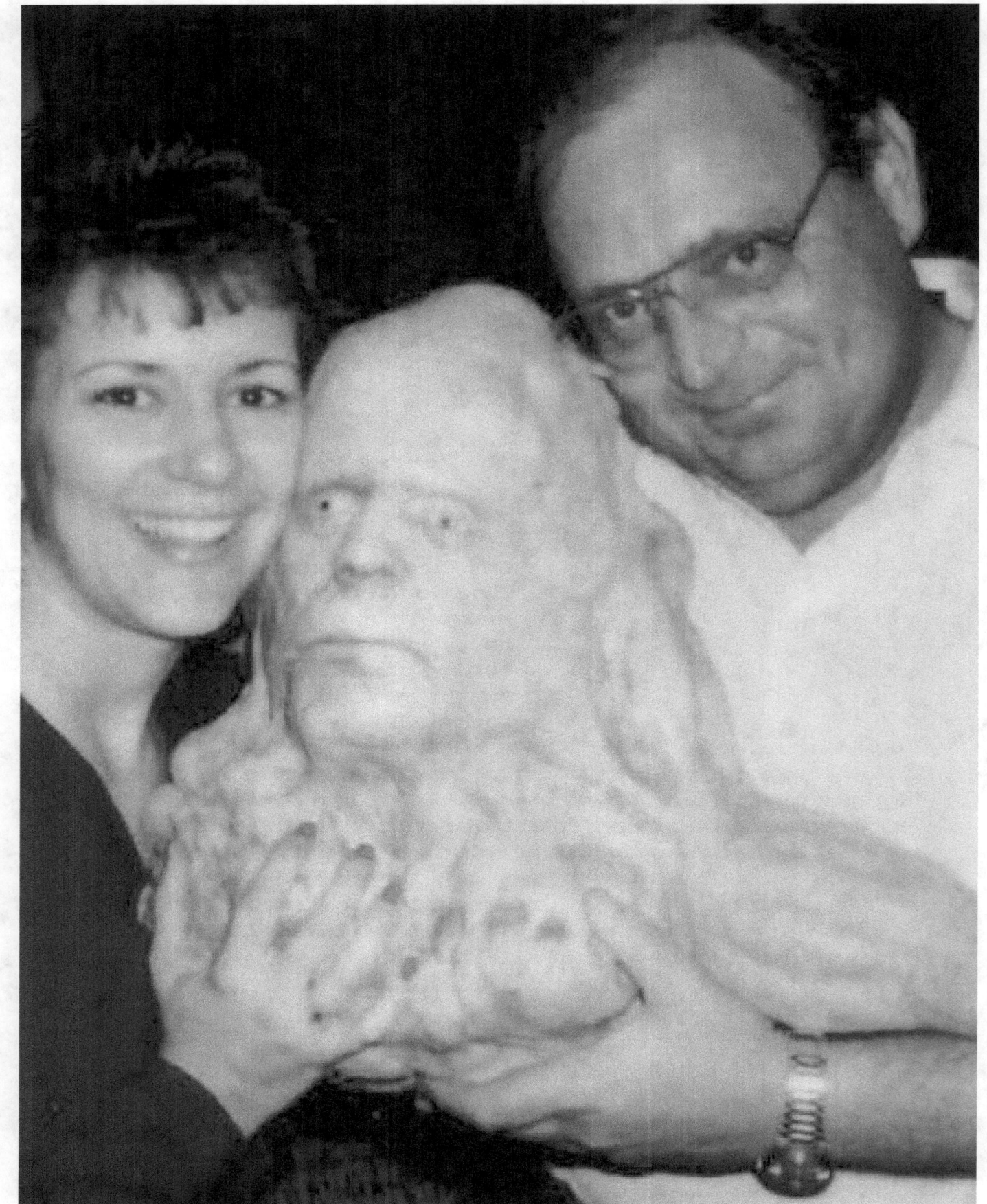

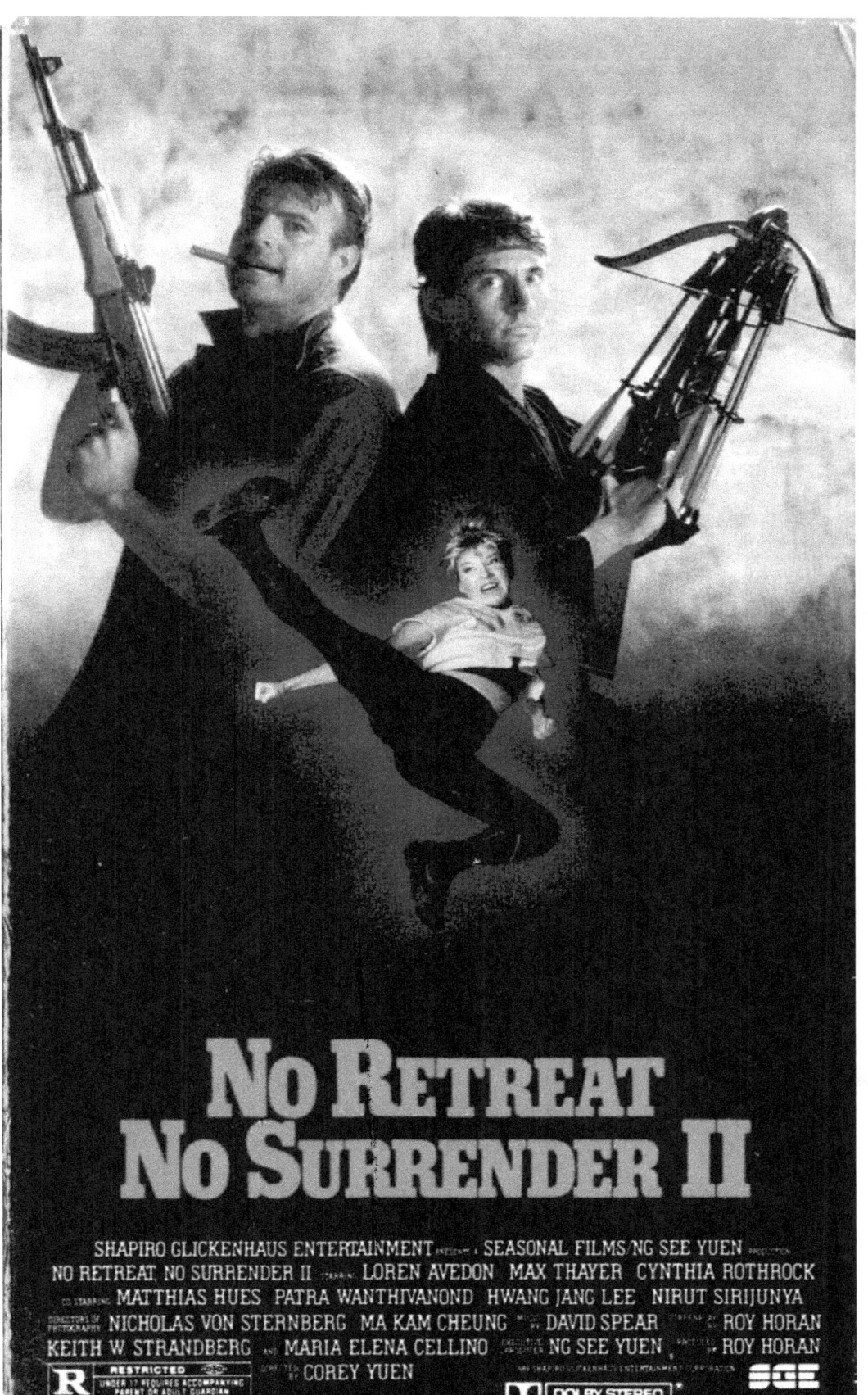

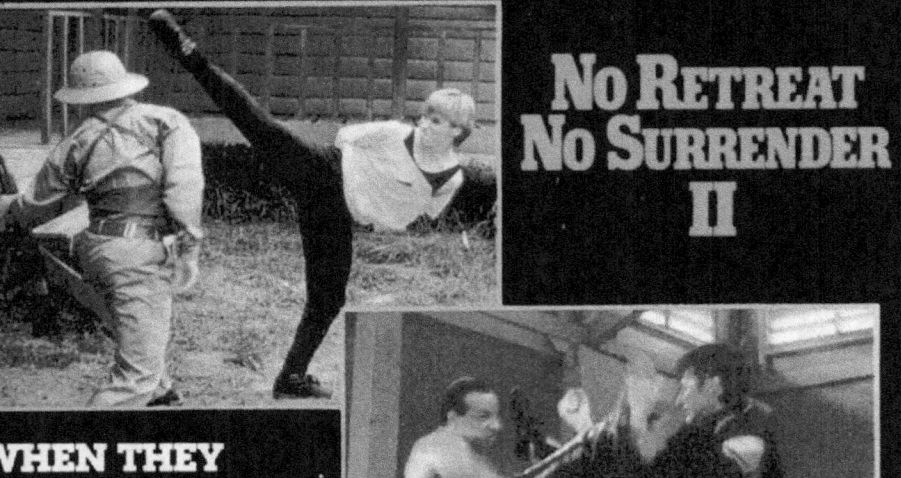

# No Retreat No Surrender II

**WHEN THEY STAND TOGETHER... NO ONE ELSE STANDS A CHANCE.**

High in the dense Vietnamese jungle a Soviet-American battle is brewing. When Scott Wylde's Thai fiancee, Sulin, is kidnapped, he vows revenge and plots her rescue. With the help of martial arts master Mac Jarvis and Terry, a real femme fatale, he sets off to battle Sulin's ruthless Soviet captors.

Fists and feet fly as Scott, Mac and Terry pummel their way through the Soviet human blockade, until they meet Yuri, the sadistic colonel who's planned a torturous death for Sulin. In a face-to-face confrontation between the "American Eagle" and the "Soviet Bear," they'll take no prisoners—in this battle there is NO RETREAT, NO SURRENDER.

- *The action-packed sequel to "No Retreat, No Surrender" in the tradition of martial arts spectaculars like "American Ninja," and "Bloodsport"*
- *1989 theatrical release*
- *From the producers of "Shakedown"*
- *Stars MAX THAYER ("Iron Eagle")*

Program Time: 92 Minutes
Program Copyright:
© 1987 Seasonal Film Corporation
Package design and summary:
© 1989 Forum Home Video,
A Unit of MCEG, Inc.
All rights reserved
Distributed by Forum Home Video
New York, New York 10017
Printed in the U.S.A.

0 23105 79283 0

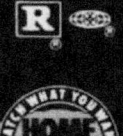
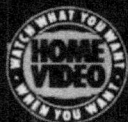

# RIGHTS AGREEMENT

THIS AGREEMENT made this 10th day of March, 1994, by and between JAMES GLICKENHAUS, an individual residing at Marble Hall, Rye, New York 10580 ("Writer") and LIBERTY BELL PRODUCTIONS, INC., a New York corporation ("Purchaser").

## WITNESSETH

In consideration of the covenants and conditions herein contained and other good and valuable consideration, the parties hereto agree as follows:

1. Grant of Rights: Writer hereby grants, sells, assigns, transfers, conveys and sets over unto Purchaser, exclusively and forever, for the entire universe, and in any and all languages and versions, all rights of every kind and nature, including but not limited to the rights hereinafter referred to in and to that certain screenplay presently entitled "TIMEMASTER", written by Writer. Writer has applied for copyright registration of said screenplay, but has, as of this date, not received a registration number. Writer warrants that no currently effective agreements have been entered into by him at any time with respect to said story. Any and all literary, dramatic and/or musical writings and materials which may be based on the titles, copyrights, adaptations, dramatizations, novelizations, songs, music, lyrics, choreography, orchestrations, arrangements and translations of any and all thereof are hereinafter referred to collectively as the "Property". Without in any way limiting the generality of any of the foregoing, the rights herein granted and conveyed to Purchaser shall include the following sole and exclusive rights in and with respect to the Property:

(A) To make motion picture versions or adaptations of the Property, or any part thereof, and to produce one or more silent, sound and talking dialogue and/or musical motion pictures (which term shall include video recordings) (including, without limitation, remakes, sequels, serials and series of two (2) or more episodes) of any type now known or hereafter to be known of any length, whether shown in one or more parts, based upon or adapted in whole or in part from the Property, or any part thereof, or any versions or adaptations (all such motion pictures, photoplays, versions or adaptations being hereinafter included and embraced in the expression "motion picture versions");

(B) To adapt, use, dramatize, arrange, change, vary modify, alter, transpose and make musical and nonmusical motion picture versions of the Property, or any part thereof, and to add to, interpolate in and subtract or omit from the Property characters, language, plot, theme, scenes, incidents, situations, action, titles, dialogue, songs, music and lyrics and to translate any of the foregoing into all languages; to include in such motion pictures and sound records such language, speech, songs, music, lyrics, dancing, choreography, sound, sound effects, action, situations, scenes, plots, dialogue, incidents, characters, characterizations, and other material whether or not based upon, or taken from, the Property and/or in conjunction with all or any part of any other work, writings or other materials, or otherwise, as Purchaser in Purchaser's uncontrolled discretion may deem advisable, it being the intention hereof that Purchaser shall have the exclusive, absolute and unlimited right to use the Property, and each and every part thereof, for motion picture purposes (and all other purposes granted hereunder) in any manner Purchaser may, in Purchaser's uncontrolled discretion, deem advisable with the same force and effect as though Purchaser were the sole author of the Property, specifically including, without limitation, the right to represent and portray any of the characters (including their names, mannerisms, habits, gestures, characterizations, and turns of phrase, situations, bits of business, gags, routines, buildings, locales, backgrounds, dialogue, animals, props, sets, costumes, drawings, designs, photographs, pictures, choreography and all other parts, elements, and components contained in the Property, or in any motion picture version or adaptation thereof) in motion pictures, as sequels or otherwise (including serials of two or more episodes) whether or not the events portrayed or the story, plot, outline or general nature of such motion pictures are the same as, or similar to, those contained in the Property, all without in any way being accountable or liable to Writer for any use which Purchaser may make thereof for any of the uses or purposes aforesaid and Writer hereby waives the benefits of any provision of law or right known as "droit moral" or any similar laws, and agrees not to institute, support, maintain or authorize any action or lawsuit on the ground that any motion pictures or sound records produced therefrom or other version or adaptation of the Property authorized by this Agreement in any way constitutes an infringement or violation of any law or right such as "droit moral" or a defamation or mutilation of any part thereof, or that Purchaser's use constitutes or contains unauthorized variations, alterations, modifications, changes or translations;

(C) To interpolate in any motion picture or other versions or adaptations of the Property authorized by the terms of this Agreement, songs, lyrics and music of all kinds; to set to music any verse, lyric, prose or part or parts of the Property and any characters thereof, and to use, print, reprint, publish, copy and record by any means and/or method, and sell, license or otherwise exploit any such copy of such music and lyrics or versions or vend such song, music and/or lyrics on any and all reproducing devices now or hereafter known (whether on film magnetic tape, wire, records or other devices of any kind and whether now or hereafter known) and to perform (for profit or nonprofit), arrange, adapt and exploit the same throughout the universe and to secure copyright therein everywhere in Purchaser's name or otherwise, and to use, superimpose and/or photograph lines, excerpts from or translations of such Property or the title, subtitles, text and dialogue of any motion picture version or other versions or adaptations;

(D) To advertise, publicize and exploit the Property and the title or titles thereof, and all motion picture versions and records and other adaptations and versions, in any manner and through any mediums that Purchaser may desire and, for the purpose thereof, to make, publish and copyright, or cause to be made, published and copyrighted, in any and all languages and in such form as Purchaser may deem advisable, including publication in newspapers, fan magazines and trade periodicals, synopses, summaries, resumes and stories of the Property and any such motion picture versions or adaptations;

(E) To produce, issue, reproduce, make, remake, reissue, distribute, exhibit, transmit, project, perform, televise, cablecast, sell, lease, rent, license, exploit, turn to account, dispose of and generally deal in and with, in any other manner or by any method whatsoever, in any and all media, whether now known or hereafter devised, one or more motion picture versions based in whole or in part on the Property, and trailers in connection therewith, including negatives, sound records, positive prints, cassettes and discs and other records thereof, of any size, color or type and any and all by-products of any thereof, in any and all parts of the universe, and to import and export any thereof, or copies thereof, into or out of any place, country or territory without limitation or restriction;

(F) To make, publish, copy, vend, license and otherwise use in any manner that the Purchaser may desire, disc or other sound records, sound on film, cassettes and any and all other mechanical, electrical and any other contrivances or devices of any nature whatsoever, for the recordation and rerecordation of the sound, talking, musical and any and all other audible portions of the soundtrack of the motion picture based on said Property and any adaptations or versions thereof, and any motion picture versions, any parts of any of the foregoing, and for the reproduction, transmission, projection and/or performance of any or all such sounds separately or as part of or incidental to or in synchronization with the exhibition or performance thereof, whether such contrivances or devices are now known or are hereafter known, invented or devised;

(G) To broadcast by means of television and radio or any process analogous thereto, whether now known or hereafter devised, all or any part of the Property or any adaptation or version thereof, including any motion picture or other version or versions thereof and announcements of or concerning said motion picture or other version accomplished through the use of living actors performing simultaneously with such broadcast or transmission;

(H) To use the title or titles by which the Property may be now or hereafter known, or any components of any such title or titles (i) as the title of motion pictures and in connection with the advertising and exploitation thereof, whether such motion picture or other versions are based in whole or in part on the Property or independent of the Property; and (ii) to use such title or titles or any components of the same in connection with songs, musical compositions, music or lyrics included in any such motion picture or other versions, and in connection with the publications, recordation, performance and any other use whatsoever thereof;

(I) To secure copyright and renewals and extensions thereof (or equivalent protections) in all parts of the universe for such motion picture versions, and any other versions or adaptations of the Property herein elsewhere mentioned, and any sound records, soundtracks, or recordings in connection therewith, in all places and countries of the world under any now existing or hereafter created laws, regulations or rules, in the name of Purchaser or any other person, firm or corporation;

(J) To use, exercise, employ, exploit and turn to account, and to license, authorize and cause others to use, exercise, employ, exploit and turn to account, all merchandising, commercial tie-up and by-product rights of any and all kinds including (but not limited to) all rights to manufacture, market, exploit and sell commercial products and

"TIMEMASTER" - Production Information                                    14


**ABOUT THE FILMMAKERS**

**JAMES GLICKENHAUS (WRITER AND DIRECTOR)**

With "TIMEMASTER," writer/director JAMES GLICKENHAUS brings to the screen his most ambitious project yet: a thrilling adventure which spans the far reaches of the universe, transcends time and space -- and explores the limitless boundaries of the imagination.

For over ten years, Glickenhaus has entertained audiences around the world with his high-action adventures. In 1980, the young filmmaker wrote and directed "The Exterminator," starring Christopher George and Samantha Eggar. Made for less than $2 million, the film went on to gross more than $15 million domestically and played equally well in most of its 62 territories worldwide. "The Exterminator" was the number one box-office draw for two weeks on Variety's charts.

Two years later, Glickenhaus wrote, produced and directed "The Soldier," starring Ken Wahl and Klaus Kinski, which was filmed on location in New York, Philadelphia, Berlin, San Antonio, Austria and Israel. In 1984 he wrote and directed "The Protector," starring international action sensation Jackie Chan and Danny Aiello, which was filmed in New York City and Hong Kong.

His company, Glickenhaus Film, merged with Shapiro Entertainment in 1987 to form Shapiro Glickenhaus Entertainment,

# INDEX

| | |
|---|---|
| Page 7 | Leonard Shapiro & James Glickenhaus |
| Page 9 | TIMEMASTER Artwork |
| Page 11 (top) | At Tippi Hedren's Ranch in Soledad Canyon, CA. Lenny is under the leopard. The woman on the right is Harriet Shapiro, Lenny's wife. *(circa 1978 - '79)* |
| Page 11 (bottom) | Leonard Shapiro with "Beethoven" the dog-star of Universal's movie of the same name, or one of its sequels. *(circa 1992 probably at VSDA Convention in Las Vegas, NV.)* |
| Page 12 | Leonard Shapiro & Lion *(circa 1978 - '79)* at Tippi Hedren's Ranch in Soledad Canyon, CA. |
| Page 13 | The front page of the entertainment trade newspaper Daily Variety *(January 8, 1981)* announcing Leonard Shapiro's promotion to Vice President at Avco Embassy Pictures. |
| Page 14 | Leonard Shapiro *(circa 1959)* playing basketball for Forest Hills High School in the Forest Hills neighborhood in the New York City borough of Queens, near Rego Park. This was published in the 'Beacon' the school newspaper. Lenny's name is misspelled. |
| Page 15-16 | Los Angeles Times article about MOONTRAP |
| Page 17 | Leonard Shapiro & Louis Feola MCA Home Video *(prior to 1991)* |
| Page 18 (top) | Leonard Shapiro, Elspeth Tavares *(editor of entertainment trade publication Screen International)* |
| Page 18 (bottom) | ^^^1Unknown man1, Leonard Shapiro with an Unknown man *(prior to 1981)* |
| Page 19 (top) | Shapiro of SGE TV with others |
| Page 19 (bottom) | Robert Rehme, Unknown man, Unknown woman, Leonard Shapiro & other. |
| Page 20-21 | Four EXTERMINATOR Stills. |
| Page 39-42 | MOONTRAP From the private Archive of Stephen A. Roberts *(Sketches & Artworks.)* |

| | | | |
|---|---|---|---|
| Page | 43 | | From the private archive of Stephen A. Roberts |
| Page | 44 | | EXTERMINATOR **Original Theatrical Poster** |
| Page | 45 | (top & bottom) | Badges from Stephen Roberts *(1985 & 1987)* |
| Page | 46 | (top) | Stephen Roberts, Kevin Tent, Stephanie Denton |
| Page | 46 | (bottom) | Pete Pidutti, Stephen Roberts, Unknowing |
| Page | 47 | | Original SGE document *(Stephen A. Roberts)* |
| Page | 48 | | EXTERMINATOR **Spotting List "Page 3"** |
| Page | 59 | | Spanish Poster Artwork PIRANHA II: THE SPAWNING |
| Page | 60 | | Original Poster Artwork PIRANHA II: THE SPAWNING |
| Page | 61 | | Original Poster Artwork POINT BREAK |
| Page | 62 | | Poster Artwork BLINDNESS |
| Page | 63 | | Original Poster Artwork TRUE LIES |
| Page | 64 | | TIMEMASTER – **Movie Still** |
| Page | 65 | | FRANKENHOOKER – **Original document** |
| Page | 79 | | Original Poster Artwork C.H.U.D. |
| Page | 80 | | Original Poster Artwork THE WIZARD OF SPEED AND TIME |
| Page | 81 | | Original Buttons THE WIZARD OF SPEED AND TIME |
| Page | 82 | | Cheque for BASKET CASE 3: THE PROGENY *(1992)* |
| Page | 83 | | Music Cue Sheet EXTERMINATOR *(1980)* |
| Page | 84 | | BASKET CASE 2 - **Certificate of Copyright Registration** *(1990)* |
| Page | 85 | | BASKET CASE 3: THE PROGENY - **Music Cue Sheet** *(1992)* |
| Page | 86 | | BASKET CASE 3: THE PROGENY - **Certificate of Authorship** *(1991)* |
| Page | 87-89 | | Six Stills from BASKET CASE 3: THE PROGENY |
| Page | 90 | | SGE Staff *(Drawing)* |
| Page | 91 | | Ted Rosenblatt Portrait Photo |

| | | | |
|---|---|---|---|
| Page | 101 | | RED SCORPION - **French Poster Artwork** |
| Page | 102-104 | | RED SCORPION - **Six Movie Stills** |
| Page | 105 | (top) | Lewis Horwitz at the FLAB *(1978)* |
| Page | 105 | (bottom) | From the private archive of Lew Horwitz |
| Page | 106 | (top) | Lewis Horwitz 2015 - Photo by Stephen A. Roberts |
| Page | 106 | (bottom) | Car Number Plate by Lewis Horwitz - Photo by Stephen A. Roberts |
| Page | 107 | | Lewis Horwitz Portrait Photo |
| Page | 108 | | Lewis Horwitz & Joan Rivers *(1980)* |
| Page | 129 | | SLAUGHTER OF THE INNOCENTS – **Movie Still** |
| Page | 130 | | FIREHOUSE - **Original Poster Artwork** |
| Page | 131 | | MCBAIN – **Movie Still** |
| Page | 132 | | BASKET CASE 3: THE PROGENY - **Key Art Detail** |
| Page | 133 | | HANGMEN - **Original Poster Artwork** |
| Page | 142 | (top) | John Alexander *(Portrait Photo)* |
| Page | 142 | (bottom) | John Alexander & Nadia Bruce Rawlings *(1982)* |
| Page | 144 | | MANIAC COP - **Key Art Detail** |
| Page | 145 | (top) | William Lustig during the shooting of VIGILANTE |
| Page | 145 | (bottom) | William Lustig during the shooting of MANIAC |
| Page | 146 | | MANIAC – **Poster Artworks** |
| Page | 147 | | William Lustig during the shooting of MANIAC COP |
| Page | 148 | | MANIAC COP – **Two Movie Stills** |
| Page | 160 | (top) | MANIAC COP – **Movie Still** |
| Page | 160 | (bottom) | MCBAIN – **Movie Still** |
| Page | 161 | (top & bottom) | From the private archive of Frank Isaac |
| Page | 162 | | MANIAC COP – **Two Stills** |

| | | | |
|---|---|---|---|
| Page | 163 | (top) | Frank Isaac during the shooting of SLAUGHTER OF THE INNOCENTS |
| Page | 163 | (bottom) | From the private archive of Frank Isaac |
| Page | 172 | | DEATHSTALKER - Original Poster Artwork |
| Page | 173 | | MANIAC COP - Theatrical Poster |
| Page | 174 | | BARBARIAN QUEEN - Original Poster Artwork |
| Page | 175 | | SLAUGHTER OF THE INNOCENTS – Credit Page from Original Press Kit |
| Page | 176 | | A personal greeting card written by Leonard Shapiro (From the private Archive of Frank Isaac) |
| Page | 177 | | FRANKENHOOKER – Synopsis |
| Page | 178 | | FRANKENHOOKER – Original document |
| Page | 179 | | Original SGE document |
| Page | 180 | | BRAIN DAMAGE – Key Art Detail |
| Page | 181 | | FRANKENHOOKER – Key Art Detail |
| Page | 182 | | Frank Henenlotter wearing a FRANKENHOOKER T-Shirt |
| Page | 192 | | BASKET CASE 2 – Key Art Detail |
| Page | 193 | (top) | BASKET CASE 2 – Crew Photo |
| Page | 193 | (bottom) | BASKET CASE 2 – Frank Henenlotter and Creatures designed by Gabe Bartolos |
| Page | 194 | | EMANUELLE 5 – Theatrical Poster |
| Page | 195 | | FRANKENHOOKER – Two Movie Stills |
| Page | 196 | | MOONTRAP – Preview Flyer (1989 / Scan by Stephen A. Roberts) |
| Page | 197 | | MOONTRAP – Original Poster Artwork (1989) |
| Page | 198 | | MOONTRAP – VHS Preview Flyer (1989) |
| Page | 199-200 | | FRANKENHOOKER – Four Movie Stills |
| Page | 201 | (top) | Kevin Tent |
| Page | 201 | (bottom) | Walter Koenig (Star of MOONTRAP) |

| | | | |
|---|---|---|---|
| Page | 219-221 | | SLAUGHTER OF THE INNOCENTS – Three Advertising Movie Stills |
| Page | 229 | | Young Jefferson Richard with Guitar |
| Page | 230 | | SLAUGHTER OF THE INNOCENTS – Flyer with Credits *(1993)* |
| Page | 231 | | Jefferson Richard - Prom Photo |
| Page | 232 | | BERSERKER – Poster Artwork |
| Page | 233 | (top) | BLACK ROSES – Reunion Snapshot |
| Page | 233 | (bottom) | BLACK ROSES – Music Cue Sheet Detail |
| Page | 234 | (top) | Director John Fasano & Cinematographer Paul Mitchnick during the shooting of BLACK ROSES |
| Page | 234 | (bottom) | John Fasano & James Glickenhaus during the shooting of SHAKEDOWN |
| Page | 235 | | BLACK ROSES - Original VHS Artwork |
| Page | 236-237 | | BLACK ROSES – Dialogue List |
| Page | 247-249 | | BLACK ROSES – Six Movie Stills |
| Page | 250 | | BLACK ROSES - Original Poster Artwork |
| Page | 251 | | SHAKEDOWN - Key Art Detail |
| Page | 252 | | THE EXTERMINATOR – Alternative Poster Artwork |
| Page | 254 | | SHAKEDOWN – Artwork |
| Page | 275 | | SHAKEDOWN – Poster Artwork |
| Page | 276-278 | | TIMEMASTER – Six Movie Stills |
| Page | 279 | | SLAUGHTER OF THE INNOCENTS – Original Poster Artwork |
| Page | 280 | | TIMEMASTER – VHS Preview Flyer |
| Page | 281 | | TIMEMASTER – VHS Pre-Pack Flyer |
| Page | 282 | | TIMEMASTER – VHS & Laserdisc Flyer |
| Page | 283 | | BEVERLY HILLS BODYSNATCHERS – Preview Flyer |

| | | | |
|---|---|---|---|
| Page | 284 | (top) | FRANKENHOOKER – **Key Art Detail** |
| Page | 284 | (bottom) | **Andi Elliot on location of making** FRANKENHOOKER **Key Art** |
| Page | 289 | (top) | **Kadeem Hardison & Cynthia Bond promoting** DEF BY TEMPTATION |
| Page | 289 | (bottom) | **SGE Home Video Crew** |
| Page | 290 | (top & bottom) | **Two Behind-The-Scenes Snapshots of Christian Ingvordsen directing** |
| Page | 291-292 | | COMRADES IN ARMS - **Two different Poster Artworks** |
| Page | 293 | | SEARCH & DESTROY – **Poster Artwork** |
| Page | 294 | | COVERT ACTION – **Poster Artwork** |
| Page | 295 | | SHOCKTROOP – **VHS Artwork Scan** |
| Page | 296 | | SIGN OF THE OTTER aka THE LITTLE PATRIOT – **Poster Artwork** |
| Page | 297 | | BACKFIRE! – **Poster Artwork** |
| Page | 298 | | AIRBOSS – **Poster Artwork** |
| Page | 299 | | SIGN OF THE OTTER – **Detail** |
| Page | 300 | | **Chris Ingvordsen nowadays** |
| Page | 319 | (top) | SIGN OF THE OTTER aka THE LITTLE PATRIOT – **Advertisement Still** |
| Page | 319 | (bottom) | THE OUTFIT – **Advertisement Still** |
| Page | 320 | | AIRBOSS IV: ECO WARRIOR – **Poster Artwork** |
| Page | 321 | | LETHAL PURSUIT – **Poster Artwork** |
| Page | 322 | | THE LOST IDOL – **VHS Artwork** |
| Page | 323 | | TC2000 – **Poster Artwork** |
| Page | 324 | | DR. CALIGARI – **VHS Artwork** |
| Page | 325 | | **Jalal Merhi - Portrait Photo** |
| Page | 333-336 | | **Documents from Jalal Mehri & others** |
| Page | 337 | | **Jalal Merhi, Cynthia Rothrock, Leonard Shapiro & others** |
| Page | 338 | (top) | TALONS OF THE EAGLE – **Crew Photo** |

| Page | 338 | (bottom) | Billy Blanks, Mathias Hues, Jalal Merhi & Bolo Yeung |
|---|---|---|---|
| Page | 341 | (top) | James Glickenhaus & Jacqueline Palmiere |
| Page | 341 | (bottom) | Nadia Bruce, Stephen Roberts, Jacqueline Palmiere, Darrin Solomon…and '80s hair! |
| Page | 342 | | Jalal Merhi Directing Cynthia Rothrock (TIGER CLAWS) |
| Page | 343-344 | | TIGER CLAWS – Two Stills |
| Page | 345 | | Cynthia Rothrock (RAGE & HONOR Artwork) |
| Page | 357-358 | | TIGER CLAWS – Four Movie Stills |
| Page | 360 | | RED SCORPION – Original BD & DVD Artwork |
| Page | 364-366 | | RED SCORPION – Six Movie Stills |
| Page | 371 | | Stephanie Denton, Nadia Bruce-Rawlings, Darby Walker |
| Page | 372 | | Nadia Bruce-Rawlings & Stephanie Denton (Nadia wearing the machete from MCBAIN) |
| Page | 378 | | Dolph Lundgren in RED SCORPION |
| Page | 379 | | MCBAIN – Two Movie Stills |
| Page | 380 | | SLAUGHTER OF THE INNOCENTS – Movie Still |
| Page | 381 | | MCBAIN – Movie Still |
| Page | 382 | (top) | Marilyn Moore's sister-in-law dressed as Frankenhooker |
| Page | 382 | (bottom) | Marilyn Moore and her father with BASKET CASE 2 T-Shirt |
| Page | 383 | | Marilyn Moore modern day |
| Page | 389-391 | | BASKET CASE 2 – Six Movie Stills |
| Page | 392 | | FRANKENHOOKER – Behind the Scene |
| Page | 393 | | RING OF STEEL – VHS Artwork Scan |
| Page | 394 | | ARMY OF DARKNESS – Original Poster Artwork |
| Page | 395 | | David Frost, Leonard Shapiro, Robert Chapin & Unknown Man |
| Page | 403 | | TIMEMASTER – Key Art Detail |

| | | | |
|---|---|---|---|
| Page | 405-406 | | Page MCBAIN – Four Behind-The-Scenes Snapshots, taken during the shootings in the Philippines |
| Page | 407 | | MCBAIN – Production Notes, taken from the Original Press Kit |
| Page | 408 | | Page MCBAIN – Dialogue Continuity Page |
| Page | 409 | | SCARS – Cover Artwork *(Book by Nadia Bruce-Rawlings)* |
| Page | 417-420 | | MCBAIN – Movie Stills |
| Page | 421 | | EXTERMINATOR – Movie Still |
| Page | 422 | | Maria Conchita Alonso in MCBAIN |
| Page | 423 | | TIMEMASTER – Movie Still |
| Page | 428 | | TIMEMASTER – Movie Stills |
| Page | 429 | | TIMEMASTER – Movie Stills |
| Page | 430 | | FRANKENHOOKER – Movie Still |
| Page | 431 | (top) | EXTERMINATOR – Movie Still |
| Page | 431 | (bottom) | MCBAIN – Movie Still |
| Page | 436 | (top) | Laurie Specter, Stephen Roberts, Darby Walker, Jacquie Palmiere, Stephanie Denton, Alan Solomon, Leonard Shapiro, Nadia Bruce-Rawlings |
| Page | 436 | (bottom) | James Glickenhaus, Alix and Alan Solomon, Leonard Shapiro, unknown, Andre Link, Jeff Sackman |
| Page | 437 | (top) | Leonard Shapiro with Lion Picture *(Photo: Stephen A. Roberts)* |
| Page | 437 | (bottom) | Leonard Shapiro 2015 *(Photo: Stephen A. Roberts)* |
| Page | 438 | | Alan Solomon Portrait Photo |
| Page | 443 | | Commemoration for Alan Solomon *(Mount Sinai Chapel, 2010)* |
| Page | 444 | | FRANKENHOOKER – Movie Still |
| Page | 445 | | Andi Elliot *(Snapshot during the marketing for* DEF BY TEMPTATION*)* |
| Page | 446 | | Nadia Bruce-Rawlings and Ron Gale at Tokyo Film |
| Page | 447 | | Burning Village – Behind-The-Scenes Snapshot during the shooting of |

| | | | |
|---|---|---|---|
| Page | 448 | | ONE MAN FORCE – **Poster Artwork** |
| Page | 449 | | TIMEMASTER – **Spanish Poster Artwork** |
| Page | 450 | | SOLDIER – **Italian Poster Artwork** |
| Page | 451 | | Alan Solomon, Nadia Bruce-Rawlings, Ron Gale & members of the Gaga Communications team at Tokyo Film Market |
| Page | 452 | (top) | Jim Glickenhaus & Cars |
| Page | 452 | (bottom) | Jim Glickenhaus & SCG Team |
| Page | 453-454 | | SLAUGHTER OF THE INNOCENTS – **Four Movie Stills** |
| Page | 455 | (top & bottom) | Leonard Shapiro, Jim Glickenhaus, Billy Blanks & others promoting TOUGH & DEADLY |
| Page | 456 | (top & bottom) | Jim Glickenhaus, Frank Isaac, Jesse Glickenhaus & Leonard Shapiro |
| Page | 457 | | THE WIZZARD OF SPEED & TIME – **Video Cover** |
| Page | 458 | | Andi Elliot, Pede Pidutti & Belial |
| Page | 459 | | NO RETREAT NO SURRENDER II – **VHS Front Cover** |
| Page | 460 | | NO RETREAT NO SURRENDER II – **VHS Back Cover** |
| Page | 461-463 | | TIMEMASTER – **Rights Agreement** |
| Page | 464 | | TIMEMASTER – **Production Information** *(taken from the Original Press Kit)* |

… Moustache's *NEXT*

¬ Find more Information's at **www.editionsmoustache.net**

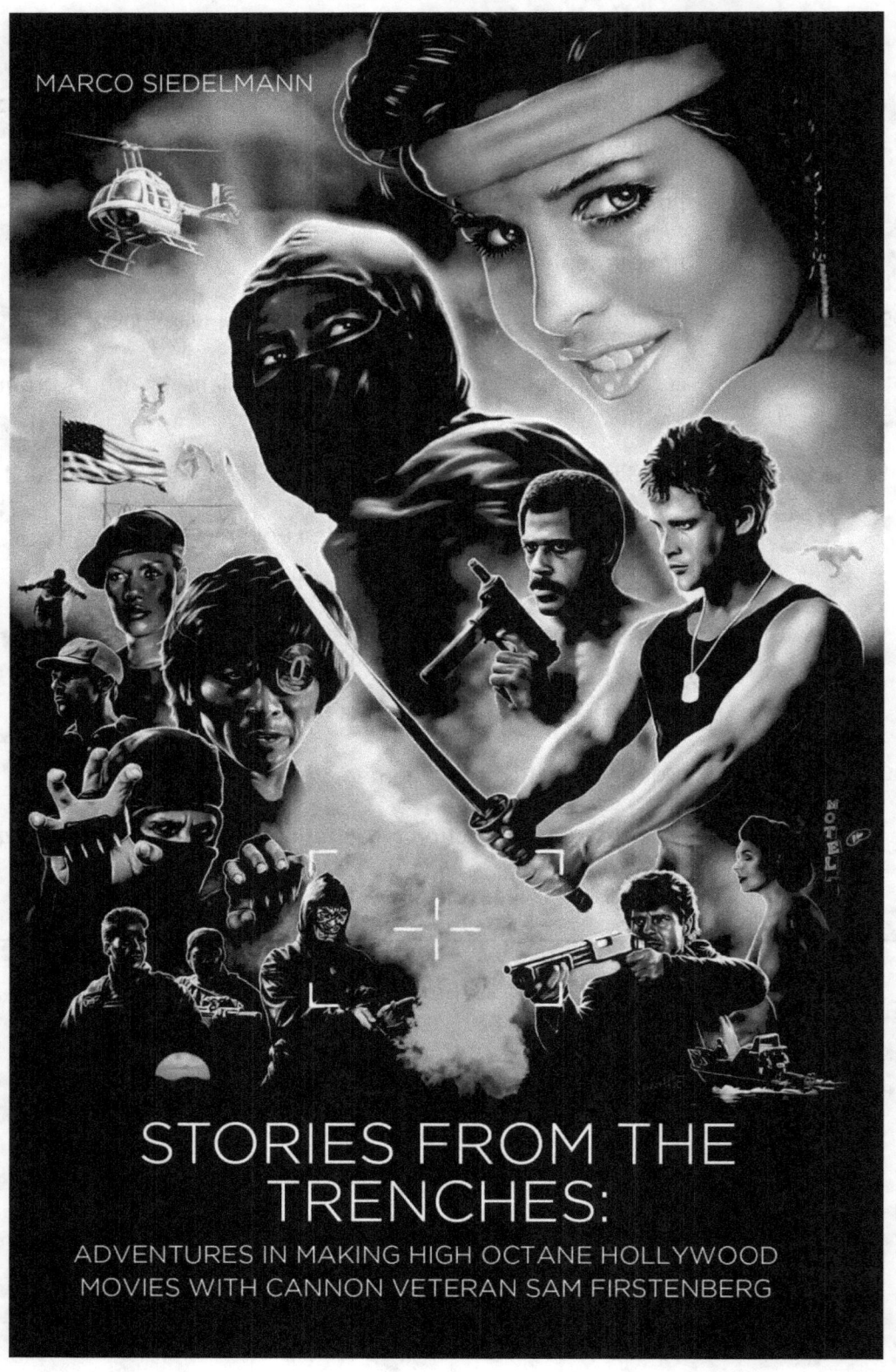

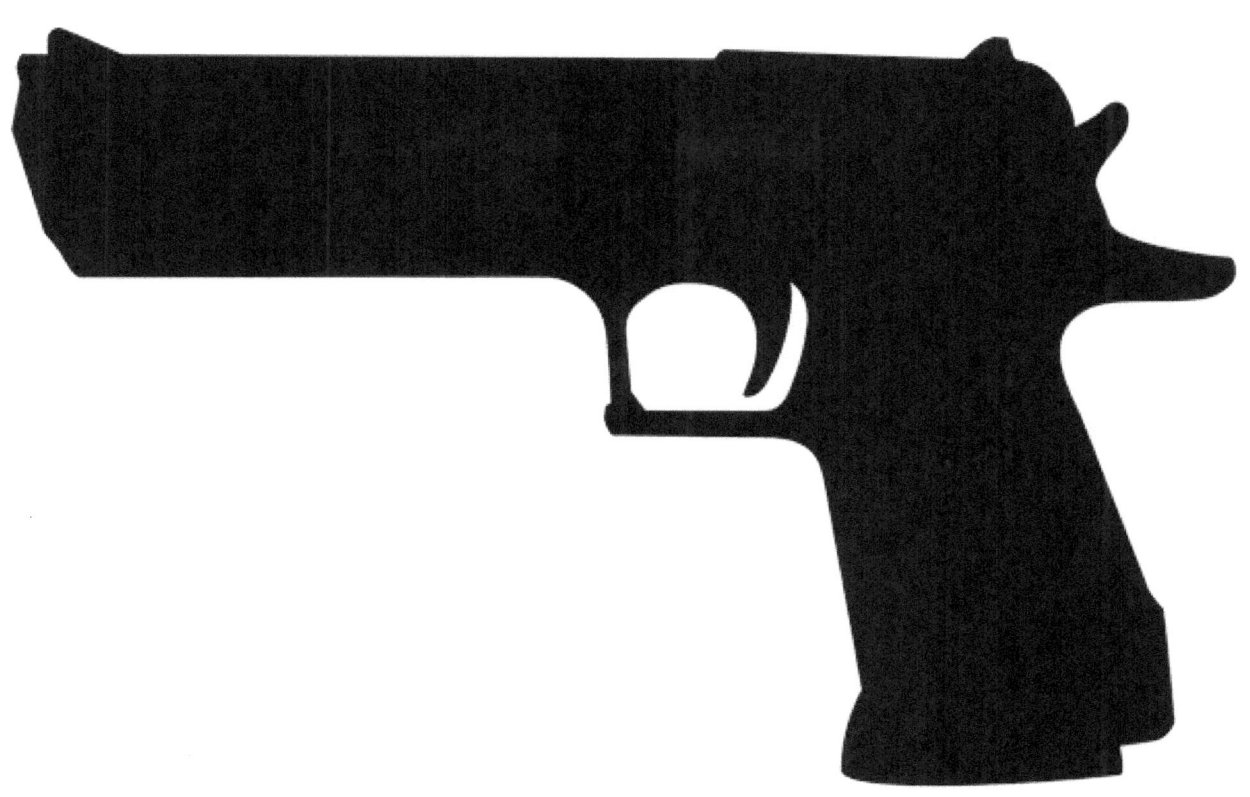

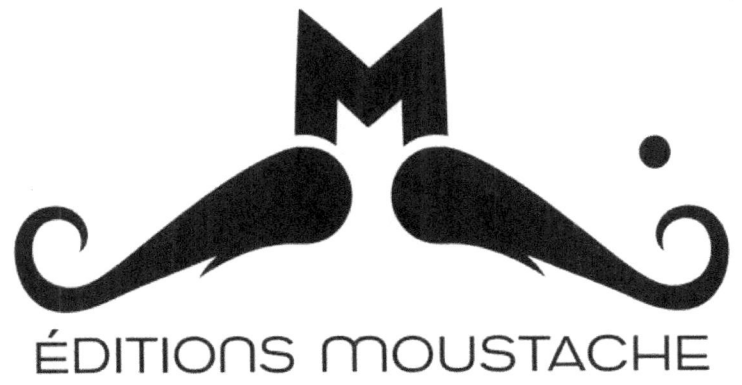